Landis on Mechanics of Patent Claim Drafting

Fourth Edition

PLI Press's
Intellectual Property Law Library

Advertising and Commercial Speech: A First Amendment Guide,
by P. Cameron DeVore and Robert D. Sack (G0-005B)

Advertising Compliance Handbook (2d ed.), by Kenneth A. Plevan and
Miriam L. Siroky (G6-2007)

Art Law: The Guide for Collectors, Investors, Dealers, and Artists (2d ed.),
by Ralph E. Lerner and Judith Bresler (G1-1028)

Copyright Law: A Practitioner's Guide, by Bruce P. Keller and
Jeffrey P. Cunard (G1-9508)

How to Write a Patent Application, by Jeffrey G. Sheldon (G6-2009)

Landis on Mechanics of Patent Claim Drafting (4th ed.),
by Robert C. Faber (G1-1025)

Likelihood of Confusion in Trademark Law, by Richard L. Kirkpatrick
(G1-1024)

*2001 Federal Circuit Yearbook: Patent Law Developments in the Federal
Circuit,* by Jeffrey G. Sheldon (G1-1036)

Patent Law: A Practitioner's Guide (3d ed.), by Ronald B. Hildreth
(G1-1923)

Patent Licensing: Strategy, Negotiation, Forms, by Mark S. Holmes
(G0-00JO)

Patent Litigation, edited by Laurence H. Pretty (G1-8901)

Trademark Law: A Practitioner's Guide (3d ed.), by Siegrun D. Kane
(G1-1029)

Trade Secrets: A Practitioner's Guide, by Henry H. Perritt, Jr. (G1-1021)

*PLI course handbooks on intellectual property law topics are also available.
Please ask for a catalog.*

PLI Press
810 Seventh Avenue
New York, New York 10019
(800) 260-4754
fax: (800) 321-0093
www.pli.edu

Landis on Mechanics of Patent Claim Drafting

Fourth Edition

Robert C. Faber

Incorporating Release No. 5

November 2001

(G9-0205)

Practising Law Institute

New York City

G1-1025

This work is designed to provide practical and useful information on the subject matter covered. However, it is sold with the understanding that the publisher is not engaged in rendering legal, accounting or other professional services. If legal advice or other expert assistance is required, the services of a competent professional should be sought.

ISBN 0-87224-096-7

Library of Congress Card Number: 00-110710

Dedication

This book is dedicated to the faculty of PLI claim-drafting tutors, who have given most generously of their time and talents in the patent bar review course, helping the students to draft better claims. The book is also dedicated to Ruth Druss, Program Attorney of PLI and founder of the PLI patent and patent bar review courses, and to Carol Faber, who encouraged the writing.

I must also dedicate this book to my partners in Ostrolenk, Faber, Gerb & Soffen, who have always set the highest standards of professionalism in all respects.

But the highest tribute goes to John L. Landis, the author of the first two editions of this book, who so thoroughly covered and so clearly presented the material that writing this edition was a pleasure.

About the Author

ROBERT C. FABER has been an intellectual property lawyer for over thirty years. He is a graduate of Cornell University and Harvard Law School. He is a partner in the New York City intellectual property law firm of Ostrolenk, Faber, Gerb & Soffen.

A member of the faculty of PLI's Patent Bar Review course, which focuses on the Agent's Examination and claims writing, for more than twenty years, of the faculty of PLI's Advanced Claim and Amendment writing course since its inception and of the faculty of PLI's Fundamentals of Patent Prosecution since its inception, Mr. Faber has lectured on intellectual property and patent matters for PLI, the Bureau of National Affairs, and other organizations.

Foreword

The enthusiastic reception of the first three editions of this book in America and abroad, including a translation into Japanese, has led to this expanded, revised version, incorporating new cases, and further discussion of developing fields.

Mr. Landis, for many years the chief lecturer for the institute in the area of drafting patent claims, passed away in 1984. His contribution, as well as the contributions of John D. Kaufmann, Bryan W. Sheffield, Myron Cohen, and Rochelle Seide will long endure.

The experienced patent practitioner will find this volume both a distillation of advanced technique and a review of the fundamentals of the field. The person new to patent practice will welcome the absence of jargon and the inclusion of texts of relevant statutes, rules, and procedural interpretations. The attorney or business person with occasional need to evaluate an existing patent should find the numerous claims, both court-approved and specially developed for illustrative purposes, convenient keys to understanding the result of the drafting process.

Table of Contents

VI Composition of Matter Claims—Chemical Cases

VII Claims of Varying Scope

VIII Nonart Rejections

IX Claiming Biotechnology Inventions

X Thoughts on Writing a Claim

Appendixes

Introduction

The primary object of this book is to present a simple and direct approach to the mechanics of claim drafting. The major emphasis in chapters I-VI is on practical techniques for composing claims to many different types of inventions. In chapters I-VI, there is also emphasis on various preferred claim-drafting practices and techniques that have grown up over the years by case law,[1] Patent and Trademark Office[2] rules and memoranda, and, simply, custom, as well as definitions and preferred usage of stylized words and phrases in the patent law, such as "comprising," "consisting," "means for," "step for," and "whereby."

There is also extensive discussion of many case law doctrines relating to nonart rejections,[3] both classic rules and modern trends. In many of these areas, there have been liberalizing trends by the courts[4] in recent years to overthrow or simplify rejections not based on prior art. In particular, this book covers both the classic and the more recent constructions of means clauses (section 34), inherent function of the apparatus doctrine (section 40), mental steps and computer programs (section 44), product-by-process claims (section 46), claims referring to drawings (section 54), new use claims and preamble limitations (section 56), *Jepson* claims (section 57), undue multiplicity (section 62),

---

1. Court or Patent and Trademark Office Board of Patent Appeals and Interferences decisions. The Board is an administrative tribunal in the Patent and Trademark Office that hears appeals from adverse decisions of the patent examiners on substantive issues. The Board usually sits in panels of three designated members.
2. Formerly the Patent Office.
3. Rejections based on doctrines other than anticipation or obviousness over prior art.
4. The Court of Customs and Patent Appeals was a special five-judge federal court having jurisdiction over appeals from Patent Office administrative tribunals, as well as customs appeals. The C.C.P.A. was succeeded in 1982 by the United States Court of Appeals for the Federal Circuit.

old combination (section 63), aggregation (section 64), and printed matter (section 65).

There are many examples of suggested claims to various types of inventions: machines (chapter III), processes (chapter IV), articles of manufacture (chapter V), compositions of matter (chapter VI), computer inventions (section 44), designs (section 47) and plants (section 48), as well as dependent claims (section 11), *Jepson* claims (section 57), generic and species claims (section 58), subcombination claims (section 59), and biotechnology (chapter IX).

Many quotations from claims on appeal and in litigation are given, so that the reader can see for himself or herself which types of limitations and phrases have been judicially approved and which not.

Unfortunately, it is too often true that the inventor or patentee wins or loses because of formal rules and language problems in the claims, not because of any lack of "invention" over the prior art. This book is intended to help the practitioner in designing claims around these myriad rules and doctrines, to draft the most effective types of claims for each type of invention.

The author would like to acknowledge Rochelle K. Seide, Esq. of Baker & Botts, and the staff of Ostrolenk, Faber, Gerb & Soffen, without whose splendid efforts the manuscript would not have been prepared, and the staff of the Practising Law Institute without whose assiduous efforts the book would not have been published.

I

Statutory Provisions—Some Basic Principles

---

§ 1 The Statute

In the beginning, 35 U.S.C. § 112:[1]

The specification shall conclude with one or more claims particularly pointing out and distinctly claiming the subject matter which the applicant regards as his invention.

This is the fundamental rule, with which all others must be consistent. It was almost ever thus; the Patent Act of 1836, which started the modern examination system, provided that the applicant "shall also particularly specify and point out the part, improvement, or combination which he claims as his own invention or discovery."[2]

The statute presents two requirements: (1) set forth the subject matter; and (2) particularly point out and distinctly claim it.[3] The

---

1. This is the section of the basic patent statutes (title 35, United States Code) relating to the patent specification, including claims. Sections of the statutes and Patent Office Rules of Practice mentioned are reproduced in appendix D, parts I and II.
2. *See* W. ROBINSON, ROBINSON ON PATENTS §§ 504-38 (Hein 1st ed. 1972).
3. MPEP 2171. MPEP stands for a looseleaf book, *Manual of Patent Examining Procedure,* which is a Patent and Trademark Office publication setting forth detailed instructions to the examiners on almost every point that could arise in practice before the Patent and Trademark Office. Sections of the Manual cited in this book are reproduced as part III of appendix D. The Manual represents the official position or opinion of the Office on practically every point of law and procedure, and is continuously amended and supplemented as changes occur. Since the Manual normally operates

first requirement is subjective and even may change during prosecution of the application.[4] But once the subject matter is selected, the second requirement for that invention must be met.[5]

Under this very broad and general statutory directive, various rules and practices have grown up by case law, Commissioner's regulations, and custom since 1836 as to how and how not to fulfill the statutory mandate of *particularly pointing out and distinctly claiming.*

In general, this means that the claims must define "the invention," meaning the claimed subject matter, in such detail that the patent examiner and, later, the world of prospective infringers and judges who construe the claims can understand what the claimed subject matter is; that is, what is forbidden territory and what is open, insofar as the particular patent is concerned.

Summary

Patent claims must particularly point out and distinctly claim what applicant (usually, you, the patent practitioner) regards as his invention after reading this book.

§ 2 Omnibus Claims

All of the specific rules and tests must be derived from, or at least not be inconsistent with, the dominating statutory provision. For example, a first rule is that "omnibus" or formal claims are not permitted in utility patents.[6] Such claims as: "A device substantially as shown and described," or "the apparatus as shown and described in figures 1–6," or the classic and all encompassing: "Any and all features of novelty described, referred to, exempli-

---

as the examiner's bible, its mandates should be followed to the letter except where one is convinced that the Manual is wrong and one's client's interests are likely to be prejudiced. In that case an appeal (35 U.S.C. § 134) or petition to the Commissioner (rule 181) will usually be necessary, in effect to reverse the Manual. When that succeeds, the Manual is amended to reflect the change.

4. MPEP 2172.
5. MPEP 2171.
6. MPEP 1302.04(b) and 2173.05(r). Utility patents are patents other than designs (section 47) and plants (section 48).

fied, or shown," are not permitted in the United States, although they are allowed in some foreign countries. Obviously, these claims do not "particularly point out and distinctly claim" anything, certainly not the "invention." The examiner rejects such claims out of hand, as being "non-statutory."

The basic concept of United States claims is that the inventor owes the public a duty to define the forbidden territory of the patent in words as precise as the circumstances permit. Correspondingly, all features disclosed but not claimed are held to be dedicated to the public,[7] at least insofar as that patent is concerned.

A customary analogy is that the patentee must stake out the precise boundaries of his claim, in a manner similar to the description of the boundaries of a plot of land. For this reason United States claims are sometimes referred to as "peripheral" claims, meaning that the outer boundaries or periphery of the patentee's claim must be stated.

This concept of claim certainty is very useful to potential infringers, but often very hard on the patentee, because the real "essence of the invention" is sometimes not fully understood until many years later—when the somewhat different structure of the accused infringer is known and when the art of the pertinent field has become developed. The doctrine of equivalents, designed by the courts to permit a finding of infringement by an equivalent that differs insubstantially from the patent claim, diminishes the harshness of claim certainty.[8]

Summary

Claims must define the invention with certainty and in detail. Omnibus claims are not permitted in utility patents.

---

7. Not normally through benevolence on the part of the patentee, but merely because the patent becomes prior art against the inventor one year after patenting. 35 U.S.C. § 102(b); *In re* Gibbs, 168 U.S.P.Q. (BNA) 578 (C.C.P.A. 1971); *In re* Bauman, 214 U.S.P.Q. (BNA) 585, 589 (C.C.P.A. 1982); and *see* MPEP 706.03(s); and it becomes prior art against others as of its earliest effective filing date in the United States, under 35 U.S.C. § 102(e). This can include the date of an earlier United States application to which the patent is entitled under 35 U.S.C. § 120, but not the date of an earlier foreign application to which the patent is entitled under 35 U.S.C. § 119.
8. Hilton Davis Chem. Co. v. Warner Jenkinson Co., Inc., 35 U.S.P.Q.2d (BNA) 1641 (Fed. Cir. 1995), *rev'd on other grounds*, 117 S. Ct. 1040, 41 U.S.P.Q.2d (BNA) 1865 (1997).

§ 3   The Statutory Classes

The statute, 35 U.S.C. § 101, sets out four main categories of technical subject matter for which utility patents can be granted. These are "process, machine, [article of] manufacture, or composition of matter," usually termed "the statutory classes." Many of the claim drafting rules to follow stem from case law definitions of the words "process," "machine," "manufacture," and "composition of matter" in the statute. No matter how novel or how valuable an "invention" may be, it cannot be patented if it cannot be fit within one of those classes. Thus, such things as mathematical formulas, or algorithms (see section 44), printed matter, and articles found in nature have been held unpatentable because they are not within the classes set up by Congress. Computer programs or software and genetically engineered live organisms, animal and vegetable, i.e., "any invention made by man," are currently patentable under Patent and Trademark Office guidelines. (See sections 44 and 71.)

It had long been accepted that a method of doing business did not fall within one of the stautory classes. But that exception was laid to rest in *State Street Bank & Trust Co. v. Signature Financial Group Inc.,*[9] which held that the test for patentability of a business method is under §§ 102, 103, and 112, not § 101. If the method is novel and unobvious and does not simply appropriate an algorithm without transforming something, it can be properly claimed. This was confirmed in *AT&T Corp. v. Excel Communications, Inc.*[10] (See section 44A.)

This leads to a second fundamental rule, that a claim, no matter how beautifully drafted, must define the invention in such a way as to fit it into one or more of the statutory classes. (See section 60A hereof concerning claiming an invention in several classes.)

With these few basic principles in mind, the following chapter concerns some details and common practices for transforming inventions, generally, into claims, after which chapters III–VI in

---

9. State Street Bank & Trust Co. v. Signature Financial Group, Inc., 149 F.3d 1368, 47 U.S.P.Q.2d (BNA) 1596, 1602-04 (Fed. Cir. 1998), *cert. denied*, 119 S. Ct. 851 (1999).

10. AT&T Corp. v. Excel Communications, Inc., 172 F.3d 1352, 50 U.S.P.Q.2d (BNA) 1447 (Fed. Civ. 1999).

turn cover particular problems encountered in the four statutory classes.

Summary

Claims must fit within the "statutory classes" of patentable subject matter, as construed by court decisions. For utility patents, these classes are machine, process, (article of) manufacture, and composition of matter. Ornamental designs and certain agricultural plants are separate statutory classes with different rules (sections 47–48).

II

Claim Forms and Formats in General

§ 4 Placement After Specification

35 U.S.C. § 112 and 37 C.F.R. § 75(a)[1] provide that the "specification shall conclude with one or more claims. . . ." Claims are placed after the specification. The practice in some countries is for the claims to precede the specification. But that is not good form for the United States. (The Patent and Trademark Office accepts and examines claims that precede the specification. But avoid that where possible.)

§ 4A Single Sentence

The only known (or at least acceptable) way so far to "particularly point out and distinctly claim" an invention in a statutory class is by means of an English sentence. This is unfortunate, because many of the problems in claim drafting stem from problems in writing English and in the meanings of words.

To begin at the beginning, the standard custom as to sentence construction is that each claim must be the direct object of a single sentence, however long, beginning with a standard introductory phrase such as "I [or We] claim," "The invention claimed is," or the equivalent. (See MPEP 608.01(m).) In an application with

---

1. The rules governing patent applications are codified in Title 37 of the Code of Federal Regulations. References herein are to "rule. . . ."

more than one claim, the introductory phrase, such as "I claim," appears only once, before the first claim.

Standard Office practice also is to insist that each claim begin with a capital or upper case letter and end with a period, so that each claim reads as a complete sentence when taken with the introductory words, e.g., "I claim," "We claim," "The invention claimed is" (preceeding examples suggested in MPEP 608.01(m)), or "what is claimed is," or the equivalent language. Except for such standard capitalization as °C.,[2] no other capital letters may appear in the body of the claim. See MPEP 608.01(m). For example:

> I claim: A pencil having an eraser fastened to one end.

The above claim is to illustrate layout and form only, not as an example of patentable subject matter. (A different claim to such a combination was held unpatentable by the Supreme Court in *Reckendorfer v. Faber*, cited and discussed in section 64 on Aggregation.)

In connection with the single sentence rule, it is important to watch grammar, particularly verb forms, to make sure the claim reads as a complete sentence. For example, "I claim: A pencil *comprises* . . . [parts A and B][3]" does not form a complete sentence. However, the generally standard phaseology, "I claim: A pencil *comprising* . . . [parts A and B]" does form a sentence.

This is sometimes troublesome in long, complicated claims with many elements, subelements, and intricate relationships between elements; in dependent claims (section 11); and in *Jepson* claims (section 57). Therefore, you should select a verb style, e.g., gerund ("ing"), third person ("es"), and use it consistently throughout each entire claim. You can switch verb styles between claims, if you wish.

Also, where possible, the verb form in a claim is preferably in the present tense, unless a past or future event is being described.

Summary

Make sure the claim forms a complete sentence forming the direct object of the phrase "I claim." Begin each claim with a capital letter and end it with a period.

---

2. Modern practice does not use a period in °C.
3. Letters ("A," "B," etc.) conventionally stand for the "elements" of the claims, such as "pencil" and "eraser" in the above example.

§ 5 Numbering and Order

Section 112 of the statute, on utility patents, provides that the "specification shall conclude with one or more claims. . . ." In design patents (section 47) and plant patents (section 48) only one claim is permitted. Almost always, more than one claim is submitted in a utility patent application. (Sometimes only one claim is allowed by the examiner, and one is lucky to obtain that one.)

When only one claim is presented, no numeral is used, as in the above example to the pencil. When more than one claim is submitted, each claim must start with an Arabic numeral (rule 75(f)). The claims must be numbered consecutively, and good practice dictates that the claims be grouped and numbered in a logical order for consideration (rule 75(f)). The usual practice is to begin with the broadest claim and proceed to the narrowest, and to group similar types of claims together.

As to preferred order, MPEP 608.01(m) provides:

> Claims should preferably be arranged in order of scope so that the first claim presented is the broadest. Where separate species are claimed, the claims of like species should be grouped together where possible and physically separated by drawing a line between claims or groups of claims. . . . Similarly, product and process claims should be separately grouped.

In view of this, as well as general good sense, the claims should be grouped in what the claim writer thinks is the most logical order for consideration. The practice occasionally seen of trying to slip in an unusually broad claim, e.g., as claim seventeen out of nineteen claims, is condemnable. For a discussion of how generic, subgeneric, and species are to be grouped, see section 58.

Special rules apply to the number of certain dependent claims (see section 11).

How many claims may be presented and how different they must be from each other are discussed in sections 60–62. For an *example of a complete claims layout:*

I claim:

1. A pencil having. . . .

2. A pencil as recited in claim I, wherein . . . [more detail].

3. A pencil comprising . . . [the most detailed combination acceptable to the applicant].

A claim number is not reused. If a claim is cancelled, its claim number is not reused in that patent application. Added claims receive the next number in sequence after the last claim. Claims are not renumbered during application prosecution. (At conclusion of prosecution, the claims are renumbered by the Patent Office for the patent to be printed.)

Summary

Present multiple claims in a logical order and number them consecutively.

§ 6 Preamble

Claims should have "preambles," or introductory statements, the purposes of which are to indicate the statutory class of the claim (often by implication from the words in the preamble) and to name or define the thing that is to be claimed. It defines the field of the invention claimed. Preambles may be quite long or very short, depending on the type of claim one is using, but a shorter preamble is preferred. For example, in *Karsten Manufacturing Corp. v. Cleveland Golf Co.*,[3.1] the patent claims all recited "an improved correlated set of iron-type golf-clubs." The court held that "correlated set" was a claim limitation, although it appeared only in the preamble. It appears that it was an unessential limitation for patentability. Had it been omitted, the claim would have been broader.

The best type of preamble for most claims is simply a general-definition of the combination to be claimed, with whatever detail or length is necessary to define what appears in the body of the claim. The preamble and the body of the claim should be consistent one with the other, two parts making up a whole. The preamble cannot be written properly until the scope of the claim-to-be is determined, and the preamble should be checked for consistency after the claim has been finished. When a claim is revised or

---

3.1. Karsten Manufacturing Corp. v. Cleveland Golf Co., 242 F.3d 1376, 58 U.S.P.Q.2d (BNA) 1286, 1288 (Fed. Cir. 2001).

amended, the preamble should be scrutinized for consistency. As to the effect of limitations in the preamble, see below and also see section 56, on new use claims; preamble limitations.

One of the best sources for the claim preamble is the title of the invention at the head of the specification. Sometimes that title is modified to conform to the claim preamble. The title of the invention is typically short, and so should be the preamble. But if the claim is to an element or a subcombination of a fuller invention, using the title as the preamble could cause the preamble to be misleading as too encompassing. Further, where the title differs from the claim preamble, the title does not define the claimed invention, as it would be reading a limitation from the specification into the claim.[3.2]

To avoid a too limited scope preamble, the claim writer might be tempted to merely recite the broad "Apparatus comprising" or use "device" or a similar non-specific noun. But, a too broad scope preamble is also not good practice, although not improper. Also, the examiner will likely require that a preamble more descriptive of the invention be substituted.

The preamble should focus on the actual subject or field of the invention and not cover too broad a field, if inapplicable. For an invention in a bicycle, for example, a preamble that says "vehicle" would appear to be of broader scope than a preamble that says "bicycle." Yet, if the invention is clearly directed to a bicycle, there is no benefit to having a preamble "vehicle" which is more encompassing than the invention itself. The preamble should be realistically narrow in scope. Conversely, if the preamble says "bicycle," but the invention is adaptable not only for bicycles but for motorcycles, and if an infringer were later to market a product which had all of the feature limitations in the claim, but which was a motorcycle rather than a bicycle, the infringer might argue that the claim does not reach the accused product because the claim is limited in scope to a bicycle. The preamble must be sufficiently broad to cover the product in the preferred embodiment to which the inventor has directed his attention (bicycle), but also to

---

3.2. Pitney Bowes Inc. v. Hewlett-Packard Inc., 182 F.3d 1298, 51 U.S.P.Q.2d (BNA) 1161 (Fed. Cir. 1999).

cover other embodiments, as "two-wheeled vehicles," to which the invention may be directed.

In general, one should avoid any unnecessary limitations or statements anywhere in the broader claims, even in the preamble. Some practitioners briefly describe an object of the invention in a preamble ("Apparatus for shaking articles to dislodge impurities"). This is unnecessary, however, as the preamble is preferably a short introduction to the body of the claim. Also, there may be other objects of the invention, and recitation of one may impliedly exclude accomplishment of others when the claim is later interpreted.

Where the invention operates upon a workpiece, some practitioners include relevant details of the workpiece in the preamble ("Apparatus for shaking articles having a soft covering over a plurality of frangible legs . . ."). Usually, description of the workpiece in the preamble is not needed. Instead, as a particular element of the apparatus acts upon the workpiece, the relevant interaction of the element upon the workpiece is described in the body of the claim, and possibly in a "whereby" clause. Sometimes, however, it is appropriate to describe the workpiece somewhat fully in the preamble as it may not otherwise be easy to comprehend the rest of the claim. In that case, the better choice is to have the fuller preamble. An example of an overlong preamble that may have confused the Board of Appeals somewhat appears in *In re Stencel.*[4]

On the other hand, the preamble may have to be longer because, in order to understand an invention, one must understand its context. Therefore, sometimes the purpose of the invention is recited in the preamble before the transition word, as in "Apparatus for treating a web to prevent tearing, the apparatus comprising. . . ."[4.1] The title of the invention at the head of the specification may be slightly different, but there is no short claim preamble that does the job.

In composition of matter claims, where the composition may have no recognized name, it may be necessary to describe certain qualities or features of the composition in the preamble in order to clearly explain or understand the elements in the following body of the claim, e.g., "A composition having a density of x and a color y

---

4. *In re* Stencel, 4 U.S.P.Q.2d (BNA) 1071 (Fed. Cir. 1987).

4.1. *See* Heidelberg Harris, Inc. v. Mitsubishi Heavy Industries, Ltd., 56 U.S.P.Q.2d (BNA) 1714, 1719 (Fed. Cir. 2000) (labeled unpublished); Pitney Bowes, Inc. v. Hewlett-Packard Co., 182 F.3d 1298, 1305, 51 U.S.P.Q.2d (BNA) 1161, 1165–66 (Fed. Cir. 1999).

with a brightness level not less than z, comprising material a, at least 10% of material b and material c." The elements of the composition are better understood with a fuller preamble. But the specifics in the preamble, between "composition" and "comprising," may alternately be included in a functional or "whereby" clause placed after the elements are recited in the body of the claim.

A statement of the purpose of the invention in the preamble will be nonlimiting, as in "A method *for reducing hematologic toxicity in a cancer patient*," because it states a purpose and the claim can be infringed even if the purpose was not always achieved.[4.2]

Long preambles mentioning elements other than the invention itself may make what the subsequent transition word refers to ambiguous (see next section). For example, in "Apparatus for shaking articles to dislodge impurities comprising . . ." clearly, the transition word "comprising" refers back to the apparatus, not the impurities. For clarity, the preamble should repeat the key word of the name of the invention in the preamble before the transition word, as "Apparatus for shaking articles to dislodge impurities, the apparatus comprising. . . ."

With the prevalence of the use of dependent claims, any dependent claim should usually cover the same invention as its preceding or parent claim. If the independent claim begins "Apparatus for shaking articles," a following dependent claim should not claim a different apparatus, e.g., "A device for containing articles to be shaken, as recited in claim 1, comprising. . . ." A dependent claim includes all of the text of its preceding claims. The dependent claim just described, however, appears to claim a different invention than or less than all of the invention of its preceding claim. Hence, a dependent claim should have the preamble of the previous claim upon which it is dependent, "The apparatus for shaking articles of Claim 1. . . ." If the previous claim is to "bicycle," the dependent claim should not be to "vehicle." Change one or the other claim for consistency.

Often the preamble of a dependent claim is shortened to the key word or words, e.g., the noun, of the preamble of its preceeding independent claim ("The apparatus of Claim 1"). As long as that leaves no ambiguity, the shortened preamble is even preferred.

4.2. Bristol-Myers Squibb Co. v. Ben Venue Laboratories, Inc., 246 F.3d 1368, 58, U.S.P.Q.2d (BNA) 1508, 1513 (Fed. Cir. 2001).

Claims of different scope are often used to describe different aspects of an entire invention, a combination and a subcombination, a genus and a species, etc. A different preamble may be used for each different claim grouping: "Apparatus for shaking articles . . ." and "Device for containing articles to be shaken. . . ." Just make each different invention or aspect of one invention subject to separate claims, each group of claims with a separate preamble.

Jepson claims under rule 75(e) have a different type of preamble, which is rather lengthy (see section 57). It includes a name of the invention and then recites the elements of that complete apparatus, process, composition, or article that is in the prior art (MPEP 608.01(m)). This is a special situation. Because the preamble of a *Jepson* claim recites elements of a claimed invention, and defines not only the context of the invention, but also its scope, a limitation which appears only at the start of the preamble is considered a claim element.[5]

The preamble is often the basis used by the Patent and Trademark Office to assign the application to a particular Examining Art Unit for review of and action on the application. Preferably, the preamble describes the field of the invention to correctly guide the invention classifiers when the application is filed and initially assigned to an Art Unit. Furthermore, the preamble defines the scope of relevant prior art. Accuracy in the preamble is recommended.

Some case precedents suggest that the content of the preamble does not limit the scope of the claim. However, in *Bell Communications Research, Inc. v. Vitalink Communications Corp.*,[6] the court said that the determination is made with reference to the specific claim and there found the preamble element limiting.

MPEP 2111.02 says that the preamble is not given the effect of a limitation unless it breathes life and meaning into the claim. Phraseology in the preamble that limits the structure must be given weight. See the cases discussed in that section of the Manual.[7]

The Federal Circuit recently restated the rule: "[T]he preamble simply states the intended use or purpose of the invention. . . .

---

5. Rowe v. Dror, 42 U.S.P.Q.2d (BNA) 1550, 1553 (Fed. Cir. 1997).
6. Bell Communications Research, Inc. v. Vitalink Communications Corp., 55 F.3d 615, 34 U.S.P.Q.2d (BNA) 1816 (Fed. Cir. 1995).
7. *See also* Corning Glass Works v. Sumitomo Electric U.S.A., Inc., 868 F.2d 1251, 1257, 9 U.S.P.Q.2d (BNA) 1962 (Fed. Cir. 1989); *In re* Burke, Inc., 786 F. Supp. 1537, 22 U.S.P.Q.2d (BNA) 1368, 1371 (C.D. Cal. 1992).

Such a preamble usually does not limit the scope of the claim unless the preamble provides antecedents for ensuing claim terms and limits the claim accordingly."[8] In *Bard*, the preamble provided antecedents by reciting the structure into which needles fit, and the claim was not anticipated or obvious over prior art, which lacked the preamble features. The preamble features saved the claim validity, but those same elements narrow the scope of the claim to be asserted against infringements.

In *Pitney Bowes, Inc. v. Hewlett-Packard Co.,*[9] the intended purpose of the invention stated in the preamble as "producing on a photoreceptor an image of generated shapes made up of spots" was held not to be a mere statement of intended field of use, but was so intimately meshed with the remaining claim language that the preamble and the remainder of the claim were to be construed as one unified internally consistent recitation of the invention.

There is nothing to gain by having an overlong preamble, with many elements recited. Each may become a claim limitation which a later copyist could avoid using.

Recommended preambles for different types of claims are set out in subsequent parts of this book.

Summary

Use descriptive preambles defining the nature of the combination claimed. Do not put unnecessary limitations even in the preamble. Assume every word you write in a claim is critical, and may some day be used against your client, to restrict the scope of his invention.

---

8. C.R. Bard, Inc. v. M3 Systems, Inc., 157 F.3d 1340, 48 U.S.P.Q.2d (BNA) 1225, 1230–31 (Fed Cir. 1998), *rehearing denied*, 161 F.3d 1380, 49 U.S.P.Q.2d (BNA) 1319 (Fed. Cir. 1998), *cert. denied*, 119 S. Ct. 1804 (1999). *See* Gerber Garment Tech, Inc. v. Lectra Sys., Inc., 916 F.2d 683, 688-89, 16 U.S.P.Q.2d (BNA) 1436, 1441 (Fed. Cir. 1990); Heidelberg Harris, Inc. v. Mitsubishi Heavy Industries, Ltd., 56 U.S.P.Q.2d (BNA) 1714, 1719–20 (Fed. Cir. 2000) (labeled unpublished).
9. Pitney Bowes, Inc. v. Hewlett-Packard Co., 182 F.3d 1298, 51 U.S.P.Q.2d (BNA) 1161 (Fed. Cir. 1999).

§ 7   Transition from Preamble to Body— "Comprising"

Most ordinary combination claims require a transitional word or phrase between the preamble (naming the thing to be claimed) and the body of the claim (defining what the elements or parts of the thing are). Two recommended forms of transition that can be employed for most claims are the phrases: "which comprises" or "comprising." The choice between the two is immaterial.

The word "comprises" has been construed to mean, in patent law, "including the following elements but not excluding others."[10] The claim is "open," not "closed."[11] Additional elements in an accused device or method do not avoid such an open claim.[11.1] Other words, less often used, have been given the same meaning in patent claim interpretation as "comprising": "including,"[12] "hav-

---

10. MPEP 2111.03; Moleculon Research Corp. v. CBS, Inc., 229 U.S.P.Q. (BNA) 805, 812 (Fed. Cir. 1986).

11. MPEP 2111.03; Burke, Inc. v. Everest & Jennings, Inc., 991 F.2d 812, 29 U.S.P.Q.2d (BNA) 1393, 1397 (Fed. Cir. 1993) (unpublished); Special Metals Corp. v. Teledyne Indus., Inc., 219 U.S.P.Q. (BNA) 953 (4th Cir. 1983); Air Prods. & Chems., Inc., v. Chas. S. Tanner Co., 219 U.S.P.Q. (BNA) 223 (D.S.D. 1983); *In re* Certain Slide Fastener Stringers, 216 U.S.P.Q. (BNA) 907 (U.S. Int. Tr. Comm. 1981). A patent claim "which uses the term 'comprising,' is an 'open' claim which will read on devices which add additional elements. . . ." Carl Zeiss Stiftung v. Renishaw PLC, 945 F.2d 1173, 20 U.S.P.Q.2d (BNA) 1094 (Fed. Cir. 1991); Abtox, Inc. v. Exitron Corp., 43 U.S.P.Q.2d (BNA) 1545, 1548 (Fed. Cir. 1997), *modified on other grounds,* 46 U.S.P.Q.2d (BNA) 1735 (Fed. Cir. 1997); Genentech, Inc. v. Chiron Corp., 112 F.3d 495, 501, 42 U.S.P.Q.2d (BNA) 1608, 1613 (Fed. Cir. 1997); *see also* T.J. Smith and Nephew Ltd. v. Parke, Davis & Co., 871 F.2d 1098, 10 U.S.P.Q.2d (BNA) 1946 (Fed. Cir. 1989); Berenter v. Quigg, 737 F. Supp. 5, 14 U.S.P.Q.2d (BNA) 1175 (D.D.C. 1988); Vehicular Technologies Corp. v. Titan Wheel International Inc., 212 F.3d 1377, 54 U.S.P.Q.2d (BNA) 1841 (Fed. Cir. 2000).

11.1. Dow Chemical Co. v. Sumitomo Chemical Co., ___ F.3d ___, 59 U.S.P.Q.2d (BNA) 1609, 1620 (Fed. Cir. 2001); Vivid Tech, Inc. v. American Science & Engineering, Inc., 200 F.3d 795, 811, 53 U.S.P.Q.2d (BNA) 1289, 1301 (Fed. Cir. 1999).

12. *In re* Certain Slide Fastener Stringers, 216 U.S.P.Q. (BNA) 907 (U.S. Int. Tr. Comm. 1981); Burke, Inc. v. Everest & Jennings, Inc., 991 F.2d 812, 29 U.S.P.Q.2d (BNA) 1393, 1397 (Fed. Cir. 1993) (unpublished).

ing,"[13] "containing," and even "wherein."[14] However, "comprising" is recommended simply because it has become a standardized word of the patent art.

Lampi Corp. v. American Power Products, Inc.[14.1] illustrates the risk a claim writer takes by using a word, here "having" rather than "comprising," as an open-ended transition word. The court spent much time analyzing the specification to see if the word "having" was open-ended in a claim. The court also relied on a dependent claim that used the word "comprising" as a basis for finding the "having" in the parent claim open-ended. So, why take a risk in claiming? The Federal Circuit yet again construed "having,"[14.2] saying that word does not presumptively "open" the body of the claim. It is not as strongly open a word as "comprising." The court therefore had to examine the claim in context to determine the limits of "having."

For example, a claim to "A writing implement *comprising* a pencil with an eraser fastened at one end" covers any type of eraser-tipped pencil: wood, mechanical, etc.; with or without a clip to hook it in one's pocket; and whether or not additional features or additions are patentable to later inventors. Thus, in patent shorthand, "the combination comprising A+B (individual elements or parts)" covers A+B+C . . . or A+B′ (a variation of element B falling under the claim definition). In general, the technique of writing broad claims is to claim the minimum number of elements that will function in the combination, each defined as broadly as the prior art and claim drafting doctrines will allow. In that manner, the main "point of the invention," or "inventive concept,"[15]

---

13. *In re* Certain Slide Fastener Stringers, 216 U.S.P.Q. (BNA) 907 (U.S. Int. Tr. Comm. 1981); Compro-Frank Corp. v. Valk Mfg. Co., 216 U.S.P.Q. (BNA) 531 (E.D. Pa. 1982). *But see* Lampi Corp. v. American Power Products, Inc., 228 F.3d 1365, 56 U.S.P.Q.2d (BNA) 1445, 1453–54 (Fed. Cir. 2000).

14. *Ex parte* Grasselli, 231 U.S.P.Q. (BNA) 395 (Bd. App. 1983).

14.1. Lampi Corp. v. American Power Products, Inc., 228 F.3d 1365, 56 U.S.P.Q.2d (BNA) 1445 (Fed. Cir. 2000).

14.2. Crystal Semiconductor Corp. v. TriTech Microelectronics International, Inc., ___ F.3d ___, 57 U.S.P.Q.2d (BNA) 1953, 1958–59 (Fed. Cir. 2001).

15. Note, some attorneys sometimes speak loosely of "the invention," meaning the point of novelty or inventive concept, rather than merely the technical subject matter to be patented, as the word "invention" is defined in the statute. This double or triple meaning for the word "invention" is confusing and should be avoided.

should be crystallized in concrete terms.

However, despite use of "comprising" as the transition, a claim can be interpreted such that all of the elements of one type have a claimed characteristic, although the claim recites that a plurality of those elements have that characteristic—suggesting to the patent owner that some of those elements in an accused product may lack that characteristic yet still be within the claim.[16]

Some form of the word "comprise" is practically always used for mechanical or method combination claims.

Although the foregoing discussion was directed at transitions following a preamble, it applies to transitional phrases throughout a claim, wherein any claim element is defined as comprising other elements.

Summary

Use the transition "comprising" or "which comprises" except in very unusual cases.

§ 8   "Consisting"—"Consisting Essentially Of"

Other transitions have more limited meanings. They are used primarily in chemical cases, where the art or other reason requires limitation.

"Consisting" or "consisting of," especially in a mechanical claim, means that the claim covers devices having the recited elements, and no more or no less,[17] and in method claims, means that the process has only the recited steps.[18] Other words may be

---

16. Texas Instruments, Inc. v. International Trade Commission, 26 U.S.P.Q.2d (BNA) 1018, 1024 (Fed. Cir. 1993).

17. MPEP 2111.03; *In re* Certain Slide Fastener Stringers, 216 U.S.P.Q. (BNA) 907 (U.S. Int. Tr. Comm. 1981); *Ex parte* Grasselli, 231 U.S.P.Q. (BNA) 395 (Bd. App. 1983); Vehicular Technologies Corp. v. Titan Wheel International Inc., 212 F.3d 1377, 54 U.S.P.Q.2d (BNA) 1841 (Fed. Cir. 2000). In *Vehicular Technologies*, the claim recited consisted of two springs, the accused device had one spring and a range of equivalents was restricted by the transition word.

18. Special Metals Corp. v. Teledyne Indus., Inc., 219 U.S.P.Q. (BNA) 953 (4th Cir. 1983).

similarly closed ended, like "composed of," "having,"[18.1] or "being." But that is not automatic and whether each is closed or open ended must be interpreted in light of the specification.[19] (In this author's opinion, "having" is an open ended word.) "Consisting of"—in chemical claims, the term excludes more than traces of other ingredients.[20] One sees greater use of "closed" claims with "consisting of" as the transition because chemical combinations are not predictable, and the addition of an element to a chemical combination could change the characteristics of the combination as they relate to the invention.

In a *Markush* grouping of elements, primarily used in chemical claims, the term "consisting of" is used to introduce the *Markush* group (see section 50).

"'Consisting essentially of' occupies a middle ground between 'closed' claims that are written in a 'consisting of' format and fully open claims that are drafted in a 'comprising' format."[21]

"Consisting essentially of" excludes other elements from having any essential significance to the combination, that is, it allows some "reading on" additional unspecified substances,[22] i.e., those which do not materially affect the basic and novel characteristics of the claimed invention.[23] Although "consisting essentially of" is typically used for compositions, it may also be used for method steps.[24] "Constituting" has the same meaning in claims as "consisting."[25]

For example, in *In re Garnero*,[26] the C.C.P.A. ruled that the phrase "consisting essentially of" excludes "additional unspeci-

---

18.1. *Cf.* Lampi Corp. v. American Power Products, Inc., 228 F.3d 1365, 56 U.S.P.Q.2d (BNA) 1445, 1453 (Fed. Cir. 2000).

19. MPEP 2111.03.

20. *Ex parte* Grasselli, 231 U.S.P.Q. (BNA) 395 (Bd. App. 1983).

21. PPG Indus., Inc. v. Guardian Ind. Corp., 156 F.3d 1351, 48 U.S.P.Q.2d (BNA) 1351, 1353–54 (Fed. Cir. 1998).

22. Special Metals Corp. v. Teledyne Indus., Inc., 219 U.S.P.Q. (BNA) 953 (4th Cir. 1983); Dow Chem. Co. v. American Cyanamid Co., 229 U.S.P.Q. (BNA) 171, 180 (E.D. La. 1985).

23. MPEP 2111.03; PPG Indus., Inc. v. Guardian Ind. Corp., 156 F.3d 1351, 48 U.S.P.Q.2d (BNA) 1351, 1353–54 (Fed. Cir. 1998); BASF Corp. v. Eastman Chem. Co., ____ F.3d ____, 56 U.S.P.Q.2d (BNA) 1396, 1404 (D. Del. 1998).

24. MPEP 2111.03.

25. American Original Corp. v. Jenkins Food Corp., 216 U.S.P.Q. (BNA) 945 (4th Cir. 1982).

26. *In re* Garnero, 162 U.S.P.Q. (BNA) 221, 223 (C.C.P.A. 1969).

fied ingredients which would affect the basic and novel characteristics of the product defined in the balance of the claim."[27] These meanings were discussed by the Patent Office Board of Appeals in *Ex parte Davis*[28] as a "code" adopted by a group of primary examiners for their guidance. These meanings are now quite stylized in the patent law. "Composed of," one might have thought, is the same as "consisting of." But the Federal Circuit, quoting MPEP 2110.03, interprets "composed of" as "consisting essentially of," which is slightly open-ended.[28.1]

These more limited claims are spoken of as "closed" or "closed ended,"[29] because other elements or other material elements are excluded from the combination.[29.1] Of course, "consisting" should be avoided in the broader claims wherever possible as it is severely limiting. The test of when "consisting essentially" is required instead of the broad "comprising" is not clear.

Other, hybrid phraseologies may be acceptable as having a scope somewhere between "comprising" and "consisting essentially." For example, *Natta et al.* patent 3,112,301 has a claim that reads, "consists prevailingly but not essentially of. . . ."

In *Ziegler v. Phillips Petroleum Co.*,[30] the court on specific facts held that "consisting essentially" permitted material additions so long as the "consisting essentially" ingredients were "necessarily present," and the composition with the additions still used the "real invention."[31]

---

27. Water Technologies Corp. v. Calco Ltd., 7 U.S.P.Q.2d (BNA) 1097, 1102 (Fed. Cir. 1988); *In re* Herz, 190 U.S.P.Q. (BNA) 461, 463 (C.C.P.A. 1976).

28. *Ex parte* Davis, 80 U.S.P.Q. (BNA) 448 (Bd. App. 1948).

28.1. AFG Industries, Inc. v. Cardinal IG Co., 239 F.3d 1239, 57 U.S.P.Q.2d (BNA) 1776, 1780–81 (Fed. Cir. 2001).

29. MPEP 2111.03; *In re* Certain Slide Fastener Stringers, 216 U.S.P.Q. (BNA) 907 (U.S. Int. Tr. Comm. 1981); Special Metals Corp. v. Teledyne Indus., Inc., 219 U.S.P.Q. (BNA) 953 (4th Cir. 1983).

29.1. In Vehicular Technologies Corp. v. Titan Wheel International Inc., 212 F.3d 1377, 54 U.S.P.Q.2d (BNA) 1841 (Fed. Cir. 2000), the claim recited "consisting of" two springs. Although the doctrine of equivalents still applied, the scope of equivalents was greatly narrowed by the use of "consisting of."

30. Ziegler v. Phillips Petroleum Co., 177 U.S.P.Q. (BNA) 481 (5th Cir. 1973).

31. *See* MPEP 2111.03.

Summary

Do not use the expressions "consisting" or "consisting essentially" unless the examiner requires them or where additional elements would not ever be expected with the claimed combination, as in a particular composition of matter. They are usually used in chemical cases due to the unpredictability of adding a new element to a chemical combination.

§ 9 Body of the Claim

The body of a combination claim, meaning the part that follows the preamble and the transitional phrase, comprises:

    a. a recitation of the "elements" of parts of the combination; and

    b. a description of how the elements cooperate with one another structurally, physically, or functionally, to make up the operative combination recited in the preamble. Where no mode of cooperation among any element and any of the other elements is described, the claim is not to a combination, is at best to an aggregation, and is improper in form.

The body of the claim is written in narrative expository prose, following the single sentence rule. The claim must be limited to a description of the technical subject matter, and surplus or laudatory statements, such as "novel," are not permitted, nor are statements of objects or advantages. Thus a claim to "A combination steam and dry iron comprising [A, B, and C], thus to iron clothes more effectively than heretofore" would be objectionable because of its last clause.

In terms of English grammar, the body of a combination claim is a series: A and B; A, B, and C; etc. The letters A, B, and C conventionally stand for the "elements" of the claim, by which is meant the main structures, steps, parts, or ingredients that form the machine, process, article of manufacture, or composition of matter recited in the preamble. See, for example, claim 1 in chapter 3.

In the rare case of a single element claim (as distinguished from a combination claim), the single element, be it a mechanism, step, article or composition, is merely described (see, for example, claim 5 in section 42). Note also the prohibition against single "means" claims, discussed in section 34, where the only element of the claim is means performing a function. Since practically all claims are to combinations of one sort or another, this book will deal primarily with combination claims except where specifically noted.

Of course, clear and intelligible wording should be used in describing the elements and how they cooperate or function, to make sure the claim "particularly points out" the invention and "distinctly claims" it (section 1). Avoid "ambiguities, vague or clumsy expressions, and unnecessary repetition of language." This latter advice is from the Patent and Trademark Office's guidelines in reviewing claims written by applicants for admission to practice before the Patent and Trademark Office in a written examination known as the Agent's Exam.

Summary

The body of the claim lists the main elements of the combination (parts, steps, chemicals, etc.) and tells how they work together or are related to each other. Most claims are directed to combinations of two or more elements. Stick to technical description, and eschew unnecessary, redundant, surplus, and any laudatory statements. Tell what the invention is, not how good it is. The claim must be readily understandable, and clear as to what it covers.

§ 10 Format and Punctuation; Subparagraph Form

Since a combination claim is a grammatical series, if three or more elements (A, B, and C) are described, which coincide with the clauses of the series, they must be set off by commas at least. Even with two element claims, punctuation should be used unless the first element contains very few words, so that it is clear where the description of the second element starts. As in any writings, semicolons should be used to set off the clauses whenever one or more of the clauses contains internal punctuation. Other punctuation, such as parentheses (except for reference numerals, MPEP 608.01(m)), dashes, etc., is not ordinarily needed or used in claims, although there is no reason expressed in the rules or in the manual why such techniques should not be used in appropriate cases.

The single paragraph form of claim (see claim 1A, section 14), with commas between the elements and no indentation, letters, or numerals to identify the elements, is the form that was used almost exclusively by practitioners in the past. It is still accepted by the Patent and Trademark Office, and may be preferable for very simple claims, such as a five-line claim with only two or three elements.

Because claims are often complex and difficult to follow, various other formats are being widely used today to make claims easier to follow and understand. The Patent and Trademark Office is known to favor most such attempts at clarity, and therefore it is recommended that some format other than a single paragraph be adopted.

One such format, the subparagraph or tabular form, is strongly favored by the Patent and Trademark Office and is recommended for most if not all claims (see MPEP 608.01(m)). Even further indentations within a subparagraph, like subsubparagraphs, are recommended in MPEP 608.01(m) to further segregate subcombination or related steps (see claim 1, section 14). This form actually helps the apprentice claim drafter, since it is easier to use and he is less likely to make mistakes in recognizing and setting out the elements of the claim. In the subparagraph form, the first word of each element, or main clause, of the claim is indented so as to distinguish clearly between each of the claimed elements.

The examples of claims in this book use versions of the subparagraph form.

Preferably, each new major claim element and subassembly is made the subject of its subparagraph. A major claim element may, in turn, be comprised of a number of other claim elements. Those other claim elements may be or need not be the subject of separate subparagraphs, as the claim drafter decides.

The colon-semicolon form, in which a colon is inserted after the transitional phrase and semicolons are used between the elements, as in claim 1, is also recommended, particularly with subparagraph claims.

Another form, termed the "outline form," involves using identifying letters, (a), (b), (c), as in an outline, before the recitation of each element, or main clause, whether or not the subparagraph form is used, Although this technique is helpful, and is recommended if the subparagraph form is not used, it ordinarily adds little to comprehension where the subparagraph form is used. Wherever the claim drafter believes letters would help in understanding the claim, particularly in complex claims, they should be used. Sometimes letters may help in referring back to elements of previous claims. For example, given a method comprising steps (a) through (e), one might refer in a dependent claim to performing an added step "after step (c)." Finally, a period (.) appears only at the end of the claim.

Summary

Use the subparagraph form for claims. Make claims as easy as possible for readers to understand and to follow what the elementsare. The examiner will appreciate it, as well as everyone else who ever reads the patent.

§ 11 Dependent Claims

Rule 75(c) defines a dependent claim:

> One or more claims may be presented in dependent form, referring back to and further limiting another claim or claims in the same application. . . . Claims in dependent form shall be construed to include all the limitations of the claim incorporated by reference into the dependent claim.

This is the single dependent claim with which practitioners are most familiar. Examples include:

The shaker of claim 1, wherein . . .

The shaker according to claim 1, wherein . . .

A shaker as claimed in claim 1, wherein . . .

The shaker as in claim 1, in which . . .

The words used to establish claim dependency in the preamble of the claim are a matter of choice, so long as the dependency of the claim is clearly set forth.

What is a dependent claim is further detailed in MPEP 608.01(n):

The test as to whether a claim is a proper dependent claim is that it shall include every limitation of the claim from which it depends (35 U.S.C. 112, fourth paragraph) or in other words that it shall not conceivably be infringed by anything which would not also infringe the basic claim.

This is the "infringement test" to determine if a claim is dependent.

Omission from a purported dependent claim of any element that had been included in the preceding claim makes the additional claim not a dependent claim. Thus, if a preceding claim has features A, B, and C, and a subsequent claim replaces feature C with feature D, so that the subsequent claim has features A, B and D, then the latter claim could not be a dependent claim, but could only be written in the form of an independent claim. For the fullest claim coverage of an invention, or if an invention includes several features whose inclusions are mutually exclusive (you can include one without having to include the other), it is preferable to add an independent claim, rather than try to somehow provide coverage through a dependent claim only. The latter claim could not refer to or incorporate the previous claims.

A dependent claim incorporates by reference everything in the parent claim,[32] and adds some further statements, limitations or restrictions. The statements added may be (1) one or more additional elements, (2) a further description or limitation of one or more of the elements of the parent claim, or (3) both.

Dependent claims enable the practitioner to thoroughly cover each invention. At least some of the independent claims should be the broadest in scope, with the least detail in their limitations. Dependent claims are used to add additional features and/or to expand upon and to detail previously claimed features. A dependent claim can only add a new element to a claim or modify and further define an element that is already present in a claim. Hence, a de-

---

32. MPEP 608.01(n).

pendent claim is narrower in scope than the claim upon which it is dependent.[32.1]

A dependent claim cannot subtract an element from a claim on which it is dependent. You cannot claim "The device of claim 3, without the shaft connected between the motor and the gear." To delete an element from one claim, a new claim is needed. That new claim may be an independent claim reciting all elements, but not reciting the element to be deleted. Alternatively, that new claim may be a dependent claim, not dependent upon the claim that had the element (shaft) which is to be deleted, but rather dependent upon an earlier claim which did not mention that deleted element, e.g., one where no shaft had been mentioned.

When an independent claim refers to several different means, while the preferred embodiment described in the specification, or even the broad description of the invention itself, includes more specifics of each means, then instead of writing one dependent claim that expands on all of the individual separately claimed features or means of the independent claim, consider using either one or more dependent claims which is/are devoted to a progressively more detailed treatment of one particular feature at a time. It may eventually turn out that the particular feature covered in one of the dependent claims is the critical one to stop an infringer. Or, because of only later discovered prior art, it may be that only that dependent claim is distinguishable from and valid in view of the prior art. Then that dependent claim covering one feature will not be burdened with other detailed limitations which an infringer may avoid, but only with details to the particular distinguishing feature.

The main advantage of dependent claims, of course, is that they require far less time to examine, and those using them should be given a financial incentive. Note that, when any claim is allowed, all dependent claims can be allowed without further examination for novelty or obviousness, other than to make sure they are de-

---

32.1. There is an apparently unresolved paradox of a structural element claim, which is dependent upon a means for performing a function element claim, receiving broader scope than the means claim. This is because the means claim element is governed by § 112, paragraph 6, while the structure claim is not, and the latter may be of broader scope (see section 34). *Cf.* IMS Technology Inc. v. Haas Automation Inc., 206 F.3d 1422, 54 U.S.P.Q.2d 1129, 1135 (Fed. Cir. 2000).

pendent claims and satisfy 35 U.S.C. § 112. In one case, *Ex parte Ligh*,[33] the Board of Appeals held that it was error to reject a dependent claim while allowing its parent. Of course, the dependent claim must be in proper form and not subject to any of the errors proscribed by the MPEP, as discussed elsewhere herein.

Section 282 of title 35 of the United States Code provides that "dependent claims shall be presumed valid even though dependent upon an invalid claim," in case there had been any doubt previously. These statutory changes have resulted in nearly universal usage of dependent claims, simplifying the jobs of everyone who must ever consider the patents.

There is no maximum limit on the total number of claims that may be included in an application, nor on the number of dependent claims. There are practical limits on the number of claims and typically of dependent claims. Attorney time spent in writing claims increases as the number of claims increases. But valuable patent protection can result from including more claims, so that the attorney time factor is of little importance, if saving it reduces the comprehensiveness of the coverage. Another practical limit is an extra Patent and Trademark Office fee for a total of more than twenty claims. That fee is relatively small, if the additional claims are of value to cover the invention.

There is no limit to the number of claims in a chain of dependent claims headed by an independant claim.

Identically worded dependent claims may be dependent from different parent claims.[34] In *Ex parte Primich*,[35] it was held improper to reject a dependent claim as adding only old elements to an allowed parent claim, as long as the total number of claims was not "unduly multiplied" (section 62).

In general, the dependent form should *never* be used unless one is sure that he really wishes to present a claim that includes every limitation of the prospective parent claim, but adds some significant element or feature. He must satisfy himself that every limitation in the first claim is also necessary in the second. There may be

---

33. *Ex parte* Ligh, 159 U.S.P.Q. (BNA) 61, 62 (Bd. App. 1967).
34. *See In re* Flint, 162 U.S.P.Q. (BNA) 228 (C.C.P.A. 1969) (discussed in section 62).
35. *Ex parte* Primich, 151 U.S.P.Q. (BNA) 737 (Bd. App. 1966).

a tendency among some who use dependent claims extensively to overuse them, by failing to present a second independent claim, where appropriate, that does not include all of the limitations of the first claim. United States practice has no requirements that any one claim be a "head claim," or otherwise dominate every other claim in the application. There may be as many head claims as the invention and the prior art permit, subject only to fees (section 13) and to restriction requirements under 35 U.S.C. § 121 and Office policy implementing that section (rule 141 and MPEP 806.04 *et seq.*). However, once it has been determined that the claim scope desired does include all elements of a preceding claim, then it is recommended that the dependent form ordinarily be used.

A dependent claim is not improper and does not cease to be a proper dependent claim because any further limitation added by it appears to change the scope of the dependent claim from the scope of the claim from which it depends.

There is no objection per se to a claim in one statutory class (e.g., product) being dependent from another claim in a different statutory class (e.g., method), as long as the dependent claim does include all the limitations of the parent claim: that is, "it shall not conceivably be infringed by anything which would not also infringe the basic claim" (MPEP 608.01(n)). This is the Patent and Trademark Office's definition of whether a claim is in fact independent, despite the fact that an alleged dependent claim might refer to another claim by numeral. Clearly, if a claim purports to be dependent, but does not comply with the requirements of the MPEP, that claim should be rewritten as independent.

MPEP 608.01(n) and 2173.05(f) provide examples of dependent claims crossing statutory classes. Thus, the preceding claim may recite a product, while the properly dependent claim recites a method of making that product in a particular manner, because the dependent claim could not be infringed without also infringing the preceding claim. Similarly, the preceding claim may recite a method of making a product and a product made by that method (product by process) could be a proper dependent claim. In contrast, if the preceding claim recites a method of making a product, a dependent claim to the product identified in the preceding claim would not be a proper dependent claim if the product could be made in other ways, i.e., there is no restriction in the dependent claim to the product produced only by the previously claimed method.

A dependent product claim should not add mere method limitations, i.e., a function or operation performed by a previously claimed feature. It should not merely make a functional recitation about something that occurs. A recitation of function does not provide a distinction over prior art.[36] Yet, it does limit the scope of the claim limitations.[37] If either adding a mere method limitation or reciting a function is desired, consider framing it in means for accomplishing the function form, either introducing a completely new element as the means or indicating that the previously named element is that element for performing the function, or using 35 U.S.C. § 112 language by saying that it is a means for accomplishing the particular function.

With respect to claims crossing statutory classes, dependent "product-by-process" claims (section 46) are very common: "A _____ produced in accordance with the method of claim 1."[38] However, a claim to "A method of making the _____ of claim 1" would not be proper because a method claim should not be dependent upon a product claim, and vice versa except product by process. Method and product claims should be separated, as by using separate independent claims.

The preceding discussion has dealt with the typical dependent claim which follows on the preceding recited claim. A claim may refer to a preceding claim to define a limitation, e.g., a product by process claim (section 46) or the example in MPEP 2173.05(f): "A method of producing ethanol comprising contacting amylose with the culture of claim 1 under the following conditions. . . ." This claim crosses statutory classes and defines only one element in the claim in terms of the claim on which the later claim is dependent. The typical dependent claim further defines the earlier claim rather than being defined by it. But both types are acceptable.

---

36. Clements Industries Inc. v. A. Meyers & Sons Corp., 712 F. Supp. 317, 12 U.S.P.Q.2d 1874 (S.D.N.Y. 1989).
37. Hollister Inc. v. E.R. Squibb & Sons, Inc., 14 U.S.P.Q.2d 2069 (Fed. Cir. 1990).
38. *See* MPEP 2173.05(f).

Dependent claims that are different in scope from each other may even relate to separate inventions and each may require a separate search by the examiner, or each may be separately classified and each may be subject to a requirement for restriction between inventions. Nonetheless, each could be a proper dependent claim, particularly for (see section 13) fee calculation purposes.

With respect to the numbering and order of dependent claims, the general rules set out in section 5 should be followed, but in addition MPEP 608.01(n) states: "A claim which depends from a *dependent* claim should not be separated therefrom by any claim which does not also depend from said 'dependent' claim." This means that the following claim patterns are permitted (arrow indicates a claim dependent from earlier numbered claim; no arrow designates a second independent claim):

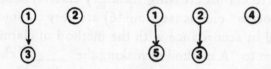

Dependent claims (3 and 5) may be separated from an *independent* parent claim (1) by any number of other claims of any kind.

The following pattern is not usually accepted:

Claim 4, here, is a claim that depends from a *dependent* claim (2), but is separated therefrom (from 2), by a claim (3), that "does not also depend from said dependent claim" (claim 2). This is not recommended.

Also, where there is a chain of dependent claims in sequence, each dependent upon a preceding claim, that chain should (but not *must*) be run out to its last claim before returning to an earlier claim in the sequence for starting another chain. Further, although not required, return to the higher number claim first to run out its sequence before returning to a lower number claim.

Note the following claim pattern in which only claims 1 and 17 are independent:

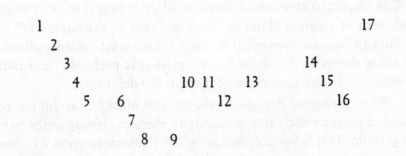

In the above sequence, for example, note that one chain from claim 6 to claim 8 is run out, then the chain back from claim 7 to claim 9, because we returned to the highest number claim first, then back to claim 6, the next highest claim, then back to claim 3, next highest and then claim 2. If an examiner allows one claim, like claim 6, it is easy to find the next claims, which are dependent upon claim 6, allowable as well.

The above rules set forth a *minimum* standard on placement of dependent claims. Beyond this, claims that depend from independent claims may be placed wherever the writer thinks most logical. However, unless unusual factors are present (such as claims in different statutory classes), it is best to group all claims dependent from a single independent claim after that claim.

One simple format for dependent claims follows (refer to example in chapter III):

14. A shaking apparatus as recited in claim 1, in which the oscillating means comprises:

(a)   a motor;

(b)   a rotary cam driven by the motor;

(c)   a cam follower engaging the cam; and

(d)   a link pivoted at one end to the cam follower and at its other end to the container, to permit oscillation of the container on the legs.

In claim 14, one of the elements of the parent claim is defined in greater detail; specifically, the "means" element is broken down into four constituent parts. Note that the new elements must be connected and related to each other and to the elements of the preceding claim, exactly as with independent claims (section 28). With respect to antecedents (section 23), it is proper to refer to an element of a parent claim as "the" or "said"; "the container" in claim 14 finds its antecedent in claim 1. One must consider all preceding claims in the chain to be certain it is perfectly clear that there is only one such element that fits the definition.

When preparing dependent claims, one must be careful not to add as an apparently new element, an element already in the parent claim. This is "double inclusion" of elements (section 21). For example, in the previous claim 14, the motor cam, etc., added by the dependent claim comprise the oscillating means of the parent claim. It would be improper to add those elements as new elements without relating them to the oscillating means of the parent claim.

In order to illustrate a dependent claim that adds an element to a preceding claim, refer to Example II in Appendix A, the take-up barrel. Assume that a photocell circuit (not shown) is provided to detect when the barrel 12 is full, and that this photocell operates (1) a pair of shears positioned between the barrel and the eyelet 20 to cut the strand 11, and also (2) an accumulator positioned between the eyelet and capstan 13 to collect the strand for a short time while a new barrel is placed on the turntable. A dependent claim to this combination might read as follows:

> 15.   A collecting apparatus as recited in claim 2, further comprising: means for detecting when a predetermined amount of strand has been collected in the barrel; a cutter, operated by the detecting means, for severing the strand when the predetermined amount has been collected; and an accumulator, operated by the detecting means, for accumulating the strand after it has been severed.

Note that "a cutter" should have a broader scope than "cutting means," so that the "means" expression, while possible, was avoided (see section 34). However, a photocell is not so broad as "detecting means" so that the means expression was used. A weight-responsive switch could equally well have been employed to sense the time when the barrel was full. But the alternatives must have been disclosed in the specification or have been recognized as equivalents at the time the application was ruled.[39]

Another format for adding an element to a claim follows: "A collecting apparatus as recited in claim 2, wherein means are provided for detecting when. . . ." There are many other acceptable styles for introducing a dependent claim.

One caution with dependent claims, particularly where elements are added, is to make certain that the larger combination is still consistent with the preamble, as discussed in section 6. Sometimes the extra elements add so many additional functions that the old preamble is no longer suitable. Although it is possible, and fairly common, to modify the preamble by a dependent claim, it is often best simply to use another independent claim.

For example, if the previous example also included automatic means responsive to the photocell to push the full barrel off the turntable and substitute an empty barrel, plus means for sensing the presence of the empty barrel on the turntable to reverse the accumulator and start collecting the strand in the new barrel, there is now significantly more than a *mere* "apparatus for collecting an advancing strand in a barrel." Instead, there is a much more impressive combination: "Automatic apparatus for continuously collecting an advancing strand in a succession of barrels." The continuous/automatic feature would undoubtedly be very important in such an invention, and should be written into the preamble. This is a main, overall feature of the combination claimed. As a dependent claim with a modified preamble, this could read: "A collecting apparatus as recited in claim 15, for automatically collecting an advancing strand in a succession of barrels. . . ." Where the dependent claim modifies the preamble of the parent, this should be stated in the preamble of the dependent claim.

An example of a form for a dependent method claim:

> A method of _____, as recited in claim _____, wherein the separating step is performed by [or comprises] distilling the aqueous solution . . . [defining a step in more detail].

---

39. 35 U.S.C. § 112, paragraph 6; see section 34.

When preparing dependent method claims, the added limitations usually relate to variations in the method steps or materials used in the case of a chemical process (section 42). Dependent method claims now sometimes add only apparatus (machine) limitations.

An example of a dependent method claim, adding steps, which is correct:

> 15A.   A method of collecting an advancing strand, as recited in claim 4, further comprising: detecting when a predetermined amount of strand has been collected in the barrel; cutting the strand when the predetermined amount has been collected; and accumulating the strand after it has been cut.

Note this corresponds in scope to dependent apparatus claim 15. For a chemical process, see claim 5 in section 42 as the parent claim:

> 5A.   A process as recited in claim 5, wherein the solution is heated to a temperature of 80° to 90°C. [adding preferred process conditions].
>
> 5B.   A process as recited in claim 5, wherein the solution also contains between 1 and 5% by weight of sodium chloride [telling more about the composition].

With respect to composition claims, dependent claims may add further materials to the composition or define one or more of the elements or radicals more specifically. For example, in the zinc-electroplating solution claim (claim 11, section 49) one could claim:

> 11A.   A zinc electroplating solution as recited in claim 11, wherein the pH modifying substance is ammonium hydroxide [specifying one ingredient in greater detail].

Note it would be wrong to add "further comprising ammonium hydroxide" if this is the pH modifying substance because the proscribed transition implies the ammonium hydroxide is a newly identified claim element and not further specifying the already identified pH modifying substance.

Another example:

> **11B.** A zinc electroplating . . ., further comprising 0.5 to 1 gram per liter of boric acid [adding a material].

One could also specify the concentrations of ingredients in more detail:

> **11C.** . . ., wherein the concentration of zinc acetate is 50–60 grams per liter, and the citric acid 100–150 grams per liter.

In claim 12 to the new molecule, one could specify the radicals in more detail:

> **12A.** A compound as recited in claim 12, wherein R is methyl and X is chlorine [Note this is a claim to one specific compound, sometimes called an "ultimate species." See section 58 on genus and species claims.]

Warning to one who amends claims. An often occurring mistake in claim drafting is made during the claim amendment process. When the claims are initially written before the application is filed, the drafter is careful about separating separate features into respective claims. During prosecution of the application, an examiner may indicate that some dependent claim, which is in turn dependent upon a chain of preceding dependent claims, would be allowable if rewritten in independent form. Sometimes the practitioner rewrites that allowable dependent claim as an independent claim by including in it all of the limitations from all of the independent and dependent claims in the claim chain leading to the allowable dependent claim. This introduces many limitations into the resulting allowable independent claim which are directed to a preferred embodiment shown in the disclosure but which are not critical to the allowability of that rewritten independent claim. The resulting unnecessarily limited independent claim is a much less effective tool against competitors and copyists. The allowable dependent claim could have been rewritten as independent by including in the original or unamended independent claim only the one or more critical limitations from the allowable dependent claim, without also adding all of the limitations from all of the dependent claims in that chain to the dependent claim. Therefore, when drafting or redrafting independent claims, both at the time of filing and during prosecution, the independent claim should be as broad in scope as the prior art permits. Limitations from other claims, which are not limitations essential to the allowance of that independent claim, should not be added into that otherwise allowable independent claim.

Summary

Use dependent claims extensively, most of the time when you wish to present a second claim that adds elements or features to a prior claim, whether the prior claim is dependent or independent. Either tell more about elements in the previous claim, or add elements to that claim, or both. But you must further restrict a previous claim in some manner. Be careful, in practice, with dependent claims, particularly those adding detailed features, that you really need every feature of the main claim for patentability. If not, stop and write a new independent claim.

§ 11A Independent Claims

Three forms of claims are used in patent applications, independent, dependent, and multiple dependent. Their use is significant for fee purposes.

An independent claim stands alone, includes all its necessary limitations, and is not dependent upon and does not include limitations from any other claim to make it complete. An independent claim is not defined in the rules or the Manual, but is part of the discussion in MPEP 608.01(n).

An independent claim can be the broadest scope claim. It has fewer limitations than any dependent claim which is dependent upon it. At least one independent claim in an application should, as much as possible, approach purely covering the inventor's invention or concept without too many structural limitations.

Sometimes an invention involves a number of different concepts. The invention simultaneously solves several different problems or has several different objectives. Sometimes different structures related to the same invention or embodiment of the invention are involved in the solution of each of the problems or achieving each of the objectives. It may not be possible to write a claim that is broad enough, in view of prior art, to be generic to and to read on the different inventive concepts in one embodiment or upon the different embodiments of one invention in one patent application. Consequently, several independent claims may be used, each covering a structure or method which solves a particular problem or achieves a particular objective within the invention or each covering a different inventive concept, possibly different cooperating sections, of one embodiment, or each covering different embodiments of one invention or inventive concept. Several independent claims in an application may share many of their claim limitations in common. But they can differ, in that others of the limitations will be specific to the particular invention, or concept or embodiment that is the subject of the particular independent claim. For fullest protection, use the number of independent claims required to cover the solutions to all problems solved by the invention. Where possible, avoid using separate independent claims for each embodiment, if a generic independent claim covering all embodiments can be written. Then the various embodiments can be covered expressly in individual dependent claims. But do not avoid coverage of all embodiments to be claimed by failing to use independent claims when no patentable generic independent claim can be written.

For more than three independent claims, there is an elevated filing fee per independent claim. This is a practical or economic limitation on the number of independent claims. But if the claim drafter gives the client the fullest independent claim protection and one of those independent claims in the issued patent happens to be an obstacle to a competitor, the increased filing fee loses significance.

§ 12 Multiple Dependent Claims

In applications filed since January 1978, multiple dependent claims have been permitted. Current multiple dependent claim practice is stated in rule 75(c) and is described in detail in MPEP 608.01(n). Rule 75(c), in pertinent part, reads:

> Any dependent claim which refers to more than one other claim ("multiple dependent claim") shall refer to such other claims in the alternative only. A multiple dependent claim shall not serve as a basis for any other multiple dependent claim. . . . A multiple dependent claim shall be construed to incorporate by reference all the limitations of each of the particular claims in relation to which it is being considered.

The Manual subsection details these points.

The multiple dependent claim should refer to the other claims on which it is dependent in the alternative ("or" not "and") only. The Manual subsection provides examples of acceptable multiple dependent claim preamble wording, which are reproduced below.

ACCEPTABLE MULTIPLE DEPENDENT CLAIM WORDING

> *Claim 5. A gadget according to claims 3 or 4, further comprising—*
> *Claim 5. A gadget as in any one of the preceding claims, in which—*
> *Claim 3. A gadget as in either claim 1 or claim 2, further comprising—*
> *Claim 4. A gadget as in claim 2 or 3, further comprising—*
> *Claim 16. A gadget as in claims 1, 7, 12 or 15, further comprising—*
> *Claim 5. A gadget as in any of the preceding claims, in which—*
> *Claim 8. A gadget as in one of Claims 4–7, in which—*
> *Claim 5. A gadget as in any preceding claim, in which—*
> *Claim 10. A gadget as in any of claims 1–3, 7–9, in which—*
> *Claim 11. A gadget as in any one of claims 1, 2 or 7–10 inclusive, in which—*

If a multiple dependent claim does not refer back to previous claims in the alternative only, it is unacceptable, as shown by the examples in the Manual:

UNACCEPTABLE MULTIPLE DEPENDENT CLAIM WORDING

A. Claim does not refer back in the alternative only
Claim 5. A gadget according to claim 3 and 4, further comprising—
Claim 9. A gadget according to claims 1–3, in which—
Claim 9. A gadget as in claims 1 or 2 and 7 or 8, in which—
Claim 6. A gadget as in the preceding claims in which—
Claim 6. A gadget as in claims 1, 2, 3, 4 and/or 5, in which—
Claim 10. A gadget as in claims 1–3 or 7-9, in which—

The multiple dependent claim, as any dependent claim, must refer back to a preceding claim, and should not refer to a claim that follows the dependent claim. Unacceptable examples of such claims appear in the Manual:

B. Claim does not refer to a preceding claim
Claim 3. A gadget as in any of the following claims, in which—
Claim 5. A gadget as in either claim 6 or claim 8, in which—

Finally, the Manual section provides an example of an unacceptable multiple dependent claim, which refers to two sets of claims covering different features and provides the following example.

C. Reference to two sets of claims to different features
Claim 9. A gadget as in claim 1 or 4 made by the process of claims 5, 6, 7, or 8, in which—

Such a claim is multiple dependent with respect to the gadget and then multiple dependent again with respect to the process. It would appear that a claim trying to accomplish the same purpose, but not doubly multiple dependent, may be acceptable, such as: "9. A gadget as in claim 1 or 4 made by the process of claim 5." It would be acceptable, as there is only one multiple dependency in that claim, either the combination of claims 1 and 5, or the combination of claims 4 and 5. Clearly, that claim 9 could easily be written as only two dependent claims, namely the combination of claims 1 and 5 and the combination of claims 4 and 5.

A multiple dependent claim cannot depend from any other multiple dependent claim. Rule 75(c) simply prohibits it. Multiple dependent claims dependent upon other multiple dependent claims are proper in other countries, but not in the United States. An example of such an improper claim is:

> *Claim 1. A widget, comprising . . .*
> *Claim 2. The widget of claim 1, further comprising. . . .*
> *Claim 3. The widget of claim 2, wherein . . .*
> *Claim 4. The widget according to either of claims 2 or 3, further comprising . . .*
> *Claim 5. The widget of either of claims 3 or 4, wherein . . .*

Claim 5 is improper as it is a multiple dependent claim dependent upon another multiple dependent claim, namely claim 4. One reason for not permitting such a claim is that the precise scope of a particular claim is rendered uncertain due to the wide variety of combinations of claim limitations that arise from multiple dependent claims dependent upon other multiple dependent claims. A second motivation for prohibiting such multiple dependent claims is that such claims cannot be clearly separated into individual claims for fee calculation purposes.

Where there are not an excessive number of possible claim combinations, an improper claim like claim 5 can be replaced by two proper claims:

> *Claim 6. The widget of claim 4, wherein . . .*
> *Claim 7. The widget according to claim 3, wherein . . .*

Claim 6 is a single dependent claim dependent upon a multiple dependent claim and is proper. A series of single dependent claims depending from a multiple dependent claim is proper. Claim 7 is a single dependent claim dependent upon another such claim and is of course proper. (Note the sequencing of claims 6 and 7. The chain of dependencies from the higher number claim 4 is run out before returning to the chain for the earlier lower number claim 3.)

Where the applicant presents a multiple dependent claim dependent upon another multiple dependent claim or one reciting the dependency in the conjunctive "and" rather than the alternative "or," examiners follow the practice under rule 75 of objecting to the claim as not being in proper form. Then examiners need not, and often do not, further treat the claim on the merits, so that the claim is not examined any further on either procedural or substantive grounds (35 U.S.C. §§ 112, 102, or 103) until it is corrected.

For purposes of examination, a proper multiple dependent claim may be treated effectively as separate claims by the examiner, so that claim 3 dependent upon claim 1 (that is 3/1) could be subject to one ground of rejection while claim 3 dependent upon claim 2 (3/2) may be allowable, because of the presence of certain limitations in claim 2.

Summary

Multiple dependent claims may be used. Their preamble form is important. A multiple dependent claim cannot be dependent on another such claim. They have high filing fees, as compared with other claim forms, as discussed next.

§ 13 Fees Payable for Claims

The distinctions among the three forms of claims (independent, single dependent, and multiple dependent) discussed in the preceding sections have significance because of filing fees paid by applicants to the Patent and Trademark Office. The official filing fees are dependent upon the number and nature of the claims included in the application. The precise fees payable for particular numbers and forms of claims is periodically changed by the Patent and Trademark Office. The amounts of the claim fees now appear in rule 16(b), (c), and (d).

In 2000, the basic filing fee for a patent application covers a total of twenty claims, whether independent or dependent, and covers a total of three independent claims, regardless of the total number of claims. Two separate claim fee computations are therefore made. For any claim in excess of a total of twenty claims, whether it be independent or dependent, there is an additional claim filing fee. For every independent claim in excess of three, regardless of the total number of claims, there is an additional claim filing fee. Thus, if there are twenty-one claims, of which only one is an independent claim, there is an additional filing fee for one additional claim. If there are fewer than twenty claims, including four independent claims, then there is an additional filing fee for one additional independent claim. If there are twenty-one claims, including four independent claims, there are two additional filing fees due, one for the one claim beyond twenty and one for the one independent claim beyond three.

It is apparent from the fees payable that the Patent and Trademark Office wishes to encourage the use of dependent claims, as the additional filing fee for independent claims arises after only three independent claims are in the application while there is no additional fee until many more dependent claims are in the application.

Multiple dependent claims have high filing fees, which tends to discourage their use. The fee calculation for multiple dependent claims is detailed in MPEP 608.01(n):

> 35 U.S.C. 41(a) provides that claims in proper multiple dependent form may not be considered as single dependent claims for the purpose of calculating fees. Thus, a multiple dependent claim is considered to be that number of dependent claims to which it refers. Any proper claim depending directly or indirectly from a multiple dependent claim is also considered as the number of dependent claims as referred to in the multiple dependent claim from which it depends.

Examples of the fee calculation for all claims appear at MPEP 608.01(n).

For example, if claim 3 in a set of claims is dependent upon both of claims 1 and 2, then for fee calculation purposes, claim 3 is counted as two claims. If claim 4 in the same set is dependent upon claim 3, then claim 4 is treated as the same number of claims as claim 3 for fee calculation purposes, whereby claim 4 is treated as two claims for fee calculation purposes. (If a multiple dependent claim were permitted to be dependent upon another multiple dependent claim, the fee calculation process would be impossible. However, the Patent and Trademark Office charges a fee of one dependent claim for an improper multiple dependent claim, one either dependent on another multiple dependent claim or one dependent upon two other claims in the conjunctive "and," rather than the alternative "or." The improper claim is rejected and not examined on the merits.) It is apparent that with multiple dependent claims, the total number of claims for fee calculation purposes rapidly can exceed twenty claims, and additional claim filing fees will thereafter become due.

Because a multiple dependent claim is treated as more than one claim for fee calculation purposes, the computation to determine when twenty claims has been exceeded for fee calculation purposes does not refer to the total number of claims, but rather to the number of claims for fee calculation purposes, and with multiple dependent claims present, an additional filing fee is due before the total number of claims exceeds twenty.

There is a separate one-time surcharge asserted on the basic filing fee on the first occasion (at filing or upon amending the claims) that the application contains any multiple dependent claims at all, that is, any number of such claims.[40] This tends to discourage the use of multiple dependent claims, but it is not a prohibition against them. If the multiple dependent claims are present when the application is filed, the surcharge is due then. If such a claim is added after filing, the surcharge is due then. If a multiple dependent claim is present in the application as filed, it can be eliminated at filing by simultaneously filing a preliminary amendment deleting or removing the multiple dependency from the claim and by noting in the remarks to the amendment that it has been made to avoid the multiple dependent claim fee.

---

40. Rule 16(d).

III

Apparatus or Machine Claims

§ 14 In General

The general rules and procedures discussed in chapter II will now be illustrated as they pertain to apparatus claims. The word "apparatus" is used generically to denote various machines and devices, including electrical circuits, computer related apparatus, hydraulic devices, anything mechanical or electrical having cooperating parts that accomplish some useful result, usually some act or operation on itself or on an article or workpiece.

Example I—Shaker

Referring specifically to the form of shaker illustrated in figures 1 and 2 of appendix A, example I, a sample independent claim specific to that structure (as distinguished from the structure in figure 3) reads as follows:

(Preamble)	1. **Apparatus for shaking articles**,
(Transition)	**which comprises**
	(a) *a container* for the articles;
	(b) *a base*;
(Body of Claim)	(c) *a plurality of parallel legs*, **each leg is**
(Elements in	connected pivotally at one end to the con-
Subparagraph	tainer and at the other end to the base to
Form)	support the container for oscillating move-
	ment with respect to the base; and
	(d) *means for oscillating the container* on
	the legs to shake the articles.

Note that the "elements" of the above claim are in italics for illustrative purposes only. The introduction "I claim" is understood, and is not normally written, except just before the first claim in a patent application.

For comparison, the same claim in single paragraph form (section 10) reads:

1A.   Apparatus for shaking articles which comprises a container for the articles, a base, a plurality of parallel legs, each leg is connected pivotally at one end to the container and at the other end to the base to support the container for oscillating movement with respect to the base, and means for oscillating the container on the legs to shake the articles.

Note that claim 1A is much more difficult to follow than the same claim in subparagraph form.

Summary

Use the subparagraph or outline claim form, and watch formal problems, punctuation, grammar, etc., as outlined in chapter II.

§ 15 Preambles for Apparatus Claims

Claim 1 illustrates one simple type of preamble, which is quite common and which can easily be used for most mechanical combination claims. Generally, this type of preamble follows the pattern: "*Apparatus for* performing a specified act or operation on a particular article or workpiece, which comprises:"

The article to be worked on, the workpiece, need not be defined in detail, unless such a description is important to the functioning of the apparatus or made necessary by the prior art.

The word "apparatus" is frequently used by patent practitioners as a sort of generic expression covering machines or other mechanical devices that perform operations on workpieces; however, phrases such as "a machine," "a device," or "a circuit" may be used where appropriate.

It should be apparent that the drafting of the body of the claim is simpler, and the claim is easier to follow, when the specific operation to be performed and the specific workpiece on which that operation is to be performed are clearly set out in the preamble.

Further examples of this type of preamble follow:

> Apparatus for coating the inside of a tubular workpiece with a liquid thermoplastic resin
>
> Apparatus for transferring articles from a first conveyor belt to a second conveyor belt running parallel to the first but in the opposite direction
>
> A device for simultaneously attaching axial leads to opposite ends of an electrical component
>
> A circuit for detecting discontinuities in the insulation of an insulated wire

In cases where the apparatus has a generic name, that may be used; for example:

> A binary computer
>
> A self-propelled lawn sprinkler
>
> A carburetor
>
> A shaker for articles [an equally acceptable preamble for claim 1]

Use of a preamble referring to apparatus by its generic name in the preamble is preferred because it may shorten the length of the preamble and it tells the reader and the Patent and Trademark Office in what technology area the invention belongs. Later searching for the patent by subject matter, e.g., by a computer search, is easier if a recognized generic name is used for the apparatus.

Other types of preambles are used for special situations, as discussed in chapter VII, and in some chemical compound cases (chapter VI).

Occasionally, one sees a claim such as "In combination, [an A, a B, and a C]." One use for this type of preamble is for inventions so broad that any attempt to name the thing to be claimed would be too narrow. Of course, if claim 1 on the shaker started out only "In combination," that would be uselessly misleading since the claim itself was intended to be limited to an apparatus for shaking articles. Therefore, there is no reason to avoid using a normal preamble.

Another use for the preamble "In combination" is when a previously claimed subcombination is joined with the remainder of a combination in a dependent claim, dependent upon a preceding subcombination claim: "In combination, the means for oscillating a container of claim 2, and a container, the container is connected with the oscillating means for. . . . "

Also, the Manual and cases[1] have held that statements in the preamble may not be disregarded in determining patentability. All of the claim is considered, including the preamble. Usually, the preamble is or includes a statement of intended purpose. Whether a preamble of intended purpose constitutes a limitation to the claim is a matter determined on the facts of each case in view of the claimed invention as a whole.[2] Thus, descriptive preambles can be quite helpful in obtaining allowance of the claim. Sometimes a statement of intended purpose is included in the body of the claim, as in a "whereby" clause (see section 32), rather than in a preamble. There the statement is considered a claim limitation. The *Duva* case is discussed in more detail in section 56 on new use claims; preamble limitations.

Summary

Select a descriptive preamble describing the overall function of the machine to be claimed, either a distinctive name, such as "power lawn mower," or a made-up phrase, such as "apparatus for [performing a specified function]."

---

1. MPEP 2111.02; *In re* Duva, 156 U.S.P.Q. (BNA) 90 (C.C.P.A. 1967); Bell Communications Res., Inc. v. Vitalink Communications Corp., 55 F.3d 615, 34 U.S.P.Q.2d (BNA) 1816 (Fed. Cir. 1995). *See* section 6 hereof.
2. MPEP 2111.02; *In re* Stencel, 4 U.S.P.Q.2d (BNA) 1071, 1073 (Fed. Cir. 1987).

§ 16 Elements of Apparatus Claims

The "elements" of an apparatus claim are the main structural parts that together make up the combination claimed. As illustrated in claim 1, the complete description of each element forms the subject matter of a separate clause, or subparagraph, of the claim.

A workpiece is a thing that the invention uses or operates upon and perhaps changes. The workpiece ("articles" in claim 1) should be identified in the preamble of the claim, but not made an element of the claimed combination.[3] The workpiece appears in the body of the claim, as it interacts with a claim element.

One of the most important technical "rules" of form in drafting claims is that it is never proper to introduce a new element of the claim in the middle of the clause describing another element, or to describe an operation or action upon or by a new element without its having been introduced. This is sometimes called "inferential claiming" (MPEP 706.03 (d)). Each new element in a product claim and each new step in a method claim should be first introduced either as (a) the subject of its own clause ("a container," "a base," etc. in claim 1 above), or (b) a previously introduced and named item or a step comprises it, has it or includes it, that is, its presence is indicated by using a verb that describes the state of being (having, comprising, including, being), as in "a container [subject] having (comprising, including, being, etc.) [a word suggesting later element is a part of earlier one] a plurality of legs [subjects]" rather than an action verb or a verb indicating something is being done to or with the element, as "is connected" in claim 1 above. Being the subject of its own clause means that it is either stated in the clause that such an element or step is present or the element or step is named at the beginning of the clause and thereafter that element or step, which has been named now for the first time, does something or has something done to it. It is important that a new item mentioned for the first time in the claim not be first mentioned as an element operated upon or cooperated with by a previous element described in the

---

3. Even if it were proper to make the workpiece an element of the combination, one would rarely wish to do so, as it would unduly narrow the claim. A machine manufacturer would rarely sell the workpiece along with the machine. Thus he would not be a direct infringer [35 U.S.C. § 271(a)] of the claim.

same clause. A clause can have more than one element as a subject, but only as limited above.

Every new element must be introduced by "a" or "an" (the part of speech called an indefinite article) or by no article at all, especially when the element is some means for performing a function (element (d) in claim 1 above), or the element is stated in the plural (e.g., "containers" or "container means"). Every subsequent mention of the previously identified element must be preceded by the definite article "the" or by "said." To repeat the same element, preceded by the indefinite article "a" or "an," or preceded by no article at all for "means" or an element in the plural, implies that a new element is being introduced in the clause. This causes undesired and inaccurate double inclusion of one element.

Although it may be quite natural, and good practice in the descriptive portion of the specification, to state: "a container which is connected pivotally to a plurality of parallel legs," it is improper in the claim. The legs are separate elements of the combination, and thus should be positively set out and defined in the claim, as in claim 1.

Another example:

Wrong:	A lever having a forked end pivoted on a pin mounted between the furcations of the forked end.

Note, the pin is not part of the lever; it is a separate mechanical element.

Better:	(a) a lever having a forked end; and
	(b) a pivot pin mounted between the furcations of the forked end
Better Still:	(a) a lever having a forked end,
	(b) the forked end comprising spaced apart furcations; and
	(c) a pivot pin mounted between furcations

The only exception to the inferential claiming prohibition is where the indefinite article "a" is used to introduce a workpiece. Because the workpiece is not an element of the claim, but rather it is only worked upon by one of the claim elements, it would not be introduced as the subject of its own clause.

A further example of improper inferential claiming is the clause "the motor being connected with *a* shaft which is connected with the gear for driving the gear." In that claim limitation, the shaft is inferentially claimed. It is not the subject of the clause. If there is a subject, it is the motor or the gear. Also, the shaft is not being described in a state of being with respect to the motor or the gear, but rather it is being described in a state of action. Proper wording might be "a shaft connected with the motor and with the gear for communicating driving motion from the motor to the gear." This says the same thing, but does not inferentially claim the shaft. (Implicit in this clause, of course, is that the motor and the gear were previously introduced in the claim, since each is preceded in the clause by the definite article "the.") Referring to the other exception, if the clause reads "the motor including a shaft extending to the gear," that would not be inferential claiming. The shaft has been first introduced in the claim in a state of being with respect to the motor, so that for an inferential claiming analysis, the shaft is now properly in the claim. Thereafter, and even in the same shaft introducing clause, the shaft can be active, and it is described as cooperating with the gear. It is no longer inferential claiming once the element with the indefinite article "a" has been properly introduced.

Four essential elements (*italicized*) were selected for the combination of claim 1 (in section 14)—(a) the container, (b) the base, (c) the legs, and (d) the oscillating means. Note that all of these parts are essential, within the framework of the scope of claim desired, to accomplish the shaking of the articles, and that nothing more is needed. If a narrower claim were desired, the motor, cam, and cam follower linkage (together making up the oscillating means) could be made elements of the claim.

For the writing of broad claims, one concentrates on the minimum number of elements essential to the invention. As stated in MPEP 706.03(f): "A claim can be rejected as incomplete if it omits essential elements, steps or necessary structural cooperative relationship of elements. . . ." It is also wise, at least in the broadest claims, to concentrate on what a potential infringer might sell, and leave out such conventional elements as power supplies, water supply hoses, compressed air sources, etc., which might not be sold as part of the combination.

There are usually four important things to tell about each element:

1. What is its name?

2. What are its constituent parts, if any, or distinctive features, that is, what features are necessary for the purposes of this claim to distinguish this element from any other element of the class?

3. How are it and its parts cooperatively associated with at least one other of the other elements or parts to accomplish the desired result? Or, what is the necessary connection and cooperation between the elements and parts?

4. Where pertinent, what does each element do and how does it do it?

5. Under (3) and (4), each element must be related structurally and/or in terms of functional cooperation or both with at least one other element.

One analogy is to think of the elements as islands, the parts of elements as peninsulas, and the statements of connection and cooperation as bridges. When the claim is done, all islands must be connected by bridges. Thus one composes a claim to a complete mechanical combination, or "machine."

Summary

Find the main elements or parts of the machine to be claimed. Make each element the subject of one clause of the body of the claim. The claim must name the elements and tell how they are related to each other either physically and/or functionally and cooperatively to be the article or to do the job stated in the preamble.

The following sections focus on how to do all this.

§ 16A Workpiece or Environmental Element

Most claimed apparatus operate upon something or use something, or are operated upon and/or used by something else. Similarly, most methods act on something or involve something that is acted upon. That workpiece or environmental element should be recited for a claim to be complete and make sense. Yet, it should not be claimed in a manner suggesting that it is one of the elements of the invention claimed.

Where the workpiece or environmental element is important in the claimed structure, it might appear in the preamble of the claim, as for example, "A juicer for squeezing citrus fruit, the juicer comprising . . ." or "A grinder for grinding rolls . . .," or perhaps have the workpiece as a modifier of the claimed apparatus as "A roll grinder comprising. . . ."

Not every workpiece or environmental element used with a claimed apparatus or method is a major element or is desirably included in the preamble. The preamble "A juicer comprising . . ." does not require mention of the citrus fruit. The preamble "A telescope comprising . . ." does not require mention of the objects observable to be recited in the claim preamble.

But, no matter whether it is recited in the preamble, a workpiece or environmental element typically is recited in the body of the claim with reference to the element of the claim that the workpiece cooperates with or acts upon or which acts upon the workpiece.

In contrast to an element of the claim, the workpiece or environmental element is introduced in the claim by words indicating that the workpiece is not one of the claim elements. Therefore, it is not written as the subject of a clause of the claim. Rather, the workpiece or environmental element is introduced inferentially in the claim, which is contrary to what is done with a claim element. An element is inferentially introduced in a claim if it first appears within the body of a claim clause as itself acting or being acted upon, without first having been introduced either as the subject of that clause or a preceding clause and without another element recited as having or being that workpiece or environmental element. (By "having or being," I mean reciting "the element comprising (being) (including) the workpiece.") For example, in an apparatus claim, the workpiece might be introduced in a clause: "the juicer including a crusher (an element of the claimed apparatus being introduced in this clause) for acting on a piece of citrus fruit (the workpiece) . . ." or "a grinding wheel acting on a roll (the workpiece is mentioned for the first time) supported in the vicinity of the wheel for grinding the surface (workpiece) of the roll (second mention of the workpiece). . . ." In these examples, the workpiece is first mentioned in the middle of a clause having another element as its main subject and the workpiece is introduced or for the first time mentioned using the indefinite article "a," whereby it is being inferentially claimed. Each succeeding mention of the same workpiece can be preceded by the definite article "the," but preferably not with the definite article "said" because that word has typically been used for referring back to a previous actual claim element.

Conventional and environmental elements present but not critical to the invention being claimed should not be mentioned as claim elements. For claiming an automobile, one would not claim environmental material that is present in the engine, such as fuel, as a claim element. For a telescope, one would not recite the celestial object being viewed as one of the claim elements, although its cooperation with the lenses and the image collector certainly is important.

However, some elements in a full combination may have to be recited positively, even if the claim drafter prefers they not be claim elements. Where a subcombination of a complete combination is claimed in terms of cooperation between elements of the subcombination and other elements of the combination which the claim drafter would prefer not to positively claim, the other elements of the combination may have to be positively recited claim elements to claim a complete apparatus. For example, if a seat back has a novel element for connection to a chair base, to claim the cooperation between the seat back and the base, it may be necessary to claim the elements of the chair positively, so that the claim would cover the chair with a seat back, and not merely the seat back. Claiming the subcombination is preferred for broader scope coverage, but may not be possible for proper claim preparation.

Conventional replaceable items that would not normally be made or sold by the party who is making the claimed invention should also preferably not appear in the claim, except perhaps by inference, as an environmental element, so as not to restrict the scope of the claim. Examples of this are discussed in section 35 below. An electrical system might include a power supply or an antenna. An automobile includes tires, or a battery. Respective supplies are used for a particular apparatus, such as fuel used to drive an engine, gas used to fill a balloon, thread in a sewing machine, etc. These should not be claim elements at all, or if they appear, they should be claimed inferentially as workpiece or environmental elements.

One would always rather catch a direct infringer under 35 U.S.C. § 271(a) than a contributory one under 35 U.S.C. § 271(c). To catch the manufacturer for infringement, you do not recite the element he would not include. If you write those elements into the claims, the manufacturer becomes only a contributory infringer, and only his customer, the retailer or the ultimate consumer, becomes the actual infringer.

Summary

Inferentially claim workpieces and environmental elements and inferentially claim elements not critical to the claimed combination which are not likely to be made and/or sold by the patentee. Do not recite them as one of the claim elements. This broadens the claim scope by not including elements not supplied by the patentee.

§ 17 Negative Limitations

In the past, negative limitations, telling what an element is not instead of what it is, were generally considered improper except in unusual cases. However, MPEP 2173.05(i) states:

> The current view of the courts is that there is nothing inherently ambiguous or uncertain about a negative limitation.

There normally would be no problem that a negative limitation per se would make a claim too broad, indefinite, etc.

Under this practice, such descriptions as "halogen other than fluorine" would presumably be acceptable. Such expressions as "noncircular," "nonmagnetic" or "colorless" have always been accepted because there is no other practical way to state the concept. In view of the former antipathy, it is suggested the negative statements still be avoided except where it seems the only way, or by far the clearest way, to state the limitation. MPEP 2173.05(i) provides as acceptable examples: "*not* in excess of 10% structure" and "incapable of forming a dye with. . . ."

In *In re Duva*,[4] a negative limitation, "absent sufficient CN [cyanide] ions to prevent deposition . . . ," was held proper even if a positive expression could have been employed, which was disputed. Further, it was held proper to claim a negative limitation even at the "point of novelty," but there were other points of novelty.

Perhaps negative limitations, under the *Duva* case and MPEP 706.03(d), could be used in some cases to avoid the limiting language "consisting" or "consisting essentially" (section 8). For example, if one's claim covered the combination comprising A+B+C, and the examiner cited A+B+C with a large amount of D, and if it were unobvious to eliminate D, the claim could perhaps be amended to read "comprising A+B+C and absent sufficient D to . . . [hurt the combination]," as in *Duva,* rather than switching to "consisting" or "consisting essentially." Then the claim would cover A+B+C+E, where E is the absence of excess D.

The negative claim limitation must have a basis in the original disclosure, i.e., the absence or negative character of the negatively claimed element must have been originally disclosed. The mere absence of a positive recitation of an element is not a basis for its exclusion in a claim.[4.1]

Summary

Avoid negative limitations except in unusual cases where you think they are the clearest way to state the limitations. But in general, tell what an element is, not what it is not.

---

4. *In re* Duva, 156 U.S.P.Q. (BNA) 90, 94 (C.C.P.A. 1967).
4.1. MPEP 2173.05(i).

§18 Support in Specification and Drawings

All terms and phrases used in the claims must find "clear support or antecedent basis in the description so that the meaning of the terms in the claims may be ascertainable by reference to the description" (rule 75(d)). That is, the claims must clearly "read on"[5] the remainder of the specification, with consistent terminology being used so that no ambiguities are present.

This rule traces from the statutory requirement that the claims "particularly point out and distinctly claim": if it is not followed, the claim will be rejected under 35 U.S.C. § 112 of the statute as "indefinite" or "vague and indefinite." Thus, one must be able to understand what the claim means, and how it is related to the example described in the detailed description.

When the claims, specification, and drawings do not correspond, the claims can be rejected. The claims should therefore be consistent with the disclosure.[5.1]

Generally, the best practice is to use the identical words of the claim somewhere in the body of the specification to ensure this requirement is met.[5.2] For example, if a fastener is used in the machine, comprising a rivet in the specific example illustrated in the application, but one wishes to claim it in some or all claims broadly as a "fastener," the descriptive portion of the specification should so describe it: "a fastener, such as a rivet 10. . . ." Thereafter it is proper merely to refer to it as "the rivet 10." It would be poor practice to refer to a certain element as a lever throughout the detailed description and then call it a bar in the claims.

One frequently observed exception to the foregoing is the use of "means plus function" language to define a claim element (see section 34). The specification may give a name to the element and also define its function. The claim may instead call the element "means" and describe the function stated in the specification or

---

5. Patentese, meaning that each technical phrase in the claim must literally describe a corresponding element or connection, etc., found in the description. Frequently, the claim is literally read word by word and the corresponding things found and checked off in the specification, or in the allegedly infringing product or drawing of the product. Thus, one's client's claim "reads on" an adverse party's product.

5.1. *See* rule 117; MPEP 2173.05(i).

5.2. *See* MPEP 2173.05(a).

clearly inherently performed thereby (specification: "hammer"; claim: "means for hammering").

Rule 81(a) requires filing of a drawing with the application where necessary for the understanding of the subject matter sought to be patented. Rule 83(a) provides that "the drawing must show every feature of the invention specified in the claims." Thus, for machines, articles of manufacture, or other inventions where an element is capable of illustration in a drawing, it must be shown; however, symbols or labeled boxes, etc., may be used if the element per se is conventional. Where an element is not shown in a drawing, it cannot be recited in a claim. Where the element is shown in the drawing and properly recited in the claim, the specification should describe or at least indicate the presence of the element in the drawing, or should be amended to add such description, in order that the specification, drawings, and claims be consistent.[5.3]

Beware of adding or amending a claim after the application has been filed which adds or relies upon new matter, i.e., elements without support in the original disclosure.[5.4]

On prior Agent's Exams, examples of lack of support have included:

1. Parts or features in the claims not described at all in the description;

2. Inconsistent descriptions of parts;

3. Misdescriptive wording in the claims;

4. Ambiguities, where it is not clear which of several elements in the description is intended by a word in the claim.

For special problems in block diagram disclosures in electrical cases, see sections 35 and 44 (computer programs and software). The key test is whether "a person skilled in the art could make and use the invention without undue experimentation."[6] In theory, that test applies equally well in all classes and types of inventions— mechanical, electrical, chemical—but the problems most frequently arise in complex electronic circuits, particularly block diagram, means-type disclosures, and most particularly, disclosures con-

---

5.3. MPEP 706.03(n).
5.4. MPEP 2173.05(a).
6. *In re* Scarbrough, 182 U.S.P.Q. (BNA) 298 (C.C.P.A. 1974).

cerned with computer software. But block diagrams can also cause "best mode problems" (under 35 U.S.C. § 112).[7]

Summary

Have clear and unambiguous support in the detailed description for all words and phrases in the claim, so that anyone can understand how the claim reads on the description. Also, all structures described in the claim must be illustrated in the drawing, even old or conventional things.

§ 19 Naming the Elements

It is good practice to analyze the structure and select the essential elements to be claimed, with whatever scope is desired, before starting to write a claim. The elements must be assigned names, such as base, container, legs, and means for oscillating in claim 1 (section 14).

The exact name selected for each element is often not critical, as long as the claim drafter is not mistaken. While applicant in theory has Humpty Dumpty's privilege of making words mean what he wants them to mean, no term may be given a meaning repugnant to its usual meaning.[7.1] This rule is often stated as "applicant may be his own lexicographer."[8] But this is still within limits. Of course, the words used must have "clear support or antecedent basis" in the specification, as mentioned in section 18. It is very important to make all parts of the specification consistent with the claims. When one wishes to impart a special meaning to a word or phrase appearing in the claims, one should define that word or phrase in the specification; for example, "As used in this description and in the appended claims, the word '_____' means '_____.'" However, do not use ridiculous words such as "gizmo" or "widget."

---

7. *See* Union Carbide Corp. v. Borg Warner Corp., 193 U.S.P.Q. (BNA) 1 (6th Cir. 1977) (box labeled "extruder" held not proper to disclosed best mode of practicing process that would include step "extruding").

7.1. MPEP 2173.05(b).

8. MPEP 2173.01; Lear Siegler, Inc. v. Aerogrip Corp., 221 U.S.P.Q. (BNA) 1025, 1031 (Fed. Cir. 1984); W.L. Gore Assocs. v. Garlock, Inc., 220 U.S.P.Q. (BNA) 303, 316 (Fed. Cir. 1983).

Frequently in mechanical apparatus, there are various expressions that could be used. For example, in claim 1, the base could have been called "a support," "a mounting plate," or the like. The container might have been designated "a box" or "a holder." The choices available frequently are descriptive names for an important function or purpose of the element named.

In most cases, the inventor or a mechanical dictionary can supply the precise name for a part in any specific embodiment. Appendix C contains a glossary of many mechanical terms commonly used in patents. For the broader claims, a generic word is usually needed. If no concrete generic name is available, often a home-made name indicating the function of the part may be used, such as "a rotary member" or "a holder," together with as much description of the part and its function as is necessary. Also "means" clauses are often used to describe an element broadly (see section 34).

New terms may be adopted by an applicant and often are used for new technology. If the claims, read in light of the specification, reasonably apprise those skilled in the art of the utilization and scope of the invention and if the language is as precise as the subject matter permits, § 112 is satisfied.[8.1]

Where practical, it is best to give two similar but different elements distinct names, such as "a holding member" and "a support member" even when in common usage those different elements might be identified by the same name. In other cases, this is not possible, in which case designations such as "first" or "second" should be used: "a first rotating member, . . . a second rotating member. . . ." Alternatively, the distinguishing adjective may refer to another element with which the named element is associated: "a base rotating member, . . . a connector rotating member. . . ." Thereafter the elements must be clearly and consistently named throughout all of the claims.

Use the same name for the element consistently throughout every claim. Do not change the noun. Do not change any adjectives. An adjective once used need not be repeated upon each subsequent appearance of its noun. But if the adjective has a subsequent

---

8.1. MPEP 2173.05(a); *In re* Burke, Inc., 786 F. Supp. 1537, 22 U.S.P.Q.2d (BNA) 1368, 1372 (C.D. Cal. 1992).

appearance, the word(s) used must remain the same. An item called a "member," as in "connecting member," is always a "member," throughout all claims dependent upon the same claim in which the element has been first named. In *Ex parte Oetiker*,[8.2] the Board of Appeals and Interferences found a claim indefinite because an element therein appeared to have been twice claimed, first as "a pan-shaped depression means" and later as "a respective depression means." Not only did the applicant change the name, he used the indefinite article "a" twice. In a claim which does not depend from one naming an element, another name may be used for the same element. For example, in one chain of claims, the element may be the broader "surface," while in another chain of claims, the element may be the narrower "anvil" of which the surface is only a part. Within each claim chain, the name of the element may never change. The "member" cannot sometimes be an "element," that is, it cannot be a "connecting element." An "element" would be a different claimed structure. If elements are named to suggest to the reader that two of them are present when in fact there is only one, this causes double inclusion of the twice-named element and the resulting claim may be held to be indefinite.[8.3]

Often, an element is described not only by the noun, e.g., "member," but by adjectives which modify the noun, as "connecting member" or "left side connecting member." After any feature is first named completely with all its adjectives in a claim, subsequent mentions of the feature in that claim or in subsequent dependent claims in the claim chain, following the first naming of the element, must use the same noun for that element, but may use fewer than all of the adjectives, thereafter calling it "member" or "connecting member," without the other adjectives "left side." The only limit on this freedom to drop adjectives is that there must be no other element whose designation, when shortened either to the noun alone or to the noun plus fewer than all of its adjectives, would be identified by the same words, because that would cause confusion as to which element was meant. Further, in a chain of claims following the one that first uses an adjective, the

---

8.2. *Ex parte* Oetiker, 23 U.S.P.Q.2d (BNA) 1651, 1655 (Board of Appeals and Interferences 1992).

8.3. MPEP 2173.05(o). *See* section 21.

adjective cannot change. It may be deleted, as just noted, but not changed. If it is "an upper engaging member," it cannot later be "the upper holding member" or the "top engaging member."

For clarity in claim writing, I recommend avoiding use of first, second, third, etc., as the adjective which distinguishes one element from another. This usage is proper and so long as the adjective is used consistently, it cannot be considered ambiguous. However, sometimes a more descriptive adjective, descriptive, e.g., as to function or location or major characteristics (left side, elongate, etc.) might help the claim reader determine which element is being identified. On the other hand, the elements designated first, second, third, etc. may be identical in structure and function and may be distinguishable only by a nondescriptive adjective, or maybe using a descriptive adjective would, in the drafter's opinion, impermissibly narrow the scope of the recited element. Further, reciting only the adjectives first, second, etc. is useful where there are two or more ways of arranging elements and the claim writer wishes to encompass all of the ways, so that one location or arrangement would be first and the other would be second, without specifiying which is which. Each element must always be described in such a distinctive manner as to clearly distinguish it from other similar or identical elements, as covered in section 16. Use the same terminology in the specification, as in the claims, even to at least once identifying the claimed elements using their distinguishing adjective, i.e., first or second, base or connector, etc.

Summary

Select a clear name for each element, based on the detailed specification description where given. Where a broad scope name is desired, functional names, such as "a fastener" or "means for moving . . . ," should be used.

§ 20 Singular and Plural Elements

The number of elements of a given type, if more than one, should also be stated where the number is material to the claim:

A pair of arms . . .

Three springs . . .

A plurality of rods . . . (used for an indefinite number, two or more). [The word "multiplicity" is often used also, but this may tend to connote a fairly large number, such as "a sieve having a multiplicity of perforations."]

At least five fingers . . . (used where there must be at least five but more would do).

The minimum (or as appropriate, maximum) number of elements necessary for the combination to function properly should be recited. The minimum number then covers a larger number where, as is customary, the word "comprising" is used (section 7). The term "a pair" will cover two or any number greater than two, but it will not cover only one. Where one or more will function, then one merely claims "a" member (singular) and this covers more than one.[8.4] However, the context of a disclosed and/or claimed embodiment may make the court interpret "a" following the transition word "comprising" to mean a single one of the elements and exclude more than one of the elements.[8.5] In *Abtox*, the court relied on the subsequent appearance of "said" before the element as evidence that only one such element was claimed. (In this author's view, that improperly restricts the claim with a "comprising" transition word and is contrary to the usual understanding of "a" and "said" in a claim.) A more correct view is stated in *Elkay Mfg. Co. v. Ebco Mfg. Co.*,[8.6] wherein "a" or "an" suggests "one," but can also mean "one or more than one" or "at least

---

8.4. Abtox, Inc. v. Exitron Corp., 43 U.S.P.Q.2d (BNA) 1545, 1548 (Fed. Cir. 1997), *modified on other grounds,* 46 U.S.P.Q.2d (BNA) 1735 (Fed. Cir. 1997).

8.5. *Id.*

8.6. Elkay Mfg. Co. v. Ebco Mfg. Co., 52 U.S.P.Q.2d (BNA) 1109 (Fed. Cir. 1999).

one," depending on the context in which the article is used,[8.7] when the claim has the open-ended transition, such as "comprising."[8.8] As the claims used the open term "comprising" in their transition phrases, the claims were not necessarily limited to a single feed tube or a single flow path, even though the preferred embodiment showed a single feed tube and a single flow path.[8.9]

Optionally, one sees "at least one _____" or "at least two _____," or "at most three _____," which are also correct. "At least one" means either one of the elements or more than one of them.[8.10]

When claiming a combination, where more than one of a certain element is included in the combination (e.g., conveyor means), the term "at least two" means the minimum number of a particular element required.[9] This interpretation gives effect to the recitation of the two distinct elements in the claimed structure. Therefore, all claims would require two or more of the conveyor structure. Since laymen are eventually considering claim language, i.e., a judge or a jury, the latter option may now be preferable, since the nuanced meaning of "comprising" may not be so easily understood as "at least two . . . ," when a claim is meant to cover any number greater than one of a particular element. An alternative statement "one or more" would ordinarily be considered improper under the rule

---

8.7. TM Patents L.P. v. International Bus. Mach. Corp., 72 F. Supp. 2d 370, 53 U.S.P.Q.2d (BNA) 1093, 1101 (S.D.N.Y. 1999); KCJ Corp. v. Kinetic Concepts, Inc., 223 F.3d 1351, 55 U.S.P.Q.2d (BNA) 1835, 1839 (Fed. Cir. 2000).

8.8. Crystal Semiconductor Corp. v. TriTech Microelectronics Int'l, Inc., ___ F.3d ___, 57 U.S.P.Q.2d (BNA) 1953, 1958 (Fed. Cir. 2001).

8.9. In Innovad, Inc. v. Microsoft Corp., ___ F.3d ___, 59 U.S.P.Q.2d (BNA) 1676, 1680–81 (Fed. Cir. 2001), "a single bi-state switch" where the main transition word after the preamble was "comprising" did not preclude the presence of other switches, even other bi-state switches, for other purposes than the stated purpose for the single bi-state switch.

8.10. Rhine v. Casio, Inc., 183 F.3d 1342, 51 U.S.P.Q.2d (BNA) 1377 (Fed. Cir. 1999).

9. Lantech, Inc. v. Keip Machine Co., 27 U.S.P.Q.2d 1906 (W.D. Mich 1993), *rev'd in part, remanded*, 32 F.3d 542, 31 U.S.P.Q.2d 1666 (Fed. Cir. 1994) *and vacating, summary judgment granted*, 1995 U.S. Dist. LEXIS 11636 (W.D. Mich. 1995).

against alternative claiming discussed in section 24. However, one case[10] allowed a claim including "a spline or splines."

Practitioners use the term "plurality." It means two or more.[10.1]

When there is a maximum number of a particular element in a claimed combination, the maximum is recited, e.g., "at most three."

An open-ended numerical range is normally definite under 35 U.S.C. § 112 unless it covers an apparently impossible situation. Particularly in chemical cases, where a composition including a range of one element could exceed 100% of the total quantity of ingredients, that claim with the open range is indefinite.[10.2]

Where the quantity of a particular element is not material to the claim, there is no benefit to reciting that there are a plurality of that element. Recite "a finger" and leave it at that, or "at least one finger," if the plurality of fingers is obviously present.

Some practitioners advocate naming the element and then following that with the word "means," such as "finger means." The latter phrasing is indefinite as to number and yet encompasses any number. However, once the word "means" is used in naming a claim element, it may be treated as a means plus function element under 35 U.S.C. § 112, paragraph 6 (see section 34). Case precedents, discussed below in the section on means clauses, may narrow the scope of means limitations, as compared with other limitations, whereby "finger means" may be more restricted in scope than "at least one finger," when a claim is interpreted for application to a possible infringement.

In an earlier claim, a single one of an element may be claimed. A later dependent claim may recite a plurality of those same elements, without redefining the features of the element, and the parent claim provides antecedent support for the dependent claim.[11]

---

10. *In re* Pavlecka, 138 U.S.P.Q. (BNA) 118 (C.C.P.A. 1963).

10.1. York Products, Inc. v. Cent. Tractor Farm & Family Ctr., 99 F.3d 1568, 40 U.S.P.Q.2d (BNA) 1619 (Fed. Cir. 1996). Plurality does not require three or more. Dayco Products, Inc. v. Total Containment, Inc., ___ F.3d ___, 59 U.S.P.Q.2d (BNA) 1489 (Fed. Cir. 2001).

10.2. MPEP 2173.05(c).

11. *Ex parte* Moelands, 36 U.S.P.Q.2d (BNA) 1474, 1475 (Bd. Pat. Interp. 1987).

For example, claim 1 at section 14 above might have claimed "a leg . . ." or "at least one leg," while claim 2 could then recite "a plurality of the legs" or "at least two of the legs."

Summary

State the minimum number of similar elements needed where more than one is necessary to the claim. If any number more than one will do, use the phrase "a plurality."

§ 21 Double Inclusion of Elements

One should be careful that precisely the same element is not included in the claim twice under two different names. See section 19 about a consistent name for each element. This is an error known as "double inclusion."[11.1] In non-chemical cases, the claim is rendered indefinite, and it may not be indefinite only in *Markush* groups, as discussed below.

Sometimes the problem arises in writing dependent claims (see section 11), where one might inadvertently add as an apparently new element something already in the parent claim or in one of several earlier claims in a chain of dependent claims. This is likely to occur in a complicated structure with many elements.

Sometimes the double recitation occurs because an element is recited broadly in an earlier claim and then mentioned in greater detail using a different name in a later claim. For example, claim 1 (section 14) calls for "means for oscillating the container." If claim 2 recited "A combination as recited in claim 1, *further comprising* a motor, . . ." it would be improper since the motor is part of the means for oscillating in claim 1. Instead, refer back to the recited element: "A combination as recited in claim 1, wherein the oscillating means comprises a motor. . . ." If two differently named elements of a claim each contain some or much common structure, but not entirely common structure, it is not double inclusion to give those elements different names so long as at least some structure is different. See further comments on this, with respect to "means" clauses, in section 34.

11.1. MPEP 2173.05(o).

Sometimes the double recitation occurs because the same element is mentioned a second time in the same claim or in a series of claims introduced by the indefinite article "a" or "an," rather than by a definite article "the" or "said," which refers the reader back to the first appearance of the element in the claim or series of claims. See section 16 above relating to how to avoid inferential claiming of elements.

MPEP 2173.05(o) describes the unique situation in a *Markush* group (section 50) wherein there may be some overlapping in the members of the group. A group including "halogens" and "chloro" appears to overlap where alternatives are recited ("or"). But decisions reported in the MPEP section suggest opposite outcomes on the indefiniteness issue.

Summary

Do not put the same element in the claim twice under two different names. Watch dependent claims so as not to add as a further element something already included in a previous claim from which the new claim depends.

§ 22 Use of Reference Numerals in Claims

Reference numerals corresponding to the specific elements or parts shown in the drawings may be used in claims. This practice, common in some foreign countries,[12] has been very rare in the United States. MPEP 608.01(m) provides for this practice on an optional and nonlimiting basis:

> Reference characters corresponding to elements recited in the detailed description and the drawings may be used in conjunction with the recitation of the same element or group of elements in the claims. The reference characters, however, should be enclosed within parentheses so as to avoid confusion with other numbers or characters which may appear in the claims. The use

---

12. For example, some countries may require numerals throughout the claim and other countries may require numerals only in the body of the claim after the preamble and transition. In the latter countries, the preamble includes material known in the art and numerals are not there required.

of reference characters is to be considered as having no effect on the scope of the claims.[13]

Although this technique may seem helpful in interpreting claims as long as the claim scope is not limited by the parenthetical numerals, it is almost never used at present, and many attorneys probably consider the practice unsafe. For example, when the claim is being interpreted for equivalents by a court, the court may still limit the scope of claim breadth due to the presence of numbers referring to drawings of an embodiment, despite the Manual's recommending (for examiners but not for judges) that the reference characters have no effect.

Summary

Do not use reference characters from the drawings in claims, but it is not wrong to do so (if placed in parentheses).

§ 23 Antecedents; Indefiniteness

The first time an element or part is mentioned, it should not be preceded by a definite article ("the") or by "said." Instead the indefinite article ("a" or "an") should be used, as in claim 1: "*a* container," "*a* base," etc.[13.1] This practice merely follows normal rules of grammar. Plural elements are not preceded by articles, as there is no plural indefinite article. Thus "containers." Sometimes an element is preceded by a numerical adjective when it is introduced in a claim, as "two containers." A "means for" clause requires no article: "means for oscillating. . . ." Note that none of these uses a definite article. When each previously identified element or part is referred to again, the definite article should be used, as "*the* container," "*the* base," or "*the* oscillating means" in claim 1; or "*the* two containers," or simply "*the* two containers." See section 16 above relating to inferential claiming.

---

13. *See also* MPEP 2173.05(s).

13.1. *See* Abtox, Inc. v. Exitron Corp., 43 U.S.P.Q.2d (BNA) 1545, 1548 (Fed. Cir. 1997), *modified on other grounds,* 46 U.S.P.Q.2d (BNA) 1735 (Fed. Cir. 1997).

If the definite article is not used for each subsequent appearance of the element and if an indefinite article is used, this will suggest to the reader that a new element is being identified, rather than the previously named element, and this will cause improper double inclusion of the element.[13.2]

The word "said" is used by many practitioners rather than "the" to refer back to previously recited elements, sometimes to a previously recited anything. This practice is unobjectionable, although perhaps overly legalistic. If "saids" or "thes" are used, one should be consistent in the usage and not alternate between those words in repetitions of the same element or among different elements. (However, one often sees alternation between "said" and "the" within a claim without any apparent reason, and there is usually no objection as to this form by an Examiner at the Patent Office.) One common style is to use "said" only for the elements themselves, and "the" for everything else. The expression "the said" which one sometimes sees is a patent redundancy and should be avoided.

When referring back to an element, it must be perfectly clear which element. The claim must be consistent within itself. For example, if two different gears have been individually described in the claim, it is improper to refer back to "said gear"; refer to "said first gear," "said drive gear," etc. Similarly, if a motor has been recited, do not refer back to "said drive means," i.e., never change the name that was first given to an element. In another example, the claim recited "a handle" and then something connected to "a handle"; thus it was not clear whether the first handle was meant or a different one. Such descriptions are "indefinite." It is also improper to describe additional details of an element when referring back to that element as an antecedent; for example, if "a gear" has been recited, it would be improper to refer to "said *plastic* gear." This is also called an "indirect limitation." To introduce the "plastic" nature of the gear, use a describing clause, "the gear is plastic" or "the gear is comprised of plastic."

13.2. MPEP 2173.05(o); *Ex parte* Oetiker, 23 U.S.P.Q.2d (BNA) 1651, 1655 (Board of Appeals and Interferences 1992).

Claim limitations are often of such length that an attempt to refer back to an earlier mentioned element may introduce an ambiguity: "a handle connected to the gear, which is supported on the axis to pivot about it." To what does "which" and "it" refer, the handle, the gear, or the axis? Better would be "a handle connected to the gear, the handle is supported on the axis to pivot about the gear"—no ambiguity there. Do not hesitate to repeat the name of an element each time it appears in a clause (the handle). Avoid using indefinite words to refer back (which or that) or pronouns that do not mention the name of the element (it) unless there can be no doubt which element is being indicated. Wherever there is a second element between a first mentioned element and a later word referring back, as occurred in the above handle/gear/axis example, use of an indefinite reference back should be avoided, as ambiguity is virtually unavoidable.

In dependent claims also, one must be careful to avoid confusion between elements in any parent claims (or claims) and elements added by the dependent claim.

All such rejections or objections on matters of claim form are based upon claim "indefiniteness" of the claim and trace from 35 U.S.C. § 112, i.e., the subject matter has not been "particularly pointed out and distinctly claimed," meaning that the examiner cannot tell what the claim covers.[14] In *In re Miller*,[15] the court held that an "indefiniteness" rejection must be based on § 112,[16] and held that the Patent and Trademark Office could not reject the claim under section 103 (obviousness) by ignoring the allegedly indefinite words.[17] The *Miller* court said: "All *words* in a claim must be considered in judging the patentabilty of that claim against the prior art."

This question arises in many contexts, such as preamble limitations (section 56), mental steps (section 44), functional language (section 31), printed matter (section 65), and others.

---

14. *See* MPEP 706.03(d); *In re* Venezia, 189 U.S.P.Q. (BNA) 149, 151 (C.C.P.A. 1976).

15. *In re* Miller, 169 U.S.P.Q. (BNA) 597, 600 (C.C.P.A. 1971).

16. MPEP 706.02.

17. Citing *In re* Wilson, 165 U.S.P.Q. (BNA) 494 (C.C.P.A. 1970).

Ex parte Schaefer[18] holds that:

> Omission of some elements of the device [the complete device described in the specification, through the use of the preamble "comprising"—Section 7] makes the claim broad, but not vague, indefinite or misdescriptive.

In other words, the court and Board are saying to the examiner: "reject broad claims on prior art, if you can find any, but not under § 112 as 'indefinite,' etc. Section 112 applies only where you cannot understand what the claim covers." See also "incomplete" claims, section 66. However, a claim that omits essentials can be rejected as incomplete under § 112. MPEP 2173.05(l) recites:

> A claim can be rejected as incomplete if it omits essential elements, steps or necessary structural cooperative relationship of elements, such omission amounting to a gap between the elements, steps or necessary structural connections. . . . Greater latitude is permissible with respect to the definition in a claim of maters not essential to novelty or operability than with respect to matters essential thereto.

Summary

Use "a" or "an" the first time you mention an element or part in a claim, where grammatical rules dictate. Use "the" or "said" after that, when referring again to the same element or part. Make sure the claim is consistent with itself, that each "the" or "said" element has one and only one clear antecedent in the claim, and that consistent, definite phraseology is used throughout the claim. In general, make sure the claim is definite and clearly understandable as to what it covers and how it reads on the detailed description and drawing.

---

18. *Ex parte* Schaefer, 171 U.S.P.Q. (BNA) 110 (Bd. App. 1970).

§ 23A Relative Terminology

Comparative words are also indefinite, that is, they are unbased comparisons, unless those words have been clearly defined in the disclosure or specification and/or the basis of the comparison, what is being compared, is stated and/or one of ordinary skill in the art, in view of the prior art and the status of the art, would be apprised of the scope of the claim.[18.1] Typically, a comparative word expresses a measure or magnitude, but has no meaning in a claim unless expressly defined in the specification: ". . . a predetermined distance of under three meters. . . ." Usually, those comparative words can mean virtually anything. If a distance is "predetermined" or a quantity is "sufficient," how much or how great are these amounts? It is best not to use such terms at all in the claims. "A claim may be rendered indefinite by reference to an object that is variable."[18.2] The Manual section provides examples decided by the Board of Appeals.

In *Norton Co. v. Bendix Corp.,*[19] a claim was held invalid for indefiniteness for inclusion of the phrases "closely spaced" and "substantial distance." Apparently, these features or relationships were important to novelty, and the specification did not define them. The testimony showed that a potential infringer could not tell, nor could the patentee, just what infringed and what did not. See *Ex parte Oetiker*[19.1] for phrases held not to define relationships, discussed in section 26A herein.

On the other hand, if the comparative word is not clearly defined in the specification, but is instead compared with something else and the relationship between them is in the claim element, then the claim element may not be indefinite.[19.2] For example, if the container of claim 1 in section 14 were capable of being filled with a "predetermined" quantity of articles, that would not say how many and the limitation would be indefinite if patentability hinged on that capability. But if the predetermined quantity were

---

18.1. MPEP 2173.05(b).

18.2. *Id.*

19. Norton Co. v. Bendix Corp., 171 U.S.P.Q. (BNA) 449 (2d Cir. 1971).

19.1. *Ex parte* Oetiker, 23 U.S.P.Q.2d (BNA) 1651, 1654–56, 1658–60 (Board of Appeals and Interferences 1992).

19.2. *Cf.* Moore U.S.A., Inc. v. Standard Register Co., 229 F.3d 1091, 56 U.S.P.Q.2d (BNA) 1225, 1238-39 (Fed. Cir. 2000).

defined as less than the quantity the legs could support, then for the critical aspect of that predetermined quantity, there is adequate definition. The claim, or one dependent on it, might recite: "the plurality of legs being adapted to support up to a predetermined quantity of the articles; the container being shaped to contain up to fewer than the predetermined quantity of the articles." Whatever is a "predetermined" quantity, its meaning as a comparative term is explained. Numerous other words suggesting magnitude can be definite in a claim if used comparatively: "more than the minimum . . .," "shorter than the preset value. . . ." MPEP 2173.05(b) provides an example of an acceptable comparative, wherein something was "dimensioned as to be insertable through the space between the doorframe . . . and one of the seats." The comparative here had a measurable standard.[19.3]

MPEP 2173.05(b) also discusses precedents relating to other comparative words, "about": yes and no; "essentially": definite; "similar": indefinite; "substantially": usually definite (and often used in claims); "type" when added to a definite expression made it indefinite. Also held indefinite were: "relatively"; "on the order of"; "or like material"; "comparable"; "superior."[19.4] Definiteness requires it be explained in the specification, be compared with something else specifically, or be a term known to one of skill in the art. But "relatively" has also been held definite.[19.5]

In *EMI Group North America Inc. v. Intel Corp.,*[19.6] a "relatively thicker layer of oxide" was not indefinite because the court found the applicant for patent had used that term to distinguish

---

19.3. In Innovad, Inc. v. Microsoft Corp., ___ F.3d ___, 59 U.S.P.Q.2d (BNA) 1676, 1680 (Fed. Cir. 2001), the court upheld the term "small volume" as meaning smaller than prior art telephone dialers. The court found no definition of "small" in this specification, but found a relationship between the "small volume" and its purpose, without relationship to any specific size. (Here, a perhaps insufficient disclosure of a claim that included an unbased comparison was saved by a court's detailed analysis. Had the actual relationship desired been claimed, the issue would not have arisen.)

19.4. *Ex parte* Oetiker, 23 U.S.P.Q.2d (BNA) 1651, 1655, 1658–60 (Board of Appeals and Interferences 1992).

19.5. Allergan Sales, Inc. v. Pharmacia & UpJohn, Inc., 42 U.S.P.Q.2d (BNA) 1560 (S.D. Cal. 1997).

19.6. EMI Group North America Inc. v. Intel Corp., 157 F.3d 887, 48 U.S.P.Q.2d (BNA) 1181 (Fed. Cir. 1998), *cert. denied*, 119 S. Ct. 1756 (1999).

from prior art during application prosecution and the court was able to use the same distinction to find noninfringement of the claim.

However, if patentability of the claim will not depend on the actual or comparative magnitude of the element described with a comparative term, then the claim will not be indefinite. It is not useful to claim that the container is fillable with a predetermined quantity of articles, as one does not know how many are in that predetermined quantity. But, it is not harmful, because patentability is not premised on that quantity.

The cases on indefiniteness can be confusing and may turn on specific facts adduced at trial, long after the claim was written and patented.

Summary

Avoid use of comparative words, unless defined in the specification or the critical aspect of the comparison is also claimed.

§ 24 Alternative Expressions

Alternative expressions are not per se indefinite. Instead, they are permitted if they present no ambiguity with respect to the question of scope or clarity of the claims.[19.7] The primary example of an acceptable alternative is a *Markush* group (section 50).

If you do not intend to claim a *Markush* group, but want to express alternatives, it must be done carefully or the alternatives will be treated effectively as a *Markush* group and, for example, prior art as to one member of the group may anticipate the entire group. In *Brown v. Air Products and Chemicals, Inc.,*[19.8] the patent claimed setting year data in a computer clock in "at least one of two-digit, three-digit, or four-digit representations." The patentee intended that the apparatus be able to perform all three alternatives. But the language used did not encompass all three, because

---

19.7. MPEP 2173.05(h).
19.8. Brown v. Air Products and Chemicals, Inc., 229 F.3d 1120, 56 U.S.P.Q.2d (BNA) 1456 (Fed. Cir. 2001).

it was merely stated alternatively in a *Markush* group. If the patentee meant the capability was as to all three alternatives, that should have been said, i.e., without "at least" and here, too, without "or."

It is ordinarily improper to use alternative expressions for a single element or part in a claim. Thus, it is improper to state: "a spring or a weight for urging the carriage against the stop [assuming the carriage and stop had been defined]." In effect, that would be two claims. Also, it is indefinite in that the reader does not know which one, the spring or the weight, infringes the claim, based on the claim language. Some case precedents suggest alternative language may sometimes be acceptable: "made entirely or in part of . . ."[19.9] But better practice says to avoid that.

The way to avoid alternative expressions is to find or invent some expression that is generic to both embodiments or species, such as "means for biasing" in the above example. (See section 50 on *Markush* expressions for a limited exception in certain types of chemical cases where an element is selectable from a list of similar ones.)

Old section MPEP 706.03(d) appeared to permit some limited use of alternative expressions:

> Alternative expressions such as "brake or locking device" may make a claim indefinite if the limitation covers two different elements. If two equivalent parts are referred to such as "rods or bars," the alternative expression may be considered proper.

Since the precise boundaries of equivalent parts often are not clear, and since alternatives were previously considered improper per se, it is suggested that this device not be used. Note the *Pavlecka* case[20] sanctioning "a spline or splines."

Similarly, attempted alternative or hedged expressions (e.g., "a drive means, such as a motor," or "a holder, preferably a perforated box") are considered improper.[20.1] "Description of examples or preferences is properly set forth in the specification rather than the claims."[20.2] These expressions are alternative and really an at-

---

19.9. MPEP 2173.05(h).

20. *In re* Pavlecka, 138 U.S.P.Q. (BNA) 118 (C.C.P.A. 1963).

20.1. MPEP 2173.05(d).

20.2. *Id.*

tempt to present two different claims—one broad, one narrower —at the same time. If it is not clear whether the claimed narrower range is a claim limitation, it is improper.[20.3] The MPEP gives examples: "R is halogen, for example, chlorine"; "material such as rock wool or asbestos"; "hydrocarbons such, for example, as the vapor"; "normal conditions, such as while in the container."[20.4] But note, while "material such as rock wool or asbestos" is improper for it is not limiting, "rock wool or asbestos" would be a proper alternative. Each claim must cover a single combination with an ascertainable scope, not several combinations of different scope.

The solution, of course, is to use the broader term for the first claim and, if important, the narrower term or alternative structure in other claims.

In *In re Wolfrum and Gold,*[21] the court expressly held that a *Markush* claim (section 50) to "patentably distinct" species A and B could not be rejected under 35 U.S.C. § 112. (See further discussion of *Wolfrum* in section 67.) The claim in question was very definitely an alternative claim to groups of compounds A or B, but the court held that § 112 would not support such a rejection, because it was clear what the applicant intended to claim, and that is all § 112 requires. Note, there would never be any indefiniteness problem per se in an alternative claim: applicant would clearly intend to claim combination A or combination B, assuming each alternative was clearly defined.

In *In re Haas,*[22] the court held that such claims could not be rejected under 35 U.S.C. § 101, defining the statutory classes of patentable subject matter. (See discussion of that case in section 50.)

It is not clear what other statutory clause might support a rejection of an alternative claim, and if all rejections of claims must be based on specific sections of the statute, the *Wolfrum* case might open up claim drafting practices to any and all definite forms of alternative claims (e.g., "a spring or a weight for biasing"). There would be no question as to what the applicant regards as the in-

---

20.3. *Id.*
20.4. *Id.*
21. *In re* Wolfrum and Gold, 179 U.S.P.Q. (BNA) 620 (C.C.P.A. 1973).
22. *In re* Haas, 179 U.S.P.Q. (BNA) 623 (C.C.P.A. 1973).

vention, the spring or the weight. By extension, one might be allowed to claim a lawn sprinkler or a popcorn popper, totally different inventions, assuming each was defined clearly, so far as § 112 is concerned. But these products are so independent that they could not appear in one claim.

Even under a doctrine permitting express alternatives, such alternative expressions as "a spring or the like" might be barred because it would not be definite what "or the like" might be.

"Optionally," as in "containing A, B and optionally C" is not considered indefinite as there is no ambiguity as to the alternatives covered in the claim. If the list of potential alternatives can vary, leading to ambiguity, the claim is indefinite under § 112, paragraph 2. This is quite a change, in the view of an experienced practitioner. But it illustrates how far MPEP 2173.05(h) goes in permitting alternatives.

Summary

Avoid alternative expressions, particularly names of parts. Make what claims cover definite.

§ 25 Parts or Features of Elements

It is necessary to describe everything about each element that is pertinent to a claim of the scope to be drafted. See sections 23 and 66 re incomplete claims. That is, where material to the claim, one must describe such features as (1) the constituent parts of the element and how they are related; (2) details of construction such as apertures, rounded ends, etc.; (3) the size, shape, and geometry of the element or any of its parts; and (4) the materials of construction used. If the orientation of an element (horizontal, vertical) or its location (above or below some other element) is important, that should be stated.

The foregoing list is illustrative, not exclusive. The rule is to describe everything about the element *that is necessary to the claim* and no more. Of course, the claim drafter must distinguish between the elements of the claim and the parts of the elements; sometimes an item of structure may be made either a separate element or a part of an element, depending on how the elements are defined. In case of doubt, make the item a separate element.

One problem comes with unbased comparatives, such as "thick," "heavy," "small." These will frequently be considered vague and indefinite by the examiner.[22.1] This was discussed in section 23A above. The remedy here usually is to relate the property to some other element or to an external standard, such as "smaller than the _____" or "having a specific gravity greater than one." In this area, there is a "rule of reason," and such qualifiers as "resilient," "flexible," etc., are usually accepted without question.

If many features of elements are essential to the claim, they should be described in some logical order, usually a matter of choice, using subordinate clauses as necessary. But watch out for grammar, particularly verb tenses, and make sure the claim continues to read as a proper sentence (section 4A). One example of a description of a moderately complex element follows:

> . . . a carriage on which the bending fingers and the article holder are mounted, the carriage being mounted in the guideway of the base for sliding movement between the first and second stops, the carriage having a transverse guide slot in its upper surface in which the article holder is mounted for relative sliding movement toward and away from the bending fingers, . . . [Note the "the bending fingers," etc., would have been described in previous clauses.]

As much detail is stated as is necessary, in the easiest way possible.

It is ordinarily best to describe all of the salient features of each element in the clause pertaining to that element, even though the purpose for a feature of the element does not appear until later in the claim. This is preferred over reciting features of one element at different points throughout the claim. It is easier to develop a mental picture of an element, and when there is a drawing, to see all of the features of the element at one time in the drawing, when the claim recites all of the features of that element before moving on to describe another element. However, this is not mandatory, and sometimes other techniques make the claim easier to understand and should be used.

Similarly, it is usually best to tell how an element moves or cooperates with other elements at the point where all of the back-

---

22.1. *See* MPEP 2173.05(b).

ground has been described, rather than waiting until the end of the claim.

The paragraphing of a claim is useful for this describing of the salient features, since a paragraph can recite all of the features of an element before moving on to the next element in the next paragraph.

It should be noted that claim 1 (section 14) does not include any features of elements, as this was not necessary to describe the simple shaker claimed. However, assume that the shaker is a popcorn popper and is to be so claimed, and that the holes in the container (figure 1) are important and must be defined.

Clause (a) of claim 1 might read:

> A container for receiving kernels of corn to be popped, the container having a perforated bottom with apertures smaller in size than the kernels;

Other examples of expressions defining features of elements:

> a disc of resilient material having a peripheral groove . . .
>
> a relay having two windings . . .
>
> a level having a forked end and a rounded end . . . [If only the forked end is important to the combination being claimed, do not mention the rounded end.]
>
> a gear of electrically insulating material . . .

If an element by definition inherently includes a certain feature, that feature need not be recited and it is proper to refer, without previous mention, to such features as: "the end of the lever . . ."; "the periphery of the disc . . ."; "the tines of the fork. . . ." In case of doubt about inherent inclusion, positively describe the feature or part.

Summary

Select those parts or features of each element that are essential to the combination being claimed. Then describe them in a logical order, preferably following the main description of the element and in the same clause of the claim. How many features need to be described and how broadly each should be recited is a matter of the claim scope (based largely on the prior art and the need to avoid an incomplete structure missing an essential component), but the principles are the same as used in selecting the elements and naming them.

§ 26 Claiming Holes

In past practice, in a claim where a hole was to be described, it was not recited positively. That is, instead of stating "a hole, groove, aperture, recess, slot, etc., in the lever," one claimed "the lever having a hole, groove, etc." The object was claimed, and then the feature of significance was recited, the hole, etc. Thereafter, one could refer to "the hole" or "said hole." This can also lead to an odd inquiry as to whether a particular feature is a claimed "hole." For example, is "a chamber in the lever" claiming a hole? Other words denoting empty space (gap, space, opening, hollow, etc.) might be subject to the same rejection. This "rule" may seem to make little sense, but it is another founded in antiquity like the single sentence rule. Perhaps someone thought that a hole, etc., is nothing—and people should not claim nothing. The author has seen objections to claiming holes, received from Examiners even in recently prosecuted patent applications.

Another approach to describing holes is an expression such as "the level having portions defining a hole, groove, etc." The hole is thus defined in terms of the structure that forms it.

However, that previous prohibition against claiming holes has not been honored, and the author has only very rarely seen a rejection of a claim for claiming a "hole," or an equivalent. One case[23] held that it was proper to claim a hole and its function as a means for performing a function, specifically "means for providing fluid communication between . . . [two members]."

Summary

You may claim holes positively and make them claim elements. Better practice is to claim "a [member] having a hole, groove, slot, aperture, etc."

---

23. *In re* Newton, 163 U.S.P.Q. (BNA) 34 (C.C.P.A. 1969).

§ 26A Words of Approximation—Substantially, et al.

There is scarcely a magnitude or quantity, a condition, or a comparison (in this section, simply called a term) that does not benefit from some softening at its edge when recited in a patent claim. A claim limitation that includes such a term often can be satisfied by a slight difference between the prior art or accused element, on the one hand, and the claimed element on the other hand. Patent practitioners use words of approximation as adjectives or adverbs for claim terms—words like "substantial," "substantially," "generally," "approximately," "about," "almost," and the like.[24] (But see section 23A.) So long as the claim element being modified does not require a precise edge or dividing line (the speed of sound is not substantially anything, it is precisely 333 meters per second at sea level), the patentee is better served by giving the claim element some degree of imprecision or fuzziness at its edge or limit.

If a claim limit were to recite 6 inches, or 6 cms, or 6 degrees, or 6 pieces, or a pH of 6, etc., would 5 of the same units meet the claim limit literally, or would 5.8 of those units meet it literally? The simple answer is "no," because the number of units is below 6. The claim limitation would not be literally satisfied. The Doctrine of Equivalents was developed to deal with this situation. But application of that Doctrine imposes considerable extra testing and comparisons, both during examination of the claim in the Patent Office (*In re Donaldson*[25]) and during an infringement tri-

---

24. A claim reciting that the claimed method "does not substantially inhibit the activity of the antimicrobial agent" is not invalid for indefiniteness. Bausch & Lomb Inc. v. Alcon Laboratories Inc., 79 F. Supp. 2d 252, 53 U.S.P.Q.2d (BNA) 1682 (W.D.N.Y. 1999). The word "substantially" gives some definitional leeway. Seattle Box Co. v. Industrial Crating and Packing, 731 F.2d 818, 829 (Fed. Cir. 1984). The word avoids undue limits to the word that "substantially" modifies. C.E. Equip. Co. v. United States, 13 U.S.P.Q.2d (BNA) 1363 (Ct. of Cl. 1989). *See* Alcon Laboratories, Inc. v. Allergan, Inc., 17 U.S.P.Q.2d (BNA) 1365, 1369 (N.D. Tex. 1990); *In re* Hauserman, Inc., 15 U.S.P.Q.2d (BNA) 1157, 1158 (1989). "About" is similar to "approximately." Syntex Inc. v. Paragon Optical, Inc., 7 U.S.P.Q.2d (BNA) 1001, 1038 (D. Ariz. 1987).
25. *In re* Donaldson, 16 F.3d 1189 (Fed. Cir. 1994).

al (*Hilton Davis Chem. Co. v. Warner-Jenkinson Co., Inc.*[26]), to find equivalence and for application of the doctrine of prosecution history estoppel, as discussed in section 34 hereof.

However, add the modifier "substantially" or "approximately," etc., before the number 6, and, unless the precision of 6 is critical, the claim limit will likely be met literally by 5.8 units and, under the particular circumstances, possibly by 5 units.[27] Proof of literal infringement of a claim limitation and of the claim which includes it is possible without also or alternatively having to prove equivalence.

Every time a claim limitation is written, whenever the claim term of magnitude, quantity, condition, or comparison need not be precise, and where that claim term would not inherently always be present in the combination (something is always to the left or the right of something else, and usually is not substantially to the left of it), then that limitation should include a word of approximation.

Terms that define one out of two or more limits or restrictions in a narrow range, e.g., terms such as "at least," "at most," "more than," "less than," "over," "under," etc., are not words of approximation since they define the end point of their particular limit quite sharply. Those limits, too, can be softened by modification with a word of approximation, e.g., "substantially at least," etc.

However, when a word of approximation is used, it must be definite as used. Either the specification explains[27.1] that term or provides a standard, or one sees a definition in the prosecution history[27.2] or one of ordinary skill in the art, in view of the prior

---

26. Hilton Davis Chem. Co. v. Warner-Jenkinson Co., Inc., 62 F.3d 1512, 35 U.S.P.Q.2d (BNA) 1641 (Fed. Cir. 1995), *rev'd on other grounds*, 117 S. Ct. 1040, 41 U.S.P.Q.2d (BNA) 1865 (1997).

27. In *Hilton Davis*, the court spent considerable time discussing whether a pH of 5 was the equivalent of a claimed pH range of 6 to 9 and performed the detailed equivalence analysis.

27.1. Zoltek Corp. v. United States, 48 Fed. Cl. 290, 57 U.S.P.Q.2d (BNA) 1257, 1265 (Fed. Cl. 2000) ("about 1300 degrees C." was claimed, and the specification explained that was a temperature at which a particular change was complete). *See* Glaxo Group Ltd. v. Ranbaxy Pharmaceuticals, Inc., ___ F.3d ___, 59 U.S.P.Q.2d (BNA) 1950 (Fed. Cir. 2001) ("essentially free from crystalline material" had restrictive limits applied from a dictionary and from the patent specification).

27.2. Viskase Corp. v. American National Can Co., ___ F.3d ___, 59 U.S.P.Q.2d (BNA) 1823 (Fed. Cir. 2001).

art and the status of the art will understand the term.[27.3] If not, that effort made to "soften" the sharp edge of a term may render the claim indefinite, an undesirable outcome. This undesired result occurred in *Ex parte Oetiker*[27.4] as to "major portion," "at least nearly flat," "non-reinforced condition," "relatively small," "generally parallel," "of the order of 5 mm," "relatively large," "relatively shallow," and "substantial part." Throughout, the court noted there were no passages in the specification to serve as a standard or guideline for ascertaining the scope of each limitation, nor any evidence that one skilled in the art would know the scope of each limitation. Make sure your specification supports your words of approximation.

§ 27 Order of Elements

The elements of the claim should be presented in some logical order. Often, there are several orders that make sense, and any one may be selected. The order used in claim 1 (section 14) is a "functional" order, starting with the element that first has contact with the workpiece (the container) and proceeding along functional lines to describe the remaining elements.

Another order that is often used is a "structural" order, starting first with the base, or the source of power, and proceeding along structural lines to describe the remaining elements. In structural order, claim 1 would read:

> 1B. Apparatus for shaking articles, which comprises:
> (a) a base;
> (b) a plurality of parallel legs, each of which is connected pivotally at one end to the base;
> (c) a container for the articles connected pivotally to the other ends of the legs, so that

---

27.3. *Id.* In *Viskase*, the claim read "below about 0.91 g/cm³." The district court used the standard scientific convention of rounding from the next decimal place, and interpreted the range as between 0.905 and 0.914. The Federal Circuit reviewed the prosecution history and narrowed the scope to 0.91, as that had been required to distinguish from prior art.

27.4. *Ex parte* Oetiker, 23 U.S.P.Q.2d (BNA) 1651, 1654–1656, 1658–60 (Board of Appeals and Interferences 1992).

the legs support the container for oscillating movement with respect to the base; and

(d) **means for oscillating the container on the legs to shake the articles.**

It should be noted that exactly the same structure and movements have been described, only more words are required. The structural order is very common, and is a fairly easy order to follow. It may be used always, or preferably, whenever no more logical order occurs to the claim drafter.

With long mechanical drives, and various electrical circuits, it is often preferable to start with the motor or power source and work toward the end of the drive or circuit, describing the elements significant to various motions or functions that must be performed by that apparatus, and describing them in the sequence in which one proceeds through the apparatus from one element to the next. In the claim, follow the action through the apparatus. Starting at the drive, for example, move through the apparatus, stopping to claim each element essential to performing the ultimate operation which the claimed apparatus performs. It is equally proper, and sometimes convenient, to start at the output and work backwards.

In many types of apparatus, a number of elements act simultaneously or in parallel. Following either the functional or structural approaches, deal with one of the elements in the proper sequence, then deal with the other elements or elements acting simultaneously, and thereafter continue the claim with other elements in sequence. When the claim writer selects one of the simultaneous or parallel action elements to recite, claim it completely and then follow the action from that element to the end point. Then return to the other simultaneous or parallel action element and claim it and then follow the action from that element to its end point.

It should be noted that claim 1 would be illogical and difficult to follow if one attempted to start with the legs or with the means for oscillating.

Summary

Describe the elements in some logical order, either along the series of actions performed by the claimed apparatus or by the sequential arrangement of its elements in the apparatus.

§ 28 Tying the Elements Together

It is very important that the essential cooperation between each element of the claim and the other elements with which it cooperates be specified. "A claim can be rejected as incomplete if it omits essential elements, steps or necessary structural cooperative relationship of elements, such omission amounting to a gap between the elements. . . ."[27.5] When complete, the claim must define the direct or indirect cooperation of each element with every other element of the combination. If no such cooperation is stated, the claim will usually be rejected for that reason alone; for example, as being drawn to "a mere catalog of elements" or, more graphically, as "reading on so many parts lying in a box." This is sometimes called an "aggregation" (MPEP 2173.05(k)), but what is really meant in such a rejection is that the combination is aggregative *as claimed*. A real "aggregation" relates to a defect in the structure (the parts do not cooperate) rather than any problem in claim drafting (see section 64). The claim must be to an assembled, operable combination, not to a mere parts list such as one might find in the corner of a production drawing. But see *In re Venezia*,[28] allowing a special form of claim to a kit of unassembled parts. The words of connection, cooperation, etc., may well be regarded as the glue that must hold the claims together.

This rule follows from court decisions construing the word "machine" in 35 U.S.C. § 101, setting out the classes of things that can be patented, as explained in section 3: machines can be; parts in a box cannot (unless the invention is the unconnected parts, as in a kit).

Of course, if one part were novel, it could be patented by itself, but not in aggregation with other parts. A "machine" is an assem-

---

27.5. MPEP 2173.05(l).

28. *In re* Venezia, 189 U.S.P.Q. (BNA) 149 (C.C.P.A. 1976).

bled, operative combination of parts or machine elements in place ready to do a job.

Example—claim 1 drafted as an aggregation or catalog of elements:

> **Apparatus for shaking articles, which comprises: a container, a base, a plurality of legs, and means for oscillating the container.**

A proper claim includes and starts with a parts list, as above, involving the selection and naming of the elements, as described in preceding sections 16–27; but it must also tie the elements together so as to make up a complete, operable machine. See the *Adams* case and others cited in section 64 on aggregation to the effect that the necessary cooperation need not be "direct mechanical interconnection"; the elements may function independently "so long as the over-all result has utility and is unobvious."

Although it is difficult to set out ground rules for writing machine claims in vacuo, a good general rule might be that each element or part of an element must be recited as physically connected, or as related functionally, or both, to at least one other element or part, and all elements must tie together in a unit through one or more such individual connections between elements. Thus, one might have five elements, A to E, connected many ways, such as

$$A-B-C$$
$$|$$
$$D-E$$

In this example, it is necessary to connect the group D-E to the previous group A-B-C, such as by connecting D to B as well as to E. There are often many connections, such as

Do not leave even one element or part hanging in the air with no apparent connection to anything else, and no apparent function in the combination. For example, do not describe "a lever having a forked end," and then fail to recite either something connected to the lever or the forked end and/or something operating on either of them or either of them operating on something else. Further, if there is no recited purpose or function for the forked end, do not recite it. It is better to err on the side of stating too much connection and cooperation between elements, rather than running the risk of defining an unintegrated or incomplete structure. Think of the elements as islands, the parts of elements as peninsulas, and statements of structural or functional connection or cooperation as bridges; then, make sure when the claim is done that each island and peninsula is connected directly or indirectly to every other island or peninsula by bridges.

One trick in making sure the elements are tied together is to draw a diagrammatic sketch, or "stick picture," of what the claim states, and only that. Make the picture as different from the specific example in the drawings as the words permit. The picture should depict more clearly than words if some element, feature, or "glue" is missing,[29] if necessary features have been omitted, if unnecessary features are included, etc.

---

29. The Patent and Trademark Office also suggests that the examiners do this in making their search. *See* MPEP 904.01, (a), (b), and (c) in appendix D. They must search for undisclosed structures that the claim also covers. Most apparatus claims cover many, usually an infinite number of, possible structures.

For example, see the stick picture of claim 1, section 14, to the shaker:

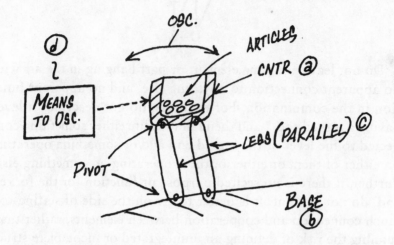

This crude sketch diagrams one simple example of the elements of claim 1, and shows how they are connected.

Summary

Tie the elements together in the claim; claim machines, not parts. Do not leave even one element with no connection to another, or with no apparent purpose in the claimed combination. If it has no purpose in the combination claimed, it can probably be left out.

§ 29 Structural Connection

A structural connection between the elements (a), (b), and(c) of claim 1 is found in the expression "each of which is connected pivotally. . . ." This ties the first three elements together mechanically.

A "means" clause automatically carries its own inherent structural and operational connection with whatever element is the object of the means clause. See section 34. Thus, it is implicit in the recitation "means for oscillating the container" that some part of such means must engage the container or something connected to the container to accomplish the function.[30] This need not be stated expressly, such as "means engaging the container for oscillating. . . ."

Some examples of structural connection statements:

a turntable on which the barrel is *mounted*;

a rotary cam *fixed to* one end of said shaft;

a cam follower *engaging* said cam . . .

a capacitor *electrically connected* to the emitter of said transistor . . .

a coil spring *positioned between* said clutch plate and said base . . .

means for mounting the bending fingers on the base *for lateral movement* with respect to the first and second clamps . . . [Note the means-for clauses inherently contain and define the necessary physical connections, particularly conventional connections, such as mounting, guiding, fastening, etc.]

a worm gear *in mesh with* the drive gear . . .

Normally, statements of physical or mechanical connection are fairly easy to write. A problem, as with elements or parts of elements, is how broadly to claim the connection, and this, of course, depends largely on the prior art. In most apparatus cases, the precise manner—or structure—of a connection is not critical to novelty or unobviousness, in which case relatively broad words are used to state the connection, such as "connected to" or "mounted on" rather than "fixed to" or "bolted to," etc. Very often, means clauses (section 34) are used for conventional mountings, connections, etc., in both machine and electrical circuit cases (section 35). But the restrictions on the breadth of means clauses causes the author to recommend avoiding means clauses where naming an element. Using another noun than "means" and describing its function relative to another element can be done while maintaining sufficient claim breadth.

---

30. 35 U.S.C. § 112, paragraph 6.

Summary

Connect the claim elements structurally, as required to make up a complete and operable combination. Use relatively broad words of connection where the prior art permits.

§ 30 Functional or Operational Expressions

A functional limitation attempts to define something by what it does rather than by what it is, i.e., its structure or ingredients. Functional language does not render a claim improper.[30.1]

In addition to the structural cooperation, it is good practice also to specify the functional or operational cooperation between the elements, where this can be done without unduly limiting the claim. When this is done, the claim not only tells what the parts are and how they are mechanically interconnected or associated, it tells how they function together and operate on the workpiece to accomplish the result stated in the preamble.[31] A functional limitation is evaluated like any other for what it fairly conveys to a person of ordinary skill in the art.

Functional or operational connectives in claim 1 are such expressions as "for the articles" in clause (a), "to support the container for oscillating movement with respect to the base" in clause (c), and "to shake the articles" in clause (d). Examples in MPEP 2173.05(g) include: "incapable of forming a dye within . . ."; "members adapted to be positioned. . . ."

Try to make each independent claim a complete, self-contained unit, comprehensible by itself. The connectives enable that.

The reader may have heard statements disparaging functional expressions, and may wonder if they should be avoided altogether. The answer is—definitely no! When properly used, statements of function or operation are usually welcomed by the Patent and Trademark Office. When not used to excess or to introduce un-

---

30.1. MPEP 2173.05(g); *In re* Swinehart and Sfiligoj, 439 F.2d 210, 169 U.S.P.Q. (BNA) 226 (C.C.P.A. 1971).

31. *In re* Swinehart, *id.*

necessary limitations into the claim, they make the claim more definite and easy to understand without having to refer to the specification.

Most problems with so-called functional statements arise when an attempt is made to predicate patentability on a purely functional statement, or to present extremely broad claims.

There is never any objection to functional statements that merely set forth the movements, actions, or results that necessarily follow from the structure previously recited. Thus, in claim 1, the capability of the container for oscillating movement follows once the double pivoted mounting of the container on the base has been stated. No magic words are necessary for functional statements. Such expressions as "so that," "for," "in order to" are typical. However, as paragraph 6 of § 112 of the statute says, means for accomplishing a function are structure claims, use of the preposition "for," as in [an article] "for" [accomplishing a function], is least likely to be an objectionable functional statement. The words "whereby" and "thereby" are often used, but have assumed stylized meanings described in section 32. Also, "means for" accomplishing a function clauses are very commonly used (section 34).

Some examples of straightforward, noncontroversial functional or cooperative statements:

> a container *for* the articles . . . ["for" is very commonly used] to *support* the container *for oscillating movement* . . .
>
> a turntable [element] on which the barrel [workpiece] is mounted [structural connection] *for rotation therewith* [cooperation or function] . . .
>
> means for *reciprocating* the strand guide *so that* it moves . . . [in a stated way]. [means clauses are very common in stating cooperative relations (section 31)].
>
> a pulse counter *responsive* to each pulse of current . . . *for counting* . . .

There are many different forms for this. Some special forms will be covered in the following sections and further examples. As usual, and as with virtually *every word in the claim,* the scope should be checked carefully. Make sure every word is really needed, particularly in the broader claims.

Watch vague and indefinite statements of cooperation, particularly the phrase "adapted to," which is likely to be objected to by the examiner as "insufficient structure to support functional statement." MPEP 2173.05(g) cites "adapted to" favorably by listing a precedent.[31.1] One precedent says "adapted for" is not a limitation[32] and one says it is a limitation.[33] But "adapted to" clauses were expressly sanctioned by the court.[34] Alternatively, use a "means for" clause under the guidelines in section 34. In *Ex parte Roggenburk*,[35] the Board held that a functional expression, "sealingly engaging," was an improper function statement, but that a "means for" clause of exactly the same scope would have been all right.

Summary

Relate the claim elements functionally to each other. That is, tell how the parts move or cooperate with each other to accomplish the overall result stated in the preamble. Tell the following things where applicable about each element:

    a. *What is it? (name, sections 16 and 19; and parts, section 25);*

    b. *Where is it? (physical cooperation or location, sections 28–29);*

    c. *What does it do? (sections 30–34); and*

    d. *How does it do what it does? (sections 30–34).*

Beware, however, of functional statements that make the claim overly broad (sections 31, 32, 34) or violate other rules, as by being vague and indefinite (section 23).

31.1. *In re* Venezia, 530 F.2d 956, 189 U.S.P.Q. (BNA) 149 (C.C.P.A. 1976).

  32. *In re* Hutchinson, 69 U.S.P.Q. (BNA) 138 (C.C.P.A. 1946).

  33. *In re* Laud and Rogers, 151 U.S.P.Q. (BNA) 621 (C.C.P.A. 1966).

  34. *In re* Venezia, 530 F.2d 956, 189 U.S.P.Q. (BNA) 149 (C.C.P.A. 1976).

  35. *Ex parte* Roggenburk, 172 U.S.P.Q. (BNA) 82 (Bd. App. 1970).

§ 31 Claiming Desired Results; Overly Broad Functional Statements

MPEP 2173.05(g) defines and also permits functional statements in a claim:

> A functional limitation is an attempt to define something by what it does, rather than by what it is (e.g., as evidenced by its specific structure or specific ingredients). There is nothing inherently wrong with defining some part of an invention in functional terms. Functional language does not, in and of itself, render a claim improper. *In re Swinehart*, 439 F.2d 210, 169 USPQ (CCPA 1971).

> A functional limitation must be evaluated and considered, just like any other limitation of the claim, for what it fairly conveys to a person of ordinary skill in the pertinent art in the context in which it is used. A functional limitation is often used in association with an element ingredient, or step of a process to define a particular capability or purpose that is served by the recited element, ingredient or step.

The main problem with so-called functional statements comes when one attempts to use them to present ultrabroad claims. One example of this is when one is trying to claim a desirable end result broadly detached from the specific mechanisms or steps for achieving that result. An example that had been cited by the Patent and Trademark Office[36] is a claim reading: "A woolen cloth having a tendency to wear rough rather than smooth," meaning that it will not become shiny as a result of wear! This tells what the cloth does, the desirable end result, but not how the result is accomplished (decreasing the animal grease content and adding silk threads). The court held, "This claim . . . describes, imperfectly and too broadly. . . . It is also functional, describing a result only and not a process." This type of claim may be variously rejected as being "functional," "too broad," or "nonstatutory" (it does not "particularly point out and distinctly claim" under 35 U.S.C. § 112).

It may be unfortunate that the phrase "functional" is sometimes used for this type of rejection, which really concerns overclaiming and not anything wrong with the functional statement itself. For example, if the claim to the woolen cloth had first described its

---

36. From *In re* Fuller, 388 Off. Gaz. Pat. Office 279, 35 F.2d 62 (C.C.P.A. 1929).

physical structure or novel properties, or even the process of manufacture, particularly if the physical structure could not be defined
or the process is significant (see section 46 on product-by-process
claims), there would have been no objection to the functional
statement about "wearing rough" following afterward. In fact,
that statement would have been most helpful to understanding the
claim and, most likely, in showing nonobviousness.

Another example: in *Knapp v. Morss,*[37] the Supreme Court stated:

> The use and purpose sought to be accomplished by the Hall
> patent was the radial expansion of the dress form, but it is well
> settled by the authorities that the end or purpose sought to be
> accomplished by the device is not the subject of a patent. The in-
> vention covered thereby must consist of new and useful means
> of obtaining that end. In other words, the subject of a patent is
> the device or mechanical means by which the desired result is to
> be secured.

Thus, the problem is not with functional statements per se, but
with claiming too broadly. In particular, in mechanical claims, the
examiner will usually argue that the recited structure itself must
contain novelty over the prior act. Unquestionably, functional recitations help to sell the claim in many cases once novel structure
has been described.

MPEP 2173.05(q) now specifically deals with "use" claims,
i.e., the use of the invention without reciting structure. The claim:
"A process for using monoclonal antibodies of claim 4 to isolate
and purify . . . interferon" was held indefinite for reciting a use
without any active positive steps of how the use is practiced.[37.1] A
use can be patented in a new use claim if the new use is nonobvious (see section 56).

Probably the classic case in claiming too broadly, and claiming
only desired results, is *O'Reilly v. Morse*[38] on the printing telegraph. Morse's claim 8 covered

> . . . the use of the motive power of the electric or galvanic cur-
> rent, which I call electro-magnetism, however developed, for
> making or printing intelligible characters, letters, or signs, at
> any distances . . .

---

37. Knapp v. Morss, 150 U.S. 221, 227 (1893).
37.1. *Ex parte* Ehrlich, 3 U.S.P.Q.2d (BNA) 1011 (Bd. of Appeals & Interp.
      1986). *See Ex parte* Dunki, 153 U.S.P.Q. (BNA) 678 (Bd. App. 1967).
38. O'Reilly v. Morse, 56 U.S. (15 How.) 62, 86 (1853).

This was held invalid by the Supreme Court; one cannot merely claim the desired end result to be accomplished, divorced from the means for accomplishing the result.

A more recent example of this doctrine, decided by the Board of Appeals, is *Ex parte Slub.*[39] In the *Slub* case, the expression "a liquefiable substance having a liquefaction temperature from about 40°C. to about 300°C. and being compatible with the ingredient in the powdered detergent composition" (broadly stated in the claim as "a powdered detergent composition") was rejected as "too broad," "functional," and also "vague and indefinite," citing cases.

While this was a process claim involving a key functional description of a composition of matter used in making a new composition of two elements, the principles of the case apply to any kind of claim: that is, any kind of technology and any class of claim. The board held this bad for several reasons:

1. Improper to recite compounds by what they do rather than what they are (*cf.* C.C.P.A. cases cited later in this section);

2. Reads on inoperative species—materials that would not work in the composition, such as low-melting metals (see section 49); and

3. Claim not supported by the disclosure, since only ten limited examples of compounds were given.

A good example of the difference between claiming a function added to a system and claiming merely the desired end result is given by Donald R. Johnson in *The Art of Drafting Patent Claims:*[40]

> I will illustrate by referring to the precipitation of solid wax from an organic solution. This precipitation of the wax is accomplished by cooling the solution in a heat exchanger. However, a problem is involved in the deposition of solid wax on the heat exchanger surfaces and in some cases the plugging up of the apparatus.
>
> What the inventor conceived as a solution to the problem was an incorporation into the system of a surface active agent which

---

39. *Ex parte* Slub, 157 U.S.P.Q. (BNA) 172 (Bd. App. 1967).

40. THE ART OF DRAFTING PATENT CLAIMS 111–12 (J. Jackson & G. Morris eds. 1966). This excellent book was an edited transcript of a PLI seminar on claim drafting in 1962, representing the combined effort of twenty-nine skilled patent attorneys. It is out of print.

would form a film on the heat exchanger surface and prevent the deposition of wax. The inventive concept here was in the form of a function to be added to the system . . .

However, the prior art situation in this case did not show the use of any surfactant in the particular system claimed. The art did show a surfactant in a related system, in which solid wax was precipitated from a liquid by cooling, but in which there were two immiscible liquid phases, and in which the surfactant and the solid wax were concentrated at the interface between the two liquid phases. In this circumstance it was, of course, necessary for the inventor to distinguish the system to which the surfactant was added from that disclosed in the art. Once this was done, it was possible to claim the surfactant generally, as one capable of forming a film on the heat exchange surface.

This illustrates a proper case of functional claiming. It also illustrates a case where the inventive concept is initially in terms of a function to be added to the system. This is a strong argument in favor of defining the added material functionally. However, it is necessary to distinguish between a function of this sort and the ultimate desired effect. In this case the ultimate desired effect was preventing the deposition of wax, and it certainly could not be claimed in this fashion, i.e., as simply a means for preventing such deposition.

Within these general rules of ultrabroad or indefinite claims, claiming only end results or desired principles, the law is not very clear as to just what kinds of broad functional statements can be permitted (patentable), and what cannot.[40.1] Examiners tend to reject broad "functional" claims for any of several reasons. General "catchword" rejections, such as "too broad," "unduly functional," "not fairly based on the disclosure," etc., will no longer suffice.

In *In re Echerd*,[41] the court held that "there is nothing inherently wrong in defining something by what it does rather than what it is." The key limitations in question were:

having sufficient flexibility and wet strength to permit . . .

and

having sufficient adhesive characteristics to firmly bond . . .

40.1. *See* MPEP 2173.05(g).
  41. *In re* Echerd, 176 U.S.P.Q. (BNA) 321 (C.C.P.A. 1973).

There are several cases to the same effect.[42] The Court of Appeals for the Federal Circuit has been holding that no limitation or wording anywhere in the claim can be ignored in determining patentability.[43] In the *Echerd* case,[44] as was typical of a great many cases in the past, the Patent and Trademark Office rejected a claim as anticipated by prior art, or as obvious, where all of the specific *structure* claimed was old and the novelty resided solely in a functional (or otherwise objectionable) statement, such as negative limitations (section 17), or mental steps (section 44). The Federal Circuit is now holding such rejections improper as not consistent with the statute.[45]

In the *Ludtke* case,[46] the claim was directed to a parachute canopy comprising old elements A and B, with:

> . . . said plurality of the lines [B] *providing* a radial separation between each of said panels [A] upon deployment [of the parachute] *creating* a region of high porosity between each of the said panels *such that* the critical velocity . . . will be less than
>
> . . . *whereby* said parachute will sequentially open and *thus* gradually deaccelerate.—

[Note the claim form uses almost all of the functional expressions known (except "means for") one after the other (in paraphrase):]

[said B]

providing . . . [a stated physical relationship, in operation],

creating . . . [a physical property]

such that . . . [a functional relationship is achieved]

whereby . . . [an effect happens]

and thus . . . [a desired end is achieved].

This may be a classic in functional language.

---

42. *In re* Hallman, 210 U.S.P.Q. (BNA) 609, 611 (C.C.P.A. 1981); *In re* Ludtke and Sloan, 169 U.S.P.Q. (BNA) 563 (C.C.P.A. 1971); *In re* Swinehart and Sfiligoj, 169 U.S.P.Q. (BNA) 226 (C.C.P.A. 1971); *In re* Fuetterer, 138 U.S.P.Q. (BNA) 217 (C.C.P.A. 1963).

43. *In re* Stencel, 828 F.2d 751 (Fed. Cir. 1987).

44. *In re* Echerd, 176 U.S.P.Q. (BNA) 321 (C.C.P.A. 1973).

45. *See In re* Stencel, 828 F.2d 751 (Fed. Cir. 1987).

46. *In re* Ludtke and Sloan, 169 U.S.P.Q. (BNA) 563 (C.C.P.A. 1971).

The court held that there was nothing wrong with the functional language, citing the *Swinehart* case,[47] but affirmed a different (anticipation) rejection that applicants had not proven that the same functions did not happen in a prior art reference. Thus, even with broad functional language acceptable under these cases, the claim must still pass other tests, particularly prior art tests, and one must be prepared to prove that the new functions are novel in view of the prior art; that is, not inherently present in the prior art.

See also section 67, vague and indefinite claims, and *In re Wolfrum and Gold*,[48] discussed therein.

In *In re Halleck*,[49] a chemical-new-use type of case, the phrase "an effective amount of [compound X] for [performing a desired function]" was held proper (see new use claims, section 56).

In the *Kockum Industries* case,[50] cited in section 34, the court held that functional expressions were proper at the point of novelty, so long as the specification was clear as to what the words meant and how the function was achieved. (See discussion of "functional at the point of novelty" rejections in section 34, on means claims.)

Summary

Beware of overly broad functional statements, particularly those claiming only desired results. In practice, scrutinize the claim language and the prior art carefully, as many kinds of functional statements may not be permissible under recent Federal Circuit cases, particularly defining an element or feature by what it does rather than by what it is.

---

47. *In re* Swinehart and Sfiligoj, 169 U.S.P.Q. (BNA) 226 (C.C.P.A. 1971).
48. *In re* Wolfrum and Gold, 177 U.S.P.Q. (BNA) 481 (5th Cir. 1973).
49. *In re* Halleck, 164 U.S.P.Q. (BNA) 647 (C.C.P.A. 1970).
50. Kockum Indus., Inc. v. Salem Equip., Inc., 175 U.S.P.Q. (BNA) 81 (9th Cir. 1972) (discussed in section 34).

§ 32 "Whereby" Clauses

"Whereby" and "thereby" clauses have come in for quite a bit of judicial construction. They are entirely unobjectionable when properly used, and are really quite helpful. A whereby clause is proper when it merely describes a function, operation, or result that *necessarily* follows from the previously recited structure or method. On the other hand, the whereby clause is given no weight if it expresses only a necessary result of the previously described structure or method.[51] Therefore, equate "whereby" with "it follows from the foregoing that. . . ." Use of such a clause should be avoided if the function does not necessarily follow, as in such a case, the claim drafter is reciting a new structural or cooperative relationship. Some cases have held that the function stated in a whereby clause cannot be considered to determine patentability of the claim.[52] Those cases and their view of "whereby" clauses have been rejected, so that the better view is that the "whereby" clause is part of the structure or method.[53] But because the usefulness of "whereby" clauses as structural has been doubted, avoid them for claiming a new structure or method limitation.

A useful test for whereby clauses is to delete the clause and substitute a period; then ask, does the claim still have structural novelty and adequate cooperation among elements? If so, the clause is probably good. If needed, the claim should be amended to add structural elements that are antecedents to the "whereby" clause. Since the "whereby" clause likely will state some objective of the invention, the fact that no element is present which would serve as an antecedent to the "whereby" clause should raise a question as to the sufficiency of the structural limitations of the claim.

---

51. *In re* Certain Personal Computers, 224 U.S.P.Q. (BNA) 270, 283 (Ct. Int'l Trade 1984).
52. *In re* Fisher, 135 U.S.P.Q. (BNA) 22 (C.C.P.A. 1962); *In re* Mason, 114 U.S.P.Q. (BNA) 127, 129 (C.C.P.A. 1957).
53. Plastic Container Corp. v. Continental Plastics, 203 U.S.P.Q. (BNA) 650 (10th Cir. 1979); *In re* Swinehart and Sfiligoj, 169 U.S.P.Q. (BNA) 226 (C.C.P.A. 1971); *In re* Fisher, 166 U.S.P.Q. (BNA) 18 (C.C.P.A. 1970), *rev'g* 135 U.S.P.Q. (BNA) 22 (C.C.P.A. 1962). *See* Eltech Systems Corp. v. PPG Industries, Inc., 710 F. Supp. 622, (W.D. La. 1988), *aff'd*, 903 F.2d 805 (Fed. Cir. 1990).

A "whereby" clause that merely states the result of the limitations in the claim adds nothing to the patentability or substance of the claim.[54] But, it may help the reader understand the claimed structure, sums it up and makes the claim more readable. Use the clause as appears appropriate. Writing claims where the description of elements of the claims includes a statement of their function or cooperation with other elements may make a "whereby" clause unnecessary, because all of the functions that might be recited in the "whereby" clause have already been recited in the descriptions of operations performed by various claim elements. However, sometimes descriptions of the functions of individual elements do not show how they fit together and function as a complete structure, and only a "whereby" clause does that.

One example of a whereby clause, used in connection with the popcorn popper discussed in section 25:

> A container for the articles, having apertured walls, the apertures of which are smaller in size than the articles to be shaken *whereby the articles are retained in the container as they are shaken;*

The retaining function necessarily follows, *whereby* the clause is proper. Contrast the foregoing clause with the following: "An apertured container for the articles *whereby the articles are retained in the container as they are shaken.*" Even though the same whereby clause has been used, it is now improper because it attempts to define a structural relationship in purely functional terms, that is, a statement of desired result without reciting structure for performing the function.

Whereby clauses, and other functional clauses, can be used (or avoided) equally well in method claims; see claim 6 in section 43 for an example of a "method whereby."

The Patent and Trademark Office should not object to "structure implying wherebys." One sees them fairly often in issued patents. A structure implying "whereby" clause was allowed in *In re Venezia.*[55]

---

54. Texas Instruments Inc. v. U.S. Int'l Trade Comm'n, 988 F.2d 1165, 26 U.S.P.Q.2d 1018 (Fed. Cir. 1993).

55. *In re* Venezia, 189 U.S.P.Q. (BNA) 149 (C.C.P.A. 1976).

In another example of an improper use of a whereby clause, the invention involved the discovery that a metal article would stick to a sheet of a particular resin, if pressed against the sheet, by a vacuum effect not clearly understood. The claim recited: "Placing the article against the sheet of . . . (X resin) whereby the article adheres. . . ." Note "whereby the article adheres. . . ." Note that "whereby" implies the manner of placing, which implies pressing or some similar positive step. "Placing the article against the sheet . . . in such manner that . . ." would be an equivalent functional expression. The latter expression might conceivably be objected to as too broad or functional, but at worst it would be no more objectionable on that score than the same type of expression via a whereby clause.

This "rule" seems entirely a matter of form not substance, based on an arbitrary definition of the word "whereby."

The same claim scope as obtained by a "whereby" clause can usually be obtained by a claim drafter using such other expressions as "for" or "means for," which have the sanction of the sixth paragraph of 35 U.S.C. § 112. Referring to the previous example, the "whereby" clause may be replaced with a no problem clause:

> A container . . . articles to be shaken *for retaining* the articles in the container as they are shaken;

But, beware of the stricter scope applied by the courts to means plus function limitations, as discused in section 34.

Since avoiding the use of a "whereby" clause for a substantive limitation is so easy, there is no point in generating controversy where none is needed.

Summary

Either avoid whereby clauses completely, or make sure the function stated as the object of the whereby clause necessarily follows from the previously recited structure in the claim. Other words and particularly "means for" limitations will do the same job, and do it as well or better in most instances.

§ 33 Location of Functional Clauses

As to claim form, cooperative or functional clauses (such as "so that," "for," "whereby" clauses) may be used either

1. At the end of the description of a particular element, provided everything necessary to the functional clause has then been set out; or

2. At the end of the claim where all that is necessary to the statement has not been set out until the last element has been described.

Type 1 is preferred, where applicable, as it makes the claim easier to follow. Also, one is less likely to be accused of functional claiming when the functions are set out one at a time, rather than, for example, when a long whereby clause is placed at the end.

Summary

Put functional clauses where you think most logical.

§ 34 The "Means" or "Step" Clauses

A "means" clause or "step" clause defines an element or feature in a product or a method claim by what it does, i.e., function, rather than by what it is, i.e., its structure.[56]

Use of a means clause is governed by 35 U.S.C. § 112, paragraph 6, as follows:

> An element in a claim for a combination may be expressed as a means or step for performing a specified function without the recital of structure, material, or acts in support thereof, and such claims shall be construed to cover the corresponding structure, material, or acts described by the specification and equivalents thereof.

The effect of "means-plus-function" language is to incorporate into the limitations of the claim the embodiment disclosed in the

---

56. Laitram Corp. v. Rexnord, Inc., 939 F.2d 1533, 1536, 19 U.S.P.Q.2d (BNA) 1367 (Fed. Cir. 1991). *See* Johnston v. IVAC Corp., 885 F.2d 1574, 12 U.S.P.Q.2d (BNA) 1382 (Fed. Cir. 1989).

specification and all equivalents of that embodiment[57] both during ex parte examination by the examiner and for an infringement analysis after a patent is granted.[58] Thus, the scope of the claim is as broad as the invention.[59] However, the same statutory language limits the scope of a means limitation, to exclude from it all equivalents not known at the time of the invention;[59.1] that is, § 112, paragraph 6 narrows claim scope, while the doctrine of equivalents broadens the scope since the doctrine extends to equivalents known at the time a claim infringement issue is considered.[59.2] Therefore, the claim writer must decide if he wants the restriction of § 112, paragraph 6.

The *Donaldson* decision affects only the manner in which the scope of a "means or step plus function" limitation in accordance with § 112, paragraph 6, is interpreted during examination of a patent application,[59.3] making consistent the way courts and the Patent Office interpret means clauses. Consequently, the means clause covers the structure disclosed and its equivalents, as discussed in the section hereof on naming a claim element.[59.4] For the means-plus-function limitation to read on an accused device, the accused device must 1) perform the identical function recited in the means limitation, and 2) perform that function using the structure disclosed in the specification or an equivalent struc-

---

57. *In re* Donaldson Co., 16 F.3d 1189, 29 U.S.P.Q.2d (BNA) 1845 (Fed. Cir. 1994) (*en banc*).

58. Pennwalt Corp. v. Durand-Wayland Inc., 833 F.2d 931 (Fed. Cir. 1987); D.M.I., Inc. v. Deere & Co., 755 F.2d 1570, 1574 (Fed. Cir. 1985).

59. Hale Fire Pump Co. v. Tokai, Ltd., 614 F.2d 1278, 1283 (C.C.P.A. 1980).

59.1. Warner-Jenkinson Co. v. Hilton Davis Chem. Co., 117 S. Ct. 1040, 1048 (1997).

59.2. Al-Site Corp. v. VSI International Inc., 174 F.3d 1308, 50 U.S.P.Q.2d (BNA) 1161, 1167 (Fed. Civ. 1999).

59.3. MPEP 2181; Interim Supplemental Examination Guidelines for Determining the Applicability of 35 U.S.C. 112 ¶6 (issued by the Patent and Trademark Office effective July 30, 1999), 64 Fed. Reg. 41392 (1999), 58 Pat. Trademark & Copyright J. (BNA) 443–45 (Aug. 5, 1999).

59.4. Valmont Indus. v. Reinke Mfg. Co., 983 F.2d 1039, 25 U.S.P.Q.2d (BNA) 1451 (Fed. Cir. 1993); Biodex Corp. v. Loredan Biomedical Inc., 946 F.2d 850 (Fed. Cir. 1991).

ture.[59.5] For an accused structure to be an equivalent under § 112, paragraph 6, it must both have an identical structure and also perform the identical function as recited in the claim limitation.[59.6]

The Patent Office did not accept that it was bound by the same interpretation of § 112, paragraph 6,[60] and instead examiners cited prior art, including any element at all that performed the claimed function irrespective of the disclosed embodiment in the application.[61] For a detailed pre-*Donaldson* history, see *Ex parte Isaksen*.[61.1] In the past, there had been a difference between the Patent and Trademark Office's view of how to interpret "means-plus-function clauses" when examining a claim for patentability and the Federal Circuit's view on how the examiner should interpret a means-plus-function clause. The Patent and Trademark Office had disregarded 35 U.S.C. § 112, paragraph 6 by applying an all inclusive analysis when interpreting a "means for" limitation. When determining equivalency, the Patent and Trademark Office would decide whether there was any element in the prior art which is capable of performing the function described in a "means for" limitation. If such an element was found, equivalency was presumed to exist. The burden would then shift to the applicant to show that the prior art element is not equivalent to the element disclosed in the specification for performing the function.

The Federal Circuit has resolved the conflict by holding that the "means" language in a means-plus-function claim is limited to the corresponding structure disclosed in the specification and equivalents thereof and that the Patent and Trademark Office must comply with 35 U.S.C. § 112(6) and construe means-plus-function claims by looking to the application's specification for structures

---

59.5. Carroll Touch, Inc. v. Electro Mechanical Systems, Inc., 15 F.3d 1573, 27 U.S.P.Q.2d (BNA) 1836 (Fed. Cir. 1993); Jackson v. Casio Phonemate, Inc., 105 F. Supp. 2d 858, 56 U.S.P.Q.2d (BNA) 1081, 1084 (N.D. Ill. 2000).

59.6. Smiths International Medical Systems Inc. v. Vital Signs, Inc., 51 U.S.P.Q.2d (BNA) 1415 (Fed. Cir. 1999).

60. *Cf. In re* Iwahashi, 888 F.2d 1370 (Fed. Cir. 1989).

61. *See* MPEP 2181; *see also In re* Lundberg and Zuschlag, 113 U.S.P.Q. (BNA) 530, 534 (C.C.P.A. 1957).

61.1. *Ex parte* Isaksen, 23 U.S.P.Q.2d (BNA) 1001, 1007–15 (Board of Appeals and Interferences 1992).

and their equivalents.[61.2] This does not require imputing limitations from the specification into the claim, but rather requires construing a limitation already in the means-plus-function clause by properly referring to the specification for the meaning of a particular word.

In response to *In re Donaldson*, the Patent and Trademark Office issued Guidelines in May 1994 for interpreting means-plus-function claims. They are in MPEP 2181. The 1994 Guidelines said it was not necessary to use the specific phrases "means for" or "step for" in order for a claim limitation to fall within the scope of § 112. It had only to be clear that the element in the claim is set forth, at least in part, by the function it performs as opposed to the specific structure, material, or acts that perform the function. The same comment applied to a step for accomplishing a function limitation. For the means or step-plus-function limitation to read on an accused device, the accused device must (1) perform the identical function recited in the means or step limitation, and (2) perform that function using the structure or process step disclosed in the specification or an equivalent structure or process.[61.3] This does not require imputing limitations from the specification into the claim, but rather requires construing a limitation already in the means-plus-function clause by properly referring to the specification for the meaning of a particular word.[62] The 1994 Guidelines said that there is no specific claim language to which § 112, paragraph 6, applies, but case precedents discussed below have construed specific language as in or out of § 112. As of 1999, the PTO's Supplemental Examination Guidelines[62.1] on applying § 112, paragraph 6 are controlling and overrule the 1994 Guidelines to the extent they are inconsistent.

61.2. *In re* Donaldson, 16 F.3d 1189, 29 U.S.P.Q.2d (BNA) 1845 (Fed. Cir. 1994); MPEP 2181.

61.3. Ishida Co. v. Taylor, 221 F.3d 1310, 55 U.S.P.Q.2d (BNA) 1449, 1453 (Fed. Cir. 2000).

62. Carroll Touch, Inc. v. Electro Mechanical Systems, Inc., 15 F.3d 1573, 27 U.S.P.Q.2d (BNA) 1836 (Fed. Cir. 1993).

62.1. Interim Supplemental Examination Guidelines for Determining the Applicability of 35 U.S.C. § 112 ¶6 (issued by the Patent and Trademark Office effective July 30, 1999), 64 Fed. Reg. 41392 (1999), 58 Pat. Trademark & Copyright J. (BNA) 443-45 (Aug. 5, 1999).

A claim limitation will be interpreted to invoke § 112, paragraph 6 if it meets the following three-pronged analysis:

(1) the claim limitation must use the phrase "means for" or "step for";

(2) the "means for" or "step for" must be modified by functional language, i.e., a specified function must be recited; and

(3) the phrase "means for" or "step for" must not be modified by structure, material, or acts for achieving the specified function.

As contrasted with the 1994 Guidelines, these controlling 1999 Guidelines are clear and precise. At present, the Guidelines control only Patent Office Examiners, and not the Federal Circuit or other courts. Court precedents discussed below determine whether the applicant intended to invoke § 112, paragraph 6 from the words chosen by the claim writer. But the 1999 Guidelines, if followed by courts interpreting claims examined under those Guidelines, will make it relatively easy to determine whether a limitation is under § 112, paragraph 6.

Under the 1999 Guidelines, if the claim writer wants § 112, paragraph 6, he must use "means for" or "step for." If he does not use those phrases, he intends that a claim limitation not be under § 112, paragraph 6.

If he wants to invoke § 112, paragraph 6, he should recite a function for the means. If no function is recited, e.g., the "means" element appears, but without a function being recited, he intends that a claim limitation not be under § 112, paragraph 6.

Finally, if the claim writer does not want the means element to be treated under § 112, paragraph 6, he should also recite the structure that performs the function; e.g., "means for redirecting air flow, comprising a surface in the path of air from the exit, the surface shaped for redirecting air toward the top side."[62.2]

62.2. When a claim recites a function and then elaborates sufficient structure within the claim to entirely perform the function, it is not in the means-plus-function form. Sage Products, Inc. v. Devon Industries, Inc., 126 F.3d 1420, 1427–28 (Fed. Cir. 1997).

To avoid § 112, paragraph 6 and at the same time to rely on it, perhaps submit two independent claims, one using the means-plus-function recital and one naming an element and structure without reciting means for performing a function.

Alternatively, the Federal Circuit has acknowledged that if an independent (or preceding dependent) claim is in means-plus-function form, a later dependent claim reciting the structure that performs the function would not be subject to § 112, paragraph 6.[62.3] Hence, filing two independent claims is not required to avoid § 112, paragraph 6. The dependent claim would simply recite: ". . . wherein the means for . . . comprises. . . ."

But the easiest way to avoid § 112, paragraph 6 is just not to use "means" in a product claim or "step" in a method claim. The presence of the word "means" triggers a presumption that the inventor meant to invoke § 112, paragraph 6,[62.4] but the recitation of structure at the means rebuts that presumption.[62.5]

Prior to the 1999 Guidelines, the Federal Circuit had held that use of the word "means" creates a presumption in favor of invoking § 112, paragraph 6 and that not using the word "means" creates the opposite presumption.[62.6] Both presumptions are rebuttable,[62.7] e.g., by the remaining words in the claim limita-

---

62.3. Medtronic, Inc. v. Advanced Cardiovascular Sys., Inc., 248 F.3d 1303, 58 U.S.P.Q.2d (BNA) 1607 (Fed. Cir. 2001).

62.4. *Sage*, 126 F.3d; Kemco Sales, Inc. v. Control Papers Co., 208 F.3d 1352, 54 U.S.P.Q.2d (BNA) 1308 (Fed. Cir. 2000).

62.5. York Prods., Inc. v. Central Tractor Farm & Family Center, 99 F.3d 1568, 40 U.S.P.Q.2d (BNA) 1619 (Fed. Cir. 1996); Cole v. Kimberly-Clark Corp., 102 F.3d 524, 531 (Fed. Cir. 1996), *cert. denied*, 118 S. Ct. 56 (1997); Envirco Corp. v. Clestra Cleanroom Inc., 209 F.3d 1360, 54 U.S.P.Q.2d (BNA) 1449, 1452 (Fed. Cir. 2000); Rodime PLC v. Seagate Technology Inc., 174 F.3d 1294, 50 U.S.P.Q.2d (BNA) 1429, 1435 (Fed. Cir. 1999), *cert. denied*, 120 S. Ct. 933 (2000).

62.6. Laitram Corp. v. Rexnord, Inc., 939 F.2d 1533, 19 U.S.P.Q.2d (BNA) 1367 (Fed. Cir. 1991); York Products, Inc. v. Central Tractor, 99 F.3d 1568, 40 U.S.P.Q.2d (BNA) 1619 (Fed. Cir. 1996); Greenberg v. Ethicon Endo-Surgery, Inc., 91 F. 3d 1580, 39 U.S.P.Q.2d (BNA) 1783 (Fed Cir. 1996); Ethicon, Inc. v. United States Surgical Corp., 135 F.3d 1456, 1463, *cert. denied*, 119 S. Ct. 278 (1998); Hester Ind., Inc. v. Stein, Inc., 142 F.3d 1472 (Fed. Cir. 1998), *cert. denied*, 119 S. Ct. 372 (1998).

62.7. Cole v. Kimberly-Clark Corp., 102 F.3d 524, 531 (Fed. Cir. 1996), *cert. denied*, 118 S. Ct. 56 (1997).

tion. The 1999 Guidelines provide rules that are clearer and easier to follow, but do not require that presumption. The Federal Circuit may not adopt the Guidelines test and may follow its precedents on the use of "means."

Under both the 1994 Guidelines and the 1999 Guidelines, if the identical function specified in the claim is found in the prior art, the examiner has the initial burden of proving that the prior art structure or step is the same as or equivalent to the structure, material or acts described in the specification which have been identified as corresponding to the claimed means or step plus function. The examiner should interpret the limitation according to the definitions in the specification including any definition of equivalents. If there is no definition, the examiner may determine the scope of the limitation.

If the claimed function is performed by a prior art element and the specification does not exclude that prior art element with an explicit definition for an equivalent, the examiner should infer that the prior art element is an equivalent and conclude that the claim limitation is anticipated.[62.8] The burden then shifts to the applicant to show that the element shown in the prior art is not an equivalent of the structure, material, or acts disclosed in the application.

However, even if the applicant shows that a prior art element is not equivalent to the structure, material, or acts described in the specification, the examiner must still make an obviousness analysis of the means-plus-function limitation, because the exact scope of an "equivalent" may be uncertain, and an anticipation/obviousness rejection would be appropriate where the balance of the claim limitations are anticipated by the prior art.

Means claims should be rejected when the function is not clearly stated, as they do not comply with § 112, paragraph 2.

Means-plus-function claim language is construed to refer to an indefinite structure, in that the language defines the structure only by the function it will perform.[63] "Means-plus-function" language may be present despite the appearance of structural language so

---

62.8. Clearstream Wastewater Systems, Inc. v. Hydro-action, Inc., 206 F.3d 1440, 54 U.S.P.Q.2d (BNA) 1185 (Fed. Cir. 2000).
  63. Haney v. Timesavers, Inc., 29 U.S.P.Q.2d (BNA) 1605 (D. Or. 1993).

long as the structural language merely defines the function.[63.1] Means-plus-function language is construed to refer to an indefinite structure and defines the structure only by the function it will perform. The court in *AMP, Inc. v. Fujitsu Microelectronics, Inc.*[64] determined that certain claims are not "means-plus-function" claims, despite the fact that the term "means" is used and function is described, because the patent in suit contained claim language which referred to very specific structure and then described the structure's function. Means-plus-function claim language refers to indefinite structure and defines the structure only by the function it will perform. This is consistent with the 1999 Guidelines.

The court in *AMP, Inc.* held the language of Claim 5 is not indefinite because it requires "bus solder tail means" rather than just any means to accomplish the function of "mounting the bus to the printed circuit board" and "securing the housing to the printed circuit board." The language of Claim 9 is even more definite, requiring "the electrically conductive element" to "constitute an additional means for establishing an electrical coupling between the printed circuit boards" and "solder tails" to "constitut[e] both the means for securing the housing to the printed circuit boards . . ." Despite the use of the term "means" and the subsequent description of a function, neither Claim 5 nor Claim 9 was held to contain "means plus function" language as contemplated by 35 U.S.C. § 112, paragraph 6.[64.1]

The Patent Office 1994 Guidelines provided several examples of limitations that fall within the scope of § 112, paragraph six. Some were not in strictly "means for" or "step for" format. But the 1994 Guidelines said that they invoked § 112, paragraph 6. This would produce uncertainty in claim interpretation, in my view. However, the 1999 Guidelines simply and without uncertainty exclude limitations without "means for" or "step for" recitations from invoking § 112, paragraph 6. Precedents that

---

63.1. AMP Inc. v. Fujitsu Microelectronics, Inc., 853 F. Supp. 808, 31 U.S.P.Q.2d (BNA) 1705 (M.D. Pa. 1994).

64. 853 F. Supp. 808, 31 U.S.P.Q.2d (BNA) 1705 (M.D. Pa. 1994).

64.1. Waterloo Furniture Components, Ltd. v. Haworth, Inc., 25 U.S.P.Q.2d (BNA) 1139, 1142–44 (N.D. Ill. 1992).

suggest the contrary[65] are not likely to be followed by the Patent Office and, for consistency, should not be followed by the courts. One pre-*Donaldson* precedent would apply here. *In re Chandler*[66] held that a "means for doing something . . . so that" clause is proper and patentable where the sole point of novelty follows the expression "so that." In other words, the general idea of means for doing the thing was old, but not for doing it in the specified way.

The clause in question read:

> . . . and *means* responsive to said movement *for regulating* the propulsive power of said engine, in accordance with said movement, so *that* said aircraft is propelled at a definite, selected speed, corresponding to the position of said engine relative to said aircraft, throughout the speed range of said aircraft.[67]

In holding the claims patentable, the court stated,

> The examiner held that the words beginning with 'so that' in the quoted expression were merely a functional expression equivalent to the "whereby" clause considered in *In re Lamb,* 64 U.S.P.Q. 241 (C.C.P.A. 1944), and hence could not have patentable significance. [Note section 32.]

> We are of the opinion that the expression beginning with "so that" is not merely functional, but constitutes a part of the definition of the "means responsive to said movement." . . . Such a definition conforms to the provision of 35 U.S.C. section 112 that an element in a claim for a combination "may be expressed as a means or step for performing a specified function without the recital of structure, material or acts in support thereof." The instant situation differs from that presented in *In re Lamb*. There the "whereby" clause did not constitute a part of the definition of any means but merely stated a function which did not necessarily follow from the apparatus recited in the claim. [Note how this decision highlights the difference between "means" and "whereby."][68]

Examples in the Patent Office 1994 Guidelines are instructive:

---

65. *See In re* Roberts, 470 F.2d 1399, 176 U.S.P.Q. (BNA) 313 (C.C.P.A. 1973); *Ex parte* Zimmerly, 153 U.S.P.Q. (BNA) 367 (Bd. App. 1966).
66. *In re* Chandler, 117 U.S.P.Q. (BNA) 361 (C.C.P.A. 1958).
67. *Id.,* 117 U.S.P.Q. (BNA) at 361 (emphasis added).
68. *See also In re* Oelrich and Divigard, 212 U.S.P.Q. (BNA) 323, 326 (C.C.P.A. 1981).

2) "printing means" and "means for printing" would have the same connotations.[69]

However, the terms "plate" and "wings," as modifiers for the structureless term "means," specify no function to be performed, and do not fall under the last paragraph of § 112.

In other words, a noun naming an object or a step that is not followed by the recitation of a function does not fall under § 112, paragraph 6, merely because it is supplemented with the word "means."

3) "force generating means adapted to provide" falls within § 112, paragraph 6.[70]

4) "call cost register means, including a digital display for providing a substantially instantaneous display for . . ." falls within § 112, paragraph 6.[71]

Other cases describing means-plus-function limitations include: *In re Bond*[72] (claim language "delay means included in said control means for delaying the seizure of said telephone line by said second circuit means for a predetermined time interval . . ." held to be "means plus function" language); *Interspiro U.S.A. v. Figgie International*[73] (claim language "means for establishing gauge pressure" held to be "means plus function" language); *but see Quantum Corp. v. Mountain Computer*[74] (claim language ". . . and correction signal generator means connected to said sample and hold circuit for generating an offset signal . . ." held not to be "means plus function" language). This case would, in this author's view, be decided differently now by the Federal Circuit. Although the claim limitation in *Quantum* describes where the means are, it does not describe structure of the means. Therefore, it appears to satisfy the 1999 Guidelines.

---

69. *Ex parte* Klumb, 159 U.S.P.Q. 694 (Bd. App. 1967).

70. De Graffenreid v. United States, 20 Ct. Cl. 458, 16 U.S.P.Q.2d 1321 (Ct. Cl. 1990).

71. Intellicall, Inc. v. Phonometrics, Inc., 952 F.2d 1384, 21 U.S.P.Q.2d 1383 (Fed. Cir. 1992).

72. *In re* Bond, 910 F.2d 831, 15 U.S.P.Q.2d (BNA) 1566 (Fed. Cir. 1990).

73. Interspiro U.S.A. v. Figgie Int'l, 18 F.3d 927, 30 U.S.P.Q.2d (BNA) 1070 (Fed. Cir. 1994).

74. Quantum Corp. v. Mountain Computer, 5 U.S.P.Q.2d (BNA) 1103 (N.D. Cal. 1987).

Recent cases show a trend in deciding what language falls within § 112, paragraph 6. *Greenberg v. Ethicon Endo-Surgery, Inc.*[75] involved the claim language: "a cooperating detent mechanism defining the conjoint rotation of said shafts . . ." The Federal Circuit held that the detent mechanism was not a means-plus-function limitation merely on the ground that the detent mechanism was defined in terms of what it does, i.e., in function terms. Here, the term "detent mechanism" had a meaning as a structure which was known in the art. The court cited other words having known meaning in the art, such as filters, brakes, clamps, and screwdrivers. "Digital detector"[76] and electronic circuit"[76.1] and "control signal generator"[76.2] are sufficiently definite.

Sometimes the words known in the art that define a structure are recited in words suggesting function, rather than being a noun or name for an element. In *Watts v. XL Systems, Inc.,*[76.3] the court interpreted the term "sealingly connected" in the clause "dimensioned such that one such joint may be sealingly connected directly with another such joint" as not falling under 35 U.S.C. § 112, paragraph 6, because the word "means" was not used and based on the specification. But the court ultimately limited the clause to what was shown in the specification in interpreting the limitation.

Conversely, if the term used in the claim does not have a generally understood meaning, use of that term in a "means" or "step" limitation might place it under § 112, paragraph 6. In *Mas-Hamilton Group v. LaGard, Inc.,*[77] the claim element was "lever moving element" and the court construed it as under § 112, paragraph 6 because it could be any device that can cause the lever to move and there was no structure in the claim limitation to remove it from § 112, paragraph 6. The test of whether the word used, e.g., detent *mechanism*, has a known meaning in the art has been sup-

---

75. Greenberg v. Ethicon Endo-Surgery, 91 F.3d 1580 (Fed. Cir. 1996).

76. Personalized Media Communications, LLC v. U.S. International Trade Comm'n, 161 F.3d 696, 48 U.S.P.Q.2d (BNA) 1880 (Fed. Cir. 1998).

76.1. Harmonic Design, Inc. v. Hunter Douglas, Inc., 88 F. Supp. 2d 1102, 54 U.S.P.Q.2d (BNA) 1273, 1275 (C.D. Cal. 2000).

76.2. *Id.,* 54 U.S.P.Q.2d at 1276.

76.3. Watts v. XL Systems, Inc., 232 F.3d 877, 56 U.S.P.Q.2d (BNA) 1836, 1838–39 (Fed. Cir. 2000).

77. Mas-Hamilton Group v. LaGard, Inc., 156 F.3d 1206, 48 U.S.P.Q.2d (BNA) 1010 (Fed. Cir. 1998).

planted by the test in the 1999 Guidelines. But the Federal Circuit has not indicated it will rely on similar rules of interpretation. The court cautioned that the use of the word "means" is not required to qualify under § 112, paragraph 6. The Patent Office Guidelines disagree. Usually, use of "means" invokes § 112, paragraph 6; but not always. The 1999 Guidelines define when use of "means" invokes § 112, paragraph 6 and when it does not.

Cole v. Kimberly-Clark Corp.[78] involved the claim limitation: "perforation means . . . for tearing the outer impermeable layer means, for removing the training brief. . . ." The court said it was not under § 112, paragraph 6 because it recited a definite structure that performs the function. Here the claim referred to "perforation" means, not "means for tearing . . ." or "means for enabling tearing. . . ." Like a detent or a filter, a perforation is a definite structure. *Waterloo Furniture Components, Ltd. v. Haworth, Inc.*[79] had claim wording which began "means for," but which was found to thereafter describe structure, rather than function, namely: "first means being mounted on said carriage means for pivotal movement relative thereto about substantially vertical hinge axis means for enabling the link means. . . ." The "first means" were not a means plus function element. Had it read "means for enabling the link means," it might have been under § 112, paragraph 6.

To be sure you are under § 112, paragraph 6, use the pure "means for . . . ." Other words lead to ambiguity and the need for a court to decide.[80]

The statute recites "means . . . *for*" performing a function. But is "for" needed to invoke § 112, paragraph 6? "Spring means

---

78. Cole v. Kimberly-Clark Corp., 102 F.3d 524 (Fed. Cir. 1996).
79. Waterloo Furniture Components, Ltd. v. Haworth, Inc., 25 U.S.P.Q.2d (BNA) 1139, 1142–44 (N.D. Ill. 1992). *See* B.F. Goodrich Flight Systems Inc. v. Insight Instruments Corp., 22 U.S.P.Q.2d (BNA) 1832, 1836 (S.D. Ohio 1992).
80. *See* York Prods., Inc. v. Central Tractor Farm & Family Center, 99 F.3d 1568 (Fed. Cir. 1996) (which appended structure after the "means," not function, the claim language reciting: "means formed on the upwardly extending liner sidewall portions including a plurality of spaced apart vertically extending ridge members protruding from the liner sidewall portions and forming load locks").

tending to keep the door . . . closed," without "for," was held to invoke § 112, paragraph 6 because the "tending" phrase pertains solely to function of the element, not its structure.[81] "Ink delivery means" was held to fall under § 112, paragraph 6 as means plus function language and "for" was not used.[81.1] "Means" or "step" is the key. The 1999 Guidelines suggest that "for" is also required. Perhaps the Federal Circuit may in the future agree.

It should be apparent that treatment under § 112, paragraph 6 applies only to the "means" within such a limitation, not to other elements or parts identified by non-means nouns within the "means for" claim limitation. In *O.I. Corp. v. Tekmar Co., Inc.*,[82] the claim limitation was "means for passing the analyte slug through a passage." The court found that the limitation invoked § 112, paragraph 6, but that § 112, paragraph 6 could not be applied to "passage" although it was in the means limitation. The same would apply to "analyte slug" in the claims limitation.

Under § 112, paragraph 6, one looks to the specification for what is disclosed, plus equivalents, to determine what is covered in a "means for accomplishing a function" limitation. What is precisely disclosed in the specification is found by reading the specification and the drawings. What is equivalent must have an equivalent structure and also perform the identical function as claimed.[83]

If the specification of the patent does not provide adequate disclosure of the § 112, paragraph 6 element, this could invalidate under § 112, paragraph 2 or make the disclosure insufficient and the patent invalid under § 112, paragraph 1.[84]

---

81. Unidynamics Corp. v. Automatic Products Int'l Ltd., 157 F.3d 1311, 48 U.S.P.Q.2d (BNA) 1099 (Fed. Cir. 1998).

81.1. Signtech USA Ltd. v. Vutek, Inc., 174 F.3d 1352, 50 U.S.P.Q.2d 1372 (Fed. Cir. 1999).

82. O.I. Corp. v. Tekmar Co., Inc., 42 U.S.P.Q.2d (BNA) 1777 (Fed. Cir. 1997).

83. Smiths International Medical Systems, Inc. v. Vital Signs, Inc., 51 U.S.P.Q.2d (BNA) 1415 (Fed. Cir. 1999).

84. Personalized Media Communications v. U.S. Int'l Trade Comm'n, 161 F.3d 696, 48 U.S.P.Q.2d (BNA) 1880 (Fed. Cir. 1998).

A court deciding infringement will look to the specification to determine what is covered by the "means for" element. The court may exclude an infringer's design if it decides that the features of that design are not encompassed in the means shown in the patent specification.[85] In *Chiuminatta*, the court studied the specification and drawings of the patent to find those elements of the disclosed product that satisfied "means connected to the saw for supporting the surface of the concrete. . . ." The court found that to be a skid plate, and the court expressly excluded other features of the skid plate which, while present, did not cooperate in performing the function.

> [S]tructure disclosed in the specification is "corresponding" structure only if the specification or prosecution history clearly links or associates that structure to the function recited in the claim. This duty to link or associate structure to function is the quid pro quo for the convenience of employing § 112, ¶ 6.[86]

Therefore, be sure the specification identifies which structure is performing the claimed function.

To assure that certain elements are or are not to be considered part of a claimed "means for" element, consider reciting in the specification the components which perform that claimed function,[86.1] and perhaps indicate other components that are present which do not participate in the function. In that way, for example, you could include a more limited number of components or elements within the "means" limitation, making it easier to have the limitation satisfied by an accused infringing product, since it needs fewer features to fall within the claim limitation.

---

85. Chiuminatta Concrete Concepts, Inc. v. Cardinal Industries, Inc., 46 U.S.P.Q.2d (BNA) 1752, 1755-56 (Fed. Cir. 1998); Globetrotter Software, Inc. v. Elan Computer Group, Inc., 236 F.3d 1363, 57 U.S.P.Q.2d (BNA) 1542, 1545 (Fed. Cir. 2001); Wenger Mfg., Inc. v. Coating Machinery Systems, Inc., 239 F.3d 1225, 57 U.S.P.Q.2d (BNA) 1679, 1684 (Fed. Cir. 2001).

86. B. Braun Medical, Inc. v. Abbott Labs., 124 F.3d 1419, 1424 (Fed. Cir. 1997).

86.1. *See* Micro Chemical Inc. v. Great Plains Chem. Co., 194 F.3d 1250, 52 U.S.P.Q.2d (BNA) 1258, 1263 (Fed. Cir. 2000); Harmonic Design, Inc. v. Hunter Douglas, Inc., 88 F. Supp. 2d 1102, 54 U.S.P.Q.2d (BNA) 1273, 1276 (C.D. Cal. 2000).

If it is unclear whether a claim limitation falls within the scope of § 112, paragraph 6, a rejection under § 112, paragraph 2, may be appropriate.

To broaden the scope of a "means" limitation in a claim at the time the specification is being prepared, the claim writer should expressly recite in the specification various alternatives which may be considered for features to be claimed in "means" limitations.[86.2] This makes those alternatives fall within the "means" limitation because they are in the specification. In effect, § 112, paragraph 6 imports the specification and drawings into the means for performing a function element.[87] Your specification is preferably broad enough to cover known and future alternatives. But including those alternatives also opens up the "means" limitation to the possibility that numerous equivalent alternatives exist, making easier a later argument by the Patent Office examiner examining the claim to find equivalent prior art (*In re Donaldson*) or a still later argument by the patentee that an accused device/process has an equivalent to the claim limitation.

Another technique for broadening the scope of a "means" limitation is to describe in the specification the part or element of an object that performs the function claimed, possibly also indicating that part is a means for performing a function. Other elements are deemed a separate subassembly or not part of the claimed means.[88] Instead of merely describing an anvil having a surface on which the workpiece is worked in the specification, the drafter describes a surface on which the workpiece is worked, that surface being on an anvil. That gives the claim drafter the argument that the means referred to in the means for limitation in the claim is not the entire anvil, but just the workpiece supporting surface. This perhaps provides a wider range of equivalents because the means in the disclosure is the surface, rather than the entire anvil.

On the other hand, the 1999 Guidelines point out that when means plus function language is employed, the specification must

---

86.2. Ishida Co. v. Taylor, 221 F.3d 1310, 55 U.S.P.Q.2d (BNA) 1449 (Fed. Cir. 2000).

87. Multiform Dessicants, Inc. v. Medzam Ltd., 45 U.S.P.Q.2d (BNA) 1429, 1433–34 (Fed. Cir. 1998).

88. Kegel Co. v. AMF Bowling, Inc., 44 U.S.P.Q.2d (BNA) 1123, 1128–29 (Fed. Cir. 1997); *Chiuminatta Concrete Concepts, Inc.,* 46 U.S.P.Q. 2d; *Micro Chemical Inc.,* 194 F.3d.

adequately disclose what is meant by that language. Failure to adequately disclose the means in the specification results in a failure to satisfy § 112, paragraph 2, requiring that you particularly point out and distinctly claim the invention. Adequate disclosure, in my opinion, means what is adequately disclosed to one of ordinary skill in the relevant art. For example, the claim may recite a "means for" and the disclosure may simply show an undetailed box described as a "microprocessor." For one skilled in the art, the disclosure of a "microprocessor" and a description of what it does may be an adequate disclosure under § 112, paragraph 1, and therefore an adequate claim limitation under § 112, paragraph 2. The 1999 Guidelines instruct examiners about clarifying the disclosure if it originally would have been understood by one skilled in the art. Best is when the specification describes the "means" elements and what disclosed features they include, such as "means for assigining" or "means for randomly selecting one of said plurality of assigned numbers."[88.1]

However, a "black box" disclosure in the specification of an element described as a means in the claim may fail to satisfy § 112, paragraph 2 because an insufficient disclosure of a specific structure has been provided, making a determination of the structure and especially equivalents impossible. This is especially the case with software patents, where claim elements are defined in device or means-plus-function form, and the specification and drawings may not have much detail, if any.[89] The only way to save such a claim is to be able to demonstrate that the "black box" is well known in the art, e.g., a computer, a microprocessor.[90] Better practice would be to disclose the computer more thoroughly in the specification, and to cover equivalents, to provide disclosure of alternative structures that can by now be contemplated.[91]

88.1. WMS Gaming Inc. v. International Game Technology, 184 F.3d 1339, 51 U.S.P.Q.2d (BNA) 1385, 1391–92 (Fed. Cir. 1999).

89. AT&T Corp. v. Excel Communications, Inc., 172 F.3d 1352, 50 U.S.P.Q.2d (BNA) 1447, 1452 (Fed. Cir. 1999). *See* Isogon Corp. v. Amdahl Corp., 47 F. Supp. 2d 436 (S.D.N.Y. 1998) (for computer software claim elements in § 112, paragraph 6 form, take "event detector for detecting," "collector for obtaining," "recorder for recording," and "correlator for correlating").

90. *In re* Dossel, 115 F.3d 942 (Fed. Cir. 1997).

91. Fonar Corp. v. General Electric Co., 107 F.3d 1543, 1551–52 (Fed. Cir. 1977), *cert. denied*, 118 S. Ct. 266 (1997).

The 1999 Guidelines set forth a process for an examiner to determine equivalence of a prior art element to a means for performing a function element during ex parte examination:

> In implementing the change in examination practice necessitated by *Donaldson*, the PTO set forth a two-step process for making a *prima facie* case of equivalence of a prior art element during *ex parte* examination. First, the examiner must find that the prior art element performs the function specified in the claim element, and, second, the examiner must find that the prior art element is not excluded by any explicit definition provided in the specification for an equivalent. This two-step process is not superseded by these interim supplemental guidelines, and is consistent with the requirement that the PTO give claims their broadest reasonable interpretation. The specification need not describe the equivalents of the structures, materials, or acts corresponding to the means- (or step-) plus-function claim element. Where, however, the specification is silent as to what constitutes equivalents, the burden is placed upon the applicant to show that a prior art element which performs the claimed function is not an equivalent of the structure, material, or acts disclosed in the specification.[92]

The Patent Office 1994 Guidelines for "means"[93] claims also guide examiners as to how to determine whether a prior art disclosure is "equivalent" to what is claimed in a claim limitation:

1) Whether the prior art element performs the function specified in the claim in substantially the same way and produces substantially the same result (the equivalents for infringement test of *Graver Tank v. Linde*[94] which is applied to Patent Office determinations as well,[95] i.e., they are functional equivalents.

2) Whether one of ordinary skill in the art would recognize interchangeability of the prior art element for the corresponding element in the specification. Clearly, the broader the scope of the disclosure in the specification, the more likely an equivalent will be found.

---

92. Interim Supplemental Examination Guidelines for Determining the Applicability of 35 U.S.C. § 112 ¶6 (issued by the Patent and Trademark Office effective July 30, 1999), 64 Fed. Reg. 41392, 41393 (1999), 58 Pat. Trademark & Copyright J. (BNA) 443, 444 (Aug. 5, 1999) (footnotes omitted).
93. MPEP 2184.
94. Graver Tank v. Linde, 339 U.S. 605 (1950).
95. Polumbo v. Don-Joy Co., 762 F.2d 969, 975 (Fed. Cir. 1985).

3) Whether the prior art element is a structural equivalent of the element disclosed in the specification,[96] again applying the function/way/result test as described in 1); or

4) The structure, materials or acts disclosed in the specification represent an insubstantial change which adds nothing significant to the prior art element.[97]

The Federal Circuit's en banc decision in *Hilton Davis Chem. Co. v. Warner Jenkinson Co., Inc.*[98] and its reversal on other grounds by the Supreme Court[99] did not negate the substance of the Patent Office guidelines, but it did change their emphasis. The test for equivalents is to determine the substantiality of the differences between the claimed and accused products and processes (see *Valmont* below). The function/way/result test and the interchangeability test may provide evidence on the substantiality of the differences.

Equivalency under 35 U.S.C. § 112 differs from the Doctrine of Equivalents as to how each is determined.[100] The Doctrine of Equivalents equitably *expands* exclusive patent rights, as *Hilton Davis* makes it easier to find equivalence. One is not restricted to a specific structure that may be claimed or to any or all of the structures in the specification, but can find equivalents anywhere, using the *Hilton Davis* tests. Equivalence is assessed as of the time that the infringement issue is considered. In contrast, § 112, paragraph 6, limits the broad language of means-plus-function limitations in combination claims to what is disclosed, plus equivalents of the structures, materials, or acts in the specification.[101] Equivalence under § 112 is assessed as of the time that the application for patent was filed, not at the later time for application of the Doctrine of Equivalents.[101.1] Therefore, not everything that could

---

96. *In re* Bond, 910 F.2d 831, 15 U.S.P.Q.2d 1566 (Fed. Cir. 1990).
97. Valmont Industries Inc. v. Reinke Manufacturing Co., 983 F.2d 1039, 25 U.S.P.Q.2d (BNA) 1451 (Fed. Cir. 1993).
98. Hilton Davis Chem. Co. v. Warner Jenkinson Co., Inc., 35 U.S.P.Q.2d (BNA) 1641 (Fed. Cir. 1995).
99. 117 S. Ct. 1040, 41 U.S.P.Q.2d (BNA) 1865 (1997).
100. Valmont Industries Inc. v. Reinke Manufacturing Co., 983 F.2d 1039, 25 U.S.P.Q.2d (BNA) 1451 (Fed. Cir. 1993).
101. *Id.*, 25 U.S.P.Q.2d at 1455.
101.1. Al-Site Corp. v. VSI International Inc., 174 F.3d 1308, 50 U.S.P.Q.2d (BNA) 1161, 1167 (Fed. Cir. 1999); Ishida Co. v. Taylor, 221 F.3d 1310, 55 U.S.P.Q.2d (BNA) 1449, 1453 (Fed. Cir. 2000).

perform the same function or that might satisfy any *Hilton Davis* tests would, with certainty, be a limitation under § 112, paragraph 6. See *In re Donaldson*. As noted above, if the claim drafter recognizes the possible equivalency issue early enough, the specification can be written to express enough alternatives to give broad scope to a § 112, paragraph 6 limitation. Although § 112, paragraph 6 restricts scope, as a practical matter, in view of *In re Donaldson* and the Patent Office guidelines, there should be no difference remaining in scope between the two types of equivalence.

A means clause is used to describe the function of a particular element, as discussed herein. However, before deciding to argue patentability based on a means-plus-function limitation in response to an examiner's rejection, remember that including a means-plus-function clause may create a prosecution history estoppel which limits the patentee's protection. The examiner will argue that the prior art of record teaches an equivalent of the disclosed means-plus-function structure and the claim writer's responsive argument will create an estoppel.

Means clauses should not be used as a vehicle to present ultra-broad or functional claims. One Patent and Trademark Office example of an overbroad means clause is the claim: "In a device of the class described, means for forcing a flow of air while preventing injury to the operator."[102] The device disclosed was a fan with soft rubber blades. This claim does not particularly point out and distinctly claim the invention. It is attempting to claim the desirable result only, not the way in which the result is accomplished. This type of case is less an adverse decision on means clauses than on overly broad claims generally. In general, one cannot use a means clause to do what one cannot do otherwise, obtain fantastic claims far broader than the invention.

Means clauses had been widely used to describe generally conventional elements of a combination. However, the more recent restrictive interpretation of clauses under § 112, paragraph 6 makes dangerous the use of such clauses even to recite conventional elements, since the claim element may be restricted in scope to what is shown in the preferred embodiment. The outer periph-

---

102. From the August 1963 Agent's Exam.

ery of permissible uses for means clauses is somewhat uncertain, and new cases on the subject appear frequently.

Because 35 U.S.C. § 112, paragraph 6 recites:

> An element in a claim for a combination may be expressed as a means or step for . . .

A single-element claim such as the following does not claim a "combination" and cannot employ means-plus-function language:

> Apparatus for shaking articles in a container, which comprises: means for oscillating the container to shake the articles.

Note that the "means for forcing air" claim was also a "single means" claim, and would also be objectionable on that score. See discussion of *In re Hyatt*, below. But adding "a base" or other conventional element would not have helped that claim.

The Federal Circuit still rejects "single means" claims, because they cover every conceivable means for achieving the desired result.[103] In *Hyatt*, the claim held unpatentable under § 112 recited:

> 35. A Fourier transform processor for generating Fourier transformed incremental output signals in response to incremental input signals, said Fourier transform processor *comprising* incremental *means* for incrementallygenerating the Fourier transformed incremental output signals in response to the incremental input signals. [Emphasis ours.]

It was a "single means" claim.

In re Donaldson[104] does not affect the holding of *In re Hyatt*[105] to the effect that a single means claim does not comply with the enablement requirement of § 112, first paragraph.[106] *Donaldson* only applies to an interpretation of a limitation drafted to correspond to § 112, paragraph 6, which by its terms is limited to "an element in a claim to a combination," as it does not affect a limitation in a claim which is not directed to a combination.

"Apparatus which shakes the container," for example, is narrative and functional, whereas "apparatus for shaking the container" would be comfortably seen as a "means . . . for."

---

103. *In re* Hyatt, 708 F.2d 712, 712–13 (Fed. Cir. 1983).
104. *In re* Donaldson, 16 F.3d 1189 (Fed. Cir. 1994).
105. *In re* Hyatt, 708 F.2d 712 (Fed. Cir. 1983).
106. MPEP 2181.

Most mechanical claims are, or can be made to be, directed to a combination of elements, in which case there is no problem on this score. A possible problem in this area is with an improvement or a *Jepson*-type claim (see section 57), where, in the body of the claim, a single new element might be claimed that cooperates with several old elements in the preamble to make up a complete machine or apparatus. As noted in section 57, it is thought that such a claim is truly a claim to a combination, so that the body of the claim following the *Jepson* transition phrase could properly consist of a single means expression. However, there may be some difference of opinion on that score, so it might be good tactics to put at least one other element, means or otherwise, in the body of the claim.

As to overly broad claims, the Supreme Court held in 1946 that a claim was invalid as indefinite and too broad where it used broad means-plus-function language at what the Court considered to be "the precise point of novelty" of the claim.[107]

The clause in question read:

> means associated with said pressure responsive device for tuning said receiving means to the frequency of echoes from the tuning collars of said tuning section to clearly distinguish the echoes of said couplings from each other.

Although the stated function apparently was technically novel, the Court felt the patentee should be limited to claiming his specific means (a tuned acoustical pipe) rather than all possible means, some of which might be later invented.

Note that this case came up before the 1952 statute, and was undoubtedly one of the items that led to the new paragraph 6 of § 112 dealing with means clauses. Means clauses were common before the statute, as a matter of practice that had grown up, but the *Halliburton* case cast doubt as to their worth. Commentators believe that the statute was intended to overrule the *Halliburton* case.

In *In re Lundberg and Zuschlag*,[108] the C.C.P.A. came close to holding that 35 U.S.C. § 112 overruled the *Halliburton* decision, though that was not necessary to the decision: "As correctly stated by appellants in their brief, this paragraph was designed, at

---

107. Halliburton Oil Well Cementing Co. v. Walker, 329 U.S. 1 (1946).
108. *In re* Lundberg and Zuschlag, 113 U.S.P.Q. (BNA) 530 (C.C.P.A. 1957).

least in part, to modify or overrule such decisions as *Halliburton....*"

In *Ex parte Ball and Hair,*[109] the Board indicated, vaguely, that "some measure of greater liberality in the use of functional expressions in the definition of elements in the proper combination claims is authorized by section 112 than has been permitted by some of the stricter decisions of the courts in the past." Some means-plus-function claims were allowed, where the function stated in the claim was "distinctly unlike any function which is or could possibly be performed" by the reference. This seems to be allowance of a means-plus-function claim at the precise point of novelty.

In *Ex parte Mayer,*[110] the Board expressly held that there is no objection to a means-plus-function clause "merely because it is at exact point of novelty in a combination claim...," citing the *Ball and Hair* case. In this case the acceptable clause was:

> means responsive to said residual of potential to disable said discharge means for a period greater than the interval between pulses and sufficient to permit normal voltage on said network to be restored before said network is again discharged by said discharge means.[111]

Note that the statute gets around what seems to be the Supreme Court's main reason for objecting to the broad clause: that it would cover nonequivalent structures, in that the coverage under 35 U.S.C. § 112 is expressly limited to the specific means shown, plus equivalents.

Means clauses are routine where it is the function of the element that is important *and* where various other specific constructions could be used. Thus, in example I, the oscillating means illustrated includes a motor, cam, and cam follower linkage, but it is obvious that various other common arrangements would be equally suitable, such as a piston and cylinder. It should be clear that the essential thing to the combination is *that* the container be oscillated, not how. Since many common structures could be employed to do that job, this is the ideal place for a means clause.

---

109. *Ex parte* Ball and Hair, 99 U.S.P.Q. (BNA) 146, 148 (Bd. App. 1954).
110. *Ex parte* Mayer, 111 U.S.P.Q. (BNA) 109 (Bd. App. 1956).
111. *See Ex parte* Roggenburk, 172 U.S.P.Q. (BNA) 82 (Bd. App. 1970).

In this example, it is difficult to draw a generic expression other than a means clause, covering both the motor-cam arrangement and a piston-cylinder arrangement, as well as any other conventional arrangement for oscillating a member. As was mentioned in section 24, an alternative expression, such as "cam or cylinder," cannot be used, even if that were considered broad enough. A generic expressions must be found. Other attempted generic expressions, such as "a mechanism for oscillating . . .," or "a mechanical device for oscillating . . .," which perhaps might have been viewed as unacceptable functional expressions, now are accepted ways of claiming apparatus, and because they are not claimed using the statutory word "means," under the 1999 Guidelines, they should not be interpreted under § 112, paragraph 6.[111.1] This raises the then unresolved question of the scope to be accorded such a non-means claim element. The Doctrine of Equivalents would apply, and that application is likely to produce a result the same as classifying the claim limitation under § 112, paragraph 6.

In writing means clauses, as many qualifying words or expressions should be employed in the means clause as are necessary to limit the claim to the scope desired. Thus, one might recite such expressions as:

> resilient means, connected between the carriage and the base, for urging the carriage against the stop;

or

> means, actuated by the carriage at the end of its forward movement, for moving the bending fingers into contact with the carriage.

In these fragmentary expressions, it should be noted that such elements as "the carriage" and "the bending fingers" must have been recited in previous elements of such claims, as mentioned in section 23 on antecedents. Where no such qualifying expressions are important, none should be used. But, as noted above, recitation of a structural element that performs a function, instead of means for

---

111.1. *See* Watts v. XL Systems, Inc., 232 F.3d 877, 56 U.S.P.Q.2d (BNA) 1836, 1839 (Fed. Cir. 2000).

performing the function, is outside § 112, paragraph 6.[112] Perhaps too much of the qualifiers noted above will remove the claim from § 112, paragraph 6, and will particularly remove the claim limitation. This occurred, for example, in *Waterloo Furniture Components Ltd. v. Haworth, Inc.*,[113] discussed above.

It is recommended that one use the exact statutory language "means for . . . (performing an act or accomplishing a result)" or "step for . . ." rather than possibly equivalent expressions that do not include "means for . . ." or "step for. . . ." Especially based on the 1999 Guidelines, limitations without "means" or "step" do not fall under § 112, paragraph 6.[113.1] Further, the statute recites only "means" or "step." A court interpreting a claim should follow the statutory words and, especially as to claims pending after the 1999 Guidelines, should follow the Patent Office Guidelines. This should not be an issue during prosecution of the application claims, because examiners should be governed by the Guidelines.

Although one should avoid the practice where possible, it is permissible to claim "means for [doing thing A], including means for [doing thing B]" if B is a part of A. For example, in patent 1,971,193, we find:

> means for causing oscillations to be produced in said polyphase circuit having a frequency dependent on the tuning in said polyphase circuit said means [assume no unclarity] including means for producing a magnetic field between said anodes and cathode.

This may be necessary to avoid double inclusion of elements (section 21) where they are partially overlapping or where one means includes another.

---

112. Greenberg v. Ethicon Endo-Surgery, Inc., 91 F.3d 1580 (Fed. Cir. 1996); Cole v. Kimberly-Clark Corp., 102 F.3d 524 (Fed. Cir. 1996); Interim Supplemental Examination Guidelines for Determining the Applicability of 35 U.S.C. § 112 ¶ 6 (issued by the Patent and Trademark Office effective July 30, 1999), 64 Fed. Reg. 41392 (1999), 58 Pat. Trademark & Copyright J. (BNA) 443 (Aug. 5, 1999).

113. Waterloo Furniture Components Ltd. v. Haworth, Inc., 25 U.S.P.Q.2d (BNA) 1139, 1142–44 (N.D. Ill. 1992).

113.1. *See* Harmonic Design, Inc. v. Hunter Douglas, Inc., 88 F. Supp. 2d 1102, 54 U.S.P.Q.2d (BNA) 1273, 1276 (C.D. Cal. 2000).

In referring back to a previously recited means element, later in the claim (see section 23, antecedents), one merely gives it a convenient distinctive name, such as "the reciprocating means" or "the container-reciprocating means" or "the means for reciprocating the container" or, less desirably, "first means," "second means." The exact choice is not critical as long as there is no possible confusion with other means elements. The use of the definite article "the" (or "said") is also required, to avoid a double inclusion of the same element in the claim language. Wherever possible, it is best to avoid identifying a means only as "first means," "second means," etc.

It is recommended that means expressions be avoided where there is a definite generic word of the same scope available and particularly where "means" is placed after the descriptive generic word. Thus, in example 1, "a base" is fully generic, and there is no need to say "base means," "means for supporting," or the like. Also "a container" is generic, so there is no need for "container means" or "means for containing." Note that, in these situations, the word "means" does not add a thing; "container means" is not a bit broader than "a container" but instead may be interpreted as narrower in scope, as invoking § 112, paragraph 6.

Sometimes there may be one or more than one, or more than two of the same type of elements disclosed, usually cooperating with each other, e.g., legs supporting the container, and the claim writer does not wish to limit the claim to a particular number, by claiming "a leg" or "a plurality of legs." Some practitioners claim "leg means" as the generic expression of any number of legs. Use of the noun "means" (or "step") following what then becomes the descriptive adjective, "leg," may ease the reader's reference to the claimed means.[114] But use of "means" in that clause is not needed. The word "comprising" or the equivalent in the claim preamble encompasses the full range of numbers of the recited elements, e.g., from one leg through many of them. Placing the generic word

---

114. Manville Sales Corp. v. Paramount Systems, Inc., 14 U.S.P.Q.2d (BNA) 1291 (E.D. Pa 1989), *modified*, 917 F.2d 544, 16 U.S.P.Q.2d (BNA) 1587 (Fed. Cir. 1990). *See* Surgical Laser Technologies Inc. v. Laser Industries Ltd., 29 U.S.P.Q.2d (BNA) 1533 (E.D. Pa. 1993) (wherein the court supported the jury's determination that "probe tip means" does not constitute means-plus-function language).

before "means" is not helpful, does not broaden claim scope, and may be harder to understand (as, how does a container differ from the container means?). Further, as noted above, in the Patent Office guidelines, merely adding "means" before a noun, without reciting a function of that means, does not convert the claim element, like "leg means," into an element governed by 35 U.S.C. § 112, paragraph 6.[115]

There are occasions where use of the word "means" following the noun is not only sensible, it is the only apparent way to cover the full range of elements that accomplish the objective. For example, if some means reflects a light beam from a source to a detector, calling the reflective device a reflector or mirror might be misdescriptive. The arrangement of disclosed elements might require two or more reflectors or mirrors, although certain angling of the light source or the detector may make only a single reflector or mirror necessary. Here, the noun "reflector" or "mirror" does not cover all apparent possibilities. The noun, e.g., "reflector" or "mirror," is now made an adjective, followed by the noun "means," and that covers the alternatives including one or more reflectors.

In addition, use of an adjective before "means" like "rod means" eases the reference, and it is a means-plus-function clause[116] if the other requirements of the Patent Office Guidelines are satisfied. But if the adjective causes a definite structure to be recited, like "perforation means," and the other Guidelines requirements are not met, then the limitation may be outside § 112, paragraph 6.[117] This is one technique the claim drafter can use to avoid § 112, paragraph 6 treatment even if he uses the "means for" format. However, use of the word "means" in a claim does not always constitute a "means-plus-function" clause. The term

---

115. *Ex parte* Klumb, 159 U.S.P.Q. (BNA) 694 (Bd. App. 1967).

116. Manville Sales Corp. v. Paramount Systems, Inc., 14 U.S.P.Q.2d (BNA) 1291 (E.D. Pa. 1989), *modified,* 917 F.2d 544, 16 U.S.P.Q.2d (BNA) 1587 (Fed. Cir. 1990); Ultrak, Inc. v. Radio Engineering Industries, Inc., 52 U.S.P.Q.2d (BNA) 1526, 1528 (Fed. Cir. 1999); Signtech USA Ltd. v. Vutek, Inc., 174 F.3d 1352, 50 U.S.P.Q.2d (BNA) 1372, 1374–75 (Fed. Cir. 1999).

117. Cole v. Kimberly-Clark Corp., 102 F.3d 524 (Fed. Cir. 1996); Envirco Corp. v. Clestra Cleanroom Inc., 209 F.3d 1360, 54 U.S.P.Q.2d (BNA) 1449 (Fed. Cir. 2000).

"means," as opposed to "means for," may be used in a non-means-plus-function claim, as when indicating a tool or device having a particular structure (recited in the claim) to carry out its intended function.[118] In *Surgical Laser Technologies, Inc. v. Laser Industries Ltd.,*[119] claim 1 contained the terms "tip means" and "securing means." The term "tip means" was determined not to be a means-plus-function term, while the term "securing means" was determined to be a means-plus-function term primarily because the term "tip means" was followed by a phrase which describes its composition, whereas the term "securing means" was followed by the phrase that describes its function. Furthermore, later claim language was "said tip means to be positioned to perform a surgical procedure on or within a patient." The jury concluded that this phrase was meant to describe the position of the tip rather than its function. Saying where the "means" is located will not invoke § 112, paragraph 6, while saying what the "means" does will invoke the statute. Additionally, the phrase "to perform a surgical procedure on or within a patient" appeared only in claim 1 while the term "tip means" appeared in other independent claims as well. The jury inferred from this that the term "tip means" was not linked to the phrase "to perform . . ." in claim 1. All these factors contributed to the jury's determination that the term "tip means" was not a means-plus-function clause.

The reader will note that the following "means" clause has been used in claim 1: "means for oscillating the container on the legs to shake the articles." As for the recitation of "legs" in claim 1, a problem in scope of claims is presented. As noted above, no benefit would have been obtained by adding "means" to the word "leg." The legs could still have been more broadly expressed as "means for mounting the container on the base for oscillating movement with respect thereto." This expression is, of course, much broader than merely claiming pivoted legs for doing the same thing. It is interesting to note that the claim now reads on the spring mounting of Figure 3 of Example I in Appendix A. However, a line was drawn

---

118. *Id.*
119. Surgical Laser Technologies, Inc. v. Laser Indus. Ltd., 29 U.S.P.Q.2d (BNA) 1533, 1535 (E.D. Pa. 1993), *subsequent appeal,* 32 U.S.P.Q.2d (BNA) 1798 (Fed. Cir. 1994).

for purposes of illustration to include the pivoted legs as elements of the claim. Figure 3 shows a simple mechanism by which the wording of claim 1 may be circumvented.

As to what specific elements are included in a means clause, the clause includes whatever elements or parts of elements are disclosed in the specification to perform the recited function, plus equivalents (35 U.S.C. § 112).[119.1] The "means for oscillating" clause stated in claim 1 covers the motor, the cam, and the cam follower attached to the container. A means clause may read on a single element or a part of an element, even a hole (section 26), or a train of fifty cooperating elements—whatever is needed to perform the recited function.

There is a limit on what "means" may encompass. In *In re Prater and Wei,*[120] the court held that a means clause did not cover a human being (a possibly mental step in that case), but that it may properly cover a programmed general purpose computer. In the *Prater* case, the clause in question of the apparatus claim was:

> means for determining that one of said scalar functions of greatest magnitude for identification of . . . [a desired mathematical relationship].

This holding was affirmed.[121] It was also amplified in the subsequent case of *In re Bernhart and Fetter*[122] (see section 44).

Further, there is no objection to having one or more specific elements of structure included as a part of two different means clauses, as long as the entire train of parts to perform each function is not identical.

For example, in *Reed v. Edwards,*[123] the court held that different parts of a single element could support two means clauses,

---

119.1. Chiuminatta Concrete Concepts Inc. v. Cardinal Industries Inc., 46 U.S.P.Q.2d (BNA) 1752, 1755–56 (Fed. Cir. 1998); IMS Technology v. Haas Automation, Inc., 206 F.3d 1422, 54 U.S.P.Q.2d (BNA) 1129, 1135 (Fed. Cir. 2000).

120. *In re* Prater and Wei, 162 U.S.P.Q. (BNA) 541 (C.C.P.A. 1969) (on rehearing).

121. *See In re* Johnston, 183 U.S.P.Q. (BNA) 172 (C.C.P.A. 1974), *rev'd on other ground (obviousness) sub nom.* Dann v. Johnston, 209 U.S.P.Q. (BNA) 257 (U.S. 1976).

122. *In re* Bernhart and Fetter, 163 U.S.P.Q. (BNA) 611 (C.C.P.A. 1969).

123. Reed v. Edwards, 40 U.S.P.Q. (BNA) 620, 622 (C.C.P.A. 1939).

quoting with approval the following language from the Board of Appeals decision:

> It has long been recognized that one element of a claim may be relied on for performing different functions . . . [W]e can see no reason why one side of a tongue or a groove in the Edwards device may not be regarded as the means for advancing the cutter, and why the other side may not be regarded as the means for limiting the rate of travel.

If the disclosure has truly one completely indivisible element for performing both functions, then classic textbook law is that the inventor cannot make the claim to separate means because of double inclusion, or double reading of elements. For example, in *Holdsworth v. Goldsmith*,[124] the court stated:

> [There is] . . . fairly well settled law on the question. If a patent disclosure shows two elements to perform two different functions and the patent claim is drawn to define both as separate elements, a disclosure which has only one element performing both functions, will not be regarded as supporting the count. (Citing cases.)

While there was never an issue as to whether a method limitation falls within § 112, paragraph 6, there are few precedents on it. *O.I. Corp. v. Tekmar Co.*[125] and *Caterpillar, Inc. v. Detroit Diesel Corp.*[126] hold that method claims fall within § 112, paragraph 6.[126.1] The statute applies when a step plus a function is recited, and without reciting definite acts. Merely claiming a step without reciting a function is not analogous to a means plus function recital. A step plus function limitation describes the result to be achieved, not specific acts which may achieve that result.[127] The presence of a purpose in the claim preamble, but not at the claim limitation itself, does not make the claim limitation within the claim into one under § 112, paragraph 6.[128]

---

124. Holdsworth v. Goldsmith, 54 U.S.P.Q. (BNA) 90, 94 (C.C.P.A. 1942).

125. O.I. Corp. v. Tekmar Co., 42 U.S.P.Q.2d (BNA) 1777 (Fed Cir. 1997).

126. Caterpillar, Inc. v. Detroit Diesel Corp., 41 U.S.P.Q.2d (BNA) 1876, 1880–82 (N.D. Ind. 1996).

126.1. Seal-Flex Inc. v. Athletic Track and Court Construction, 172 F.3d 836, 50 U.S.P.Q.2d (BNA) 1225, 1233 (Fed. Cir. 1999).

127. *Id.*

128. O.I. Corp. v. Tekmar Co., 42 U.S.P.Q. 2d (BNA) 1777 (Fed. Cir. 1997).

Neither *O.I. Corporation v. Tekmar Company* nor *Caterpillar, Inc. v. Detroit Diesel Corp.* included a method claim limitation that used the words "step for." The method claim in *O.I.* is quoted in the note below.[129] The Federal Circuit held the claim to be under § 112, paragraph 6 because of the broad recital of purpose in the preamble. The court then concluded that the individual steps within the method claim were not governed by § 112, paragraph 6 because the "passing" step was not related to functions performed by the step. The author believes that the court's decision is correct, especially in view of the 1999 Guidelines, which, while they do not control here, provide clear guidance as to when a claim limitation invokes § 112, paragraph 6. Similarly, in *Caterpillar*, the court viewed the individual steps in the process, "providing," "determining," "retrieving," and "using," as not describing the achieved results but as acts in themselves. Therefore, these limitations did not invoke § 112, paragraph 6.

In *Serrano v. Telular Corp.*,[130] the Federal Circuit found that a "determining" element did not invoke § 112, paragraph 6 because the claim element did not recite a function.[130.1]

Practical advice to a claim writer who wants to avoid § 112, paragraph 6 is not to use claims with "means" or "step" in them. Alternatively, supply two sets of claims, one with "means" or "step" limits and one using generic nouns and verbs. As to the former group of claims, this will demonstrate an intent to invoke § 112, paragraph 6, and the contrary for the latter group of claims.

---

129.   9. A method for removing water vapor from an analyte slug passing between a sparge vessel, trap and gas chromatograph, comprising the steps of:

> (a) passing the analyte slug through a passage heated to a first temperature higher than ambient, as the analyte slug passes from the sparge vessel to the trap; and

> (b) passing the analyte slug through the passage that is air cooled to a second temperature below said first temperature but not below ambient, as the analyte slug passes from the trap to the gas chromatograph.

    Id. at 1779.

130. Serrano v. Telular Corp., 42 U.S.P.Q.2d (BNA) 1538 (Fed. Cir. 1997).

130.1. *Cf.* Seal-Flex Inc. v. Athletic Track and Court Construction, 172 F.3d 836, 50 U.S.P.Q.2d (BNA) 1225, 1233 (Fed. Cir. 1999).

Summary

Means clauses are proper in combination claims. They are a simple way to define functions performed broadly. They are governed by 35 U.S.C. § 112, paragraph 6. To invoke that statute, you need use only the statutory language "means" or "step" for performing a specified function; that is, an act or operation such as "means for reciprocating the container." A "means" or "step" clause may cover one element, 10,000 elements, half of one element, or even a hole; it covers whatever is described in the specification, plus equivalents. However, because the scope of the means or step may be restricted, as just indicated, it is recommended that the claim writer avoid these claim limitations and instead give the element or step an appropriate descriptive name not including the words "means" or "step."

Example II—Take-Up Barrel

In the take-up barrel (see Appendix A, Example II), the object is to collect an advancing strand 11 in a barrel 12. The strand is advanced toward the barrel by a conventional advancing means known as a "capstan" 13. The barrel is rotated on a turntable 14 by a motor 15, pulley 16, belt 17, and pulley 18. This operates to vary the point of strand collection circularly with respect to the bottom of the barrel, as shown in figure 2. An eyelet 20 is reciprocated by the same drive motor 15, a pulley 21, a belt 22, a pulley 23, a cam 24, and a cam follower 25 on a shaft 26 of the eyelet 20. This varies the collection point radially with respect to the barrel bottom. The particular strand is a flexible "tinsel" conductor, which forms itself into loops, as shown, as it hits the bottom of the barrel; however, the invention would be useful with other types of strand, which would form other patterns.

A fairly broad claim to the combination follows:

> 2. Apparatus for collecting an advancing strand in a barrel, which comprises:
>
> (a) *a turntable* on which the barrel is mounted for rotation therewith;
>
> (b) *a strand guide* positioned above the barrel for guiding the advancing strand into the barrel;

(c) *means for rotating the turntable* so that the point of collection of the strand varies circularly with respect to the bottom of the barrel; and

(d) *means for reciprocating the guide* so that the point of collection varies radially with respect to the bottom of the barrel.

This claim illustrates the use of two means clauses having some common elements, that is, both the rotating means (c) and the reciprocating means (d) include the motor 15 and its shaft. However, they also include many different elements, starting with the two pulleys 16 and 21 on the motor shaft. For this reason, two separate clauses are proper.

From a function standpoint, the elements (c) and (d) could equally well have been driven from separate motors. Therefore, the claim would be unnecessarily limited if a single drive motor for both were recited. The invention obviously is not in using a single drive motor to drive two moving parts synchronously—that is a common industrial expedient. The invention must relate to the fact of simultaneous rotation and reciprocation. Note how that is accomplished.

Claim 2 further illustrates such general principles of mechanical combination claims as preparing the preamble, selecting the essential elements (including means expressions), listing them in a logical order, and tying them together structurally and functionally to accomplish the result stated in the preamble.

These are the most important elements of mechanical claim drafting.

Further examples of mechanical claims of various kinds are presented in Appendix B.

§ 35 Electrical Circuit Claims (Bryan W. Sheffield, John L. Landis, & Robert Faber)

Substantially all of the precepts discussed in this chapter on apparatus claims apply to electrical circuits. The major difference is that the elements, or some of them, are electrical devices instead of mechanical parts, and the association or cooperation is or may be electrical, not mechanical. One simple example follows:

> 3.   A circuit for counting the number of faults in the insulation on an insulated wire, which comprises:
> (a)   means for applying a test potential between a selected portion of the insulation and the underlying wire;
> (b)   means for moving the insulated wire relative to the potential-applying means; and
> (c)   a pulse counter, associated with the potential-applying means and responsive to each pulse of current between the insulation and the underlying wire, for counting the number of faults in the insulation.

Means clauses are frequently used in electrical cases, both for the electrical elements and for associated mechanical structure, even to cover portions of a programmed general purpose computer. Note that the above claim covers a combination of electrical and mechanical structure. This is quite common and normally presents no problem.

In writing broad claims in electrical cases, it is desirable where possible to focus on what combination a prospective infringer might sell, and to avoid including as elements conventional items, such as power sources or batteries, that such a person might not include with the device. This theory applies to all types of cases.

Thus, in claim 3, above, element (a) is recited as:

> means for applying a test potential between a selected portion of the insulation and the underlying wire.

and not, for example,

> a d.c. battery for applying a test potential between a selected portion of the insulation and the underlying wire.

But even the element (a) means for applying might suggest to a reader the inclusion of the actual power source. To avoid that possibility, recite the means for receiving or connecting to the conventional means, so it is clear you are not claiming that conventional means. For example, claim it as:

> means for receiving and applying a test . . .

clearly avoiding any implication of inclusion of the power source there.

As another example, if one were writing a broad apparatus claim to the simple radio receiver shown in example IV of appendix A, one should not write:

> an antenna connected to the tuning coil of said receiver . . .

because ordinarily such a receiver would not be sold with an antenna attached. It would be better practice to claim,

> means for supplying the radio frequency signals to be detected . . .

and would be even better, to avoid any undesirable interference to claim:

> means for receiving the radio frequency signals to be detected and for supplying the radio frequency signals to the . . .

which, of course, reads on the antenna input terminals, etc., without an antenna attached, as well as reading on the complete, operating combination with the antenna attached.

The importance of not positively reciting conventional elements, or elements that are not customarily sold with the claimed apparatus, cannot be overstressed. Not claiming power supplies, signal sources, and other conventional elements is in many respects analogous to not claiming the workpiece in a machine claim (see section 16).

A Cautionary Note—In complex electrical cases, for example, in telephone switching or computer applications, it is customary to use block diagrams of the claimed circuitry rather than describe in detail each resistor, capacitor, etc. (See section 18 on support for claim elements in the specification and drawings.)

This is a practice of long standing and is perfectly acceptable, provided that the requirements of 35 U.S.C. § 112 are at all times satisfied. The patent attorney who uses such block diagrams must always be prepared to demonstrate to the examiner that what is contained within each block is per se known in the art, for example, by reference to another issued patent or to a publication, such as a textbook or to a supplier's data sheet or catalog. Also see the final portion of section 18 with reference to block diagrams, since block diagrams must themselves be or be coupled with adequate disclosures for supporting a claim limitation.

Of course, a block diagram should *never* be used as the sole disclosure of the contents of a block when what is inside the block is novel and comprises the claimed invention or a subelement thereof.

Another problem arises when what is inside the block is a programmable logic element or computer, admittedly old, but the novel program itself is not disclosed. Such was the case in *In re Brandstadter*,[131] which dealt with a message retrieval system for a "store and forward" communications system. A key element of the invention, which was recited in each of the apparatus claims, was a programmable control circuit, which the specification stated could be the stored program-controlled structure disclosed in an also pending "jumbo" patent application.

The Patent and Trademark Office rejected the claims, under 35 U.S.C. § 112, stating:

> . . . How and by what means (specifically) are the rectangles shown . . . caused to perform their functions, and (to) do so at the appropriate time? . . . A review of the instant disclosure reveals little more than a system diagram consisting of three sheets of labeled rectangles, accompanied by statements of a myriad of desired results. . . . The instant disclosure is completely devoid of any . . . program or even a flow chart to indicate the functions to be performed, the sequence in which they are to be performed, and the conditions which must be present at the time of performance. . . .

The applicants submitted affidavits from three experts stating that, in their opinion, it would be readily apparent to systems and circuit designers of ordinary skill in the art how to build *and program* the disputed control unit. Importantly, the applicants failed to supply the missing software, stating that, "More information regarding these programs is not submitted herewith because the detailed information is considered proprietary."

Nor surprisingly, the C.C.P.A. affirmed the rejection of all claims, stating:

> The Affidavits . . . do not convince us that the examiner's challenge to enablement was unreasonable or has been met. Appellants have not submitted to the examiner even flow charts of the

---

131. *In re* Brandstadter, 179 U.S.P.Q. (BNA) 286 (C.C.P.A. 1973).

programs which they admit . . . (they have) developed for the practice of their invention, and the examiner correctly observed that he (has) been given no circumstances pertaining to this accomplishment . . . such as the number of programmers involved, the number of man-hours involved and the level of skill of the programmers involved.

Thus, to satisfy the standards laid down in *Brandstadter,* any application involving a programmable logical element or computer should include a flow chart and, preferably, the entire program listing if the claim, apparatus, or method is to satisfy § 112.

See also section 43 on electrical methods and section 44 on computer programs for further discussion of questions and problems in electrical claims.

Further Examples—Other examples of typical electrical circuit elements and connections:

—first and second field effect transistors having gate, source, and drain electrodes; means for connecting the drain electrode of the second transistor to the gate electrode of the first transistor; means for connecting a source of clock pulses to the gate of the second transistor;—[Note, these claim elements are specific circuit components.]

This claim part illustrates an important point, made elsewhere about mechanical elements claims, that applies to electrical apparatus claims. No matter how broadly the elements are claimed, they should be recited to interact with, cooperate with, or be connected to each other, so that unconnected elements are not claimed.

Other examples of electrical circuit element claims are:

—a shift register connected to [or responsive to] said data input signal—; [Note, the shift register is a complex element, like a "means for."]

—means for sensing a difference between the output voltage from the capacitor under test and that from the reference capacitor, and for providing an error signal proportional to the difference [Note, a double means plus function for a complex element]; a servomotor responsive to the error signal for . . .;

—means, responsive to a change in light intensity between the light source and the photocell, for generating an output signal related to the—[electro-optical cooperation].

Considering the familiar Wheatstone Bridge circuit of Appendix A, Example III, a fairly specific claim to the circuit illustrated reads as follows:

3A. Apparatus for measuring the electrical resistance of an unknown resistor R_x, which comprises:

a four-terminal electrical network (A, B, C, D) including a first resistor having a known resistance R_1 connected between the network terminals (A) and (B), a second resistor having a known resistance R_2 connected between the network terminals (B) and (C), the resistance of the second resistor being selectively variable in value up to the maximum resistance R_2, a third resistor having a known resistance R_3 connected between the network terminals (C) and (D), and the unknown resistor being connected across the network terminals (A) and (D) for measurement;

means for impressing a source of potential from an external source across the network terminals (A) and (C); and

means, connected across the network terminals (B) and (D), for detecting when the voltage developed there across falls to zero, as the resistance of the variable second resistor is adjusted, whereby the resistance of the unknown resistor is determined from the equation:

$$R_x = \frac{R_1 R_3}{R_2}$$

Note the specific language connecting the four resistors into the bridge circuit, combined with the broad "means for impressing" and "means for detecting" language for conventional circuit elements such as batteries and meters. Note the "whereby" clause is proper (section 32) because the functional relationship and equation necessarily follows from the previously recited structure and connections. Note the use of reference characters (A), (B), etc. from the drawing (section 22). These must be placed in parentheses.

Finally, note the presence of an equation in the claim, which is acceptable when accurate. Formulas, equations, and the like frequently appear in claims, and especially in chemical claims (section 49) and in claims to a computer program or software where an algorithm is recited (section 44). Remember, you usually do not claim the formula, just the product, composition, apparatus, or method using the formula.

A sample claim to the basic radio receiver (crystal set) shown in Appendix B, Example IV, follows:

> **3B. A radio receiver, which comprises:**
>
> > a radio-frequency transformer having a primary and a secondary winding, said primary winding being connected between an external antenna and ground to receive (or "for receiving") radio frequency signals transmitted through the other;
> >
> > a variable capacitor connected across said secondary winding to form a tuned L-C circuit which rejects (or "for rejecting")all but the particular radio frequency signal to which the circuit is tuned;
> >
> > means, connected to said tuned L-C circuit, for rectifying said particular radio frequency signal;
> >
> > transducing means, serially connected with said rectifying means, for rendering audible audio frequency signals priorly modulated on said radio frequency signal; and
> >
> > a capacitor, connected in parallel with said transducer, to prevent (or "for preventing") the a.c. component in said rectified radio frequency signal from passing therethrough.

This claim further illustrates the selection of elements, broad ("transducing means") or narrow ("a capacitor"), and connecting the elements together both structurally ("connected to said tunnel L-C circuit) and functionally ("for rectifying") to do the job stated in the preamble. Note the frequent use of language other than in "means for" words which have the same effect (see section 34).

Further examples of electrical circuit and structure claims are given in Appendix B.

Summary

Electrical circuit claims follow the same rules as machine claims. The claim elements can be circuit components, or partly circuit components, partly mechanical structure. Means clauses are used frequently. For broader claims, focus on the combination as it would likely be sold. The connection or cooperation between elements can be electronic, electromagnetic, electrooptical, mechanical, or any mixture. Be careful of block diagrams in the drawings, and attendant lack of description in the specification—the man skilled in the art must know how to build each block, without exercising ingenuity and without undue experimentation. On support in specification (section 18) for block diagram, means-type disclosures, see In re Scarbrough,[132] *and cases cited in section 44 on computer programs.*

As with mechanical claims, one recites in broad claims the minimum number of elements that will work in the combination, defining each element and the necessary connections as broadly as the prior art will permit.

---

132. *In re* Scarbrough, 182 U.S.P.Q. (BNA) 298 (C.C.P.A. 1974).

IV

Method or Process Claims

§ 36 In General

Method, or process, claims are generally easier to write than mechanical claims. The reason for this is that method claims by their very nature do not require as much structural "connecting up" nor as many detailed statements of the mechanical cooperation of parts as do mechanical claims. Also, selecting the elements (steps) is easier, and there is less problem in giving the elements names, broad or narrow.

As to form, the body of a method claim is rarely much more difficult to write than a cookbook recipe: "Preheat an oven to 350°F; sift 1 1/2 cups of sugar; sift 1 cup of cake flour; sift together the sugar and the flour; add 1/2 teaspoon of salt to the sifted sugar and flour; beat . . . eggs . . . ; add the beaten eggs; . . . ; bake in the preheated oven for 45 minutes." As easy as pie (or angel cake)!

The words "method" and "process" are interchangeable in the patent law, although "process" is perhaps more frequently used in chemical cases, while "method" is more usual in mechanical and electrical cases. To provide uniformity, this statutory class is now called "process" in 35 U.S.C. § 100(b) and is defined therein to mean "process, art or method."

Most of the general rules previously given apply also to method claims. They may be broad or narrow; may be chemical, mechanical, or electrical; and may have most of the other variations (e.g., genus/species) found in mechanical claims. The terms in the claim must find support in the specification; reference numerals may be used; appropriate antecedents are necessary; logical order is also necessary; steps must be "tied" together; "whereby" clauses may be used. However, even if a drawing of the invention is part of the disclosure, the steps of the method need not be shown in the drawing, in contrast to elements of a product claim. It is not necessary to provide a flow diagram of the claimed steps in the drawings, although such a diagram might be helpful in some cases for making a process more easily understandable.

A very important rule to remember is that the "elements" of a method claim, instead of being structural parts, are, and must be, *acts* or manipulative steps that are performed upon an article, workpiece, or chemical substance. It is the transformation or reduction of the article, workpiece, or chemical substance to a different state or thing that is the essence of a method claim—and the key to its patentability. This is especially true when the claimed method includes no particular machine or apparatus.[1]

There is no per se objection to claiming a single-step method,[2] except where a broad functional step is claimed, as noted in section 34. However, most claimed methods do involve combinations of steps, as is the case with machines and circuits. Of course, the claim must *particularly point out and distinctly claim* what the applicant regards as his invention (section 1), which is the basic requirement of 35 U.S.C. § 112 (see section 31).

In re Kuehl[3] announced a liberal philosophy toward granting method or process claims of various kinds, even where the point of novelty appears to the examiner to reside in other statutory classes (new compound in that case), so long as the process is unobvious to one of ordinary skill in the art. This was further defined in *In re Durden*.[3.1]

A process claim may be patentable if an otherwise conventional process *uses* either a novel material or an old material whose use in the claimed process would have been unobvious.[4] In either case, the test is whether the process is found to be unobvious.

---

1. Gottschalk v. Benson, 409 U.S. 63 (1972) (discussed in section 44).
2. *Ex parte* Kelly and Ford, 173 U.S.P.Q. (BNA) 743 (Bd. App. 1971); *Ex parte* Britton, 154 U.S.P.Q. (BNA) 321 (Bd. App. 1967); *Ex parte* Macy, 132 U.S.P.Q. (BNA) 545 (Bd. App. 1960).
3. *In re* Kuehl, 475 F.2d 658, 177 U.S.P.Q. (BNA) 250 (C.C.P.A. 1973).
3.1. *In re* Durden, 763 F.2d 1406 (Fed. Cir. 1985).
4. *In re* Ochiai, 71 F.3d 1565 (Fed. Cir. 1995).

Durden held that use of a novel or unobvious starting material or producing a novel or unobvious end product was not enough. The process had to be unobvious to one of skill in the art. Thus a claim:

> A process for making a soap comprising mixing water with compound X.

would be a patentable claim if compound X is as above.[5] But a process claim for *making* a novel material using a conventional process and conventional materials is not patentable.[6] Finally, *making* a known material but in an unobvious manner is a patentable process.[7] Some aspect of the making, not of the result, must be novel.

Summary

Method claims involve one or more acts or steps performed on an article, workpiece, or chemical substance to achieve some result in the useful or technical arts. The elements of a method claim must be steps or acts, expressed as verbal statements or phrases.

§ 37 Elements of Method Claims

Generally, the verbs in a method claim need not be phrased in any particular voice or tense as long as there is no ambiguity and the requirements of § 112 are met.[8] Nevertheless, it must be remembered that the elements of a method claim are method *steps,* which should usually be verbal (gerundial) phrases, introduced by a gerund or verbal noun (the "-ing" form of a verb), such as (the gerunds are italicized):

(a) *reciprocating* the guide . . .

(b) *punching* a series of holes . . .

---

5. *Ex parte* McAdmans, Wu, and Joyner, 206 U.S.P.Q. (BNA) 445, 447 (Bd. App. 1978); *In re* Maucy, 182 U.S.P.Q. (BNA) 303, 306 (C.C.P.A. 1974).
6. *Id.*
7. *In re* Hirao, 190 U.S.P.Q. (BNA) 15 (C.C.P.A. 1976).
8. *Ex parte* Lewin, 154 U.S.P.Q. (BNA) 487 (Bd. App. 1966).

(c) *impressing* a signal . . .

(d) *coating* the sheet with an adhesive . . .

(e) *heating* the mixture to a temperature of . . .

(f) *separating* the alcohol from the aqueous solution . . .

(g) *distilling* the aqueous solution to separate the alcohol therefrom . . .

(h) *fractionally crystallizing* the aqueous solution to separate the alcohol therefrom . . .

(i) *permitting* the mixture to cool . . .

The three steps ("separating," on the one hand, and "distilling" or "crystallizing," on the other) illustrate, respectively, generic and two species method steps (see section 58).

One should be aware that as to the format of step (g), examiners sometimes express a preference for language similar to the following: (g') *separating* the alcohol from the aqueous solution *by distilling* the solution . . ." The argument favoring such wording is along these lines: "Regarding the phrase 'distilling . . . to separate,' [as in step (g)] one *could* distill the solution, yet never achieve alcohol separation. Such separation being the ultimate goal of the step, it (separation) should be *more positively recited* by being made the introductory gerund of the clause ["separating . . . by distilling," as in step (g')] which sets forth the step."

It is believed that this is fallacious reasoning. First, steps (g) and (g') may be seen to cover exactly the same territory logically and semantically. Second, an objection to the *form* of a step written as step (g) ignores the expressly stated *substantive* limitation therein of "distilling . . . *to* separate." This limitation *requires* that the distillation effect the separation. Third, an administrative preference for one or the other form of the step ignores the reasonable latitude permitted by decisions such as *Lewin*,[9] cited at the beginning of this section. Fourth, seemingly ignored are the principles set forth in the next paragraph.[10]

---

9. *Id.*

10. If the two formats, (g) and (g'), however, truly *are* the same, one would usually be foolish to "fight" the examiner on the point. There are usually more important issues present, and a firm stand by the applicant on one particular format may not, in the words of Cicero, "render the audience [here, the examiner] benevolent" as to more substantive issues.

The choice of which word (gerund) to use for introducing a method step is similar to the choice of which word to use for describing elements in apparatus claims. Generally, one chooses the broadest word the prior art will allow. Thus, in step (g), "distilling" is narrower than step (f) "separating." One may recite a generic or broad step, such as "separating," that is really a function or result of a more specific act such as "distilling" or "crystallizing." Moreover, it is permissible for a method step to recite some condition or property without reciting in the claim every step necessary to obtain or achieve that condition or property.[11] For example, "distilling" alone in step (g) should be sufficient. There should usually be no need, in place of "distilling," to recite "*placing*" the aqueous solution in a (certain) container . . ."; "*heating* the solution to a (certain) temperature . . ."; "*condensing* the alcohol vapors . . . "; etc. Of course, the terms used must find some antecedent in the disclosure. Preferably, therefore, the word appearing in the claim can be found in the specification, where it will have also been defined or explained or how it relates to the subject of the invention will have been described. Often, the word used is itself so clear in its meaning, like "heating" or "separating," that explanation of the word is not needed and its simple or mere mention by use of the precisely same word or a clearly equivalent word in the supporting specification is a sufficient antecedent. However, where the step or process procedure is not clear from the word used (e.g., distilling in a particular context, like wine or petroleum, needs more explanation), the mere word "distilling" is not detailed enough, and its component parts, heating and separating, may also have to be recited.

Pragmatically, the choice of what gerund to use is really of little moment as to the form of the claim. Moreover, 35 U.S.C. § 112 states (in the same paragraph sanctioning "means plus function" clauses) that:

---

11. *In re* Roberts and Burch, 176 U.S.P.Q. (BNA) 313 (C.C.P.A. 1973); *In re* Alul and McEwan, 175 U.S.P.Q. (BNA) 700 (C.C.P.A. 1972); *In re* Rainer, 134 U.S.P.Q. (BNA) 343 (C.C.P.A. 1962). Of course, either the specification must disclose, or a person skilled in the art must know, how to achieve the condition or property.

> An element in a claim for a [method] combination may be
> expressed as a . . . step for performing a specified function
> without the recital of . . . acts in support thereof, and such
> claim shall be construed to cover the corresponding . . . acts
> described in the specification and equivalents thereof.

Thus, the statute expressly sanctions the use of broad functional
steps, such as "separating," where the prior art permits, rather
than the specific *act,* "distilling." The interpretation of this language is similar to that described under "means claims" in section 34: the claim "*shall* be construed to cover the corresponding
. . . acts described . . . and equivalents. . . ." Consequently, as
with means clauses, the scope of protection afforded is exactly as
broad as "the invention" disclosed in the specification, plus
equivalents. Although "step of" clauses may be used whenever
the prior art permits, their scope may be more restricted under
applicable precedent than a clause with more specific language
on the method step. For example, in (f) or (g) above, one could
recite "the step of separating" or "performing a step separating"
or other equivalent language which could be governed by § 112.
Better now would be to use the actual recital of a process step,
"separating" or perhaps "distilling to separate" or "distilling for
separating." The latter two phrases would now likely be governed by § 112, and might be restricted merely to the steps disclosed in the specification and their equivalents (see section 34).

The distinction between acts and steps is probably more academic than real, as very few, if any, cases focus on the difference in concept between a functional step and the act done to perform the step.
As with "means claims," such functional step clauses must be limited to claims to *combinations*. In concept, a single step method
claim is all right (see section 36) only when the step is an act.

The preamble of a method claim may be almost the same as that
of a mechanical claim. Generically, the following preamble format
is usually appropriate: "A *method of* (or process for) performing a
specified act (or operation) on a particular article (or workpiece
or chemical substance) which comprises: . . ." Except for the
words "a method" this format is identical to the format proposed
in section 15 for apparatus claim preambles. Note that the workpiece is properly placed in the preamble, just as it is in the apparatus claims (see section 16). In the broader claims, avoid

describing the workpiece or article any more narrowly than the prior art requires, which would be an "unnecessary article limitation" in the words of the Patent and Trademark Office comments on grading Agent's Exam method claims. The preamble is not locked into a particular format, and can be shorter than the above suggestion, as the invention warrants.

Another similar preamble format ends with the transition words "which comprises *the steps of:* . . ." The choice between these and equivalent forms is a matter of style. Equivalents of "comprises" are used: "includes," "has." The words "the steps of" or equivalents might not be used (see Example II below).

Referring again to the take-up barrel of Example II (Appendix A) a method claim relating thereto might read:

4. A method of collecting an advancing strand in a barrel, which comprises:

   (a) *guiding* the advancing strand into the barrel;
   (b) *rotating* the barrel so that the point of collection of the strand varies circularly with respect to the bottom of the barrel; and
   (c) *reciprocating* a guide point above the barrel so that the point of collection varies radially with respect to the bottom of the barrel.

Note the similarity in form to the apparatus claim in section 34. If the title of claim 4 were changed to "Apparatus for . . ." and the phrase "means for" were inserted before each step, one would have a proper apparatus claim (at least as to form). This is typical of most method claims: Add the words "means for" to transform a method step into an apparatus element. Similarly, where an apparatus element is expressed in "means for" fashion, deletion of that phrase usually results in a proper (as to form) method step. Thus, method and apparatus claims can be of comparable scope and equally broad or narrow. Where the practitioner elects to include both apparatus and method claims in a specification, it would not be unusual to have at least some of the two types of claims analogous, that is, the method steps in a method claim become "means for" clauses in the analogous apparatus claim. As is elsewhere recommended, where an invention permits, different classes of claims should be used to cover an invention. Where an apparatus accomplishes something in a series of operations, the series can be claimed in a series of steps in a method claim.

Further examples of method claims of many kinds are given in Appendix B.

Summary

The elements of a method claim are acts or steps, customarily phrased as gerunds ("heating"). They can be broad or narrow, depending on the prior art, and functional step clauses ("separating") can be used, corresponding to means clauses where the function performed, not the act used to do it, is the important thing. Single step method claims are permitted where the step is an act, not a functional step.

§ 38 Order of Steps

The elements (steps) of a method claim must, of course, also be set forth in some logical order. The order of listing the elements in method claims is usually clearer than in mechanical claims. The elements of a method claim are typically recited in the sequence in which the steps are performed. If the claim does not expressly indicate that steps are performed simultaneously or in a different order than the sequence in which the elements appear, the reader of the claim will assume the steps are performed in the sequence of their appearance. But unless the sequence of steps is expressed in the claim, the sequence is not being claimed and another sequence may be either prior art to the claim or an infringement of the claim. If the nature of the method requires a sequence different than the order of the elements, then the reader will not read the claim in the usual way. (Of course, mechanical claims have their logical sequence of elements too, as noted above at section 27.)

In the method of claim 4, all three steps ("guiding," "rotating," and "reciprocating") occur simultaneously, each to accomplish its respective result and all to accomplish the intended result stated in the preamble so that, as written, either clause (b) or (c) could immediately follow step (a). It would be illogical to put step (a) last or in the middle. Steps (b) and (c) each modify the activity described in step (a). If one step modifies what is being done in or what has been accomplished by another step, the step modified should precede the modifying step. While a reader familiar with claim 4 herein and the disclosure in the specification supporting that claim would realize that steps (b) and (c) should be performed simultaneously, better claim form would be to tell the reader, by reciting at the beginning of element (c) "while rotating the barrel, . . ." or "simultaneously" or beginning element (b) with "simultaneously," but finishing element (b) without the ";" so as to connect it with element (c) rather than element (a).

Quite often, the steps, or some of them, must be performed in a given sequence. In this event expressions indicative of the order should be used, such as: "first," "second," "then," "subsequently," "after the embossing step," "between steps (c) and (d)," etc.[12]

Where all of the steps must be performed in a specific order, then all should be tied in chronologically, either by sequence words associated with the description of each step, as previously discussed, or by a preamble statement such as: "A method of _____, comprising the following steps in the order named: . . ." or " . . . in the sequence set forth: . . ." These are useful ways of stating a necessary order of steps, particularly for claims with many steps.

Sometimes the description of a particular step inherently implies the order, such as "(a) depositing a film of zinc on a substrate; (b) depositing a film of platinum *on the zinc film.*" In this case, the order need not be further expressly stated, because step (a)'s precedence in time over step (b) is *required* by the phrase "on the zinc film" in step (b). Step (b), therefore, cannot, within the wording of the claim, be performed until the zinc film is deposited by step (a).

Where the claim does not expressly state or necessarily imply the sequence of all or some steps, it would cover the steps performed in any order or simultaneously. (For example, the patentability of the claim or the question of its infringement would not be determined by an unspecified sequence of the steps.) Then, as with the barrel take-up method, the order of description is a mat-

---

12. Note that use of the outline form of claim, with each step labeled with a number or letter, permits reference back to, e.g., "step (c)," instead of to "the mixing step."

ter of logical convenience. However, where a required sequence of steps is not stated, it is conventional among practitioners, and logical to claim readers, to assume that steps are performed in the order of their appearance in the claim, unless the claim language indicates otherwise (rotating the barrel and reciprocating the guide point, and then only as to that step).

Summary

Where the steps, or some of them, must be performed in sequence, one after the other, the sequence should be described. Otherwise, the steps should be set out in any logical order in which they should be performed, but with no sequence precisely stated. As with all other limitations in any claim of any kind, make sure every word and every phrase is necessary in the broader claims. Consequently, do not expressly state the sequence unless it is important to the claim.

§ 39 Obvious Method Using Novel Starting Material or Producing Unobvious Product

It is possible to obtain a United States patent claim to a process, even though the general process steps are obvious, when the process uses a novel or unobvious starting material or is for producing an unobvious product.

In re Ochiai[12.1] holds that the United States Patent and Trademark Office (PTO) had misinterpreted a prior Federal Circuit decision, *In re Durden*[12.2] to establish a rule of per se obviousness, that an obvious chemical process can never be patentable even when it uses a novel starting material or produces an unobvious product. The Federal Circuit in *Ochiai* rejected the Patent Office argument that a process is obvious if prior art references disclose the same general process using "similar" starting materials.

Ochiai sought to patent a process for converting an acid into a cephem compound. Both the acid and cephem were subjects of oth-

---

12.1. *In re* Ochiai, 37 U.S.P.Q.2d (BNA) 1127 (Fed. Cir. 1995).
12.2. *In re* Durden, 226 U.S.P.Q. (BNA) 359 (Fed. Cir. 1985).

er Ochiai patents. The examiner rejected the application claims on the ground that they claimed conventional process and that the only difference from the prior art was the selection of a slightly different starting material to make a slightly different final product. The Board of Patent Appeals and Interferences of the PTO affirmed the examiner based on controlling prior decisions, *In re Larsen,*[12.3] *In re Albertson,*[12.4] and *In re Durden.*[12.5]

The Patent Office took an expansive view of the 1985 *Durden* decision. If a claimed process involved prior art steps and merely used reactants which were "similar" to the prior art reactants, examiners held such a process unpatentable based on *Durden.*

In re Pleuddemann[12.6] was another case involving the so-called *Durden* rule. The court held that the *Durden* case did not concern patent claims covering a method of using a material, but only concerned claims covering a method of making the material.

In 1995, Congress enacted 35 U.S.C. § 103(b), which allowed an obvious biotechnical process of using or making an unobvious biotechnical product to be patented so long as the claims to the obvious process co-existed with valid claims to the unobvious product in the same patent. This law is limited to biotechnology patents.

In *Ochiai,* the Federal Circuit reversed the examiner. It found that the acid starting material was not known to the prior art and that a person having no knowledge of the acid could hardly find it obvious to make a product using this acid as a reactant. The court pointed out that the test of obviousness is statutory and requires the comparison of the claimed "subject matter as a whole" with the prior art. It pointed out that this inquiry is highly fact specific, regardless of whether the claimed invention is directed to a process of making, a process of using, or some other process. The Federal Circuit found that the PTO examiner had used Ochiai's disclosure of the acid starting material in his own application as if the acid was in the prior art and this was not correct. The court also held that no prior decision had established a per se rule of unpatentability and

---

12.3. *In re* Larsen, 130 U.S.P.Q. (BNA) 209 (C.C.P.A. 1961).
12.4. *In re* Albertson, 141 U.S.P.Q. (BNA) 730 (C.C.P.A. 1964).
12.5. *In re* Durden, 226 U.S.P.Q. (BNA) 359 (Fed. Cir. 1985).
12.6. *In re* Pleuddemann, 15 U.S.P.Q.2d (BNA) 1738 (Fed. Cir. 1990).

noted that its prior decision in *Durden* had expressly cautioned "not to generalize or make rules for other cases."

The Patent Office argued that the courts' prior decisions in *Durden, Pleuddemann,* and other cases had been inconsistent. The Federal Circuit rejected this argument and pointed out that all of the prior decisions were based on fact-intensive comparisons of the claimed processes with the prior art, as required by the patent statute.

The Federal Circuit concluded by stating that when "any applicant properly presents and argues suitable method claims, they should be examined in light of all . . . relevant factors, free from any presumed controlling effect of *Durden* or any other precedent." In other words, after considering what is being claimed, what exists in the prior art and the level of skill of those practicing in the art, the obviousness or nonobviousness of the method claimed should be determined.

Summary

Method claims to a known method starting with a novel or unobvious starting material or producing an unobvious product may be patentable if the subject matter of the claim as a whole is unobvious.

§ 40 Claims to Both Method and Apparatus; Method is Function of Apparatus

Until 1968, there was a fundamental principle that, to be patentable, a method must be more than the "inherent function of the apparatus" that was disclosed to effect the method. As stated in the first *Guidelines of Patentability* memorandum:[13]

> A rejection on this ground is proper where the disclosed machine will inherently carry out the steps of the process set forth in the process claims regardless of whether an apparatus claim is allowed, unless it appears that the process

---

13. 792 Off. Gaz. Pat. Office 3 (June 17, 1963).

claimed can be carried out by some machine which is not the functional equivalent . . . or by hand. . . .[14]

The Patent and Trademark Office instead now relies on *Tarczy-Hornoch,* cited in MPEP 2173.05(v), which reads:

2173.05(v) Mere Function of Machine

In view of the decision of the Court of Customs and Patent Appeals in In re Tarczy-Hornoch, *397 F.2d 856, 158 U.S.P.Q. 141 (C.C.P.A. 1968), process or method claims are not subject to rejection by Patent and Trademark Office examiners under 35 U.S.C. 112, second paragraph solely on the ground that they define the inherent function of a disclosed machine or apparatus.*

The Federal Circuit has left no doubt that *Tarczy-Hornoch* is controlling law.[15]

The inherent function was of the disclosed apparatus, whether or not it was claimed at all and, if claimed, whether or not the apparatus itself was unobvious and patentable. In *Tarczy-Hornoch,* the method was unpatentable, although the disclosed device used therein was not.

In any event, the previous claim 2 (section 34) would easily satisfy even the old rule, because the strand could be manually guided, the barrel could obviously be turned by hand, the guide could be similarly reciprocated, any two steps could be manual, or all three steps could be.

Summary

Method claims cannot be rejected as merely drawn to the inherent function of a machine. Where possible, detach the method from the machine so far as possible and try to define novelty in the steps performed.

---

14. *See* Federal Sign & Signal Corp. v. Bangor Punta, Inc., 177 U.S.P.Q. (BNA) 737 (S.D.N.Y. 1973).

15. Union Carbide Corp. v. American Can Co., 220 U.S.P.Q. (BNA) 584, 591 (Fed. Cir. 1984); *see In re* King, 801 F.2d 1324 (Fed. Cir. 1986).

§ 41 Apparatus Limitations

Of necessity, there will be product or apparatus limitations in a method claim. The method is usually performed upon or acts in conjunction with the product or apparatus. This is analogous to the functions performed by the various elements of an apparatus (as in the article shaker example claim) which frequently appear in a product or apparatus claim.

Although there is no per se objection to including structural (mechanical, electrical, or both) apparatus limitations in the elements (steps) of method claims, when the steps are properly phrased in method language, the use of such limitations should be avoided insofar as possible for at least two reasons.

First, apparatus limitations will often unduly limit the claim. Second, and more important, the "black letter" law is that the patentability of a method claim cannot be predicated *solely* on the structure of a mechanism used in practicing the method.[16] Accordingly, there is usually no point in including the structure except where the method necessarily involves manipulation of apparatus. There is no objection to including composition-of-matter or chemical limitations in method claims, and in fact these are frequently relied on for patentability, as noted in section 42.

See *In re Kuehl*,[17] where the claim was to an old method of cracking gasoline, so far as the steps were concerned, using a new catalyst.[18]

In dependent method claims (section 11), avoid adding *only* apparatus limitations. Limitations added in dependent method claims are preferably phrased as method steps, except where further defining compositions of matter or chemicals (section 49). Thus, it would be poor form to depend a claim from the take-up method in claim 4 setting forth: "A method . . . as recited in claim 4, further comprising a *turntable*. . . ." One example of proper form along this line would be: "A method . . . as recited in claim

---

16. *See Ex parte* Dammers, 155 U.S.P.Q. (BNA) 284 (Bd. App. 1961), which nevertheless points out that structural apparatus limitations are not per se objectionable, and, to the extent necessary to carry out the claimed method, are permissible in a method claim.
17. *In re* Kuehl, 177 U.S.P.Q. (BNA) 250 (C.C.P.A. 1973).
18. *See In re* Schneider, 179 U.S.P.Q. (BNA) 46 (C.C.P.A. 1973).

4, wherein the step of rotating the barrel includes mounting the barrel on a turntable and rotating the turntable."

Note that this is primarily a matter of form, not substance. Although the claim drafter is entitled to include the turntable in the claim, there is no good reason to do so in a broad claim, because it is not essential to the method. Thus, claim 4 might have included:

rotating *a* turntable on which the barrel is mounted . . .

reciprocating *a* strand guide positioned above the barrel . . .

Note the form (inferential) for bringing in apparatus limitations, where they are used, such as "rotating a turntable. . . ."

As in apparatus claims (section 20), antecedents are important. Support for "*the* guide" must have been provided in a previous clause of the claim (in the clause above). However, because the claim is to a method that is a series of steps, the product or apparatus or composition, etc., with which a method step is practiced may be inferentially claimed in that step. Therefore, that product, etc. may have been introduced as the object ("a guide") on which a previous step was performed, usually in the middle of a clause, and that product, etc. should not have been made the subject of a clause.

See also section 56 on new use claims, for method claims where the novelty resides in a new use for an old material.

Summary

Avoid apparatus limitations (machine or circuit) in method claims so far as possible. When necessary, bring them into the claim inferentially, i.e., "rotating a turntable." There is no problem with chemical or materials limitations; they can be relied on for patentability, and frequently are, in "new use" claims, such as killing insects by exposing them to DDT.

§ 42 Chemical Processes

An example of a chemical process claim follows:

> 5.   **A process for treating a surface of a polyethylene article to increase its receptivity to printing ink, which comprises:**
>
> **exposing the surface of the article to a saturated solution of sodium dichromate in concentrated sulfuric acid.**

As previously noted in section 36, there is no objection to a single step method. Claim 5 illustrates the rare case of a claim that is not to a combination.

With chemical processes, it is proper to include a dependent process claim adding only details of the materials used. For example, if claim 5 had recited "an acid," a dependent claim could cover: "A process . . . as recited in claim 5, wherein the acid is sulfuric acid."

It is standard in chemical process cases that the process may distinguish by the compositions recited, as well as the actual manipulative step, which is often trivial per se. In the example of claim 5, the manipulative step "exposing" an article to a reagent is of course prehistoric; the sole novelty resides in the composition of the reagent. Eminently logically, it is considered that exposing to reagent X is not the same step as exposing to reagent Y. (See also section 56 on new use claims.)

Where the process can be practiced, or used, with more than one related material or chemical, *Markush* phraseology may be used under the rules set out in section 50. Also, alternative expressions (A or B—section 24) may sometimes be permitted in describing different chemical substances that can be used in the process. In *Ex parte Pantzer and Feier,*[19] during prosecution, claim 16 was rejected under 35 U.S.C. § 112, without the citation of any references. Claim 16 recited a method of dyeing fibers wherein the dye used to prepare the dyeing solution was defined as the product of the reaction of "one or both of [A'] and [B'] with [C] under [certain] alkaline conditions." Other claims used the phrase "one *or*

---

19. *Ex parte* Pantzer and Feier, 176 U.S.P.Q. (BNA) 141 (Bd. App. 1971, 1972).

more of." Claim 1, from which all of the claims ultimately depended, recited A and B, certain amino phenols, of which A' and B' were species. Claim 1 was not limited to only one of A or B, because it called for a method that "comprises" dispersing A and B in an aqueous medium. The board reversed the rejection, holding that the phrases "one *or* both" and "one *or* more" were not so broad as to be indefinite and did not encompass "an infinite number,"[20] etc.

Chemical processes can be to methods of making chemical compounds (new or old); methods of using chemicals, as in claim 5 above or such as killing insects or treating baldness; or any other process or subject having industrial utility.

A typical method of use claim:

> 5A. The method of treating baldness, which comprises applying to the scalp an aqueous solution of sodium chloride[21] having a concentration of 30–40 percent by weight[22] of sodium chloride.

A typical claim to a method of making a chemical compound:

> 5B. The method of manufacturing sodium hydroxide, which comprises electrolyzing an aqueous solution of sodium chloride at a current density sufficient to decompose the sodium chloride into elemental chlorine and sodium, the sodium reacting with the water present in the solution to form sodium hydroxide and hydrogen gas.

Note this process is one of the oldest, and still most common, ways to make sodium hydroxide, as well as chlorine and hydrogen gas. Since the circuit parameters would not be critical, they can be stated broadly (section 31).

The Federal Circuit has held in *In re Ochiai*,[22.1] that the patentee/applicant may premise patentability of a chemical process

---

20. *See, e.g., Ex parte* Pontius, Endres, and Van Akkeren, 169 U.S.P.Q. (BNA) 122 (Bd. App. 1970).

21. Salt water.

22. This avoids reading on ocean bathing.

22.1. *In re* Ochiai, 37 U.S.P.Q.2d (BNA) 1127 (Fed. Cir. 1995).

claim on the use of a novel and unobvious starting material or on the novel and unobvious product obtained by the process.[23] The process may be new or novel and also unobvious due either to the choice of starting material or final product. An obviousness determination for the claim as a whole is required. See Section 36.

Other examples of chemical process claims are given in appendix B, cases 13, 18, 20, 21, and 24.

In re Kuehl,[24] a predecessor of *In re Ochiai*, held that patentability of a process can reside in the use of a novel and unobvious material in the process, though the single process step (section 36), contacting X with catalyst Y, is notoriously old per se. In *Kuehl*, one of the claims in question read:

> A hydrocarbon conversion process which comprises contacting a hydrocarbon charge under catalytic cracking conditions with the composition of claim 6.

Claim 6, a composition of matter claim to a group of new zeolites, had been allowed. The court held it would be unobvious to crack gasoline with the new zeolite, even though cracking with other, generally similar, zeolites was very well known in the prior art and would have been obvious *after* one knew about applicant's new zeolite. However, the Court held that to one of ordinary skill in the art, selection of the particular zeolite for cracking hydrocarbons would not have been obvious. The Federal Circuit in *In re Durden* affirmed and distinguished *In re Kuehl*. In *Durden*, use of the novel starting material would have been obvious, while in *Kuehl*, use of the novel starting material would not have been obvious. Guidance in drafting a particular claim is difficult to obtain from these precedents. Since the claim drafter cannot know for certain that the process will be found non-obvious, try to also protect the novel starting material and, if applicable, the final product. The patentee is entitled to both types of claim when one invents (a) a new compound and (b) an unobvious process for using that compound.

---

23. *In re* Durden, 763 F.2d 1406 (Fed. Cir. 1985).
24. *In re* Kuehl, 475 F.2d 658; 177 U.S.P.Q. (BNA) 250 (C.C.P.A. 1973).

Summary

Chemical process claims are the same as other method claims as to claim-drafting techniques. Often the novelty is in the chemicals used, not the act itself (treating, exposing). Use of a novel and unobvious starting material and/or producing a novel and unobvious end product is enoughto make a process unobvious.

§43 Electrical Methods (Bryan W. Sheffield & John L. Landis)

As an example of electrical method, consider the following claim which covers the use of the Wheatstone Bridge shown in example III of appendix A to measure an unknown resistance.

6.   A method of measuring the electrical resistance of an unknown resistor R_x, which comprises:

connecting the unknown resistor R_x between terminals (A) and (D) of a four-terminal electrical network (A, B, C, D), said network including a first known resistor R_1 between terminals (A) and (B), a second known resistor R_2 between terminals (B) and (C), and a third known resistor R_3 between terminals (C) and (D), at least one of said known resistors being a variable resistor;

impressing a potential across terminals (A) and (C) of said network;

detecting the voltage developed across terminals (B) and (D) of said network as a result of said impressed potential; and

varying the resistance of at least one of said known resistors until the voltage detected across terminals (B) and (D) falls to zero, whereby[25] the resistance of the unknown resistor R_x is determined from the equation:

$$R_x = \frac{R_1 R_3}{R_2}$$

Claim 6A is another example of an electrical method claim and covers use of the Marconi crystal radio illustrated in example IV of appendix A.

6A.　　A method of demodulating a radio frequency carrier wave priorly modulated with an audio frequency signal, which comprises:

applying said modulated carrier wave to a resonant L-C circuit;

adjusting the resonant frequency of said L-C circuit until it equals the frequency of said carrier wave;

rectifying the voltage developed across said resonant L-C circuit to recover said audio frequency signal;

passing said rectified voltage through a transducer to render said audio frequency signal audible; and

filtering out the radio frequency components present in said rectified voltage to prevent same from entering said transducer.

---

25. Note the proper "whereby" clause (section 29), since this function indubitably follows from the previously recited steps. Whereby clauses can be used as well in method claims as in apparatus claims.

Summary

Electrical methods present no special problems so far as claim drafting techniques are concerned. The only difference from mechanical methods is that the steps, or some of them, are electrical rather than mechanical. Typical steps or acts are "amplifying," "charging," "connecting," "impressing a potential," "detecting," "rectifying," "sensing," etc. The acts (amplifying) need not be do-able by a human being, circuit components do nicely.

§ 44 Claims to a Computer Program or Software-Related Invention

Computer programs or software stated either as a series of means for performing function elements (apparatus) or as a number of method steps (process) are patentable.[25.1] The tests for the presence of patentable subject matter under § 101 in a computer program, formerly applied under prior precedents of the Federal Circuit and the district courts, have been made unnecessary by the Federal Circuit in the *State Street Bank* case (see section 44A). So long as the apparatus or method is transformative in some manner—so long as it accomplishes something other than merely appropriating an algorithm or manipulating numbers—the elements in means-plus-function form, or the steps for performing a function, provide statutory subject matter under § 101, and the patentability of such claims is to be judged under §§ 102, 103, and 112.

A computer program or software-related invention is an apparatus or process that employs a computer or that is adapted for employing a computer as an operative component of the device or process. In particular, it relates to an invention in computer software, the program that drives the computer to perform a series of steps. The invention lies in the series of steps, not in the program itself. It

---

25.1. State Street Bank & Trust v. Signature Financial Group, 149 F.3d 1368, 47 U.S.P.Q.2d (BNA) 1596 (Fed. Cir. 1998), *cert. denied*, 119 S. Ct. 851 (1999); AT&T Corp. v. Excel Communications, Inc., 172 F.3d 1352, 50 U.S.P.Q.2d (BNA) 1447 (Fed. Cir. 1999).

has become well settled that a computer related invention can be a useful process or machine and a patentable invention under 35 U.S.C. § 101. Computer related inventions often include a series of steps. When those steps result in the solution of a problem, or there is a procedure, process, or rule for the solution of a problem in a finite number of steps, that is, an algorithm. Thus, a statement of a step-by-step procedure for solving a problem is an algorithm, and one for solving a mathematical problem, which might be or include a mathematical formula, is a mathematical algorithm.

Courts have excluded certain subject matter areas from patent protection under § 101, including principles or laws of nature, ideas and mathematical expressions of scientific truths. See *Gottschalk v. Benson*[26] and see *Diamond v. Diehr*,[27] which stated that an "algorithm, or mathematical formula, is like a law of nature, which cannot be the subject of a patent."[27.1] As many computer-related inventions, and particular computer programs and software, employ mathematical principles and mental thought processes, it became necessary to define how such programs and software could be protected when they constituted an invention.

Although there had been doubt as to the patentability of a computer related invention that included an algorithm, that doubt has been dispelled through a long series of decisions by the United States Supreme Court, the United States Court of Customs and Patent Appeals and its successor, the United States Court of Appeals for the Federal Circuit, by the district courts and by the Patent Office Board of Interferences and Appeals.

This section is devoted to explaining how claims to a computer-related invention might be written. The Patent and Trademark Office established guidelines in 1995 to instruct examiners how to examine applications drawn to "computer-implemented inventions." The examiner's guidelines have been modified and are instructive for writing claims for computer-implemented inventions. Before writing such a claim, reading MPEP 2106 is recommended.

---

26. Gottschalk v. Benson, 409 U.S. 63 (1972).
27. Diamond v. Diehr, 450 U.S. 175, 186 (1981).
27.1. *See* AT&T Corp. v. Excel Communications, Inc., 172 F.3d 1352, 50 U.S.P.Q.2d (BNA) 1447, 1450 (Fed. Cir. 1999).

MPEP 2106.II.C. requires the examiner to correlate each claim element to a relevant portion of the written description. Each element of the claim must have antecedent support in the specification. Further, elements of such an invention may be defined in the means plus function format.

Different classes of claims that may be written on such inventions. A computer or other programmable apparatus whose actions are directed by a computer program or other software is a "machine."

Consider a computer-readable storage medium and a specific physical configuration of the substrate of that medium that represents data, e.g., the program where that storage medium causes the computer to operate in a specific and predefined manner. The composite of these two elements is a storage medium with a particular physical structure and function, e.g., it will impart the functionality that is represented by the data onto the computer. That is an "article of manufacture."

A "process" is a series of steps that is performed on or with the aid of a computer. A claim that defines a computer-implemented process but which is neither cast as an element of a computer-readable memory or implemented on a computer should be classified as a process. For example, a claim that is cast as "a computer program" but which recites specific steps to be implemented on or to be performed using a computer is classified as a process. On the other hand, a claim to a "computer program" that does not define the invention in terms of steps is not a process. A "process" requires reciting at least one physical element recited that would place the invention in one of the two product categories, machine or article of manufacture ((c)(iii)). That element might be unnecessary in view of *State Street Bank*, so long as the process steps together are transformative.

The guidelines also identify claims that would be nonstatutory. In light of the *State Street Bank* decision, this list should be shortened. These include (1) a compilation or arrangement of data, independent of any physical element; (2) a known machine-readable storage medium which is coded with creative or artistic expression, because they represent the expression of the program and are literary creations; (3) a "data structure" independent of a physical element, i.e., not implemented on a physical component of a computer, such as a memory, because it is necessary to render the component capable of causing a computer to operate in a particular manner (not correct under *State Street Bank*); or (4) a process that merely manipulates abstract ideas or concepts; an example of this is a series of steps for solving a mathematical problem, i.e., a mathematical algorithm. A claim to a method consisting solely of steps necessary to converting one set of numbers to another set of numbers would be nonstatutory if it is not transformative.

The claim must be written in recognizable English language. Computer program code, in either source or object format, cannot be included in the claim as a limitation. A claim which attempts to define elements using computer program code, rather than English language description of actual functional steps which are to be performed, is rejected under 35 U.S.C. § 112. If there is no other way to define a claim element except by reference to code, then code should be used. This is analogous to situations where special trademarks, coined names, etc. (sections 51 through 54 hereof) are used for elements not claimable using normal English language. But then the specification should make clear the terms or code used in a claim element.

Nonstatutory subject matter, i.e., abstract ideas, laws of nature, or natural phenomena, does not become statutory merely through claiming it in a different manner.

The Federal Circuit in *State Street Bank* has swept away the former requirement that a claim to a computer apparatus or process be subjected to a two-part test. Under that test, the claim was first tested to see whether it appropriated an algorithm. Next, if a mathematical algorithm was found, the claim as a whole was further analyzed to determine whether the algorithm was applied in any manner to physical elements or process steps, and if it was so applied, the claim was under § 101.[28] One determined if there was any significant pre- or post-algorithm solution activity, i.e., whether the invention involved (as the district court in *State Street Bank* put it) the transformation or conversion of subject matter that is representative of or that constitutes physical activities or objects.[29]

---

28. 47 U.S.P.Q.2d (BNA) at 1601.
29. State Street Bank & Trust Co. v. Signature Financial Group Inc., 38 U.S.P.Q.2d (BNA) 1530, 1541 (D. Mass. 1996).

The district court in *State Street Bank* held that the claim in suit was directed to a nonstatutory computer implemented invention because it compiled, processed, and stored business data,[30] and that changing one set of numbers into another set of numbers without more is insufficient for patent protection. It is the mere solution of a mathematical algorithm.[31]

In reversing the district court, the Federal Circuit stated that claim 1 of the patent in *State Street Bank* concerned a machine and was proper statutory subject matter under § 101.

The court agreed that certain mathematical algorithms, standing alone, would fall into the category of unpatentable abstract ideas until and unless the algorithms were reduced to some type of practical application, i.e., a useful, concrete, and tangible result.[32] However, an algorithm can be patentable if it is applied in a useful way.[33] The court extended its holdings of previous cases:

> Today, we hold that the transformation of data, representing discrete dollar amounts, by a machine through a series of mathematical calculations into a final share price, constitutes a practical application of a mathematical algorithm, formula, or calculation, because it produces "a useful, concrete and tangible result"—a final share price momentarily fixed for recording and reporting purposes. . . .[34]

The court rejected the two-part test that had been followed in practice.

The court continued by stating that after *Diamond v. Diehr*[35] and *In re Alappat*,[36] the mere fact that a claimed invention involves inputting numbers, calculating numbers, outputting and storing numbers, in and of itself, would not render it nonstatutory subject matter, unless, of course, its operation does not produce a useful, concrete, and tangible result.

---

30. *Id.*
31. *Id.*
32. 47 U.S.P.Q.2d (BNA) at 1600–01.
33. *Id.* at 1601.
34. *Id.*
35. Diamond v. Diehr, 450 U.S. 175 (1981).
36. *In re* Alappat, 33 F.3d 1526 (Fed. Cir. 1994).

Those portions of the Guidelines in the MPEP, which state that converting one set of numbers into another set of numbers does not manipulate appropriate subject matter and thus cannot constitute a statutory process, were held to be incorrect practice.

The *State Street Bank* decision removes the requirement for physical transformation. Physical transformation is merely one example of how a mathematical algorithm may bring about a useful application.[36.1] Even a transformation of numbers with practical result appears to fall within § 101, based upon the holding of and the fact pattern of the case. It is necessary, however, that the claimed product or process produce some transformation—not a mere manipulation of numbers, but some transformation in something, even if it be data only.

Decisions following on *State Street Bank* will further explain its scope and limits. At present, however, if an invention in connection with computer software is stated either as a machine with a series of means for performing a function limitations or as a process as a series of manipulative steps, and if the machine or process transforms something into something else, even if the transformation is wholly within the computer and nothing physical outside the computer is involved, i.e., no pre- or post-solution activity is in a claim element, so long as the claimed software or process is transformative in some manner, it will be statutory subject matter under § 101.[36.2]

The court in *AT&T* focused its inquiry on "whether the mathematical algorithm is applied in a practical manner to produce a useful result."[36.3] The court criticized some of the earlier decisions because the panels of the court did not look to see if a practical result had been obtained.

A good example of a computer software claim stated in means-plus-function language is claim 1 of U.S. Patent 5,193,056 in the *State Street Bank* case:[37]

36.1. AT&T Corporation v. Excel Communications, Inc., 172 F.3d 1352, 50 U.S.P.Q.2d (BNA) 1447, 1452 (Fed. Cir. 1999).

36.2. *Id.*

36.3. *Id.,* 50 U.S.P.Q.2d at 1453.

37. Bracketed material is the court's explanation of the claim.

1. A data processing system for managing a financial services configuration of a portfolio established as a partnership, each partner being one of
a plurality of funds, comprising:

(a) computer processor means [a personal
computer including a CPU] for processing
data;

(b) storage means [a data disk] for storing
data on a storage medium;

(c) first means [an arithmetic circuit configured to prepare the data disk to magneti-
cally store selected data] for initializing the
storage medium;

(d) second means [an arithmetic logic circuit
configured to retrieve information from a
specific file, calculate incremental
increases or decreases based on specific
input, allocate the results on a percentage
basis, and store the output in a separate
file] for processing data regarding assets in
the portfolio and each of the funds from a
previous day and data regarding increases
or decreases in each of the fund's, assets
and for allocating the percentage share
that each fund holds in the portfolio;

(e) third means [an arithmetic logic circuit
configured to retrieve information from a
specific file, calculate incremental
increases and decreases based on specific
input, allocate the results on a percentage
basis and store the output in a separate
file] for processing data regarding daily
incremental income, expenses, and net
realized gain or loss for the portfolio and
for allocating such data among each fund;

(f) fourth means [an arithmetic logic circuit
configured to retrieve information from a
specific file, calculate incremental
increases and decreases based on specific

input, allocate the results on a percentage basis and store the output in a separate file] for processing data regarding daily net unrealized gain or loss for the portfolio and for allocating such data among each fund; and

(g) fifth means [an arithmetic logic circuit configured to retrieve information from specific files, calculate that information on an aggregate basis and store the output in a separate file] for processing data regarding aggregate year-end income, expenses, and capital gain or loss for the portfolio and each of the funds.

The patent claim is generally directed to a data processing system for implementing an investment arrangement. A hub party is an administrator and an accounting agent for several mutual funds, which are the spokes. In the patented hub-and-spoke system, mutual funds pooled their assets in an investment portfolio. The patented system provided means for daily allocation of assets for the spokes that invested in the mutual fund hub.

In the opinion of this author, the court in *State Street Bank* has interpreted the law to avoid the need for elements (a) and (b) of this claim. Apparatus (a system) starting with element (c) meets the transformative criterion of *State Street Bank*.

These claims are likely to be treated as invoking 35 U.S.C. § 112, paragraph 6, since they claim "means," plus the function it performs, not recognized structures. In *Isogon Corp. v. Amdahl Corp.*,[37.1] the court found claim terms which used a descriptive noun followed by a function in a patent claim to software to be under § 112, paragraph 6, even though "means" was not expressly recited. Those terms were "event detector for detecting," "collector for obtaining," "recorder for recording," and "correlator for correlating." One should expect that the usually used means-plus-function style claim limitations will be interpreted under that statute[37.2] (see section 34). The disclosure in the specification will

---

37.1. Isogon Corp. v. Amdahl Corp., 47 F. Supp. 2d 436 (S.D.N.Y. 1998).
37.2. S3, Inc. v. nVIDIA Corp., ___ F.3d ___, 59 U.S.P.Q.2d (BNA) 1745, 1746–47 (Fed. Cir. 2001).

govern.[37.3] It should be sufficient to teach one skilled in the art what the claimed elements are.[37.4] Then the claim will not be indefinite under 35 U.S.C. §112, paragraph 2.[37.5]

Another example of a claim that would be statutory now, in the opinion of this author, is the process claim previously held non-statutory by the Federal Circuit in *In re Schrader*.[38] The court had found that the claim failed the now discarded two-part test for patentability of an algorithm. But the claim is transformative and statutory according to the holding of *State Street Bank*.

Summary

A claim to a computer program or software, either as a series of means for performing function elements or as a number of method steps, is patentable under § 101, so long as the program or the method is transformative of something, in some manner—i.e., it accomplishes something other than merely appropriating an algorithm or manipulating numbers.

37.3. AT&T Corp. v. Excel Communications, Inc., 172 F.3d 1352, 50 U.S.P.Q.2d (BNA) 1447, 1452 (Fed. Cir. 1999).

37.4. S3, Inc. v. nVIDIA Corp., ___ F.3d ___, 59 U.S.P.Q.2d (BNA) 1745, 1747 (Fed. Cir. 2001); Atmel Corp. v. Information Storage Devices, Inc., 198 F.3d 1374, 1381, 53 U.S.P.Q.2d (BNA) 1225, 1229 (Fed. Cir. 1999).

37.5. S3, Inc. v. nVIDIA Corp., ___ F.3d ___, 59 U.S.P.Q.2d (BNA) 1745 (Fed. Cir. 2001).

38. *In re* Schrader, 22 F.3d 290 (Fed. Cir. 1994) ("A method of competitively bidding on a plurality of items comprising the steps of identifying a plurality of related items in a record, offering said plurality of items to a plurality of potential bidders, receiving bids from said bidders for both individual ones of said items and a plurality of groups of said items, each of said groups including one or more of said items, said items and groups being any number of all of said individual ones and all of the possible combinations of said items, entering said bids in said record, indexing each of said bids to one of said individual ones or said groups of said items, and assembling a completion of all said bids on said items and groups, said completion identifying a bid for all of said items at a prevailing total price, identifying in said record all of said bids corresponding to said prevailing total price.").

§ 44A Business Methods

Although there had been no statutory prohibition against patent claims directed to business methods, until the United States Court of Appeals for the Federal Circuit ruled that patent claims to business methods are within the statutory classes of invention under 35 U.S.C. § 101 and could be patented, in *State Street Bank & Trust Co. v. Signature Financial Group, Inc.,*[39] claims to business methods were rejected as nonstatutory. In *State Street Bank*, the court held that a process will receive statutory protection "if it is limited to a practical application of the abstract idea or mathematical algorithm in the technological arts (i.e., involves some species of physical transformation of input data)." The physical transformation need not produce a physical product. In a business method, it may simply involve the manipulation of data and information according to an algorithm entirely within a computer or the like apparatus.

After the *State Street Bank* decision, the issue of whether an invention is patentable is whether it transforms intangible or tangible material to produce a practical or useful result. A system or process that transforms information itself produces a practical and useful result. Only an abstract idea that lacks any useful transformation remains unpatentable.

To further dispel doubt as to the patentability of a business method, the Federal Circuit in *AT&T Corp. v. Excel Communications, Inc.*[40] pointed out that the inquiry is whether a useful, concrete, and tangible result is obtained, rather than a physical act being performed. In the *AT&T* case, the invention related to the generation of information in an electronic record for long-distance telephone calls to permit differential billing treatment of subscribers. Prior to the *State Street Bank* decision, the district court in *AT&T* had granted summary judgment of invalidity under 35 U.S.C. § 101, holding that the method claims implicitly recited a mathematical algorithm. Following the *State Street Bank* decision, the Federal Circuit on appeal held that the claims, which were directed to a method for generating a particular data field in

---

39. 149 F.3d 1368, 47 U.S.P.Q.2d (BNA) 1596 (Fed. Cir. 1998).
40. 172 F.3d 1352, 50 U.S.P.Q.2d (BNA) 1447 (Fed. Cir. 1999).

an electronic record, were not invalid under § 101 and that business method claims are patentable.

Following these two court decisions, the patentability of claims to business methods is determined by the same tests as for any other process or apparatus.

The Patent Office has issued a "White Paper" on business method patents, which attempts to place them in historical context and provides patenting statistics.[41] The White Paper notes that business method patents are now classified by the Patent Office in U.S. inventions subject matter classification class 705 (although one finds those patents also classified in other classes). That class includes a collection of over twenty financial and management data processing areas including insurance, securities trading, health care management, reservation systems, postage metering systems, and certain general enterprise functions such as electronic shopping, auction systems, and business cryptography. Groupings of patents include identifying the potential customers of a business and determining their need for its products and services; informing customers that the business exists and trying to get them to buy its products and services; exchanging money and credit related to a business transaction; and tracking resources, money, and products. These are the typical types of business methods. Numerous other business methods in use or to be developed may be claimed.

Since business methods have been held patentable, the number of filings for them has increased. The White Paper indicates that for fiscal year 1999, they represented only about 1% of the total patent applications filed, and that 2,658 applications filed were classified in class 705. Nearly 600 such patents were issued in that year. An increase in the number of filings and the patents granted is expected due to the continuing growth and development in electronic commerce. Not only are electronic and data processing hardware and software now claimed, but the business method performed with them is claimed as well.

The prevalence of method claims that relate to some data storage and manipulation apparatus results from e-commerce, be-

---

41. www.uspto.gov/web/menu/busmethp.

cause e-commerce inventions are typically directed to systems or methods that use a computer and/or software. But not every patentable business method is directed to e-commerce and not every business method involves computers.

A business method should be claimed like any other method, in a series of method steps. The rules and practices for method claiming apply to methods of doing business. Expanding on what appears to be claimable, any method involving several steps that brings about a practical result would appear to be able to satisfy the requirements of Title 35 of the U.S. Code.

From a claim-drafting viewpoint, it is possible also to claim some business methods using an apparatus claim for apparatus that performs the method. The claim elements may most likely be stated as means for performing particular functions. This would be especially the case where the apparatus inputs certain information or materials in order that the process be performed and/or outputs certain information or materials following performance of the process. This is analogous to computer-related or computer-implemented inventions discussed in section 44. The Federal Circuit in *State Street Bank*[41.1] said that machine claims having "means" clauses are viewed as process claims if there is no supporting structure in the written description that corresponds to the claimed "means" elements. The court found claim 1 to be to a machine, with the terms "computer processor means" and "first means for initializing the storage medium."

Even a method of preparing a patent application is covered by a patent, as illustrated by U.S. Patent 6,049,811. Its broadest method claim recites:

> 10.   A method by computer for drafting a patent application having at least sections including claims, a summary of the invention, an abstract of the disclosure, and a detailed description of a preferred embodiment of the invention, said method comprising the steps of:

41.1. 149 F.3d at 1371, 47 U.S.P.Q.2d (BNA) at 1599. *See Ex parte Donner,* 53 U.S.P.Q.2d (BNA) 1699, 1701 (Bd. of App. & Interferences 1999) (unpublished).

requesting and storing primary elements (PE) of the invention that define the invention apart from prior technology before drafting the claims;

drafting the claims before drafting the summary of the invention, abstract, and the detailed description of a preferred embodiment of the invention; and

drafting the sections in a predetermined order prohibiting jumping ahead to draft a latter section.

This claim covers preparation of a conventional patent application using a computer and then recites a series of steps. In the opinion of this author, these are standard steps and standard sequencing of steps performed in preparing an application. They differ in that some part of the method is performed using a computer. Dependent method claims of the patent indicate that the computer, rather than the person, is performing some steps. Presumably, every practitioner has prepared patent applications using the claimed steps in the claimed sequence. But if we now perform the known steps using a computer that causes the practitioner or the computer to perform the claimed steps in the particular manner claimed, the patent claim would reach them.

Preparing a patent application is not "business" because it does not involve a monetary or business transaction. Nonetheless, in this author's opinion, the patent falls with the broad method-of-doing-business category.

As is typically found in many business method patents, this patent also includes machine claims, and the first machine claim is quoted below. The machine claims may be machine analogs to the method elements of the method claim, and vice versa:

1. A machine for drafting a patent application having at least sections including claims, a summary of the invention, an abstract of the disclosure, and a detailed description of a preferred embodiment of the invention, said machine comprising:

one or more input devices, one or more output
devices, and a computer with memory for receiving and storing data from the input devices, transmitting data to the output devices, and storing
program steps for program control and manipulating data in memory;

the computer, through input and output devices,
requests and stores primary elements (PE) of the
invention that define the invention apart from
prior technology before the claims are drafted;

the claims are drafted before the summary of the
invention, abstract, and the detailed description of
a preferred embodiment of the invention is
drafted; and

the computer requires drafting the sections in a
predetermined order prohibiting jumping ahead
to draft a latter section.

Yet another example of a method that appears to be a comput-
er-accomplished series of steps that one could otherwise perform
manually, and that possibly were performed manually before the
patent was granted, is claimed in U.S. Patent 4,890,228, which
provides a loan to a taxpayer based upon his or her anticipated
tax refund. The claim is quoted below:

7.   A method of operating at least one programmable
electronic data processing machine comprising the
programmed steps of:

(a) receiving inputted tax preparer data, tax
return data and loan application data;

(b) creating electronic tax return data files
from said tax return data;

(c) creating deposit/loan account files related
to said tax return data and said loan application data at an unauthorized financial
institution;

(d) transmitting said electronic tax return data
files to at least one tax collecting authority;

(e) processing said tax return data files and said deposit/loan account files and authorizing payment by said authorized financial institution from said deposit/loan account files of a tax refund loan amount based on said tax return data prior to completion of tax return processing and refund payment by said tax collecting authority; and

(f) authorizing receipt by said authorized financial institution of tax refund electronic fund transfers, based on said tax return data, from said tax collecting authority.

A patent practitioner or a tax specialist might say that a process or apparatus that performs the steps that the practitioner regularly performs in his or her practice should not be protected by grant of a business method patent. One frequently hears such a comment from business people confronted with a business method patent claim, which includes claims often tied to a computer or other machinery in the claim, and which accomplishes, via computer, a process that had previously been done without reliance upon a computer. Nonetheless, such a claim is statutory and its validity must be determined under sections of the Patent Act other than § 101, namely § 102 for anticipation or § 103 for obviousness, as well as § 112.

In an interesting essay on the patenting of business methods,[42] James Gleick correctly points out that business method patent claims are possibly too expansive in scope. He illustrates his point by citing U.S. Patent 5,965,809, issued in 1999, which is entitled "Method of Bra Size Determination" and involves a measuring step followed by a fabrication step, and U.S. Patent 5,453,036, issued in 1995, for a "Method of Exercising a Cat" using a laser. One must look to the prior art for restrictions on the scope of claims in those patents. Unless the claims are anticipated or obvi-

---

42. James Gleick, *Patently Absurd,* New York Times Magazine, Mar. 12, 2000, at 44.

ous in view of the prior art, they are valid as much as claims to any other invention.

Amazon.com acquired a high-profile method-of-doing-business patent on its "one click" system for ordering goods, U.S. Patent 5,960,411. The claims of this patent were interpreted in *Amazon.com, Inc. v. Barnesandnoble.com Inc.*[43] Claim 1 of the patent is a method claim with a series of steps, tied to some electronic means. Again, the patent has product claims that are analogs of the method, and vice versa. The independent method claim and the independent product claim of the patent are reproduced:

> 1.   A method of placing an order for an item comprising:
>
> under control of a client system, displaying information identifying the item; and
>
> in response to only a single action being performed, sending a request to order the item along with an identifier of a purchaser of the item to a server system;
>
> under control of a single-action ordering component of the server system;
>
> receiving the request;
>
> retrieving additional information previously stored for the purchaser identified by the identifier in the received request; and
>
> generating an order to purchase the requested item for the purchaser identified by the identifier in the received request using the retrieved additional information; and
>
> fulfilling the generated order to complete purchase of the item whereby the item is ordered without using a shopping cart ordering model.
>
> 6.   A client system for ordering an item comprising:
>
> an identifier that identifies a customer;

---

43. 73 F. Supp. 1228, 53 U.S.P.Q.2d (BNA) 1115, 1126–28 (W.D. Wash. 1999).

a display component for displaying information identifying the item;

a single-action ordering component that in response to performance of only a single action, sends a request to a server system to order the identified item, the request including the identifier so that the server system can locate additional information needed to complete the order and so that the server system can fulfill the generated order to complete purchase of the item; and

a shopping cart ordering component that in response to performance of an add-to-shopping-cart action, sends a request to the server system to add the item to a shopping cart.

A method of doing business does not require inclusion of a computer, or a server, or the like apparatus in the method claim. The method may include a series of steps that without the computer, or server or apparatus, would be a set of novel and unobvious steps. A hypothetical claim that is not tied to an apparatus, data processor, computer, server, etc., might read:

A method for performing a financial transaction comprising:

obtaining information concerning the financial transaction from several sources;

comparing and sorting the information according to an algorithm;

selecting displayable information that has been sorted according to the algorithm;

displaying the selected displayable information; and

making a financial transaction based upon the displayable information displayed.

As written above, the claim would be unpatentable under §§ 102 and 103. It is provided as one form to show how a method of doing business claim might be written without reference to any apparatus. Depending upon the type of financial transaction being performed, the information gathered, the algorithm, and the criteria of the algorithm for selecting information, the claim could be novel, unobvious, and patentable under §§ 102, 103, and 112.

That method should, where possible, also be claimed in a product claim. A product analog claim to the method claimed above might be:

> Apparatus for performing a financial transaction comprising:
>
>> means for storing inputted information from several sources concerning the financial transaction;
>>
>> means for comparing and sorting the information according to an algorithm consisting of ...;
>>
>> means for selecting displayable information that has been sorted according to the algorithm;
>>
>> means for displaying the selected displayable information; and
>>
>> means for making the financial transaction based upon the displayable information displayed.

For nearly every business method, the various classes and types of claims should be considered for use.

When the practitioner drafts claims on a business method invention, the claims can include the method itself, a system or apparatus employing the method, signal claims, data structure claims, program claims directed to the software program and even claims to the graphical user interface. Claim each novel aspect of the business method, which means that the method may be claimed in various ways, e.g., directed to novelties in the information gathering, the information assembly or sorting and selecting, and the information presentation. There may be different approaches, like different groups of steps, available to perform the method. All of these approaches may be claimed in separate independent claims if the approaches are to an extent mutually exclusive, i.e., at least one step is not generically used in all approaches, or may be claimed in dependent claims, if appropriate.

Many new business enterprises in any field involve some novel activity when the developer seeks to differentiate the business from competitors or existing business models. Each such activity may be a patentable business method, if it avoids §§ 102 and 103 of the Patent Act.

Summary

Business methods are patentable as are any other methods. Consider also claiming the method using apparatus claims.

V

Article of Manufacture Claims

§ 45 In General

Claims to an article of manufacture (termed a "manufacture" in 35 U.S.C. § 101)[1] differ little in principle from apparatus claims, and most of the general rules previously given apply. Basically, the article will ordinarily be a combination of elements, which must be named and tied together as with the elements of a mechanism. However, *In re Venezia*[2] allowed a carefully drawn claim to a kit of unassembled parts as a properly claimed article of manufacture. Articles of manufacture usually have no moving parts—examples are an ashtray, a hammer, or an electric battery—whereas machines (even though they *are* manufactured articles) generally have moving parts, as well as some "rule of operation"—examples are a stapler or a typewriter. In some borderline cases, it may be hard to tell whether a specific structure is an article of manufacture or a machine. Which (an article or a machine) is a pair of scissors? Fortunately, the difference is academic only, as no one ever questions whether an invention is in the class "machine" or the class "manufacture" for claim purposes.

Ordinarily, the preamble of an article claim merely names the product to be claimed, such as:

---

1. "Manufacture" and "article of manufacture" mean the same thing. *In re* Hruby, 153 U.S.P.Q. (BNA) 61 (C.C.P.A. 1967); *In re* Hadden, 20 F.2d 275 (D.C. Cir. 1927).
2. *In re* Venezia, 189 U.S.P.Q. (BNA) 149 (C.C.P.A. 1976).

A resistor

A soap dish

A girdle

If there is no generic name, one can use a functional preamble such as "A device for _____," similar to machine claims.

The elements of an article claim are the constituent parts that go to make up the article being claimed. One simple article claim follows:

7. A resistor which comprises:
   (a) a ceramic core;
   (b) a coating of carbon on the core; and
   (c) a stripe of conductive material at each end of the core in electrical contact with the carbon coating.

Further examples of article claims are given in Appendix B, cases 22 and 23.

Means-plus-function clauses (section 34) may also be used in article claims, such as "means for attaching element A to element B . . . [in some particular manner, or perhaps so that some function is accomplished]."[3] There is nothing intrinsically wrong in

---

3. *In re* Roberts and Burch, 176 U.S.P.Q. (BNA) 313 (C.C.P.A. 1973) (claim 1: "Corrugated polyethylene terephthalate film having a surface coefficient of friction of less than about 0.40 *as determined by the Bill test*."); *In re* Echerd and Watters, 176 U.S.P.Q. (BNA) 321 (C.C.P.A. 1973) (claim 12: "A . . . pipe lagging material . . . having sufficient flexibility and wet strength to permit [it] to be be wrapped when wet around insulated pipe surfaces . . . and having sufficient adhesive characteristics to firmly bond itself to such surfaces upon subsequent drying"); *In re* Swinehart and Sfiligoj, 169 U.S.P.Q. (BNA) 26 (C.C.P.A. 1971); *In re* Ludtke and Sloan, 169 U.S.P.Q. (BNA) 563 (C.C.P.A. 1971). Moreover, such functionality may be expressed *negatively*, such as in "formed by mixing together [A and B] at a temperature whereat [A and B] are *incapable* of forming [certain undesirable compounds]. . . ." *In re* Barr, Williams, and Whitmore, 170 U.S.P.Q. (BNA) 330 (C.C.P.A. 1971). *See also* section 17 and MPEP 706.03(c). One should be aware, however, of the many non-C.C.P.A. infringement decisions that seem to state that the patentability of apparatus and article claims depends on structural limitations and not on "mere" statements of function, whatever that means. *See, e.g.,* Bowles Fluidics Corp. v. Mossinghoff, 228 U.S.P.Q. (BNA) 512 (D.D.C. 1985); Scott Paper Co. v. Fort Howard Paper Co., 167 U.S.P.Q. (BNA) 4 (7th Cir. 1970); Galland-Henning Mfg. Co. v. Dempster Bros., 165 U.S.P.Q. (BNA) 688 (E.D. Tenn. 1970). To avoid this problem, use the § 112-approved means for accomplishing a function claim format.

defining something by what it does (i.e., functionally) rather than by what it is (i.e., structurally).[4] The sixth paragraph of 35 U.S.C. § 112 specifically allows the use of such functional language as a claim limitation in defining an invention to distinguish over prior art. The Patent and Trademark Office may, however, properly require proof that the functional limitations are not inherent in the prior art.[5] Otherwise, the claim could be unpatentable under 35 U.S.C. §§ 102 or 103, even if proper under § 112. Moreover, the means-plus-function language, to be "accorded structural significance," must encompass a means "which possesses a *presently existing* function [*in the article*] or a *presently existing capability to* perform [the stated] function [*in the article*]."[6]

An article claim may distinguish from the prior art by the shape or arrangement of parts, by the materials used in construction[7]

---

4. *In re* Hallman, 210 U.S.P.Q. (BNA) 611 (C.C.P.A. 1981). *See* section 31.

5. *In re* Hallman, 210 U.S.P.Q. (BNA) 611 (C.C.P.A. 1981); *In re* Ludtke and Sloan, 169 U.S.P.Q. (BNA) 563 (C.C.P.A. 1971); *In re* Swinehart and Sfiligoj, 169 U.S.P.Q. (BNA) 226 (C.C.P.A. 1971).

6. *In re* Bozek, 163 U.S.P.Q. (BNA) 545 (C.C.P.A. 1969). In *Bozek,* a "rib means" in a pulltab-type can top was claimed as performing the function of absorbing excess metal resulting from the formation, during the manufacture of the can top, of the score line defining the pulltab. The score line formation was effected by pressing the can top between two dies, which extruded metal (i.e., caused it to flow) out and away from the formed score line—thus the excess. The only function served by the rib means *in the completed top* was to strengthen the top; the prior art showed similar strengthening ribs in can tops. The function of excess metal absorption was accorded no structural significance because the rib neither performed its absorbing function *in the completed top* nor had the capability of *presently* performing that function. International Tel. & Tel. Corp. v. Union Carbide Corp., 210 U.S.P.Q. (BNA) 496, 512 (D.S.C. 1981), similarly found unpatentable a claim whose distinguishing feature was "means providing means for retaining liquid insulating compound about said terminal means during the in site solidifying" because it referred to manufacturing history, not a present structural feature or existing function.

7. *See* further discussion in section 53 on new use claims. In *In re* Andrews, 168 U.S.P.Q. (BNA) 360 (C.C.P.A. 1971), the court held that the rejection of a claim because it set forth a "device according to Claim 1 . . . made from CR-MO-W steel material" was impermissible where the specification asserted that the use of such materials gave the device improved properties, and where the examiner had neither questioned the assertion nor shown the obviousness of the improved properties.

and sometimes even by the manner in which it was made,[8] as discussed in the next section. Special considerations apply when it is attempted to distinguish an article from the prior art by printed matter appearing on the article (see section 65).

Summary

Article of manufacture claims list the parts of the article and connect them where applicable. Means clauses and other permissible function descriptions may be used.

---

8. Article claims are not indefinite simply because they include process limitations. *In re* Certain Steel Rod Treating Apparatus, 215 U.S.P.Q. (BNA) 237, 251 (Ct. Int'l Trade 1981); *In re* Brown and Saffer, 173 U.S.P.Q. (BNA) 685 (C.C.P.A. 1972) ("In order to be patentable, a product must be novel, useful and nonobvious. In our law, this is true whether the product is claimed by describing it, or by listing the process steps used to obtain it."); *Ex parte* Clark and Summering, 174 U.S.P.Q. (BNA) 40 (Bd. App. 1971); *In re* Garnero, 162 U.S.P.Q. (BNA) 221 (C.C.P.A. 1969); *In re* Pilkington, 162 U.S.P.Q. (BNA) 145 (C.C.P.A. 1969). Moreover, to the extent such process limitations distinguish the article from the prior art, they must be given the same consideration relative to patentability as traditional limitations. And that is true even though what the process uses or operates on is not present in the final article. *In re* Luck and Gainer, 177 U.S.P.Q. (BNA) 523 (C.C.P.A. 1973). Accordingly, where an article claim includes elements A and B "bonded together by being contacted in the presence of X at a temperature of 200°F," the process limitation ("by being contacted . . .") is entitled to patentable significance even though X is not present in any form in A, B, or the A/B bond.

Although the existence of an old or obvious method of producing an article does not *necessarily* negate the article's patentability, such a method is a factor to be considered along with similarities in and differences between the structure and properties of the article and the prior art. *In re* Lewis, 172 U.S.P.Q. (BNA) 238 (C.C.P.A. 1972); *In re* Hoeksema, 158 U.S.P.Q. (BNA) 596 (C.C.P.A. 1968). On the other hand, the general rule is that an article must *itself* meet the tests of 35 U.S.C. §§ 102 and 103 to be patentable. It is usually insufficient for patentability that the article is manufactured by a novel or unobvious method. *In re* Pilkington, 162 U.S.P.Q. (BNA) 145 (C.C.P.A. 1969); Thomson Indus., Inc. v. Nippon Thompson Co., 160 U.S.P.Q. (BNA) 318 (E.D.N.Y. 1969); *Ex parte* Edwards, 162 U.S.P.Q. (BNA) 64 (Bd. App. 1968). But the development of a new process, especially in the face of previous unsuccessful efforts by others, is evidence of nonobviousness of the product eventually developed. Phillips Petroleum Co. v. U.S. Steel Corp., 6 U.S.P.Q.2d (BNA) 1065, 1096 (D. Del. 1987).

§ 46 Product-by-Process Claims

A product-by-process claim is one where an article or at least one element of an article is claimed by reciting the process for fabricating the article or its element.[8.1] Typically, the article or element is recited in the form of a method claim or a method limitation, preferably by using the gerund form for the process step in which the product or its element is formed. The simplest form of such a claim might be:

5C. Sodium hydroxide produced according to the process of claim 5B

Using a dependent claim form to refer back to an earlier claim and to cross statutory classes is proper here. See section 11 and MPEP 2173.05(f).

As an example of product-by-process, assume that in the resistor of claim 7 the carbon coating was deposited on the ceramic core by decomposition of a hydrocarbon gas. In this instance, claim 7 might read:

7A. A resistor which comprises:
- **(a) a ceramic core;**
- **(b) a coating of carbon *deposited* on the core by *decomposition of a hydrocarbon gas in the presence of the core;* and**
- **(c) a stripe of conductive metal . . . etc.**
- **or, preferably, (b) . . . *by decomposing a hydrocarbon gas in the presence of the core* . . .**

(Italics indicate typical product-by-process phraseology.)

This type of process description of a product element would be necessary to define the novel feature if carbon-coated resistors were old with the carbon applied in some other way, such as by lacquering. It would be permissible as to form *if* the carbon coating produced by decomposition of the hydrocarbon gas were different mechanically or electrically than the prior art coating, and if the nature of the mechanical or chemical differences was not known or could not be stated.

8.1. MPEP 2113, 2173.05(p).

This type of claim covers the product *only* when made by the specified method, so the claims are not so broad as regular or "pure product" claims. Prior to April of 1974, a product-by-process claim was permissible as to form only where the product "cannot be described in any other manner" than by the process by which it was made.[9] The applicant was not allowed such claims where he also presented regular product claims. This seems unreasonable in that one might have a patentable invention on two levels: one on a generic level, covering the article produced by any method, and one on a specific level, covering the article produced by the particular method. For example, in the carbon resistor example, one might have invented the basic carbon-coated resistor of claim 7 and also the deposited-carbon resistor of claim 7A. This would be one typical example of generic and species inventions (section 58). In any event, no such restriction exists now.

In addition, the old Patent Office manual permitted only one product-by-process claim, with rare exception. No such restriction exists now.

In *Leutzinger v. Ladd,*[10] the court allowed both a straight product claim and dependent product-by-process claim, such as:

> 7. The subject matter of claim 1, in which the linseed oil is heated to 200°F.; the waxes are then added and the temperature is held for four to nine days.

The court found that the product of claim 7 was not the same as the generic product of claim 1, and both were patentable.

The product-by-process claim must satisfy both 35 U.S.C. § 102 and 35 U.S.C. § 103. As to unobviousness of a product-by-process claim, it must reside solely in the final product, not the process that produced it.[11.1] The process is immaterial except as it affects the characteristics of the product. This means that the process can be patentable while the product made by the patentable process may be unpatentable. *In re Pilkington,*[12] quoting from *In re Dilnot,*[13] says:

---

9. *See Ex parte* Donahey, 126 U.S.P.Q. (BNA) 61 (Bd. App. 1959); *In re* Moeller, 48 U.S.P.Q. (BNA) 542 (C.C.P.A. 1941); *see also In re* Dreyfus, 24 U.S.P.Q. (BNA) 463 (C.C.P.A. 1935).

10. Leutzinger v. Ladd, 139 U.S.P.Q. (BNA) 196 (D.D.C. 1963).

11. *In re* Brown and Saffer, 173 U.S.P.Q. (BNA) 685, 688 (C.C.P.A. 1972).

11.1. MPEP 2113; *In re* Thorpe, 277 U.S.P.Q. (BNA) 964, 966 (Fed. Cir. 1985).

12. *In re* Pilkington, 162 U.S.P.Q. (BNA) 145, 147 (C.C.P.A. 1969).

13. *In re* Dilnot, 133 U.S.P.Q. (BNA) 289, 292 (C.C.P.A. 1962).

"The addition of a method step in a product claim, which product is not patentably distinguishable from the prior art, cannot impart patentability to the old product." Citing *In re Moeller,* 48 U.S.P.Q. 542; *In re Lifton,* 89 U.S.P.Q. 641; *In re Shortell,* 81 U.S.P.Q. 359; and *Tri-Wall Containers, Inc. v. U.S.,* 161 U.S.P.Q. 116.[14]

Referring to claims 7 and 7A above as to a resistor, prior art resistor having its coating deposited by applying a lacquered-on layer of carbon, rather than by decomposing a hydrocarbon gas, would make unpatentable or invalid, under § 102 or § 103, both of claims 7 and 7A. Claim 7A, while involving performing a process not known in the art to deposit the coating, produced a resistor known in the art. The process used to make the resistor would be patentable and valid over the prior art, while the resistor made using that process would not be patentable or valid.

Steppan,[15] cited in *Pilkington,* involved a claim to:

> 25. An acid phosphate of *a condensation product* of formaldehyde with a salt of a compound selected from the group consisting of . . . [A and B], the acid phosphate having the general formula[16] . . . [C].[17]

Pure product (structural formula) claims were also presented, but were held obvious by the court, affirming the examiner and the board.

As to claim 25, the court held it was not a product-by-process claim at all. Words such as "condensation product," while telling the process (condensation) are not purely process limitations; they are also structural. (Obviousness was not considered, as the claim was rejected only as being an "improper" product-by-process claim.)

Some apparent process limitations, such as "etched," "welded," "interbonded by interfusion," are considered structural limitations not subject to the product-by-process rules. See *In re Garnero,*[18] where the following claim was considered:

---

14. *See In re* Brown and Saffer, 173 U.S.P.Q. (BNA) 685 (C.C.P.A. 1972).
15. 156 U.S.P.Q. (BNA) 143 (C.C.P.A. 1967).
16. A general formula tells what elements are involved and in what proportions, but not how connected.
17. *In re* Pilkington, 162 U.S.P.Q. (BNA) 145, 147 (C.C.P.A. 1969) (emphasis added).
18. *In re* Garnero, 162 U.S.P.Q. (BNA) 221, 223 (C.C.P.A. 1969).

> A composite, porous, thermal insulation panel characterized by dimensional stability and structural strength consisting essentially of expanded perlite particles which are *interbonded to one another by interfusion* between the surfaces of the perlite particles *while in a pyroplastic state* to form a porous perlite panel. (Emphasis added to stress limitations in question.)

The court held that:

> . . . the recitation of the particles as "interbonded one to another by interfusion between the surfaces of the perlite particles" is as capable of being construed as a structural limitation as "intermixed," "ground in place," "press fitted," "etched," and "welded," all of which at one time or another have been separately held capable of construction as structural, rather than process, limitations.

The court found it unnecessary to consider the further process limitation, "while in a pyroplastic state," because the claim was already held unobvious in view of the "interbonded" limitation. However, with respect to process limitations generally, the court remarked:

> . . . the mere presence of a method limitation in an article claim which is otherwise allowable would not so poison the claim as to render it unpatentable. *Ex parte Lindberg,* 157 U.S.P.Q. 606, 607 (P.O. Bd. App. 1967).[19]

Similarly, "chemically engraved," read in context, described the product more by its structure than the process used to obtain it.[20]

Another example where a product-by-process claim could be used is the treated polyethylene article of claim 5 (section 42), where the surface was treated with a solution of sodium dichromate in sulfuric acid. One might claim:

> 8. A polyethylene article having a surface treated in accordance with the process of claim 5.

---

19. *In re* Certain Steel Rod Treating Apparatus, 215 U.S.P.Q. (BNA) 237, 252 n.88 (Ct. Int'l Trade 1981).
20. Hazani v. U.S. Int'l Trade Comm'n, 126 F.3d 1473, 44 U.S.P.Q.2d (BNA) 1358, 1363 (Fed. Cir. 1997).

This claim also illustrates claims in two statutory classes for the same invention, and a dependent claim that crosses statutory classes (see section 11).

How many claims applicant wants to present, and how many different types of claims, are covered by the general rule set out in sections 61 and 62, not by any special rules for product-by-process.

Every method claim which produces or modifies any object should be considered for preparation of a corresponding product-by-process claim, including independent and dependent method claims. There is no restriction on the quantity of product-by-product process claims permitted in one application.

Therefore, the examiner should consider whether the product is novel as made by X process and, if so, then whether such a new product would have been obvious. Of course, these are merely the standard statutory tests for patentability of any claim on the merits, once the formal barriers have been passed.

The basic rule remains, however, that the product itself must be novel and unobvious, when made by process X, and the fact that process X may be patentable is not material to patentability of the product per se. This conforms to the basic rule that there must be novelty and unobviousness in each statutory class of subject matter in which claims are sought.

In 1991, a Federal Circuit panel stated that "the correct reading of product-by-process claims is that they are not limited to product prepared by the process set forth in the claims."[21] The claim read:

> Highly purified and concentrated human or porcine VIII:C prepared in accordance with the method of claim 1.

The court held that sufficiently purified VIII:C would infringe even if not prepared by the method of claim 1.

One year later, in *Atlantic Thermoplastics v. Faytex,*[22] another Federal Circuit panel ruled that "process terms in product-by-process claims served as limitations in determining infringement." The claim at issue in *Atlantic* read:

> The molded innersole produced by the method of claim 1.

---

21. Scripps Clinic & Research Foundation v. Genentech, 927 F.2d 1565, 1583 (Fed. Cir. 1991).
22. Atlantic Thermoplastics v. Faytex, 970 F.2d 835, 846–47 (Fed. Cir. 1992).

The court held that the same innersole would not infringe unless the method of claim 1 were used in its manufacture. To the author, *Atlantic* seems to be the better law. Why have claim language if it is to be ignored? The Federal Circuit has yet to issue a clarification. As a result, at least one district court has felt constrained to follow the earlier *Scripps* precedent, despite the district court's apparent disagreement with it.[22.1]

Summary

Product-by-process claims may be obtained whenever the product has novelty and is unobvious over prior art products. These are claims reciting a product or composition of matter or its elements by the process by which it was made, rather than by its structural or chemical characteristics. Mixed claims are also permitted, defining some features in "regular product" phraseology, and one or more features in product-by-process language. It is up to the applicant to describe what he thinks his invention is, and he can use product-by-process language whenever he thinks necessary or best for a particular claim.

§ 47 Design Claims

For design patents (35 U.S.C. sections 171–173), only one claim, in formal terms, is permitted: "The claim shall be in formal terms to the ornamental design for the article (specifying name) as shown, or as shown and described. More than one claim is neither required nor permitted" (rule 153).[23]

Thus, a design claim attempting to describe the article verbally is improper. The claim may only incorporate the specification (drawing) by reference.

22.1. Columbia University v. Roche Diagnostics GmbH, 126 F. Supp. 2d 16, 57 U.S.P.Q.2d (BNA) 1825, 1837–38 (D. Mass. 2000). *See* Tropix, Inc. v. Lumigen, Inc., 825 F. Supp. 7, 27 U.S.P.Q.2d (BNA) 1475 (D. Mass. 1993).

23. MPEP 1503.03.

When the name of the article is specified, it should be the title of the invention as stated in the title of the specification. (Further, that same term should be used in the description of figure 1 in the specification.)

The claim ends with "as shown" when the specification only describes the direction of view of each drawing figure.

The claim ends with "as shown and described" when there is a special description of the design in the specification or a showing of a modified form of the design, or there is other descriptive matter.[24]

For example, when the specification describes more than the direction of view for every drawing figure. For example, the description of one figure may note that it is a view of one side, and that the opposite view is a mirror image; or the specification may say that the side not illustrated is plain or may say that the application is a continuing one.

One example, from Design Patent No. 215,546:

> "9. The ornamental design for a cover for data communications apparatus, substantially as shown and described."

However, use of "substantially" in the claim is not the best form. Thus, the claim is better written:

> 9. **The ornamental design for data communications apparatus, as shown and described.**

As with any other claimed invention, a claimed design must be novel and unobvious. The overall aesthetic effect (*tout ensemble*) of the design must be viewed as a whole in determining whether these qualities are present.

A design may be embodied in an entire article or only in part of it. *In re Zahn*[25] found patentable a design embodied only in the shank portion of a drill. Further, a design is not "of" an article, but "for" an article and includes ornamental designs of all kinds, including surface ornamentation as well as configuration of the goods.[26] It has been held that a portion of a water fountain that is composed entirely of water in continuous motion (i.e., the spray!)

---

24. *Id.*
25. *In re* Zahn, 204 U.S.P.Q. (BNA) 995, 998 (C.C.P.A. 1980).
26. *Id.*

is an "article of manufacture" within 35 U.S.C. § 171 and may be the subject of a design patent.[27]

§ 48 Plant Patent Claims

A rule similar to that for design claims holds for a plant patent claim (35 U.S.C. §§ 161–164). Only one claim is permitted, except that "the principal distinguishing characteristics" may be recited (rule 164),[28] and usually are, in rather flowery language. The following example is from plant patent 2,866 (Feb. 25, 1969):

> 10. **A new and distinct variety of chrysanthemum plant of the thick decorative class, substantially as herein shown and described, characterized particularly as to novelty by the unique combination of a hardy and free habit of growth, a large bloom size, a very durable flower petalage, and a distinctive and attractive general color tonality of the flowers corresponding to Apricot Yellow, very lightly overcase with Light Cadmium.**

Plant patent claims frequently appear to violate the general rule that laudatory statements are not permitted therein.

The disclosure of a plant patent may not fully comply with 35 U.S.C. § 112, but yet be adequate under 35 U.S.C. § 162. For example, plant patents require no "how-to-make" disclosures.[29] Nevertheless, there must be a sufficient disclosure (e.g., of alleged

---

27. *In re* Hruby, 153 U.S.P.Q. (BNA) 61, 64 (C.C.P.A. 1967):
    [T]he permanence of any design is a function of the materials in which it is embodied and the effects of the environment thereon. Considering the fact that the Romans and the French built now-famous fountains hundreds of years ago which still produce the same water designs today, the notion that a fountain is "fleeting" [and, therefore, not an article of manufacture] is not one which will "hold water. . . ."
28. MPEP 1605.
29. Jessel v. Newland, 195 U.S.P.Q. (BNA) 674, 677 (Bd. Pat. Interp.), 195 U.S.P.Q. (BNA) 678, 683-84 (Comm. 1977); Yoder Bros. v. California-Fla. Plant Corp., 193 U.S.P.Q. (BNA) 264, 290 (5th Cir. 1976); *In re* LeGrice, 133 U.S.P.Q. (BNA) 365 (C.C.P.A. 1962).

characteristics present in the plant that are absent in closely related varieties of the prior art) to establish the inventive characteristics.[30]

The plant invention must be novel in conception, rather than novel in use: must be not only new, but not existing in nature; and cannot merely be newly found; must be nonobvious;[31] and, finally, must have been asexually reproduced.[32] The scope of a plant patent differs from that of other patents, because an infringer must not merely copy; he must use stock obtained from, presumably directly or indirectly, the patentee.[33]

§ 48A Provisional Applications

A provisional application receives a filing date when a written description, necessary drawings, and the names of the inventors have been supplied to the Patent and Trademark Office. No claim is required.[34] Because the applicant must file a nonprovisional application within one year of filing the provisional application, the applicant may first file the claim when the nonprovisional application is filed.

As a provisional application filed without a cover sheet identifying it as a provisional application is treated as nonprovisional,[35] some practitioners recommend including a claim in the provisional specification. Also, preparing a claim may aid in preparing the specification of the provisional application, as it will help the claim drafter be sure that the disclosure of the provisional application provides antecedent support for every element in the claim.

A claim in the provisional application can be in any form, since the provisional application claim is not required and therefore is not examined for compliance with any statutory section, § 112 or §§ 102 or 103.

---

30. *In re* Greer, 179 U.S.P.Q. (BNA) 301 (C.C.P.A. 1973).
31. Yoder Bros. v. California-Fla. Plant Corp., 193 U.S.P.Q. (BNA) 264, 293 (5th Cir. 1976).
32. *Id.*
33. *Ex parte* Weiss, 159 U.S.P.Q. (BNA) 122 (Bd. App. 1967) (particularly cases cited at 124); Yoder Bros. v. California-Fla. Plant Corp., 193 U.S.P.Q. (BNA) 264, 293 (5th Cir. 1976).
34. MPEP 601.01(b).
35. MPEP 506.

VI

Composition of Matter Claims—
Chemical Cases

---

§ 49 In General

Compositions of matter are products where the chemical nature of the substances or materials used, rather than the shape or form of a product, is the distinguishing characteristic. As with machines versus manufactures, there is no need to determine the statutory pigeonhole between manufacture and composition. If one had a situation where both the form and composition of a material were required for novelty, or otherwise to be claimed, it would not be necessary to designate into which class the claim fell.

As in the other classes, most composition claims are combination claims, except where a new compound or molecule per se is claimed. Even those involve combinations of the chemical elements, and groups of elements, or radicals. Composition claims are usually fairly easy to prepare, as to formulating a claim; the main problems relate to the allowable scope of the claims, such as: How many examples are needed to support a generic claim?[1] How close can one come to the prior art? Problems in broad functional definitions of materials (section 31) are especially acute.[2]

---

1. *See In re* Marzocchi, 169 U.S.P.Q. (BNA) 367 (C.C.P.A. 1971); *Ex parte* Laiderman, 175 U.S.P.Q. (BNA) 575 (Bd. App. 1971). Note also the possibility of "reading on inoperative species." *In re* Cook and Merigold, 169 U.S.P.Q. (BNA) 298 (Bd. App. 1971). Although *Cook* was not a "chemical case" (optical lens), the problem most often arises in chemical-type cases.
2. *See Ex parte* Slub, 157 U.S.P.Q. (BNA) 172 (Bd. App. 1967) (discussed in section 31); *In re* Koller, 204 U.S.P.Q. (BNA) 702 (C.C.P.A. 1980).

One simple example of a composition claim to a combination of materials follows:

11. A zinc electroplating solution, comprising:

(a) an aqueous solution of zinc acetate, from 30 to 90 grams per liter;

(b) citric acid, from 1.5 to 3 times the zinc acetate concentration; and

(c) an alkaline pH-modifying substance in an amount sufficient to adjust the pH[3] to a value of from 4 to 5.5.

Note that the "elements" of a composition claim are chemical elements or compounds, described either broadly (element c) or narrowly (elements a and b), depending on the prior art. Note that the "pH modifying substance" clause is very similar to a "means clause" in that it tells what function the element performs, not what it is. Presumably, any alkaline substance would work in the combination, and the point of invention concerned establishing the stated pH range, not how to establish it. Means clauses are not often if ever used in composition claims, but the author sees no theoretical reason why they could not be, as: "means for adjusting the pH of the solution to a value of from 4 to 5.5. or perhaps "a substance for . . ." because it is not necessary to use only the word "means" to meet 35 U.S.C. § 112, paragraph 6 (see section 34). As described in section 31, the statute says "an element in a claim for a combination"; it does not limit this to any particular type of combination.

In a composition claim, it is usually not essential to state the intended use for the composition in the preamble. Under classic rulings, a label such as "zinc electroplating solution" will not save the claim if the composition per se is old for another use. (See further comments in section 56, new use claims.)

A composition of matter, claimable under the patent law, may be a new molecule, compound, solution, mixture, and even a living being (section 55), etc., although, in the case of a mere physical mixture of materials, an obviousness question is very likely to be raised. However, the test should be whether it would have been

---

3. A measure of acidity, numbers below 7 being acid.

obvious to associate the materials, not *how* they are associated. *Ex parte Dubsky and Stark*[4] is one case allowing claims to a physical mixture. Although the components of the mixture (a polymerizable compound and a chelate) were intended to react to form a compound, the mixture had a substantial shelf life and thus could be claimed. The Board implied that, if the reaction were instantaneous, the mixture could not be claimed because it would have no substantial existence.

Special problems come up in the metallurgical arts in claiming new alloys, usually nowadays including changes in proportions of known ingredients to achieve new properties or advantages. Also, as discussed in section 54, it is often permissible to refer to an area of a component diagram shown in the drawings to define proportions of ingredients in metallurgical cases.

In the early 1960s, the Board of Appeals settled a long-standing philosophical debate by allowing claims to new atoms. Claim 1 of patent 3,156,523 reads "Element 95" (now called americium) and Claim 1 of patent 3,161,462 reads "Element 96" (curium).[5] The Board of Appeals held that the claims were directed to proper statutory subject matter, but that both elements were anticipated as having been inherently produced in the prior art (Enrico Fermi *et al.* patent), etc. The C.C.P.A. held the elements were neither anticipated nor obvious in view of the prior art, and that any prior production was minuscule and unknown. (Many might question the basic conclusion as to the obviousness of a new atom per se.[6])

A typical type of claim to a new organic molecule:[7]

> 12.   A compound having the formula:
>
> R-CH = N-S-X,
>
> wherein
>
> R is an alkyl group selected from the group consisting of methyl, ethyl and isopropyl; and

---

4. *Ex parte* Dubsky and Stark, 162 U.S.P.Q. (BNA) 567 (Bd. App. 1968).
5. *See In re* Seaborg, 140 U.S.P.Q. (BNA) 659 (C.C.P.A. 1964); *In re* Seaborg, 140 U.S.P.Q. (BNA) 662 (C.C.P.A. 1964).
6. *See also In re* Bergstrom, 166 U.S.P.Q. (BNA) 256 (C.C.P.A. 1970).
7. See also section 50 for further examples of formula claims to organic molecules and groups of molecules.

X is a halogen selected from the group consisting of chlorine and bromine.

Note that the foregoing claim covers a total of six specific compounds, for any use to which they can be put. This illustrates the very common class of inventions in which new molecules are claimed by structural formula. It also illustrates the use of what is termed *"Markush,"* or alternative, terminology to cover several different compounds with a single claim (see section 50).

See section 11 for comments on dependent composition claims, and section 57 on *Jepson*-type claims in this area.

Summary

Composition of matter claims list the chemical ingredients (compounds, elements or radicals) making up the composition or compound. The ingredients or elements may be claimed narrowly (specific named components), with intermediate scope (a group of similar elements functionally equivalent), or broadly as to function performed, where the prior art permits. Where necessary to novelty, etc., the proportions or other conditions or parameters of the compound are stated, usually in ranges of concentration of ingredients. The intended use for the composition (rust inhibition, antibiotic) may or may not be stated in the preamble. (See section 56 for details on the effect of preamble limitations.) The problems in chemical practice come primarily with obviousness questions over prior art and how much disclosure is needed in the specification, not primarily in the techniques of drafting claims.

§ 50 "Markush" Expressions

Markush expressions are alternative expressions described in MPEP 2173.05(h):

> ... a *Markush* group, recites members as being 'selected from the group consisting of A, B, C.' *Ex parte Markush,* 1925 C.D. 126; sanctions claiming a genus expressed as a group consisting of certain specific materials. Inventions in metallurgy, refractories, ceramics, pharmacy, pharmacolo-

gy and biology are most frequently claimed under the *Markush* formula but purely mechanical features or process steps may also be claimed by using the *Markush* style of claiming, *see Ex parte Head,* 214 U.S.P.Q. 551 (Bd. Appl's 1981); *In re Gaubert,* 187 U.S.P.Q. 664 (C.C.P.A. 1975) and *In re Harnisch,* 206 U.S.P.Q. 300 (C.C.P.A. 1980).

Further, as to the form of language for a *Markush* grouping MPEP 2173.05(h) says: "It is improper to use the term 'comprising' instead of 'consisting of'." In other words the group must be recited as closed ended.

Rather than using "selected from the group consisting of," one can simply list the group members, with "or" preceding the final member (see below in this section).

Furthermore, *Markush* grouping can lead to possible double inclusion of a claimed element. An example in the MPEP 2173.05(h) is a *Markush* group: "selected from the group consisting of . . . halogen . . . chloro . . ." The group is acceptable although "halogen" is generic to "chloro." The claim itself must be evaluated for indefiniteness.

The *Markush* expression is commonly used in chemical cases as it deals with naming a selected group of materials. However, practitioners sometimes use them in nonchemical, e.g., mechanical and electrical cases, where the rationale for the use of such an expression will equally apply. The Manual section says it may be used for "purely mechanical features," like simple screws or staples, or even individual large, complex structures. It may be used for "process steps," e.g., gluing or stapling.

A *Markush* is a sort of homemade generic expression covering a group of two or more different materials (elements, radicals, compounds, etc.), mechanical elements, or process steps, any one one of which will work in the combination claimed.

Treatment of a claim element as a *Markush* group occurs even if that treatment was not intended.[7.1] For example, prior art teaching one member of the group will be prior art as to the entire *Markush* group. If you do not intend to claim a *Markush* group,

---

7.1 *See* Brown v. Air Products & Chemicals, Inc., 229 F.3d 1120, 56 U.S.P.Q.2d (BNA) 1456 (Fed. Cir. 2001).

do not use alternative language for a series of related alternative elements.

A typical example, from the previous section, Claim 12:

> . . . *a* halogen *selected from the group consisting of* chlorine and bromine.

Note that this covers either chlorine or bromine, either of two specific elements out of five in the halogen group, in apparent violation of the "rule" against alternative claiming discussed in section 24. The *Markush* doctrine originated out of necessity. In the previous example, there is no generic word for the specified group of two halogens out of five. To refuse a generic claim because of a paucity of language seems unreasonable. Thus, *Markush* language is used to create an artificial generic expression.

Mr. Markush's claim in question involved: "a material selected from the group consisting of aniline and halogen substitutes of aniline."

Markush terminology may be used in claims in any of the statutory classes of utility patents; wherever several alternative types of material are involved. Thus, although the claim may be to a mechanical structure, an article of manufacture, the particular element of that structure that is described by a *Markush* expression may be a chemical type limitation. As an example of an article of manufacture, in the resistor of section 45, if the only materials that would work for the terminal stripes were copper, silver and aluminum, or if for any other reason a claim limited to those three materials were desired, clause (c) of Claim 7 could read as follows: "a stripe of *a conductive metal selected from the group consisting of* copper, silver and aluminum at each end of the core in electrical contact with the carbon coating."

For a process claim including a series of materials or elements that may be used as alternatives, consider the example in section 42 of treating polyethylene articles, and suppose that the acid could be only concentrated sulfuric, nitric, or phosphoric acid.

The claim would then read:

5A.   A process for treating the surface of a polyethylene article to increase its receptivity to a printing ink, which comprises:

exposing the surface of the article to a saturated solution of sodium dichromate in *an acid selected from the group consisting of* concentrated sulfuric, nitric and phosphoric acids.

Markush group claiming can be extended to alternative process steps. In a process limitation, the *Markush* group consists of a group of steps: ". . . weakening the bond by a process selected from the group consisting of heating, freezing, and pulling the pieces apart. . . ." In claim 5A above, the exposing step may be written as an additional *Markush* grouping, "wherein the exposing is performed by a process. . .," or "wherein the exposing step is selected from the group consisting of dipping, spraying and painting" or even "wherein the exposing is done by dipping, spraying or painting," since the "or" alternative is also permitted, see below.

In the foregoing examples, the italics indicate the *Markush* phraseology. The precise format should, but not must, be followed exactly. The *Markush* expression preferably has the form "a _____ selected from the group consisting of _____ . . . and _____." Note that the word "consisting" limits the claim to the named group, as mentioned in section 8.

An interesting example is from Stebbings patent 3,234,948 on a cheese filter cigarette: "2. A cigarette filter according to claim 1, in which the cheese comprises grated particles of cheese selected from the group consisting of Parmesan, Romano, Swiss and cheddar cheeses." This illustrates the use of a *Markush* expression to define one element of an article of manufacture claim.

The claim in which the expression appears may have the transition word "comprising" after the preamble, but the *Markush* expression of the claim may never include "comprising." Instead, the *Markush* expression must begin only with "the group consisting of."

Further, the group members are listed separated by commas. Where the *Markush* expression is introduced by "selected from the group consisting of," the final member of the group is preceded by the conjunction "and."[7.2] Proper practice also permits claiming in the alternative using "or," if a *Markush* group would have been proper, but then you omit the formulaic "selected from the group consisting of":

> When materials recited in a claim are so related as to constitute a proper *Markush* group, they may be recited in the conventional [Markush] manner, or alternatively. For example, if "wherein R is a material selected from the group consisting of A, B, C and D" is a proper limitation, then "wherein R is A, B, C or D" shall also be considered proper.[7.3]

Under this modification, in the example of claim 7, one could recite a "stripe of copper, silver or aluminum. . . ." This is much simpler and covers the same thing as the regular *Markush* form.

There once was a policy against *Markush* claims of diminishing or varying scope (claim 1—the group A, B, C, and D; claim 2—A, B, and C), but this is now considered proper *unless* ". . . such a practice renders the claims indefinite [this would be rare] or if it results in undue multiplicity."[8]

Markush claims also may be allowed as subordinate ("subgenus") claims under a broader ("genus") claim not naming particular materials[8.1] (see section 58 on generic and species claims). Under this liberalized practice, for example, claim 1 could cover conductive materials broadly; claim 2, a *Markush* group of five materials; claim 3, a limited group of three preferred materials; etc.

When claiming specific compounds per se (that is, molecules), questions have arisen in how closely related the members of the *Markush* group must be for the claim to be proper: could one claim such disparate things as air, earth, fire, or water? Polypropylene, benzene hexafluoride, tantalum sesquinitride, or undiscovered element 117? MPEP 2173.05(h) requires that the materials in the *Markush* group must ordinarily "belong to a recognized physical or chemical class or an art-recognized class." Air, earth, fire, and water would not suffice.

7.2. MPEP 2173.05(h).
7.3. *Id.*
8. MPEP 2173.05(h); section 62.
8.1. MPEP 2173.05(h).

Unlike *Markush* groupings that recite materials or a compound, *Markush* groups in a claim reciting a process or a combination need not belong to one class.[9] MPEP 2173.05(h) says "it is sufficient if the members of the group are disclosed in the specification to possess at least one property in common which is mainly responsible for their function in the claimed relationship, and it is clear from their very nature or from the prior art that all of them possess this property." This lends itself to making a broad range of mechanical equivalents, sharing one common property, part of a *Markush* grouping: "a resting surface selected from the group consisting of a chair, a bench and a stool." The *Markush* grouping is more easily explained if the clause including it includes the property that the members of that group possess, e.g., "a resting surface." Alternatively, that property may be recited in a preceding claim without the *Markush* group and the specified group may then be recited in a following dependent claim, as "wherein the resting surface is selected. . . ."

In mechanical cases, there would usually be some generic word available, often a "means for" clause, avoiding the need for *Markush* claiming and making its use optional. Yet, the *Markush* claiming is also available. For example, the *Markush* grouping a "fastener selected from the group consisting of nail, rivets and screws" may instead be preceded by the generic claim reciting "a fastener" or a "means for fastening."

MPEP 803.02 concerns restriction requirements for *Markush* groups and permits such requirements when members of a group present independent and distinct inventions. Then the examiner may require provisional election of a single species. As MPEP 803.02 says:

> Broadly, unity of invention exists where compounds included within a Markush group (1) share a common utility and (2) share a substantial structural feature disclosed as being essential to that utility.

The above appears to relate only to claims for two different compounds. When claiming a process or a combination of materials, standard Patent and Trademark Office practice is more liberal:

---

9. *In re* Harnisch, 206 U.S.P.Q. (BNA) 300 (C.C.P.A. 1980).

it is sufficient if the members of the group are disclosed in the specification to possess at least one property in common which is mainly responsible for their function in the claimed relationship and it is clear from their very nature or from the prior art that all of them possess this property.[10]

Also, where a *Markush* expression is applied only to a portion of a chemical compound (for example, claim 12, a radical such as methyl, ethyl, etc.), the propriety of the grouping is determined by consideration of the compound as a whole, and does not depend on there being a community of properties in the members of the *Markush* expression per se.[11]

Summary

Markush claims define alternative chemical ingredients that can be used in a compound, composition, alternative steps in a process, or alternative choices for an article. Where claiming alternative compounds, they must not be "patentably distinct" under present Office practice; otherwise, they need only have a common property useful in the combination claimed. The standard format is "a _____ selected from the group consisting of A, B, and C." There are many detailed rules on Markush *practices described in the preceding section, and modern Patent and Trade Office practice may be to restrict use of* Markush *claims and to require restriction between inventions the examiner thinks are independent and distinct.*

§ 51 Trademarked Materials; Arbitrary Names

Where an ingredient in a composition to be claimed is known only by a trademark or by an arbitrary name used in trade, according to the Patent and Trademark Office,[12] such a name may be used in the application and claims *only* where the term has a fixed and definite meaning, either well known in the literature or defined in the application, if necessary by describing the process

10. MPEP 2173.05(h).
11. MPEP 2173.05(h); *see Ex parte* Price, 150 U.S.P.Q. (BNA) 467 (Bd. App. 1965).
12. MPEP 608.01(v); 2173.05(u).

of manufacture. Where available, a generic name should be used. If the description is not sufficiently definite to enable one skilled in the art to practice the invention (35 U.S.C. § 112), the claim may be rejected.

A trademark does not identify a particular product, because the product or its characteristic to which the trademark is applied is changeable.[13] Thus, claim the product by its relevant generic name or its characteristics as disclosed on the specification or drawings.

A different type of term is a name used in trade. That is a name for a product used in a particular art and is nonproprietary. Names used in trade can be used in the claim if they have a sufficiently well known definition in the literature or are accompanied by a precise definition.

In a leading article,[14] F. Prince Butler reviewed many prior cases and publications on the subject, and deduced the following general rules and summary:

> Rule #1–A Trade Term is properly used in a specification if those skilled in the art can make the product designated by the trade term at the time the application is filed, using the specification and/or published literature that is implicated by the specification.
>
> Rule #2–A trade term is also properly used in a specification if the product is generally known to persons skilled in the art and is readily obtainable at the time the application is filed, provided the composition of the product is a trade secret and there is reason to believe that whenever the composition of the product is modified the trade term will also be changed.
>
> Rule #3–A trade term is also properly used in a specification if it designates a component of the embodiment which is not essential to the invention.
>
> Rule #4–A trade term can be used in a claim only if its meaning has been adequately defined in the specification, whereby it imparts specific limitations to the claim.

---

13. MPEP 608.01(v); *Ex parte* Bickell, 122 U.S.P.Q. (BNA) 27, 28 (Bd. App. 1957).
14. Butler, *Rules Defining the Use of Trade Terms in Patent Applications*, 51 J. Pat. Off. Soc'y 339 (1969).

SUMMARY

Generally, it is undesirable to use trademarks and trade names in patent applications; however, courts have allowed their use under a variety of factual circumstances. Because of the divergence of such decisions it is difficult for patent attorneys and patent office examiners to appraise whether or not particular trade terms have been properly used in patent applications. This note presents four rules which embody all the known cases involving the use of trade terms in patent aplications.

The proper test should be the rule of reason, derived only from 35 U.S.C. § 112. Has the applicant disclosed everything about the material he or she reasonably can? If so, that is enough.

If "Amberlite IRC 50" is a critical material in a process or composition, and if the applicant does not know what it is and the trademark owner will not say, why should he be denied a patent, assuming the invention is unobvious, etc.? If, as the board or courts worry, the trademark owner goes out of business or so modifies the formula that the invention no longer operates, then the patent would be useless. Validity would not come into question, because no one could practice the invention. However, if, as more normally happens, the trademark owner does not go out of business, the patent would then remain operative and useful as long as the material stayed available. A patent with an effective life of five years is preferable to no patent at all. Also, since the disclosure of the trademarked material by name is a description of an existing thing, it should not be held "new matter" to add a further description of that material if it subsequently becomes available at any time before the patent is granted and perhaps even after the grant of the patent. The only thing that should be required is an affidavit or statement of *identity*—that the later description indeed describes the composition mentioned in the application—nothing else. The rule against the new matter[15] should really have nothing to do with this mere identification question.

---

15. 35 U.S.C. § 113 ("No amendment shall introduce new matter into the disclosure of the invention.").

Of course, trademarks should always be properly designated, by capitalizing them in upper case type and placing them between quotation marks. (See MPEP 608.01(v) and other sources on correct trademark usage for details.)

Summary

Avoid defining compositions used in practicing an invention by trademark or trade name so far as possible. Where there is no other way, describe everything known about the material in the application. If rejected under 35 U.S.C. § 112, appeal.

§ 52 Special Claims for Chemical Cases— Fingerprint Claims

In chemical composition claims, special forms of claims are sometimes permitted on an emergency basis. One important situation is where a new composition has been produced, such as a new or modified form of a material, but where the differences from previous forms *cannot* be explained in terms of physical or chemical structure. In that situation, so-called fingerprint claims are sometimes permitted, defining the material in terms of its properties, such as X-ray diffraction patterns, solubility, melting point, etc.[15.1]

One famous example follows, from the Aureomycin patent, Duggar 2,482,055. Claim 1 reads:

> Substances effective in inhibiting the growth of Gram positive and Gram negative bacteria selected from the group consisting of a substance capable of forming salts with acids, containing the elements carbon, hydrogen, nitrogen, chlorine, and oxygen, being very soluble in pyridine, soluble in methanol and in acetone and being slightly soluble in ethanol and in water, its crystals having a refractive index parallel to elongation between about 1.674 and 1.694, and exhibiting characteristic absorption bands in the infra red region of the spectrum when suspended in a hydrocarbon

---

15.1. *See* MPEP 2173.05(t).

oil in solid form at the following frequencies expressed in reciprocal centimeters: 3420, 1643, 1609, 1580, 1523, 1302, 1231, 1209, 1121, 1080, 1050, 969, 943, 867, 844, 825, 805, 794, 788, 733, 713 and the acid salts of said substance.

This was a new chemical compound, but the inventors did not know what the structure was at the time. They described it as to every property known, as well as providing considerable detail in the specification on methods of production with a newly discovered strain of bacteria named *"Streptomyces aureofaciens,"* because it produced the new chemical Aureomycin.

Note that the proper test for this type of claim should be whether it "distinctly claims" the invention under section 112 of the statute. In other words, do the listed properties so uniquely identify the novel composition, as do fingerprints, that they (1) distinguish from old compositions and (2) cover the new composition with sufficient certainty that potential infringers can tell when they have the patented compound and when they do not.

In *Benger Labs, Ltd. v. R.K. Laros Co.,*[16] the court held:

> . . . nothing in the law requires the courts to deny a patent to the inventor of a new and useful product merely because . . . the chemical structure cannot be recognized and described. All that is necessary is that the patentee make as full disclosure as he reasonably can and that he describe the product with sufficient particularity that it can be identified and that those who are interested in its manufacture are enabled to determine what will and what will not infringe.

Claim 1 in question was: "A composition comprising a substantially nonionic complex of ferric hydroxide with a dextran having an average intrinsic viscosity at 25°C. at about 0.025 to about 0.25, said complex being stable in contact with water."[17] The court held that precise enough: "whatever its chemical formula may be, it can be distinguished from both mixtures and compounds."[18]

---

16. Benger Labs, Ltd. v. R.K. Laros Co., 135 U.S.P.Q. (BNA) 11, 14 (E.D. Pa. 1962), *aff'd,* 137 U.S.P.Q. (BNA) 693 (3d Cir. 1963).
17. *Id.,* 135 U.S.P.Q. (BNA) at 13.
18. *Id.,* 135 U.S.P.Q. (BNA) at 14.

In at least some cases, the claim may be simplified by referring to a spectrum shown in a drawing. For example, Donouick *et al.* patent 2,982,689 (May 2, 1961):

> A substance effective in inhibiting the growth of gram-positive bacteria, selected from the group consisting of thiostrepton and the salts thereof, said thiostrepton being
>
> *a weakly basic substance*
>
> *having the following elementary analysis . . . ;*
>
> *has an antibacterial spectrum including . . . ;*
>
> *possesses a crystalline structure in the pure state;*
>
> *is substantially soluble in . . .,*
>
> *and relatively insoluble in . . .;*
>
> *darkens at . . and*
>
> *melts at . . .;*
>
> *has an absorption spectrum . . .;*
>
> *and an infra spectrum when suspended in hydrocarbon oil in*
>
> *solid form substantially as shown in the drawing.*

See section 54 on claims referring to drawings generally, and section 53 on coined name claims. This seems to be a hybrid claim, defining first the coined name and then its distinctive properties, telling what the coined name means.[19]

See also *In re Miller*[20] for an allowable fingerprint claim to polytetrafluoroethylene particles defined by size, molding properties (use), strength, and many other factors. Note this claim is to the form of a product, as a molding compound, not to its chemical composition.[21]

---

19. *See also* Waksman *et al.* patent 2,992,162 (July 1961; Cataldi *et al.* patent 3,015,607 (Jan 2, 1962); PLI THE ART OF DRAFTING PATENT CLAIMS 220–26, 333–35 (J. Jackson & G. Morris eds. 1966) (out of print).
20. *In re* Miller, 169 U.S.P.Q. (BNA) 597 (C.C.P.A. 1971).
21. *See Ex parte* Gring and Mooi, 158 U.S.P.Q. (BNA) 109 (Bd. App. 1967).

§ 53 Coined Name Claims

A somewhat similar form of claim is the "coined name" claim. For example, in Conover patent 2,699,054, claim 2 simply reads "Tetracycline."[22] While this patent has been much in litigation, the form of claim—one word—was not attacked. Tetracycline was alleged to be a new organic molecule (whether or not it was new was part of the dispute), which was identified in the specification as to structure, properties and method of production. Of interest, it was a chlorinated form of Aureomycin discovered in the course of the research that finally determined the structure of Aureomycin. Presumably, the antibiotic tetracycline had become known by that name in the literature, so that the mere name did identify the compound, and drawing the long organic molecule was unnecessary.

Apparently, the Patent and Trademark Office has held that coined name claims are proper only where the name was known to the art before the application was filed. That would be rare.

In *Ex parte Brian,*[23] the Board held that a claim to "An alkali metal salt of gibberellic acid" was improper since the coined name was not art recognized, although defined in the specification.

Citing authority, the Board stated: "Since these claims do not recite the . . . necessary physical and chemical characteristics [as in other "fingerprint" claims] . . . to properly identify the acid, they do not adequately define the invention."[24] Fingerprint claims to the unknown structure were allowed as discussed in section 52. Product-by-process claims (section 46) were rejected because the material could be otherwise defined, i.e., by the fingerprint claims.

It is not clear whether such a claim could be used instead of a fingerprint claim in such a case as Aureomycin, where the structure was unknown at the time, but the name was known. The method claims in the Duggar patent do refer to "A process for the production of Aureomycin," without repeating all the characteristics. Perhaps a coined name claim to an unknown structure, if allowable, would not be as valuable as a fingerprint claim because,

---

22. Its full name is "4-dimethylamino-1, 4a, 5, 5a, 11, 12a-octahydro-3, 6, 10, 12, 12a-pentahydroxy-1, 11-dioxo-2-naphthacenecarboxamide."
23. *Ex parte* Brian, 118 U.S.P.Q. (BNA) 242 (Bd. App. 1958).
24. *Id.,* 118 U.S.P.Q. (BNA) at 245.

from the claim, it would not be clear which of all the properties listed in the specification would be required to infringe the coined name claim, whereas each of the fingerprint claims lists specific key properties that must be met, but not all properties mentioned in the specification. If the claim is to one specific molecule, the number of properties listed would presumably be immaterial because the compound is the same regardless of the number of properties listed.

For fullest protection, the practitioner can use both a fingerprint claim and a coined name claim.

In Altman *et al.* patent 3,382,053 (May 7, 1969), the Office allowed both a coined name claim "A composition of matter comprising beta tantalum" and several fingerprint claims describing the material in terms of its properties and characteristics. The Altman patent involved a new form of the element tantalum of unknown physical structure, but the distinct properties of which could be stated in terms of crystallographic analysis, etc.

In all of these situations, whether or not the structure is unknown, a product-by-process claim might also be proper—as noted in section 46—to define the new material. Note the process would necessarily be different, and almost always unobvious, if a new material were produced. However, such a claim would not necessarily be as valuable as a fingerprint or coined name claim, since the product-by-process claim would cover the material only when made by that process, and there might be other processes to produce the material. Sometimes, fingerprint and product-by-process recitations are combined in a single claim further to identify the material.

As to presenting more than one type of claim to the same material, the board in the *Brian* case, previously discussed in this section, rejected all claims for "undue multiplicity" (sections 61–62), since applicants were attempting to claim the same material three different ways (coined names, fingerprint, and product-by-process). This ruling seems unduly harsh, and should not be proper today.

§ 54 Claims Referring to Drawings

Another example of an emergency situation is a claim referring to a drawing Figure or a table.[24.1] Citing *Ex parte Fressda*,[24.2] the MPEP says such claims are "permitted only in exceptional circumstances where there is no practical way to define the invention in words and where it is more concise to incorporate by reference than duplicating a drawing or table into the claim." Incorporation by reference is a necessity doctrine, not for applicant's convenience. There is no restriction to chemical cases, and it is useful in mechanical, electrical, etc. cases as well as chemical ones.

One example of this comes up in three-element compositions, such as alloys, where the proportions of one element may be varied and the other two may then be varied for each concentration of the first element. This can readily be depicted on a three-element triangular diagram, but is extremely difficult to define in words. Thus, where practical necessity dictates, claims with limitations such as the following have been allowed: "with said manganese content restricted to amounts beneath the curve in the accompanying diagram. . . ."[25] The diagram was a series of curves in a drawing showing maximum amounts of manganese for various amounts of chromium.

Similarly in a process, claim 1 of Stauch patent 3,248,173 (April 26, 1966) reads:

> A process for testing female urine to determine pregnancy which comprises heating in the urine at a pH below 6.5 a paper strip impregnated with a predetermined amount of iodine, the amount of iodine being related to the specific gravity of the urine sample and to the volume thereof in the manner shown on the accompanying graph, to produce a raspberry pink color on said strip indicating pregnancy when the test is positive.

The graph was a three dimensional perspective drawing, depicting operable amounts of iodine as a function of volume and specific gravity.

24.1. MPEP 2173.05(s).

24.2. *Ex parte* Fressda, 27 U.S.P.Q.2d (BNA) 1608, 1609 (Bd. Pat. App. Interf. 1993).

25. *In re* Tanczyn, 97 U.S.P.Q. (BNA) 150 (C.C.P.A. 1953).

In 1961 this doctrine was extended to a mechanical case. In *Ex parte Squires*,[26] the Board of Appeals allowed a claim to "A font of numerals as shown in Fig. 1," reproduced below:

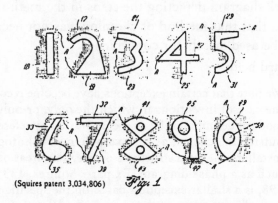

(Squires patent 3,034,806)   *Fig. 1*

As is apparent, it is extremely difficult, probably impossible, to describe the characteristics of the numerals in words.

Applicant alleged that this font was particularly superior to previous numerals in low intensity red light encountered in submarines, which increased the readability of the numerals. That was not denied by the examiner.

The Board found this to be: "the best, most accurate way of defining the invention which depends on . . . the precise configuration of the numerals and their interrelation in a set."[27] Claim 2 of the Squires patent (the only other claim allowed) reads: "In an environment of low brightness of red light, a font of numerals as shown in Fig. 1."

As to what equivalents are covered by such a truly "picture claim," no one may ever know, since it is a United States government patent intended for use in submarines. For further discussion of the principles, see an article by the attorney for Mr. Squires, L. B. Applebaum.[28]

In 1966, the Board of Appeals refused to extend the *Squires* doctrine,[29] holding that it is a doctrine of necessity only, not one

---

26. *Ex parte* Squires, 133 U.S.P.Q. (BNA) 598 (Bd. App. 1961).
27. *Id.*, 133 U.S.P.Q. (BNA) at 600.
28. Applebaum, *The One Line Picture Claim,* 44 J. Pat. Off. Soc'y 379 (1962).
29. *Ex parte* Lewin, 154 U.S.P.Q. (BNA) 487 (Bd. App. 1966).

for applicant's convenience. In *Lewin,* a claim to an electrical method as "The method set forth in Figure 15 of retrieving words from a content-addressed memory" was held improper. Figure 15 was a block diagram depicting the steps in the method. The reasoning was that that method of claiming was not necessary, and could not be used merely for convenience.

The Board held:

> We note that certain exceptions have become recognized in the case of inventions in which the only, or only feasible mode of definition is by an incorporation by reference from outside the claims, as for example microphotographs of metallurgical grain structures or irregular areas of a graph, such as a phase diagram. Ex parte Squires, 133 U.S.P.Q. 598, is a similar exception based on the specific nature of the subject matter of that invention, a font of numerals, which the Board found to be the most accurate way of defining the invention in view of the "poverty of words to properly point out and distinctly claim the invention."

In *Ex parte Gring and Mooi,*[30] the Board permitted reference to the drawing, which was there a photomicrograph submitted pursuant to MPEP 608.02. The Board permits "reference in a claim to a figure of an application drawing where such reference points out with sufficient clarity what could be set forth in words only with prolixity and less clarity."

Summary (Sections 52–54)

In emergency cases involving impossibility of words accurately to define an invention, special techniques may be employed, such as the fingerprint claim (section 52); more rarely, the coined name claim (section 53); or the claim referring to drawings (section 54). These are emergency doctrines only, and normally one has to show there is no other possible or practical way. Normally these are limited to chemical cases, although there is no necessary reason they have to be, as in the "font of type" case.

---

30. *Ex parte* Gring and Mooi, 158 U.S.P.Q. (BNA) 109 (Bd. App. 1967).

§ 55 [Reserved]

§ 56 Use Claims and New Use Claims; Preamble Limitations

One may not simply claim a new use for an existing object or composition, by stating the object or composition and then stating its use.[31] Two examples of improper "use" claims appear in the Manual: "A process for using monoclonal antibodies of claim 4 to isolate and purify . . . interferon" and the "The use of a[n] . . . iron alloy . . . as a vehicle brake part subject to stress by sliding friction." Use claims are common in patents in other countries. A product or process is recited in one claim. Another dependent claim then recites the use of the product or process for a stated purpose, or something does not even state the purpose. This is indefinite and nonstatutory under § 101 or § 112.[31.1]

A new use claim is instead a process of using the object or composition or process, which includes steps in the process. The claimed process must be directed to a new use. If the claimed new use is only a newly discovered result of a known process directed to the same purpose, it is not a patentable new use, as it is inherent in the known process.[31.2]

At least until 1969, standard textbook law and routine Patent Office rulings were that one could not rely for novelty on a statement of intended use in the preamble of a composition claim, sometimes called a "label claim."

For example, if the zinc-electroplating solution of claim 11 (section 49) were old for some other (and, it was hoped, unrelated) purpose, the label "a zinc electroplating solution" would not render the claim to the old material patentable. Instead, one would need to employ a "new use" claim, which is nothing more than an ordinary method claim, the main difference being that the novel

---

31. MPEP 2173.05(q).
31.1. *Id.*
31.2. Bristol-Myers Squibb Co. v. Ben Venue Laboratories, Inc., 246 F.3d 1368, 58 U.S.P.Q.2d (BNA) 1508, 1514 (Fed. Cir. 2001) (Bristol claimed the result of an infusion in cancer patients, the same purpose as previously, treating cancer); *In re* May, 574 F.2d 1082, 1090, 197 U.S.P.Q. (BNA) 601, 607 (C.C.P.A. 1978).

feature is not, or need not be, in the manipulative steps of the method. Rather, the novelty may reside in the use of the old composition for a new purpose. Such a claim might read:

> 13.   A method of electroplating zinc, which comprises the step of electrolyzing a solution comprising:
>
> (a)   an aqueous solution of zinc acetate, from 30 to 90 grams per liter;
>
> (b)   citric acid, from 1.5 to 3 times the zinc acetate concentration; and
>
> (c)   an alkaline pH-modifying substance in an amount sufficient to adjust the pH to a value of from 4 to 5.5.

Note that this claim recites the same composition defined in claim 11, but the invention is now phrased as a method. The test of patentability becomes obviousness of the new use, since a novel process is defined. Even though the only manipulative step, "electrolyzing," is notoriously old, the novelty of a process step may reside in the material being treated as well as in the nature of the step itself (see section 42). If the composition were previously used as a cleaning solution, it presumably would be unobvious to employ it as an electroplating solution.

The doctrine that one cannot claim an old material as a composition by stating an intended new use in the preamble has sometimes been stated as being that one cannot patent a new use for an old material. That is misleading because new uses have long been patentable as methods; in fact many method claims inherently involve new uses for old materials. Since 1952, the statute (35 U.S.C. § 100(b)) has expressly covered this by stating that the word "process" includes "a new use of a known process, machine, manufacture, composition of matter, or material."[32]

As another example of a new use for an old material, the method of treating polyethylene of claim 5 (section 42) is also a new use claim if the treating solution (sodium dichromate and sulfuric acid) is known for other uses, such as cleaning test tubes.

---

32. *See* Gottchalk, *The Term "Process" Includes a New Use,* 40 J. PAT. OFF. SOC'Y 451 (1958); Hewitt, *The New Use Patent,* 51 J. PAT. OFF. SOC'Y 634 (1969).

Although the statute expressly refers to new uses for old materials, etc., a new use for a new material is equally patentable as a process under standard interpretation of the term "process." In other words, as far as a process claim, such as claim 13, is concerned, it matters not whether the material is old or new. For the composition claim, such as claim 11, the composition per se must be novel under conventional tests.

Where the new use is properly claimed as a process, the claim must be written as a normal process or method claim (see sections 36–37), including steps or acts. In *Clinical Products, Ltd. v. Brenner*,[33] an attempted hybrid claim to "the use of X (an old chemical) as a Y (use)" was held improper as not a true process claim. A proper method claim would have been: "the process of (doing thing Y), which comprises administering (compound X) to the body (or object in question)."

Under statute 35 U.S.C. § 100(b), there can be a patentable new use for every class of invention. Thus, for a new use for a known process, a claim might read:

> A process for [the new use] comprising [performing the known step(s)] on a [previously unselected, different, known object, but unobvious to select that object].

For a new use for a known machine, manufacture, composition or matter or material, a claim might read:

> A process for [the new use] of a [the known machine, manufacture, composition or material] comprising [performing one or a series including at least one previously unselected step, whether that step is known or unknown as a step, but unobvious to select that step] on [a workpiece] [or] for [accomplishing a specified objective, possibly relating back to the new use].

The following text discusses claiming a known product with a new use in other than method claim form.

Perhaps the leading case on the "new use" product claim is *In re Thuau*[34] in which the court held that a claim to a therapeutic agent, which was an old compound for tanning, was not patent-

---

33. Clinical Products, Ltd. v. Brenner, 149 U.S.P.Q. (BNA) 475 (D.D.C. 1966).
34. *In re* Thuau, 57 U.S.P.Q. (BNA) 324 (C.C.P.A. 1943).

able as a compound. A typical claim read: "A new therapeutic product for the treatment of diseased tissue, comprising a condensation product of metacresolsulfonic acid condensed through an aldehyde." Method claims were not involved or mentioned in the decision. This case led to the "rule" that "a new use of an old compound, without modification, is not patentable," meaning as a composition. How much "modification" is needed is a subject of much controversy, and many cases have appeared on the details. For example, is it enough to:

1. **Add a carrier or a solvent?** Generally, no, unless perhaps some particular solvent cooperates specially with the composition.[35] Note also the Müller DDT claim discussed later in this section.

In *Ex parte Douros and Vanderweff,*[36] the Board considered a claim to:

> A composition for use as an effective algaecide which comprises . . . [a named compound] dissolved in a solvent selected from the group consisting of water, ethyl alcohol and mixtures of water and ethyl alcohol.

The compound was held obvious over the art, but the use was not. With respect to the solvent, the Board held: "It is clearly obvious to add a carrier or a solvent to an unpatentable compound, [citing many cases]." With respect to the statement of use, it held: "The recital in the claims of the intended use of the composition does not patentably distinguish it from an aqueous solution thereof. *In re Sinex* . . . 135 U.S.P.Q. 302."[37]

In *Ex parte Billman,*[38] claim 24 read:

> A plant stimulant composition containing as an essential active ingredient . . . [X chemical] in a water soluble diluent selected from the class consisting of . . . [generally old materials] . . . in the proportions of 10 to 20 grams for each pound. . . .

35. *In re* Rosicky, 125 U.S.P.Q. (BNA) (C.C.P.A. 1960).
36. *Ex parte* Douros and Vanderweff, 163 U.S.P.Q. (BNA) 667 (Bd. App. 1968).
37. *Id.,* 163 U.S.P.Q. (BNA) at 668.
38. *Ex parte* Billman, 71 U.S.P.Q. (BNA) 253 (Bd. App. 1946).

X chemical was old for other (unstated) purposes, selection of the solvent apparently was trivial, and the proportions were not alleged to be critical (nor probably were they). The claim was rejected as a direct consequence of *Thuau*. One could not, at least in 1946, avoid the *Thuau* doctrine by adding obvious limitations so as to define a technically novel chemical composition.

> 2. **Make the material into a tablet or capsule; (the so-called dosage-form claims)?** Probably not if the tablet is the pure material, but if the dosage form requires a particular unobvious concentration of the pharmaceutical, effective for a certain disease, then, often, yes.

In re Craige[39] considered:

> 13. A veterinary antihelminthic [tapeworm killer] composition containing an essential active ingredient [X, an old chemical] and a solid carrier therefor and in the form of a compressed tablet.

The court held that (1) the label was no help under *Thuau*, which was merely a "restatement of the well established rule 'that a patent for a new use for an old substance quite unchanged is not authorized.' . . ."; (2) adding a carrier, making into a tablet, or doing both was not inventive:

> While it is true that in certain cases invention might be present in a very slight alteration and the *Thuau* doctrine avoided, such alteration must always amount to more then mechanical or professional skill.

In *In re Halleck*,[40] however, the court allowed a claim to "an improved *growth stimulating* composition for animals which comprises an animal feed and *an effective amount* of [old compounds] contained therein for *growth stimulation*." Other than the *italicized* phrases, the mixture was old.

All of this has been very confusing and involves hypertechnical consideration of apparent flyspecks.

---

39. *In re* Craige, 90 U.S.P.Q. (BNA) 33 (C.C.P.A. 1951).
40. *In re* Halleck, 164 U.S.P.Q. (BNA) 647 (C.C.P.A. 1970).

In 1967, the C.C.P.A. cast grave doubt on the entire basis of the *Thuau* doctrine. In *In re Duva*,[41] the court held that one could not ignore the preamble limitation, "a composition *for* chemically depositing gold," and that *all* statements in the claim must be considered in determining obviousness.

The court stated:

> Thus, all *factual* differences which may be properly noted in any portion of a claim must be included within the basis for comparison with the prior art if we are to properly evaluate the *differences* between the invention defined in a claim and the teaching of a reference. The command of 35 U.S.C. section 103 is to compare the invention *as a whole* with the prior art. Absent a failure of the applicant to comply with 35 U.S.C. section 112, we think every portion of the appealed claims must be considered in determining the invention as a whole in arriving at our decision as to obviousness required by a rejection under section 103.[42]

See also *In re Miller*[43] and *In re Wilson*,[44] cited in section 23, to the effect that "*All words* in a claim must be considered in judging the patentability of that claim . . ." Although those cases arose in other contexts (indefiniteness, etc.), the quoted language fits exactly with the *Duva* case, and should be applicable in many situations. In *Union Carbide v. Filtrol*,[45] the district court expressly followed the *Duva* case and held that "non-obviousness of novel compositions requires consideration of limitations in the preambles of the claims." The claims in question were not quoted.[46]

As to the materiality of preamble limitations generally, prior to the *Duva* case, that was a matter of great confusion. No one could say with any degree of certainty whether a particular preamble limitation was to be counted or not, and the test might be different

---

41. For additional discussion of these specific problems, *see* Fellner, *Method Claims for New Use and Their Enforcement*, 41 J. Pat. Off. Soc'y 54 (1968). For detailed discussion of problems in pharmaceutical practice, *see* Wolk, *Pharmaceutical Patent Practice*, in Calvert, Encyclopedia of Patent Practice 622 (1964).
42. *In re* Duva, 156 U.S.P.Q. (BNA) 90 (C.C.P.A. 1967).
43. *Id.*, 156 U.S.P.Q. (BNA) at 94.
44. *In re* Wilson, 169 U.S.P.Q. (BNA) 597 (C.C.P.A. 1971).
45. Union Carbide v. Filtrol, 165 U.S.P.Q. (BNA) 494 (C.C.P.A. 1970).
46. 170 U.S.P.Q. (BNA) 482 (C.D. Cal. 1971).

depending on whether the applicant/patentee wanted the words counted to make the claim patentable, or ignored so as to copy someone else's claim for interference, or to catch an infringer.[47]

In *Union Carbide*, the body of the claim also contained some novelty, so it might not have been necessary for the court to throw out, if it did, that ancient doctrine. In view of this case, the future of "label-claims" is uncertain. It might be dangerous to rely on any silent overruling of the old *Thuau* doctrine. Thus, it is recommended that claims of the various types permitted, i.e., product, process, new use, be sought.

Suppose one were permitted simply to claim: "An insecticide comprising . . . [DDT],"[48] DDT being known for other uses. When another party merely makes DDT, it *is* an insecticide comprising DDT, but this cannot be an infringement because DDT is old. It might be difficult to tell when infringement arises. Is it when sold to a farmer in a bottle labelled DDT, but with no instruction as to what to do with it? Would whoever put a label "insecticide" on the bottle be an infringer?

The DDT patent, finally Reissue 22,922, was involved in a second application for reissue in *Ex parte Müller*[49] before the Board of Appeals. At issue were new use claims sought for the first time in the second reissue application, such as claim 5:

> The method of killing insects which comprises dissolving the chemical compound [DDT] in a solvent liquid and spraying the liquid so as to bring the [DDT] into contact with the insects.[50]

This claim and a somewhat broader one were allowed as proper new use method claims. The original and first reissue claims were for "A contact insecticide composition comprising" a similar composition, the scope being narrowed in the first reissue. After the first reissue, the patentee learned that the composition was old, in an obscure thesis at the University of Basel, Switzerland, use as an insecticide not being suggested. The Board held that that

---

47. *See In re* Stencel, 4 U.S.P.Q.2d (BNA) 1071, 1073 (Fed. Cir. 1987).
48. The broadest label claim, claim 4, actually reads: "A contact insecticide comprising the chemical compound . . . [DDT] in an aqueous emulsion."
49. *Ex parte* Müller, 81 U.S.P.Q. (BNA) 261 (Bd. App. 1948).
50. *Id.*, 81 U.S.P.Q. (BNA) at 261.

was a proper reason for reissue, since the product claims were doubtful at best. Interestingly, the product claims were not rejected, although one concurring Board member would have taken them away under the *Thuau* case.

The object of the claim drafter in these cases should be to get as many different types of claims as possible. For example, in Buzas *et al.* patent 2,827,418 (Mar. 18, 1958), claim 2 covers a new compound per se (but this might be found in obscure prior art); claim 3 is to an intermediate (which could be unobvious if the compound turns out to be old); claim 4 is for the process of making the intermediate (in case that material turns out to be old, the process might not be); claim 6 is for an injectable preparation containing a certain amount of the compound of claim 2 in water; and claim 7 is for a tablet containing the required dose (0.15 gram) of the compound of claim 2. Any of these different claims, as well as use claims, might be very important, depending on prior art later developed and on the court's feelings about the *Thuau* case and extensions to composition and dosage form claims.

Note that the method new use claims are usually far less desirable, and in many cases may be worthless, because the patentee, to enforce the patent, would usually have to sue each individual farmer, doctor, etc., which would normally be impractical. Those users are usually also the customers of the patentee. And who wants to sue a customer?[51] However, the possibilities of also suing the supplier of a dedicated component or material having no substantial noninfringing use as a contributory infringer or suing the supplier for inducing the customer's infringement of the new use claim should be explored as a particular fact pattern develops.

It is interesting to note that the "new use" doctrine has been held not to apply to cases where the use results in a technically novel article of manufacture. This "technical novelty" doctrine was promulgated chiefly by Judge Learned Hand in *Traitel Marble Co. v. Hungerford Brass & Copper Co.*[52] and *Old Town Ribbon & Carbon Co. v. Columbia Ribbon Mfg. Co.*[53] Those cases

---

51. 18 F.2d 66, 68 (2d Cir. 1927).
52. Traitel Marble Co. v. Hungerford Brass & Copper Co., 72 U.S.P.Q. (BNA) 57, 60 (2d Cir. 1947).
53. *See* Kropa v. Robie and Mahlman, 88 U.S.P.Q. (BNA) 478 (C.C.P.A. 1951); *In re* Stencel, 4 U.S.P.Q.2d (BNA) 1071, 1073 (Fed. Cir. 1987).

hold that, as long as there is *any* structural change, the patentable concept can reside in the realization of the new use in the new article, claimed in a claim directed to that article.

§ 57 Improvement or "*Jepson*-Type" Claims

A *Jepson* claim recites all or some of the elements of a known article, process, composition, or combination in the preamble to the claim, includes a transition that states "wherein the improvement comprises" or "the combination with the old article, etc., of," and recites in the body of the claim only the new or modified elements, or tells there of new forms of connection or cooperation between old elements, i.e., recites the improvement. Such claims are frequently used where there is an improvement in one or more elements of an otherwise old and unchanged combination, or where one or more new elements are added to an old combination.[54] This type of claim should avoid or help avoid an "old combination" rejection (see section 63).

These types of claims are frequently used in some European country patent applications and are required in some countries. Where this type of claim is used, the preamble relates all elements and relationships in common with the closest reference. U.S. rule 75(e) states:

> Where the nature of the case admits, as in the case of an improvement, any independent claim *should* contain in the following order, (1) a preamble comprising a general description of all the elements or steps of the claimed combination which are conventional or known, (2) a phrase such as "wherein the improvement comprises," and (3) those elements, steps and/or relationships which constitute that portion of the claimed combination which the applicant considers as the new or improved portion. (Emphasis added.)

The word "should" was apparently meant to be strong urging, but not mandatory. At a hearing on the proposed rule, the Assis-

---

54. *See* Wells Mfg. Corp. v. Littelfuse Inc., 192 U.S.P.Q. (BNA) 256 (7th Cir. 1976); Johns Manville Corp. v. Guardian Indus. Corp., 221 U.S.P.Q. (BNA) 319 (E.D. Mich. 1983).

tant Commissioner stated that it was not intended as compulsory. Although the Patent and Trademark Office recommends that "*Jepson*-type" claims be used, they are still seen infrequently in United States patents and applications and examiners seldom, if ever, object to their absence. Further, they tend to focus too much attention on too few features, and de-emphasize that a typical invention is a combination of cooperating elements. The more usual claim form makes the combination protection clearer. Also, at a later time, the patentee may realize that some other feature in the claim or some unnoted interactions among elements have inventive significance. The *Jepson* format may have precluded reliance upon these.[55]

The danger of a *Jepson* format is that "the preamble elements in a *Jepson*-type claim . . . are impliedly admitted to be old in the art, but it is only an implied admission."[56] That implication can be overcome by appropriate explanation, e.g., *Jepson* format was used to avoid double patenting.[57]

In *In re Bernhart,*[58] the *Jepson* format was considered optional with no mention of rule 75(e).[59] See further discussion in section 63.

The original *Jepson* claim[60] was:

> [16.]   *In an* electrical system of distribution of the class wherein a variable speed generator charges a storage battery and when the battery becomes sufficiently charged a voltage coil becomes effective to regulate the generator for constant potential, *the combination with* said voltage coil *of* a coil traversed by current flowing to the battery which is acted upon by decreasing the battery current to

---

55. *See* Medtronic, Inc. v. Cardiac Pacemakers, Inc., 220 U.S.P.Q. (BNA) 97, 110 (Fed. Cir. 1983); Biuro Projektor v. UOP, Inc., 203 U.S.P.Q. (BNA) 175 (N.D. Ill. 1979).

56. *In re* Ehrenreich, 200 U.S.P.Q. (BNA) 504, 510 (C.C.P.A. 1979).

57. MPEP 2129.

58. *In re* Bernhart, 163 U.S.P.Q. (BNA) 611 (C.C.P.A. 1969).

59. *But cf.* Dollar Elec. Co. v. Syndevco, Inc., 205 U.S.P.Q. (BNA) 949, 955 (E.D. Mich. 1979), *aff'd,* 214 U.S.P.Q. (BNA) 241 (6th Cir. 1982); *see also* D. CHISUM, PATENTS section 8.06[1][c] (1978 & Supp. 1986).

60. *Ex parte* Jepson, 243 Off. Gaz. Pat. Off. 525 (Ass't Comm'r 1917).

reduce the potential maintained constant by the voltage coil. [Emphasis added.]

Generalized, the original *Jepson* form is "In a _____ having [old elements A, B, C] the combination with [A] *of* [new element D]." Under Rule 75(e), the words "the combination with" might be replaced with "wherein the improvement comprises combining a coil . . ." Note that the new element is defined both as to structure and how it cooperates with the old element A, B, or C to accomplish a useful result.

Various other formats (known as "*Jepson*-type") are permissible, no magic words being necessary. One suitable and straightforward form follows: "In combination with an [A] of the type wherein [conventional elements B and C are provided for doing something], the improvement which comprises. . . ."

The new or modified elements then follow as in any other claim, related structurally and functionally both to each other and to the elements in the preamble.

There are three distinctive parts of the *Jepson* claim, the preamble, the formatted transition phrase and the body of the claim. The preamble may begin with the same preamble as a usual claim, naming the subject of the invention. However, there are two preferred alternatives to tell the reader it is a *Jepson*-type claim. The first starts with the word "In" followed by the name of the subject of the claim, as in claim 16, above. The second starts with the words "An improved" followed again by the name of the subject of the claim; as in claim 17, below. The transition phrase would be worded to make good English usage with the preamble words. It is advantageous to work the word "combination" into the preamble somewhere, where appropriate and not awkward in the claim. That is because rule 75(e) expressly mentions "combination."

There is sometimes an issue as to whether a claim preamble is considered an element of the claim.[61] But in a *Jepson* claim, the preamble defines not only the context of the invention, but also its scope. Therefore, a preamble limitation is considered a claim element.[62]

---

61. *See* MPEP 2111.02; section 6.
62. Rowe v. Dror, 42 U.S.P.Q.2d (BNA) 1550, 1553 (Fed. Cir. 1997).

The transition phrase is suggested in the specific language from rule 75(e)—"wherein the improvement comprises"— for example, "An improved A of the type having a B and a C, wherein the improvement comprises. . . ." Other possibilities for a transition phrase include: "In a machine of the type having . . ., the improvement which comprises: . . ." or even "A machine having [old elements named], charcterized in that: . . ." It is recommended that the word "improvement" be included in the transition phrase to avoid objection for non-compliance with rule 75(e).

In European country applications, including claims separating prior art elements from the inventive contribution by a transition phrase, the transition phrase is usually translated into English as something like "characterized in that" or "characterized by comprising." The "characterized" form is acceptable in the United States although not very commonly used. This language is frequently objected to by examiners, but the original claim form can be retained through substituting a more typical *Jepson* claim language transition phrase.

Except when the "characterized" form is used, the body of the *Jepson* claim starts after the transition word "comprises" or "comprising" as in normal United States claims. Thus, that magic word is a code word or trigger, telling the reader where the allegedly novel part of the claim starts. For this reason, it is recommended that the word "comprising" not be used in the *Jepson* preamble; instead use "having," "including," or the like in the preamble. For example, "An improved A comprising B and C, wherein the improvement comprises D" could be confusing.

For a specific example, consider again the barrel takeup of example II, but assume this time that all of the elements shown in the drawing are quite old and well known. Assume that the client's only invention is in the addition of the detector, cutter and accumulator of claim 15, section 11.

A *Jepson*-type claim to the improved combination might read as follows:

17.   An improved strand-collecting apparatus of the type in which an advancing strand is collected in a barrel mounted on a rotating turntable, and in which a reciprocating strand guide is positioned

above the barrel to guide the advancing strand into the barrel, wherein the improvement comprises:

(a)   means for detecting when a predetermined amount of strand has been collected in the barrel;

(b)   a cutter, operated by the detecting means, for severing the strand when a predetermined amount has been collected; and

(c)   an accumulator, operated by the detecting means, for accumulating the strand after it has been severed.

It should be noted that the body of this claim is identical with that of dependent claim 15, the only difference being in the preambles. It is a significant difference. In claim 15, the client invented both the basic system of claim 2 and the photocell system of dependent claim 15, whereas in claim 17 the client invented only the photocell as an improvement on the basic system.

Note that the preparation of the body of a *Jepson*-type claim is very similar to a dependent claim, except that the part that would be the parent claim is the preamble of the *Jepson*-type claim rather than a different claim.

The Patent and Trademark Office interpretation of these claims is set out in MPEP 608.01(m):

> The form of claim required in rule 75(e) is particularly adapted for the description of improvement type inventions. It is to be considered a combination claim. The preamble of this form of claim is considered to positively and clearly include all the elements or steps recited therein as a part of the claimed combination.

With this description of the entire claim as being a combination, there should be no objection per se to the body of the claim comprising a single means element, as mentioned in section 33.

Also, in *Jepson*-type claims, there is less need to tie the preamble elements together as described in section 27, as long as the elements of the body are adequately tied to each other *and to* the preamble elements with which they cooperate. However, a bald preamble catalog is not recommended as sound practice. (See section 64 on aggregation.)

While the foregoing example relates to a machine claim, *Jepson*-type claims may also be used for methods, articles of manufacture, and compositions.

An example of a method:

> 18.   In a method of collecting an advancing strand in a barrel, of the type wherein the advancing strand is guided into the barrel and the barrel is rotated to vary the point of collection circularly with respect to the bottom of the barrel, the improvement comprising:
>
> reciprocating the guide point back and forth above the barrel so that the point of collection varies radially with respect to the bottom of the barrel.

Note that this claim covers the same combination as claim 4, chapter IV, except that two of the elements of claim 4, acknowledged to be old, have been put in the preamble.

A composition of matter:

> 19.   An improved zinc-electroplating solution of the type containing an aqueous solution of zinc acetate, from 30 to 90 grams per liter; citric acid, from 1.5 to 3 times the zinc acetate concentration; and an alkaline pH modifying substance in an amount sufficient to adjust the pH to a value of from 4 to 5.5, wherein the improvement comprises:
>
> 0.5 to 1 gram per liter of boric acid.

Note that the preamble of this claim is identical in scope to claim 11, section 49, with added material.

Summary

Use Jepson-*type claims for improvement-type inventions, where new or modified elements are added to an otherwise old and unchanged combination. Describe the old elements from the closest single reference in the preamble. Usually the old things can be described fairly broadly. Describe the new or modified elements in the body of the claim after a transition such as "wherein the improvement comprises," or "the improvement comprising." Connect or relate the new elements to each other and to the preamble elements, as with any other claim, particularly in mechanical combination (machine) claims as outlined in chapter II.*

§ 58 Generic and Species Claim

In some inventions, there are two or more alternative and mutually exclusive embodiments of the invention; that is, where two or more different structures, steps, parts or compounds, called "species," may be used interchangeably to accomplish a desired result.[63] Examples of this are the legs and springs in Figures 2 and 3 of Example I (Appendix A), which may generically be referred to as "a support"; the copper, silver, or aluminum stripe of the resistor in section 50, which may be generically referred to as "a conductive stripe" or even "a stripe"; the separation of alcohol from a water solution by fractional distillation or by solvent extraction in section 37, which may be generically recited as "separating."

A generic claim is one that defines the element in question with sufficient breadth to cover all of the species claimed, which is also usually all of the disclosed species, and often also covers additional undisclosed species (see MPEP 806.04(d)), while the species claims cover the separate embodiments one at a time. There may be subgeneric claims that cover some, but not all, of the species. Note that, if no allowable generic claim is presented, a requirement for restriction among disclosed species is likely, called "election of species."[64] After election, all claims readable on the species are examined. The ones not elected are not examined, but may be made the subjects of divisional applications. However, if a generic claim is eventually found allowable, the restriction requirement is typically withdrawn. Therefore, the practitioner should not be concerned about whether a claim is a generic or species claim. Just

---

63. *See* MPEP 806.04(a)-(j).
64. 35 U.S.C. § 121; rules 141, 142, 146.

write claims seeking the broadest scope of protection that the disclosed invention and the prior art will allow. Some claims should also be broad enough to cover all species, if possible.

If no concrete generic word is apparent, a means-plus-function clause may be appropriate to provide a generic expression, as outlined in section 34. In all technologies, but particularly chemical cases, a *Markush* group is always a generic expression of the listed members of the group, as discussed in section 50. Of course, alternative expressions cannot be used to make a generic claim, as set out in section 24, except under the *Markush* practice in section 50.

There is no special form for drafting generic and species claims. The species claims may be either dependent or independent, although the dependent claim form is especially useful and common in this situation. The practitioner makes an element of the generic claim more specific in one way for species I and in a different way for species II.

The words genus and species, in most cases, have significance relative to a particular set of claims; a generic expression (electrically conductive *metals*) may be a species of a more generic expression (electrically conductive *materials,* which also includes carbon). The words genus and species in patent law can be totally arbitrary. The breakdowns are made in whatever way suits the invention. Some species, which cannot practically be further divided (sodium chloride) are referred to as "ultimate species." In mechanical cases, there would theoretically never be an ultimate species, because an element (a spring, for example) could be a species of biasing means, but would be generic to particular kinds of springs (coil springs, leaf springs), and each of these could be further defined in parallel, mutually exclusive ways.

These distinctions are not too significant as far as writing claims is concerned. They relate primarily to the question of whether one can obtain one patent (with an allowable generic claim) or several patents (in most cases where no allowable generic claim is presented).

Summary

Generic claims cover two or more mutually exclusive species, A or B, and possibly also C or D, etc., not all of which may be disclosed. Claims to the individual species cover less than the whole group of things, either one at a time, or less than all at one time. There are no special problems in writing such claims. Such claims may come up in any statutory class of utility invention: machine, process, article of manufacture, or composition of matter.

§ 59 Combination and Subcombination

Thus far, we have been considering primarily combination claims; that is, claims to complete machines, processes, manufactures, etc. A subcombination is some element or group of elements that forms a part of the main combination (MPEP 806.05(a)). A subcombination includes fewer elements than the combination of which the subcombination may be a part. Hence, the subcombination claim is broader than the combination, as it includes fewer elements and limits. If the subcombination has utility by itself, it may be separately claimed, although restriction between the two claimed inventions, combination and subcombination, and election of inventions will often be required if the combination is also claimed. (See MPEP 806.05(c) as to requirement for restriction between combination and subcombination.) Subcombinations usually relate to machines, but may also be present in methods, compositions, or articles of manufacture.

As one example, the details of construction of the accumulator used with the barrel take-up arrangement of claim 17 of section 57 would comprise such a subcombination. If new, it could be separately claimed. Such a subcombination claim might start out: "Apparatus for accumulating an advancing strand, which comprises: . . ."

Note that, in that case, the subcombination is a complete mechanism or machine in itself, serving its own function, but which would always be used with other machines to make a combination machine.

Restriction would probably be required since the subcombination may obviously be used in other combinations and is separately classified (see MPEP 806.05(c)).

Other examples of subcombinations are a carburetor for a car, and such other major subassemblies as tires, headlights, etc. A subcombination method might be a method of accumulating strand in a take-up method, or a method of separating chemical X from Y as a part of a complete process for making Z, wherein X is a byproduct and useful to be recovered. In a composition, a subcombination might be a new compound per se, useful in killing insects, while a combination would be an insecticide containing the new compound with other materials.

Note that subcombination claims of this sort offer no special problems in claim drafting.

Another common format for subcombination claims is: "In an apparatus for doing something, an A, a B, and a C."

Note that, as written, this type of claim is an exception to the general "rule" about having a transition word or phrase between the preamble and the body (section 7). But it is preferred to include a standard transition word. Also, in this type of claim, it is less important to list all elements necessary to make a complete combination, since by definition the claim need only be to some part of the combination.

The author is not certain how far one can go in drafting fragmentary "In a" claims, covering only certain portions of a combination, where less than a complete functional subcombination is claimed. In his experience, such claims have been rejected as "incomplete" (section 66) or lacking in utility in that they would lack sufficient structure to themselves make a complete combination, machine or process, etc. Elements from the full combination may be added to the subcombination claim until a complete structure is claimed. Alternatively, the claim preamble may be modified to name the subcombination, rather than the combination of which the subcombination is a part.

Another format combines the subcombination with a *Jepson* approach (section 57): "An improved A for an X-type system having old elements Y and Z, wherein the improved A comprises: . . ." (for example: "An improved accumulator for a strand-collecting apparatus of the type having a barrel . . ., wherein the improved accumulator comprises: . . .").

See further discussion in section 63 on old combinations, and the claim involved in *In re Rohrbacher and Kolbe*.[65] That discussion is to the effect that a claim to "a cooling liquid pump *for* engines" of a certain type, is properly a subcombination claim to the pump.

See also *In re Dean*,[66] to the effect that a claim to "in a camera having . . ., a shutter-timing apparatus . . . comprising:" is a proper subcombination claim to the timer, not an (allegedly old) combination of the timer and a shutter. See also section 56 on new uses and preamble limitations generally.

A claim that might fit a definition of a subcombination was instead held to be for a combination. The claim in *In re Allen*,[67] read: "A waler bracket for concrete wall forms . . . comprising: a metal bracket . . ." The claim was held to be a bracket, which is an element of a combination, and not a subcombination. The court said: "The bracket is a single integral entity whose shape is defined, rather than a combination of parts which is the usual nature of a subcombination."[68] Not much turns on this, except for the issue of restriction and election of claims (MPEP 806.05(a), (c)).

With respect to applicant's right to obtain subcombination claims, see *Special Equipment Co. v. Coe*,[69] discussed further in section 66 on incomplete claims.

Summary

Subcombination claims cover parts or portions of a complete combination or system, where the subcombination has utility in itself. There are no special problems in writing such claims, and they may be necessary in some cases to avoid an old combination rejection.

---

65. *In re* Rohrbacher and Kolbe, 128 U.S.P.Q. (BNA) 117 (C.C.P.A. 1960).
66. *In re* Dean, 130 U.S.P.Q. (BNA) 107 (C.C.P.A. 1961).
67. *In re* Allen, 145 U.S.P.Q. (BNA) 147 (C.C.P.A. 1965).
68. *Id.*, 145 U.S.P.Q. (BNA) at 149.
69. Special Equipment Co. v. Coe, 64 U.S.P.Q. (BNA) 525 (U.S. 1945).

VII

Claims of Varying Scope

§ 60 In General

In drafting claims of varying scope, whether dependent or independent claims are used, the claim drafter should make certain that there is "a mere difference in scope" between the claims (MPEP 706.03(k)). Significant differences in scope are not required. But if two claims are so close that they cover the same thing, despite different wording, one can be rejected. This usually does not occur if there are only "a few" claims. Of course, the differences between the claims need not amount to patentable differences, but they should be as substantial as the situation permits and related to the areas of novelty. Such practice ordinarily makes the problems of duplicate or redundant claims (section 61) and undue multiplicity of claims (section 62) fairly easy to avoid. Dependent claims also help in that regard.

The narrowest claim is usually a sound "picture claim," which should probably recite by name all of the significant structure disclosed, omitting only the nuts and bolts. This should describe the commercially most effective way to carry out the invention, including all preferred conditions.

This not only protects against the copyist, but, wherever possible, it is desirable to assert a narrow claim against an alleged infringer, because such a claim is harder to invalidate either on newly discovered prior art or on formal grounds (too broad, etc.). Furthermore, the narrowest scope claim is more likely allowable than the broadest, so that you will initially be presenting and obtaining some patent protection.

The narrowest claim should be fairly easy to write if the structure and operation are understood. The broad claims are the most difficult to prepare, in that the claim drafter must analyze the structure, pick out its essential elements, and decide how broadly to state them. Intermediate claims should be fairly easy to prepare in that some significant elements or details of construction are either added to a broad claim or omitted from a narrow claim. Although there is no prohibition against a dependent claim adding only prior art features, there may be little value to including such a claim. However, if it covers a preferred commercial design you want to specifically protect, then such a dependent claim has some value.

Any one of the claims may be written first, whichever seems easiest. Different practitioners advocate different methods of beginning. Perhaps a flexible approach is best: if the claim drafter has a clear idea for a broad claim, he should start with that; if not, he should simply write *a claim* and work it over. Having any claim done helps one think of variations. Then elements may be (1) added or described in more detail to make a narrower claim, or (2) omitted, combined or broadened to make a broader claim. It is probably best if at least several, if not all, claims are prepared before starting to write the remainder of the specification, because then the specification can better be written to point out the claimed invention, and the words in the claim will naturally find clear support in the remainder of the specification (see section 18).

While it is important to provide at least mere differences between the claims, the terminology and form should be as consistent as possible except where the differences occur. Do not give the same part different names in two successive claims, except intentionally to change the scope of the claim. However, beware of a common limitation in all claims. If there is one, make certain that it is absolutely essential to patentability.

With respect to preferred numbering and order of multiple claims, refer to section 5, numbering and order.

See also the discussion in section 11, that there need be no one head claim, or dominating claim in the application. One is entitled to claim every possibly novel combination, subcombination, method, apparatus, etc., that one wants to, subject only to restriction practice that one might have to get two patents instead of a single patent.

Summary

Present a "reasonable" number of claims, given the nature and scope of the invention over the prior art. This varies widely from case to case. Avoid extra claims adding only things old in the art. The narrowest claim or claims should be quite detailed, including all significant structure, both to clearly catch copyist infringers and also to try to get some claims allowed on the first Office action. In that case, you will then be arguing only allowable scope of the invention, not whether or not it is patentable.

§ 60A Claiming Different Classes of Invention in One Patent

Section 3 hereof identifies the four statutory classes of inventions which may be claimed, process, machine, [article of] manufacture or composition of matter.

Each of the classes of invention should be the subject of a separate claim, to the extent that the invention encompasses several classes of claims.[1] An application may have any or all of each of the different classes of claims. Never mix claim types to different classes of invention in a single claim.[2] An apparatus claim covers what a device is, while a method claim covers what a device does.[3] They are different. Avoid method limits in a product claim, except in the correct way of describing some element for perfoming a particular function and in a "whereby" (necessary result of the structure or process claimed) clause. Avoid product limits in a method claim, except where the method involves a workpiece which is being described or the method describes operating some means to act on the workpiece.

---

1. *Ex parte* Lyell, 17 U.S.P.Q.2d 1548 (Bd. Pat. App. & Interferences 1990).
2. *Ex parte* Lyell, *supra.*
3. Hewlett-Packard Co. v. Bausch & Lomb, Inc., 909 F.2d 1464, 15 U.S.P.Q.2d 1525 (Fed. Cir. 1990).

An invention to a product, article of manufacture or composition (three of the classes) may be claimed in any of several ways, depending on the individual product. It may be claimed as (1) a product, (2) a process for producing the product, (3) a process for using the product, and (4) a machine for producing the product. The remaining statutory class of a process may be claimed as (5) a process, (6) a machine which performs or uses the process, or (7) a product which is produced by the process. For fullest protection wherever an invention is capable of being claimed in more than one of the different ways, it is recommended that that be done. However, it is likely that an examiner will issue a restriction requirement as between different statutory classes of claims, on the one hand, and even with one statutory class, between different types of processes, e.g., (2) and (3) above, on the other hand, so that coverage of each of the different types of claims will require the filing of a respective divisional application. There may be practical economic considerations in avoiding having to file divisional applications which may cause the claim drafter to avoid using multiple types of claims. But, at least, consider using them initially.

When preparing claims of more than one of the types (1)-(7) noted above, avoid mixing claim limitations in one claim directed to different ones of the types of processes (2) and (3) noted above. Avoid mixing limitations of different types of processes (2), 3), (6) above) with different apparatus (1) or (7)) in one claim.

VIII

Nonart Rejections

The following sections cover some formal rejections to claims not previously discussed in detail. By "formal" is meant rejections other than anticipation, obviousness, or lack of statutory subject matter (e.g., rejections of methods of doing business, naturally occurring articles, scientific principles, etc.). See MPEP 706.03(a).

§ 61 Duplicate Claiming

"Duplicate claiming" (MPEP 706.03(k)), refers to two claims that are "so close in content that they both cover the same thing, despite a slight difference in wording." The manual also provides that "it is proper after allowing one claim to reject the other as being a substantial duplicate." In *Ex parte Primich*,[1] the Board seemed to have renounced this doctrine, at least where the second claim was a dependent claim. But MPEP 706.03(k) continues.

In practice, a claim that adds, subtracts, or changes one small feature from every other claim would not even be rejected as a duplicate claim. Just reciting an element using a different term, perhaps using a more or less generic expression for the element, is these days accepted as an adequate difference.

The basis for a ground of rejection of duplicate claiming is rule 75(b): "More than one claim may be presented *provided they differ substantially from each other* and are not unduly multiplied."

---

1. 151 U.S.P.Q. (BNA) 737 (Bd. App. 1966).

(Emphasis added to indicate the basis for the duplicate, or redundant claiming, doctrine.) This doctrine theoretically applies regardless of the total number of claims presented, although in practice it is not used often unless "too many" claims are also presented, as discussed in the next section.

Summary

Avoid claims that are "substantial duplicates" as to what is covered, particularly independent claims. Avoid claims that differ only by items clearly old in the art, or highly conventional.

§ 62 Undue Multiplicity

A separate but related doctrine of "undue multiplicity" derives from the same rule 75(b), second part: "provided . . . they *are not unduly multipled.*" Theoretically, this means that too many claims are presented, whether or not any two meet the "duplicate" test of the previous paragraph. According to MPEP 2173.05(n):

> An unreasonable number of claims, that is unreasonable in view of the nature and scope of applicant's invention and the state of the art, may afford a basis for a rejection on the ground of multiplicity. A rejection on this ground should include all the claims in the case inasmuch as it relates to confusion of the issue.

The boundaries of this rejection are not very clear and it is not used very often. When used, it is usually combined with a duplicate claims rejection.

In an undue multiplicity rejection, the examiner will set a number of claims he thinks is reasonable under the circumstances, and one can then elect that many claims to prosecute on the merits. Then, after prosecution is completed on the elected claims, one can appeal the multiplicity rejection, along with any other rejections, if one still believes it is unreasonable.

In *Ex parte Birnbaum,*[2] the board reversed an undue multiplicity rejection stating:

---

2. 161 U.S.P.Q. (BNA) 635, 637 (Bd. App. 1968).

All of the claims [twenty-four] have been rejected on the ground of multiplicity. While forty pages of claims may seem to be unnecessarily prolix, the mere psychological reaction to this amount of material does not, in and of itself, constitute a legal basis for rejection. The examiner must show either that the claims are so unduly multiplied that they are difficult to understand, or that the claims are for the most part duplicates.

See also *Ex parte Joyce*[3] for a Board opinion affirming such a rejection and applying a "rule of reason" test (forty-two claims covering thirty pages for a "relatively simple and not complex" invention).

The C.C.P.A. was not sympathetic to a multiplicity rejection. In 1969, *In re Flint*[4] held such a rejection improper on the merits. That case reviews many previous cases on the subject.[5]

Of course, there is a substantial filing fee for a large number of claims and of independent claims, which provides another reason for avoiding multiplicity. (The fees conversely provide a reason against a multiplicity rejection. If you are willing to pay the extra fee, you should have the extra claims examined too.)

Summary

Avoid presenting "too many" claims in total, and where a large number of claims must reasonably be presented, make sure there are clear-cut differences between the claims. Dependent claims will help in avoiding multiplicity rejections. Basically, be reasonable, particularly where more than ten claims are thought necessary.

§ 63 Old Combination; Overclaiming

Damages for patent infringement are awarded based on the claimed invention. The larger the claimed invention, i.e., the more elements it contains, the greater may be the base upon which dam-

---

3. 168 U.S.P.Q. (BNA) 373 (Bd. App. 1969).
4. 411 F. 2d 1353, 162 U.S.P.Q. (BNA) 228 (C.C.P.A. 1969).
5. *See In re* Wakefield, 422 F.2d 897, 164, U.S.P.Q.2d (BNA) 636 (C.C.P.A. 1970).

ages are calculated. Hence, one claims an entire machine or installation or article or process, not just a component part. Of course, one can write separate claims to a fuller combination and to a sub-combination or component part of the combination.

MPEP 2173.05(j) sets out the Patent and Trademark Office's view of § 112 of the statute that "old combination" is no longer a valid basis of rejection of a claim, if the claim otherwise complies with § 112, para. 2. The rejection was based on the principle that an inventor who improves one element of an old combination should not patent the entire combination including the new element. The Patent Office acknowledges that the Federal Circuit has held the doctrine to no longer be viable.[6]

A prior edition of the Manual provides an example:

> Example [of old combination]: An improved carburetor claimed in combination with a gasoline engine.

The combination of a carburetor and an engine is old and in the invention and the reference, the engine and the carburator cooperate in the same way.

Although the Patent Office guidelines in the Manual are neither law nor rules, they indicate how the Office will act and will surely influence courts in deciding the issue. But precedents still in effect have invalidated a claim based on its covering an old combination (although the Federal Circuit has more recently said the doctrine is gone).[7]

In *Holstensson v. V.M. Corp.*,[8] the patentees had invented the modern offset-spindle type of phonograph record changer, which replaced the prior slicer blade structure and achieved great commercial success. While the judge indicated this was a very significant invention, he held the claims not only included the novel record dropping mechanism, but also included all of the old and unchanged elements of a complete automatic record player: turntable, pick-up arm and cycling mechanism. Neither did the specification point out what was old and what was new.

---

6. Radio Steel & Mfg. Co. v. MTD Prods., Inc., 731 F.2d 840, 221 U.S.P.Q. (BNA) 657 (Fed. Cir. 1984).
7. *Id.*
8. 139 U.S.P.Q. (BNA) 401 (6th Cir. 1963), *cert. denied,* 377 U.S. 966 (1964).

The claim in question called for the following elements (old except where italicized):

1. In a talking machine,

(a) a rotatable *hollow* shaft,

(b) a turntable . . .,

(c) *a post extending through the shaft and having an upper extension which is offset . . . for forming a shoulder for supporting a stack of records . . .,*

(d) *steadying means . . .,*

(e) *a lever pivotally mounted in said supporting post . . .,*

(f) a pickup arm . . .

(g) means . . . for swinging the pickup arm . . ., said means also rocking said lever, and

(h) means for then returning the pickup arm inwards to playing position.

The five generally old elements, (a), (b), (f), (g), and (h), were defined only very broadly, while the new elements, (c), (d), and (e), were described in substantial detail. Unquestionably, the new record dropper cooperated with the old cycling mechanism in no basically new way.

The sole issue was the formal ground of old combination or overclaiming. The court even held that "the spindle type record dropper was new and constituted invention [meaning it was unobvious]."

The court then held the claim invalid (emphasis added):

> We come, finally, to the critical question for our decision, namely, will the owner of a patent which, *in part, contains patentable invention,* be denied recovery from one who clearly infringes the part of the patent which is invention, merely because the patent is not a true combination and claims as part of the invention that which is old and disclosed in a prior patent? We are of the opinion that we must answer in the affirmative. Such a holding appears unfair unless there is a policy of patent laws which, in its effect, visits total forfeiture upon a patent which attempts to extend its monopoly to something already patented. There is such a policy.

Claiming more than the invention had been called "overclaiming." But that term seems inaccurate, since a subcombination claim to A+B+C is *broader* than a combination claim to

A+B+C+D+E+F, etc. Thus, it seems the big combination claim would be *under*claiming the invention. In fact, had Holstensson *et al.* attempted to file for reissue, to eliminate the old elements, the Patent and Trademark Office would have held that to be a *broadening* reissue.

Regardless of any theoretical discussion of the word "overclaiming," the *Holstensson* case is a strict decision clearly teaching that one should be very careful to claim *only his new invention,* detached from a lot of old things. This type of case, as well as rule 75(e), should point the way toward *Jepson*-type claims (section 57) or subcombination claims (section 59), whichever are appropriate.

Claim writers pursue claims to large combinations, and particularly narrower claims to large combinations, because royalties or damages might be based on the value of the large combination including the invention instead of "the Invention."[9]

In keeping with its custom of discarding or drastically liberalizing nonart rejections[10] the C.C.P.A. threw out the classic "old combination" doctrine in 1969.[11] The invention concerned computer programs. Certain claims were rejected as "drawn to the old combination of a programmed computer and a plotting device, which combination is shown to be old by . . . [a reference]." Here the novelty was strictly in the computer program.

The court quoted the previous Manual section stating that the MPEP "statement has the support of many cases."

The court then held that there was no statutory basis for the rule, as stated, and rejected it. The court discussed the cases calling this "overclaiming" and rejected that, as suggested above by this author.

> Such statements [about overclaiming] are indeed puzzling in view of the fact that the addition of elements to a claim *narrows* its scope and thereby creates a lesser monopoly. Others have said that

---

9. *See* Crisman, *Vending an Old Combination: A Patent Misuse-Antitrust Problem,* J. Pat. Off. Soc'y 649 (1969) (further discussion of doctrine and problems generated in licensing subcombination patents).

10. *See* method function of apparatus (section 40), product-by-process claims (section 46), new-use claims and preamble limitations (section 55), mental steps (section 57), aggregation (section 61), printed matter (section 62).

11. *In re* Bernhart and Fetter, 163 U.S.P.Q. (BNA) 611 (C.C.P.A. 1969).

the combination is not new, or is obvious, if no new coaction or result is obtained. This too is unsound, since it is not the result which is to be patented but the recited machine, composition, etc. If the prior art does not show or suggest that improved element itself, it defies logical reasoning to say that the same prior art suggests the use of the improved element in a combination.

The court next reasoned that, under the present statute, the old combination rejection could only be based on 35 U.S.C. section 112, lack of "particularly pointing out and distinctly claiming." The court then held that the claims in issue were particular and distinct. Note, there is nothing peculiar about old combination claims that would make them as a class nonparticular or indistinct. The court thought that, if the plotter were put in the preamble à la *Jepson* (section 57), it would "greatly increase the number of words"; and, if eliminated (as a subcombination claim, section 59), it would not make the claims "more particular or distinct, since the monopoly . . . would be substantially broadened." In *Ex parte Barber*,[12] the Board held that *In re Bernhart* had abolished the old combination doctrine.

The classic "old combination" rejection did not apply where the subcombination was only *intended* for use in the combination, but the old elements were not positively recited in the claim.

For example, in *In re Rohrbacher and Kolbe*,[13] claim 1 in question was directed to a special cooling pump designed for use with a particular kind of engine, but the engine parts were not made positive elements of the claim. Claim 1 read:

1. A cooling liquid pump *for engines having parallel rows of liquid cooled cylinders* and comprising

an elongated pump casing *adapted to extend between said rows of cylinders and to be secured at the opposite ends thereof to the liquid cooling cavity walls of said rows of cylinders*,

said casing being formed to provide . . . [certain chambers defined in detail], . . .

said casing ends being formed to provide outlet ports . . . [defined] and being *adapted to provide communication between* said discharge chamber *and the cooling liquid cavities within said cav-*

---

12. 187 U.S.P.Q. (BNA) 244 (Bd. App. 1974).
13. 128 U.S.P.Q. (BNA) 117, 119 (C.C.P.A. 1960).

ity walls of said rows of cylinders. . . . (Paragraphing and emphasis added to show relation to the engine.)

In reversing an old combination rejection, the court held:

> The first ground of rejection is based on the board's holding that the claims are not drawn merely to pump structure, as contended by appellants, but that the engine forms a part of the claimed combination.
>
> It is clear that the engine is not positively recited as an element of any of the claims. It is referred to only by such statements as that the pump is "for" engines of a particular type and that the pump chambers are "adapted" to communicate with certain portions of the engine. We are of the opinion that such statements are intended merely to define the structure of the pump itself and that, as stated in appellants' brief:
>
>> "The pump defined by the claims may be separated from the engine and carried away from the engine. The claims still read on the pump after it has been carried away . . . ."
>
> The appealed claims do not state that the article claimed is an engine or includes an engine, but merely that it is for an engine or is adapted to be connected therewith. Such statements of adaptation for an intended use have been held not to limit the claims to the particular use specified. Brown Mfg. Co. v. Deere et al., 61 F. 972 (C.C.A. 7).
>
> While the device recited in the appealed claims is intended to be used with an engine and has a particular structure adapting it for such use, the claims define only the structure of the pump itself and not a combination of the pump with an engine.

Another example of how to avoid the "old combination" doctrine, while retaining some aspects of the combination in the claim, is to use an "In a" claim discussed under section 59 on combination and subcombination. One can claim the subcombination for use in the combination, with the subcombination elements *adapted* to do things to the elements of the combination. Dean's claim 3 in *In re Dean*[14] trod a very fine line to avoid old combination:

> In a camera having a shutter mechanism, including two independently operable shutter-actuating elements, a *shuttering apparatus for* effecting a precisely predetermined camera exposure *comprising:*

---

14. 130 U.S.P.Q. (BNA) 107 (C.C.P.A. 1961).

[1] a pair of electro-responsive devices adapted to be individually coupled to said [shutter-actuating] elements; . . .

[7] and an electrical time-constant circuit responsive to . . . for rendering said discharge device conductive to develop a delayed pulse . . . to cause its associated electro-responsive device to *complete an exposure.* (Emphasis and paragraphing added).

The claim had been rejected, among other grounds, as drawn to an old combination of a timing circuit and an old shutter mechanism.

The C.C.P.A. ruled that the claim was a subcombination claim to the timer per se, not a claim to the combination of the timer and shutter. The preamble limitations "In a camera" and "for effecting a camera exposure" were not considered positive elements of the claim. With respect to "adapted to be coupled," the court stated:

To state mere *adaptability* of these parts of the timer to perform the coupling function does not import into the claim the shutter . . . . The above clause is a limitation of element [1] but not an inclusion of shutter elements.

Similar comments were made with respect to such clauses as "to cause its associated . . . device to complete an exposure." This was merely a statement of the *reason* why the pulse is developed at all, a statement which, together with the preamble we think improves the clarity of definition of the elements of the timer, and nothing more.

These types of claims, then, are really only special forms of subcombination claims, sort of hybrids spelling out inferentially enough of the combination details to give meaning to the subcombination elements, but not including such details in the claim. This seems to be a highly useful type of claim in an appropriate case. (See further discussion in section 59 — combination and subcombination. Compare also, with the discussion in section 56 of new use claims, concerning preamble statements of intended use.)

Summary

---

*The old-combination rejection should no longer be received. But,
nonetheless, claim the new things your inventor contributed, not
in combination with a lot of old and unchanged things. Point out
what your inventive contribution is, not the old environment
where it is used. Use* Jepson *claims (section 57) or subcombination
claims (section 59) to avoid this problem. In addition to avoiding
invalidity on a purely technical defense, claims to "the invention"
are better received by the examiner and more likely to be allowed.
But because the measure of a damages award for an infringement
can be based on the entire claimed invention, there can be additional claims to the entire combination, which may be cancelled if
rejected.*

§ 64 Aggregation

A claim to an aggregation is unfortunately very easy to draft.
The word "aggregation" is defined in MPEP 2173.05(k):

> Rejections on the ground of aggregation should be based upon a
> lack of cooperation between elements of the claim.

> Example of aggregation: A washing machine associated with a
> dial telephone.

The statutory classes, particularly the class "machine," are limited by court decisions to "combinations": that is, structures in
which the parts cooperate to achieve a result. It has been said[15]

---

15. Skinner Bros. Belting Co. v. Oil Well Improvements Co., 12 U.S.P.Q.
(BNA) 61, 63 (10th Cir. 1931):

> A rough analogy, that cannot be pressed too far, has repeatedly occurred
> to me in considering this question. I think of a football team as a combi-
> nation; one passes, one receives, another blocks, another runs, and still
> others hold the line. Eleven men are doing different things, each in his
> own way, and not always simultaneously; yet they are working to a com-
> mon end, to advance the ball; and they co-act as a unit. I think of a track
> team as an aggregation; one runs, another hurdles, another jumps, anoth-
> er throws. They all work for a common general end, to amass points for
> their alma mater, but there is lacking the vital spark of cooperation or co-
> ordination. They work, not as one unit, but as several. In the case at bar,
> we have no doubt that the device is a combination and not an aggrega-

that an aggregation is like a track team, while a true combination is like a football team. In a famous case,[16] a pencil with an eraser on the end was held to be unpatentable, at least in part because it was an aggregation of parts and the statute did not authorize such claims. MPEP 2173.05(k) states:

> A claim is not necessarily aggregative because the various elements do not function simultaneously, e.g., a typewriter. *In re Worrest,* 40 C.C.P.A. 804, 96 U.S.P.Q. 381 (1953). Neither is a claim necessarily aggregative merely because elements which do cooperate are set forth in specific detail.

Reanalyzing *Reckindorfer,* aside from the major commercial success of pencils with erasers, there is an obvious advantage in being able to correct written material using the same instrument that had originally written it. Just as each typewriter key and associated linkage could be viewed as a separate unit, their cooperation makes a more useful whole. The same applies to that pencil with the eraser on it.

A true aggregation relates to a defect in the structure, and a well-written claim will not help. In section 28, it was noted that a valid combination may be rejected as "aggregative as claimed" when the cooperation between the elements is not properly described in the claim.

In 1964, the C.C.P.A. cast doubt on the propriety of aggregation rejections,[17] suggesting that the sole test should be obviousness under 35 U.S.C. section 103.

MPEP 2173.05(k) concludes:

> A rejection on aggregation should be made only after consideration of the court's comments in *In re Gustafson,* 51 C.C.P.A. 1358, 141 U.S.P.Q. 585 (1964).

About all this cryptic paragraph does is to alert a diligent examiner that there may be some sort of problem with aggregation rejections, but does not identify what it is.

---

tion. A single object is to be accomplished—to prevent escape of the oil from the well. All the elements coordinate in working to that end. It is not a relay of horses from London to Bath; it is a three-horse hitch to the same coach. We conclude that the first patent is valid.

16. Reckindorfer v. Faber, 92 U.S. 347 (1875).
17. *In re* Gustafson, 331 F.2d 905, 141 U.S.P.Q. (BNA) 585 (C.C.P.A. 1964).

See *In re Venezia*,[18] allowing a claim to an unassembled kit of parts. Expressly, no physical connection was recited between claimed elements.

In *Ex parte Nolden*,[19] the Board of Appeals cited the *Gustafson* case as rejecting the old aggregation (lack of cooperation) doctrine, stating that the *Gustafson* court suggested that: "the term 'aggregation' as a ground of rejection is nebulous and has no basis under the Patent Act of 1952."

The examiner had rejected the claim as an aggregation under section 112 of the statute, saying that the lack of co-action made the claims indefinite, but citing the "classic aggregation" cases, including *Reckindorfer v. Faber.* That was, of course, the wrong section of the statute. The board quickly held that it was quite clear what subject matter (aggregation or combination) the applicant was claiming. There is nothing about an aggregation claim per se that makes it indefinite under 35 U.S.C. section 112. But, just as plainly, there is no section of the statute that supports a pure aggregation rejection — it was a common law doctrine not mentioned in the statute.

In *Ex parte Davie*,[20] the Board reversed an "aggregation" rejection by name, following the *Gustafson* case. But the board held the claim unpatentable under sections 112 and 103 of the statute. Aggregations are often obvious. Note, this was a composition-of-matter claim, involving a noncooperating mixture of compounds.

In *Ansul Co. v. Uniroyal, Inc.*,[21] the court held that "aggregation" applies to a chemical mixture of A and B, where no new function was performed by A or B (a wetting agent). A use (new use) claim was held patentable (section 56).

As to a textbook aggregation, there is nothing one can do to improve a claim if the structure itself lacks cooperation. In marginal cases, include as much co-action and cooperation in the claim as the structure permits.

---

18. 189 U.S.P.Q. (BNA) 149 (C.C.P.A. 1976).
19. 149 U.S.P.Q. (BNA) 378, 380 (Bd. App. 1965).
20. 175 U.S.P.Q. (BNA) 122 (Bd. App. 1971).
21. 169 U.S.P.Q. (BNA) 759, 761 (2d Cir. 1971).

Aggregation-like rejections, involving alleged lack of cooperation between elements (sections 28 and 29), can come up in other frames of reference than a classical aggregation rejection. For example, in *Ex parte Adams and Ferrari*,[22] a claim to a "combination" of a fireplace, damper, and assertedly novel means to indicate when the damper is closed was rejected as obvious over prior art under 35 U.S.C. section 103, the examiner stating that "no cooperation is present between the fireplace and the pendant except for what the user may eventually choose to indicate. . . ." The Board reversed, holding:

> We know of no requirement in the statute of direct mechanical interaction between the elements of a combination. As long as the over-all result has utility and is unobvious, the elements of a patentable combination may function independently.

See also sections 28–29 on tying the claim elements together.

Summary

Avoid claiming "aggregations" insofar as possible, particularly in mechanical combination cases; combinations where the elements do not cooperate. Tie the elements together insofar as possible (sections 28–30). If the invention is an unobvious aggregation, appeal any rejection under the Gustafson case.

§ 65 Printed Matter

One of the ancient general rules is that "printed matter" is not patentable, primarily because it is not within the interpretation of the class "manufacture" of 35 U.S.C. section 101, discussed in section 45. MPEP 706.03(a) states: "a mere arrangement of printed matter, though seemingly a 'manufacture,' is rejected as *not being within the statutory classes*." Clearly this means that such things as books, menus, tables of scientific data, etc., are not patentable subject matter even through, broadly, they are manufactured articles.

---

22. 177 U.S.P.Q. (BNA) 21 (Bd. App. 1972).

But when printed material is associated with a structural article for some utilitarian purpose, the rule becomes very cloudy. Note the omnipresent word "mere" in the Manual section. Under this rule, the test is whether the printed matter is mere or not. "Non-mere" printed matter is all right, whatever that is. It would be permissible to include printed matter in the claim, but the patentably novel portion could not reside solely in the nature of the printed matter.

In *In re Miller,*[23] the court clarified this "rule" in what seems a clear and reasonable fashion: "The fact that printed matter *by itself* is not patentable subject matter, because non-statutory, is no reason for ignoring it when the claim is directed to a combination."

Claim 10 was directed to:

> A measuring device comprising:
>
> a spoon for measuring ingredients;
>
> and volume measuring *indicia* . . . on said spoon . . . , and
>
> a *legend attached to said spoon.* . . .[24]

The spoon was ostensibly an ordinary measuring spoon, the indicia were things such as "1 teaspoon," and the legend was, for example, "1/2 recipe." The spoon marked "1 teaspoon" for "1/2 recipe" was really only a half teaspoon. The novel feature resided solely in the proper relation between the indicia and the legend.

Thus, it seems the nature of printed matter on an article of manufacture can be considered in determining patentability. In this case, the court considered the printed matter and found the invention highly unobvious.

In re Gulack[25] dealt with printed matter on a substrate, wherein the only difference over prior art under 35 U.S.C. section 103 resided in the printed matter. The court said that the claim must be viewed as a whole, that the printed matter was functionally related to the substrate, and that the claims were, therefore, patentable.

---

23. 164 U.S.P.Q. (BNA) 46, 49 (C.C.P.A. 1969).
24. *Id.,* 164 U.S.P.Q. (BNA) at 47 (emphasis added).
25. 217 U.S.P.Q. (BNA) 401 (Fed. Cir. 1983).

Claim printed matter related functionally to other nonprinted matter elements in the claim.

The "printed matter" rule is also discussed in detail in *In re Bernhart and Fetter,*[26] although the claims did not involve printed matter in any way. The general principles of *Bernhart,* on nonstatutory class rejections, seem to apply equally to "printed matter" cases. The general import is that, even though certain items are nonstatutory by themselves, it is proper to include them and rely on them for novelty and unobviousness if combined with other items that are in the statutory class. The "other" items may all be old. The *Miller* case[27] is a perfect example of this reasoning. If true, this is a new and rather beneficient "rule" for inventors.

Summary

Avoid including printed matter in claims where possible. Where necessary to patentability, include the printed matter in combinations with mechanical elements under the Miller *case.*

§ 66 Incomplete

On completeness, the Office states, MPEP 2173.05(l)):

> A claim can be rejected as in*complete* if it omits essential elements, steps or necessary structural cooperative relationship of elements, such omission amounting to a gap between the elements, steps or necessary structural connection. . . . Greater latitude is permissible with respect to the definition in a claim of matters not essential to novelty or operability than with respect to matters essential thereto.

There have been few cases in recent years. The Manual section discusses *In re Collier,*[28] wherein the court found that essential structure connecting elements in the claim had not been recited.

If a claim were so rejected, it would be far easier to put in more elements or connections than argue against the rejection. This

---

26. 163 U.S.P.Q. (BNA) 611 (C.C.P.A. 1969).
27. 164 U.S.P.Q. (BNA) 46 (C.C.P.A. 1969) (discussed above).
28. 397 F.2d 1003, 158 U.S.P.Q. 226 (C.C.P.A. 1968).

completeness doctrine, if applied, would set some sort of limit on subcombination or fragmentary claims discussed in section 59 such as "in an A, a B, and a C."

In view of this provision, and for general reasons as discussed in sections 28–30, it is recommended that all claims define complete, operable combinations unless highly exceptional circumstances are present.

Ex parte Schaefer[29] is cited in section 23 to the effect that omission of elements from a claim makes it broad, but not vague, indefinite, or misdescriptive. Although the word "incomplete" was not actually used, it clearly was implied.

There is elsewhere in this book a suggestion as to how to prepare a claim related to apparatus or a machine. The writer moves through the apparatus, stopping to recite any element essential to operation of the machine to achieve the objective of the invention. Each element is named, and it is described to cooperate either physically or functionally, or both, with at least one other previously claimed element. That avoids an incomplete claim and also avoids a mere aggregation of elements.

A claim too broad in scope might be incomplete, or might be too broad in view of the prior art.[30]

Summary

To the extent feasible, claim complete combinations of elements. But, it is perfectly proper and advisable to claim a novel subcombination under the cases cited above and in section 59.

§ 67 Vague and Indefinite

In addition to being incomplete, a claim can be rejected or invalidated because it is vague and indefinite. This derives from 35 U.S.C. section 112, paragraph 2, that the claim does not particularly point out the invention or distinctly claim it. Various formal

---

29. 171 U.S.P.Q. (BNA) 110 (Bd. App. 1970).
30. *See* MPEP 2173.04.

sources of indefiniteness were pointed out earlier, such as lack of antecedents (section 23) or failure to read on the embodiments disclosed (section 18). Too little detail in a claim renders it indefinite; too much detail is too limiting for infringement. In *Shatterproof Glass Corp. v. Libbey Owens Ford Co.,*[31] failure to recite the size of the glass sheets or the quantity or quality of the coating did not render the claims indefinite. Words of degree, if defined in the specification, do not render claims indefinite,[32] and not indefinite if understood by an expert witness.[33]

The claim in toto may also be so peculiarly worded that it is unknown just what it covers, even though a patent lawyer may be able to read the claim word for word on the structure disclosed. It may bear no relation to the real point of the invention. That is somewhat similar to a rejection as being too broad, discussed in various sections (particularly section 31), but it is also somewhat different.

Examiners are encouraged to suggest amendments to assure definiteness.[34]

One example is *Laitram Corp. v. Deepsouth Packing Co.,*[35] involving what the judge considered to be a worthwhile and unobvious *invention* of a shrimp deveining machine. However, all but one of the claims of Lapeyre et al. patent 2,825,927 were held invalid as "hopelessly vague and indefinite."

Claim 12[36] was an example:

> A shrimp vein remover comprising: hook-like vein engaging means, shrimp moving means operatively associated with said vein engaging means, and means associated with at least one of said above named means for effecting relative movement therebetween.

The court held that such claims "do not accurately describe and are not limited to the scope of the . . . invention." Also, "a patent must be a certain guide; not a congeries [collection] of pregnant

---

31. 225 U.S.P.Q. (BNA) 634 (Fed. Cir. 1985).
32. Seattle Box Co. v. Industrial Coating & Packaging Inc., 221 U.S.P.Q. (BNA) 568 (Fed. Cir. 1984) ("substantially equal to").
33. Rosemount Inc. v. Beckman Indus., Inc., 221 U.S.P.Q. (BNA) 1 (Fed. Cir. 1984) ("close proximity").
34. *See* MPEP 2173.02.
35. 162 U.S.P.Q. (BNA) 14 (E.D. La. 1969).
36. *Id.,* 162 U.S.P.Q. (BNA) at 30.

suggestions." Further "enterprise and experimentation must not be discouraged by an area of uncertainty as to the scope of the invention."

Although this type of case could come up in any statutory class, it normally occurs primarily in the class "machine." In this case, structural and functional connections (sections 28–30) were stated, but only in incomprehensible fashion. For example, the shrimp-moving means is "operatively associated" with the vein-engaging means. How? Why? For what purpose? How does a shrimp get deveined? The "glue" mentioned in section 28 is nominally present, but the wrong brand of glue was used.

Fortunately for the patentee, claim 1 was more specific; it was held valid and infringed. For comparison, claim 1[37] (162 U.S.P.Q., at p. 30) included:

> In a shrimp vein remover, a supporting member, a lip projecting at an acute angle from the supporting member and having a smooth rounded free edge for engaging beneath the vein of a shrimp and for wedging the vein between the lip and the supporting member, and means operatively associated with said supporting member for relatively moving the shrimp with respect to said member to cause separation of the vein from the shrimp meat.

While the judge thought that this "can claim no prizes for clarity or artistry," he also held[38] the claim sufficiently definite:

> . . . it is impossible to suppose that anyone who really wished to respect the patent would have any difficulty in identifying what the claim covered. . . . (Quoting from *Musher Foundation v. Alba Trading Co.,* 66 U.S.P.Q. 183 (2d Cir. 1945).)

This case well illustrates the point about obtaining intermediate and narrow claims, section 60. In view of the ultrabroad claim 12, one might be tempted not to concentrate on the more pedestrian claims, such as claim 1; but ultrabroad claims can be shot down for a great many reasons; specific claims cannot be.

In *In re Wolfrum and Gold,*[39] discussed in section 50 on *Markush* claims, the court held that a *Markush* claim to groups of compounds A or B was not rejectable under 35 U.S.C. section 112, and that 112 rejections of claims were limited to cases where

---

37. *Id.*
38. *Id.*
39. 179 U.S.P.Q. (BNA) 620 (C.C.P.A. 1973).

the claim was not "precise and definite" as to what it covered; that is, the examiner could not understand what *the applicant* regarded as the invention. "An applicant is free under that provision [section 112] to set the metes and bounds of 'his invention' as he sees them,. . . ."

Thus, in effect, the court held that section 112 cannot be used as a basis for formal rejections of claims, such as the problem of *Markush* claims covering "patentably distinct" species.

Summary

Avoid "vague and indefinite" claims. Make claims certain as to what they cover and how they relate to the example or examples described in the detailed description.

§ 68 Prolixity

In the previous sections, we stated that claims must be complete and definite; now one must also learn that a claim can be *too* complete and *too* definite. According to a doctrine known as "prolixity," MPEP 2173.05(m):

> Claims are rejected as *prolix* when they contain long recitations of unimportant details which hide or obscure the invention. *Ex parte Iagan,* 1911 Dec. Com. Pat. 10; 162 O.G. 538, expresses the thought that very long detailed claims setting forth so many elements that invention [now including unobviousness] cannot possibly reside in the combination should be rejected as prolix.[40]

Although this doctrine is probably used relatively rarely, one should know it exists. A string of dependent claims might well help overcome the "problem," if one wanted to present such a total claim, in that no one claim would be all that long and detailed. Also, once one claim in the string was allowed, the further dependent claims would most likely be allowed without extensive consideration (section 11).

---

40. *See In re* Swinehart and Sfiligoj, 169 U.S.P.Q. (BNA) 226 (C.C.P.A. 1971); *In re* Wakefield, 104 U.S.P.Q. (BNA) 636 (C.C.P.A. 1970).

A claim suffering from prolixity likely includes so many features that its infringement is likely easily avoided, which means it would be of little value to the client. Breaking out numerous features into dependent claims will preserve valuable claim breadth for the broader claims in the string.

Summary

The overall rule on claim scope is simple to state but often hard to follow:

"The claim should not be too broad nor too narrow, not incomplete nor too complete; it should be just right."

§ 69 New Matter

New matter is any element added either to the specification, the drawings or the claims after the application has been filed that discloses recites elements without support in the original disclosure. MPEP 706.03(o). Anything disclosed in the specification and drawings or claimed in the original claims is by definition not new matter.

A claim cannot itself recite new matter or be based upon any element not disclosed or claimed in the application as filed. A claim cannot be based upon subject matter not found anywhere in the disclosure nor upon new subject matter added after filing. Furthermore, a claim cannot be amended to be narrower or more restricted than the original disclosure or to eliminate something that the disclosure suggests is mandatory. MPEP 706.03(o) says:

> New matter includes not only the addition of wholly unsupported subject matter, but may also include adding specific percentages or compounds after a broader original disclosure, or even the omission of a step from a method.

IX

Claiming Biotechnology Inventions

by Rochelle K. Seide

§ 70 In General

Biotechnology may be defined as the use of living organisms to make commercially and therapeutically valuable products and processes, including, inter alia, therapeutic compositions and agricultural and industrial products. Many scientific disciplines are involved in biotechnology, such as genetics, molecular biology, biochemistry, microbiology, virology, cell biology, enzymology, immunology, neurobiology, receptor biology, and fermentation techniques.

Genetic engineering involves the use of recombinant DNA[1] ("rDNA") technology to alter the genes of a particular organism (e.g., to insert the gene coding for human growth hormone into a bacterium) to allow the now altered organism to make the particular gene product (protein) encoded by the inserted gene.

---

1. Deoxyribonucleic acid. DNA comprises the genetic information of most living organisms. A related molecule, ribonucleic acid (RNA) is involved in translating the genetic information contained in DNA. Some viruses, such as the AIDS virus or HIV, utilize RNA, rather than DNA as their genetic material. DNA and RNA code for amino acids, which are the building blocks of proteins or polypeptides found in living organisms. The sequence of the DNA or RNA molecule specifies the amino acid sequence of the protein.

Related technology allows for the production of highly specific monoclonal antibodies[2] which can be used to isolate and target specific cellular antigens. MAbs can also be useful as therapeutic and diagnostic agents, for diseases such as various cancers.

The results of genetic engineering and monoclonal antibody production may constitute patentable subject matter. The table sets forth a non-exhaustive list of categories of possible claimable subject matter in biotechnology. Depending on the nature of a particular invention, one or more of these categories may be present in a particular patent application.

Representative Subject Matter for Biotechnology Claims
cDNA, recombinant (r) DNA, synthetic DNA, DNA fragments
Protein, Polypeptide or Peptide (Product) & fragments
Ribozymes, Catalytic RNA
Monoclonal Antibodies (MAbs) vs. Protein
Neutralizing or Blocking MAbs
Engineered MAbs — Fab, F_V, V_L, V_H, SC, etc.; Humanized MAbs
Cell Surface Receptor for Protein
Anti-Sense DNA, RNA
Recombinant Vectors; Expression Vectors
Host Cells; Transformed Cell Lines
GeneSequencing Techniques, PCR - related diagnostics

---

2. Antibodies are serum proteins produced by the immune system in animals. Antibodies are reactive to foreign antigens and specifically bind to regions on such antigens termed "epitopes." Monoclonal antibodies, or MAbs, are the product of a single antibody producing clone derived from a single cell.

Methods of Producing Protein via Expression; Methods of Using Protein
Transgenic Animals
Diagnostics/Kits
Pharmaceutical Compositions and Therapeutic Methods
Gene Therapy Protocols and Materials

§ 71 Claims to Living Organisms, e.g., Animals and Plants

The U.S. Supreme Court has held living organisms to constitute patentable subject matter under 35 U.S.C. section 101,[3] saying that statutory subject matter includes "anything under the sun that is made by [wo]man."[4]

Following the Supreme Court's holding in *Chakrabarty*, the PTO Board of Patent Appeals and Interferences ("the Board") held that seeds and plants could be covered by utility patents, not just under the Plant Patent Act of 1930 and the Plant Variety Protection Act of 1970.[5] The Board subsequently held that multicellular organisms, such as animals, were patentable subject matter under 35 U.S.C. section 101.[6] After *Allen*, the PTO issued a statement that it would grant patents on non-human multicellular animals.[7] Shortly thereafter, in 1987, U.S. Patent No. 4,736,866 was issued for the so-called "oncomouse," a transgenic mouse that had an activated oncogene inserted into its germline DNA, which

---

3. Diamond v. Chakrabarty, 447 U.S. 303 (1980).

4. *Id.* at 309.

5. *Ex parte* Hibberd, 227 U.S.P.Q. 443 (Bd. Pat. App. 1985). The Plant Patent Act of 1930, 35 U.S.C. §§ 161-64 (1992), protects plants reproduced via asexual means. The Plant Variety Protection Act of 1970, 7 U.S.C. §§ 2321-2582 (1992), protects sexually reproduced plants - those that are propagated via seeds.

6. *In re* Allen, 2 U.S.P.Q.2d 1425 (Bd. Pat. App. 1985) (the claimed invention was a non-naturally occurring oyster induced into polyploidy).

7. *See, e.g.*, Seide et al., *Patent Protection for Animal Inventions*, 1 J. PROPRIETARY RTS. 7 (Nov. 1989) for review.

makes it susceptible to neoplasms. The subject mice are useful for testing compounds that (1) induce cancers or (2) could treat or slow the disease. The claims of the '866 patent were directed to the animals per se:

> 1. A transgenic non-human mammal all of whose germ cells and somatic cells contain a recombinant activated oncogene sequence introduced into said mammal, or an ancestor of said mammal, at an embryonic stage.[8]
>
> 11. The mammal of claim 1, said mammal being a rodent.
>
> 12. The mammal of claim 11, said rodent being a mouse.

After a hiatus of a number of years, the PTO has issued several additional patents directed to transgenic animals.[9]

The PTO has also granted patents on processes by which new animal life may be created.[10] Thus, the only potential biological

---

8. *Id.* Today it is unlikely that the PTO would issue such a broad claim (to a "mammal") based solely on the disclosure of mice.

9. *See, e.g.*, U.S. Patent Nos. 5,175,383 ("Animal Model for Benign Prostatic Disease"), 5,175,384 ("Transgenic Mice Depleted in Mature T-Cells and Methods for Making Transgenic Mice") and 5,175,385 ("Virus-Resistant Transgenic Mice") issued on December 29, 1992; U.S. Patent No. 5,221,778 ("Multiplex Gene Regulation") issued June 22, 1993.

10. *See, e.g.*, U.S. Patent No. 4,873,191 issued to T. Wagner in which the genetic transformation of zygotes is covered. Claim 1 of the '191 patent reads:

> 1. A method of obtaining a mammal characterized as having a plurality of cells containing exogenous genetic material, said material including at least one gene and a control sequence operably associated therewith, which, under predetermined conditions, express said gene under the control of said control sequence in a cell of said mammal, which comprises:
>
> (a) introducing exogenous genetic material into a pronucleus of a mammalian zygote by microinjection, said zygote being capable of development into a mammal, said genetic material including at least one gene and a control sequence operably associated therewith, thereby obtaining a genetically transformed zygote;
>
> (b) transplanting an embryo derived from the genetically transformed zygote into a

subject matter prohibited patent protection is human beings.[11]

Animal patent disclosures, however, provide some unique problems relating to the written disclosure, enablement and best mode provisions of 35 U.S.C. section 112,[12] and animal claims can present particular problems of indefiniteness under section 112, second paragraph. This can occur where the animal is claimed in terms of its "phenotype" rather than its "genotype."[13] While an animal's genotype may be defined with particularity, its phenotype cannot.[14] Thus it is important to define the animal in terms of genotype.

The following are representative examples of possible animal claims:

> 1. A method of producing a nonhuman animal which comprises introducing into at least some cells of a recipient animal a vector comprising gene G, said gene being operably linked to a promoter that is functional in at least some of the cells into which said vector is introduced, such that a genetically modified animal is obtained which can express gene G.

> 2. A nonhuman animal produced by the method of claim 1, and progeny thereof, wherein at least some cells retain gene G in expressible form.

---

pseudopregnant female capable of bearing the embryo to term; and
    (c) allowing the embryo to develop to term; where said gene and control sequence are selected so that the gene is not activated in such manner and degree as would prevent normal development of the embryo to term.

11. *See* U.S. CONST. amend. XIII. More than 200 applications directed to transgenic animals are believed to be pending before the PTO.

12. *See generally* Seide et al. *Patent Protection for Animal Inventions*, 1 J. PRO-PRIETARY RTS. 7 (November 1989) for review.

13. An organism's genotype is the sum total of its genetic information. Genotype is often described, however, with respect to one or few physical locations (genes) on a chromosome, e.g., an individual may be homozygous (identical copies) for the gene coding for normal hemoglobin. The organism's phenotype describes all of the observable characteristics, or traits, produced in the organism by the interaction of its genotype and the environments, e.g., sickle cell anemia in individuals homozygous for the gene coding for sickle cell hemoglobin, when red blood cells containing such hemoglobin are exposed to low amounts of oxygen. *Id.* at n.36.

14. This is because a single phenotype can result from different genotypes.

3. A transgenic mouse whose somatic and germ cells contain and express a DNA molecule coding for human alphabet protein at a level sufficient to provide antiviral activity in said mouse, said DNA molecule having been introduced into said mouse at an embryonic stage, and wherein said DNA molecule is operably linked to an at least partially constitutive non-alphabet protein promoter.[15]

4. A transgenic mouse that carries in the genome of its somatic and germ cells a transgene which comprises a gene of interest operably linked to a promoter sequence which is regulated by a viral gene product of virus X.[16]

Moreover, as noted above, transgenic plants can also constitute patentable subject matter. For example, fertile transgenic *Zea mays* (corn) plants that stably express a heritable heterologous (foreign) DNA are the subject of U.S. Patent Nos. 5,484,956 and 5,508,468.

U.S. Patent No. 5,484,956 is directed to *Zea mays* plants containing a DNA encoding *Bacillus thuringiensis* endotoxin which confers resistance to insects. The claims are directed to the plants themselves and the following are representative.

1. A fertile transgenic *Zea mays* plant of the R0 generation containing heterologous DNA encoding *Bacillus thuringiensis* endotoxin, wherein said DNA is expressed so that the plant exhibits resistance to an insect, wherein said expression is not present in said plant not containing said DNA, and wherein said DNA is transmitted through a complete normal sexual cycle of the R0 plant to the R1 generation, and wherein said DNA is introduced into said plant by microprojectile bombardment of *Zea mays* callus cells.

2. The transgenic plant of claim 1 wherein said DNA comprises a promoter.

3. The transgenic plant of claim 1 which is selected from the group consisting of field corn, popcorn, sweet corn, flint corn and dent corn.

4. A seed produced by the transgenic plant of claim 1 which comprises a replication of said heterologous DNA.

U.S. Patent No. 5,508,468 is directed to corn plants which contain and express a foreign DNA encoding a seed storage protein to

---

15. *See* U.S. Patent No. 5,175,385.
16. *See* U.S. Patent No. 5,221,778.

improve the amino acid profile of the corn. The following claims are representative.

1. A fertile transgenic *Zea mays* plant containing an isolated preselected DNA construct comprising a promoter and encoding a *Zea mays* seed storage protein under the control of said promoter, wherein the DNA construct is expressed as said seed storage protein so that the level of a seed storage protein amino acid in the seeds of said transgenic plant is substantially increased above the level in the seeds of a *Zea mays* plant which only differ from the seeds of said transgenic *Zea mays* plant in that said DNA construct is absent and wherein said DNA construct is transmitted through a complete normal sexual cycle of the transgenic plant to the next generation.

2. The plant of claim 1 selected from the group consisting of field corn, popcorn, sweet corn, flint corn, and dent corn.

3. The plant of claim 1 wherein said preselected DNA construct further comprises and expresses a selectable marker gene or a reporter gene.

5. The transgenic *Zea mays* plant of claim 1, wherein the seed storage protein is the 10-kD zein protein, which is expressed so that the level of the whole kernel methionine is substantially increased above the whole kernel methionine level in the corresponding *Zea mays* plant which only differs from said transgenic *Zea mays* plant in that said DNA construct is absent.

11. The transgenic *Zea mays* plant of claim 1 wherein the amino acid is methionine.

Patents for methods of producing recombinant or transgenic plants have also been granted, as, for example, U.S. Patent No. 5,384,253:

1. A method for producing a transgenic *Zea mays* plant comprising:

a) incubating a population of cultured *Zea mays* cells with at least one pectin-degrading enzyme in an aqueous osmoticum so as to partially degrade the walls of said cells to yield a population of transformation-competent *Zea mays* cells;

b) electroporating the population of transformation-competent *Zea mays* cells in a buffered aqueous osmoticum comprising recombinant DNA to yield a population of transgenic *Zea mays* cells stably transformed with said DNA;

c) growing transgenic *Zea mays* callus tissue from said cells; and

d) regenerating a population of fertile transgenic *Zea mays* plants from said transgenic callus tissue; wherein said plants comprise said DNA which is heritable.

2. The method of claim 1, wherein the culture of *Zea mays* cells is derived from a culture of embryogenic *Zea mays* callus tissue.

§ 72 Claims Based on a Biological Deposit

Certain biological inventions, for example those that may involve the use of a microorganism, hybridoma,[17] animal embryos, or tissue culture material may not be readily known or available to the public, or cannot be adequately described in words to satisfy the written description and enablement provisions of 35 U.S.C. section 112, paragraph 1.[18]

In such cases, a biological deposit may be used to satisfy 35 U.S.C. section 112, paragraph 1. 37 C.F.R. sections 1.801-1.809 (and MPEP 608.01 (p)(c)) set forth the PTO Rules of Practice relating to a biological deposit. However, the Federal Circuit has clarified that a deposit of a preferred cell line in a patent claiming transformed cells is not necessarily required to satisfy the best mode requirement if the specification adequately teaches those skilled in the art how to make the cell line.[19] Examples of patent

---

17. A hybridoma is a cell line that makes and secretes a monoclonal antibody.

18. *See Ex parte* DeCastro, 28 U.S.P.Q.2d 1391 (Bd. Pat. App. 1993)(application rejected as non-enabled, inter alia, where microorganisms from which claimed theophylline utilizing enzymes were obtained had been deposited (but subsequent to application filing date), but the specification provided no further description of the physical characteristics of the enzyme, and did not adequately describe how to isolate the enzymes from the deposits).

19. *See* Amgen, Inc. v. Chugai Pharmaceutical Co., Ltd., 927 F.2d 1200, 1209-12 (Fed. Cir.), *cert. denied*, 116 S. Ct. 169 (1991) (Note this best mode issue was the basis for Genetic Institute's unsuccessful petition for certiorari to the Supreme Court) and Fritsch v. Lin, 21 U.S.P.Q.2d (Bd. Pat. App. 1991) (The Board's review of Federal Circuit's best mode holding). *See also* Scripps Clinic & Research Fdn. v. Genentech, Inc., 927 F.2d 1565, 1578-80 (Fed. Cir. 1991). *But see* Halluin, A., *Withholding Patent Biocultures from Public Depositories: Will the Trend Harm Medical Progress?*, 4 J. PROPRIETARY RTS. 9, 7-10 (Sept. 1992).

claims based upon such deposits are quoted below along with their corresponding specification descriptions. Note the references to the deposited microorganisms in the claim in place of a physical description, composition description, or the like of the deposited material:

U.S. Patent 4,292,406 describes the microorganisms by their deposits:

> The newly discovered thermophilic anacrobes were isolated in biologically pure cultures and designated as *Thermoanaerobacter ethanolicus.* A representative strain of this new microorganism in a biologically pure subculture, designated JW 200, has been deposited in the patent strain collection of the American Type Culture Collection, Rockville, Md., USA. ATCC 31550 is the accession number assigned by the American Type Culture Collection to this strain.

> A newly isolated representative strain of *C thermocellum* designated JW 20 has been deposited in the patent strain collection of the American Type Culture Collection, Rockville, Md., USA. ATCC 31549 is the accession number assigned to this strain of *C. thermocellum.* . . .

Claims 1 and 2 of the patent rely on those microorganisms:

> 1. . . . Thermoanaerobacter ethanolicus, having the identifying characteristics of ATCC 31550 and a Clostridium thermocellum, having the identifying characteristics of ATCC 31549 . . .

> 2. . . . , having the identifying characteristics of ATCC 31550 and 31549 . . .

U.S. Patent 4,166,112 also describes microorganisms by their deposit:

> The present inventor devised an empirical method for locating and isolating microorganisms having unique, high larvicidal activity and in the instant case succeeded in isolating the microorganism herein referred to as ONR-60A. He further devised a unique carrier for dispersal of the new larvicide.

> A sample of the microorganism has been deposited with the International Culture Depository, Columbus, Ohio 43210. In subsequent screening and analysis by WHO, it has been identified as a unique strain of *Bacillus thuringiensis* and has been granted an accession number within this depository as WHO/CCBC 1897.

The spores of ONR-60A were successfully isolated and a pure biological strain obtained the following way. . . .

Claim 1 of the patent also recites the microorganisms:

1. . . . pure biological strain of *Bacillus thuringiensis* var U.S. Patent 3,984,575, also describes a microorganism:

The growth and use of *Lactobacillus lactis* NRRL-B-5628 are described in detail. Set forth in Table 1 are the characteristics of *Lactobacillus lactis* strain NRRL-B-5628. The culture is deposited at Peoria, Illinois Northern Region U.S. Department of Agriculture laboratory and is freely available to public. . . .

Claim 1 of the patent relies on that disclosure:

1. . . . live *Lactobacillus lactis* NRRL-B-5628 mixed with a growth . . . . On the other hand, if the microorganism has a recognized name, then that name should be used in the claim.

§ 73 Claims to Nucleic Acids and Proteins

Proteins are the building blocks and functional materials of living organisms — from viruses to man. Proteins are composed of amino acids that are strung together in a sequence like beads in a necklace. There are twenty (20) different amino acids found in proteins and their sequence provides the protein with its individuality and specifies its functions.

The unique sequence of amino acids in a protein is encoded by a gene, which specifies the order of the amino acids in the protein. In most organisms, genes are composed of DNA (except in certain viruses where the genes are composed of RNA).

DNA is a double helix, formed from two complementary strands, each of which is composed of nitrogenous bases — adenine (A), thymine (T), guanine (G) and cytosine (C) — linked to a sugar (deoxyribose) and a phosphate group to form a nucleotide. The complementary DNA strands are held together by hydrogen bonds formed between specific base pairs: A binds only to T and G binds only to C. The sequence of the bases in DNA is "read" by a cell's protein synthetic machinery in groups of three. These three bases are called "codons," each corresponding to a specific amino acid. Because there are 64 (4^3) possible codon triplets and there are only 20 amino acids, some amino acids are specified by multiple codons. This phenomenon is known as the degeneracy of the genetic code.

The degeneracy of the code gives rise to a unique situation, which, as discussed below, has implications for claiming DNA and proteins. Once the nucleotide sequence of a DNA molecule has been determined, the amino acid sequence of the encoded protein is readily determined. However, because of the code's degeneracy, the reverse is not necessarily true. A protein having a known amino acid sequence may be encoded by millions of possible codon combinations.

The use of recombinant DNA technology has allowed the development of new, purified or modified proteins and polypeptides, such as structural proteins, antibodies, hormones and enzymes, that previously could only be isolated from natural sources with great difficulty. Usually today, complete characterization of the protein or polypeptide and its encoding nucleic acids requires chemical and physical characterization, including determining the amino acid sequence of the protein or polypeptide and/or the nucleotide sequence of its encoding gene. Various manipulations of these structures, for example a change in an amino acid or nucleotide sequence, so that the sequences are different from those in the art, may be the basis for patentability.

One way of claiming a protein or nucleic acid can be by reciting its sequence. If adequate support for a broader claim is provided in the specification, a claim reciting a sequence may depend from the broader claim as in U.S. Patent No. 5,443,825:

> 1. Purified and isolated human leukemia inhibitory factor (LIF) which is substantially free of other human proteins.
>
> 2. Purified and isolated human LIF, according to claim 1, having the amino acid sequence set forth in FIG. 26A and B.
>
> 3. Purified and isolated human LIF, according to claim 1, as an expression product of a transformed host cell containing a DNA molecule coding for human LIF.
>
> 5. Purified and isolated human LIF according to claim 3, wherein the DNA molecule has a nucleotide sequence as set forth in FIG. 25A-C or FIG. 29A and B.

8. Purified and isolated human LIF having the amino acid sequence set forth in FIG. 26A and B beginning at Ile at position
4.

The isolation, purification and use of human LIF and its encoding DNAs were discussed in the specification. The recited DNA
sequences in one of the figures recited in claim 5 was the sequence of the genomic DNA coding for human LIF, while the
other was a cDNA sequence. Moreover, claim 8 specifies a trun-
cated version of LIF.

Claims directed to methods for recombinant production of a
protein may also be patentable as in U.S. Patent No. 5,427,925:

1. A method of producing human leukemia inhibitory factor
(LIF) comprising the steps of

a) transforming or transfecting suitable host cells with a recombinant DNA molecule comprising a nucleotide sequence
which codes for human LIF,

b) culturing the host cells of step (a) under conditions in
which said cells express the recombinant DNA and produce
human LIF, and

c) recovering said human LIF.

2. The method of claim 1 in which said recombinant DNA
molecule codes for human LIF having the amino acid sequence
set forth in FIG. 26.

4. The method of claims 1, 2, or 3, wherein the recombinant
DNA molecule further comprises a promoter sequence operably linked to said nucleotide sequence to allow expression of
the recombinant DNA and production of human LIF by said
host cells.

The above claims recite the specific amino acid and nucleotide
sequences in terms of the sequences set out in figures in the patent.
This had been a common way of defining such sequences, which
are often quite lengthy. Now, however, such sequences must be set
forth in a "Sequence Listing" which must comport with the parameters set forth in the PTO's Rules of Practice relating to amino
acid and nucleotide sequences set forth in 37 C.F.R. sections
1.821 -1.825. Patent applications that disclose (and claim) nucleotide and amino acid sequences must assign each such sequence in
the application a Seq. ID No. and list them in the sequence listing.

Also the applicant must provide the sequence information to the PTO in computer readable form (i.e., on a disk) to facilitate searching the sequence for novelty and unobviousness. It is also preferable to claim sequences in terms of a Seq. ID No., rather than by reference to a figure or by setting out the complete sequence.

Often the search for a DNA sequence that codes for and expresses a protein begins by determining at least a portion of the amino acid sequence of the protein (automated amino acid sequencers and amino acid analyzers have been available for nearly 30 years). DNA probes complementary to degenerate DNA sequences encoding a particular amino acid sequence may be chemically synthesized and then used to "fish out" the gene that codes for the protein from, for example, a "DNA library."

However, in recent years, spawned by automated DNA sequencing machines that can churn out high quality nucleotide sequence information, the approach can be reversed. The field of genomics is directed at determining DNA sequences from particular organisms and, in turn, using this information to find, isolate and purify the encoded protein.

Such an approach has led to patents for the enzyme, superoxide dismutase -4 (which cleaves molecular oxygen in cells) (U.S. Patent No. 5,506,133), macrophage inflammatory proteins -3 and -4 (U.S. Patent No. 5,504,003) and human osteoclast-derived cathepsin (U.S. Patent 5,501,969). In each of these patents, the genes were isolated and sequenced before identifying the encoded proteins. The claims are directed to the nucleic acids and to the encoded proteins.

U.S. Patent No. 5,506,133 is representative:

1. An isolated polynucleotide comprising a member selected from the group consisting of:

(a) a polynucleotide encoding a polypeptide comprising amino acid 1 to amino acid 255 set forth in SEQ ID NO:2; and

(b) a polynucleotide which hybridizes to and which is at least 95% complementary to the polynucleotide of (a).

2. The polynucleotide of claim 1 comprising the polynucleotide of (a).

3. The polynucleotide of claim 2 comprising nucleotide 1 to nucleotide 1080 of SEQ ID NO:1.

4. The polynucleotide of claim 1 comprising polynucleotide (b).

5. The polynucleotide of claim 2 wherein the polynucleotide is DNA.

6. The polynucleotide of claim 2 wherein the polynucleotide is RNA.

7. The polynucleotide of claim 3 wherein the polynucleotide is DNA.

8. The polynucleotide of claim 3 wherein the polynucleotide is RNA.

9. An isolated polynucleotide comprising a member selected from the group consisting

(a) a polynucleotide encoding a polypeptide comprising amino acid 31 to amino acid 255 as set forth in SEQ ID NO:2; and

(b) a polynucleotide which hybridizes to and which is at least 95% complementary to the polynucleotide of (a).

10. The polynucleotide of claim 9 comprising polynucleotide (a).

Moreover, because of the nature of biotechnology inventions, several interesting issues have arisen regarding novelty, obviousness and adequate disclosure, a few of which are discussed here.

§ 74 Novelty

As biotechnology has matured, lack of novelty has become a greater problem for DNA and protein inventions as a block to the issuance of patents, as a limit to the scope of issued claims and as a basis for attacking the validity of patent claims. For example, a claim for a naturally-occurring protein that has been produced by means of recombinant DNA ("rDNA") technology may be denied for lack of novelty if the existence of the natural protein, even if not fully characterized, is known from the literature.[20] In one

---

20. *See, e.g., In re* Spada, 911 F.2d 705 (Fed. Cir. 1990), in which the Federal Circuit held that where the PTO has shown a sound basis for believing that

sense, claims to recombinant versions of a naturally occurring known protein may be treated as "product-by-process" claims which may be deemed unpatentable unless the recombinant product can be shown to be different somehow from the native protein.[21]

A disclosure of a DNA sequence in a prior art patent was found to anticipate claims to DNA in a later filed application under 35 U.S.C. section 102(e) when the application which matured into the prior art patent enabled one skilled in the art to practice the invention.[22]

Another example involved the alleged infringement of a product-by-process claim for purified Factor VIII, where the product per se had been deemed unpatentable (not novel) by the PTO, since it was already known from the literature.[23] During the litigation, neither side challenged this point or that one may claim a purified form of the natural product. Thus, with adequate disclosure, proteins produced by recombinant technology, the DNA sequences encoding them and monoclonal antibodies ("MAbs") directed against such protein may all be patentable.

---

the products of an applicant and the prior art are the same, the applicant has the burden of showing the products are not the same (e.g., by way of evidence presented in the specification or in a declaration under 37 C.F.R. § 1.132). Claims to the DNA coding for the protein may be obtainable, however. *See In re* Bell, 911 F.2d 781 (Fed. Cir. 1993), and *In re* Deuel, 51 F.3d 1552 (Fed. Cir. 1995).

21. *See, e.g., Ex parte* Gray, 10 U.S.P.Q.2d 1992 (Bd. App. 1989); *In re* Thorpe, 777 F.2d 695 (Fed. Cir. 1985).

22. *See Ex parte* D, 27 U.S.P.Q 2d 1067 (Bd. App. 1993), in which a prior art patent covering DNA encoding tissue plasminogen activator (t-pa) was deemed an effective reference under section 102(e), even though the t-pa DNA sequence in the original application leading to the prior art patent differed from the sequence in the issued prior art patent.

23. Scripps Clinic & Research Fdn. v. Genentech, Inc., 927 F.2d 1565 (Fed. Cir. 1991), *rev'd in part*, Atlantic Thermoplastic Co. v. Faytex Corp., 970 F.2d 834, *reh'g denied*, 974 F.2d 1279 (dissent), *concurring*, 974 F.2d 1299 (Fed. Cir. 1992). A representative process claim (claim 1) and a product-by-process claim (claim 13) of the patent in suit are set forth:

> 1. An improved method of preparing Factor VIII procoagulenty activity protein comprising the steps of (a) adsorbing a VIII:C/VIII:RP complex from a plasma or commercial concentrate source onto particles bound

In *Fiers v. Sugano*,[24] the Federal Circuit addressed novelty of a DNA invention in determining conception and priority of an invention under 35 U.S.C. section 102(g) directed to a claimed DNA coding for ß-interferon in an interference proceeding. In *Fiers*, the Court reiterated its holding in *Amgen Inc. v. Chugai Pharmaceutical Co.*[25] that "conception of a DNA, like conception of any chemical substance requires a definition of that substance other than by its functional utility."[26] Thus, for some biotechnology inventions (such as claims to DNA and proteins), conception may not be achieved until the invention has been actually reduced to practice and there is some practical way of defining the invention (e.g., by a nucleotide or amino acid sequence or other physical properties), other than by reciting its function.

§ 75 Obviousness of DNA Inventions

A controversial issue regarding patentability of DNA claims is whether prior art disclosing general methods of obtaining a DNA molecule ("cloning") may be cited against claims to specific DNA sequences encoding for specific proteins. The Federal Circuit decision in *In re Bell*[27] appeared to answer the question in the negative. In *Bell*, the court held that a claimed DNA sequence was not prima facie obvious in view of references setting forth the full amino acid sequence of the polypeptides (insulin-like growth factors I and II) encoded by the claimed DNAs, and a reference providing a general method for cloning DNA.

---

to a monoclonal antibody specific to VIII:RP, (b) eluting the VIII:C, (c) adsorbing the VIII:C obtained in step (b) in another adsorption to concentrate and purify same, (d) eluting the adsorbed VIII:C, and (e) recovering the highly purified and concentrated VIII:C.

13. Highly purified and concentrated human or porcine VIII:C prepared in accordance with the method of claim 1.

24. 984 F.2d 1164 (Fed. Cir. 1993).
25. 927 F.2d 1200 (Fed. Cir. 1991).
26. *Id.* at 1206.
27. 991 F.2d 781 (Fed. Cir. 1993).

The *Bell* claims are directed to DNAs coding for insulin-like growth factors ("IGF") I & II.[28] In finding the invention not obvious, the court noted that for DNA inventions, a "vast number of nucleotide sequences might code for a specific protein" due to the degeneracy of the genetic code, and that one could not predict beforehand whether a particular amino acid sequence would be encoded by a particular DNA sequence.[29] Thus, the established relationship in the genetic code between a particular DNA and the protein it encodes does not necessarily make the gene prima facie

_____

28. Claim 25 of the *Bell* application was found to be representative of the claims in issue in the appeal:

25. A composition comprising nucleic acid molecules containing a human sequence encoding insulin-like growth factor (hIGF) substantially free of nucleic acid molecules not containing said hIGF sequence, wherein said hIGF sequence is selected from the group consisting of:

(a) 5'-GGA CCG GAG ACG CUC UGC GGG GCU GAG CUG GUG GAU GCU CUU CAG UUC GUG UGU GGA GAC AGG GGC UUU UAU UUC AAC AAG CCC ACA GGG UAU GGC UCC AGC AGU CGG AGG GCG CCU CAG ACA GGU AUC GUG GAU GAG UGC UGC UUC CGG AGC UGU GAU CUA AGG AGG CUG GAG AUG UAU UGC GCA CCC CUC AAG CCU GCC AAG UCA GCU-3', wherein U can also be T;

(b)5'-GCU UAC CGC CCC AGU GAG ACC CUG UGC GGC GGG GAG CUG GUG GAC ACC CUC CAG UUC GUC UGU GGG GAC CGC GGC UUC UAC UUC AGC AGG CCC GCA AGC CGU GUG AGC CGU CGC AGC CGU GGC AUC GUU GAG GAG UGC UGU UUC CGC AGC UGU GAC CUG GCC CUC CUG GAG ACG UAC UGU GCU ACC CCC GCC AAG UCC GAG-3', wherein U can also be T;

(c)nucleic acid sequences complementary to (a) or (b); and

(d)fragments of (a), (b) or (c) that are at least 18 bases in length and which will selectively hybridize to human genomic DNA encoding hIGF.

29. 991 F.2d at 784.

obvious in the same way that a prima facie case may be made for homologs, analogs and isomers in a chemical case.[30]

Since the *Bell* claims covered only the specific DNA sequences of IGF I and II which are naturally occurring in humans, rather than all of the 10^{36} possible degenerative DNA sequences which could theoretically encode the polypeptides, the claims were deemed patentable over the prior art.

A subsequent decision by the Board indicated its willingness to disallow the holding in *Bell* and continue to allow examiners to cite prior art disclosing methods of cloning against claims to DNA molecules per se in order to render DNA claims obvious. For example in *Ex parte Deuel* (*Deuel I*),[31] the appellant's claims were directed to DNA sequences coding for heparin-binding growth factor (HBGF). The Board upheld the examiner's obviousness rejection based on prior art references disclosing a partial amino acid sequence (the N-terminal sequence) of the protein and a general method for cloning genes which code for proteins having a known N-terminal sequence. The Board relied heavily on statements by the examiner indicating that cloning is routine in the art.[32]

The Board tried to distinguished *Deuel I* from *Bell* by stating that, in *Bell*, the prior art actually taught away from the method of cloning used by the appellants.[33] Based in part on this observation, the Board interpreted *Bell* as being limited to its specific facts,[34] despite the fact that the issue in each case was stated in broad terms and was virtually identically framed.[35] Furthermore,

---

30. The court noted, however, that a gene may be obvious in view of the known amino acid sequence of the encoded protein, if it was *known* that the protein was encoded by "unique" codons (i.e., that there was only one DNA sequence coding for the protein). *Id.*

31. 33 U.S.P.Q. 2d 1445 (Bd. Pat. App. 1993).

32. *Id.* at 1447.

33. *Id.* at 1449.

34. *Id.*

35. The *Bell* court framed the issue as follows:

> The issue before us is whether the Board correctly determined that the amino acid sequence of a protein in conjunction with a reference indicating a general method of cloning renders the genes *prima facie* obvious; *In re* Bell, 991 F.2d 781, ... (Fed. Cir. 1993), whereas the Board in *Deuel I* framed the issue as: Whether or not

the *Deuel I* Board dismissed the statement in *Bell* pointing out the impropriety of focusing on the method of isolation when the issue was "the obviousness of the claimed composition, not the method by which they are made." It did so by noting that intelligent guesses at the DNA sequence can be made from the amino acid sequence, and that the appellant had not provided any evidence that the cited method required undue experimentation.[36]

The Board's reasoning in *Deuel I*, however, was explicitly rejected by the Federal Circuit in *In re Deuel* ("*Deuel II*").[37] The Federal Circuit asserted that the relationship (i.e., the genetic code) between proteins and nucleic acids does not render a particular DNA (sequence) obvious from a disclosed amino acid sequence. Furthermore, relying on its previous decision in *Bell*, the court stated that "the existence of a general method of isolating cDNA or DNA molecules is essentially irrelevant to the question of whether the specific molecules *themselves* would have been obvious, in the absence of other prior art that suggests the claimed DNA."[38] The court emphasized that the fact that it would be *obvious to try* (i.e., an incentive) to isolate a DNA sequence (corresponding to a known amino acid sequence), and that a known method existed for doing so, does not render the claimed sequence itself obvious until the compound has been definitively isolated.[39]

As a result of the Federal Circuit's opinion in *Deuel II*, it appears that the previously problematic question of whether prior art disclosing general methods of DNA cloning may be cited against DNA composition claims with regard to obviousness determinations has been answered in the negative.[40]

---

knowledge of the amino acid sequence of a protein, in conjunction with a general method of cloning, renders the invention, as a whole, *i.e.*, the gene, *prima facie* obvious.

Ex parte Deuel, 33 U.S.P.Q.2d at 1449.

36. *Id.* at p. 1450.
37. 51 F.3d 1552 (Fed. Cir. 1995).
38. *Id.* at 1559 (emphasis added).
39. *Id.* at 1559-60 (emphasis added).
40. Perhaps the major beneficiary of the Federal Circuit's *Deuel II* decision will be in regard to claims to monoclonal antibodies ("MAbs"). (See below.) Generally the PTO has taken the position (like in *Deuel I*) that a MAb is obvious if it is directed to a known antigen (particularly if the sequence or structure is known) (i.e., the "relationship" question), given the known

§ 76 Obviousness of Biotechnology Process Claims

For a number of years, biotechnology inventions dealing with processes were almost always subject to obviousness rejections in view of the Federal Circuit's decision in *In re Durden*.[41] The question of patentability of such claims was framed as whether an old process becomes new and nonobvious due to the presence of either or both a new starting material in the process or a new product resulting from the process (so-called "analogous processes"). While *Durden* involved the patentability of a chemical process,[42] its major impact has been on patentability of biotechnology inventions, where *Durden* has been often cited, almost by rote application, to deny patentability of process claims, even though the Federal Circuit admonished that each determination had to be based on the facts of the particular case.

For a long time *Durden* had a chilling effect on the pursuit of process patent protection and delayed issuance of patents. *Durden* rejections could be overcome, only at great expense, such as in U.S. Patent No. 4,766,069 which claims rDNA coding for interleukin 1B (IL-1b), and a process for making the interleukin. The issued claims of the patent include:

> 1. A recombinant DNA cloning vehicle comprising a DNA sequence comprising human [IL-1] IL-1 beta gene sequence.

> 12. A process for preparing human [IL-1B] IL-1 beta which comprises culturing a microbe hosting a cloning vehicle comprising DNA encoding human [IL-1B] IL-1 beta and recovering human [IL-1B] IL-1 beta.

However, the process claims in Amgen's original erythropoietin (EPO) application that ultimately matured into U.S. Patent No. 4,703,008 (the Amgen patent in suit in the various EPO litigations) could not be obtained because of *Durden* and Amgen elected to prosecute the DNA, vector and host claims in the application leading to the '008 patent. Amgen process claims for

---

methods for making MAbs. The rationale of *Deuel II* may be applied, however, if the MAb is clearly defined and circumscribed.

41. 763 F.2d 1406 (Fed. Cir. 1985).

42. Both the starting material for the process and the resulting product of the process were deemed novel and patentable.

making EPO by recombinant DNA technology were left for another application.[43] Representative DNA claims of the '008 patent include:

> 1. A purified and isolated DNA sequence encoding erythropoietin, said DNA sequence selected from the group consisting of: (a) the DNA sequences set out in Figs. 5 & 6 or their complementary strands; and (b) DNA sequences which hybridize under stringent conditions to the DNA sequences defined in (a).

> 7. A purified and isolated DNA sequence consisting essentially of a DNA sequence encoding a polypeptide having an amino acid sequence sufficiently duplicative of that of erythropoietin to allow possession of the biological property of causing bone marrow cells to increase production of reticulocytes and red blood cell, to increase hemoglobin synthesis or iron uptake.[44]

The Federal Circuit limited the holding in *Durden* to cases dealing with the patentability of a process of *making* a product, not a process of *using* one in *In re Pleuddemann*.[45] The Board, citing *Durden*, had rejected Pleuddemann's claims covering a method of *using* novel and patentable silane coupling agents in bonding methods. In reversing, the Federal Circuit stated that one could claim an invention in different ways: (1) the compound per se; (2) the method or process of making the compound; and (3) the method or process of using the compound.[46] The court reiterated

---

43. As a result of the '008 patent not having claims covering the method of making recombinant EPO, Amgen was deemed to have no recourse to prevent Chugai, which was manufacturing EPO abroad, from bringing its rEPO into the U.S. pursuant to either 35 U.S.C. § 271(g) or 19 U.S.C. § 1337(a). *See* Amgen, Inc. v. Chugai Pharmaceutical, Ltd., 13 U.S.P.Q.2d 1737 (D. Mass. 1989) and Amgen, Inc. v. U.S. Int'l Trade Comm'n, 902 F.2d 1532 (Fed. Cir. 1990). The PTO has since allowed Amgen's process claims, which became involved in an interference with an application from Genetics Institute. The Board determined priority in Amgen's favor. *See* Fritsch v. Lin, 21 U.S.P.Q.2d 1739 (Bd. Pat. App. 1991). After further appeals, these cases have now been settled. Amgen has recently been issued its patent covering the method for making EPO using the DNA of the '008 patent. *See* U.S. Patent No. 5,441,868.
44. U.S. Patent No. 4,703,008. The validity of a number of claims of the '008 patent was upheld in Amgen v. Chugai Pharmaceutical Co., Ltd., 927 F.2d 1200 (Fed. Cir.), *cert. denied*, 112 S. Ct. 169 (1991). However, claim 7 was invalidated for lack of enablement. See discussion, *infra*.
45. 910 F.2d 823 (Fed. Cir. 1990).
46. *Id.* at 826 (citing *In re* Kuehl, 475 F.2d 658 (C.C.P.A. 1973)).

the prohibition of using an applicant's invention against the inventor to show obviousness of his invention against the inventor. *Pleuddemann* follows the rationale and holding of *In re Mancy*, a C.C.P.A. decision dealing with biological subject matter, where a claim for the use of a new product was distinguished from a claim for its manufacture and a finding of obviousness overturned.[47]

Durden type rejections primarily affected three types of biotechnology claims: (1) purification process claims; (2) claims to preparation of MAb for a specific antigen; and (3) claims to methods of making an identified gene product, e.g., a recombinant protein or plant, via genetic engineering techniques.

Drafting around *Durden* rejections was difficult, for example, because of the uncertain patentability of the product itself (e.g., a protein). A recombinant protein may be deemed already known (anticipated) under 35 U.S.C. section 102 or obvious under section 103 where the natural protein is known, or where some of its basic properties are known, even if the protein is not fully characterized or purified.[48]

Moreover, without process of *making* claims, biotechnology inventors cannot take advantage of the Process Patent Amendments Act of 1988.[49] Specifically, without such claims neither 19 U.S.C.

---

47. *Application of Mancy*, 409 F.2d 1289 (C.C.P.A. 1974). Claims to the use of a culture of *Streptomyces bifurcus*, which had been supplied by the patentee, to make the antibiotic doxorubicin were deemed patentable. Although, similar culture techniques had previously been used to produce the antibiotic with other strains of bacteria, the court upheld the process claims. In other words, patentability of the novel strain of bacteria imparted patentability to the method of using it to make the antibiotic. Many commentators have indicated that *Mancy* is more applicable than *Durden* to the patentability of method of making claims in biotechnology.

48. *See, e.g., Ex parte* Gray, 10 U.S.P.Q.2d 1922 (Bd. App. 1989). In *Gray*, the Board essentially treated claims to a recombinant protein (nerve growth factor – "NGF") as unpatentable "product-by-process" claims under 35 U.S.C. §§ 102 and/or 103, in view of art directed to purified NGF.

49. Pub. L. No. 100-418, title IX, subtitle A, 101 Stat. 128 (1988) codified at 19 U.S.C. § 1337 (1991). This section empowers the International Trade Commission to issue an exclusion order of a product made, produced or processed abroad, if the product was made by a process covered by a valid and enforceable patent.

section 1337 nor 35 U.S.C. section 271(g)[50] would prevent foreign manufacturers located abroad from using a process of making a product (patented in the U.S.) to produce the products, such as medically useful proteins, and then importing them into the U.S.[51]

However, in the Biotechnology Patent Process Protection Act of 1995 (the "Biotechnology Act"),[52] Congress added a new section (b) to 35 U.S.C. section 103 to deal with the obviousness of process of making claims in biotechnology inventions:

> (b)(1) Notwithstanding subsection (a), and upon timely election by the applicant for patent to proceed under this subsection, a biotechnological process using or resulting in a composition of matter that is novel under section 102 and nonobvious under subsection (a) of this section shall be considered nonobvious if —
>
> (A) claims to the process and the composition of matter are contained in either the same application for patent or in separate applications having the same effective filing date; and
> (B) the composition of matter, and the process at the time it was invented, were owned by the same person or subject to an obligation of assignment to the same person.
>
> (2) A patent issued on a process under paragraph (1) —
>
> (A) shall also contain the claims to the composition of matter used in or made by that process, or
> (B) shall, if such composition of matter is claimed in another patent, be set to expire on the same date as such other patent, notwithstanding section 154.
>
> (3) For purposes of paragraph (1), the term "biotechnological process" means —

---

50. Pub. L. No. 100-412, 35 U.S.C. § 271(g), which provides that "[w]hoever without authority imports into the United States or uses or sells within the United States a product which is made by a process patented in the United States shall be liable as an infringer."
51. For just such an example, *see* Amgen, Inc. v. U.S. Int'l Trade Comm'n, 902 F.2d 1532 (Fed. Cir. 1990). *See also* Seide, *Durden Debate*, AIPLA BULLETIN, at 525-527 (Apr., May, June 1991).
52. Pub. L. No. 104-41, § 1, 109 Stat. 351 (Nov. 1, 1995), 35 U.S.C. § 103(b).

(A) a process of genetically altering or otherwise inducing a single- or multi-celled organism to —

(i) express an exogenous nucleotide sequence,

(ii) inhibit, eliminate, augment, or alter expression of an endogenous nucleotide sequence, or

(iii) express a specific physiological character-is-
tic not naturally associated with said organism;

(B) cell fusion procedures yielding a cell line that expresses a specific protein, such as a monoclonal antibody; and

(C) a method of using a product produced by a process
defined by subparagraph (A) or (B), or a combination of
subparagraphs (A) and (B).

Also, the Federal Circuit issued two decisions, *In re Ochiai*[53]
and *In re Brouwer*,[54] directed to the patentability of process
claims in general. In view of the passage of the Biotechnology Act,
Ochiai, and *Brouwer*, the PTO issued a Notice regarding examination of product and process claims in biotechnology.[55] In view
of *Ochiai* and *Brouwer*, however, it is believed that reliance on
section 103(b), which is specific for biotechnology, will be minimized. The effect of the Notice, cases, and statutes, however,
should be increased issuance of claims to biotechnology process.

§ 77 Sufficient Written Description of DNA Inventions

The description requirement dictates that an inventor describe
with particularity the claimed features of the invention. In a three-
party interference dealing with who was the first to invent a DNA
coding for ß-interferon, *Fiers v. Sugano*,[56] the Federal Circuit discussed the legal standard for a sufficient written description for a
claimed DNA:

---

53. 71 F.3d 1565 (Fed. Cir. 1995)
54. 77 F.3d 422 (Fed. Cir. 1995)
55. *See* 51 PTCJ 626 (BNA) (March 21, 1996).
56. 984 F.2d 1164 (Fed. Cir. 1993).

> On reconsideration, the Board correctly set forth the legal standard for sufficiency of a description: the specification must "reasonably convey [ ] to the artisan that the inventor had possession at that time of the [making of the invention that he had possession of the] claimed subject matter." (citations omitted).[57]

The court went on to say that

> An adequate written description of a DNA requires more than a mere statement that it is part of the invention and reference to a potential method for isolating it; what is required is a description of the DNA itself . . .
> A bare reference to a DNA with a statement that it can be obtained by reverse transcription is not a description; it does not indicate that Revel was in possession of the DNA.[58]

The court reaffirmed its holding in *Amgen v. Chugai* that an adequate disclosure of a DNA invention is more than "a wish, or arguably, a plan for obtaining the DNA."[59] The court found that the claim in issue, which purported to cover all DNAs coding for ß-interferon, was analogous to a single means claim and, thus, did not comply with the requirements of 35 U.S.C. section 112, paragraph 1.[60] The court found Revel's application was attempting to "preempt the future before it arrived" by "claim[ing] all DNAs that achieve a result without defining what means will do so," and, as such, was not in compliance with the written description requirement.[61]

---

57. *Id.* at 1170.
58. *Id.* at 1170-71.
59. *Id.* at 1171.
60. *See In re* Hyatt, 708 F.2d 712 (Fed. Cir. 1983)("the enabling disclosure [must] be commensurate in scope with the claim under consideration").
61. 984 F.2d at 1171.

§ 78 Enablement for DNA and Protein Claims

Often an inventor wishes to obtain claims not only to a protein or DNA having one specific sequence, but also to proteins or DNAs whose sequences have been modified. Because the PTO considers biotechnology to be highly unpredictable technology with simple changes in amino acid or nucleotide sequences possibly giving rise to altered functions, we must take great care to provide adequate enablement for broader claims.[62]

One way to enable broader protein or DNA claims is to provide some functional language in the claim to define the modified protein or DNA. For example, in *Ex parte Mark*,[63] the Board determined that appealed claims directed to cysteine-depleted muteins[64] of biologically active proteins, which required the mutein to retain the biological activity of the native protein, to be enabled. Claim 1 is representative:

> 1. A synthetic mutein of a biologically active native protein in which native protein has at least one cysteine residue that is free to form a disulfide link and is nonessential to said biological activity, said mutein having at least one of said cysteine residues substituted by another amino acid and said mutein exhibiting the biological activity of said native protein.

The Board found that the record established, inter alia, via a Declaration under 37 C.F.R. section 1.132, that for a given cysteine-containing protein, one skilled in the art would be able to determine in a routine fashion (i.e., without undue experimentation) whether replacement or deletion of a cysteine residue would result in a mutein covered by the claims (i.e., retain biological activity of native protein).[65]

---

62. The enablement provision of 35 U.S.C. § 112, ¶ 1, requires that the specification provide sufficient information to permit one skilled in the art to make and to use the invention without the exercise of undue experimentation.

    See Hybritech, Inc. v. Monoclonal Antibodies, Inc., 802 F.2d at 1384. Enablement is not precluded if some experimentation is necessary — it must not, however, be undue. *Id.* Furthermore, the patent does not have to teach and preferably omits what is well known in the relevant art. *Id.*

63. 12 U.S.P.Q. 2d 1904 (Bd. Pat. App. 1989).

64. A "mutein" is a protein in which one amino acid (naturally occurring) is replaced by another.

65. *Id.* at 1906-07.

Moreover, as discussed above, genetic engineering and immunological inventions are considered highly unpredictable technologies, requiring more than a single embodiment to afford a broad scope of enablement.[66]

The Federal Circuit reviewed the scope of enablement for claims to DNA in regard to claim 7 of Amgen's U.S. Patent No. 4,703,008:[67]

> 7. A purified and isolated DNA sequence consisting essentially of a DNA sequence encoding a polypeptide having an amino acid sequence sufficiently duplicative of that of erythropoietin to allow possession of the biological property of causing bone marrow cells to increase production of reticulocytes and red blood cell, to increase hemoglobin synthesis or iron uptake.

The court construed claim 7 as a generic claim covering "all possible DNA sequences that will encode any polypeptide having an amino acid sequence 'sufficiently duplicative' of EPO to possess the property of increasing production of red blood cells."[68] The district court had determined that over 3600 different EPO analogs could be made by substituting at only one amino acid in the polypeptide chain, and over one million if three amino acids in the polypeptide were changed.

The Federal Circuit noted that the district court had erred in its analysis by focusing on EPO *protein* analogs, rather than on the *claimed DNAs*, but nonetheless found that there was insufficient disclosure to enable one skilled in the art to carry out the invention commensurate with the scope of the claim.[69] The court noted that Amgen's claim was directed to DNA sequences and that

---

66. *See, e.g., Ex parte* Hitzeman, 9 U.S.P.Q.2d 1821 (Bd. Pat. App. 1987). ("[T]he) scope of enablement provided to one having ordinary skill in the art of appellants' specification disclosure is to [sic] commensurate with the scope of protection sought by the appealed claims . . . [A]ppellants' specification fails to provide those having ordinary skill in the art reasonable assurance, *as by* adequate representative examples, that vectors and yeast transformants falling within the scope of the appealed claims can be prepared and used.") (Emphasis in original).

67. Amgen, Inc. v. Chugai Pharmaceutical Co., Ltd., 927 F.2d 1200, 1212-14 (Fed. Cir.), *cert. denied*, 112 S. Ct. 169 (1991).

68. *Id.* at 1212.

69. *Id.* at 1213.

"Amgen has not enabled preparation of DNA sequences sufficient to support its all-encompassing claims."[70]

The rationale in *Amgen* was followed by the Board in *Ex parte Ishizaka*,[71] which found claims to nucleic acids coding for polypeptides exhibiting glycosylating inhibiting factor activity, defined in terms of the nucleotide sequence and homologues thereof, to be unpatentable under both 35 U.S.C. section 112, paragraphs 1 and 2. The Board determined that, although the claims superficially appeared to be definite, their intended scope could not be determined, nor was there sufficient enablement for the apparent breadth of the claims.[72]

Similarly, in *Ex parte Maizel*,[73] the Board reviewed and upheld for lack of enablement rejected claims directed to a recombinant DNA vector coding for human B-cell growth factor ("BCGF") protein or a "biologically functional equivalent thereof."[74]

---

70. The court noted that with regard to DNA claims:

> What is necessary is that he provide a disclosure sufficient to enable one skilled in the art to carry out the invention commensurate with the scope of his claims. For DNA sequences that means disclosing how to make and use enough sequences to justify grant of the claims sought.

> The court further stated that it did "not intend to imply that generic claims to genetic sequences cannot be valid where they are of a scope appropriate to the invention disclosed by an applicant. That is not the case here, where Amgen has claimed every possible analog of a gene containing about 4,000 nucleotides, with a disclosure only of how to make EPO and a very few analogs." *Id.* at 1214. *See also In re* Deuel, 51 F.3d 1552, 1560 (Fed. Cir. 1995).

71. 24 U.S.P.Q. 2d 1621 (Bd. App. 1992).

72. *Id.* at 1625-26.

> At present, there is no case from the Board or Federal Circuit discussing the scope of enablement required to support broad claims intended to generically encompass homologues, analogues, fragments, etc. of peptides, polypeptides, and proteins. However, in view of *Amgen* and *Ishizaka*, it is believed that there must be more than a mere allegation in the specification that such derivatives may be made (without undue experimentation) to obtain (or uphold) broad claims.

73. 27 U.S.P.Q.2d 1662 (Bd. Pat. App. 1993).

74. Claim 1 of Maizel's application reads as follows:

> 1. A recombinant DNA vector comprising a DNA sequence which encodes a protein exhibiting a molecular weight between about 8 and about 14 kiladaltons upon gel exclusion chromatography, said protein having an amino acid sequence which includes the non-B-galac-

Among other grounds, the claims were rejected as being broader in scope than the enabling disclosure (under section 112, paragraph 1) and as being directed to subject matter not described in the specification (new matter).

In affirming the scope of enablement rejection, the Board analogized the rejected claims to "single means" claims, which have been disparaged by the Federal Circuit.[75] The applicants had chosen to claim the DNA, not by what it is, but by what it does (functionally), i.e., encoding a protein (BCGF) having particular biological and structural characteristics, or a biologically functional equivalent thereof.[76] The Board commented:

> The problem with the phrase "biologically functional equivalent thereof" is that it covers any conceivable means, i.e., cell or DNA, which achieves the stated biological result while the specification discloses, at most, only a specific DNA segment known to the inventor.[77]

Since the specification provided, at most, only a specific DNA segment, the Board concluded that the scope of the claims was "far in excess of that warranted by the scope of the enablement set forth in the specification."[78]

§ 79 Claims to Monoclonal Antibodies (MAbs)

The potential subject matter of MAb (and hybridoma) inventions may be divided into several categories: (1) the hybridoma cell line per se; (2) the MAb secreted by the hybridoma of interest;

---

tosidase derived sequence of amino acids displayed in Figure 4, or a biologically functional equivalent thereof, and having a **BCGF** biological activity characterized by an ability to stimulate the incorporation of thymidine into **DNA** of BCGF-dependent B-cells, or an ability to stimulate the comitogenesis of anti-μ activated B-cells, when said protein is cocultured in effective concentrations with said respective B-cells *in vitro* (emphasis in original).

75. *See In re* Hyatt, 708 F.2d 712 (Fed. Cir. 1983).
76. 27 U.S.P.Q.2d at 1665.
77. *Id.*
78. *Id.*

(3) methods of making MAbs; (4) methods of using MAbs, including immunoassays; and (5) immunoassay kits incorporating MAbs.

Protection for the product MAb would provide the inventor with the right to exclude others from making and using the MAb. Preferably, MAb claims should cover the inventor's MAb, as well as others that possess the same inherent properties. The problem becomes how to avoid narrowly defining the MAb (e.g., "MAb RKS 123."). MAbs may be defined in terms of their binding characteristics if the antigen is known (e.g., "MAb reactive with leukocyte interferon"). If the antigen is unknown, the MAb might be claimed more generally in terms of function (e.g., "MAb that binds to human breast adenocarcinoma cells, but not to normal human breast epithelial cells"). Another approach is to claim the MAb in terms of the specific antigenic determinant or "epitope" with which it reacts.

However, the outcome of several decisions from the Board, e.g., *Ex parte Erlich (Erlich I)*,[79] *Ex parte Erlich (Erlich II)*,[80] *Ex parte Sorg*,[81] has circumscribed the patentability of monoclonal antibody claims. In view of these decisions, MAb claims are usually subject to a rejection for obviousness, once the antigen with which the MAb reacts has been identified, purified or otherwise characterized.

However, this rejection may be overcome by a clear showing (e.g., by way of a declaration under 37 C.F.R. section 1.132) that either an inventive process was used to make the MAb or that the MAbs exhibit novel specificity for a particular antigen.[82] Moreover, as discussed above, the decision in *In re Deuel*[83] is highly relevant to the patentability of MAbs directed to known antigens and has been used successfully in securing such claims.

---

79. 3 U.S.P.Q.2d 1011 (Bd. Pat. App. 1986).
80. 22 U.S.P.Q.2d 1463 (Bd. Pat. App. 1992).
81. 22 U.S.P.Q.2d 1958 (Bd. Pat. App. 1992).
82. *See, e.g.*, U.S. Patent No. 5,109,115 (the selection of a bombesin antigen conjugate was non-obvious) and U.S. Patent No. 5,134,075 (a MAb that has novel specificity to L45, a tumor antigen, is non-obvious). For a further discussion *see* McGough, K. and Burke, D., *The End of Monoclonal Patents*, BIOTECHNOLOGY, vol. 10, 1082 (Oct. 1992).
83. 51 F.3d 1552 (Fed. Cir. 1995).

The following are some forms for MAb claims that have been successful:

> 1. A monoclonal antibody which specifically binds to a peptide having an amino acid sequence identical to carboxy terminal heptapeptide of protein X and has the same antigen-binding specificity as antibodies produced by the deposited cell line having the ATCC number HB 0000.[84]

> 2. A monoclonal antibody produced by hybridoma cell line ATCC No. HB 0000, which antibody binds to a determinant site on a cell surface glycoprotein antigen of human tumor cells and antibodies which bind to the same antigenic determinant as does the monoclonal antibody produced by ATCC No. HB 0000 and compete with the monoclonal antibody produced by HB 0000 for binding at that antigenic determinant, Fab, $F(ab^1)_2$, and Fv fragments and conjugates of said antibody.[85]

> 3. A continuous cell line which produces a monoclonal antibody, wherein said monoclonal antibody binds to the same antigenic determinant as monoclonal antibody LAX produced by hybridoma cell line ATCC No. HB 0000, said cell line produced by the process of fusing a lymphocyte derived from a mouse immunized with carcinoma cells or an immunogenic determinant thereof and a mouse myeloma cell.[86]

> 4. A continuous cell line which produces a monoclonal antibody, wherein said monoclonal antibody binds to the same antigenic determinant as monoclonal antibody LAX produced by hybridoma cell line ATCC No. HB 0000, said cell line produced by the process of fusing a lymphocyte derived from a human with carcinoma and a myeloma cell.[87]

> 5. A process for the determination of the presence of or concentration of an antigenic substance in a fluid comprising the steps:

>> (a) contacting a sample of the fluid with a measured amount of a soluble first monoclonal antibody to the antigenic substance in order to form a soluble complex of the antibody and antigenic substance present in said sample, said first monoclonal antibody being labelled;

---

84. *See* U.S. Patent No. 5,109,115.
85. *See* U.S. Patent No. 5,134,075.
86. *Id.*
87. *Id.*

(b) contacting the soluble complex with a second monoclonal antibody to the antigenic substance, said second monoclonal antibody being bound to a solid carrier, said solid carrier being insoluble in said fluid, or order to form an insoluble complex of said first monoclonal antibody, said antigenic substance and said second monoclonal antibody bound to said solid carrier;

(c) separating said solid carrier from the fluid sample and unreacted labelled antibody;

(d) measuring either the amount of labelled antibody associated with the solid carrier or the amount of unreacted labelled antibody; and

(e) relating the amount of labelled antibody measured with the amount of labelled antibody measured for a control sample prepared in accordance with steps (a)-(d), said control sample being known to be free of said antigenic substance, to determine the presence of antigenic substance in said fluid sample, or relating the amount of labelled antibody measured with the amount of labelled antibody measured for samples containing known amounts of antigenic substance prepared in accordance with steps (a)-(d) to determine the concentration of antigenic substance in said fluid sample, the first and second monoclonal antibodies having an affinity for the antigenic substance of at least about 10^8 liters/mole.[88]

§ 80 Claims to Therapeutics

Claims to therapeutic biotechnology compositions or methods of treating a disease using the composition should be supported by *in vitro* or *in vivo* evidence of usefulness.[89] *In vitro* evidence alone should be sufficient, as in *Cross v. Iizuka*,[90] which involved

---

88. *See* U.S. Patent No. 4,376,110 at issue in the *Hybritech* cases.

89. However, for methods of treatment using products of biotechnology, *in vitro* data alone have in the past been deemed insufficient to show utility, especially when the treatment is for diseases such as cancer, neurodegenerative and other neurologic diseases and viral diseases, particularly AIDS; *see infra*.

90. 753 F.2d 1040 (Fed. Cir. 1985).

claims to imidazole derivative compounds having general pharmacological effects.[91]

The Federal Circuit upheld the Board in finding that practical utility was established on the basis of *in vitro* evidence alone, even though this evidence did not establish a specific therapeutic use. The court stated that:

> there was a reasonable correlation between the disclosed *in vitro* utility and an *in vivo* activity, and therefore a rigorous correlation is not necessary where the disclosure of pharmacological activity is reasonable based upon the probative evidence.[92]

Reasoning that *in vitro* testing is usually a prerequisite to, and indicative of, therapeutic value in humans, the court further articulated its position by stating:

> We perceive no insurmountable difficulty, under appropriate circumstances, in finding that the first link in the screening chain, *in vitro* testing, may establish a practical utility for the compound in question.[93]

In this case, additional evidence was presented indicating a correlation between the claimed drug and its parent compound, which had previously demonstrated the pharmaceutical activities being claimed.

Despite *Iizuka*, the PTO had taken an increasingly narrow and stringent view, particularly with regard to claims to therapeutic benefits. For example, a decision from the Board, *Ex parte Balzarini*,[94] involved claims to pharmaceutical compositions that recited broad pharmaceutical activity for treatment of retroviral diseases, including AIDS, in both animals and humans. The specification supported this utility with only *in vitro* testing.

The Board rejected Balzarini's claims for lack of utility, stating that the evidence did not indicate that those skilled in the art would find the *in vitro* evidence predictive of *in vivo* utility. This determination was reached even though the Board conceded, as in

---

91. *See also In re* Brana, 51 F.3d 1560 (Fed. Cir. 1995).
92. 753 F.2d at 1050.
93. *Id.* at 1051.
94. 21 U.S.P.Q.2d 1892 (Bd. Pat. App. 1991).

Iizuka, that *in vitro* testing is useful as a screening tool for further *in vivo* testing. The Board went on to make the remarkable statement that with regard to the field of anti-viral compounds, while it is not requiring human clinical trials, "it may very well be that in 1987 or even now those skilled in this art would not accept anything short of such human clinical trials."[95]

With regard to claims to products having useful "pharmaceutical activity" which are supported only by *in vivo* testing in animals, in *In re Krimmel*[96] the U.S. Court of Customs and Patent Appeals held that such evidence is sufficient to satisfy the utility requirement so long as the animals on which the tests are performed are "usually used by those skilled in the art to establish the particular pharmaceutical application in question," and the condition treated occurs both in humans and in lower animals.[97]

Krimmel involved a compound which was alleged to be effective in treating inflammation of the iris. The court found that, even if the applicant's *ultimate* purpose for the claimed invention was for treatment of the human condition, lack of proof of effectiveness in humans was not determinative of the patentability.[98] In reaching its conclusion, the court stated:

> There is nothing in the patent statute or any other statutes called to our attention which gives the Patent Office the right or the duty to require an applicant to prove that compounds or other materials which he is claiming, and which he has stated are useful for "pharmaceutical applications" are *safe, effective, and reliable for use with humans.*[99]

The court held that the application satisfied the utility requirement since the invention was sufficiently useful in the art, regardless of whether it was ever proven to be useful for treating a human ailment.[100]

---

95. *Id.* at 1897.
96. 292 F.2d 948 (C.C.P.A. 1961).
97. *Id.* at 952-953.
98. *Id.* at 953.
99. *Id.* at 954 (emphasis added).
100. *Id.* at 953.

Moreover, in *Nelson v. Bowler*[101] the C.C.P.A. held that pharmacological or therapeutic inventions that provide *any* "immediate benefit to the public" satisfied the utility requirement of section 101. Thus, the *identification* of the pharmacological activity of a compound and its relevance to a specific pharmacological use are sufficient. As the court stated in *Nelson v. Bowler*:

> Knowledge of the pharmacological activity of any compound is obviously beneficial to the public. It is inherently faster and easier to combat illnesses and alleviate symptoms when the medical profession is armed with an arsenal of chemicals having known pharmacological activities. Since it is crucial to provide researchers with an incentive to disclose pharmacological activities in as many compounds as possible, we conclude the adequate proof of any such activity constitutes a showing of practical utility.[102]

In response to perceived problems relating to the inability to obtain claims to therapeutic biotechnology products and process, the PTO promulgated a new set of guidelines on utility for biotechnology inventions that must be followed by examiners.[103] These guidelines specifically address certain aspects of the PTO's controversial position on utility. For example, the guidelines explicitly state, inter alia, that:

- an examiner should accept any reasonable use that can be viewed as providing a public benefit;
- evidence of a pharmacological activity of a compound which has a reasonable correlation to an asserted therapeutic use is sufficient; and
- data from human clinical trials or evidence of safety for treatment in humans is not required.

The guidelines also place a clear burden on the examiner to show by a "well-reasoned" factually-supported statement why an asserted utility is *not* credible. Under the guidelines, demonstrated *in vitro* or animal data should be sufficient to show utility.

---

101. 626 F.2d 853, 856 (C.C.P.A. 1980).
102. *Id.*
103. *See* 60 Fed. Reg. 36263 (1995) and associated Legal Analysis.

Citing PTO's utility guidelines with approval, the Federal Circuit in *In re Brana*[104] explicitly rejected the Board's pre-guideline position on utility. Stating that the Commissioner "confuses the requirements under the law for obtaining a patent with the requirements for obtaining government approval to market a particular drug for human consumption,"[105] the court unambiguously held that human testing of pharmacologically active compounds (having anti-tumor activity) was *not* required to establish utility of the compounds for purposes of patentability under 35 U.S.C. section 101.[106]

In view of the new utility guidelines and supporting Federal Circuit opinions, the recent trend in the PTO of requiring a higher utility standard under section 101 for biotechnology applications is likely to cease.[107] Demonstrated *in vitro* or animal data should once again be sufficient to establish utility. Clinical studies in humans, if at all possible, are of course preferable. Evidence, by way of a declaration under 37 C.F.R. section 1.132, may also be used to support the claims.

§ 81 Claims for Gene Therapy

Gene therapy, in general, is directed to the introduction of a gene encoding a specific protein into a cell for the purpose of producing such protein in the body for therapeutic effect. Gene therapy claims can be directed, inter alia, to gene transfer techniques, improved vectors (e.g., retroviruses, adenovirus, AAV, lipid carriers), targeting specific diseases and cell types. For example, U.S.

---

104. *In re* Brana, 51 F.3d 1560 (Fed. Cir. 1995).
105. *Id.* at 1442.
106. 34 U.S.P.Q.2d at 1442-1443.
107. However, some examiners in the biotechnology examining group are issuing similar types of rejections under 35 U.S.C. § 112, ¶ 1 for failing to teach "how to use" the claimed invention. The guidelines, however, are explicit that determining utility under § 112, ¶ 1 follows the same parameters as under § 101. *See also In re* Brana, 51 F.3d 1560 (Fed. Cir. 1995) in which the utility question was couched as a rejection under § 112, ¶ 1, not § 101.

Patent No. 5,436,146 provides for methods of preparing AAV vectors for use in gene therapy. Claim 1 is representative:

1. A method for producing a helper-free stock of recombinant adeno-associated virus comprising:

a) cotransfecting cells permissive for adeno-associated virus replication, in the presence of helper virus infection with i) a recombinant adeno-associated virus vector which contains a portion of foreign DNA sequence and which can be incorporated into an infectious virion and ii) a recombinant helper adeno-associated virus DNA which provides viral functions sufficient for the replication and packaging into infectious virions of said recombinant adeno-associated virus vector, and recombinant adeno-associated virus vector, and which comprises a nucleotide sequence not found in wild-type adeno-associated virus which promotes expression of adeno-associated virus genes which results in the viral functions provided, but which lacks adeno-associated virus terminal repeat sequence and shares no adeno-associated virus sequences with said vector, and which cannot itself be incorporated into an infectious virion in said cotransfected cells; and

b) collecting virions produced.

Therapeutic applications in the gene therapy field may be directed to *ex vivo* (*in vitro*) and/or *in vivo* approaches for the introduction of genetic material into cells.

Briefly, the *ex vivo* approach involves removal of target cells from the body, followed by introduction of a particular gene of interest into the cells and subsequent transplantation back into the body, where the inserted gene produces a desired product and result. For example, the *ex vivo* approach is the subject matter of U.S. Patent No. 5,399,346 to Anderson et al. Claim 1 of the '346 patent reads as follows:

1. A process for providing a human with a therapeutic protein comprising:

introducing human cells into a human, said human cells having been treated in vitro to insert therein a DNA segment encoding a therapeutic protein said human cells expressing in vivo in said human a therapeutically effective amount of said therapeutic protein.

While the above-recited claim appears quite broad in its face, the '346 patent is highly controversial and may not withstand likely challenges.[108]

The *in vivo* approach to gene therapy involves direct administration of the genetic material to an individual, either through administration at the site of interest or through the use of a targeting mechanism (e.g., a virus vector or a lipid) to ensure that the introduced gene enters the cells of interest, where it can be expressed to produce a therapeutic effect. As of the present, there are no issued U.S. patents relating to *in vivo* therapy.

---

108. *See, e.g.*, Brisbee, C.A., *Will The Broad Ex Vivo Gene Therapy Patent Be Challenged: An Appraisal,* GENETIC ENGINEERING NEWS (May 15, 1995) at 22-23. Indeed, the '346 patent is currently involved in a three-party interference.

X

Thoughts on Writing a Claim

The author now describes a preferred process he would use in writing claims. Following afterward is advice on claim writing from another experienced practitioner.

These comments are primarily directed to mechanical claims on a mechanical apparatus or an article of manufacture, and to mechanical methods. However, many of these comments apply to claims of all types.

Patent claim writing is an art, not a precise science. There is no correct or best claim. So long as the goals of claim writing are achieved, any claims will suffice. But, through practices of patent attorneys and agents, the Manual of Patent Examining Procedure (MPEP) requirements of the Patent and Trademark Office, precedents in the district courts and the courts of appeals, what may be viewed as good claim form has evolved. This paper seeks to state in words what experienced practitioners have learned and put into practice.

I. GOALS OF CLAIM WRITING

A. Covering the Invention

The inventor/client's invention has been disclosed in the specification and drawings of the application. The object or goal of the invention has been understood. The concept of the invention is understood. The claims should cover the disclosed invention.

1. The coverage should be as broad as possible, as discussed below. The claims should cover the inventor's concept.[1] Some claims should cover the concept as broadly as possible.

---

1. *See* Corporate Communications Consultants, Inc. v. Columbia Pictures Industries, Inc., 576 F. Supp. 1429, 221 U.S.P.Q. 883 (S.D.N.Y. 1983), *rev'd without opinion,* 776 F.2d 1064 (Fed. Cir. 1985).

2. The claims should also protect the specific disclosed embodiments. Some claims should be sufficiently detailed that even if the broad claims covering the inventor's concept are held invalid, anyone who copies any of the inventor's disclosed preferred embodiments will infringe a valid detailed claim.

B. Claims Coverage Should Be as Broad as Possible

Broad coverage means not only that every particular preferred disclosed embodiment is protected in the claims, but that the claims cover all expected and unanticipated equivalents that competitors and others may later develop and all intentional and unintentional copies of the claimed invention which embody the inventor's concept. The inventor/client will compare a competitive or a similarly functioning product or process with the patented embodiments. If the client sees similar structure, operation and/or result, he will want to be able to use his patent to halt an infringement. It is the claim drafter's job to have written the claims in the application to not only cover what the attorney and the inventor/client could at the time of application prosecution have envisioned as competing products, but to cover competitive products which neither the inventor nor the attorney thought of or could even have imagined at the time, but which employ the concept of the invention.

C. Cover Competing Products or Methods

1. A claim should cover a product that is identical to the invention, particularly identical to the preferred embodiments.

2. A claim should cover a product or a method that is similar to the claimed invention in that:

    a. the similar product or method to be covered is different than that disclosed in the disclosure, specification and drawings of the patent, but embodies the same inventive concept and/or,

    b. the competitive product or method achieves the same result. Patent claims typically are not result dependent, that is, they do not merely claim an apparatus or method for achieving a particular result. Instead, they claim several product elements or a series of method steps which achieve a particular result. Nonetheless, the claims should be broad enough to reach to a competitive product or method which is substantially similar to, or which has no substantial differences from or is interchangeable with or which accomplishes substantially the same result in substantially the same way (a restatement of the Doctrine of Equivalents which has evolved through judicial precedents, most recently, *Hilton Davis v. Jeakins Co., Inc.*[2]), possibly by using the same or a related structure or process. The attorney should envision and write the claims to cover various undisclosed, even unimagined equivalents of the embodiments of the invention that are disclosed in the application and that are included in the inventor's concept.

D. Avoid the Prior Art

The claims should be as broad in scope as the prior art permits, should not read on the prior art, but should improve upon it. The prior art establishes the maximum breadth of claim scope.[3] The concept of the invention typically is its distinguishing feature over the prior art. The claims should be broad, but should include the concept of the invention which distinguishes it from the prior art.

E. No Unnecessary Limits

Coupled with the avoidance of the prior art is the avoidance of unnecessary limitations in the claims, those not dictated by prior art or by proper form under the rules and practices of claim drafting which are in part set out in the Manual of Patent Examining Procedures and are required by 35 U.S.C. section 112 of the Patent Act.

II. HOW TO WRITE THE BROAD CLAIM

A. Use Different Classes of Claims

Mechanical inventions are of numerous types. Some inventions can be covered by different classes of claims:

1. Nearly all mechanical inventions, except methods, can be expressed in product or apparatus claims which describe the structure in terms of its elements, their relative locations and their cooperation. Product claims should be used for mechanical inventions where possible.

---

2. 35 U.S.P.Q.2d F.3d (BNA) 1641 (Fed. Cir. 1995)
3. Corporate Communications Consultants, Inc. v. Columbia Pictures Industries, Inc., 576 F. Supp. 1429, 221 U.S.P.Q. 883 (S.D.N.Y. 1983), *rev'd* 776 F. 2d. 1064 (Fed. Cir. 1985); Beale v. Schuman, 212 U.S.P.Q. 291 (Bd. Interferences 1980).

2. Even method inventions may have a novel, unobvious product analog, so that some method inventions can be stated in product terms, and vice versa. A broad example of that would be a method claim comprising various steps, each of which is performed by respective machine elements, and a corresponding analog claim to an apparatus comprising the various machine elements that perform the various steps.

3. Sometimes a unique structure, or workpiece, or component element, or starting material, etc. is used during the performance of the method. Product claims can be directed to that feature used in the method. The claim writer should review any method invention to see if a product claim could be written on any aspect of the method.

4. A method claim is a series of steps of manipulation, whether the steps would be performed wholly by machine or partly by a person, so long as they are not purely mental steps (an algorithm, which is dealt with in connection with electronics and computer claims). Any invention which lies in the manipulation of an object is susceptible to a method claim, which should be written.

5. As noted above, certain product inventions include different respective means which perform different manipulative steps. Maybe a method analog claim can be written wherein each means for performing a step in a product claim can be included in a method claim as a recitation of the performance of that step.

6. A product covered in a product claim may in part perform, or may have some subassembly which performs, a novel process or method, and that may be included in a separate method claim.

7. Where the method is solely the function performed by the product covered in a product claim, and the method would not otherwise be unobvious, then the method should not be claimed.

8. Product by process claims should also be considered to claim a product where a novel, hopefully patentable, method is used to produce or fabricate a particular product. The patentability of the resulting product itself as a product is judged under sections 102 and 103 of the Patent Act, not by the patentability of the method by which the product is produced. If a new method is used to produce an existing product, a product by process claim would not be allowable under sections 102 or 103.

B. The Goal or Object of the Invention

Every invention has a purpose, to improve upon something, or to achieve a particular objective or goal. All claims should be directed toward that. Claims to an invention should not be written merely to describe the structure disclosed, as this will lead to inclusion of unnecessary claim limitations. Before writing any claims, try to articulate to yourself the objectives or goals of the invention.

1. An invention may have more than one objective or goal, or it may solve more than one problem. These may be related. A good set of claims would include respective claims directed to each objective or goal.

2. To cover the inventor's solution to each objective, consider using a separate independent claim. Focus on one goal or objective and claim it completely. Thereafter switch to the other goal or objective and claim that completely. Similarly, the apparatus under consideration has several different features, whose existence in the final product may be mutually exclusive, i.e. one feature need not be present when the other is. Two separate sets of claims will be developed, possibly headed by two independent claims each directed to a different objective, or each directed to a final product with not all of the mutually exclusive features. But the invention will be fully covered. It is possible that an Examiner examining the application may issue a restriction requirement on the ground that two or more separate and distinct inventions have been claimed. But that should not dissuade the drafter from preparing the groups of claims.

C. The Inventor's Way of Achieving the Objective or Goal

Before beginning to write the claim, also state to yourself the inventor's way of achieving each goal or objective. In other words, state the invention. By first articulating the inventor's way of achieving the goal, the drafter avoids detailing many of the unnecessary specific disclosed structures, and recites only those which achieve the objective. Sometimes, the articulated goal or objective and the articulated way it is achieved are the same and, by doing one, you do both.

D. Writing the Claim

1. While writing the claim, observe a preferred embodiment of the invention. For a mechanical invention, look at a primary drawing Figure which shows the embodiment that is the subject of the claim, also consider the specification, as needed. Throughout the claim writing, keep referring to the embodiment. You want to claim the invention without naming elements that are not disclosed. You also want to describe elements accurately. The claim drafter is also the specification writer and is in charge of amending the drawings. While writing the claims, you may recognize that certain elements essential for inclusion in the claim are not in the disclosure. Hence, the claim writing stage is also important to enable the claim drafter to assure that every element claimed can be found in the drawings, as required by Rule 83(a).

2. Move through the illustrated embodiment. In the broadest independent claim, recite only each element of the embodiment which is critical to the inventor's way of achieving the goal or objective of the invention.

3. A complete structure for achieving the objective and which covers the invention must be claimed. Do not omit necessary elements, as that would make the structure incomplete and inoperative. If you are claiming a gear and a wheel that is to be driven by the gear, there must be some connection between the wheel and the gear or the structure is incomplete.

4. Omit mentioning elements that, while shown in the preferred embodiment, are not critical to the inventor's way of achieving the objective.

5. A product claim has a number of interacting or connected elements, whether it be a claim to an apparatus or to an article of manufacture. The claim drafter must start somewhere.

   a. With an operating apparatus, you start somewhere and write a claim moving along the action or motion.

      i. With an apparatus that accomplishes or does something, you might start at the drive or the motor and move through the apparatus in the direction toward its output element or, you might start at the final output element and move backward through the apparatus to the drive.

ii. Because of simultaneous actions or interactions, while you are claiming elements as you move through from the drive to the output, in order that the claim make sense, you may have to break off your sequence of describing elements through the apparatus and pick up the description elsewhere in the apparatus. For example, if the invention concerns two separate types of motion controlled from a single drive, and the types of motion are interacting, you may carry a description of elements from the drive outward to the first means causing the first motion, and then carry a description of elements from the drive out to the second means that is causing the second motion. Then the cooperation between the two motions is described. But a logical sequence should be used.

iii. A claim on a mechanical apparatus, when well written, often can be understood by a reader even without seeing any drawing disclosure and should usually be understood when it is read by a patent practitioner familiar with that art, in conjunction with a drawing depicting the embodiment claimed. A logical sequence of recited claim elements enables a reader somewhat familiar with that art to read a well-drafted claim without having first studied the disclosure in detail. Were the elements seemingly randomly named in the claim, it would be more difficult to follow and understand the claim.

b. The guidelines provided above would apply equally to a claim directed to an article of manufacture, which does not move. With an article of manufacture, start at one part and move through the article. There is a logical sequence of reciting elements through the article, e.g., typically from the base out to whatever is supported on the base, or vice versa. Writing in a logical sequence will enable the reader to understand the claimed article without needing to study the disclosure in detail.

6. There is an art to selecting the elements to be named in the broadest claim. The preferred embodiment has many more elements than need be recited in the broadest claim. While the absence of a need to recite many of the illustrated elements for a complete structural recitation of an invention will be apparent (for example, the number of screws used, or even the presence of

a screw, for holding elements together, may not be necessary to re-cite), the decision about inclusion of other elements may not be so easily made.

7. I have found it helpful to use an essentially method step anal-ysis of the apparatus to be claimed. In any machine or product, each element performs some function or operation which makes its presence in the apparatus necessary. However, when writing the broadest claim and determining which elements are necessary to achieve the inventor's objective, not all of these functions are necessary. As you move through the disclosure, e.g., move through a primary drawing Figure, consider not only the elements you observe, but the function that each element performs in the observed structure. If that function is necessary to achieving the inventor's objective, whether it be an active function or just a function of being present, then whatever performs that function probably should be recited in the broadest claim. I say only prob-ably should be included because certain functions that you will believe are necessary may be parts of a larger group of functions which together may be defined by a broader claimed description of an element that satisfies an overall objective of the particular sub-assembly of elements.

8. When a function believed critical to achieving the inventor's objective is seen, the elements which must be recited to perform that function are recited. This is true in an apparatus claim. It is also true for an article of manufacture claim, which describes el-ements that are there, although usually are not active. Various el-ements in a product claim can be described in the claim in terms of the function each performs.

E. Claiming Individual Claim Features

Every element in a claim must be properly identified and de-scribed, or else the claim is improper under section 112. To iden-tify a claim element:

1. Name the element.

a. Usually the element is given the name that it has in the specification as a noun. This enables the reader of the patent to understand the claimed element on two levels. First, the name in the specification is or perhaps should be sufficiently descriptive that when the claim is read without, or perhaps with, reference to the drawing and without reference to the specification, the claim element referred to can be understood. Secondly, when the element is read in conjunction with the specification in which it is already named, antecedent support for that element is found in the specification.

b. Using the name for the element that appears in the specification does not give that claim element all of the characteristics of that element which are disclosed in the preferred embodiment in the specification and drawings. The element has only the characteristics recited in the claim itself.

c. The name given to the element should be related to the primary function which the element performs in the claimed combination. The element may have a different name in the specification, which is the name by which the element is usually known. But, some feature of that element may be important and it is that feature of the element which would be named in the claim. If a particular name is selected for an element in writing a claim because, for example, of the function that the element performs in the claimed structure, the specification should be reviewed to add that name for the element into the specification.

For example, the item disclosed in the disclosure may be an anvil on which a workpiece is worked. But it is not an anvil or any other product used in lieu of an anvil that is significant for the claim. It is instead the presence of the surface of the anvil on which the workpiece is worked that is significant. Hence, the claimed element should be a "surface," rather than an "anvil." The specification may have only described an anvil, and may not have mentioned the surface. But, because the writer is probably drafting the specification along with the claim, the writer would not only recite "a surface" in the claim, he would return to the specification previously prepared and modify it so that it recites ". . . an anvil having a surface on which the workpiece is worked . . . ." or the equivalent, so that you could then claim the surface as the critical element, and not the needlessly limiting "anvil." This is an example of looking for the function that the element of interest performs and then claiming the element in terms of the part of it that performs the necessary function, rather than claiming the element in its entirety.

d. Often, and especially if you use a functional analysis, the tendency might be to describe each element as means for accomplishing a function, rather than giving that element a name that appears in the specification. This is permissible under the statute. But it is not always or even usually necessary to do that, and using another noun, e.g., "a surface on which the workpiece is worked" as contrasted with "means on which the . . ." makes the claim more easily understood. The occasions to use "means for performing a function" language are addressed in section 34 of this book.

2. After naming the element, the claim drafter describes where the element is in the apparatus or the article. In particular, describe to which previously named element the new element is connected or with which it co-acts, e.g., a gear connected with the shaft, a gear on the shaft, or two shafts near each other.

a. Avoid reciting an unplaced or unrelated element, which makes it impossible to know where the element is in the complete structure.

b. In this regard, the recited physical relationship or placement of the claim elements should be capable of being drawn or diagrammed. Some practitioners like to be able to draw a claim combination based not upon the drawing in the disclosure of the application, but rather based upon the word description in the claim. If no physical relationship or relative placement between two elements appears in a claim, the person making the diagram should not be able to diagram the connection or relative placement, and that may provide an indication that a necessary relationship should be described.

c. Recitation of a placement or connection is not needed for the first named element in the broadest claim (the housing in claim 1 at II above).

d. Sometimes, to logically explain the cooperation among various elements, describing the connection of a newly named element to others on the first appearance of the new element, may make the claim difficult to understand. It is possible to name an element earlier in a claim and to, for the first time, refer back to the earlier named element later in the claim when describing the physical relationship between a later named element and the earlier named element. Two separate elements may cooperate with a third one. One element must be named first, and there would be no way to relate it physically to the other elements until all three are named. This is an example of a situation where the physical relationship between two elements is described sometime after at least one of the elements has been identified. But it is preferable to describe the physical relationship of an element to others at the time the element is first named. That makes the claim more easily comprehended than to list a catalog of elements and later describe the various connections among and between them.

e. It is not required to recite the physical relationship or placement of an element with respect to others. Sometimes, a description of the functional relationship between two elements sufficiently suggests their physical relationship, so that a specific recitation of the physical relationship is not needed. For example, the claim limitation "a motor for driving the shaft," which is a mere functional description of the relationship between those two elements, serves equally well as would "a motor connected with the shaft for driving the shaft." As discussed below, a description of the physical connection between elements, without some indication of the reason for the connection, while accurate in terms of what is disclosed, tends to make the claim more difficult to read and understand. For another example, "a motor connected with the shaft," without reciting the reason for that connection ("for driving the shaft") may be accurate. But, it makes the particular relationship and, thus, the claim difficult to understand. Where the claimed functional description of the cooperation between elements satisfactorily also suggests their physical relationship, the physical relationship need not also be claimed. Yet, describing the physical relationship is still helpful to the reader. Sometimes, the actual physical relationship between an element and all others is irrelevant and only their functional relationship is important. In that case, the physical relationship need not be mentioned at all, and only that functional relationship need be mentioned.

f. Every claimed element of a mechanical claim must appear in the drawing of the application. If a claim includes an element that the claim drafter feels must be in the claim, that element must also be found in the drawing of the disclosure. 37 C.F.R. section 1.83(a). If the element is missing from the drawing, the drawing should be amended by the drafter of the claim to include the element. Probably, the specification should be amended to describe the new element shown in the drawing and recited in the claim, because there should be an antecedent for the element in the specification, including the name for the element recited in the claim. 37 C.F.R. section 1.75(d)(1). If the original disclosure at the time of filing lacked a particular element, and the claims as filed lacked the element, it is not possible to later add that element to the claim, because to do so would be to introduce new matter.

3. The description of where an element is with reference to others is often joined with a description of the function of that combination of two elements, as in "a motor connected with the shaft for driving the shaft to rotate."

a. In addition to naming an element and saying where it is with reference to other claimed elements, the function of the element in the entire claimed structure or at least with respect to another element with which it cooperates is recited, as mentioned above in the description of the cooperation between the motor and the shaft. Sometimes, the function performed is not related to any physical relationship between the elements. As discussed in the preceding part hereof, in that case there need be no description of the placement or physical relationship of the elements. Only a description of the cooperation and joint functioning is recited in the claim.

b. Essentially, the claim drafter is describing what the claimed element does. You describe the function of the element either for itself, i.e., what it does, and/or you describe what it does in cooperation with or does to another element, and/or you describe how it affects another element, and/or you describe how it acts on or affects a workpiece which is not one of the claimed elements of the structure. For example, "a hammer for flattening the workpiece against a surface" describes the function of one claim element, the hammer, in terms of another claim element, the surface, and in terms of the workpiece. Sometimes the workpiece is not on the surface, so that the description would be "a hammer for banging the workpiece," and that could be an adequate description, especially if the presence of the surface is not critical to action by the hammer on the workpiece. (What moves the hammer or what the hammer is connected to has not been recited, but that is presumably described in the claim.)

F. Revising the Claim after Writing It

1. After each claim is written, and again after all of the claims have been written, remove all elements from every claim that are unnecessary for achieving the inventor's goal or objective. This clearly applies to the broad independent claims. It also applies to the dependent claims. A dependent claim may add details as to a previously broadly claimed limitation. But, sometimes the dependent claim adds too much detail. Each further detail covered in a dependent claim perhaps should be added in respective successive dependent claims. If there are two details of one particular feature that are to be claimed or a particular feature is to be further claimed in detail in a later dependent claim, consider breaking up the dependent claim into two or three dependent claims, each adding one further detail.

2. Review each claim, limitation by limitation. Keep in mind the inventor's goal or objective and the inventor's way of achieving that goal. Remove, especially from the broader claims, any elements that are not essential for achieving that objective. Strike an element from the independent claim and consider whether to insert it in another dependent claim to be added. Similarly, in every dependent claim directed to one particular feature, consider dividing up the dependent claim and moving any other extra feature to yet another dependent claim, which further details the subject of the dependent claim or adds a new limitation.

3. When a limitation is removed from a claim, it may also remove the recitation of the physical relationship between a remaining element and the removed element or it may remove a description of a cooperative functional relationship between two of the remaining claimed elements. Correct the amended claim to re-establish a physical and/or functional relationship between remaining elements.

4. Consider whether any set of cooperating elements can be combined together into a more generically claimed element which performs an overall function that the individual elements perform in combination. Be sure that all necessary functional limitations still remain. Sometimes a broader encompassing generic descrip-

tion of two previously separately named elements adequately claims them, without also making the claim an unacceptable functional recitation of an intended result without the supporting structure for accomplishing that result.[4]

G. Alternate Claim Drafting Techniques

1. The above described technique of moving through the apparatus and claiming each relevant element as it is encountered may be viewed by some claim readers as making a claim difficult to understand. Some readers may find it helpful to see a general picture of the invention and to have an outline of the whole structure that will be claimed before reading about its details. For an improved telephone, for instance, one might first recite, in the first independent claim, the main subassemblies of the telephone, including a base unit, a handset and a connecting cord between them. Then the claim recites each subassembly in more detail, in the manner discussed above. This provides a claim of a similar scope as the prior technique, with a slight modification at the beginning portion of the claim.

2. There is a catalog of elements approach to claim writing. A list of all of the various elements in the preferred embodiment in the disclosure, i.e., in the drawings and the specification, is prepared by reciting the descriptive nouns and adjectives of the features. Then with the drawing and/or the specification at hand, the main claim is prepared by selecting, out of the catalog of elements, those elements which are deemed critical for the invention. Other elements are saved for inclusion in dependent claims.

There is much to recommend this approach. Before the claims are written, the drafter can assure that there is a complete catalog of all of the elements to be considered, even if some are not eventually recited in a claim. This prevents omission of critical elements, although it has the potential to cause inclusion of unessential elements. No matter which claim writing technique is used, the inventor's objective and the way of achieving it should be kept in mind so that elements relevant to attainment of the objective of the inventor are selected for inclusion in the claims.

---

4. *See* Clements Industries, Inc. v. A. Meyers & Sons Corp., 712 F. Supp. 317, 12 U.S.P.Q.2d 1874 (S.D.N.Y. 1989).

A claim written to include all of the elements in the catalog would be a picture claim directed to the most preferred disclosed embodiment. Such a claim well protects that preferred embodiment. But its breadth is not sufficient for fullest protection of an invention against others who decide to adopt the inventor's concept, but not his precise embodiment, for achieving that objective. Further, with the catalog of elements approach, avoid aggregation or listing of elements that are not connected to each other.

III. CLAIMING PLURAL EMBODIMENTS

An inventor of a mechanical invention often conceives various embodiments for practicing the inventive concept. The specification and drawings of the patent include disclosures of preferred embodiments. The embodiments should be adequately protected in the claims.

A. The Generic Claim

The claim drafter should consider the inventor's objective and the way in which the objective is accomplished, consider all of the disclosed embodiments and find a common thread running through all of them which defines a single solution or way of achieving the objective or goal. Then, the claim drafter should write a generic claim, with minimal structural limitations, yet claiming a complete structure, that is directed to the generic invention and generic structure found in all of the embodiments disclosed.

1. The primary generic claim written on all embodiments would be an independent claim. The generic claim may have limitations which can be further developed and detailed, or there may be additional limitations or features of all of the embodiments that are not included in the first generic claim. It is not unusual to provide dependent generic claims on those features, which claims are generic because they cover all of the embodiments.

2. There may be some features in one embodiment that are not present in others and that prevent preparation of a generic claim which covers all embodiments, which avoids prior art, which also has sufficient structural limitations and which is not a mere statement of the desired objective without a supporting structure. In that case, no generic claim can be written. Separate independent

claims on the separate embodiments can be written. To the extent possible, a subgeneric claim, generic to some of the embodiments, would be written and another subgeneric claim generic to others of the embodiments would be written. Sometimes those subgeneric claims may be so different that they may really recite separate and independent inventions that should be covered in separate patent applications. However, if they are different embodiments of what the inventor has identified as the same invention, then it is recommended that they initially be included in the single application, that as claims as broad as possible on all of the embodiments be written, and that the applicant await a restriction requirement, if any, as to the claims to different inventions, rather than from the outset filing a number of applications on different embodiments, which may not be needed.

3. Following each generic claim, it is recommended that an individual dependent claim and, more usually, a group of dependent claims, be written to cover specific features of each embodiment which are directed to the inventor's way of achieving the general goal or objective of the invention. For each individual embodiment, therefore, there will be generic claims and claims specific to that embodiment.

B. Use enough Claims to Completely Cover the Invention

1. If there are several embodiments, cover all of them in enough claims. This has been reviewed in earlier sections hereof.

2. Some limitations may have been stricken out of earlier claims to keep those claims broader. Those limitations can be added back in respective additional dependent claims. This also has been discussed earlier.

3. Several elements may have been combined in one more generic claim limitation to make an earlier claim broader in scope and less particularly limited. Each such element may be specified individually in a later dependent claim. Where two elements had been combined to make a broader claim, one dependent claim may recite, "wherein the generic feature is comprised of both of the elements." Where appropriate, one dependent claim may recite that "the generic feature is comprised of one of the elements," and another dependent claim may recite that "the generic feature is comprised of the other element," and yet another dependent

claim may recite that "the generic feature is comprised of both of the elements." The latter claiming technique gives broader coverage.

4. A dependent claim should recite elements which relate to accomplishment of the objective or goal of the invention. Numerous features in any preferred embodiment could each be made the subject of a dependent claim. But it is not useful to have a claim just adding details that are not related to the accomplishment of the ultimate objective of the invention. There is a contrary view, perhaps somewhat cynical, on this. The validity of claims is eventually judged in view of prior art. More detailed claim limitations may not be found in primary cited prior art, but only in other secondary references. Invalidating a very detailed claim under 35 U.S.C. section 103 may require combining several references, so many that it could be said that claim would not have been obvious in view of the combined prior art.

5. Dependent claims are used to cover the specific commercial embodiment. Narrower claims are needed to cover the preferred design because:

a. That protects against a copyist copying the precise preferred embodiment. To avoid the patent claim, the copyist must make changes.

b. A more detailed claim is more difficult to invalidate over prior art, while protecting against a copyist. Of course, the ultimate is a picture claim, which in words recites the details of the preferred embodiment. But there is no reason to go that far in claiming details.

c. Dependent claims are used to cover the detailed features of the embodiments illustrated in the specification and drawings.

IV. CLAIMING AN IMPORTANT FUNCTION IN A PRODUCT CLAIM

A. Do not simply claim a result, that is, a claim having a preamble naming a device or product simply stated as being for accomplishing a particular result.

1. The MPEP gives as an example of such a forbidden claim, "A woolen cloth having a tendency to wear rough, rather than smooth." Note that such a claim lacks any structure for accomplishing the stated ultimate objective.

2. Before claim writing, as noted above, the drafter should determine the ultimate objective, e.g., those features of a woolen cloth. Thereafter, determine the technique disclosed by the inventor for accomplishing that objective, e.g., multiple layers of short filaments. Then claim a structure which accomplishes that ultimate objective by using the inventor's invention "A woolen cloth comprising a first layer of woven wool cloth, the first layer having projecting filaments, a second layer . . . ." That is a claim to a structure, not a claim merely to an ultimate objective.

3. Correspondingly, of course, do not merely claim some means for accomplishing the ultimate result.

4. Instead, claim a series of related elements, as discussed above. Some of these elements may comprise means for accomplishing a particular function or step. But wherever the means for accomplishing that step is claimed, the drafter does not simply claim the step functionally as its own objective, the drafter claims some means for accomplishing that step, which is permitted by 35 U.S.C. section 112, paragraph 6.

B. Whereby Clauses (Sec. 32)

1. "Whereby" or statement of ultimate result clauses are permitted. Such statements should be used to state only the necessary outcome or result of the previously described structure. *In re Certain Personal Computers*, 224 U.S.P.Q. 270 (Ct. Int'l Trade 1984). They are functional clauses. The "whereby" clause should not be relied upon to add a structural limitation, whether or not that structure is critical to accomplish the inventor's objective. Some precedents suggest that "whereby" clauses can be used to add structural limitations. They are effective in a claim. See *Eltech Systems Corp. v. PPG Industries, Inc.*, 710 F. Supp. 622, 11 U.S.P.Q.2d 1174 (W.D. La. 1988), *aff'd*, 903 F.2d 805, 14 U.S.P.Q. 1965 (Fed. Cir. 1990). But, that is not good form to examiners. Therefore, it is dangerous to rely on the "whereby" functional clause to add structure.

When a "whereby" clause is written in a claim, the claim should be reviewed to make sure that it recites structure to support that "whereby" clause. If needed, the claim should be amended to add structural elements that are antecedents to the "whereby" clause. Since the "whereby" clause likely will state some objective of the invention, the fact that no element is present which would serve as an antecedent to the "whereby" clause should raise a question as to the sufficiency of the structural limitations of the claim.

A "whereby" clause that merely states the result of the limitations in the claim adds nothing to the patentability of substance of the claim. *Texas Instruments Inc. v. U.S. Int'l Trade Comm'n*, 988 F.2d 1165, 26 U.S.P.Q. 2d 1018 (Fed. Cir. 1993). But it may help the reader understand the claimed structure, sum it up, and make the claim more readable. Use them as appears appropriate.

2. Writing the claims as suggested above, where the description of elements of the claims includes a statement of their function or cooperation with other elements, may make a "whereby" clause unnecessary, because all of the functions that might be recited in the "whereby" clause have already been recited in the descriptions of operations performed by various claim elements. However, sometimes descriptions of the functions of individual elements do not show how they fit together and function as a complete structure, because only a "whereby" clause does that.

V. THE MEANS CLAUSE (Sec. 34)

A. Avoid Overbroad Means Clause

Recitation in a claim of a means to perform the ultimate function or objective of the invention is too broad. "Means for causing a woolen cloth to wear rough, rather than smooth," would not be a proper claim as this statement merely indicates there is some means for accomplishing the final objective. A complete structure must be claimed, moving through the apparatus or the article and describing each element essential to accomplishing that final objective.

B. Use of Means Clauses

A means clause is used to describe the function of a particular element, as discussed herein. However, before deciding to argue patentability based on a means-plus-function limitation in response to an examiner's rejection, remember that including a means-plus-function clause may create a prosecution history estoppel which limits the patentee's protection. The examiner will argue that the prior art of record teaches an equivalent of the disclosed means-plus-function structure, with no guidelines to support that assertion. Although the *In re Donaldson* case provided no guidelines to determining what is an equivalent, the Federal Circuit and the Supreme Court recently gave that term better definition in *Warner-Jenkinson Co. v. Hilton Davis Chem. Co.*, discussed below.

1. Review the inventive structure and select each element that performs a function for accomplishing the ultimate objective. If appropriate, recite that element as a means for performing its particular function in the entire structure.

2. A means clause to be effective as such should be written in the "means for . . ." style. If a noun other than "means" is used to name the element, then it may not be treated as a "means for" clause governed by 35 U.S.C. section 112. *In re Donaldson* and the Patent Office guidelines on means claims, discussed in section 34 hereof, indicate that the Patent Office, at least, will not require that a claim recite "means for" or "step for" before treating that claim as one under section 112, paragraph 6. But, court and Federal Circuit precedents have not yet appeared dealing with the Patent Office's proposed change in application of section 112, paragraph 6. However, bear in mind that use of the word "means" will not necessarily make the claim a means-plus-function limitation. *Cole v. Kimberly-Clark Corp.*, 102 F.3d 524 (Fed. 1996). *See Surgical Laser Technologies, Inc. v. Laser Industries Ltd.*, 29 U.S.P.Q.2d 1533, 1535 (E.D. Pa. 1993). Use of an extra adjective before "means," like "rod means," eases the reader's reference to the element being claimed and is usually a means-plus-function limitation covered by 35 U.S.C. section 112. *Manville Sales Corp. v. Paramount Systems Inc.*, 14 U.S.P.Q.2d 1291 (E.D. Pa. 1989), *modified,* 917 F.2d 544, 16 U.S.P.Q.2d 1587 (Fed. Cir. 1990), unless the resulting claim term describes a definite structure that performs the function, rather than an indefinite "means."

Equivalency under 35 U.S.C. section 112 differs from the Doctrine of Equivalents. *Valmont Industries Inc. v. Reinke Manufacturing Co.,* 983 F.2d 1039, 25 U.S.P.Q.2d 1451 (Fed. Cir. 1993). The Doctrine of Equivalents equitably expands exclusive patent rights, while section 112, paragraph 6, limits the broad language of means-plus-function limitations in combination claims to equivalents of the structures, materials, or acts in the specification. *Id.* at 1455. The Doctrine of Equivalents turns on the "substantiality" of the differences between the patented and accused products or processes, and that the evidence that the accused device or process "performs substantially the same overall function or work, in substantially the same way, to obtain substantially the same overall result as the claimed invention," *Warner-Jenkinson Co. v. Hilton Davis Chemical Co.*, 35 U.S.P.Q.2d 1641 (Fed. Cir. 1995), *rev'd on other grounds*, 117 S. Ct. 1040, 41 U.S.P.Q.2d (BNA) 1865 (1997); *See also Pennwalt Corp. v. Durand-Wayland, Inc.*, 833 F.2d 931, 934, 4 U.S.P.Q.2d 1737, 1788 (Fed. Cir. 1987) (en banc), *cert. denied*, 485 U.S. 961, 1009 (1988).

In applying the Doctrine of Equivalents, one determines the range of equivalents when analyzing the prosecution history, pioneer status of the invention, and the prior art. Then one must determine whether the particular element of the accused device or process is "equivalent" (as defined above) as to fall within that range. *Warner-Jenkinson Co. v. Hilton Davis Chem. Co.*, 117 S. Ct. 1040, 41 U.S.P.Q.2d (BNA) 1865 (1997). When applying section 112, the only issue is whether the single means in an accused device which performs the claimed function is the same as or equivalent to the structure in the specification which performs that same function. *D.M.I., Inc.*, 755 F.2d at 1575.

Although the decision in *In re Donaldson Co.*, 16 F.3d 1189, 29 U.S.P.Q.2d 1845 (Fed. Cir., 1994), does not explain how to examine for equivalency when dealing with a means-plus-function clause. However, the opinion did state in footnote 8 that the term "equivalent," as used in 35 U.S.C. section 112, paragraph 6, is not to be interpreted as an equivalent under the Doctrine of Equivalents, citing *D.M.I., Inc.*, 755 F.2d at 1575, 225 U.S.P.Q. at 239 and *Pennwalt Corp.*, 833 F.2d at 933-934, 4 U.S.P.Q.2d at 1741 (en banc). *See Warner-Jenkinson Co. v. Hilton Davis Chem. Co.*, 117 S. Ct. 1040, 41 U.S.P.Q. 2d (BNA) 1865 (1997). However, the Patent Office guidelines to examiners tries to explain how the Patent Office should examine for equivalency.

The Federal Circuit has recently explained the term "equivalent" by holding that a trial court had properly instructed a jury regarding the interpretation of "means" clauses in combination claims, including an instruction that such clauses must be interpreted to cover structure disclosed in the specification as corresponding to the "means" clause, as well as equivalents thereof, and that an "equivalent" means under 35 U.S.C. section 112 is one that "functions identically and is merely an insubstantial change that adds nothing of significance" to the device disclosed in specification. *Durable Inc. v. Packaging Corp. of America*, 31 U.S.P.Q.2d 1513 (Fed. Cir. 1994). The court in *Durable* relied on *Valmont* in its analysis. But *Warner-Jenkinson* provides the full court's current opinion on scope of equivalence.

3. It presents no problem if the means clause is at what is known as the point of novelty, that is, it recites the feature that distinguishes the claim from prior art. The claim may have a number of limitations that are in the prior art and one distinguishing feature. The means clause may be that distinguishing feature.

 (Faber, Rel. #1, 11/97)

4. A means clause is used especially where the function or action, rather than the specific structure that causes or accompanies the action, is important to the claim.

5. A means for performing a function clause is useful where there are actually two separate functions being performed and the two functions accomplish a further broader objective, so that the "means for performing the further function" encompasses both of the more specific functions. The "means for performing a function" clause is also useful where there is a partial overlap in functions between two structures. For example, a shaft may have two functions, to drive a propeller and to drive a wheel. Merely claiming that shaft as one element could be too limiting, since that does not deal with the objectives of that shaft, which are to drive a propeller and to drive a wheel. However, the claim recites "means for driving the propeller and means for driving the wheel," (the purest means style), or "first means for driving the propeller and second means for driving the wheel," or "propeller driving means connected to drive the propeller (not in means style) and wheel driving means for driving the wheel," then the overlapping functions of the shaft are covered by use of the means for language covering both of the functions. Additionally, should an infringer not use the single shaft for two purposes, but instead provide two shafts, one for each driving purpose, or even use other means than a shaft to drive one of the propeller or the wheel, the claiming of two separate means for performing respective functions covers it, if the infringer's structure is equivalent to what is disclosed.

6. As noted above, do not add the word "means" after a generic descriptive noun describing the element. However, if there are either one or more than one of the same type of units that cooperate, as noted above, such as one of a series of mirrors or blades, etc., then use of the word "means" following the descriptive word, mirror, blade, etc., can cover either one or several of those items that cooperate and together perform a function. This is because use of the noun "means" after what then becomes the descriptive adjective, "mirror," "blade," etc., eases the reader's reference to the claimed means. *Manville Sales Corp. v. Paramount Systems, Inc.*, 14 U.S.P.Q.2d 1291 (E.D. Pa. 1989), *modified,* 917 F.2d 544, 16 U.S.P.Q.2d 1587 (Fed. Cir. 1990). See the

previous discussion of *Surgical Laser Technologies Inc. v. Laser Industries Ltd.*, 29 U.S.P.Q.2d 1533 (E.D. Pa. 1993), wherein the court supported the jury's determination that "probe tip means" does not constitute means-plus-function language; whereas "securing means" does.

7. A means clause can differ from a prior art reference that applies to it only in the means feature. A means limitation at the point of novelty, although proper, could be found unpatentable, because of prior art showing something else that performs the same function. The Patent Office gave a "means" limitation the "broadest reasonable interpretation." Now under the examining guideline for "means" claims, MPEP 2181, the "means or step plus function" limitation is to be limited to the corresponding structure, material or acts described in the specification and their equivalents. This was designed to be more restricive than previous examining practice.

8. A problem in interpreting apparatus claims arises in computer-arts inventions (section 44) when the structure in the claim is defined only as "means for" performing a specified function. In computer-related inventions, the means often perform the function of solving mathematical algorithms and making calculations. Consequently, the applicant has the burden of showing that the claims are drawn to a specific apparatus rather than other apparatus capable of performing the same functions.

The recent Federal Circuit decision, *In re Alappat* 33 F.2d 1526, reversed, *Ex parte Alappat*, 23 U.S.P.Q.2d 1340 (Bd. Pat. App. & Interferences 1992), by holding that "it was error for the Board majority to interpret each of the means clauses in claim 15 so broadly as to "read on any and every means for performing the functions" recited, . . . and then to conclude that claim 15 is nothing more than a process claim wherein each means clause represents a step in that process." 31 U.S.P.Q.2d 1545, 1554 (Fed. Cir. 1994). The court stated that precedents do not support the Board's view that the particular apparatus claims at issue should be viewed as nothing more than process claims for which when one determines patentability, the issue would be whether the method is statutory subject matter under 35 U.S.C. section 101. The Federal Circuit's decision in *In re Donaldson* confirms *Alappat*.

For example, the court in *In re Alappat* stated that when independent claim 15 is construed in accordance with 35 U.S.C. section 112, paragraph 6, claim 15 reads as follows, the subject matter in brackets representing the structure which *Alappat* discloses in his specification as corresponding to the respective means language recited in the claims:

15. A rasterizer [a "machine"] for converting vectors in a data list representing sample magnitudes of an input waveform into antialiased pixel illumination intensity data to be displayed on a display means comprising:

(a) [an arithmetic logic circuit configured to perform an absolute value function, or an equivalent thereof] for determining a vertical distance between the endpoints of each of the vectors in the data list;

(b) [an arithmetic logic circuit configured to perform an absolute value function, or an equivalent thereof] for determining an elevation of a row of pixels that is spanned by the vector;

(c) [a pair of barrel shifters, or equivalents thereof] for normalizing the vertical distance and elevation; and

(d) [a read only memory (ROM) containing illumination intensity data, or an equivalent thereof] for outputting illumination intensity data as a predetermined function of the normalized vertical distance and elevation.

Claim 15 recites a machine, or apparatus, made up of a combination of known electronic circuitry. The court held that because claim 15 is directed to a machine, which is one of the four categories of patentable subject matter, it appears to be patentable subject matter. The Board had held that the claimed subject matter falls within the "mathematical algorithm" exception. The court stated that the claimed subject matter in this case does not fall within the exception.

The court held that, although all of the means elements recited in claim 15 represent circuitry elements that perform mathematical calculations, the claimed invention as a whole is directed to a combination of interrelated elements which combine to form a machine for converting discrete waveform data samples into antialiased pixel illumination intensity data to be displayed on a display means. The court found this is not a "disembodied mathematical concept which may be characterized as an 'abstract idea,' but rather a specific machine to produce a useful, concrete, and tangible result. The fact that the four claimed means elements function to transform one set of data to another through what may be viewed as a series of mathematical calculations does not alone justify a holding that the claim as a whole is directed to non-statutory subject matter." *In re Alappat*, 31 U.S.P.Q.2d at 1557-8. *See In re Iwahashi*, 888 F.2d 1370, 1375, 12 U.S.P.Q.2d 1908, 1911 (Fed. Cir. 1989). Claim 15 is limited to the use of a particular claimed combination of elements performing the particular claimed combination of calculations to transform, i.e., rasterize, digitized waveforms (data) into anti-aliased, pixel illumination data to produce a smooth waveform.

The court also found that the Board majority erred in stating that claim 15 is unpatentable merely because it "reads on a general purpose digital computer 'means' to perform the various steps under program control." *Alappat*, 23 U.S.P.Q.2d at 1345. The Board majority had assumed that the stored program digital computer was within the range of equivalents, under section 112, paragraph 6, of the structure disclosed in the specification. Precedent has held that programming a general purpose computer to carry out the claimed invention, i.e., function, creates a new machine which may be patentable subject matter.

VI. METHOD CLAIM (Secs. 36-41)

A method claim covers a manipulative process which converts, changes, or operates on a workpiece in some manner.

A method claim is particularly valuable because it is not usually tied to a particular structure for accomplishing its objective. As a technical art evolves, new products and hardware are developed. But a basic method continues to be used, and new product technology may continue to perform the patented method long after the product disclosed and perhaps also claimed in the patent has been superseded.

A. Sample Method Claim

A product like the steam and dry iron shown in example 27 in appendix B of this book, does something to a workpiece, like a cloth. It is capable of being covered in a method claim. Sample method claims for the iron appear below. Note how the method limits are analogs, to an extent, for product limits.

Method Claim On "Steam And Dry Iron":

10. A method of ironing comprising:

applying an ironing surface to a cloth to be ironed for applying ironing pressure to the cloth; moving the ironing surface in a first direction while delivering steam to a first leading side of the ironing surface which leads movement of the ironing surface in the first direction;

moving the ironing surface in a second direction while delivering steam to a second leading side of the ironing surface which leads movement of the ironing surface in the second direction;

blocking delivery of steam to the second leading side of the ironing surface while delivering steam to the first leading side, and blocking delivery of steam to the first leading side of the moving surface while delivering steam to the second leading side;

whereby steam leads and may pass under the ironing surface as it moves in either of the first and second directions.

11. The method of claim 10, wherein the ironing surface is part of an iron;

the method further comprising generating steam in the iron and transmitting the steam to be delivered to the then leading side of the ironing surface.

12. The method of claim 11, wherein the steam generating comprises heating water in the iron.

13. The method of claim 12, further comprising heating the ironing surface.

14. The method of claim 13, wherein the heating of water in the iron and the heating of the ironing surface are performed in the same step.

15. The method of claim 11, wherein the iron includes a rockable handle thereon and a valve for directing steam to the then leading side of the ironing surface, the valve being connected with the handle for being operated by rocking of the handle;

the delivery and blocking delivery of steam comprising rocking the handle to operate the valve to selectively deliver steam to the then leading side of the ironing surface.

16. The method of claim 10, further comprising selectively blocking delivery of steam to both leading sides of the ironing surface simultaneously while the iron is moved.

17. The method of claim 10, wherein the ironing surface first leading side is at the front end of the ironing surface and the ironing surface second leading side is at the rear end of the ironing surface.

B. The Elements Of A Method Claim

1. A method claim recites a series of steps, typically not apparatus features, article of manufacture features, or characteristics of components. A method claim names each method step. A product claim names each structural element. *See Hewlett Packard Co. v. Bausch & Lomb, Inc.*, 909 F.2d 1464, 15 U.S.P.Q.2d 1525 (Fed. Cir. 1990).

2. The step in a method claim is recited in the verb gerund or "ing" form. (See claim 10 at A. in this section.) It is an active form of a verb. Even non-action verbs are used actively, e.g., "waiting." Other verb forms are avoided, such as a passive form. For example, use "introducing," not "is introduced." The gerund form typically causes the verb to be the first word in the method limitation, but not always.

3. Typically, a method step in a claim is described in terms of operating on something, either on an apparatus (the ironing surface, above) that in turn operates on the workpiece (the object being ironed, above) or directly on the workpiece, for accomplishing a particular objective.

4. A method limitation names the step by using an appropriate descriptive verb word from the specification (moving, delivering, blocking). As with a product claim, if the needed verb is not in the specification, it is recommended that the word from the claim be added into the specification by the claim drafter.

5. The step is described by indicating what object or workpiece the step is performed on, e.g., "striking the workpiece . . . ." An invention seldom performs a step without acting on something.

6. Where possible, a function or purpose for performing each step is indicated, e.g., "striking the workpiece for flattening" it. (See claim 10 above, first "applying" limitation.)

a. As with product claims, sometimes the function need not be described if an adequate description is provided by naming the step performed and indicating what the step is performed on.

b. On other occasions, there is an adequate description of the claimed function by naming the step and indicating the function that the step is performing without indicating the structure or workpiece on which the step is being performed, e.g., "hammering for flattening the workpiece" or "hammering the workpiece for flattening it." This, the process equivalent of a "means for" limitation, is permitted under 35 U.S.C. section 112, and is discussed briefly below.

C. In a Method Claim, a Product Is Not Being Claimed

1. A product recited in a method claim is a structure which performs some or all of the steps indicated in the claim "rotating two fingers of the machine . . ." and/or performs those steps on the workpiece "rotating two fingers against the workpiece . . .," or broadly "contacting the workpiece . . . ." The last mentioned clause is a broad method clause just indicating what is happening without specifying the product that participates in accomplishing it.

2. A narrow method limitation has a method verb acting on some machine element to act on the workpiece. Broader still is to have the method step acting on the workpiece without reciting a particular machine element that does that action. Possibly broader still would just be reciting a process step for accomplishing a result which is on the way to accomplishing the objective of the method, without specifying the nature of the particular step that accomplishes it. That is, the method analog of a means for accomplishing a function claim limitation.

3. The Patent and Trademark Office has released proposed new examination guidelines for evaluating the patentability of computer-related inventions. The examiners, when classifying the invention defined by each claim as to its statutory category, should presume that a series of specific operational steps to be performed in or with the aid of a computer is a statutory "process." The computer is an apparatus performing a process.

D. A Dependent Method Claim

1. A dependent method claim either adds additional limitations (claim 13 in A. above in this section) or details or further defines previous limitations (claim 14 in A. above). The comments made above concerning dependent product claims apply to dependent method claims.

2. A dependent method claim can add an additional step (claim 13 above), or can define a previously broadly described step (claim 12 above) as a more detailed precise step, or can recite a set

of separate steps that make up a previously broadly claimed method step (see claim 15 above).

3. A dependent method claim can include product limitations only (see claim 17 above). In contrast, a dependent product claim should not include only method limitations, as discussed above. In a method claim, for example, where the method is performed using a particular structure or using a particular substance that acts upon something else than, for example, the product, or even the tool element used for performing the process, or the substance or material used in performing the process can be recited in a separate dependent method claim.

4. Claimed methods work on a workpiece to modify it in some way. There would not be a separate claim defining or altering the workpiece, because the workpiece is by definition not one of the claimed elements.

5. Where a method claim has a more broadly stated step and that more broadly stated step is defined in terms of a more narrowly stated step, both of the steps may be recited in a single limitation and both should be recited in the gerund form. The broader step is recited prior to the narrower step in the method claim (if claims 11 and 12 above were combined into one claim). For example, a claim might read "separating [the broader step] by distilling [narrower step]" rather than reciting "distilling to separate." Staying with that example, the distilling and separation may be also viewed in the sense that separation is the objective while distilling is the step, so that the claim limitation could also be written as "distilling for separating . . . ." But where a step is a narrow, more specific way of doing a step that is broader in scope, then the broader scope step should precede the narrower scope step in the claim limitation.

In this example of a broader step encompassing a narrower one, the claim writer should consider separating the "distilling" and "separating" steps into two claims, with the earlier claim reciting the broader "separating" and the later dependent claim reciting the "distilling," as in "wherein the separating comprises distilling [the workpiece]."

E. A Step for Accomplishing a Particular Function

35 U.S.C. section 112, paragraph 6, says that a recitation of a step for accomplishing a function is construed to cover what is disclosed in the specification and equivalents. Therefore, the "step for" limitation (see first limitation in claim 10 at A. above) covers equivalents. Case precedents have required use of the words "means for" to fall under 35 U.S.C. section 112. Patent Office guidelines MPEP 2181 and 2184 have eased that strict language requirement. Few cases have commented on the corresponding wording for process steps. *See O.I. Corp. v. Tekmar Co.,* 42 U.S.P.Q.2d (BNA) 1777 (Fed. Cir. 1997). But if you were solely to rely upon the language "step for" performing function, you might recite "performing a step for pressing the workpiece." That appears awkward. Another way of reciting the same method would be "pressing the workpiece." Case precedents establish that § 112, para. 6 applies to the step for limitation, but not that that "pressing the workpiece" limitation which is outside § 112, para. 6.

F. No Physical Interrelationship of Claimed Steps

1. In contrast to product claims, an interrelationship or connection of method claim steps to one another and their connection need not be recited.

2. Typically, method steps are performed in a sequence (see claim 10 above). Other than that sequence, they may bear no physical relationship to each other. But the claim steps must act in some logical sequence to lead to the final objective. Sometimes the various steps in the method are performed simultaneously (claim 10 above). But they too lead to the final goal.

3. Although the method steps are not necessarily related physically or by function to each other, they are usually related to the workpiece to which the method claim is directed (item being ironed in claim 10 above). Any method step not somehow directly or indirectly related to the workpiece probably does not belong in the method claim.

4. The method steps should always be related to attaining the final objective. Any steps not directed toward accomplishment of that objective clutter the method claim with unnecessary limitations which ease avoidance of the claim by an infringer.

G. Review the Claim after Writing

Method claims should be reviewed as described above to be certain that every limitation relates to the invention and is necessary for accomplishment of the objective. Detailed limitations which are not essential to the broadest way of claiming the method to achieve the ultimate objective should be removed from the broad claim and perhaps should be moved to narrower dependent method claims.

VII. ARTICLE OF MANUFACTURE CLAIMS

A. An article of manufacture is an object which exists and may do something, but it does so without claimable motion. An electric battery, a shoe, a window screen are articles of manufacture. They have practical uses, but no parts whose relative movements are relevant to the claimed invention. The actual article disclosed in the specification may have moving parts. But the article itself, not the action that the article is capable of performing with reference to a workpiece, is the subject of an article of manufacture claim.

B. Means for accomplishing a function limitations can be used in an article of manufacture claim. For example, such a claim includes "means for attaching A to B" or "means for closing the open end of . . ." or some other state of being between components of the article which can be described in "means for" language.

C. An article of manufacture claim could differ from the prior art by its shape, arrangement of parts, materials used, an inventive part included in an apparatus and sometimes by the manner in which it is made, although that typically is the subject of a product by process claim, discussed below.

D. The Patent and Trademark Office has released proposed new examination guidelines for evaluating the patentability of computer-related inventions. These Guidelines were released on June 1, 1995. In reviewing the written description and the claims, the examiners must "classify the invention defined by each claim as to its statutory category (i.e., process, machine, manufacture or composition of matters)." Examiners making that classification should presume the following, according to the guidelines:

     (Faber, Rel. #1, 11/97)

A computer-readable memory that can be used to direct a computer to function in a particular manner when used by the computer is a statutory "article of manufacture."

VIII. PRODUCT-BY-PROCESS CLAIMS (Sec. 46)

A. A product-by-process claim defines a product in the terms of the process used to make the product.

The most common situations in which claims use both product and process terms are: (1) when a product is new and unobvious, and incapable of independent structural definition; (2) the product is old and obvious, but the process is new; and (3) the product is new and unobvious, but has a process-based limitation. *Atlantic Thermoplastics Co. v. Faytex Corp.*, 974 F.2d 1279, 23 U.S.P.Q.2d 1801, 1803 (dissenting from denial of rehearing en banc) (Fed. Cir. 1992).

B. Occasionally, a product-by-process recitation is used to define one component part of a product in a claim rather than used for the entire claim. For example, a product may have a number of components, including a particular structure that is described in the terms of the process by which it is made, i.e., an electrical product may have a new structure which includes a contact made by a particular process. That contact would be covered by a respective product-by-process limitation within the body of the claim.

C. A product-by-process claim can be used in an application having a regular product claim. *In re Certain Steel Rod Treating Apparatus and Components Thereof*, 215 U.S.P.Q. 237 (Ct. Int'l Trade 1981). There is no limit on the number of product-by-process claims that may be used in one application.

D. A product-by-process claim is particularly useful when there are method claims, or method steps in an article of manufacture, or in product claims where the method or the steps cause something to be produced. In this case, the item that has been produced, or even the feature of the claimed structure that has been produced, may be made the subject of a product-by-process claim. Such a claim would recite a product [naming the product itself] made by the process comprising steps: . . . and then reciting the steps as in a method claim.

E. Product-by-process claims in a patent reciting a method for producing a "random faded effect" on fabric were held invalid because they were directed to non-patentable subject matter under 35 U.S.C. section 101. The court found the claims were more similar to claims in a design patent as the appearance of the random faded effect on jeans attracts attention, but does not affect the utility of the jeans. *Levi Strauss & Co. v. Golden Trade S.R.L., DCSNY*, No. 92 Cin. 166) (RPP) (4/14/95). But, if the product is the jeans, the process of producing them should be claimable and so should the process used in producing jeans with that effect. The issue is more likely whether the process is novel or unobvious (section 102 or section 103) over existing jeans, rather than a subject of patenting at all. (See F. below)

F. A product-by-process claim must satisfy 35 U.S.C. sections 102 and 103. Therefore, it is possible to have a completely new process, while the resulting product made by the process may not be patentable, because it is old. *In re Marosi*, 710 F.2d 799, 218 U.S.P.Q. 289 (Fed. Cir. 1983); *Ex parte Edwards*, 231 U.S.P.Q. 981 (Bd. Pat. App. and Interferences 1986). For example, there could be a new process for the assembly and packaging of cigarettes, but the resulting product, the cigarette itself is well known. Therefore, a product-by-process claim on such a cigarette would not be patentable.

G. A process limitation describing how a product is used, rather than how the product is made, does not result in a product by process claim, and thus does not fall within the holding of *Scripps Clinic & Research Foundation v. Genentech, Inc.*, 927 F.2d 1565, 18 U.S.P.Q.2d 1001 (Fed. Cir. 1991), *clarified on reconsideration*, 18 U.S.P.Q.2d 1896 (Fed. Cir. 1991). *Mentor Corp. v. Coloplast, Inc.*, 998 F.2d 992, 27 U.S.P.Q.2d 1521 (Fed. Cir. 1993).

H. The Federal Circuit is split on whether the process terms in a product-by-process claim serve as limitations when determining infringement. In *Scripps*, the court held:

> [T]he correct reading of the product by process claims is that they are not limited to product prepared by the process set forth in the claims.

Shortly, after the *Scripps* decision, the Federal Circuit rendered what appeared to be a decision contrary to *Scripps*. In *Atlantic*

Thermoplastics Co. v. Faytex Corp., 970 F.2d 834, 23 U.S.P.Q.2d 1481 (Fed. Cir.), *reh'g en banc denied.* 974 F.2d 1299, 24 U.S.P.Q.2d 1138 (concurring opinion); 974 F.2d 1279, 23 U.S.P.Q.2d 1801 (dissenting opinions) (Fed. Cir. 1992), the Federal Circuit held:

> Process terms in product-by-process claims serve as limitations in determining infringement.

The *Atlantic* court determined that the product-by-process claim at issue was not infringed by a product made by a process different from the one recited in the claim.

A recent District Court decision follows *Atlantic* by holding that product-by-process claims cover only the process, not the product, when determining infringement, so that the *Scripps* decision distinguishing between a process which produces a totally new substance and a novel process applied to a product which exists in prior art, is not controlling. *Tropix, Inc. v. Lumigen, Inc.*, 825 F. Supp. 7, 27 U.S.P.Q.2d 1475 (D. Mass. 1993).

The District Court stated that it appears that "a majority of the judges of the Federal Circuit would rule that *Atlantic* states the controlling law." *Tropix, Inc.*, 27 U.S.P.Q.2d at 1478.

However, the dissent in *Atlantic* provides a rationale to resolve the conflict between *Scripps* and *Atlantic*. They support drawing a distinction between (1) product-by-process claims used to describe a new and unobvious product which is incapable of independent structural definition (i.e., similar to "Fingerprint" claim rationale) and product claims having process limitations which were argued to be a basis for patentability over the prior art. *See* the dissenting opinion of Judge Newman in *Atlantic*, 23 U.S.P.Q.2d 1801. *Scripps* refused (for infringement purposes) to apply a process limitation of the former type. *Atlantic* applied a process limitation of the latter type.

In *Scripps*, the product was difficult to describe for patentability purposes. Consequently, a product-by-process claim was used. Hence, the court held that an accused product could infringe the patent even though it was made using a different noninfringing process. In *Atlantic*, in contrast, the product-by-process claim appeared to have been added to avoid rejection of the patent. Hence, the court determined, in order to find infringement, not only must the product be the same, but the product must be made by the same process claimed.

The Federal Circuit has not yet resolved the conflict between its two precedents, nor has it clarified whether their decision in *Atlantic* was intended to overrule *Scripps*. Consequently, when drafting product-by-process claims, one should be aware that process language could limit the claim, as in *Atlantic*. Therefore, when deciding whether to use a product-by-process claim, one should be cautious that it may limit the usefulness of the patent at a later date when trying to have other products, made by different processes, held to infringe the claim.

For patentability purposes, use of product-by-process claims allows one to patent products which are structurally difficult to describe. But they may limit one's ultimate ability to obtain a judgment for infringement if a party makes the same product via a different noninfringing process.

I. An example of a product-by-process claim used to describe a structurally difficult product is taken from *Scripps*, 18 U.S.P.Q.2d at 8005:

Claim 13 is representative of the product-by-process claims:

13. Highly purified and concentrated human or porcine VIII:C prepared in accordance with the method of claim 1.

Claim 1 is:

1. An improved method of preparing Factor VIII procoagulant activity protein comprising the steps of

(a) adsorbing a VIII:C/VIII:RP complex from a plasma or commercial concentrate source onto particles bound to a monoclonal antibody specific to VIII:RP,

(b) eluting the VIII:C,

(c) adsorbing the VIII:C obtained in step (b) in another adsorption to concentrate and further purify same,

(d) eluting the adsorbed VIII:C, and

(e) recovering highly purified and concentrated VIII:C.

IX. THE *JEPSON* CLAIM (Sec. 57)

A. The *Jepson* claim format can be used for method claims as well as product claims. The *Jepson* format is good and proper. *See*

In re Jepson, 1917 C.D. 62, 243 O.G. 525 (Ass't Comm'n Patents 1917). But the occasion is rare when it is the recommended format. The Patent and Trademark Office encourages its use in independent claims. 37 C.F.R. section 1.75(e). Its use is optional. It is seldom used in practice.

B. Examples of a *Jepson* claim now appear. They are based on the steam and dry iron product in example 27 in appendix B.

18. A steam and dry iron comprising:

a housing having an ironing surface; the ironing surface having a front side and a rear side with respect to motion of the ironing surface over an article to be ironed;

steam ports at the ironing surface for delivery of steam to the ironing surface;

a steam supply for delivering steam to the steam ports;

wherein the improvement comprises:

the steam ports including a front steam port at the front side of the ironing surface and a rear steam port at the rear side of the ironing surface;

a valve connected between the steam supply and the front and the rear ports, the valve being selectively moveable to a first position opening communication from the steam supply to the front port while closing communication between the steam supply and the rear port, and to a second position opening communication between the steam supply and the rear port while closing communication between the steam supply and the front port;

a valve operator connected with the valve for moving the valve to the first position as the iron is moved toward the front side of the ironing surface and for moving the valve to the second position as the iron is moved toward the rear side of the ironing surface;

whereby steam will exit the front and rear ports, respectively, to lead the iron in its motion toward the front and the rear sides of the ironing surface.

19. The steam and dry iron of claim 18, wherein the improvement further comprises the valve having a third position at which the valve closes communication from the steam supply to the front and the rear ports.

20. The steam and dry iron of claim 18, further comprising a heating element at the ironing surface for heating the ironing surface.

C. The *Jepson* format claim recites all or at least some elements of a known article, process, or combination in its preamble.

Medtronic, Inc. v. *Cardiac Pacemakers, Inc.,* 721 F.2d 1563, 220 U.S.P.Q. 97 (Fed. Cir. 1983): *Johns-Manville Corp.* v. *Guardian Industries, Corp.* 586 F. Supp. 1034, 221 U.S.P.Q. 319 (E.D. Mich. 1983); *amended,* 223 U.S.P.Q. 974 (E.D. Mich. 1984), *aff'd.,* 770 F.2d 178 (Fed. Cir. 1985). The preamble is usually rather lengthy, in contrast to the short preamble recommended for other product and process claims. The preamble may recite: "An apparatus comprising . . .," reciting prior art elements in proper claim style.

D. Following its preamble, the *Jepson* claim includes a transition clause that states, "wherein the improvement comprises," or "the combination with the old article, etc. of."

E. The following body of the claim recites only the new elements or the modified elements or tells of the new forms of connection or cooperation between all of the elements by reciting the improvements.

F. *Jepson* claims may be used when there is an improvement in one element of an otherwise old combination.

G. A dependent *Jepson* claim may be used to define only a known or prior art element.

H. A *Jepson* claim is similar to the claim form used in some European countries.

I. In the preamble, the various elements should be properly named and interrelated, as is done in other format claims. Similarly, in the part of the claim defining the improvement, the elements also should be properly named and related either to elements in the preamble portion or in the improvement portion, so that the *Jepson* claim meets all the other claim drafting requirements.

J. One danger of the *Jepson* claim format is that it emphasizes some elements of a combination over the others. It suggests to a reader that one should not look at the novelty and unobviousness of the entire combination, but rather at only a part of the combination. It may encourage a court which is later assessing the validity of the patent to combine a prior art reference directed to the preamble material of the claim with another prior art reference directed to the material following the transition and to suggest that these two references are properly combined to render the claim obvious and invalid. *See In re Fout*, 675 F.2d 297, 213 U.S.P.Q. 532 (C.C.P.A. 1982) and *In re Ehrreich*, 590 F. 2d. 902, 200 U.S.P.Q. 504 (C.C.P.A. 1979). While such a combination of prior art in a validity determination would be proper even if the usual claim format were used, the fact that a prior art reference is found, which shows all of the features that are recited in the *Jepson* claim to be the novel features, may weigh strongly in the mind of a trier of fact in deciding if that claim is invalid.

X. PARTICULAR POINTS RELATED TO GOOD CLAIM DRAFTING

A. Preamble (Sec. 6)

1. The preamble of a claim is its first words. It identifies the field of the invention. Preferably, that is all it should recite.

2. For an invention in a bicycle, for example, a preamble that says "vehicle" would appear to be of broader scope than a preamble that says "bicycle." Yet, if the invention is clearly directed to a bicycle, there is no benefit to having a preamble "vehicle" which is more encompassing than the invention itself. The preamble should be realistically narrow in scope. Conversely, if the preamble says "bicycle," but the invention is adaptable not only for bicycles but for motorcycles, and if an infringer were later to market a product which had all of the feature limitations in the claim, but which was a motorcycle rather than a bicycle, the infringer might argue that the claim does not reach the accused product because the claim is limited in scope to a bicycle. The preamble must be sufficiently broad to cover the product in the preferred embodiment to which the inventor has directed his attention (bicycle), but also to cover other embodiments, such as "two-wheeled vehicles," to which the invention may be directed. (In claim 1 in II above, the preamble is a steam and dry iron. Yet claim 1 only claims the steam iron aspect. The dry iron aspect is introduced in dependent claim 2. The preamble of claim 1 may be too narrow and an accused infringer may say that it excludes the two directional steam irons of claim 1. Perhaps the preamble should merely have been "An iron" or "A steam iron."

3. To avoid a too limited scope preamble, the claim writer might be tempted to merely recite the broad "Apparatus comprising" or use "device" or a similar non-specific noun. But a too

broad preamble is also not good practice, although not improper. Some writers use a statement of ultimate purpose or field of use with the non-specific noun, e.g., "Apparatus for flattening a workpiece" [statement of objective], or "Apparatus for ironing" (II above), or "Apparatus for improving a vehicle transmission" [field of use].

4. Typically, a preamble is either identical to or a slight adaptation of the title of the invention that appears at the head of the specification (which is why the claims in II above have their stated preamble). The title in the specification and the preamble of the claims should be correlated and consistent. If one is changed, the claim writer should consider changing the other.

5. A good preamble is short. It does not tell a story. It does not typically describe the ultimate purpose of the invention. (But see above.) It does not typically describe the workpiece on which the invention operates. (Again, see above.) A preamble limited to the title of the invention as it appears at the head of the specification should always be enough.

On the other hand, the preamble may have to be longer because in order to understand an invention, one must understand its context. Therefore, sometimes the purpose of the invention is recited in the preamble before the transition word, as in "Apparatus for treating a web to prevent tearing, the apparatus comprising . . . ." The title of the invention at the head of the specification may be slightly different, but there is no short claim preamble that does that job. Consideration should be given to keeping the preamble short in length, avoiding noting the ultimate objective of the invention and avoiding noting the workpiece, unless that is the only way to define a field for the invention, which is what the preamble does.

6. The preamble should not be longer for providing a basis for elements which appear in the body of the claim, except for the unusual *Jepson* claim preamble. Even a *Jepson* claim preamble has its own introductory portion or preamble which defines the field of the invention. Also, the preamble does not mention or distinguish the prior art.

7. The preamble of an independent claim may be a full statement of the field or the full title of the invention, longer, as in the

apparatus preambles noted above. The preamble of the dependent claims need not be as lengthy as the preamble of the independent claim. Often, the preamble of the dependent claim merely consists of the major noun of the preamble of the independent claim. In the above example, the dependent claim preamble may simply be "The apparatus of claim . . . ." But the preamble of any dependent claim can have more details.

The preamble of the dependent claim must be consistent with that of the claim from which it depends. If the previous claim is to "apparatus," the dependent claim should not be to "device." If the previous claim is to "bicycle," the dependent claim should not be to "vehicle." Change one or the other claim for consistency.

8. Depending upon how it reads, the preamble may or may not provide elements in the claim which limit or restrict its scope, other than the normal purpose of a preamble to define the field of the invention.

B. Subparagraph Claim Form (Sec. 10)

In an effort to improve U.S. claim clarity, the subparagraph claim form is preferred. The subparagraph format is not required. Preferably, each new major claim element and subassembly is made the subject of its subparagraph. A major claim element may, in turn, be comprised of a number of other claim elements. Those other claim elements may be or need not be the subject of separate subparagraphs, as the claim drafter decides.

Some claim drafters use numbers or letters to indicate the different elements and subparagraphs. This, too, is optional.

C. Multiple Dependent Claims (Sec. 12)

1. A multiple dependent claim refers back to more than one preceding claim.

2. A special one-time fee is payable for any multiple dependent claim in the application. In addition, each multiple dependent claim is treated as the number of claims on which it is dependent, so that a multiple dependent claim dependent on two other claims is treated as two claims.

3. It is not permissible to have a multiple dependent claim dependent upon another multiple dependent claim. A multiple dependent claim can be dependent only upon a number of single dependent claims. In turn, only a single dependent claim can be

dependent upon a multiple dependent claim. Each single dependent claim dependent upon a multiple dependent claim is for fee purposes treated as the same number of claims as the multiple dependent claim.

4. It is almost always possible to break a multiple dependent claim into single dependent claims. For fee reduction purposes and clarity of claiming, in the United States form, it is better to have single dependent claims, rather than multiple dependent claims. But the claim drafter may use multiple dependent claims which are acceptable.

D. Inferential Claiming

1. Each new element in a product claim and each new step in a method claim should be first introduced either as (a) the subject of its own clause (the "housing" in claim 1, line 2, at II above), or (b) a previously introduced and named item or a step comprises it, has it or includes it, that is, its presence is indicated by using a verb that describes the state of being (having, comprising, including, being), rather than an action verb (see the introduction of the "ironing surface" in claim 1, line 2 at II above). Being the subject of its own clause means that it is either stated in the clause that such an element or step is present or the element or step is named at the beginning of the clause and thereafter that element or step, which has been named now for the first time, does something or has something done to it. It is important that a new item mentioned for the first time in the claim not be first mentioned as an element operated upon or cooperated with by a previous element described in the same clause.

2. The indefinite article "a" may be used where it is preceded by either of the words "comprises," "includes," "has," or "being" or the equivalent, which indicates a state of being, rather than some activity involving that element being named.

3. A new element or step is introduced with an indefinite article "a" or "an." (Some plural items have no introductory article "a" and are introduced by the plural noun itself. But, from the context, the silent introductory indefinite article can be inferred.) On the other hand, when a previously identified element or step is repeated, it is introduced by a definite article "the" or "said".

4. The claim drafter should look at the claim to see that each element or step is introduced with an indefinite article. Then note whether that element or step is the subject of the clause or whether it is being acted upon or is itself acting upon another object or step. If it is being acted upon or acting upon another object, then it should be the subject of that clause.

5. The only exception to the inferential claiming prohibition is where the indefinite article "a" is used to introduce a workpiece. Because the workpiece is not an element of the claim, but rather is only worked upon by one of the claim elements, it would not be introduced as the subject of its own clause.

6. An example of improper inferential claiming is the clause "the motor being connected with *a* shaft which is connected with the gear for driving the gear." In that claim limitation, the shaft is inferentially claimed. It is not the subject of the clause. If there is a subject, it is the motor or the gear. Also, the shaft is not being described in a state of being with respect to the motor or the gear, but rather it is being described in a state of action. Proper wording might be "a shaft connected with the motor and with the gear for communicating driving motion from the motor to the gear." This says the same thing, but does not inferentially claim the shaft. (Implicit in this clause, of course, is that the motor and the gear were previously introduced in the claim, since each is preceded in the clause by the definite article "the.") Referring to the other exception, if the clause reads "the motor including a shaft extending to the gear," that would not be inferential claiming. The shaft has been first introduced in the claim in a state of being with respect to the motor, so that for an inferential claiming analysis, the shaft is now properly in the claim. Thereafter, and even in the same shaft introducing clause, the shaft can be active, and it is described as cooperating with the gear. It is no longer inferential claiming once the element with the indefinite article "a" has been properly introduced. (See the introduction of the water chamber in claim 5 at II above.)

Review of Some Basics

by Myron Cohen

Preface

MR. LANDIS: The following remarks were prepared by Myron Cohen [then] of Hubbel, Cohen & Stiefel, as advice to our PLI Agent's Exam students at claim drafting clinics, in which the students prepare claims to sample structures for criticism by our tutors, including Mr. Cohen. Many such problems appear in appendix B.

Mr. Cohen's half-time pep talk to his students not only summarizes and highlights many of the most important portions of this book on how to write mechanical claims, it contains very sage advice on how to write broad claims generally. Although some of the advice is intended for the rank beginner, and other parts focus on particular kinds of Agent's Exam questions, all can learn from these self-styled "random thoughts"[5] of Mr. Cohen.

Random Thoughts on How to Draft Claims to Mechanical Apparatus

MR. COHEN: A claim is a one-sentence definition of the structure of the defined invention. It defines that invention with the same particularity and precision as the description of a parcel of land in a deed. The analogy to the deed is a good one because United States claims serve to define the outer limits or boundaries of the invention in the same fashion as the description of land in a deed defines the outer limits of the land monopoly. Thus, United States claims do not define the spirit or heart or central theme of an invention. Much of this does not shed any light on how to draft claims, but it is important to recognize that claim language must be extremely precise. The precision of the language has nothing whatsoever to do with the breadth or narrowness of the claim, for the broad claim must be drawn with the same precision as the nar-

---

5. These thoughts were composed over some ten years of practice in tutoring novice claim drafters. They are decidedly not random; they hit the students' problems on the head.

row claim. The point is that there are very few if any chores in the area of legal draftsmanship that are as demanding of language as the chore of drafting a claim.

Throughout the balance of these remarks, I intend to speak principally of apparatus claims. I shall touch on method claims briefly and on composition claims not at all. However, the truly tough job in drafting mechanical claims is the preparation of a broad claim to apparatus, and that is what we are going to concentrate on.

Most commentators in the field of United States claim drafting usually state that an apparatus claim is *not merely a catalog of parts*.[6] They are absolutely correct in saying this. Unfortunately, they usually overlook the fact that, while an apparatus claim is not *merely* a catalog of parts, it *absolutely must include a catalog of* parts. It is the cataloging of the parts that gives rise to what we call the positive recitation of the elements. That is, each structural element in the claim must be set forth directly and independently of every other element.

Thus, if an apparatus is to be claimed that includes three elements, A, B, and C, then the claim must have as a part of itself language that states "an A" and language that states "a B" and language that states "a C."

However, as the commentators told us, a United States claim is not merely a catalog of parts. What distinguishes a United States claim from a mere catalog is the inclusion in the claim of language that directly or indirectly interrelates each element in the claim with each other element. The interrelationship can be (1) by connection, either a dynamic connection (such as "rotatably mounted on") or a static connection (such as "fixed to"); (2) by definition of relative position between two elements (such as element B being disposed above element A); or (3) by setting forth yet another element in the catalog that interrelates two elements, (such as a gear train drivingly connecting element B to element A).

Thus, when one drafts a claim, perhaps the simplest way to do it is first to set forth a catalog of the major parts. After this has been done, one can either add additional parts to interrelate the

---

6. Sections 28 and 29.

major parts or modify the major parts to put in language of relationship. For example, a claim can read as follows:

A gadget comprising:

an A;

a B interrelated with A; and

a C interrelated with B.

It will be seen in the example that by interrelating A with B and by interrelating B with C you have indirectly interrelated C with A. Thus, all three elements, A, B, and C, are directly or indirectly interrelated and you have a complete claim. If, on the other hand, the claim called for:

A gadget comprising:

an A;

a B interrelated with A; and

a C.

you would not have a complete claim, as C would not be interrelated with either A or B. Such a claim would not be complete and would be rejected as being indefinite.[7]

Perhaps a more common way of writing a United States claim is to interrelate the main elements with additional structural elements that must also be positively recited or catalogued. Thus a perfectly proper claim would be:

A gadget comprising:

an A;

a B;

a C;

means interrelating A with B; and

means interrelating B with C.

This example meets all of the tests of a complete claim: all the elements are positively recited and each element is directly or indirectly interrelated with each other. The form of this last claim

---

7. Section 67; or "incomplete," section 66; or drawn to an aggregation; section 61; or not properly drawn to a machine: sections 28–29. Whatever the exact name of the ground of rejection, the examiner will usually object to such a claim. [JLL]

can prove rather sterile: generally speaking, a skilled claim drafts-man would write the claim in slightly different form. The preferred form would probably be:

A gadget comprising:

an A;

a B;

means interrelating A with B;

a C; and

means interrelating B with C.

In apparatus claims, we are concerned solely and exclusively-with a definition of structure. By structure I mean hardware, something you can touch, something you can feel, something you can manipulate. We are not interested in function, and the function of an element cannot be used as a substitute for the definition of the structure of the element itself.

However, there is one exception to the rule concerning the avoidance of the definition of an element by virtue of its function. In the last paragraph of section 112 of the statute, there is a statutory authority for defining an element as "a means for performing a function."[8] Now you may very well think that is ridiculous, that merely saying "means for performing a function" is as functional as defining the element by the function itself. Well, your logic may be good, but if you believe that you fail as a lawyers. The Congress of the United States has said that "means for performing a function" is structural, it is not functional.[9] So, by act of Congress, such language meets all of the statutory requirements for the definition of a structural element. In this connection, I would like to urge you not to avoid the use of the expression, "means for." It is a perfectly fine expression, and gives rise to the writing of claims of substantial breadth.

There is one place that "means for" cannot be used. You cannot define a structure by a single element that is defined in terms of a means for performing a function. That is what is meant by a "single means claim" and it is regarded as being functional. How-

8. *See* section 34.
9. *See* section 31.

ever, when you have more than one element in a claim, there is nothing wrong with defining one, several or all of the elements in terms of "means for." I might say that there have been times when I have actually done this and have secured the allowance of such claims. When the prior art permits it, it is the best kind of claim you can get.

There are a couple of specific rules that I would like to set forth for your guidance in connection with taking the examination. These rules, in some instances, you may shed after you have become a licensed practitioner; but I think they should be followed at this point in your career.

The first rule is *never use the expression, "adapted to" or "adapted for."* Both of these expressions tend to be somewhat functional and may lead to an objection on the ground of the claim's being indefinite.[10] There is a perfectly simple solution to the problem of proper language to be used in lieu of "adapted to" or "adapted for." The proper linguistic solution is the word "for." Thus never say, "a base adapted to support a table." It is much preferable to say, "a base for supporting a table."

The second rule, which I think should be followed through the examination, is *never use the word "whereby"*[11] *in a claim.* Now I know that you have been told that "whereby clauses" are perfectly good, and I, for one, use them regularly.

However, I think you have to know when to use them and when not to use them, and I seriously doubt that you have reached the point in your development as claim drafters at which you can use them with consistent propriety. Generally speaking, my experience has been that when a novice claim drafter uses the word "whereby," he or she generally uses it to introduce a lengthy functional expression to cover up or blur the fact that he or she has not

---

10. *See* sections 23 and 30. But see Patent Office guidelines of 1994, which broaden the range of the claim language that falls under section 112, paragraph 6 so that "adapted to " or "adopted for" would not necessarily be rejected as functional. However, on the agent's exam and before an experienced examiner during prosecution, you are better advised to adhere to the more traditional approach, pre-guidelines, of using "for." [Faber]
11. Section 32.

setforth the necessary structure. My advice to you is when you are drafting a claim and you suddenly see the word "whereby" jump out of that paper, stop! Go back and write the claim again. If the word "whereby" is going to be used, I think you are going to have a claim that is going to cost you a considerable number of points.

The third rule relates to the definition of holes, grooves, and other absences of material.[12] Just as I have said that every structural element, every hardware element, must be recited positively, I can give you an equally inflexible rule concerning *holes, grooves, slits, and slots. They cannot be recited positively;* they must always be recited inferentially. Thus, you cannot say "a doughnut, a hole in the center of a doughnut." That would positively recite the hole in the doughnut and would be considered improper. The proper way to handle this is to write "baked goods comprising: a cylinder of dough having a hole in the center thereof." Note that the hole just is not positively set forth or catalogued. It is "impositively" or inferentially recited by the use of the word "having." In the same manner, you might call for "a tube having a circumferential groove therein" or "a link having an axially extending slot therein."

Everything that I have discussed above relates to independent claims, that is, to claims that are wholly self-contained as to the structure set forth herein. There is another breed of claim called a "dependent claim,"[13] which is a claim of narrower scope than the claim from which it depends. A dependent claim is one that incorporates by reference all of the structure of the claim from which it depends. Thus, a dependent claim is not self-contained, but relies for some of the structure defined therein on a claim that is referred to in the preamble of the dependent claim.

The Patent and Trademark Office greatly prefers dependent claims to a series of ever narrower independent claims. The Office has found them easier to examine, as such dependent claims highlight the points of difference between successive claims. For this reason the Patent and Trademark Office charges less for each excess dependent claim than for each excess independent claim.

---

12. *See* section 26.
13. *See* section 56.

That being the case, when you take the exam, if you are asked to write three claims of differing scope defining a particular structure, you should write one broad independent claim and two dependent claims. When you are asked to write "broad, intermediate, and narrow," claims, you should make claim 2 depend from claim 1 and claim 3 depend from claim 2, whereby[14] claim 1 must logically be the broadest, claim 2 must be the intermediate claim, and claim 3 must be the narrowest.

But beware. The first rule of taking any exam is reading the exam carefully. One year, for no discernably good reason that I have ever conjured up, the Patent and Trademark Office, notwithstanding its own preference for dependent claims, specifically instructed the examinees to write three *independent* claims of different scope. Many of the students wrote a single independent claim and two dependent claims and lost many points on the two dependent claims. So, please read the exam and follow the instructions. If no instructions are given, then follow the formula given of one independent broad claim followed by a first dependent claim that depends on number 1 and a second dependent claim which depends on number 2. Dependent claims are quick and easy to write, as you will see in a moment, and conform with Patent and Trademark Office preference.

As I told you, a dependent claim incorporates by reference the entire subject matter of the claim from which it depends. If a dependent claim depends from a dependent claim, then it incorporates everything set forth in the claim from which that claim in turn depends. The chain of incorporation by reference can go on indefinitely.

There are only three things a dependent claim can do: it can add structure to the claim from which it depends; it can more particularly define structure already set forth in the claim from which it depends; or it can do both of those things.[15]

In order for a claim to add additional structure, the dependent claim must have the following language:

---

14. Note the purpose of a "whereby" clause (section 32), since the function necessarily follows from the previously recited structure [JLL].
15. A dependent claim cannot eliminate a feature of a previous claim.

The gadget as defined in claim 1, *further comprising* . . .

After the words "further comprising," you set forth the additional structural elements. Thus, for example, suppose you have a main or independent claim that states:

A gadget comprising:

an A;

a B interrelated with A; and

a C interrelated with B.

If in a narrower claim, you wish to add an element D to the claimed combination, then you would write a dependent claim in the following form:

The gadget as defined in claim 1, *further comprising* a D interrelated with (A or B or C).

Do not forget, even in a dependent claim every element must be directly or indirectly interrelated in some fashion with every other element that is contained in the claim either by express language or by incorporation by reference.

If, however, rather than adding an additional element D, you wish to define more particularly that the element B is actually made up of subelements E, F, and G, then you would be performing the second function of a dependent claim. You would be more particularly defining an element already set forth. To do this, the dependent claim would read as follows:

The gadget as defined in claim 1, *wherein* element B includes E, F, and G interconnecting E and F.

Please note this example sets forth more particularly just what is the construction of element B. Note that this dependent claim adds no additional element to the structure. Thus, when confronted with defining B as we have done in the immediately preceding example it would be improper to set forth this definition in the following fashion:

The gadget as defined in claim 1, further comprising an E, an F, and a G interrelating E and F.

The reason for this claim's being improper is that E, F, and G make up B. By using the "further comprising" language you have included element B twice in the structure, once as "B" and once as

"E, F, and G," when in fact B only appears once in the gadget. It is for this reason that the language "wherein" must be employed more particularly to define an already claimed element rather than "further comprising."[16]

All that I have said above relates to claims directed to structure, to apparatus. Apparatus claims are clearly more difficult to write than method claims. I am not going to spend much time on method claims other than to say that a method claim is merely a recitation of the manipulative steps necessary to perform the process.[17] Note the emphasis on the word "manipulative." By manipulative steps, we mean steps that can be performed directly or indirectly by hand or by machine controlled by the hand. Generally speaking, you cannot include mental steps, in such processes. In setting forth the manipulative steps you invariably use the "-ing" form of the verb such as "placing, gouging, sawing, heating, cooling, drilling," etc. In method claims you generally set forth the series of steps in the preferred sequence of performance.[18] However, be careful not to limit yourself to that sequence unless the particular sequence is critical. Be very wary of direct or indirect temporal limitations, such as, for example, the word "then" preceding the verb at the beginning of the step. Also be wary of performing a particular step implicitly after another step. For example, if a method calls for hollowing out a bar, and also heating the bar, be careful not to call for the heating step as "heating said hollowed bar," because then you would be required to perform the heating after the hollowing in order to infringe the claim. However, if this particular sequence is necessary to a successful practicing of the process, then naturally you must include it.

Finally, I thought I might tell you just how I go about writing a broad claim in my day-to-day practice.[19] The reason I stress the broad claim is that once you have written a broad claim, that is, a

---

16. *See* section 21 on (double inclusion of elements.) This point is to assure that the claim language is clear. Words other than "wherein" may achieve the same purpose and may be used: "In the gadget of claim 1, element B comprising [or further comprising] an E . . ."[Faber]
17. *See* sections 36–38 on (method claims, generally.)
18. Section 38.
19. Sections 16, 19, 60, etc.

claim as broad as the prior art will permit, it really is very simple through the mechanism of dependent claiming to write narrower claims.

The first thing you must do in writing any broad claim is to arrive at the decision as to what is and what is not essential to "the invention," meaning in this sense the patentable invention over the prior art. In this connection, and I speak principally to the chemists in the room, do not be afraid of making the wrong decision. If you do not know what really constitutes the invention, then decide on something and write three claims to it. You will get points for doing that.[20] You will get no points if you leave your paper blank. As a matter of fact, I must tell you that when I took this examination, all too many years ago, I actually wrote three claims to a cutting machine having a shock absorbing means, when, in fact, what I thought was a shock absorbing means was a safety guard. But I wrote three good claims, and I passed the exam. So do not panic on the assessment of where the invention is. Make a decision as to where the invention is and then write a broad claim using the following technique.

After I have decided what the invention is, what I do is, on a piece of scratch paper (do not put it in the notebook or the exam book yet, put it on a piece of scratch paper) I write a claim of indeterminate breadth. That is, some of my elements come out very broadly and some of my elements come out very narrowly, and I really do not care. All I am concerned with is getting something on paper from which to work. Once I have written down this claim of indeterminate scope I conduct what I call my schizophrenic dialogue. That is, I actually talk to myself and ask myself two series of questions. The first series of questions relates to each of the major elements in this claim of indeterminate scope. I read over each element and I ask myself if this element is necessary to the invention as I have perceived it. Thus, if I have included as an element

---

20. This advice applies to the type of Agent's Exam question given some years ago, where the examinee was required to write three claims to a mechanical structure (can opener, electric shaver, etc.) given only the drawing, with no description of the parts or how the device worked; and little if any indication of what might be the novel features. Examples of this type of question are given in appendix B. [JLL]

of my draft claim "a housing surrounding the drive shaft" and I know that the machine will work without the housing as well as with the housing, then I cross out that entire element. I do not need it and I do not want it to limit my claim unduly. By carrying on the first series of questions, I get rid of any unnecessary major elements in the claimed combination. Once I have done that I go back and check to see that each element remaining in the claim is in fact interrelated with each other element. If it is not, I add language to interrelate the unrelated elements.

Once I perform this second step to make sure that everything is interrelated, I go through the claim again. This time I go word-by-word and ask if the word is necessary. When I do this, I look for all words of limitation, such as "rigid, flexible, elongated, round," etc. Does the element have to be rigid? If it does, leave "rigid" in; if it does not, take it out. I look for "s's" on the ends of words because unless I need a plurality of the element, I have limited the claim to having the plural and have given up on the possibility of preventing someone from using the combination with a single one of those pluralized elements. In this fashion, I proceed through the claim word-by-word to measure the necessity of each word. If I do not need the word, I take it out. If I think that a given noun without modification is simply too broad or a modifier is necessary for the invention to be operative, I include the modifier.

When I get done with this second scanning of the claim, I have a broad claim, and it is as simple as that. Do not be bashful to talk to yourself and ask "is this element necessary" or "is this word necessary" and then say "yes" or "no." That is the way you are going to broaden your claim in the simplest, most direct fashion. After you have completed all of this crossing out and interlineating, then your claim is in shape to be copied it into your exam book, and you have yourself a broad claim.

With respect to the narrower claims, I have already told you that I strongly urge you to write them in dependent form unless expressly told otherwise. I would also urge you, *if possible,* to narrow your claims in the area that you really consider to be novel in the combination. Thus, for example, if what is new is the addition of an element D to an old combination of A, B, and C, then it is preferable for the second claim to define the new element D more particularly and the third claim to define the same element even more specifically.[21] But in writing your narrower claims please be sure that there is *substantial difference* between them. For example, do not try to distinguish one claim from another by saying "wherein the means for securing element A to element B is a nut and a bolt." That is simply not a substantial limitation, and you will lose points on it.

---

21. The dependent claims should cover those elements which contribute to achieving the objectives of the invention. Detailing elements of the disclosed apparatus which are unrelated to the invention is unnecessary and gives the patentee little of value. On the other hand, you want to protect the likely commercial embodiment of the invention, and claims to that may include those unrelated elements, for fullest patent protection. [Faber]

EXAMPLE I – SHAKER

FIG.-1

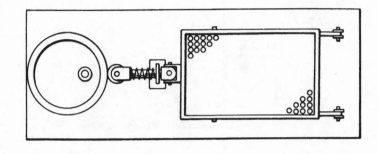

FIG.-2

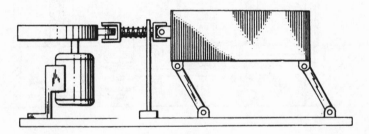

FIG.-3

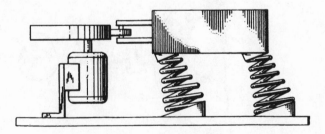

EXAMPLE II - TAKE-UP BARREL

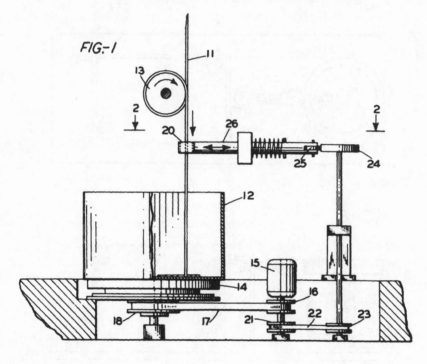

FIG.-1

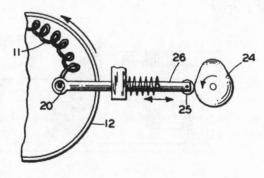

FIG.-2

EXAMPLE III– *WHEATSTONE BRIDGE*

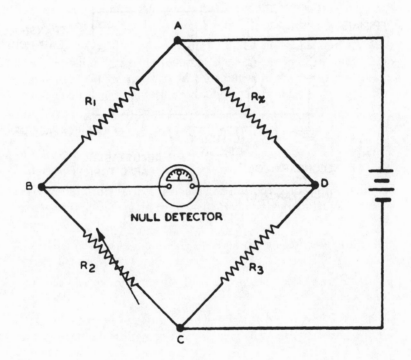

EXAMPLE IV - RADIO SIGNAL

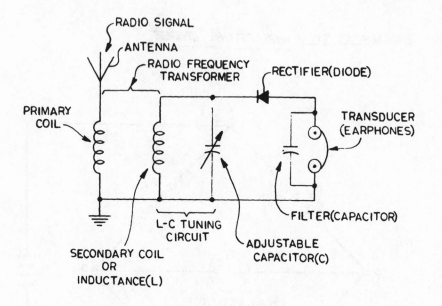

Appendix B

FURTHER EXAMPLES OF
CLAIM-DRAFTING PRINCIPLES AND PRACTICE
IN CLAIM-DRAFTING TECHNIQUES

The following material is selected from examples used in the Practising Law Institute's Patent and Trademark Office Agent's Examination Review Course. These examples are intended to provide practice in drafting claims of various kinds, and in criticizing poorly written or "sloppy claims." Many examples are from prior Agent's Exam questions.

The sample claims and the comments are intended primarily for students planning to take the Agent's Exam, and do not represent sophisticated claim-drafting practices or possibly controversial claim writing techniques that might be permissible and advantageous under modern court decisions cited in this book. The comments are intended to reflect Patent and Trademark Office practices and preferences, as understood from the Manual of Patent Examining Procedure, Patent and Trademark Office published remarks of acceptable answers to Exam questions, and generally conservative practice.

The sample claims in most cases are intended to be fairly moderate in scope, primarily to teach techniques of drafting relatively sound claims; in most cases not the broadest claims that might be allowable. In most real-life situations, drafting of really broad claims requires an exact knowledge of the prior art and, usually, a chance to argue such claims extensively in an amendment, because they are usually rejected the first time round. In all but a few of the examples, the prior art is not given, or not given precisely; thus the object of these examples is to give an intermediate-scope sample claim that an Examiner reviewing a student's paper would like and be willing to accept fairly readily as allowable and conforming to good, standard claim-drafting techniques and practices.

If the student wishes to use these examples for practice, he should study the problem or question, then write claims or other answers as directed. Then he should compare his claims and answers with the sample claims and comments to look for major differences. In most cases, there are many acceptable claims and approaches, almost as many as there are patent attorneys. Claim-drafting is an art, not a science, after all. Thus there are no right or wrong answers. The best bet is to ask an experienced patent attorney to review your claim in detail. On the mechanical structure cases, particularly those given only a drawing, read again the advice in Appendix C on describing mechanisms and Chapter X on writing claims to mechanical structures.

The following is a list of the cases in Appendix B and what problems they illustrate.

List of Cases

I Drafting of Claims

Case 1 Stephen — Apparatus for Propelling Articles
Apparatus claims and relation of apparatus and method claims

Case 2 Keltner — Traveling Lawn Sprinkler
Apparatus claims given the specification
Dependent claims

Case 3 Tonn — Nutcracker
Apparatus claims given only a drawing

Case 4 Wood—Hose Nozzle
Same

Case 5 Brown—Glue Container and Spreader
Same

Case 6 Chambers—Can Opener
Same

Case 7 Washington—Sowing Device
Same

Case 8 Wenstrand—Turntable
Same

Case 9 Kokeisl—Apparatus for Storing and Delivering
Granular or Like Flowable Materials
Apparatus claims given the specification

Case 10 McBride—Power Propelled Water Craft Apparatus
claims, given a drawing

Case 11 Optical Sound Reproduction
Electrical circuit claim (mixed circuit and
mechanical structure)

Case 12 Unijunction Pulse Generator
Detailed electrical circuit claim

Case 13 Gunderman—Polymer Latex Films
Method claims given the specification
Markush claims—Generic and species claims

Case 14 Bickel—Brush Making
Mechanical method claims, given specification
Generic and species claims

Case 15 Hiers—Straightening Flock
Method claims, given specification

II Criticizing "Sloppy Claims"

I Drafting of Claims

Case 1

PREPARING APPARATUS CLAIMS—RELATION OF APPARATUS CLAIMS TO METHOD CLAIMS

July 25, 1961   W. F. STEPHEN   **2,993,737**

APPARATUS FOR PROPELLING ARTICLES

Filed Feb. 23, 1960   3 Sheets—Sheet 1

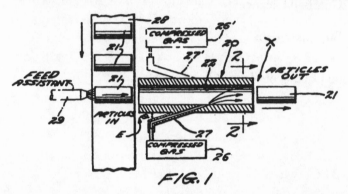

FIG. 1

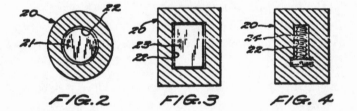

FIG. 2   FIG. 3   FIG. 4

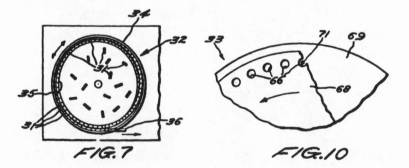

FIG. 7   FIG. 10

App. B-6

Problem

Draft an apparatus claim to the structure of Fig. 1 (assuming it to be new): A vacuum exists at the left end of tube 20, which tends to draw articles 21-21 into the tube, while high pressure exists at the right end thereof which forces the articles out of the tube. Assume the prior art is a standard blowgun or peashooter. Query: Would method claims be proper? If so, write a method claim.

Case 1

PREPARING APPARATUS CLAIMS—RELATION OF APPARATUS CLAIMS TO METHOD CLAIMS

SAMPLE CLAIMS— APPARATUS FOR PROPELLING ARTICLES

Moderate Scope

1. Apparatus for propelling an article, which comprises:

a tube having a bore extending therethrough, the tube bore having an entrance end and an exit end, the bore being shaped for closely receiving and passing the article therethrough;

a source of compressed gas;

a conduit extending from the source of compressed gas and terminating in the bore at an acute angle directed toward the exit end of the tube for discharging a partial vacuum at the entrance of the bore; and

means for feeding the article to a position immediately adjacent to and, in alignment with, the entrance end of the tube for sucking the article into the entrance end of the tube and for blowing it out the exit end.

Fairly Broad

2. Apparatus for propelling an article, which comprises:

a tube having a sidewall defining a bore through the tube for closely receiving and passing the article through the tube; and

3. Apparatus for propelling an article, which comprises:

a tube etc.

means for injecting a gas under pressure into the bore through the side wall of the tube at an angle such that a partial vacuum is created at a first end of the tube and the gas is discharged out the other end of the tube so that an article placed adjacent to and in alignment with the first end of the tube is sucked into the tube and is blown out the other end of the tube.

COMMENTS

This is a simple example, not from an Agent's Exam, illustrating some of the main principles in drafting apparatus claims. Claim 2 is about as broad in scope as one would want to go in the main claim; claim 1 about as narrow.

Note, "a tube having a bore," an example of how to claim holes, section 26. Note the references, apparently inferential, in claim 2 to "a first end" and "the other end" of the tube. As any tube inherently includes ends, the inferential reference to features inherently present in the element "a tube" is not improper inferential claiming. Better might be to first have recited, "the tube having a first end and another [or 'an opposite'] end."

In claim 1, the source of gas and conduit can readily be combined into "means for injecting gas," as in claim 2. In claim 2, the "means for injecting a gas . . . such that . . ." clause follows *In re Chandler*, cited in section 34.

The "means for feeding" clause in claim 1 is obviously appropriate, particularly since the structure of the means (air blast 29) is probably not important to the inventive concept. This element is more broadly phrased in claim 2, which would be superior in practice, "so that an article placed. . . ." Thus, claim 2 would cover the case where a human places the article 21 in the appropriate position, as in a pneumatic transport system, which uses this principle. Literally, the "means for" clause does not cover a human being, as noted in section 34.

ANSWERS TO QUERY ON METHOD CLAIMS

Method claims would be proper, assuming the invention, with a scope such as in claim 2, is novel. Such a claim, following the scope of claim 2 could read:

3. The method of propelling an article, which comprises:

injecting a gas under pressure through a side wall of a tube having a bore therethrough for closely receiving and passing the article therethrough, the gas being injected at an angle to the tube such that a partial vacuum is created at a first end of the tube and the gas is discharged at the other end of the tube; and

placing the article adjacent to and in alignment with the first end of the tube so that the article is sucked into the first end of the tube and is blown out the other end of the tube.

Note how an apparatus claim (2) can be turned into a method claim by finding the actions or steps—"injecting gas" and "placing the article." Otherwise, claim 3 is of essentially the same scope as claim 2. Note how the minimum necessary apparatus limitations are brought into the claim (see section 41); for example, injecting a gas . . . through *a wall of a tube*. Of course the mechanical structure recited in the claim should be minimized so far as possible. It would seem that "a tube" of the right size is indispensable in practicing the method.

Note finally how a broad product claim is, in effect, generally a series of functions or steps recited in structure (elements, elements of composition terms), whereby important elements of a broad product claim are those which perform a vital step in a method, and those elements not performing a vital step may possibly be eliminated from the product claim, or possibly may be stated more broadly or generically.

Case 2
PREPARING APPARATUS CLAIMS, GIVEN
A SPECIFICATION—DEPENDENT CLAIMS

Sept. 22, 1959

H. R. KELTNER

2,905,392

TRAVELLING LAWN SPRINKLER

Filed Dec. 16, 1955

2 Sheets—Sheet 1

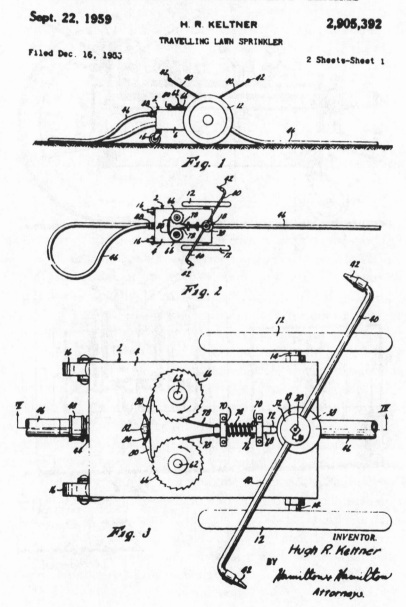

Fig. 1

Fig. 2

Fig. 3

INVENTOR.
Hugh R. Keltner
BY
Hamilton & Hamilton
Attorneys.

App. B-11

Sept. 22, 1959　　　　　　H R KELTNER　　　　　　2,905,392
TRAVELLING LAWN SPRINKLER

Filed Dec 16. 1955　　　　　　　　　　　　2 Sheets-Sheet 2

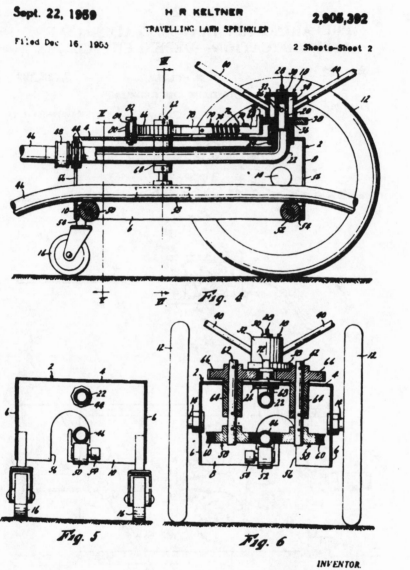

Fig. 4

Fig. 5　　　　　　Fig. 6

INVENTOR.
Hugh R. Keltner
BY
Hamilton & Hamilton
Attorneys.

2,905,392
TRAVELING LAWN
SPRINKLER
Hugh R. Keltner,
Johnson County, Kans.
Application December 16, 1955,
Serial No. 553,453
1 Chatm. (Cl. 239—110)

This invention relates to new and useful improvements in lawn sprinklers, and has as its principal object the provision of a lawn sprinkler comprising a sprinkler head mounted on a wheeled frame and attached to a pressure water supply, and having means operable by the pressure of the supply water to propel said wheeled frame over the ground.

Another object is the provision in a lawn sprinkler of the character described wherein the sprinkler head rotates to distribute water evenly over a wide area, and wherein said propelling means operates mechanically from the rotation of said head.

A further object is the provision of a lawn sprinkler of the class described wherein said propelling means operates by traction on an elongated member, which may be the water supply hose, laid out on the ground. The frame is steerable, so as to follow the elongated member around curves.

Other objects are simplicity and economy of construction, efficiency and dependability of operation, and adaptability for uses other than the watering of lawns.

With these objects in view, as well as other objects which will appear in the course of the specification, reference will be had to the drawing wherein:

Fig. 1 is a side elevational view of a lawn sprinkler embodying the present invention, shown in operative relationship to a water supply hose,

Fig. 2 is a plan view of the parts as shown in Fig. 1,

Fig. 3 is an enlarged plan view of the sprinkler,

Fig. 4 is a sectional view taken on line IV—IV of Fig. 3, and

Figs. 5 and 6 are sectional views taken respectively on lines V—V and VI—VI of Fig. 4.

Like reference numerals apply to similar parts throughout the several views, and the numeral 2 applies to a frame formed of sheet metal and having generally the form of a hollow rectilinear box. It has a top wall 4 and depending side walls 6, front wall 8, and rear wall 10, and is open at the bottom. It is supported at each of its forward corners by a ground-engaging wheel 12 rotatably mounted on a stub axle 14 fixed in the adjacent side wall 6, and at each of its rearward corners by a caster wheel 16, whereby the frame is rendered steerable.

Carried on top wall 4 of the

frame, adjacent the forward edge thereof, is a sprinkler head 18. As best shown in Fig. 4, said sprinkler head includes a vertical tubular body member 20 closed at its upper end and threaded at its lower end to a pipe 22, extending upwardly through said wall. Said body and pipe are fixed relative to the frame by a nut 24 threaded on said pipe below wall 4. Body member 20 is provided adjacent its upper end with a plurality of apertures 26, and at its upper end with a threaded axial extension 28. Mounted rotatably on said extension, and secured thereon by nut 30, is an inverted cup-shaped member 32 the depending skirt of which is disposed concentrically about body 20, and is of larger diameter than said body member whereby to form a chamber 34 therebetween. At its lower end, member 32 is provided with a sealing ring 36 which engages body member 20 to seal chamber 34, and with an external circular flange 36 which is disposed eccentrically to the axis of body member 20. Flange 38 serves as a cam as will be fully described below.

Fixed in the skirt portion of member 32, in communicating relation with chamber 34, are a plurality of upwardly and outwardly inclined tubes 40, at the outer end of each of which is mounted a nozzle 42. It will be noted in Figs.

2 and 3 that the nozzles are angled to direct streams of water substantially tangentially to the orbit of the nozzles, in the same relative angular direction. Hence when water under pressure is delivered to sprinkler head 18 through pipe 22, it passes outwardly through holes 26 of body 28 into chamber 34, and thence through tubes 40 to nozzle 42. The reactive force of the streams leaving the nozzles causes cup 32 of the head to rotate, this rotation being clockwise as shown although the direction of rotation is immaterial. This rotation distributes the water evenly over a relatively large ground area, and also causes rotation of cam flange 38, which operates the frame propelling mechanism to be described below.

Pipe 22 extends horizontally and rearwardly just below frame wall 4, and extends through rear wall 10, being secured therein by a pair of nuts 44. A flexible water supply hose 46 is secured to the outwardly extended end of said pipe by a suitable coupling 48. The hose is then looped as shown in Figs. 1 and 2 and passed beneath the frame 2 parallel to the line of travel thereof. The hose is then lifted from the ground and laid over a pair of rollers 50 and 52 carried rotatably at the inner face of rear wall 10 and front wall 8 respectively, said rollers being mounted on axles fixed to said frame walls by brackets 54. As best shown in Figs. 5 and 6, said rear and front frame walls are each provided with an inverted J-shaped notch 56 through which the hose may be moved transversely to engage the associated roller, and which serves to hold the hose centered over said roller.

Intermediate rollers 50 and 52, the hose is gripped between a pair of drive wheels 58, each of said wheels having a thick soft rubber facing 60 whereby to grip the hose frictionally. The drive wheel faces are concave whereby to conform closely to the hose. However, the wheel facings are sufficiently yieldable that the hose may be crowded therebetween. Each of the drive wheels is fixed on a vertical shaft 62 which extends upwardly through top frame wall 4 and is journalled in a bearing member 64 affixed to said frame wall. To the upper end of each of shafts 63, above wall 4, is affixed a ratchet wheel 66.

Ratchet wheels 66 are operated by a cam follower mechanism including a bar 68 disposed horizontally above frame wall 4 and carried slidably in a pair of brackets 70 fixed to said frame wall. Said bar is movable longitudinally along a line intersecting the axis of sprinkler head 18 and passing between ratchet wheels 66. It is provided at its forward end with an upright finger 72 which bears

slidably against the rim of flange cam 38 of the sprinkler head, and which is urged yieldably against said cam by a coil spring 74 encircling bar 68. Said spring bears at one end against one of brackets 70, and at its opposite end against a pin 76 inserted transversely through bar 68. At its rearward end, a pair of leaf springs 78 are affixed to bar 68, and extend rearwardly therefrom. Said springs extend between ratchet wheels 66, and are tensioned outwardly so that each spring engages in the teeth of one of the ratchet wheels, as best shown in Fig. 3.

Thus it will be seen that as sprinkler head 18 rotates as previously described, cam 38 thereof will rotate and urge cam follower bar 68 rearwardly against spring 74, and leaf springs 78, acting as pawls, will turn ratchet wheels 66 in the direction indicated by the arrows in Fig. 3. The throw of cam 38 is such that the ratchet wheels will be turned one tooth for each revolution of the sprinkler head. The ratchet teeth, and the cam throw, may obviously be made much smaller than shown, in order to provide slower rotation of the ratchet wheels, but are enlarged somewhat in the drawing for clarity. Springs 18 are sufficiently stiff to function as pawls, but are also sufficiently flexible that they will be deflected transversely to ride over the ratchet teeth as the bar 68 is moved rearwardly by spring 74. The rotation of ratchet wheels 66 of course also turns drive wheels 58, and since the drive wheels are in frictional engagement with the hose, the frame is pulled forwardly along the hose. The hose may be laid out on the ground ahead of the sprinkler in any desired pattern, so long as any curves therein are of sufficiently large radius, and the frame will follow the hose. In this manner, even an irregularly shaped lawn may be watered thoroughly and evenly without necessity of attendance on the sprinkler.

It has been found that the work which must be performed by the frame in lifting the hose from the ground applies a braking force to the frame sufficient to prevent the frame from coasting forwardly by gravity, which could occur if the ratchet wheels overran the pawls 78, on any slope usually encountered in lawns. The ratchet wheels are secured against following pawls 78 on their retracting stroke, which could otherwise occur particularly on upslopes, by a pair of dogs 80 pivotally mounted on a bolt 82 fixed in frame wall 4 and engaging respectively the two ratchet wheels 66 (Fig. 3). Said dogs are urged yieldably into engagement with said ratchet wheels by a coil spring 84 disposed on bolt 82 and having its end portions extended to engage said dogs intermediate their ends.

Although I have shown and described a specific embodiment of my invention, it will be apparent that many minor changes of structure and operation could be made without departing from the spirit of the invention as defined by the scope of the appended claim.

Problem

Given the specification, write three claims of varying scope, indicating "broadest," "intermediate" and "narrowest." Assume that it is old in the art to use the power provided by the rotation of the sprinkler head to cause movement of the sprinkler along the hose supplying water to the sprinkler. In narrowing your claims, do not rely on immaterial limitations.

Case 2

PREPARING APPARATUS CLAIMS—GIVEN A SPECIFICATION—DEPENDENT CLAIMS

SAMPLE CLAIMS—TRAVELING LAWN SPRINKLER

Broadest

1. An improved traveling lawn sprinkler of the type having a wheeled carriage, a rotary sprinkler head mounted on the carriage, and a fitting on the carriage to connect a water supply hose to the sprinkler head, wherein the improvement comprises:

(a) a pair of friction drive wheels mounted rotatably on the carriage for gripping the supply hose therebetween;

(b) a rotary cam mounted on the sprinkler head for rotation thereby;

(c) a cam follower mounted reciprocally on the carriage and driven by the cam; and

(d) a one-way drive linkage actuated by the movement of the cam follower in one direction to rotate the drive wheels intermittently in order to cause the carriage to travel along the hose.

Intermediate

2. An improved traveling lawn sprinkler as recited in claim 1, in which the one-way drive linkage comprises:

a pair of ratchet wheels fixed to and rotatable with the friction of drive wheels; and a pair of spring pawls carried by the cam follower, each pawl engaging one of the ratchet wheels, for driving the ratchet wheels.

Narrowest

3. An improved traveling lawn sprinkler as recited in claim 2, in which the cam comprises an eccentric circular flange formed integrally with the sprinkler head and having an eccentricity designed to rotate the ratchet wheels through a distance equal to the space between successive teeth of the ratchet wheels for each revolution of the sprinkler head.

COMMENTS

This structure was used on the November 1962 Agent's Exam.

When used on the Exam, the statement in the problem about "assume it is old" was given.

In view of the statement that traveling lawn sprinklers with rotary heads, etc., are old, an improvement or Jepson-type claim might appear preferable. (See Rule 75(e), discussed in section 57.) But, see below for examples of usual style claims which cover the same ground.

It is difficult in this case to tell what specific structure to put in claim 1, and what to leave for claims 2 and 3. This is particularly tough in this case, since there is no real "summary of the invention" in the specification, and the statements in the object clauses (col. 1, lines 15-25) are generally old according to the question.

It appears that the purpose in stating that "it is old to use the power, etc." was to force the student to claim at least some mechanical structure, and not present merely "means responsive to . . . for driving . . ." types of claims. Sample claim 1 is only one of several possible arrangements, specifically reciting some of the mechanical details; many other combinations seem equally good. Note that, if too much structural detail is put in claim 1, then the student is hard put to add *significant* details for claims 2 and 3. (See section 11.)

These claims further illustrate principles of selecting and naming claim elements (section 19), and connecting or relating the elements (sections 28-30) to make up a complete combination. For example, the friction drive wheels are "mounted rotatably on the carriage," "for gripping the hose." This relates them both structurally and functionally to the cooperative preamble elements, carriage and hose (the workpiece).

Claims 2 and 3 illustrate dependent claims, adding further detail of elements from the parent claim 1 (section 11). Note, claim 2 defines element (d) of claim 1 in more detail, while claim 3 tells more about element (c) of claim 1, and ties this structure in with the material added in claim 2. This is perfectly proper, and would be proper even if the matter added in claim 3 did not cooperate with the structure added in claim 2. Then, it would be the claim drafter's option whether to make claim 3 depend from claim 2 or claim 1.

Since the question asked one to label "broadest," "intermediate" and "narrowest," claim 3 should depend from claim 2, not claim 1. Otherwise it might not necessarily be narrower than claim 2. But if claim 3 recites all of the limitations of claim 2 and adds yet more limitations, claim 3 would be yet narrower than claim 2.

SAMPLE CLAIMS—TRAVELING LAWN SPRINKLER— Claim Set 2

Broadest

1. A traveling lawn sprinkler comprising:

a carriage; wheels supporting the carriage; the wheels being rotatable to move the carriage;

a rotary sprinkler head rotatably mounted on the carriage, the sprinkler head being shaped such that spraying from the head rotates the head on the carriage; means for connecting a water supply hose to the sprinkler head for supplying water thereto;

at least one friction drive wheel rotatably mounted on the carriage and for engaging the supply hose as the drive wheel is rotated;

a rotary cam mounted on the sprinkler head for rotation thereby; a cam follower reciprocably mounted on the carriage and placed for being engaged by and for being reciprocably driven by the cam as it rotates;

a one way drive linkage connected with the cam follower for being actuated by movement of the cam follower in one direction and connected with the one drive wheel for intermittently driving the drive wheel to rotate for causing the drive wheel to move along the supply hose and moving the carriage along the hose.

Intermediate

2. The traveling lawn sprinkler of claim 1, in which the one-way drive linkage comprises: [see rest of prior claim 2].

Narrowest

3. The traveling lawn sprinkler of claim 2, in which [see rest of prior claim 3].

COMMENTS

Note that the regular claim form may be used. All elements, old and new, cooperate to make the invention operate.

Only one friction drive wheel is needed, although two such cooperating wheels are preferred. Claim 1 here recites only one. A dependent claim could recite the second drive wheel.

The supply hose is not a positively recited element, but is instead inferentially claimed. The sprinkler is a separate entity from the hose and the hose may be supplied separately. Yet, one may treat the hose as an element and positively claim it, for so much of the operation relies upon that hose.

The claim requires that the same supply hose that supplies water also defines the track for the friction drive wheel. Query, must that track be only the supply hose? The invention does not appear to require that, especially as the inventive features are found in the drive elements on the carriage.

Case 3

PREPARING APPARATUS CLAIMS
GIVEN ONLY A DRAWING

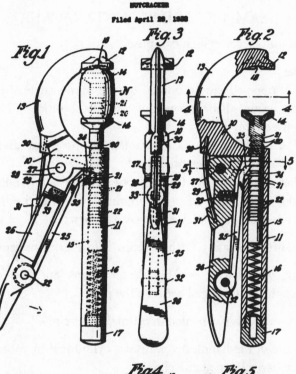

Dec. 10, 1940. G. J. TONN 2,224,415
NUTCRACKER
Filed April 29, 1938

Fig.1 Fig.3 Fig.2

Fig.4 Fig.5

Spring 16 urges plunger 15 "up" to hold nut between jaws.
Ratchet 20 and Pawl 25 operate to advance Jaw 14 one small
step at a time to crack nut without crushing.

PROBLEM

Prepare three claims of varying scope.

Case 3

PREPARING APPARATUS CLAIMS
GIVEN ONLY A DRAWING

SAMPLE CLAIMS—NUTCRACKER

1. A nutcracker, which comprises:

a frame;

a pair of opposed jaws mounted on the frame, at least one of the jaws being mounted for movement toward the other to crack a nut placed between the jaws;

a pair of operating handles mounted on the frame and movable toward and away from each other; and

a ratchet-and-pawl drive linkage connected to one handle and one jaw for closing the jaws a limited amount each time the handles are closed to crush a nut positioned between the jaws.

2. A nutcracker as recited in claim 1, further comprising:

a spring mounted in one handle for urging one jaw toward the other to clamp a nut placed between the jaws.

3. A nutcracker as recited in claim 2, wherein:

a first one of the handles comprises a cylindrical member having a cylindrical bore closed at one end;

the spring comprises a compression spring positioned in the bore against the closed end of the bore;

a first one of the jaws comprises a cylindrical member having a shaft portion slidably received in the bore against the spring and a jaw portion protruding from the first handle, the cylindrical member having a ratchet surface formed along a portion of its length and comprising part of the ratchet-and-pawl drive linkage;

the second jaw is pivotably mounted to the second handle; and

a pawl pivotably mounted to the second jaw for engagement with the ratchet surface.

COMMENTS

From the February 1962 Exam. No description was given. Claim 1 illustrates one of several possible approaches, picking out 3 or 4 main elements, defined fairly broadly, and then connecting them together to form an operable nutcracker. Then pick out relatively significant details for claims 2 and 3.

Case 4

PREPARING APPARATUS CLAIMS
GIVEN ONLY A DRAWING

May 14, 1957

H. A. WOOD

2,792,260

HOSE NOZZLE

Filed Dec. 12, 1956

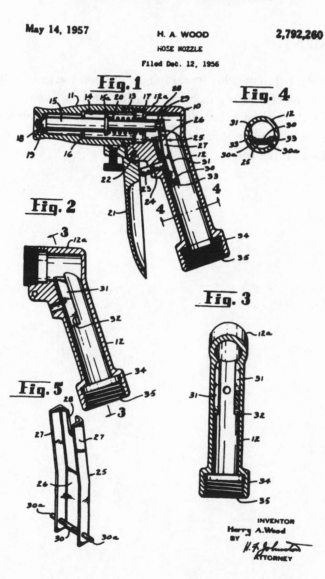

INVENTOR
Harry A. Wood
BY
H. F. Johnston
ATTORNEY

Problem

Write three claims of varying scope, indicating "broadest" "intermediate" and "narrowest." Hand-held, trigger-operated hose nozzles are old.

Case 4

PREPARING APPARATUS CLAIMS
GIVEN ONLY A DRAWING

SAMPLE CLAIMS—HOSE NOZZLE

Broadest

1. A trigger-operated hose nozzle, which comprises:

(a) a casing having a barrel section with a rear end and a front end, the casing having a handle section with an entrance end, the handle section being so connected to the barrel section that, in use, the handle section depends from the rear end of the barrel section, the two sections being shaped and oriented to have a continuous passage therethrough designed to permit flow of fluid into an entrance end of the handle section and out through the front end of the barrel section, the barrel section having a valve seat near the front end;

(b) a valve member slidably mounted in the barrel section, the valve member having a front portion designed for reception in the valve seat, the valve member having a rear portion;

(c) resilient means for urging the valve member into engagement with the seat to seal the nozzle against discharge of fluid;

(d) a trigger pivotably mounted to the casing and spaced from the handle section a distance such that the handle section and trigger may be gripped and the trigger squeezed toward the handle section;

(e) a lever pivotably mounted within the handle section and engaged with a rear portion of the valve member; and

(f) means for translating movement of the trigger toward the handle section into pivoting movement of the lever to open the valve.

Intermediate

2. A hose nozzle as recited in claim 1, wherein:

the valve member includes an elongated cylindrical stem centered within the barrel section, the stem having a rear end and a center and having a circumferential groove near the rear end thereof and an enlarged flange near the center thereof;

the barrel section includes an inwardly projecting portion, the resilient means comprises a coil spring mounted within the barrel section between the inwardly projecting portion of the barrel section and the flange of the valve stem; and

the lever comprises a flat bar mounted wholly within the handle section and having a U-shaped groove at its upper end designed to receive the groove of the valve stem.

Narrowest

3. A hose nozzle as recited in claim 2, further comprising:

a pair of pivot pins secured to the lever and extending transversely therefrom near the lower end thereof;

the handle section having a pair of internal projections and the projections having U-shaped recesses in which the ends of the pivot pins are received to permit pivoting of the lever;

the movement-translating means comprises a cylindrical plunger engaging both the trigger and a middle portion of the lever; and

the handle section having a cylindrical bore in a front wall thereof, for receiving the plunger closely but slidably through that wall, the bore also being provided with a fluid tight seal about the plunger for preventing leakage of fluid between the plunger and bore.

COMMENTS

This structure was used on the November 1965 Exam.

As usual, it is difficult or impossible to tell exactly what if anything is *the* point of novelty. To do this, one would really need to know the exact state of the trigger-type hose nozzle art as of December 1955.

On reading the patent, one discovers that the primary point of novelty apparently resided in the specific construction of the pivot mounting for the lever 25 inside the handle 12. This is seen at best only dimly in fig. 4. This the examinee could not possibly realize.

Therefore, the only sensible approach is to recite what appear to be the main structural parts of the combination in claim 1, leaving some structural details for claims 2 and 3. Sample claim 1 represents one such approach, but many others would be equally good, depending on the way the reader viewed the structure. Some details should be regarded as obviously noncritical and thus left out of claim 1, such as whether the casing is one piece or two, the angle of the handle to the barrel, or the shape of the valve seat.

In view of the statement in the question, we cannot assume that this is *the* basic patent on the trigger-operated squirter and claim it as broadly as

—a casing, a valve, and a trigger for operating the valve. —

The point of the question was to force us to claim some details of structure, not merely means for A, plus means for B.

It is recommended that at least some structural details be put in claim 1; however, such details as the structure of the plunger 23 for converting motion of the trigger 21 into movement of the lever 25 are presumably not critical, and could well be expressed as "means for translating . . ." as in sample claim 1.

Claim 1 is one typical example of many claims that could be written, and is on the narrow side. Substantially broader claims can be written, so long as some significant structural detail is included.

Case 5
PREPARING APPARATUS CLAIMS
GIVEN ONLY A DRAWING

Jan. 14, 1936.   S. A. BROWN   2,028,084

GLUE CONTAINER AND SPREADER

Filed April 3, 1933

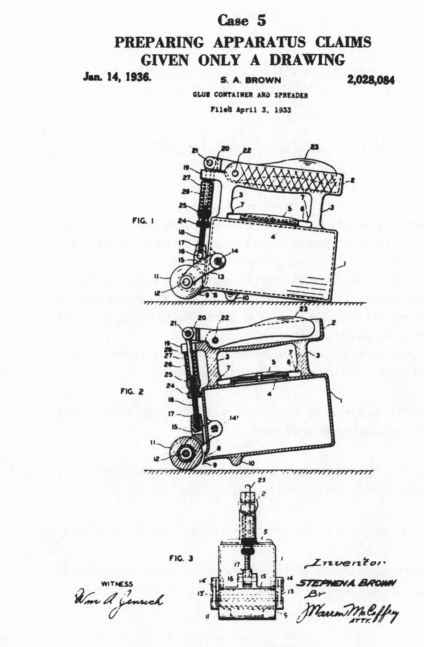

PROBLEM

Write three claims of varying scope.

Case 5

PREPARING APPARATUS CLAIMS
GIVEN ONLY A DRAWING

SAMPLE CLAIMS—GLUE APPLICATOR

1. A liquid applicator which comprises:

a container for the liquid, said container having a lower frontal edge and a discharge opening extending along the lower frontal edge;
a rotatable, liquid-applying roller;
means for mounting said roller to said container for movement from a first position closing the discharge opening to a second position uncovering said discharge opening to receive liquid issuing from said uncovered discharge opening; and
an actuator connected to said mounting means for selectively moving said roller between said first and second positions.

2. An applicator in accordance with claim 1, wherein said mounting means comprises:

an arm hingedly connected to said container for pivotally moving said roller between said first and second positions.

3. An applicator in accordance with claim 2, further comprising:

a spring connected to said roller mounting means for resiliently urging said roller into said first position to close said discharge opening.

COMMENTS

This is from an old Agent's Exam. No description was given, and it is impossible or nearly so to figure out all the structural details. One must claim what he can understand or guess at. Rarely if ever would the main features of novelty be in structural details such as the springs and levers in the actuating mechanism. It is better to focus on the main functions performed, with some structural detail, in this type of case.

Note, it is not necessary to make the claim preamble "liquid applicator" conform to the title of the patent "glue applicator." The claim preamble can be broader whenever one wishes, but of course must be consistent with the title. For the Agent's examination, however, it is preferable to have the claim preamble conform to the name of the invention, the title of the specification, as that is where the invention lies. In practice, you have control over the title and specification also, so you can amend them consistent with the claim preamble and the selected breadth of the claims.

Note also the use of "said" rather than "the" for references to antecedent expressions and elements. Either word is acceptable. Consistency of choice is preferred for style and ease of reading.

Case 6

PREPARING APPARATUS CLAIMS
GIVEN ONLY A DRAWING

July 12, 1955   S. W. CHAMBERS   **2,712,689**

ELECTRICALLY OPERATED AUTOMATIC CAN OPENER

Filed Sept. 28, 1954

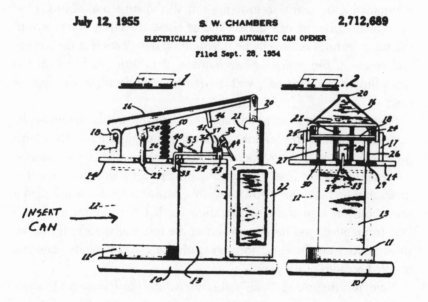

INSERT
CAN →

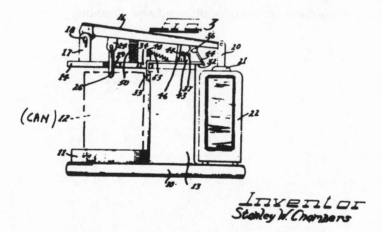

(CAN)

Inventor
Stanley W. Chambers

By Hill, Sherman Meroni, Gross & Simpson
Attys

Problem

Write three claims of varying scope and label them "Broadest," "Intermediate" and "Narrowest."

Case 6

PREPARING APPARATUS CLAIMS
GIVEN ONLY A DRAWING

Broadest: Sample Claims—Can Opener

1. A can-opener, which comprises:

a frame having a can-receiving space;
a can punch;
means for mounting the punch on the frame above the can-receiving space for movement into and out of engagement with the top of a can positioned in the space;
a can-sensing member movably mounted on the frame and having a portion thereof normally projecting into the space for engagement and movement by a can inserted in the space; and
means, responsive to the engagement and movement of the can-sensing member by a can positioned in the can-receiving space, for moving the punch into engagement with the can top for perforation thereof.

Intermediate

2. A can-opener as defined in claim 1, wherein the mounting means comprises:

a lever pivotally mounted on the frame, the punch being pivotally mounted on the lever and depending toward the can-receiving space.

Narrowest

3. A can opener as defined in claim 2, wherein the moving means comprises:

a solenoid for pivoting the lever; and

a switch, operated by a predetermined movement of the can sensing member, for energizing the solenoid.

COMMENTS

From the August 1966 Exam. This one is very difficult, as the drawing is poor, many would not know what some of the parts are in any event (solenoid 22, mercury switch 36, etc.). Also, the title may be misleading in can "opener," rather than punch.

But, if one had to try to claim this without any description, he would have to look for the main functions performed and omit the structural details of how it works. The solenoid and switch actuating mechanism are probably conventional anyway.

In this kind of case, where you are not sure exactly what is going on, study the drawings carefully (colored pencils help, to locate the same element by number in different views). Comparing the before and after pictures of FIGS. 1 and 3, it should be apparent, or almost so, that the can 12 goes in a space at the left, above a base or frame 11. Since the title says "electrically operated automatic," the can must hit or actuate something (tip 33 of arm 32, note how it has moved to the right in fig. 3 from fig. 1), to turn on the electrical gadget 22. This is a good time for "means responsive to insertion of a can . . . for moving the punching [or opening] means . . . ," since the details of what 22 is and how the switch works probably are not important, at least to claim 1.

It should be clear, in any case, that rod 20 moves down to pivot lever 16 down, thus lowering punch 29 into the can top. There are actually two punches 29, 30 as seen with difficulty in FIG. 2, but this is not important.

Sample claim 1 is a fairly broad claim to the main functional elements, which seems appropriate here: some sort of frame or support to locate the can; a punch, or punching means; something to mount the punch for movement into and out of the can top; something to sense the can ("automatic"); and something to operate or actuate the punch after ("*in response to*") sensing.

Since there is a combination of several cooperating means functions here, there would be no problem with a claim of all means elements, since no one of them would by itself constitute "means plus function at the point of novelty" (section 34), assuming that were improper or dangerous. However, to play safe and not include all means clauses, it costs nothing to specify a frame, a can punch, and a sensing *member*. These expressions are just as broad as "punching means" or "sensing means."

Case 7

PREPARING APPARATUS CLAIMS
GIVEN ONLY A DRAWING

SOWING DEVICE

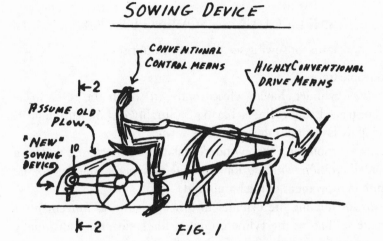

FIG. 1

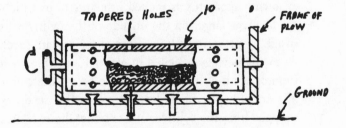

FIG. 2

PROBLEM

Object is to sow seeds behind plow blade. Holes are spaced to sow optimum numbers of seeds per acre. Draft three claims of varying scope.

Case 7

PREPARING APPARATUS CLAIMS
GIVEN ONLY A DRAWING

SAMPLE CLAIMS—SOWING DEVICE

1. Apparatus for sowing seeds, which comprises:

a movable frame;

a hollow cylinder, having closed ends, in which the seeds to be sown are placed, the cylinder having a plurality of holes through its walls slightly larger than the seeds to be sown;

means for mounting the cylinder rotatably on the frame and in a horizontal position with its longitudinal axis perpendicular to the direction of movement of the frame; and

means for rotating the cylinder in timed relation to movement of the frame so that, as the cylinder rotates, the seeds drop individually to the ground through the holes in the cylinder.

2. A sowing apparatus as recited in claim 1, in which the holes are tapered, larger on the outside of the cylinder than on the inside, to prevent the holes from clogging with seeds.
3. A sowing device as recited in claim 1, in which a plurality of funnels are mounted on the frame below the cylinder and in alignment with the holes to collect the seeds as they are dropped from the cylinder and conduct them to the ground.

COMMENTS

This invention was by George Washington.

The problem stated three claims of "varying scope," thus it is permissible to make claims 2 and 3 both dependent from claim 1.

A subcombination claim (section 56) would also be in order:

1A. In combination with a wheeled plow, a device for sowing seeds into the freshly plowed ground, which comprises:
[here recite claim 1, with "frame" changed to ". . . plow . . ."]

Claim 1 illustrates claiming holes (section 26), and a "means for doing something so that . . ." clause (section 34).

Claim 2 illustrates a dependent claim adding details of an element of the main claim.

Claim 3 adds a new element to the main combination (section 11 on dependent claims).

Case 8

PREPARING APPARATUS CLAIMS
GIVEN ONLY A DRAWING

May 30, 1961   L. D. WENSTRAND   2,986,261
APPARATUS FOR TRANSFERRING ARTICLES FROM AN ARTICLE-FEEDING
DEVICE TO AN ARTICLE-RECEIVING DEVICE

Filed Dec. 21, 1959   4 Sheets-Sheet 1

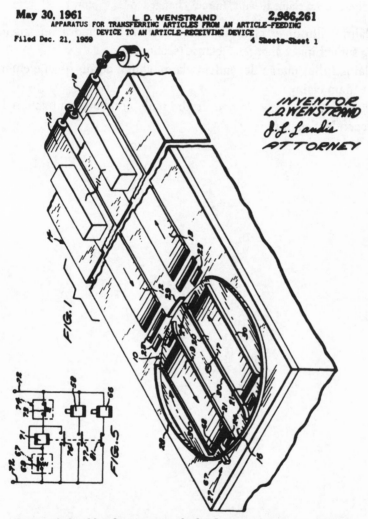

INVENTOR
L.D. WENSTRAND
J.L. Landis
ATTORNEY

FIG. 1

FIG. 5

An article 11 advances to left from a conveyer 12 onto
a conveyor belt 19 on a turntable 16, hits a switch actuator
68 which initiates 180° rotation of the turntable, after which
the article is discharged onto another conveyor 13 running in
the opposite direction while a second belt 20 on the turntable
16 is in position to receive a following article 11.

Problem

Draft an apparatus claim.

Case 8

PREPARING APPARATUS CLAIMS
GIVEN ONLY A DRAWING

SAMPLE CLAIM — APPARATUS FOR
TRANSFERRING ARTICLES

Apparatus for transferring an article from an article-feeding device to an article-receiving device, which comprises:

a turntable mounted adjacent to the receiving device and to a discharge end of the feeding device;

a conveyor mounted on the turntable for selective alignment with one of the feeding device and the receiving device, depending on the position of the turntable;

means for positioning the turntable initially to align the conveyor with the feeding device to receive an article therefrom;

means, responsive to the presence of an article on the conveyor, for rotating the turntable from the initial position to a discharge position in which the conveyor aligns with the receiving device; and

means for actuating the conveyor to transfer the article from the conveyor to the article-receiving device after the turntable has been rotated to the discharge position.

COMMENTS

This claim covers what are believed to be the essential elements of the invention: the turntable, one conveyor and drive, and means responsive to the article on the conveyor to rotate the turntable. The responsive means could have been a photocell, weight sensor or the like; one conveyor on the turntable is all that is absolutely essential; and the main conveyors 12 and 13 could be any feeding and receiving devices.

The preamble, while lengthy, conforms to the title of the invention in the specification.

In the "conveyor" feature, the description of two positions . . . "with one of the feeding device and the receiving device . . ." avoids use of an undesired alternative "or" while providing a limitation having the meaning: ". . . with the feeding device or the receiving device."

This was not an Agent's Exam question.

Case 9

PREPARING APPARATUS CLAIMS
GIVEN THE SPECIFICATION

T. KOKEISL PATENT 3,125,256

APPARATUS FOR STORING AND DELIVERING
GRANULAR OR LIKE FLOWABLE MATERIALS

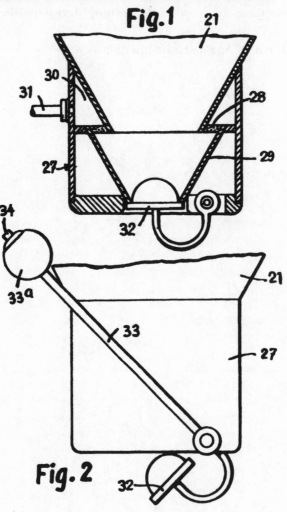

Fig.1

Fig.2

APPARATUS FOR STORING AND DELIVERING GRANULAR OR LIKE FLOWABLE MATERIALS

This invention relates to an apparatus with at least one container for storing and delivering measured quantities of granular or like flowable bulk materials and, more particularly, foods in powder form, such as flour, caster sugar, etc., the container having a funnel-shaped bottom part with a discharge device, a locking member and a porous filter element for introducing a gaseous medium into the container for loosening the granular material and preventing arch formations therein.

In embodiments of the type known heretofore, the inner wall of the funnel-shaped bottom part of the container is lined with porous filter elements which are at a distance from the inner wall to form an interspace, through which compressed air is supplied; this air penetrates through the porous elements into the granular material to loosen the same. Now such a construction is particularly disadvantageous because the granular material must flow out along the porous elements and its movement is hindered by the comparatively high coefficient of friction of the surface of these filter elements. In order that the

material can move over the filter elements with as little frictional engagement as possible, the gaseous medium must be blown in at a correspondingly high pressure which, however, results in a relatively large part of the air escaping through the funnel throat with formation of eddy currents, whereby not inconsiderable quantities of the material are carried along, thereby leading not only to loss of material but also to the formation of dust and contamination of the environment. The amount of material blown out of the container in this manner reaches unacceptable proportions if the filter elements, as is usually the case in prior art embodiments, extend into the range of the funnel throat. Said shortcomings are naturally not only encountered in embodiments in which the air is blown in through filter elements carrying the granular material, but in all constructions, in which the inlets of the air supply open into the slide way of the material, whereby the associated air slots and air holes as such offer a high resistance to the flow of the material so that a particularly high air pressure is necessary.

The primary object of the invention is to obviate the drawbacks mentioned and to create the possibility of taking from the container or its funnel-shaped bottom part any desired quantity of material, down to the very smallest measure, without any appreciable amount of dust being formed thereby. According to the invention this is achieved in that the funnel-shaped bottom part of the container has a cross-sectional enlargement in at least one location between the inlet and outlet of the funnel, and that the porous filter element for the inflow of the gaseous medium is arranged outside the slide way of the granular material. The porous filter disk can thus have no influence upon the flow of the granular material. Since, moreover, the filter element, lying outside the slide way of the granular material, is preferably disposed in the range of the cross-sectional enlargement situated between the inlet and outlet of the funnel, hence at a point located some distance from the outlet of the funnel, the air cannot escape directly through the funnel outlet and thereby blow out any part of the material. The air flowing out through the porous filter element, thereby not only penetrates into the material to loosen the same, but, moreover, pushes the goods and acts in aiding relationship with, the action of gravity to force the bulk material through the funnel part beneath the filter element towards the throat of the funnel, so that minimum pressure is required to ensure proper outflow of the material. Preferably

the funnel-shaped bottom part, at the location of said cross-sectional enlargement, may exhibit an annular gap having the filter element set therein and coextensive therewith, the gap communicating with an annual distribution chamber for the gaseous medium, which chamber, at the location of said enlargement, surrounds the funnel-shaped part of the container.

The accompanying drawing shows, by way of example, one embodiment of the invention; in the drawing.

FIG. 1 is a vertical cross-sectional view of the funnel-shaped bottom part of the container of the apparatus, with the outlet closed, and

FIG. 2 is an elevational view of the apparatus with the funnel outlet open.

Referring to the drawing, the funnel-shaped bottom part 21, 29 of the surmounted storage container (not shown) has, at a location between the inlet and outlet of the funnel, a cross-sectional enlargement receiving porous filter body 28 for the inflow of the gaseous medium; this body being located out of the slide way of the granular material, so that the same upon discharging of the container, does not pass over the filter element 28. The arrangement according to the invention is such that the funnel-shaped bottom part, at the location of the cross-sectional enlargement, has an annular gap filled with the filter element 28, which communicates with an annular distribution chamber 30 for the gaseous medium, said chamber at said enlargement extending round the funnel-shaped bottom part or feed means of the container. The chamber 30 may be connected through a pipe 38 to an air compressor (not shown) that supplies conditioned compressed air to the apparatus. The outlet of the funnel-shaped chute means 21, 29 is closable by a locking member designed as a swivably mounted plug 32 which, by means of a lever 33, can be pivoted into either the closed or open position. The lever 33 at one end is provided with a spherical headpiece 33a having mounted therein a push-button switch 34 adapted to close a circuit to start the driving motor of the air compressor. Thereby the funnel-shaped bot-

tom part is surrounded by a casing 27, whose top part laterally defines the annular distribution chamber 30, and whose lower part has the lever 33 pivoted thereon.

If it is required to take material from the container, the lever 33 is swung in a sense opening the outlet of the funnel-shaped bottom part 21, 29, after the push-button 34 has previously been pressed down to switch on the air compressor motor. The compressed gaseous medium is pressed through the filter element 28, whereby the material will be loosened and, at the same time, be pushed towards the outlet of the bottom part; it does not slide over the filter element which, as being porous, has a correspondingly rough surface, but over the smooth wall of the funnel part 29, whereby a relatively low pressure ensures continuous emptying without the formation of any appreciable amount of dust.

Problem

Draft three claims of substantially varying scope covering the apparatus for storing and delivering granular or like flowable materials described in the preceding specification. Claims in dependent form may be used. The claims should not distinguish from each other by merely immaterial limitations and should distinguish over any prior art described in the specification.

Case 9

PREPARING APPARATUS CLAIMS
GIVEN THE SPECIFICATION

SAMPLE CLAIMS—KOKEISL PATENT 3,125,256

1. An improved apparatus for storing and delivering flowable bulk material, the apparatus being of the type having a vertically disposed funnel-shaped member with an inlet opening at the top for receiving the material and an outlet opening at the bottom for delivering the same, a closure member for selectively opening and closing the outlet opening, and a porous filter element for introducing a gaseous medium under pressure into the funnel-shaped member to loosen the material and assist in discharging it, the improvement wherein:

the funnel-shaped member is formed with a cross-sectional enlargement between the inlet and the outlet openings thereof; and

the filter element is mounted at the cross-sectional enlargement outside of the slide path of the material, to deliver the gaseous medium into the funnel-shaped member in the direction of the outlet opening.

2. An improved apparatus for storing and delivering bulk material as recited in claim 1, wherein:

the funnel-shaped member comprises two similar conically tapered funnels mounted one above the other so as to define an annular gap between the lower end of the upper funnel and the upper end of the lower funnel; and

the filter element is mounted in and fills the annular gap, so that the gaseous medium may be delivered generally downward through the filter element into the upper portion of the lower funnel.

3. An improved apparatus for storing and delivering bulk material as recited in claim 2, wherein:

a generally cylindrical casing is provided for mounting the funnels and the closure member, the casing defining in conjunction with a portion of the outer wall of the upper funnel an annular distribution chamber for the gaseous medium which is closed except for the space occupied by the filter element; and

means are provided for selectively admitting the gaseous medium under pressure into the annular chamber.

COMMENTS

This patent was used on the February 1968 Exam in the form reproduced here. As sometimes is done, a choice was given between writing claims to this patent and a chemical process, Crowell patent 2,308,588 on purifying maleic anhydride (Appendix B, Case 20).

The specification states, paragraphs 1 and 2, that the general combination of a funnel, a closure and a filter element is old for the same general purpose. In paragraph 3, it states that the main point of novelty consists in (1) providing a cross-sectional enlargement, and (2) in locating the filter element in a particular stated fashion. Thus, claim 1 should focus primarily on these factors. Statements in the specification such as "preferably the funnel-shaped bottom part . . . may exhibit an annular gap . . ." (p. 2, lines 3-10) indicate preferred but not critical features. Things such as this are good to include in claims 2 and 3, but should not be in claim 1.

Sample claim 1 indicates one approach to this structure, using the Jepson form to put the elements stated to be old in the preamble. This is probably not necessary for this case, but should be helpful both to better point out the invention and avoid a possible "old combination" rejection. (See sections 57 and 63.) Various other approaches are possible, the main points being to limit details of description of the admittedly old elements and concentrate on the portions stated to be new.

As usual, the additional claims should be devoted primarily to the new features and not merely add elements or features stated to be old in the art. See section 58, citing MPEP 706.03(k); ". . . it is possible to reject one claim on an allowed claim if they differ only by subject matter old in the art . . ." Although this "rule" may be questionable and is probably little used, it indicates Patent and Trademark Office policy on the subject.

In addition, items such as the shape of the closure member 32, while not expressly stated to be old, have no real bearing on the subject invention and would be best not to describe in detail.

Also, note that since the container from which the granules come and the source of compressed air are not shown, they should not be positively recited in the claim (Rule 83).

Since the question said to write three claims of *substantially varying scope*, claim 3 need not be dependent from claim 2. The choice would depend on whether you were adding in claim 3 items closely related to those added in claim 2 (in series) or items related to the elements of claim 1 and not particularly important to the additions of claim 2 (in parallel).

Case 10
PREPARING APPARATUS CLAIMS AFLOAT

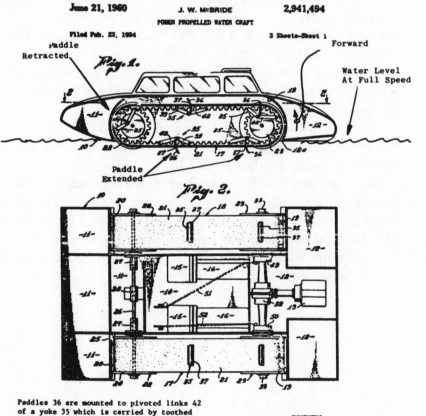

June 21, 1960   J. W. McBRIDE   2,941,494
POWER PROPELLED WATER CRAFT

Filed Feb. 23, 1954   3 Sheets-Sheet 1

Fig. 1.

Paddle Retracted

Forward

Water Level At Full Speed

Paddle Extended

Fig. 2.

Paddles 36 are mounted to pivoted links 42
of a yoke 35 which is carried by toothed
endless belts 21-21. The belts pass
around sprocket wheels 22-23. As the
links travel around the sprocket
wheels, they pivot to retract the
paddles inward through slots 37 in the belts.
The object is to eliminate turbulence as the
paddles enter and leave the water, by retracting the paddles.

INVENTOR
JOHN W. McBRIDE,

June 21, 1960   J. W. McBRIDE   2,941,494

POWER PROPELLED WATER CRAFT

Filed Feb. 23, 1954   3 Sheets-Sheet 2

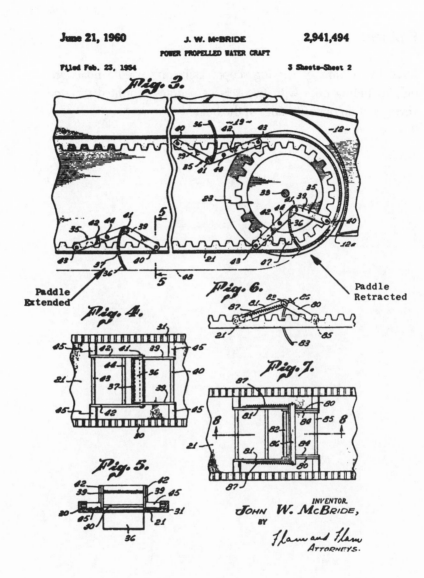

INVENTOR.

JOHN W. McBRIDE,

BY

Flam and Flam

ATTORNEYS.

Problem

Draft two claims of varying scope, assuming paddle boats are old, including ones with two sets of paddles mounted to conveyor belts on opposite sides of the boat.

Case 10

PREPARING APPARATUS CLAIMS AFLOAT

SAMPLE CLAIMS—McBRIDE PATENT 2,941,494

Fairly Broad Claim

1. A propelling mechanism for a water craft, which comprises:

(a) an endless belt carried by the craft, the belt having a lower run extending substantially horizontally beneath the craft, the belt having a plurality of transverse slots therethrough at intervals along the length thereof:

(b) means for driving the belt along horizontally;

(c) a plurality of paddles movably mounted to the belt at intervals along the length thereof for movement therewith; and

(d) means for setting the position of each paddle with respect to the belt so that (1) each paddle extends outward beneath the belt, thereby to extend into the water to propel the craft, when the paddle is traveling with the lower run of the belt, and (2) each paddle is retracted to above the belt at the ends of the lower run of the belt.

COMMENTS

This rather broad claim covers what are believed to be the main elements of the invention: the belt, belt drive, paddles and position-governing or setting means. Various other means could be employed to extend and retract the paddles, the essential thing being that a means be provided. On the "means + function so that . . ." clause, note *In re Chandler*, 117 U.S.P.Q. (BNA) 361, 364 (C.C.P.A. 1958), discussed in section 34.

Another Claim

    2. In a drive for propelling a boat:

  a hull on the boat which always will float; a wheel at the bow and one at the stern, and a belt 'round the wheels which moves with a turn; and for driving a wheel, a motor in tote;

  a set of strong oars from a tree, extending in slots through the belt to the sea; on the belt, for each oar, in pivot a yoke, for retracting these oars at the end of each stroke to stop any splash and to set the oars free.

COMMENTS

  This claim covers the main elements in somewhat different order. It may be too broad in the last two lines, in that "a yoke for" performing the function might not be considered as entitling one to the same breadth as a statutory "means for" clause as in claim 1. (See section 34.) With relatively broad, functional clauses such as this it is probably safer to use the exact statutory language "means for," for example "Yoke means mounted pivotally on said belt. . . ."

Case 11

PREPARING ELECTRICAL CIRCUIT CLAIMS

OPTICAL SOUND REPRODUCTION

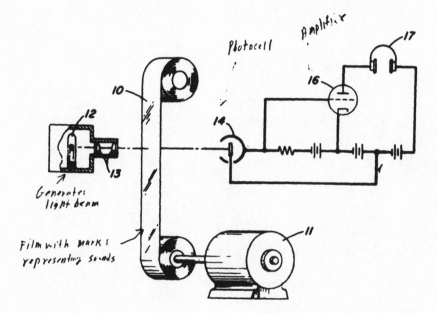

Problem

Sound movie patent—draft a claim to the system.

Case 11

PREPARING ELECTRICAL CIRCUIT CLAIMS

SAMPLE CLAIM—
OPTICAL SOUND PRODUCTION

A system for producing audible sounds in accordance with a varying visual pattern formed on a transparent film, which system comprises:

means for projecting a beam of light;

a photoelectric detector for receiving said beam of light and for generating an output signal which varies as the amount of said light received by said detector;

means for advancing said film between said projecting means and said detector to vary the amount of light received by said detector in accordance with the variations in said visual pattern; and

means responsive to variations in said output signal for producing audible sounds.

COMMENTS

Note, this claim is a mixture of electrical, optical and mechanical elements, which is OK. "Means for" clauses are very common in circuit claims, since the specific circuit components are rarely critical in combination claims.

The "means for projecting a beam" of light can also be as broadly claimed by reciting "a projector of a beam of light" or "a light beam projector" or even "a light projector." The film and the visual pattern are workpieces, so that they are inferentially claimed.

In a claim, name an item, physically locate it and/or say what it does.

Case 12

PREPARING ELECTRICAL CIRCUIT CLAIMS

UNIJUNCTION PULSE GENERATOR

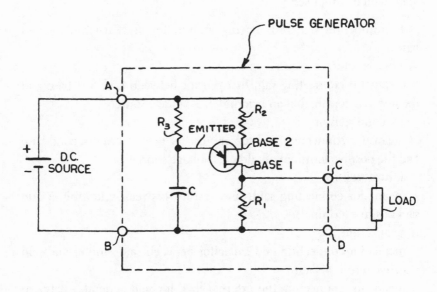

DRAFT A SPECIFIC CLAIM TO THIS CIRCUIT

PROBLEM

Draft a specific claim to this circuit.

Case 12

PREPARING ELECTRICAL CIRCUIT CLAIMS

SAMPLE CLAIM—
UNIJUNCTION PULSE GENERATOR

A pulse generator for generating voltage pulses across an external load, which comprises:

a unijunction transistor having an emitter and first and second bases;

a first resistor;

means for connecting said first resistor between said first base and the negative terminal of an external d.c. voltage source;

a second resistor;

means for connecting said second resistor between said second base and the positive terminal of said d.c. voltage source;

a third resistor;

means for connecting said third resistor between said emitter and said positive terminal;

a capacitor;

means for connecting said capacitor between said emitter and said negative terminal; and

means for connecting the external load for said generator between the first base and the negative terminal of said d.c. voltage source;

said transistor, resistors and capacitor having parameters selected so that, when said source and said load are connected to said pulse generator by said connecting means, said capacitor repetitively charges from said d.c. source through said third resistor until the voltage across said capacitor reaches a value that causes said unijunction transistor to conduct, and then discharges through said transistor, and the parallel paths of said first resistor and the external load, whereby each discharge of said capacitor generates a voltage pulse across the external load.

COMMENTS

This claim further illustrates practice in composing detailed circuit claims (section 35); listing the elements and parts, and connecting them together both structurally (section 29) and operationally (section 30).

Note that the power source and load are not made elements of the claim, as the pulse generator would normally be sold including only the components in the phantom-line box, up to terminals or connectors A, B, C, D. The purchaser or user would usually add the battery and load. The clauses such as "means for connecting said first resistor between said first base and the negative terminal of *an* external d.c. source" illustrate one way to claim the subcombination (pulse generator) as it is connect*able* to operate, without expressly claiming the battery. The "means for connecting" would always include a terminal (clip or post) such as B; thus the claim covers the circuit in the phantom box as a subcombination (section 59). The claim also covers the complete unit connected as shown in the drawing, in which case the "means for" clause also includes the lead or wire connecting terminal B to the battery.

The operational clause (section 30) was placed at the end of the claim (section 33) since it requires the presence of all of the recited circuit components connected in the stated manner. This was made a separate clause since it relates to the operation of all of the elements, not just the last named one (means for connecting the capacitor). Note the "whereby clause" (section 32) is proper since the pulse-generation function necessarily follows from the previously recited structure. If the structure had novelty, the clause about selecting parameters (R_8, C, and turn-ON voltage of the transistor) would clearly not be unduly functional under the cases cited in section 31. Given some novelty, any "man skilled in the art" would know how to select the components to generate the desired pulse.

In all probability, if the circuit had novelty and was not obvious in the connection of the components in the stated manner, the last clause of the claim, telling how the circuit works, would not be necessary and could be omitted. Circuit claims are frequently patented with only statements of physical connection. Whether a final clause telling how it works should be included is largely up to the judgment of the claim writer, and to some extent the Examiner. Such a clause may help make the claim more definite and help convince the Examiner it is novel and unobvious, and may avoid an "accidental anticipation" — type rejection on a circuit that looks structurally similar but works entirely differently.

Case 13

PREPARING METHOD CLAIMS
MARKUSH CLAIMS—GENERIC AND SPECIES CLAIMS

April 7, 1959   R. E. GUNDERMAN ET AL   2,880,466

PROCESS FOR PREPARING FILMS FROM POLYMER LATEXES

Filed Jan. 14, 1957

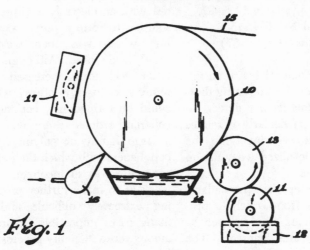

Fig. 1

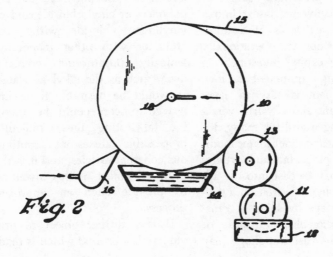

Fig. 2

2,880,466
PROCESS FOR PREPARING FILMS FROM POLYMER LATEXES

Roland E. Gunderman, Clare, and Max E. Elder, Midland, Mich., assignors to The Dow Chemical Company, Midland, Mich., a corporation of Delaware

Application January 14, 1957,
Serial No. 634,125
7 Claims. (Cl. 18—57)

This invention relates to an improved process for preparing thermoplastic films from polymer latexes. More particularly it relates to such a process involving the continuous localized coagulation of the latexes.

Polymer latexes are particularly useful forms from which to prepare continuous articles, such as films, tapes, and filaments. The number of procedural steps required to convert a latext into a continuous article is at a minimum, the steps are operationally simple, the capital investment in film forming equipment is low, the equipment is easy to clean and maintain and is fairly versatile in being useful for many different latexes without major modification. In preparing such articles the latex may be cast into the approximate shape desired on a supporting surface by suing a transfer roll, doctor blade, air knife, or the like. The cast wet shape may be then dried and fused either sequentially or simulanteously. That method or technique, however, is limited to a relatively few latexes which are capable of film formation by air drying. More recently a technique was developed whereby a film forming latex was cast on a supporting surface wetted with an electrolyte coagulant solution to form a porous coagulum which was then washed, dried, and fused. Although the latter technique increased the number of useful latexes which could be formed into continuous coherent articles, there was still a large family of polymers and copolymers with which the porous coagulum was so incoherent and weak as to make further processing extremely difficult and in many cases impossible. Included among those difficulty processable latexes are the polymers and copolymers of cinyl chloride and of vinylidene chloride with each other or with other monoethylenically unsaturated comonomers, such as the alkyl acrylates. It would be desirable if an improved process could be found for fabricating these difficulty processable latexes into continuous coherent articles, and it is the principal object of this invention to provide such an improved process.

It is a further object to provide such a process which is readily adaptable to existing equip-ment.

The above and related objects are realized with a process where-in an electrolyte-coagulable poly-mer latex is cast and electrolyte coagulated into approximately the desired shape as a continuous, co-herent, porous coagulum which is washed to remove substantially all of the electrolyte coagulant, the excess water removed without destroying the porosity of the co-agulum, and the coagulum then dried and fused. The improve ment in the above process which is contemplated by this invention is the subjecting of the freshly cast porous coagulum to relatively mild beating prior to washing. By the use of this improvement poly-mer latexes which could not be fashioned by prior procedures into continuous coherent articles are capable of such fabricaton.

Although any film-forming elec-trolyte-coagulable, polymer latex may be used in the process of this invention, it has been found to be especially useful and necessary with the latexes of the polymers and copolymers of vinyl chloride and vinylidene chloride with each other or with other monoethyen-ically unsaturated comonomers, such as the alkyl acrylates, and acrylonitrile. Within this family of difficultly processable polymer latexes it has been found that those latexes of the normally crys-talline vinylidene chloride copoly-mers are particularly troublesome and such latexes accordingly rep-resent preferred materials for use in the process. The useful latexes must be electrolyte coagulable into a continuous, coherent co-agulum. It is not essential that the continuous, coherent coagu-lum be self-supporting, imperme-able, transparent, or commercially useful by air drying, but it is necessary that the coagulum be a unitary integral article, however weak it may be. It is known that some latexes require minor treat-ment to aid their inherent film forming characteristics, their cast-ing ability, or their coagulability. For example it is frequently ad-vantageous to add a very small amount of a hydrophilic, colloidal thickener, such as the water-sol-uble cellulose ethers, and to ad-just the pH of the latex prior to casting. Such techniques which enhance the film formability of the latex are intended to be with-in the scope of the invention.

The latexes may be prepared by any of the known procedures for polymerization in aqueous emulsion. Typically the monomer or monomers are dispersed in an aqueous solution of from about 0.05 to 5 percent polymerization catalyst, such as potassium per-sulfate or hydrogen peroxide, and from about 0.05 percent of a sur-face active agent as an emulsifies.

Polymerization is initiated by heating the emulsified mixture usually between 35 degrees C. and 100 degrees C. and continued by maintaining the polymerizing emulsion at the selected temperature. After the polymerization has reached the desired conversion of monomer to polymer, the latex is filtered to remove any precoagulum and stabilized to storage by the addition of a small amount of a surface active agent.

Latexes which are to be used in forming continuous coherent articles, such as films, should preferably contain from about 30 to about 50 percent by weight of non-volatile solids. When less than about 30 percent of weight of non-volatile solids are present in the latex, no useful, continuous coherent articles can be produced by simple deposition of the latex. Latexes having appreciably more than 50 percent by weight of non-volatile solids are difficult to prepare and are extremely sensitive to mechanical shear and to storage and may coagulate prematurely.

It is also known that the quality of continuous coherent articles prepared by the deposition of a latex is dependent upon the latex particle size. The particle size is a function of the kind and concentration of emulsifier, the temperature of polymerization, and the rate of agitation used in forming the initial dispersion. Most latexes will generally not form films by simple deposition unless substantially all of the particles are under 3000 angstrom units in diameter. Most desirable results are obtained when the majority of the dispersed particles have diameters between 400 and 2000 angstrom units. Means for making latexes whose particles are of those dimensions are known.

The coagulents useful for coagulating polymer latexes are well-known. Typically they consist of aqueous solutions of bi- and polyvalent inorganic salts, such as calcium chloride, magnesium chloride, and aluminum sulfate. It has been found that a solution of from about 5 to about 20 percent concentration provides the best coagulating characteristics. The greater the concentration that is used, the more extensive will the washing step have to be to remove residual electrolyte. Such electrolytes frequently have a deleterious effect on the stability of the polymer. It has also been found to be desirable to add a small amount of surface active agent to the aqueous coagulant solution to improve the wetting qualities of the solution.

The operation and advantages of this process will be more apparent from the following description and annexed drawings which represent schematically a preferred and illustrative apparatus for carrying out the steps of the process.

In the drawing:

Figure 1 represents a schematic elevation of an apparatus employing external heating means, and

Figure 2 represents a schematic elevation of an apparatus employing internal heating means.

In the embodiment illustrated in Figure 1 a large rotatably driven, smooth-surfaced drum 10 is used as a casting surface. The surface 10 of the drum is first wetted with aqueous electrolyte coagulant solution. The wetting is conveniently accomplished using a transfer roll technique wherein a pickup roll 11 rotating partially in a coagulant bath 12 is in contact with a transfer roll 13 which in turn is in contact with the drum 10. The transfer roll technique assures a constant wetting of the drum surface 10. As the drum 10 rotates further the wetted surface dips into or touches a latex bath 14 forming a wet latexcoagulant film 15. Excess water and latex is removed from the wet film by a planiform air blast, sometimes called an air knife 16, which is directed at a slight angle to the surface of the wet film 15. The rotating drum surface 10 next passes under a radiant heating means 17 such as a quartz bar heater, which strengthens and conditions the film 15 without destroying its porosity. It is only necessary that the

temperature of the wet film 15 be raised to about 35 to 70 degrees C. to achieve the desirable result. If the film 15 is not raised to at least 35 degrees C., there is little improvement noticed in the coagulum characteristics. If temperatures of much over 70 degrees C. are used, there is a danger that much of the porosity will be lost, and the other processing steps made more difficult. It should be apparent that the actual temperature to be used to give optimum results will depend upon the polymer composition, the latex characteristics, the thickness of th wet film and other variables. An investigator will be able to make a judicious choice of temperature by examining the coagulum following the beating step.

Following the warming step the continuous, coherent, porous coagulum is stripped from the drum surface, washed, dried, and fused.

In the embodiment represented in Figure 2 the apparatus consists of the same elements in the same relative positions except that the external radiant heating means 17 is omitted. In this embodiment the axis of drum 10 is fitted with a conventional rotary union 13 and heat transfer fluids circulated therethrough to maintain the drum surface at a temperature of from 35 to about 70 degrees C.

The drum or other supporting

surface should be contacted with the latex as soon as possible after wetting with coagulant to avoid drying of the coagulant on the drum surface. This is particularly important when a heated drum or supporting surface is employed as in the embodiment of Figure 2 since that heat increases the drying problem. Dried coagulant does not provide good continuous localized coagulation characteristics.

Plasticizers, stabilizers, dilers, pigments, and the other additives commonly incorporated into polymer components may be employed in this process by water blending them into the latex prior to casting or by passing the wet washed coagulum through a solution of the additive prior to fusion.

The thickness of the continuous, coherent article is easily controlled by the setting of the air knife, doctor blade, or other device, by the time of contact of the drum with the latex, by the concentration of the coagulant, and by the latex compositions. The process operates best when the article has a thickness of from 0.001 to 0.003 inch. When it is attempted to prepart articles of much greater thickness than 0.003 inch by the continuous localized coagulation of a latex, it is found that it is difficult to achieve uniform coagulation, the coagulant is difficult to wash away, and the wet article is difficult to dry and fuse.

In a specific example an aqueous latex prepared by the emulsion polymerization of 91 percent by weight of vinylidene chloride and 9 percent by weight of acrylonitrile and having 40 percent solids was formulated by stirring in 5 percent by weight based on the weight of nonvolatile solids of ethyl phthalyl ethyl glycolate as a plasticizer. One percent of the dioctyl ester of sodium sulfosuccinic acid was added to reduce the surface tension of the latex to 38.8 dynes. An 8 inch steel drum having a Heresite surface was wetted with a 10 percent aqueous calcium chloride solution containing 0.4 of a nonionic wetting agent. The wet drum surface was then rotated through a bath of the formulated latex and then through the blast of an air knife. The drum was maintained at a temperature of 60 degrees C. by circulating hot water therethrough. Also the drum was rotated to give a peripheral speed of 20 feet per minute. The coagulum formed on the roll was continuous and coherent, could be stripped from the roll and passed through a water bath, then air dried, and finally fused at 170 degrees C.

By way of contrast when the process was repeated omitting the heating of the drum, the coagulum could not be stripped from the drum without breakage.

In a further example a latex prepared by the emulsion polymerization of 30 percent by weight of vinylidene chloride and 70 percent by weight of vinyl chloride and containing 47.4 percent by weight of non-volatile solids was formulated with 1 percent of the dioctyl ester of sodium sulfosuccinic acid and 10 percent plasticizer. The drum, without any fluid circulating therethrough, was wetted with 10 percent aquous calcium chloride solution then passed through the latex bath, finally subjected to the air knife blast. The west drum surface was passed under a 1000 watt quartz bar heater placed 2 inches from the drum at a speed of 14 feet per minute. The porous coagulum was stripped from the drum, washed, then dried and fused into a continuous coherent film.

Similar results are observed when latexs of copolymers of vinylidene chloride and ethyl acrylate are processed in this manner.

The process of this invention allows the preparation of films, filaments, and other continuous, moherent articles from latexes which heretofore could not be used in the continuous, localized coagulation technique because of the inherent weakness of the coagulum.

We claim:

？　？　？　？

Problem

Part I — Write three method claims of varying scope, based on the specification as written.

Part II — Write a Markush claim covering the specific coagulants mentioned at the start of the ninth paragraph of the specification.

Part III — Write two method species claims to the two ways of heating described.

Case 13

PREPARING METHOD CLAIMS
MARKUSH CLAIMS—GENERIC AND SPECIES CLAIMS

SAMPLE CLAIMS—
PROCESS FOR PREPARING FILMS

Part I

1. In a process for preparing a continuous coherent article from a film-forming, electrolyte-coagulable polymer latex, the process being of the type including the steps of

(a) wetting a moving supporting surface with an electrolyte coagulant solution,

(b) casting a film of the polymer latex on the wet surface to form a continuous, coherent, porous coagulum of the polymer and coagulant solution,

(c) washing the coagulum so formed to remove the electrolyte, and

(d) drying and fusing the washed coagulum into a continuous coherent article;

the improvement which comprises:

(e) heating the coagulum prior to step (c) to a temperature sufficient to strengthen and condition the coagulum without destroying its porosity, and below the fusion temperature of the coagulum.

Claim 1 is in a *Jepson* format. For the agent's examination, this is a difficult and thus less preferred format. Claim 1 can be written in more usual form without separating out the feature believed to distinguish over the art:

1. A process for preparing a continuous coherent article from a film-forming, electrolyte-coagulable polymer latex, the process including the steps of

   (a) wetting a moving supporting surface with an electrolyte coagulant solution,

   (b) casting a film of the polymer latex on the wet surface to form a continuous, coherent, porous coagulum of the polymer and coagulant solution,

   (c) heating the coagulum to a temperature sufficient to strengthen and condition the coagulum without destroying its porosity, and below the fusion temperature of the coagulum.

   (d) washing the coagulum so formed to remove the electrolyte, and

   (e) drying and fusing the washed coagulum into a continuous coherent article.

Other claims to follow:

2. A process as recited in claim 1, wherein the polymer latex is selected from the group consisting of the polymers and copolymers of vinyl chloride and vinylidine chloride with each other and with other monoethylenically unsaturated comonomers.

3. A process as recited in claim 2, wherein the coagulum is heated to a temperature of about 35 to 70°C. in step (e).

Part II

4. A process as recited in claim 2, wherein the coagulant solution is an aqueous solution of an inorganic salt selected from the group consisting of calcium chloride, magnesium chloride, and aluminum sulfate.

Part III

A—First Species—fig. 1:

5. A process as recited in claim 3, wherein the heating step is accomplished by localized radiant heating of the outer surface of the coagulum after step (b).

B—Second Species—fig. 2:

6. A process as recited in claim 3, wherein the heating step is accomplished by uniformly heating the supporting surface.

COMMENTS

In preparing method claims from a specification, there should be no problem in understanding the method or in naming the parts or steps. Usually, the names given in the specification will suffice, such as "wetting," "casting," etc. A problem might be in figuring out what is most fundamental to the method for inclusion in claim 1, and what details should be left for other claims. Since the specific question asked in Part I was to write three claims of "varying scope," it is not necessary (but would not hurt) to make each claim include all of the limitations of the preceding claim.

In this case, the specification states very clearly (especially Col. 1, lines 34-43 and 55-67) that the "Invention" in this case involves an improvement in a prior known process which is *otherwise unchanged*. Specifically, the "Invention" involves adding a single step, heating (e of sample claim 1), to the several conventional steps (a thru d) of the prior process.

This factual situation should point the way toward using a "Jepson," or improvement-type, claim, one form of which is employed in sample claim 1. (See section 57.) Rule 75(e) which reads as follows:

"Where the nature of the case admits, as in the case of an improvement, any independent claim should contain in the following order,

(1) a preamble comprising a general description of all the elements or steps of the claimed combination which are conventional or known, (2) a phrase such as 'wherein the improvement comprises,' and (3) those elements, steps and/or relationships which constitute that portion of the claimed combination which the applicant considers as the new or improved portion."

From the use of the word "should," it would appear that the Office would like to force or at least strongly urge the use of Jepson claims for improvement inventions. It is not quite certain what "should" means, when "may" is used in some rules and "must" in others. But, in practice, Examiners seldom request or suggest the *Jepson* format, and its use is rare.

As to the format for a Jepson claim, section 57 gives several alternatives, the exact choice of which is not critical. However, for the transition between the preamble and the body of the claim, it might be advisable to use the exact language of rule 75(e)—"wherein the improvement comprises."

As to the scope of claim 1, a question is presented as to whether the specific temperature range (35-70°C.) should be recited. From the way this is discussed in Column 3, lines 31-45, it appears that the precise temperature is noncritical, and will vary for different latexes to give optimum results. Therefore, it would appear satisfactory to define the amount of heating functionally, in terms of the result effected, even though the heating step per se is the "heart of the invention." Of interest, claim 1 of the patent did issue in functional terms in this respect, as follows:

> In a process for preparing . . . (etc.) . . . , the improvement consisting of subjecting said coagulum to heating below the fusion temperature . . . prior to said washing step . . .

Note that sample claim 1 tried to be a little more specific, without reciting a temperature range, by telling everything about the heating step mentioned in the specification.

Whether to recite specific latexes is another problem. The way the specification is written, one would not think this necessary since the class of resins is said to be known as is the basic process of preparing such coagula. However, claim 1 of the patent does recite a class of resins.

Sample claims 2 and 3 add what appear to be important subfeatures of the invention. If one or both of these items were included in claim 1, subclaims could be drafted to specify the way or ways of heating, the type of coagulants, the "air knife" step, etc. If the "moving" supporting surface were omitted from claim 1, this could also be added.

It is acceptable to use submethod claims which add only mechanical structure such as:

> The method as recited in claim X, wherein the supporting surface is a rotary drum.

Subordinate method claims preferably add method steps, tell more about previously recited steps, or add details of the materials being worked on, such as the composition of the latex, etc. In general, avoid structure insofar as reasonably possible in writing method claims (see Part IV). Of course, there is no objection to describing the article or materials being worked on in whatever detail is necessary to the method being claimed.

Part II was intended to familiarize the student with *"Markush"* language. (See section 50.)

Part III was intended to test knowledge of genus and species expressions. (See section 58.) On some exams, the examinees have been asked to prepare genus and species claims on the disclosure. When this disclosure was used on the November 1965 examination, genus and species claims were requested. Presumably, species would have been acceptable directed either to the two methods of heating, as in Part III, or to two specific latexes.

The most important point to remember about species claims is that they must define two or more alternative and mutually exclusive variations on an element of the generic claim.

Case 14
PREPARING METHOD CLAIMS

Feb. 15, 1938.   F. J. BICKEL   2,108,742

BRUSH

Filed July 13, 1936

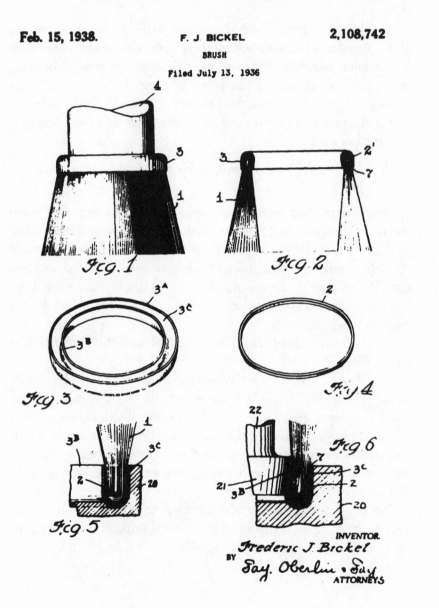

Fig. 1

Fig. 2

Fig. 3

Fig. 4

Fig. 5

Fig. 6

INVENTOR.

Frederic J. Bickel

BY Fay. Oberlin . Fay

ATTORNEYS

1,108,742
BRUSH
Frederic J. Bickel, Cleveland,
Ohio, assignor to The Osborn
Manufacturing Company, Cleve-
land, Ohio, a corporation of Ohio
Application July 13, 1936,
Serial No. 90,306
6 Claims. (Cl. 300—21)

This invention pertains to the brush art and particularly aims to improve the manufacture and construction of hollow center end brushes.

Among the aims and purposes are: the production of brushes which present certain advantages particularly for use as elements of vacuum cleaning tools; absence of rough projections or irregular junctions, edges, points and so on, which would cause difficulty in placing the bristles during manu- facture or cause injury to furni- ture, draperies, household orna- ments and the like, by catching, pulling or scratching; firm grip- ping of the bristles without dam- age thereto; simplification of the manufacture of such brushes: adaptability to manufacture with economical materials and methods of construction.

To the accomplishment of the foregoing and related ends, said invention, then consists of the means hereinafter fully described and particularly pointed out in the claims.

The annexed drawing and the following description set forth in detail certain means and one mode of carrying out the inven- tion, such disclosed means and mode illustrating, however, but one of various ways in which the principle of the invention may be used.

In the accompanying drawing:

Fig. 1 is a side elevation of my brush on the end of a vacuum cleaner attachment;

Fig. 2 is a median section through the brush on an axial plane;

Fig. 3 is a perspective of the brush channel;

Fig. 4 is a perspective of a pre- ferred form of retaining ring;

Fig. 5 is a cross section through The brush, as completed, com- o fassembly; and

Fig. 6 is a cross section through the brush, showing the final as- sembly step.

The brush, as completed, com- prises a filling of bristles 1, looped about a ring 2 or 2′ and secured in an annular channel 3, which is of slightly modified U-shape when seen in cross section in its final form, and which has its opening pointed endwise, that is, in such a direction that the bristles 1 form a cylinder instead of a disc. In use the brush is mounted on or se- cured to suitable holder means, the principal intended purpose being to use it on a tube such as

4 which represents part of a vacuum cleaner attachment. The inner surface of the channel 3 is placed on the tube by a sliding forced fit, or otherwise, as may be most suitable. As best shown in Figs. 2 and 6 the rim channel is somewhat narrowed at the open end to constrict the bristles at 7 and thus firmly anchor the bristles and the retaining ring against withdrawal.

In the manufacture of this brush I have found it preferable to use an annular channel in the shape 3A, having straight inner and outer sides 3B and 3C respectively, Figs. 3 and 5. This channel is designated by the reference character 3 when the brush is in its completed form.

A preferred method of constructing the brush is to fit the channel 3A with the wall of the bristles 1 looped upon the retaining ring 2 or 2'. In the manufacture of the brush a die 20, Figs. 5 and 6, shaped to support the bottom and the outer wall 3C, is used. The filled channel A3 is placed therein, or the empty channel may be placed therein and the die also used to serve the purpose of a holder during the filling of the channel.

Fig. 5 shows, in a partly sectional fragment, the channel in the die, there filled, ready for the next step, shown in Fig. 6. A central expanding tool, such as 21,

Fig. 6, conically sided with an outward upward taper, is moved down by a suitably guided and driven actuating plunger 22 to expand the inner wall 3B of the channel 3A, thus contricting the channel top at 7. My preference is to leave the wall 3C straight both for the reason that this makes a simpler manufacturing operation, and also that it avoids excessive narrowing of the top of the channel and danger of damage to or wear upon the bristles at the portion 7. The completion of construction by the forming tool 21 is shown in Fig. 6.

It will be observed that the retaining ring, as shown in Figs. 4, 5 and 6, is of rectangular cross section, the specific showing being square. I do not confine myself to this shape of retaining ring, but may use a ring of ordinary wire as at 2', Fig. 2. My preference for the ring of rectangular cross section is that it may be more cheaply made than a wire ring, by cutting off successive ends of a seamless tube of proper diameter and wall thickness. The use of square cut sections of a seamless tube has been found in practice not to be injurious to the bristles, and is more economical than making rings of round section.

From the foregoing it will be seen that I have invented a brush of simple and durable construction, free from rough or projecting parts, junctions or seams, wherein the bristles are held firmly, but without injurious pressure at the point of construction, and have likewise invented a method of making such a brush which is simple, economical and quick and in some measure permits utilization of less expensive material than has heretofore been deemed necessary, but without lowering the quality of the product.

Problem

Part I — Write three method claims of varying scope, based on the specification as written.

Part II—Assume that specification disclosed that, for some applications, it was desirable to bend the inner and outer walls 3B and 3C equally toward the center of the channel. With this in mind, prepare a generic claim and two species method claims (using claims from Part I where possible).

Case 14

PREPARING METHOD CLAIMS

SAMPLE CLAIMS—BRUSH MAKING

Part I:

1. A method of making a brush, which comprises:

assembling a plurality of bristles with a core member and a channel having a U-shaped cross section by placing the core member in the channel so that the bristles are lopped about the core member with the ends of the bristles projecting from the open end of the channel; and

partially closing the open end of the channel to secure the bristles and the core member in the channel.

2. A method as recited in claim 1, for making a hollow cylindrical brush, wherein the assembling step comprises:

looping a plurality of the bristles about a ring-shaped core member; and

inserting the core member and bristles into an annular channel having a U-shaped cross section of such size as to receive the core member and bristles therein.

3. A method as recited in claim 2, wherein the channel is partially closed by bending the edge of the inner wall of the channel toward the outer wall thereof while maintaining the outer wall fixed.

Alternate 3. A method as recited in claim 2, wherein the partial closing of the channel comprises bending the edge. . . .

Part II:

Claims 1 and 2 are generic. Claim 3 is directed to the first species, that disclosed in the specification. The following claim covers the second species:

> 4. A method as recited in claim 2, wherein the channel is partially closed by bending the edges of the inner and outer walls of the channel toward each other.

COMMENTS

This disclosure was used on the November 1956 Agent's Exam. As is customary for the method claims, the entire specification (minus claims) was given. In some instances, an examinee has been requested to compose genus and species method claims.

In preparing method claims from a specification, there is usually no problem in understanding the method or in naming the parts or steps. Usually, the names given in the specification will suffice, such as "looping," "annular channel," etc. A problem is in figuring out what is most fundamental to the method for inclusion in claim 1, and what details should be left for other claims. Since the specific question asked in this case was to write three claims of "varying scope," it is not necessary (but would not hurt) to make each claim include all of the limitations of the preceding claim.

Claim 1 covers what appears to be the most important steps— assembling the elements and closing the channel. This claim covers other possible methods of assembling the core, bristles and channel, such as laying the bristles in the channel first and then inserting the core. In this case, some details must be left out of claim 1 because the method is so simple that there would otherwise be a problem in preparing three claims of *materially* different scope.

Another approach to claim 1 would be to claim the looping and inserting steps separately perhaps along the following lines:

". . . looping a plurality of bristles about a core member; inserting the core member and bristles into a channel. . . ."

Probably the most important thing in writing method claims is to make certain that the "elements" of the claim are manipulative steps or acts (looping, inserting, closing, bending, etc.). Apparatus used in carrying out the method should not be mentioned insofar as it is possible to avoid it; thus, in this case, there is no need to recite the die 20 or the expanding tool 21. Of course, there is no problem in describing as much of the *article* being worked on as is essential to the method being described, such as the core member, channel and bristles.

On the species claims 3 and 4, see section 58.

Case 15

PREPARING METHOD CLAIMS

Sept. 7, 1943.   G. S. HIERS   2,328,904

METHOD OF ATTACHING AND STRAIGHTENING FLOCK

Filed April 2, 1941

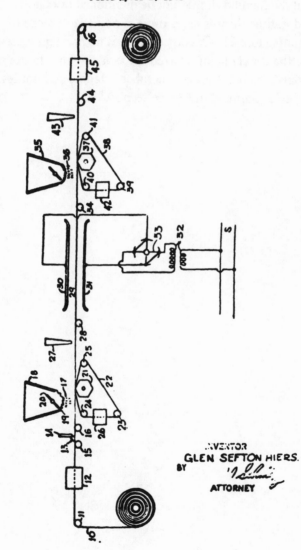

INVENTOR
GLEN SEFTON HIERS.
BY
ATTORNEY

G. S. HIERS PATENT 2,328,904
SPECIFICATION

This invention relates to a method of and apparatus for producing flocked pile fabrics.

High voltage electrostatic methods have heretofore been used in the production of flocked pile fabrics, but fabrics so produced, while having a great number of pile fibers per unit area and hence sufficient density of face coverage as well as excellent erectness of pile, have been characterized by deficient anchorage of the fibers to the adhesive with the result that the durability of the fabric has been unsatisfactory. In addition, the great number of pile flock fibers per unit area is undesirable for many purposes, as too great density of the pile face, particularly with straight fibers of equal length, causes stiffness which interferes with the draping properties of the fabric. As it is exceedingly difficult to control the regular deposition of pile forming flock when less than an excess of the amount actually secured to the base fabric is introduced into the electrostatis field or positioned on portions of the base fabric, as by sifting, prior to those portions of the base fabric entering the electrostatic field, prior flocked fabrics were produced which were relatively costly because of the amount of flock used and yet undesirable because of their lack of desired draping quality and softness of appearance.

Beater methods have also been employed in the production of flocked pile fabrics, but in fabrics so produced, while the anchorage of the fiber to the adhesive is good, the erectness of pile and density of coverage is not all that is desired for some uses.

According to my improvements, I overcome these prior difficulties and deficiencies and produce a flocked pile fabric having a desired erectness of pile, density of coverage and excellence of anchorage of fiber to adhesive and hence a fabric which is superior to fabrics produced by either the beater or the high potential electrostatic methods alone or prior combinations of these methods. It will be understood, of course, that wool fibers which are cured or crescent shaped, will not have the erectness of the straighter fibers, but the wool fibers will be oriented to the extent permitted by their shape.

I accomplish the above desirable result by subjecting the adhesively coated fabric successively to a rapid beater operation and to high potential electrostatic forces. The successive steps of first rapidly beating or otherwise vibrating the fabric upon which fibers have been or are being deposited and then positioning the flocked fabric within a high potential electrostatic field may be repeated as often as and to the extent that is necessary to produce the desired result. During the rapid beating step a low potential electrostatic field may be generated by frictional engagement of the beating means with a material other than the base fabric and/or with the base fabric itself, although beating alone will form a pile face.

The generation of the low potential electrostatic field is not essential to the broad concept of the present improvements and the particular methods will be the subject matter of separate applications. The rapid beating alone will cause the pile forming flock to stand on end in a known manner, although the erectness and density of pile is less than exists in fabrics produced by high potential methods. The beating step, aside from embedding the end of the flock in the adhesive, also uniformly distributes it over the face of the base fabric. The adhesive is not yet set and the pile fibers are adjustable therein, as will be explained. In cases where the adhesive has set it may be treated with a solvent to soften it to tackiness. This latter step is not essential to the continuous process. The loose or excess fibers resulting from the beating step may be removed by a vacuum device or other convenient means.

In the initial operation flock fibers are dropped upon the adhesively coated surface of a cotton or other base fabric which is vibrated rapidly preferably under the beats of a rapidly rotating polygonal bar or bars which may be in actual contact with the back of the base fabric or which may be in engagement with a flexible apron interposed between the beater and the base fabric and in contact with both.

Following the rapid beating and excess flock removal operations or a softening operation, the flocked fabric is placed within a high potential electrostatic field to cause the deposited fibers to assume a more erect position in the adhesive and to thereby create openings into which additional flock may subsequently be dropped. I prefer that the high potential field be used solely for straightening the position of fibers previously applied without additional flock being deposited while the fabric is within the high potential field. Additional flock may, however, be introduced within the field if desired.

Upon removal from the high potential electrostatic field, the flocked fabric is brought into contact with a beating means which may be similar to or somewhat different from that used in the initial step, and during the second beating operation additional flock of the same or different kind and/or length is dropped upon the rapidly vibrating fabric. Following this operating, the fabric may again be placed within a high potential electrostatic field and this sequence of steps may be continued until the desired result is obtained. Ordinarily, two applications of flock will suffice.

It is an object of this invention to provide a method of and apparatus for producing a flocked pile fabric having good anchorage of fiber to base, erectness of pile and sufficient density of face coverage.

Another object is to provide a means of controlling the amount and uniformity of an application of pile flock fibers before their entrance to a high potential electrostatic field.

Another object is to provide a method of producing flocked pile fabrics which includes the steps in sequence of depositing flock fibers upon an adhesively coated base fabric by a beater method, and then by means of a high potential electrostatic force causing the deposited fibers to assume a more erect position in the adhesive.

Another object is to anchor flock fibers in the adhesively coated surface of a base fabric by heating and to thereafter subject the flocked fabric to a high potential electrostatic force to cause the anchored fibers to assume a more erect position and thereby create openings in the face of the fabric, and then to anchor additional fibers by a subsequent beating operation.

Another object is to subject an adhesively coated base fabric to a plurality of flocking operations by beater methods and interpose between the flocking the step or steps of pulling the deposited fibers to more erect position in the adhesive.

A further object is to deposit upon an adhesively coated base fabric as much flock as can be secured by a single beating operation, and then by high potential electrostatic methods to cause the fibers to assume a more erect position and thereby create openings into which additional flock may be dropped and anchored by a subsequent beating operation.

These and other objects of invention will clearly appear from the following description of a preferred embodiment, in which:

The figure depicts schematically apparatus suitable for flocking a base fabric in accordance with my improvements.

Referring to the drawing, reference numeral 10 depicts a base fabric of cotton or other suitable material which is carried over guide roll 11 to drier 12, in which moisture may be removed from the fabric to the point of bone dryness if desired, after which an adhesive 13 of rubber cement, pyroxylin, or other composition, may be applied to the face side of the fabric as by doctor blade 14 positioned between guide rolls 15 and 16. Flock fibers 17 of wool, mohair, cotton, viscose, casein, acetate, or other textile material, and of desired length may be deposited upon the adhesively coated surface as from hopper 18, having screen bottom 19 and rotating blade 20 for forcing the flock through the screen.

Polygonal beater bar 21, positioned beneath the fabric and apron 22 at a point preferably just beyond that at which the fibers are dropped upon the fabric, may be rotated by conventional means (not shown) at a speed sufficient to cause rapid vibration of the base fabric.

The apron 22 may be supported as by rollers 23, 24 and 25 and may be dried as by can drier 26 if desired. The beating bar 21 may be of all metal or metal with a surface covering of lucite, Bakelite, hard rubber, or other good dielectric material, and should be rotated at a speed which will produce at least three thousand beats per minute.

Fibers dropped upon the rapidly vibrating base fabric are forced into the adhesive in somewhat erect position by the mechanical forces alone or together with the electrostatic forces present the degree of erectness being dependent somewhat upon the intensity of the electrostatic field. The fabric so flocked is then passed beneath suction tube 27 which extends across the fabric to remove the excess flock, after which the fabric supported by guide roller 28 passes into high voltage electrostatic field 29, established between electrodes 30 and 31 by the impression thereupon of voltages on the order of from 20 to 100 k. v. The high potential field may be of alternating polarity if desired, but is preferably unidirectional and its energy may be supplied from low voltage alternating current line supply S through step-up transformer 32 and mechanical rectifier 33. One of the electrodes is preferably grounded.

Within the high potential field in the previously deposited fibers are caused to assume a more erect position in the still soft adhesive thereby creating openings which are more or less uniformly distributed over the face of the fabric and which may be later filled by the deposit of additional flock. Such additional flock may if desired be applied while the fabric is still within the high potential field, but I prefer that the high potential field be used solely for fiber straightening purposes.

Upon leaving the high potential field, the flocked fabric is passed over guide roller 34 and beneath hopper 35 containing additional fibers 36 of the same or different kinds and/or lengths as those initially applied and which may be sifted upon the fabric while it is being rapidly vibrated by rapidly rotating polygonal bar 37. As in the first beating operation, apron 38 of wool may be interposed between the bar 37 and the base fabric. The apron may be supported as by rollers 39, 40 and 41 and may be dried as in can drier 42 if desired.

The fibers deposited in this second beating step will fill the openings created when the fibers were straightened up in the high potential field. Following the second application of flock, the excess may be removed as by suction tube 43, or by other conventional means.

If for any reason further straightening of deposited fibers and application of additional flock is desirable, the fabric may be passed through a second high potential field similar to the first and then to another flocking and beating operation. These steps may, of course, be continued until the desired result is attained. Ordinarily, two flockings interposed by a single straightening operation will be sufficient.

After the final flocking and/or straightening operation, the fabric may be passed over guide roller 44 to drier 45 where the adhesive is set and thence over roller 46 to roll up of the finished fabric.

I have found that fabrics made in accordance with my improvements have excellent anchorage of fiber to base, erectness of pile and density of face coverage.

My invention also contemplates the application of flock of different kinds, colors, and/or lengths, whereby pleasing effects may be attained.

Problem

Write three method claims of varying scope, given the specification.

Case 15

PREPARING METHOD CLAIMS

SAMPLE CLAIMS—METHOD OF ATTACHING AND STRAIGHTENING FLOCK

1. A method of attaching and straightening flock fibers on a base material, which comprises the steps of:

depositing flock fibers upon an adhesively-coated base while the adhesive is soft,
vibrating the base to attach an end of some of the flock fibers to the still soft adhesive,
removing unattached flock fibers, and then
electrostatically *attracting* the attached fibers into erect positions on the still soft adhesive.

2. The method according to claim 1, including the additional steps of:

depositing additional flock fibers upon the still soft adhesive,
vibrating the base material to attach the ends of some of the additional flock fibers to the still soft adhesive to fill any openings on the face thereof, and *removing* unattached flock fibers.

3. The method according to claim 2, including the additional steps of:

electrostatically *attracting* the attached fibers into erect positions on the still soft adhesive, and
setting the adhesive to fix the fibers to the base material in their erect positions.

COMMENTS

Action words have been italicized for illustration (only). Instead of "depositing," there could be recited two steps, *viz.*,

    (a) *coating* the base with an adhesive, and
    (b) *depositing* . . .

The written description states that the additional "depositing" and "vibrating" steps of claim 2 may be repeated until a desired density of flocking is achieved. Thus, an additional claim could take the form of:

2A. The method according to claim 2 wherein the steps thereof are continuously repeated in sequence until a predetermined density of the flock fibers is achieved.

Note how the main claim 1, can often be lifted from the "Summary of the Invention" (rule 73) given in the specification prior to the detailed description. In this case, the "summary" appears in the first full paragraph on page 2 of the specification, where the patentee tells what he thinks his invention is, in a relatively broad sense. These summaries are required by rule 73, but cannot always be relied on in practice to define the scope of the invention accurately. But in claim-drafting practice, this is usually the best guideline one has.

Case 16

PREPARING METHOD CLAIMS

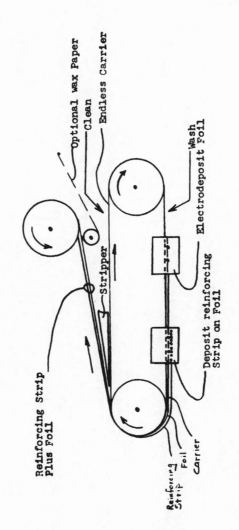

METHOD OF MAKING FOIL

Problem

Write three claims of varying scope on the depicted process. Prepare a fourth claim covering zinc, tin or aluminum as the material of the foil.

Case 16

PREPARING METHOD CLAIMS

SAMPLE CLAIMS—METHOD OF MAKING FOIL

1. A method of making a continuous strip of metal foil, which comprises:

advancing an endless carrier through a metal-deposition chamber;
depositing a layer of metal foil on the carrier as it passes through the chamber;
stripping the layer of foil from the advancing carrier; and then returning the stripped carrier to the metal-deposition chamber.

2. A method as recited in claim 1, for making a continuous composite strip of the metal foil having a backing sheet, which further comprises:

depositing a continuous adherent backing sheet on the layer of foil prior to stripping the foil from the carrier.

3. A method as recited in claim 2, further comprising:

winding the composite strip of foil and the adherent backing sheet into a coil with the layer of foil exposed; and
inserting a protective layer of wax paper between the convolutions of the coil as it is wound.

4. A method as recited in claim 1, wherein the foil metal is selected from the group consisting of zinc, tin and aluminum.

331

COMMENTS

Claim 1 covers the endless feature without defining the reinforcing strip, which is one approach. Another equally good approach would be to cover the step of adding the reinforcing strip, in which case the endless feature could be omitted from claim 1.

Claim 2 is a dependent claim varying the preamble of the parent claim.

Claim 3 adds preferred details, and claim 4 illustrated Markush practice (See section 50).

Case 17
PREPARING METHOD CLAIMS

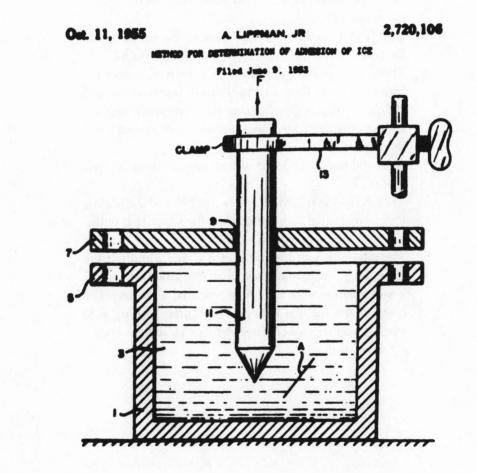

Oct. 11, 1955 A. LIPPMAN, JR 2,720,106

METHOD FOR DETERMINATION OF ADHESION OF ICE

Filed June 9, 1953

Problem

Draft three method claims of varying scope, given the drawing and the following:

1. First, the container 1 is filled with a solidifiable liquid, preferably water.
2. Next, the sliver 11 is inserted through the opening 9 in the cover 7, and the sliver 11 is placed in the liquid.
3. Then, the liquid is solidified as at 3, preferably from the bottom up, so that no unsolidified liquid is trapped within the solid during freezing and to minimize the formation of faults or cleavage points, as at A, during solidification.
4. The solidified body 3 is confined within the cover 7 via clamp 13.
5. The sliver 11 is pulled up with a force F, and the pulling force is measured at the time when the sliver 11 is pulled from the solidified, confined body 3.
6. The difficulty with the prior art was that it did not use the cover 7, with the result that the solidified body 3 would fracture at the fault A, giving a false reading. The object of the method is to get an accurate reading as to when the adhesion between the sliver 11 and the body 3 is broken by the force F.

Case 17

PREPARING METHOD CLAIMS

SAMPLE CLAIMS—TESTING ADHESION

1. A method of determining the adhesion of one solid material to another solid material, which comprises the steps of:

(a) inserting a member formed of one of the materials into a liquid mass of the other material, the member being inserted into the mass with a portion thereof extending therefrom;

(b) solidifying the mass;

(c) confining the entire external surface of the solidified mass;

(d) applying a gradually increasing, separative force to both the solidified mass and the member; and

(e) measuring the force at which separation is effected to determine the adhesion of the one solid material to the other.

2. A method as recited in claim 1, wherein the member is a metal and the solidified mass is ice.

3. A method as recited in claim 2, wherein the mass is solidified by freezing it in stages from the bottom thereof to the top thereof.

COMMENTS

In practice, claim 1 is of proper scope. For the examination, claim 1 may be overly broad. The title of the invention in the specification is Method for Determination of Adhesion of Ice. But claim 1 describes adhering one solid material to another. Thus, for the examination, claim 1 might better read:

1. A method of determining the adhesion of ice, comprising:

(a) inserting a solid sliver into water;
(b) solidifying the water to ice by freezing;
(c) confining the external surface of the ice through which the sliver is accessible;
(d) pulling the sliver from the ice through the external surface by applying a gradually increasing force to the sliver while the external surface of the ice is confined;
(e) measuring the pulling force at which the sliver separates from the ice.

Case 18

PREPARING METHOD CLAIMS

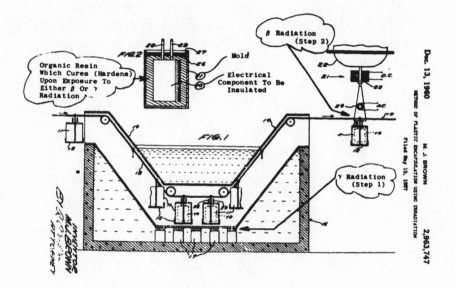

Problem

The object is to encapsulate the component in a soft body of plastic having a hard outer shell. The gamma radiation cures the plastic only to the soft state and is then stopped. The beta radiation is much less penetrating, and hardens only the outer surface of the resin, so that the interior remains soft and gelatinous.

Draft a claim to this method. Assume both gamma and beta radiation, per se, are known to cure such resins for encapsulation purposes.

Case 18

PREPARING METHOD CLAIMS

SAMPLE CLAIM—ENCAPSULATION METHOD

A method of encapsulating an article, which comprises:

positioning the article in a body of liquid resin of a type that cures gradually upon exposure to both gamma and to beta radiation;

irradiating the body of resin with gamma radiation until the body has been partially cured to form a gelatinous body surrounding the article; and

irradiating the gelatinous body with beta radiation so that an outer layer thereof is cured to form a hard protective shell of the resin on the surface of the gelatinous body.

COMMENTS

Structural (apparatus) elements, such as the mold, are not needed in a method claim (section 41), and should be omitted insofar as possible. The main method steps are "irradiating" and then "irradiating" in the prescribed sequence.

Note the phraseology "irradiating . . . until . . . cured. . . ." As discussed in section 37, this follows the format "performing an act [irradiating] to accomplish a step or function [curing]." This could equally well have been phrased "partially curing . . . by irradiating" or "by exposing," etc. This is the form of reciting the overall step performed by the act.

The first and second steps could be combined: "irradiating a body of a liquid resin . . . having the article positioned therein. . . ."

Case 19

PREPARING METHOD CLAIMS

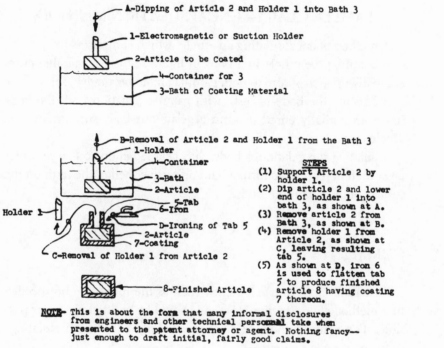

Problem

Part I—Draft one generic and two species method claims to the method shown.

Part II—Would it be proper to present claims to the coating apparatus or the finished article? Assume there are no restriction requirement problems.

Case 19

PREPARING METHOD CLAIMS

SAMPLE CLAIMS — COATING METHOD

Generic and Species Claims

1. A method of coating an article with a thermoplastic material, which comprises:

supporting the article with a holder;

coating the article and adjacent portions of the holder with the thermoplastic material in liquid form, and allowing the coating material to solidify;

withdrawing the holder from the article so as to leave a tab of solidified coating material projecting from the article at the portions formerly engaging the holder; and

heating and forming the tab so as to coat the portion of the article formerly engaging the holder.

2. A coating method as recited in claim 1, wherein the supporting step includes applying a partial vacuum between the holder and portions of the article, and wherein the partial vacuum is released prior to the withdrawing step.

3. A coating method as recited in claim 1, for use with a paramagnetic article, wherein the supporting step includes applying an electromagnetic force to the holder to support the article, and wherein the electromagnetic force is released prior to the withdrawing step.

COMMENTS

Step 2, "coating . . . and allowing to solidify," is a perfectly proper *step*, allowing something to happen—that is, just sitting there doing nothing. Also, the coating and allowing steps are clearly related, and can be put in the same subparagraph of the claim. They could equally well have been separated. The "allowing" concept could also have been put into the following clause instead: "withdrawing . . . after the coating has solidified." In clause 4, the "heating and forming" steps are done together and can be combined.

Query

1. Apparatus claims are not proper, because there is nothing new in the magnetic or vacuum holder. The sole novelty is in the manipulation (new use) of such old equipment as part of a novel coating process. New uses for old devices may be claimed only as methods. (See section 56.)

2. Article claims are not proper, because the coated article is the same as that produced in any other manner. It has no distinguishing characteristics based on the novel method of manufacture. But, a product-by-process claim is proper. (See section 46.)

Case 20

PREPARING CHEMICAL PROCESS CLAIMS

MALEIC ANHYDRIDE
PURIFICATION
CROWELL PATENT 2,308,588

This invention relates to purification of maleic anhydride and particularly to a method for refining maleic anhydride produced by catalytic vapor phase oxidation and containing colored and/or color-forming impurities.

In the catalytic vapor phase partial oxidation of organic compounds, such as, for example, benzene, methyl-naphthalene, phenol, cresol, benzophenone, furane, diphenyl, toluene, butene, furfural, and naphthalene, to produce maleic anhydride, various methods for recovering maleic anhydride from the gaseous reaction mixtures resulting from such processes have been employed; for example, the gases have been subjected to controlled preliminary cooling to effect a partial condensation therefrom of maleic anhydride before further treatment of the gases to effect removal of remaining condensible vapors; or the gases have been conducted through an organic solvent to absorb maleic anhydride and the anhydride then has been recovered from the resulting solvent solution, as described in United States Patent 2,140,140; or the gases have been conducted into water to form an aqueous solution of maleic acid from which the acid has been recovered and converted to maleic anhydride by a dehydration process such as that described in United States Patent 1,066,853 or that described in United States Patent 2,205,402. Maleic anhydride recovered by some methods is very dark; that recovered by others is less so; but an attribute common to all such products is the presence therein of colored and/or color-forming impurities.

Hereinafter, in the specification and in the claims, maleic anhydride which contains colored or color-forming impurities to be removed will be termed "crude maleic anhydride," and colored and color-forming impurities will be designated genetically by the term "chromogenic impurities."

While it might be presumed that processes applicable to the removal of chromogenic impurities which are present in crude phthalic anhydride obtained from the catalytic vapor phase partial oxidation of organic compounds, e.g., napthalene, should be suitable also for the purification of crude maleic anhydride, such has not been found to be the case. Thus, while a treatment with sulfuric acid at high temperature followed by distillation to recover the purified product has been employed successfully to produce colorless phthalic anhydride products which are surprisingly stable, and remain colorless for long periods of time, the same process when applied to crude maleic anhydride has been found to produce products which are only temporarily colorless.

In my United States Patent 2,-129,166 of September 6, 1938, I have described and claimed a process for purifying maleic anhydride by maintaining the anhydride at an elevated temperature for a sufficient time to convert chromogenic impurities to products differing greatly in volatility from the anhydride, and separating the anhydride and reaction products by volatilization. This "aging" process accomplishes as effective purification, but when a product characterized by a commercially acceptable standard of color is required from a not particularly good grade of crude maleic anhydride, it entails heating for so many hours that the process becomes an excessive burden to maintenance of low production costs.

The present invention is in the nature of an improvement over and upon the hot-aging process of my United States Patent 2,129,166. Objects of the present invention are to provide a more rapid method of purifying crude maleic anhydride than methods hitherto available, and to effect more complete purification of crude maleic anhydride and thereby produce a purified maleic anhydride product distinguished by its unusual stability to the development of color.

In accordance with the present invention, crude maleic anhydride is subjected to a hot-aging in liquid phase in contact with an oxide of boron, or a hydrated oxide of boron, to convert the chromogenic impurities contained in the crude maleic anhydride to products which are relatively non-volatile compared with maleic anhydride, and maleic anhydride is separated from such products by fractional distillation.

The process of the present invention accomplishes the purification of even refractory types of crude maleic anhydride rapidly and at relatively low temperatures, and produces from highly impure and highly colored grades of crude maleic anhydride excellent yields of purified maleic anhydride characterized by excellent color and stability to development of color during storage.

The crude maleic anhydride may be treated either alone in molten condition or in the form of a solution in an organic solvent which is inert to the maleic anhydride and to the reagent employed. As examples of solutions may be mentioned solvent naphtha solutions or chlornaphthalene solutions containing from 50% to 70% by weight of maleic anhydride.

Pressure, aside from its effect upon the boiling point of maleic anhydride, is substantially without effect on the present treatment, and the process may be carried out under superatmospheric, normal, or reduced pressure under otherwise like conditions with substantially identical results.

The mixture of maleic anhydride and purifying reagent may be maintained at the selected treatment temperature until the mixture or a sample thereof brought to its refluxing temperature under the pressure at which the distillation is to be effected, produces a distillate or reflux condensate, the color of which is equal to or better than a desired color standard. The mass then may be subjected to distillation to obtain a very high yield of purified maleic anhydride of the desired color standard. However, the stability of the product towards development of color may be further improved by prolonging the hot-aging period beyond the minimum time required to attain the desired color of distillate. Hence the hot-aging may be regulated to provide the desired degree of stability.

I have found that with otherwise like conditions, to effect a particular degree of purification in a particular mixture of molten maleic anhydride and a purifying reagent of the type hereinbefore described, the necessary period of treatment diminishes as the temperature of treatment is increased.

In general, with other conditions equal, an increase in the amount of the reagent employed permits a reduction in the time required to effect a commensurate purification. On the other hand, with the addition of an amount of solid reagent such as B_2O_3 greater than 30% of the crude maleic anhydride, it has been found difficult to maintain the mixture as a homogeneous mass; and when such a mixture is distilled, this lack of homogeneity appears to cause an impairment of heat transfer which results in excessive decomposition and loss of yield of refined maleic anhydride.

It is preferable to employ an amount of purifying agent not exceeding about 10% by weight of the crude maleic anhydride.

Examples of suitable compounds for effecting the purification are boric oxide and metaboric and orthoboric acids, which are hydrated boric oxide.

When the crude maleic anhydride to be treated contains free water or maleic acid, the crude product is preferably dehydrated by rectification prior to applying the purification treatment.

The purification treatment of a crude maleic anhydride which contains only a small proportion of chromogenic impurities may be effected by mixing the molten maleic anhydride with the purifying reagent, agitating the mixture for a short time, for example 10 minutes, at a temperature above the melting point of the maleic anhydride, and thereupon distilling the mixture.

However, when the crude maleic anhydride is contaminated by a relatively large content of chromogenic impurities, a short treatment with the purifying reagent may be insufficient to produce more than a small recovery of maleic anhydride exhibiting a commercially acceptable standard of color or stability towards development of color during storage. In such cases, the first part of the distillate may contain excessive proportions of chromogenic impurities, while as the distillation proceeds and thus prolongs the duration of action of the purifying agent on the crude maleic anhydride, more extensive purification takes place and the distillate becomes progressively lighter and in general has a decreasing tendency to develop color during storage. Thus, a late portion of the distillate may be actually satisfactory in color and stability to development of color on standing, but the yield of acceptable maleic anhydride so obtained may be comparatively small. Hence in the treatment of such refractory crude maleic anhydride products the crude is heated in the presence of the purifying reagent for at least three hours and usually considerably longer prior to distillation of maleic anhydride.

A good grade of crude maleic anhydride which is intermingled with a limited quantity of boron oxide can be purified to produce a distillate of a commercial standard of "whiteness" by maintaining the mixture before distillation at a suitable temperature, for example, at 150° C., for substantially less than the time necessary to effect the same degree of decolorization employing an aging treatment in the absence of the boron oxide at the same temperature; and, in general, stability against development of color during storage of the purified maleic anhydride obtained with the aid of the treatment with boron oxide is greater than that of the maleic anhydride purified by the aging treatment without the aid of the boron oxide.

Preferably the aging treatment is conducted at temperatures between 140° C. and 200° C.

The following examples further illustrate the purification process of the present invention. In these examples, deviation from colorlessness of the shade of the purified maleic anhydride in the molten state is expressed in terms of a scale of color standards wherein each color standard bears a number which is synonymous with the shade of a specific dilution of a stock aqueous solution of potassium chlorplatinate and cobalt chloride. The stock solution is prepared by adding 100 cc. of concentrated hydrochloric acid to a solution of 1.246 grams of potassium chlorplatinate (K_2PtCl_3), corresponding at 0.50 gram of platinum, and 1.00 gram of cobalt chloride hexahydrate ($CoCl_2.6H_2O$), corresponding to 0.25 gram of cobalt, in distilled water, and diluting the resulting solution with distilled water to a volume of one liter. The stock solution thus prepared is given a color number of 500 and the remaining color numbers of the scale are ascribed to solutions obtained by specific degrees of dilution of the stock solution as follows:

Color number	Dilution (parts by volume of distilled water per part of stock solution)
10	48
20	24
40	11.50
60	7.30
80	5.25
100	4.00
150	2.30
200	1.30
300	0.67
400	0.25
500	0.00

To determine the color number of a purified maelic anhydride, a molten sample of the latter is compared, under substantially identical conditions, with standard solutions which correspond to these identified by the numbers in the foregoing color scale; the number of the solution whose color is most closely approximated by the color of the molten anhydride is said to be the color number of the latter.

In the following examples "parts" signifies parts by weight.

Example 1

In the catalytic vapor phase oxidation of benzene by means of air, a crude maleic anhydride product may be obtained by contacting the reaction gases with solvent naphtha. The resulting solvent naphtha solution of maleic anhydride may be fractionally distilled to expel the solvent naphtha and yield a crude maleic anhydride.

To 100 parts of such a crude product 6 parts of boric acid were added and the mixture was heated. The boric acid dissolved and when a temperature of about 135° C. was reached, water vapor came off from the hot mixture; the maleic anhydride began to boil at a temperature between 160° and 170° C. and water was gradually expelled until the boiling point of maleic anhydride was reached. Maleic anhydride was thereupon distilled from the mixture and collected as a substantially colorless product.

A second portion of the sam crude maleic anhydride, treated by the same procedure except for omission of boric acid, yielded a deep orange-colored distillate.

Example 2

To 100 parts of crude maleic anhydride obtained in the same manner as the anhydride employed in the preceding example, 10 parts of boric anhydride (B_2O_3) were added. The mass was refluxed at atmospheric pressure for 30 minutes and then distilled. A substantially colorless distillate was obtained.

By subjecting another portion of the same crude anhydride to the same treatment except for omission of boric anhydride an orange distillate was obtained.

Example 3

Crude maleic anhydride obtained by direct partial condensation in the absence of solvents from the hot reaction gases produced by catalytic air oxidation of benzene was refluxed in a glass still fitted with a reflux condenser until no further water distilled off from the product.

100 parts by weight of the dehydrated crude anhydride were mixed with 1 part by weight of metaboric acid. The mixture was agitated in a glass vessel at 150° to 160° C. at atmospheric pressure for about four hours and then was transferred to a glass distillation flask and fractionally distilled at an absolute pressure of 60 mm. to 70 mm. of mercury. A distillate comprising 75% by weight of the still charge and a distillation residue comprising 25% thereof were obtained. The color of the distillate immediately after

distillation and after standing 20 and 50 days was 40, 100, and 100+, respectively.

A control run was conducted using the same type of dehydrated crude anhydride alone but under otherwise like conditions and fractionally distilling the product as described for the metaboric-acid-treated anhydride. The control distillate comprising about 83% by weight of the still charge had a color of 100 which darkened to 300 after only 20 days of standing.

Example 4

Boric acid (H_3Bo_3) is an amount equal to 10% by weight of the dissolved maleic anhydride, is added to a solution of maleic anhydride in solvent naphtha. The mass is refluxed at a temperature between about 120° C. and 130° C. for 30 minutes, during which time any water vapors in the reflux vapors are not condensed but allowed to escape. The mixture is then distilled. The distillate has a color equal to about 3.5 on the Barrett scale. (The Barrett scale consists of a series of fifteen standard color solutions. It is described in the Journal of Industrial and Engineering Chemistry, 1918, vol. 10, page 1008. The color number as obtained above is that of the standard color solution most nearly approximating the color of a sample of the distillate when both distillate and color solution are observed under the same conditions.)

A distillate possessing a color equal to 6.5 (Barrett scale) is produced if the addition of boric acid is omitted.

Problem

Draft three claims of substantially varying scope covering the method described in the specification. Claims in dependent form may be used. The claims should not distinguish from each other by merely immaterial limitations and should distinguish over any prior art described in the specification.

Case 20

PREPARING CHEMICAL PROCESS CLAIMS

SAMPLE CLAIMS—
MALEIC ANHYDRIDE PURIFICATION

1. A process of purifying crude maleic anhydride containing chromogenic impurities, comprising:

subjecting crude maleic anhydride to a hot-aging process in liquid phase;

conducting the hot-aging process in the presence of a compound selected from the group consisting of the oxides and hydrated oxides of boron to convert the chromogenic impurities to products which are relatively nonvolatile compared to maleic anhydride; and then

separating the maleic anhydride from such products by fractional distillation.

2. A process as recited in claim 1, wherein the hot-aging process is carried out at a temperature between about 140° C. and 200° C.

3. A process as recited in claim 2, wherein: the compound is selected from the group consisting of boric oxide, metaboric acid and orthoboric acid, in an amount not exceeding 10 percent by weight of the crude maleic anhydride.

COMMENTS

This patent was used on the February 1968 Exam. A choice was given between this patent and a mechanical structure on apparatus for delivering granular materials, Kokeisl patent 3,125,256 (Appendix B, Case 9).

Note the specification, first five paragraphs, describes the prior art, particularly the patentee's own "hot-aging" process. In paragraphs six to eight (the "summary of the invention," required by Rule 73), he tells one exactly what the invention is in a broad sense. In preparing claim 1, it is best to abstract this summary in claim language, as was done for example in claim 1.

The *Jepson* form (section 57) may be used for claim 1 in this case (Rule 75-e) because it is pellucid from paragraphs 5 and 6 of the specification that this "invention is in the nature of an improvement over . . . the hot-aging process of my . . . [prior] patent. . . ." The *Jepson* form can be used, with the elements of the old process set out in the preamble. (See sections 57 and 63 (on "old combination")).

Note how phrases such as "crude maleic anhydride," "chromogenic impurities," and "hot-aging," which are defined in the specification, can and should be lifted out of the specification and used in the claim without further definition. (See section 18 on "Support in the specification" for words used in the claims, and section 19, that applicant can be his own lexicographer, define the words as he chooses so long as he is not using a meaning repugnant to the customary meaning of the word.)

For the Agent's examination, it is recommended to not attempt to claim any broader than the patentee says is in the invention the summary, nor much narrower. In practice, when writing the specification, initially write the summary as broadly as the broadest claim. Note that process details such as "preferably, the aging treatment is conducted at temperatures between 140° C. and 200° C." should be left for subordinate claims. These the patentee says are important but not critical.

In chemical process claims, useful things to add in dependent claims are temperatures, pressures, times, proportions, specific materials, etc.

Case 21

PREPARING CHEMICAL PROCESS CLAIMS

PURIFICATION OF PHENOL

This invention relates to a novel process for the purification of phenol prepared by decomposition of cumene hydroperoxide.

Phenol is prepared by the partial oxidation of cumene and subsequent decomposition of the resulting cumene hydroperoxide. The decomposition reaction mixture comprises phenol, acetone, and unreacted cumene. The phenol, recovered from the cumene hydroperoxide decomposition reaction mixture by distillation methods, contains acetone condensation products, principally mesityl oxide as well as other carbonyl compounds. Although present in only minute quantities, the carbonyl compounds have color-forming tendencies which render the phenol product commercially unacceptable in many instances.

It is therefore an object of this invention to present a novel process for the purification of phenol containing carbonyl compounds as impurities therein.

In one of its broad aspects, this invention embodies a process which comprises contacting the carbonyl compound contaminated phenol with a nitrogen compound hereinafter described, forming reaction products of the said carbonyl compounds and the said nitrogen compounds and thereafter separating phenol from the said reaction products, the aforesaid nitrogen compound being represented by the formula

$$\overset{\displaystyle H}{\underset{\displaystyle R_1-N-R_2}{|}}$$

wherein R_1 and R_2 are selected from the group consisting of hydrogen, alkyl, cycloalkyl, aryl, alkaryl, aralkyl, hydroxyalkyl and polymethylene radicals, said polymethylene radicals together forming a heterocyclic ring in combination with the nitrogen atom to which they are attached.

Other objects and embodiments of this invention will become apparent in the following detailed specification.

In accordance with the process of this invention, the carbonyl compound-containing phenol is contacted with a nitrogen compound of the formula:

$$H$$
$$|$$
$$R_1{-}N{-}R_2$$

R_1 and R_2 can be polymethylene radicals which in combination, and together with the nitrogen atom through which they are attached, form a heterocyclic ring. Also, R_1 and R_2 may be independently selected from the group consisting of hydrogen, alkyl, cycloalkyl, aryl, alkaryl, aralkyl and hydroxyalkyl.

Thus it will be seen that the nitrogen compound can be ammonia, and one of the more specific embodiments of this invention relates to a process for the purification of phenol containing carbonyl compounds as impurities, which process comprises contacting the phenol with ammonia, forming reaction products of the said carbonyl compounds and ammonia, and separating phenol from the said reaction products.

Nitrogen compounds with which the phenol can be contacted pursuant to the process of this invention further include alkyl primary amines like methylamine, ethylamine, propylamine, isopropylamine, n-butylamine, secbutylamine, beta-ethylbutylamine, amylamine, isoamylamine, alpha-methylamylamine, n-hexylamine, isohexylamine, n-heptylamine, heptadecylamine, etc., and also dialkyl secondary amines, for example, dimethylamine, diethylamine, ethylmethylamine, diisopropylamine, di - n - butylamine, di-sec-butylamine, bis(beta-ethylbutyl)amine, morpholine, and the like. One of the embodiments of this invention relates to a process for the purification of phenol containing carbonyl compound as impurities, which process comprises contacting the phenol with an alkyl primary amine, preferably methylamine, and forming reaction products of the said carbonyl compounds and the said amine and thereafter separating phenol from the said reaction products. In another embodiment, a dialkyl secondary amine, preferably diethylamine, is utilized.

Still another embodiment of this invention concerns a process for the purification of phenol containing carbonyl compounds as impurities wherein the nitrogen compound is an alkanolamine, preferably ethanolamine. Other suitable alkanolamines include 3-hydroxy-n - propylamine, 2 - hydroxy - n - propylamine, 4 - hydroxy - butylamine, 3 - hydroxy - n - butylamine, and the like, and also dialkanol amines such as diethanolamine, etc.

In still another embodiment, the nitrogen compound is benzylamine. Other such aralkyl amines like beta - phenylethylamine, alpha-phenylethylamine, beta-phenylethylamine, alpha-phenylethylamine, beta-phenylpropylamine, etc., and also diaralkylamines like di-beta-phenylethylamine and the like, are also operable.

Other nitrogen compounds of the described formula

$$\begin{array}{c} H \\ | \\ R_1{-}N{-}R_2 \end{array}$$

which can be utilized include cycloalkyl amines like cycyopentylamine, cyclohexylamine, etc., and also dicycloalkylamines such as dicyclopentylamine, dicyclohexylamine, and the like. Arylamines like aniline, 1-naphthylamine, 2-naphthylamine, N-methylaniline, N-ethylaniline, etc., as well as diarylamines including diphenylamine, di-2-naphthylamine and the like, and also alkarylamines, for example, toluidine, xylidine, o-ethylaniline, etc., are also operable. Piperidine, pyrrolidine, and other like compounds of the formula

$$\begin{array}{c} H \\ | \\ R_1{-}N{-}R_2 \end{array}$$

wherein R_1 and R_2 are polymethylene radicals which, together with the nitrogen atoms to which they are attached, form a heterocyclic ring, can also be utilized.

The required amount of any particular nitrogen compound herein described is dependent on the concentration of the carbonyl compound impurities in the phenol product to be treated. In the usual case, from about .02% to about 0.2%, based on the weight of the phenol to be treated, is adequate although larger amounts can be utilized. The optimum amount in any particular case is in part dependent on the nitrogen compound being utilized and in part on the concentration of carbonyl compounds, the latter being readily determined by routine experimentation. The reaction products of the nitrogen compound and the carbonyl compounds, as well as any excess nitrogen compound utilized, can be separated from the phenol by acid extraction methods, distillation methods, or other suitable means. When the phenol is recovered by distillation methods, any excess of ammonia or other nitrogen compound may distill over with the phenol. This can be obviated by including only the required amount of nitrogen compound in the phenol, which amount may be readily determined by experiment. Alternatively, the excess nitrogen compound as well as the reaction products of the nitrogen compound and carbonyl compounds can be retained in the distillation bottoms by treatment with an equivalent amount of an acid, for example sulfuric acid. However, since the addition of any excess acid tends to decompose the nitrogen compound-carbonyl compound reaction products, it is preferred to avoid the use of an acid altogether and to utilize instead a higher boiling nitrogen compound, for example diethanolamine (B.P. 270° C.), to achieve the same effect.

The phenol is preferably contacted with the nitrogen compound at liquid phase reaction conditions. While this can be accomplished at normal room temperature of about 25° C., for example in the case where phenol and ammonia are contacted in aqueous solution, it may be desirable to utilize an elevated temperature within the melting and the boiling point range of phenol, i.e. from about 41° C. to about 182° C. Although the temperature is not a critical aspect of this invention, reaction rates are accelerated at higher temperatures and the necessary contact time between phenol and the nitrogen compound is thereby minimized.

The following examples are presented in illustration of the process of this invention and are not intended as an undue limitation on the generally broad scope thereof.

Example I

104 grams of phenol prepared by decomposition of cumene hydroperoxide was analyzed by gas-liquid chromatography methods and found to contain 0.16 wt. percent mesityl oxide and 0.17 wt. percent of a carbonyl compound described as an acetone trimer, as well as 0.02 wt. percent of unknown impurity. The phenol was therefore 99.65% pure. About 5 grams of ammonia in dilute aqueous solution was added to the phenol and the resulting solution was thoroughly mixed at room temperature. Thereafter, phenol was separated from the ammonia and the impurity products by distillation. Gas-liquid chromatography analysis of the recovered phenol indicated a product purity of 99.91%. There was no evidence of "acetone trimer" and mesityl oxide had been reduced to about 0.02 wt. percent.

Example II

150 grams of a phenol sample prepared by decomposition of cumene hydroperoxide was analyzed by gas-liquid chromatography methods and found to contain 0.11 wt. percent acetone, 0.13 wt. percent mesityl oxide, 0.08 wt. percent acetophenone and 0.34 wt. percent of undetermined impurity. The phenol sample was

therefore 99.34% pure. About 1.5 grams of ammonia in dilute aqueous solution was added to the phenol and the resulting solution was heated at 70° C. with stirring. Thereafter, the phenol was separated from the ammonia and the impurity products by distillation. Gas-liquid chromatography analysis indicated a product purity of 99.93%. The melting point of the product was 40.89° C.

Example III

In the purification of phenol containing carbonyl substances as impurities, the phenol is heated in mixture with about 0.2% ethanol amine, based on the weight of the phenol, at reflux conditions for a period of about 4 minutes. Thereafter, a phenol fraction substantially free of carbonyl impurities is separated from the impurity products by distillation.

Example IV

Phenol, prepared by decomposition of cumene hydroperoxide and containing carbonyl compounds as impuriities, is mixed with .02% ethylamine, based on the weight of the phenol, in aqueous solution. The solution is thoroughly mixed for about 2 hours at room temperature. Thereafter, the impurity products are extracted from the solution with dilute hydrochloric acid. The phenol is recovered substantially free of carbonyl substances.

Example V

In the purification of phenol containing carbonyl impurities, about .02% dimethylamine, based on the weight of the phenol, is prepared in aqueous solution and admixed with the phenol. After about 1 hour of mixing at room temperature, the impurity products are extracted with dilute hydrochloric acid and phenol is recovered substantially free of carbonyl impurities.

Example VI

In the purification of phenol containing carbonyl impurities, the phenol is heated in mixture with about 0.2% benzylamine, based on the weight of the phenol, at a temperature of about 70° C. for a period of about 5 minutes. Thereafter, the impurity products are extracted with dilute hydrochloric acid and phenol is recovered substantially free of carbonyl substances.

Problem

Draft three claims of substantially varying scope covering the process described in the disclosure. The three claims should be in *independent* form. The claims should not distinguish from each other by merely immaterial limitations and should distinguish over any prior art described in the disclosure.

Case 21

PREPARING CHEMICAL PROCESS CLAIMS

SAMPLE CLAIMS—PURIFICATION OF PHENOL

1. A method of purifying phenol in a mixture containing phenol and carbonyl-compound impurities, the method comprising contacting said mixture with a nitrogen compound of the formula R_1-NH-R_2 wherein R_1 and R_2 are selected from the group consisting of hydrogen, alkyl, cycloalkyl, aryl, alkaryl, aralkyl, hydroxyalkyl, and a polymethylene radical which taken together with the nitrogen atom forms a heterocyclic ring, with the carbonyl compounds, and separating the phenol from the resulting reaction products.

2. A method of purifying phenol in a mixture containing phenol and carbonyl-compound impurities, the method comprising contacting said mixture *in the liquid phase* with a nitrogen compound of the formula R_1-NH-R_2, wherein R_1 and R_2 are selected from the group consisting of hydrogen, alkyl, cycloalkyl, aryl, alkaryl, aralkyl, hydroxyalkyl, and a polymethylene radical which taken together with the nitrogen atom forms a heterocyclic ring, the amount of the nitrogen compound being *from about 0.02 to about 0.2* percent by weight of the weight of the phenol present in the mixture, to thereby react the nitrogen compound with the carbonyl compounds, and separating the phenol from the resulting reaction products.

3. A method of purifying phenol in a mixture containing phenol and carbonyl-compound impurities, the method comprising contacting said mixture with *ammonia at a temperature from*

about 41° to 182° C, the amount of ammonia being from about 0.02 to about 0.2 percent by weight of the weight of the phenol present in the mixture, to thereby react the ammonia with the carbonyl compounds, and separating the phenol from the resulting reaction products by *distillation.*

COMMENTS

The question asked for three independent claims; otherwise dependent claims would be more suitable here. Since claims of varying scope were requested, claim 3 need not include everything in claims 1 and 2, but this would not hurt either. Italicization in claims 2 and 3 is solely to show what was added.

Case 22
PREPARING ARTICLE OF MANUFACTURE CLAIMS

Sept. 18, 1962   **L. MORRIS**   3,054,212

SOAP DISH

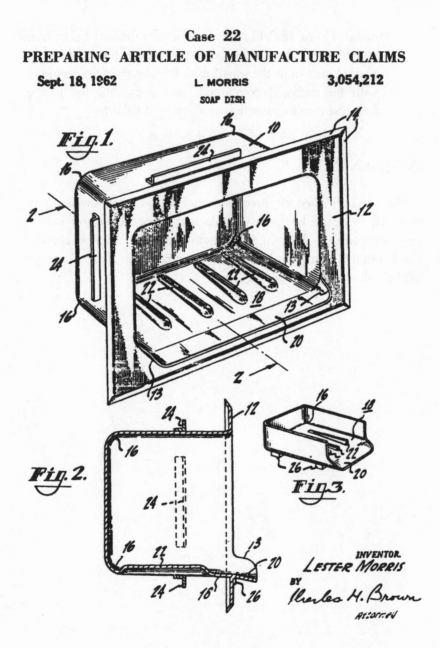

Fig.1.

Fig.2.

Fig.3.

INVENTOR.
LESTER MORRIS

BY

Charles H. Brown

ATTORNEY

PROBLEM

Draft three claims of varying scope. Label them "broad," "intermediate" and "narrow."

Case 22

PREPARING ARTICLE OF MANUFACTURE CLAIMS

SAMPLE CLAIMS—SOAP DISH

BROAD

1. A soap dish, which comprises:

a housing having a bottom wall and a frontal opening, the bottom wall being slanted downward from the back toward the frontal opening; and

a plurality of spaced projections extending upward from the bottom wall, the upper surfaces of the projections being shaped for defining a generally horizontal surface for supporting a cake of soap out of contact with the bottom wall, the projections being spaced to define channels therebetween such that water on a cake of soap placed on the projections drains downward between the projections and then along the slanted bottom wall out the frontal opening.

INTERMEDIATE

2. A soap dish as recited in claim 1, wherein the projections comprise spaced parallel ribs running from the back toward the front of the housing.

NARROW

3. A soap dish as recited in claim 2, for mounting into a recess in a wall, wherein:

the housing also includes three side walls and a rear wall, all shaped to fit in the recess with the frontal opening substantially flush with the wall; and

the housing further includes means for mounting the housing in the recess, and

a downwardly turned lip forming a continuation of the bottom wall and projecting forward beyond the frontal opening to permit water to drain out of the dish and away from the wall.

COMMENTS

Claim 1 illustrates typical technique in preparing article of manufacture claims. The procedure is essentially the same as for machine claims, but usually much simpler:

1. Select a preamble—"soap dish"—pretty easy.
2. Find and name what you think are the essential elements (A) "housing," or base, support, frame, etc.; (B) "projections," or ribs, etc. (see sec. 19 on "naming"). Best to make projections separate element, as they would not have to be integral with housing.
3. Select essential features of elements (sec. 25). Slanted bottom wall and opening (sec. 26 on claiming holes) for base (the side walls and wall mounting are not vital to operation); and horizontal surface, with channels, formed by projections.
4. Connect elements together (sec. 28-29) and with workpiece (soap), "extending upward from the bottom wall," "for supporting a cake of soap."
5. Preferably, tell what elements do and how, as in last three lines of claim 1. This is effectively a "whereby" clause.

Claim 2 further defines the "projections" as "ribs," which hopefully is fairly significant. See section 60 on claims of varying scope, and section 11 on dependent claims.

Claim 3 is a dependent claim adding one element and also further defining one element of a parent claim. Claim 3 also contains a revised preamble, adding further details of the setting for the dish (See sec. 11). Note the wall into a recess of which the dish is placed should *not* be an element of the claim. See sections 15 and 16. Put the workpiece or background in the preamble; and try to claim the combination in the form in which it would be sold, not as it would be used, wherever possible.

Case 23
PREPARING ARTICLE OF MANUFACTURE CLAIMS

March 16, 1954   E. HASLETT   2,672,250

COASTER

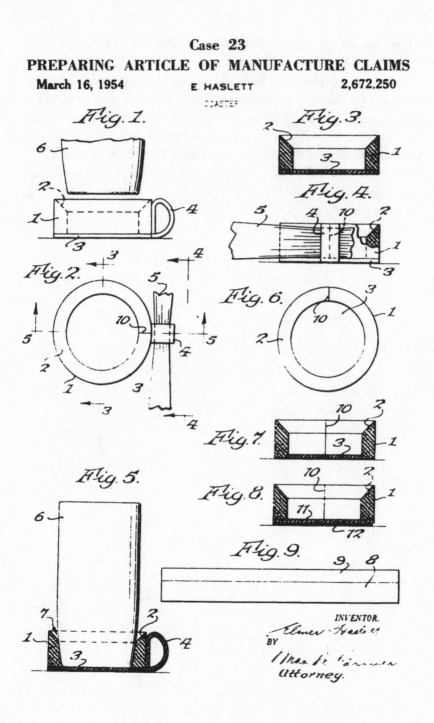

Fig. 1.

Fig. 2.

Fig. 3.

Fig. 4.

Fig. 5.

Fig. 6.

Fig. 7.

Fig. 8.

Fig. 9.

INVENTOR.
Elmer Haslett
BY
Max H. Farmer
Attorney.

Problem

Draft three claims of varying scope to the coaster shown in the drawings. Following are some of the disclosed features and characteristics of the coaster:

1. It will remain attached to the bottom of a glass even when picked up.
2. It fits glasses of different sizes.
3. It is light in weight.
4. It absorbs condensate that runs down the side of the glass.
5. Its outside surface will not mar a surface on which it is placed.
6. The annular ring 1 and the disc-like bottom 3 are made of a cellular, elastic material.
7. The upper end of the annular ring 1 is bevelled as at 3.
8. The loop 4 may hold a napkin 5.
9. The ring 1 and the bottom 3 may be molded as a unit, or may be separate items which are adhesively attached.
10. The bottom 3 may also be made of an elastic material such as rubber, but in any event its outer surface is liquid impervious.
11. The cellular, elastic material of the ring 1 and the bottom 3 is liquid absorbent.
12. The basic shape is old.

Case 23

PREPARING ARTICLE OF MANUFACTURE CLAIMS

SAMPLE CLAIMS—COASTER

1. A coaster for a glass, which comprises:

a cup-shaped glass-receiving member having a flat bottom of liquid-impervious, elastic material, and an upstanding side wall of an elastic, liquid-absorbent material.

2. A coaster as recited in claim 1, wherein the side wall has an interior rim that is so bevelled inwardly that as the glass container is inserted into the coaster, the bottom edge of the glass engages the rim and expands the side wall outwardly, allowing entry of the container into the coaster.
3. A coaster as recited in claim 2, further comprising a handle formed integrally with the bottom and attached to the exterior of the side wall.

COMMENTS

Similar to the previous problem, this rather easy-to-write claim involves selecting a preamble and essential elements, here a "glass-receiving member" which includes a "bottom" and a "side wall." Note that while the shape of the "member" is per se old (see item 12 above) the characteristics of the bottom ("liquid-impervious" and "elastic") and the side wall ("elastic" and "liquid-absorbent") result in a novel coaster. The glass (workpiece) is set forth in the preamble. Claim 2 adds mechanical detail about the side wall and claim 3 adds a new element ("handle") both in independent fashion.

Case 24

PREPARING COMPOSITION OF MATTER, CHEMICAL PROCESS AND METHOD OF USE CLAIMS

PARABANIC ACID DERIVATIVES

ABSTRACT OF THE DISCLOSURE

Compound of the formula

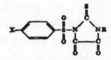

wherein X is selected from the class consisting of amino, nitro and alykyl of not more than 4 carbon atoms, and R is selected from the class consisting of hydrogen, alkyl and alkenyl of not more than 12 carbon atoms are useful as phytotoxicants.

This invention relates to parabanic acid derivatives which are useful as biological toxicants, particularly phytotoxicants.

The parabanic acid derivatives of this invention can be represented by the formula

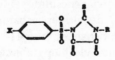

wherein X is selected from the group consisting of nitro, alkyl of not more than 4 carbon atoms and amino, and R is selected from the group consisting of hydrogen, alkyl of not more than 12 carbon atoms and alkenyl of not more than 12 carbon atoms.

The parabanic acid derivatives of this invention can be prepared by reacting axolyl chloride with para - substituted benzenesulfonyl thioureas having the R substituent. The substituted thioureas can be prepared by reacting para-substituted benzenesulfonyl iso-thiocyanate with a primary amine or a secondary amine having the R substituent. Many of the thioureas which are reacted with oxalyl chloride in accordance with this invention can be prepared by processes disclosed in Martin et al. U.S. Patent No. 2,411,661.

The reaction is usually carried out at temperatures from about 40° C. to about 150° C. in the presence of an aromatic hydrocarbon medium. Suitable aromatic hydrocarbon media include benzene, toluene, xylene and the like. The reaction is preferably carried out by slowly adding oxalyl chloride to an admixture of para-substituted benzenesulfonyl thiourea and aromatic organic media, and heating the reaction mixture at reflux until the emulsion of hydrogen chloride substantially ceases.

The desired product can be separated from the reaction mixture by conventional means for example distillation, extraction and the like.

The following examples will illustrate the invention. In these examples, as well as in the specification and appended claims, parts and percent are by weight unless otherwise indicated.

EXAMPLE 1

About one mole of oxalyl chloride is added dropwise to about one mole of p-nitrobenzenesulfonyl thiourea in benzene at about 25° C. Upon evolution of hydrogen chloride, the reaction mixture is heated at reflux for about two hours. The product is l - (p-nitrobenzenesulfonyl) thioparabanic acid.

EXAMPLE 2

A solution of l - (p-aminobenzenesulfonyl) - 3 - ethyl thiourea in ethylene dichloride is treated by dropwise addition of oxalyl chloride and the mixture heated to reflux. After the evolution of

hydrogen chloride has substantially ceased, the following crystalline product is recovered from the reaction mixture:

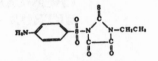

[1-(p-aminobenzenesulfonyl)-
3-ethylthioparabanic acid]

EXAMPLE 3

The procedure of Example 1 is repeated using 1-(p-methylbenzenesulfonyl) - 3 - (2-ethylhexyl) thiourea in place of p-nitrobenbenesulfonyl thiourea to form 1-(p-methylbenzenesulfonyl) - 3 - (2-ethylhexyl)thioparabanic acid.

Following substantially the same procedure as in the foregoing examples, the following compounds of this invention are prepared:

1-(p-aminobenzenesulfonyl)-
3-n-butylthioparabanic acid
1-(p-ethylbenzenesulfonyl)-
3-ethylthioparabanic acid
1-(p-n-butylbenzenesulfonyl)-
3-methylthioparabanic acid
1-(p-aminobenzenesulfonyl)-
3-allylthioparabanic acid
1-(p-nitrobenzenesulfonyl)-
3-dodecylthioparabanic acid
1-(p-nitrobenzenesulfonyl)-
3-(2-pentenyl)thioparabanic acid

The parabanic acid derivatives of this invention are useful for controlling or modifying the growth of plants. They are effective as general phytotoxicants including postemergent phytotoxicants and preemergent phytotoxicants, but their most outstanding utility is as preemergent phytotoxicants. Furthermore, these compounds are characterized by a broad spectrum of herbicidal or phytotoxic activity, i.e., they modify the growth of a wide variety of plant systems including both monocotyledonous and dicotyledonous plants. For the sake of brevity and simplicity the term "active ingredient" will be used hereinafter in this specification to describe the parabanic acid derivatives of the above formula.

When operating in accordance with the present invention, effective amounts of the active ingredients are dispersed in soil or plant growth media and applied to plant systems in any convenient fashion. Application to the soil or growth media can be carried out by simply mixing with the media, by applying to the surface of the soil and thereafter dragging or discing into the soil to the desired depth, or by employing a liquid carrier to accomplish the penetration and impregnation. The application of liquid and particulate solid phytotoxic compositions to the surface of soil or to plant systems can be carried out by conventional methods, e.g., power dusters, boom and hand sprayers and spray dusters. The compositions can also be applied from airplanes as a dust or a spray because of their effectiveness at low dosages. In a further method, the distribution of the active ingredients in soil can be carried out by admixture with the water employed to irrigate the soil. In such procedures, the amount of water can be varied with the porosity and water holding capacity of the soil to obtain the desired depth of distribution of the phytotoxicants.

The exact amount of active ingredient to be employed is dependent upon the response desired in the plant as well as such other factors as the plant species and stage of development thereof, the specific soil and depth at which the active ingredients are distributed in the soil and the amount of rainfall as well as the specific active ingredient used. In foliat treatment for the control or modification of vegetative growth, the active ingredients are supplied in amounts from about 1 to about 50 or more pounds per acre. In applications to soil for the control or modification of the growth of germinant seeds, emerging seedlings and established vegetation, the active ingredients are applied in amounts from about 0.01 to about 25 or more pounds per acre. In such soil applications, it is desirable that the active ingredients be distributed to a depth of at least 0.2 inch and preferably in amounts from about 0.01 to about 5 pounds per acre.

The active ingredients can be uesd alone or in combination with a material referred to in the art as a phytotoxic adjuvant in liquid or solid form. The phytotoxic compositions are prepared by admixing the active ingredient with an adjuvant including diluents, extenders, carriers and conditioning agents to provide compositions in the form of finely divided particulate solids, granules, pellets, solutions and aqueous dispersions or emulsions. Thus the active ingredient can be used with an adjuvant such as finely divided particulate solid, a liquid or organic origin, water, a wetting agent, dispersing agent, an emulsifying agent or any suitable combination of these.

Typical finely divided solid carriers and extenders which can be used in the phytotoxic compositions include for example, the talcs, clays, pumice, silica, diatomaceous earth, quartz, fuller's earth, salt, sulfur, powdered cork, powdered wood, walnut flour, chalk, tobacco dust, charcoals, volcanic ash, and the like. Typical liquid diluents include for example water, kerosene, Stoddard solvent, hexane, benzene, toluene, acetone, ethylene dichloride, xylene, alcohols, Diesel oil, glycols and the like.

The phytotoxic compositions, particularly liquids and wettable particles, usually contain as a conditioning agent one or more surface-active agents in amounts sufficient to render a given composition readily dispersible in water or in oil. By the term "surface-active agent" it is understood that wetting-agents, dispersing agents, suspending agents, emulsifying agents and the like are included therein.

Surface-active agents which can be used in the phytotoxic compositions of this invention are set out, for example, in Searle U.S. Patent 2,426,417, Todd U.S. Patent 2,655,447, Jones U.S. Patent 2,412,-510, and Lenher U.S. Patent 2,-139,276. A detailed list of such agents, is also set forth by J. W. McCutcheon in "Soap and Chemical Specialties," November 1947, page 8011 et seq., entitled "Synthetic Detergents"; "Detergents and Emulsifiers—Up to Date" (1960), by J. W. McCutcheon, Inc., and Bulletin E-607 of the Bureau of Entomology and Plant Quarantine of the U.S.D.A. In general, less than 15 parts by weight of the surface active agent is present per 100 parts by weight of phytotoxic composition.

Although the invention is described with respect to specific modifications, the details thereof are not to be construed as limitations except to the extent indicated in the following claims.

The embodiments of the invention in which an exclusive property or privilege is claimed are defined as follows.

Problem

Draft three claims in *independent* form which distinguish over any prior art described in the specification. Claim 1 should cover broadly the parabanic acid derivatives of the invention. Claim 2 should cover broadly the method of making parabanic acid derivatives of Examples 1 and 2. Claim 3 should cover a method of using the compound of Example 2.

Case 24

PREPARING COMPOSITION OF MATTER, CHEMICAL PROCESS AND METHOD OF USE CLAIMS

SAMPLE CLAIMS— PARABANIC ACID DERIVATIVES

1. A compound having the formula:

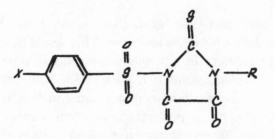

wherein X is selected from the group consisting of nitro, amino, and alkyl of not more than four carbon atoms, and

wherein R is selected from the group consisting of hydrogen, alkyl of not more than 12 carbon atoms, and alkenyl of not more than 12 carbon atoms.

2. A method of preparing a compound selected from the group consisting of 1-(p-nitrobenzenesulfonyl) thioparabanic acid and 1-(p-aminobenzenesulfonyl)-3-ethylthioparabanic acid, which comprises:

(a) reacting oxalyl chloride with a material selected from the group consisting of p-nitrobenzenesulfonyl thiourea and 1-(p-aminobenzenesulfonyl)-3-ethyl thiourea, at a temperature sufficient to form the corresponding compound and to drive off hydrogen chloride; and

(b) recovering said compound from the mixture.

3. A method of modifying plant growth, comprising dispersing in plant growth media an amount of 1-(p-aminobenzene-sulfonyl)-3-ethylthioparabanic acid effective to modify the plant growth.

COMMENTS

From the September 1970 Agent's Exam. Claim 1 must be "a broad claim" to the derivatives of the invention. This should be very simple, given the specification. In fact, one can practically copy the "summary of the invention," column 1, lines 35-48. Note—do not claim any broader than the specification clearly states, such as by imagining that X could just as well be pentyl (5 carbons) or benzene.

Claim 1 follows the general form in the book, section 49, and various modifications of form are possible. However, "a compound having the formula" or "of the formula" is a very common, standard form for claims to new compounds, or molecules. One could equally well claim "parabanic acid derivatives having the formula. . . ." Avoid any statement of use in a "pure compound" claim, such as "phytoxicants having the formula. . . ." There is no need to state the preferred use in a compound claim. In this problem, as given, the compounds are presumably novel; thus, claim 1 should cover the compounds per se, for any use.

Note the classic Markush phraseology, "wherein R is selected from the group consisting of. . . ." (See section 50.) It is now equally correct to use the "alternative" phraseology provided in MPEP 706.03(y): "wherein X is nitro, amino, or alkyl. . . ."; and "wherein R is hydrogen, alykyl of . . . , or alkenyl of. . . ." Note that this use of the alternative is limited by the Manual to materials "so related as to constitute a proper Markush group," as in this problem.

Of interest, this claim covers 150 individual compounds (not counting isomers), 25 R substituents with any of six X substituents. Note also, that it is not necessary to know what parabanic acid is, or "nitrobenzene sulfonyl. . . . ," etc. to write this claim. One can safely copy the pertinent language in the specification, where the patentee is supposed to state what the claimed invention is as well as giving examples, etc.

Claim 2

This requires more care, as one wants a *broad* method (as to the steps performed) for making the two specific compounds of Examples 1 and 2. Thus, the preamble should be limited to the method of preparing the two named compounds (not a broad Markush group), and preferably using the named reactants, oxalyl chloride and the particular thiourea precursors. The examinee could not conceivably know what if any other precursors or chlorides could be substituted, and would be very ill advised to guess.

As to the process steps, these should be phrased fairly broadly since a broad method claim was requested. The common steps of examples 1 and 2 appear to be mixing (or adding, treating, reacting), heating (or refluxing), and recovering. These can be combined into two or even one step the choice is optional so long as the scope is correct.

A single step process could be phrased as "reacting [A] with [B] at a temperature sufficient to form [C]." There would be no problem in including the broad temperature ranges (40-150° C) from column 1, lines 59-60, but most preferred process details should be omitted since this is to be a broad claim to the process, and it does not appear from the specification that process parameters are critical to success.

Note, on the law (not part of *this* question), that a process for making a novel compound, such as in claim 2, is not necessarily patentable (nonobvious) merely because the compound is patentable. (See section 39.) The courts have held (over vigorous dissent and with much adverse criticism by the bar) that a so-called "obvious method" of making a new compound or product of any kind is not patentable merely because the compound or product is patentable.

Claim 3

This claim is to cover a method of using the specific compound of Example 2, which should be specifically named in claim 3. The preamble could be "controlling" or "modifying" plan growth (not both in the alternative), as indicated in column 2, line 44. The only possible step can be "dispersing" (col. 2, lines 57-58) or contacting, treating, etc. This claim typifies the relatively rare case of a single-step method (section 33), which is perfectly permissible.

Note that this method of using claim is a "new use" claim (section 56), and that such claims can be patentable for new uses for new compounds as well as for old compounds. If the compounds turned out to be old for other purposes, the "use claims" such as claim 3 could still be patentable if the use was unobvious. This happened in the DDT case (*Ex parte Muller*) cited in the book, section 56.

Note that claim 3 specifies "an amount . . . effective to . . ." Cases hold that the recitation ". . . an effective amount . . ." is *not* indefinite. This is particularly true in this case, where the specification defines the term "effective amount" (col. 2, lines 56, etc.) and gives many examples of effective amounts. Obviously, in the present case, the invention as to use of the compounds resides in discovering that the parabanic acid derivatives *are* plant growth modifiers (inhibitors or poisons), rather than in the determination of particular amounts needed to effect such modification. As stated in the specification, the amount can vary quite widely based on particular plants, soils, even rainfall, for a particular one of the compounds.

Note that this question asked for all claims in *independent form*, as sometimes is requested. Make certain to follow directions! In this case, because of the specific nature of the claims requested, including varying statements of the compounds involved in each successive claim, it would be difficult and highly cumbersome to use a dependent claim anyway.

Dependent claims "crossing statutory classes" (process, compound), such as "A method of preparing the compounds related in claim 1 . . . ," or "A method of modifying . . . comprising dispersing . . . a compound as recited in claim 1. . . ." are not correct. Product and process type claims should be separate. The only exception is a product-by-process claim.

For those interested in the chemical details, parabanic acid is:

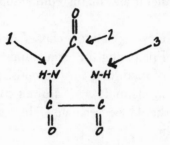

This is a cyclic diacid formed by oxidation of uric acid. *Thio* parabanic acid substitutes $= S$ for the $= 0$ in the 2 position. The thiourea radical is:

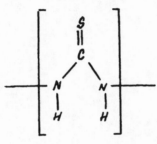

Oxalyl chloride is:

Thus, with HCl driven off, the amine nitrogens of the thiourea bond to the carbons of the oxalyl radical to form the parabanic ring.

Case 25

PREPARING BIOTECHNOLOGICAL CLAIMS

UNITED STATES PATENT 4,237,224

Process for Producing Biologically
Functional Molecular Chimeras

Inventors: Stanley N. Cohen, Herbert W. Boyer

BACKGROUND OF THE INVENTION

1. Field of the Invention

Although transfer of plasmids among strains of *E. coli* and other Enterobacteriaceae has long been accomplished by conjugation and/or transduction, it has not been previously possible to selectively introduce particular species of plasmid DNA into these bacterial hosts or other microorganisms. Since microorganisms that have been transformed with plasmid DNA contain autonomously replicating extrachromosomal DNA species having the genetic and molecular characteristics of the parent plasmid, transformation has enabled the selective cloning and amplification of particular plasmid genes.

The ability of genes derived from totally different biological classes to replicate and be expressed in a particular microorganism permits the attainment of interspecies genetic recombination. Thus, it becomes practical to introduce into a particular microorganism, genes specifying such metabolic or synthetic functions as nitrogen fixation, photosynthesis, antibiotic production, hormone synthesis, protein synthesis, e.g., enzymes or antibodies, or the like—functions which are indigenous to other classes of organisms—by linking the foreign genes to a particular plasmid or viral replicon.

SUMMARY OF THE INVENTION

Methods and compositions are provided for genetically transforming microorganisms, particularly bacteria, to provide diverse genotypical capability and producing recombinant plasmids. A plasmid or viral DNA is modified to form a linear segment having ligatable termini which is joined to DNA having at least one intact gene and complementary ligatable termini. The termini are then bound together to form a "hybrid" plasmid molecule which is used to transform susceptible and compatible microorganisms. After transformation, the cells are grown and the transformants harvested. The newly functionalized microorganisms may then be employed to carry out their new function; for example,· by producing proteins which are the desired end product, or metabolites of enzymic conversion, or be lysed and the desired nucleic acids or proteins recovered.

DESCRIPTION OF THE SPECIFIC EMBODIMENTS

Preparation of Plasmid Chimera

In order to prepare the plasmid chimera, it is necessary to have a DNA vector, such as a plasmid or phage, which can be cleaved to provide an intact replicator locus and system (replicon), where the linear segment has ligatable termini or is capable of being modified to introduce ligatable termini. Of particular interest are those plasmids which have a phenotypical property, which allow for ready separation of transformants from the parent microorganism.

A wide variety of plasmids may be employed of greatly varying molecular weight. The desirable plasmid size is determined by a number of factors. First, the plasmid must be able to accommodate a replicator locus and one or more genes that are capable of allowing replication of the plasmid. Secondly, the plasmid should be of a size which provides for a reasonable probability of recircularization with the foreign gene(s) to form the recombinant plasmid chimera. Desirably, a restriction enzyme should be available, which will cleave the plasmid without inactivating the replicator locus and system associated with the replicator locus. Also, means must be provided for providing ligatable termini for the plasmid, which are complimentary to the termini of the foreign gene(s) to allow fusion of the two DNA segments.

The original plasmid should desirably have a phenotypical property which allows for the separation of transformant bacteria from parent bacteria. Particularly useful is a gene, which provides for survival selection. Survival selection can be achieved by providing resistance to a growth inhibiting substance or providing a growth factor capability to a bacterium deficient in such capability.

Conveniently, genes are available, which provide for antibiotic or heavy metal resistance or polypeptide resistance, e.g., colicin. Therefore, by growing the bacteria on a medium containing a bacteriostatic or bacteriocidal substance, such as an antibiotic, only the transformants having the antibiotic resistance will survive.

Growth factors include the synthesis of amino acids, the isomerization of substrates to forms which can be metabolized or the like. By growing the bacteria on a medium which lacks the appropriate growth factor, only the bacteria which have been transformed and have the growth factor capability will clone.

In preparing the plasmid for joining with the exogenous gene, a wide variety of techniques can be provided, including the formation of or introduction of cohesive termini. Flush ends can be joined. Alternatively, the plasmid and gene may be cleaved in such a manner that the two chains are cleaved at different sites to leave extensions at each end which serve as cohesive termini. Cohesive termini may also be introduced by removing nucleic acids from the opposite ends of the two chains or alternatively, introducing nucleic acids at opposite ends of the two chains.

To illustrate, a plasmid can be cleaved with a restriction endonuclease or other DNA cleaving enzyme. The restriction enzyme can provide square ends, which are then modified to provide cohesive termini or can cleave in a staggered manner at different, but adjacent, sites on the two strands, so as to provide cohesive termini directly.

Where square ends are formed such as, for example, by HIN (Haemophilus influenzae RII) or pancreatic DNAse, one can ligate the square ends or alternatively one can modify the square ends by chewing back, adding particular nucleic acids, or a combination of the two. For example, one can employ appropriate transferases to add a nucleic acid to the 5' and 3' ends of the DNA. Alternatively, one can chew back with an enzyme, such as a λ-exonuclease, and it is found that there is a high probability that cohesive termini will be achieved in this manner.

An alternative way to achieve a linear segment of the plasmid with cohesive termini is to employ an endonuclease such as EcoRI. The endonuclease cleaves the two strands at different adjacent sites providing cohesive termini directly.

With flush ended molecules, a T_4 ligase may be employed for linking the termini. See, for example, Scaramella and Khorana, J. Mol. Biol. 72: 427–444 (1972) and Scaramella, DNAS 69: 3389 (1972), whose disclosure is incorporated herein by reference.

Another way to provide ligatable termini is to leave employing DNAse and Mn^{++} as reported by Lai and Nathans, J. Mol. Biol, 89: 179 (1975).

Problem

Draft three method claims of varying scope, given the specification. Direct the narrower claims to the formation of "staggered and cohesive termini."

Case 25

PREPARING METHOD CLAIMS, BIOTECHNOLOGY SAMPLE CLAIMS, METHOD FOR REPLICATING A BIOLOGICALLY FUNCTIONAL DNA

1. A method for replicating a biologically functional DNA, which comprises:

    transforming under transforming conditions compatible unicellular organisms with biologically functional DNA to form transformants; said biologically functional DNA prepared in vitro by the method of:

    (a) cleaving a viral or circular plasmid DNA compatible with said unicellular organism to provide a first linear segment having an intact replicon and termini of a predetermined character;

    (b) combining said first linear segment with a second linear DNA segment, having at least one intact gene and foreign to said unicellular organism and having termini ligatable to said termini of said first linear segment, wherein at least one of said first and second linear DNA segments has a gene for a phenotypical trait, under joining conditions where the termini of said first and second segments join to provide a functional DNA capable of replication and transcription in said unicellular organism;

    growing said unicellular organisms under appropriate nutrient conditions; and

    isolating said transformants from parent unicellular organisms by means of said phenotypical trait imparted by said biologically functional DNA. (1)

2. A method according to claim 1, wherein said predetermined termini are staggered and cohesive. (6)

3. A method according to claim 2, wherein said cohesive ends are formed by staggered cleavage of said viral or circular plasmid DNA and a source of said second segment with a restriction enzyme. (8)

or

3. A method according to claim 2 wherein said cohesive termini are formed by addition of nucleotides. (9)

COMMENTS

The above claims are from the Cohen and Boyer patent as issued; the number of the claims as they appeared in the patent are provided in the parentheses. The Cohen and Boyer patent describes the method behind what is commonly called recombinant DNA or genetic engineering, that is, a method of transferring genetic material from one organism into the cells of another organism, across species lines if desired.

Though biotechnology is a relatively new field, techniques previously used to write claims for chemical or microbiology cases can be used for biotechnology cases as well. Note, for example, that claim 1 is a series of action steps arranged in a logical order (see Sections 37 and 38).

One goal in biotechnology cases is covering the variability introduced by the use of living organisms and their biochemical systems. Anticipating future developments in a field for the next seventeen years and writing claims broad enough to encompass them has always been challenging; but with biological systems, it is possible that a new organism or protein will be discovered that performs the same or similar reactions as those described in the patent. The question then becomes how similar is the new organism or protein to those disclosed in the patent. Devising generic categories are not always satisfactory, because living systems are notoriously difficult to categorize. For example, witness the continuing debate as to whether humans' closest cousin is the chimpanzee, orangutan, or gorilla.[1]

One approach to the issue of biological variability is to claim a feature functionally (see Sections 27 and 28). Note that in claim 1, the termini (ends) are primarily defined as ligatable (connectable) to one another. The dependent claims set out details such as the "staggered and cohesive" variation of the termini, which can be formed by chemical or enzymatic means. Another claim in the patent[2] refers to "blunt end" termini, a form of the termini created by the use of enzymes isolated from organisms different from the organisms that are the source of the enzymes used to create the "staggered and cohesive" termini.

II Criticizing "Sloppy Claims"

The following examples are from Agents' Exams given between August 1966 and September 1970, where the student was given a specification and a set of claims, and asked to comment on errors or possible errors in those claims.

This required a detailed knowledge of the law, rules and Patent Office practices on many points of claim-drafting law and practice.

---

1. R. Holmquist et al., "Higher-Primate Phylogeny—Why Can't We Decide?" *Molecular Biology and Evolution*, 5:201 (1988); A. Wilson, "The Molecular Basis of Evolution," *Scientific American*, 253:164 (1985).
2. "A method according to claim 1, wherein said predetermined termini are blunt end and said joining conditions include enzymatic ligation."

Case 26
CRITICIZING "SLOPPY CLAIMS"
(Suction Cleaner)

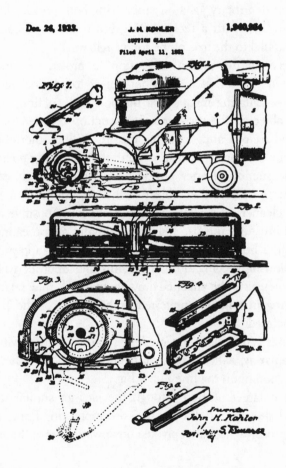

Specification

The present invention relates to suction cleaners and particularly to new and improved agitating means in suction cleaners. More specifically the invention comprises the provision, in a suction cleaner, of the combination of a rotary agitator, embodying both positive beating and brushing means, with a reciprocating brush whose direction of movement is parallel to the axis of the rotary agitator.

It is an object of the present invention to provide a new and improved suction cleaner. It is a further object to provide new and improved surface-agitating means in a motor-driven suction cleaner. A still further object is the provision, in a suction cleaner, of combined rotary and reciprocating agitating means. Still another object is the provision of a suction cleaner in which rotary agitating means are provided in the suction cleaner nozzle from which a reciprocating brush is driven. A still further object is the provision, in a motor driven suction cleaner, of a rotary agitator embodying positive agitating means and brushing means, and a horizontally reciprocating agitator comprising a brush. These and other objects will appear upon reading the following specification and claims and upon considering in connection therewith the attached drawing to which they relate.

In the drawing in which a preferred embodiment of the present invention is disclosed:

Fig. 1 discloses a side view of a modern suction cleaner, with certain parts broken away, with the present invention embodied therein;

Fig. 2 is a section upon the line 2-2 of Fig. 1;

Fig. 3 is an enlarged section through the cleaner similar to that shown in Fig. 1 showing, in dotted lines, the supporting frame of the rotary and reciprocating agitators pivoted downwardly from the nozzle mouth;

Fig. 4 is a view in perspective of a reciprocating brush element;

Fig. 5 is a partial view in perspective of the agitator-supporting frame showing the reciprocating brush set;

Fig. 6 is a view in perspective of the pivoted luatch or retaining cover of the brush seat;

Fig. 7 is a view in perspective of the pivoted brush supporting frame.

The present invention is disclosed embodied in a modern suction cleaner which comprises a main casting or casing including a nozzle 1, a fan chamber 2, which is interiorly connected to the nozzle 1 by means of the air passageway 3, and an exhaust outlet 4 to which is detachably connected a dust bag 5. A motor casing 6 is positioned upon the main casing immediately above the fan chamber 2 and houses a suitable driving motor, which is not shown, but the shaft 7 of which extends downwardly thru the fan chamber 2 where the fan 3 is mounted thereon. The shaft 7 extends into the rear end of the air passageway 3 where it carries a suitable pulley 9. The cleaner is movably supported by means of front wheels, of which one is shown resting upon a supporting surface being indicated by reference character 10, and by means of a rear wheel 11. A pivoted handle 12 is mounted on the casing of the cleaner and provides means by which the operator can propel the machine over the surface covering undergoing cleaning.

Within the nozzle 1 of the cleaner and extending thereacross is a rotary agitator which, in its general appearance, differs but slightly from a common and well known type. This agitator comprises a large diameter cylindrical body 13 on the surface of which are mounted helically-extending rigid beater elements 14, 14 which extend substantially the length of the agitator, with the exception of a small central portion which is reduced in diameter to form a pulley 15. Carried by the cylindrical body 13 of the agitator and seated within the periphery thereof are longitudinally-extending brushes 16, 16 which are of a common and well-known type and which are removably secured in their seats in any suitable manner. Upon the surface body 13 of the agitator, immediately adjacent the sides of the pulley 15, which is connected to the driving pulley 9 on the motor shaft 7 by a suitable belt 21, are encircling cam races positioned below the periphery of the body. These cam races are designated by the reference characters 22, 22 and have a function which will be apparent from the following description. A shaft 17, which extends through the agitator with each of its ends resting in a seat 20 in the side member 19 of the frame 18, rotatably supports the agitator.

Between the side members 19, 19 of the frame 18, which is pivoted within the nozzle 1 at a point somewhat in the rear of the rear nozzle lip 23, is a front cross member 24 which extends closely adjacent and parallel to the front wall of the nozzle 1, being secured thereto, and holding the frame 18 within the nozzle, by ordinary and suitable means which form no part of the present invention. This cross member 24 slopes downwardly from the lower end of the front wall of the nozzle 1 and forms the front lip of the nozzle thereby cooperating with the rear nozzle lip 23 in defining the nozzle mouth. The lip 24, however, differs from the usual nozzle lip thru being provided with two transversely-extending openings or apertures 25, 25, each of which extends parallel to the axis of the rotary agitator and has a length substantially equal to half the length of the agitator. Seated upon the lip 24 with their bristles projecting downwardly thru the apertures 25, 25 are brush elements 26, 26 which comprise rigid backs having the flexible brush bristles mounted therein. The length of each brush element 26 is slightly less than the length of the aperture 25 in the nozzle lip 24 thru which the bristles extend, thereby permitting the brush a limited range of movement transversely of the agitator mouth, that is, parallel to the longitudinal axis of the agitator itself. To make use of this permissible movement of the brushes 26, 26 in order to obtain the maximum agitation of the surface covering undergoing cleaning, each brush element 26, 26 is provided at its inner end, with an upstanding lug 27 on which is mounted a roller or head 28 of such size that with the brush seated upon the front lip 24 the roller 28 extends within the adjacent cam race 22 in the cylindrical body 13 of the rotary agitator, with the result that upon the rotation of that body the brush 26 will be reciprocated back and forth as the roller 28 is moved by the cam. To insure the permanent positioning and the correct alinement of each brush 26 with the aperture 25, relative to which it must slide, a pivoted cover element 29 is provided which is pivotally mounted upon a pin 30 carried by the side of the transverse member or lip 24. The cover member 29 is adapted to closely enclose the sides and top of the brush 26 to hold it in contact with the upper surface of the lip 24. To prevent the unintentional displacement of the cover relative to the lip the forward edge of the lip is curved upwardly, as at 31, and is adapted to resiliently clamp the forward edge of the cover which extends against it in the closed position.

In the operation of a suction cleaner constructed in accordance with the present invention, the suction-creating fan within the fan chamber is rotated by the driving motor resulting in a decrease in the pressure existing within the nozzle thereby effecting the lifting of the surface, covering undergoing cleaning against the nozzle lips, as is clearly indicated in Figure 1. With the surface covering suspended against the nozzle lips the rotary agitator is rotated at high speed by the driving belt 21 which is connected, as aforedescribed, between the pulleys 15 and 9, the latter carried by the motor shaft. The beating elements 14, 14 upon the agitator function to violently vibrate the surface covering to dislodge the embedded foreign matter which is positioned therein. The longitudinally-extending brushes 16, 16 upon the agitator surface cooperate with the rigid beating elements 14, 14 and assist in the removal of the light dirt. As the agitator is revolved the brushes 26, 26, which are carried by the front nozzle lip 24 of the cleaner, are reciprocated transversely or parallel to the longitudinal axis of the rotating agitator and, thru extending below the nozzle lip, contact the surface covering which is positioned adjacent thereto and function to deflect, bend and agitate the pile of that covering in a direction as right angles to the direction of vibration and bending effected by the beating elements 14, 14 and the brush elements 16, 16 carried by the rotary agitator.

To effect the removal of the agitators constructed in accordance with the present invention from the nozzle, it is only necessary to pivot the supporting frame 18 downwardly to the position shown in dotted lines in Figure 3. With the frame so positioned the rotary agitator may be lifted therefrom, the supporting shaft 17 sliding outwardly from its open ended seat 20 in each end plate 19 of the frame. With the rotary agitator removed it is then possible to pivot each brush-holding cover 29 on its supporting pin 30, a recess 32 being conveniently provided in the forward edge of the nozzle lip into which an instrument such as a screw driver may be inserted to wedge the cover free from the retaining forward edge of the lip. With the cover pivoted back it is then possible to remove the brush 26 by merely lifting it from the lip and withdrawing the bristles through the aperture 25 through which they were extended, there being two brush elements, the same operation is necessary to release the other element.

If desired, a single brush element extending across the full width of the nozzle may be used instead of two brush elements.

Problem

Part I—Given the specification and drawings, comment on the "Problem Claims" following.

Part II—Assuming you were asked to write three claims of varying scope, and indicate "broadest," "intermediate" and "narrowest." Write *only* the first such claim ("broadest"), and indicate what features you might include in the other two claims.

PART I—PROBLEM CLAIMS

Below is the statement of the question from the April 1967 Exam:

This part of the examination consists of three claims drawn to a suction cleaner apparatus proposed to be added to an application having the accompanying specification and drawings. Certain words and phrases in the claims have been italicized and numerically designated. *Most, but not all*, of the italicized portions represent instances wherein the claims fail to comply with United States patent law or accepted claim writing practice. In addition to the 10 numbered items in the claims, there are two additional instances involving deficiencies in the claims in substance or form. These instances should be listed as items 11 and 12 in your answer. For each number in each claim and for items 11 and 12, make a short statement as to why the underlined portion does represent a defect, if such is the case.

NOTE: For this exercise, try to find *four* more major errors (11), (12), (13), (14) and discuss.

Case 26

CRITICIZING "SLOPPY CLAIMS"
(SUCTION CLEANER)

SAMPLE CLAIMS TO BE CRITICIZED

6. A suction cleaner comprising a body supported by wheels, a drive motor mounted on said body forward of *the rear pair of wheels* (1), *the nozzle* (2), formed on the front portion of the body having a lip, *a flexible* (3) agitator roll mounted in said nozzle, and drive means connecting said motor and agitator to cause it to rotate. Said nozzle being further provided with a rear lip, a supporting frame for the agitator pivotally mounted adjacent *said lip* (4), a single brush agitator mounted on said other lip and extending across the full width of said nozzle, *adapted to reciprocate* upon rotation of said rotary *agitator* (5), drive means for said reciprocating agitator including *a cam race* (6), on said rotary agitator.

7. The suction cleaner of this invention *includes* (7) a motor, a suction creating means, a rotary agitator, and an additional brush agitator mounted to reciprocate relative to the surface being cleaned.

8. A suction cleaner according to *claims 6 or 7* (8) in which the nozzle has mounted therein forward of the rotary agitator *two reciprocating agitators* (9) having brush elements made of nylon to ensure long *wear* (10).

COMMENTS ON PART I—PROBLEM CLAIMS

1(a). There is *no antecedent* in the claim for the "rear pair" of wheels. The claim has previously stated only that there are wheels.[1]

1(b). Also, there is *no support in the disclosure* for the rear "pair" of wheels. The specification discloses "a rear wheel 11." A claim may not be contrary to, or inconsistent with, the specific example(s) disclosed.[2]

2. There is *no antecedent* in the claim for "the nozzle."[3]

3. There is no support in the disclosure for a "flexible" agitator roll. The agitator 14 is shown as a solid member.[4]

4. "Said lip" is indefinite because two different lips have previously been recited.[5]

5. "Adapted to reciprocate . . ." was stated by the Patent Office to be improper "functional language without supporting structure." The "adapted to" phrase attempts to imply the mounting of the brush element (26) and its driving connection to the rotary agitator (13).[6]

---

1. These notes are not part of the suggested typical answers, but rather further comments and suggestions for students. *See* section 23.
2. See rule 75(d) and section 15:
   > The . . . claims must conform to the invention as set forth in the remainder of the specification and the terms and phrases used in the claims must find clear support or antecedent basis in the description. . . .

   In these problem claims, when the specification is given, watch very carefully for discrepancies between the specification and the problem claims. It would help to find the place in the specification where each term in the claim is described and underline, so as to locate ambiguities and misdescriptions. Even though the number of wheels probably is not important, it would not be *improper* to claim a pair if supported by the description.
3. *See* section 23. This should have been "*a* nozzle."
4. *See* note 2, *supra*.
5. *See* section 23.
6. *See* section 31. This may be a debatable point, as "adapted to" phrases are used fairly often in practice, but quite obviously such usage should be avoided on the Agent's Exam. Make certain that sufficient structure is included to support functional statements.

6. "A cam race" was considered "OK."[7]

7. The wrong verb form, "includes," is used. The claim must form a *complete sentence*, being the direct object of the (understood) phrase "I claim. . . ."[8]

8. "Or 7" is improper recitation of a multi-dependent claim. [See section for various forms of multidependent claims.][9]

9. "Two reciprocating agitators" is improper. If this claim is dependent from claim 6, the recitation of *two* agitators is *inconsistent* with "a *single* brush agitator" in the parent claim. A dependent claim may not add statements inconsistent with the structure of the parent claim.[10] If claim 7 is the parent claim, "an additional brush agitator" is already an element of the parent claim, so that it would be improper to add two more, apparently as new elements. This would be *double inclusion* of elements.[11]

10. There is no support in the disclosure for "nylon."[12] The specification does not state of what material the brushes are made.[13]

---

7. The drive means does *include* a cam race (22), as well as other elements. There is nothing wrong with claiming a cam race when two are shown, if the invention can work with one. *See* section 20. Also, this is not an attempt to claim "a hole" positively (section 26), since the *race* can be considered a structural unit including the walls of the groove, which actually do the guiding.

8. This should read "including" rather than "includes." "Which includes" would be a satisfactory alternative. There is nothing wrong with the transitional phrase "including" rather than "comprising," although the latter is much more common, and is almost conventional for mechanical cases. *See* section 7. Note: watch for little things (section 4A), capital letters, periods, punctuation, verb tenses.

9. Rule 75(c). *See* section 11.

10. *See* section 11.

11. *See* section 21.

12. *See* note 2, *supra*.

13. This would probably be immaterial to the invention, but it is not improper in this context to claim too narrowly.

OTHER ERRORS

11. Claim 7 is directed to a catalog of elements. There is no connection or cooperation whatever between the elements.[14]

12. Claim 6 is composed of two sentences, and is thus improper under Patent Office practice.[15]

13. There is no antecedent in claim 6 for "said *other* lip." Nothing in the claim would tell which of the lips referred to is meant by "other."

14. In claim 6, "a *single* brush agitator" is not illustrated in the drawings.[16] Every feature of the invention specified in the claims must be shown in the drawings.[17]

The foregoing were the four other specific errors identified by the Patent Office. There may be other errors of a lesser or more technical nature. For example:

15. Claim 6 does not have sufficient elements or cooperation between elements to make the complete combination stated in the preamble. Specifically, the combination claimed is a "*suction cleaner*," but nothing is recited in the claim to produce suction.[18]

16. In claim 6, "a body supported by wheels," the term "by wheels" is inferential claiming, as the wheels were not previously introduced. Better would have been ". . . a body, wheels supporting the body . . ."

---

14. *See* section 28.
15. *See* section 4A.
16. Although it is described in the last paragraph of the description as an alternative.
17. Rule 83. *See* section 18.
18. Even though the suction elements are *per se* conventional, either they should be included or, preferably, the claim should be in Jepson form. *See* section 57.

17. "Of this invention," in claim 7 appears to be surplusage. The same could be said of "to ensure long wear" in claim 8.[19]

SOME GENERAL NOTES ON ANSWERING SLOPPY CLAIMS QUESTIONS

Be quite specific as to the error; don't just say "no antecedent" or "indefinite," etc. For example (1) item (3) *"flexible* agitator," point out that the description does not state that the agitator is flexible and, if you noted it, that the agitator is illustrated as being solid. If you remembered that the rules of practice provide that all terms in the claims must find clear support or antecedent basis in the description, you could mention this. There is no need to cite rule number[20] or the exact language so long as the substance is correct.

At the other extreme, there is no need for a long essay or any discussion of philosophy or policy. Up to two or three short sentences along the lines of the suggested answers are sufficient.

Normally, do not volunteer how you would do it correctly. This can hardly gain, and might lose if you are wrong.

Where you think there are two things wrong, mention both in the order you think most important. For example, if you thought (as many do) that "nylon" (item 10) is a trademark and might be improper for that reason,[21] mention also that there is no support in the descrip-

---

19. *See* section 9.
20. Rule 75(d).
21. Section 51.
    *Reprinted as given on the Feb. 13, 1968, Exam.
    *Note: there are fewer errors here than in the previous two problems, but they are more sophisticated. Also, many more require knowledge of the law.
    *Reprinted as given on the Nov. 19, 1968, Exam.
    *Note: some of these errors required careful study of the specifications and a good knowledge of how the device works.
    *Reprinted as given on Aug. 26, 1969, Exam.

tion (since nylon is not a trademark and you might get most of the credit for having the right answer, as well as an incorrect statement).

PART II—SAMPLE CLAIMS AND COMMENTS (SUCTION CLEANER)

From the specification, it is quite clear that the general arrangement of the suction cleaner, including the motor, fan (8), rotary agitator (13), beaters (14) and rotary brushes (16) is conventional. The invention is stated to relate to adding the transversely reciprocating brushes 26 to this old structure. Thus, an improvement or *Jepson*-type claim could be used.

Such a claim follows, of fairly broad scope:

1. An improved suction cleaner of the type including a movable casing, a rotary agitator mounted in the casing for rotation about an axis transverse to the direction of movement of the cleaner, and drive means for rotating the agitator and producing suction within the casing; wherein the improvement comprises:
   (a) a brush element mounted in the casing for reciprocating movement parallel to the axis of rotation of the agitator; and
   (b) means for reciprocating the brush element in timed relation to the rotation of the agitator.

Note section 57, and rule 75(e) with respect to *Jepson*-type claims. It would probably not be necessary in claim 1 to specify the mechanical details of the cam-type drive linkage between the agitator and the reciprocating brushes. This per se is generally conventional. The main point of novelty, so the specification states, is in adding the transverse brushes. This should be claimable fairly broadly, within the general combination of the suction cleaner.

Claims 2 and 3 could add details of the cam drive, and the specific mounting and positioning of the reciprocating brushes with respect to the agitator.

It would be best not to use dependent claims adding *only* matters that the specification (or any instructions given with the problem) says are old. Thus, such things as the helical beater (15) structure would not be appropriate to add via a dependent claim since it is part of the old structure *and* does not coact in any new way with the new structure.

Case 27

CRITICIZING "SLOPPY CLAIMS"
(Steam and Dry Iron)

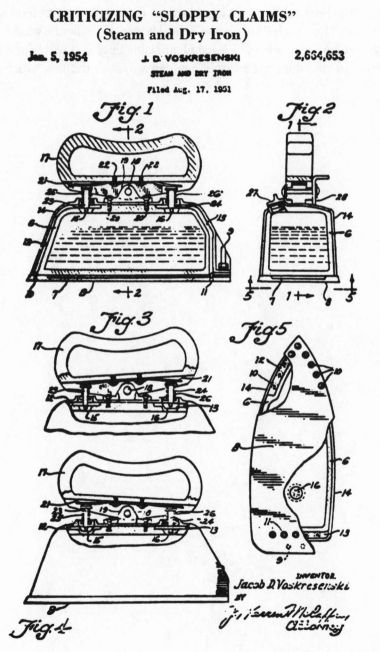

Jan. 5, 1954   J. D. VOSKRESENSKI   2,664,653

STEAM AND DRY IRON

Filed Aug. 17, 1951

Fig. 1

Fig. 2

Fig. 3

Fig. 5

Fig. 4

INVENTOR.
Jacob D. Voskresenski
BY
Attorney

Excerpts from Specification

The feature of this invention is the supplying of steam to the article being ironed in advance of, and while moving the iron across the article whether in a frontward or backward direction.

However, if the operator desires to iron dry, he may shut off the supply of steam and use the device of this invention as a dry iron.

An equally important feature of this invention is the controlling of the supply of steam through either the front or rear ports of the iron to the article being ironed as desired. The operation of the means for controlling the supply of steam is simple and coincides with the normal movement by hand of any iron over an article to be ironed.

The water chamber of the steam iron is indicated as 6 and the upper section of the chamber becomes a steam dome when the water is heated sufficiently by electrical element 7. The heating element is encased in the bottom of the iron by a flat ironing surface 8 and connection between usual electric cords and the heating element 7 is made by wiring not shown to the electrical terminals 9.

A plurality of steam ports represented by 10 are located in the flat ironing surface 8 around the front end of the iron and a similar plurality of ports 11 are located in the flat surface 8 around or across the back end of the iron. The front ports 10 lead to the forward steam chamber 12 while the rear ports 11 connect with the rear steam chamber 13. The front steam chamber 12 may encircle the forward part of the iron and back along the sides of the iron as far as desired. Similarly the back steam chamber 13 may extend across the back as shown and also extend back along the sides of the iron as desired. However, in order to accomplish one of the features of the iron of this invention the front and rear steam chambers cannot be connected. The chambers are formed between the wall of the combination water and steam chamber 6 and the outside casing 14 of the iron. In areas of the side walls beyond the limits of front steam chamber 12 and rear steam chamber 13 the casing 14 and wall 6 of the combined steam and waterchamber are contiguous as seen in Figures 2 and 5 of the accompanying drawing.

A steam valve 15 controls the passage of steam from the steam and water chamber 6 to the front steam chamber 12 and a similar valve 16 controls passage of steam into the rear chamber 13. In Figure 1 the two steam valves 15 and 16 are shown in closed positions. In Figure 4 valve 15 is open and 16 is closed which would be their relative positions when the iron is being moved forward. In Figure 3 front valve 15 is closed while rear valve 16 is open which would be their relative positions when the iron is being moved backward. The operation of these steam valves 15 and 16 is accomplished by handle 17 which is free to rock on pin 18 in trunnion 19 which is bolted by means 20, or in any other way connected to casing 14.

A strip of spring steel 21 is fastened to the underside of handle 17 by any means, such as bolts 22, and is preformed so that its two end sections bear down on the heads of valve stems 23 and 24 so as to keep steam valves 15 and 16 closed as shown in Figure 1.

When the operator of the steam iron decides to move it forward, he naturally presses on the rear of the handle so that the front of the iron will slide over the article being pressed. Thus in the normal operation of the iron he inclines the handle down in the rear and it rocks on pin 18 so that the forward part of the handle is up. This movement of the handle causes steam valve 15 to open up whereas steam valve 16 is firmly shut as shown in Figure 4.

Similarly if the operator decides to pull the iron backwards across the article being ironed, he bears down on the forward end of the handle, and thus on the front of the iron, thereby releasing pressure on the back end of the rockable handle and the back of the iron, so that the iron will slide backward over the article being ironed. This manipulation of the handle in turn closes steam valve 15 tight and allows steam valve 16 to open as shown in Figure 3.

The obvious reason for so operating the handle of the steam iron is to simultaneously operate the steam valves and thus supply moist steam through ports 10 when moving the iron forward while ironing, and through ports 11 when moving the iron backward. Thus supplying moist-steam to the article being ironed eliminates otherwise sprinkling or wetting the article before ironing.

Problem

Given the drawings and excerpts from the specification, criticize errors in the following "sample" claims 1-7.

SAMPLE CLAIMS TO BE CRITICIZED

1. A combination steam and dry iron, comprising a body having a water chamber therein and front and rear steam chambers. The iron includes a bottom member, a first plurality of openings formed in the forward portion of the bottom plate and communicating with the front steam chamber, a second plurality of openings formed in the rear section of the bottom plate, and a toggle member connected to alternately activate the valve means whereby the iron may be operated either forwardly or backwardly to iron clothes more effectively than heretofore.

2. An iron including push-pull valve means for automatically spraying steam ahead of the iron when moving forwardly and behind the iron when moving backwardly.

3. Apparatus as recited in claims 1 or 2, wherein the water chamber is omitted and steam is supplied directly to the iron from a central steam boiler through a flexible hose.

4. A base 8, a heater 7, a plurality of valves 15-16, a selective actuator 21 for the valves selected from the group consisting of springs, weights, and levers, a plurality of steam ports 10-11, and a handle 17.

5. A method as recited in claim 4, further comprising the step of moving the iron alternately forward and back to iron the clothes.

6. A method as recited in claim 5, further comprising a pair of leaf springs for actuating the valves when the handle is pivoted.

7. Any and all novel features described, referred to, exemplified or shown.

Case 27

CRITICIZING "SLOPPY CLAIMS"
(STEAM AND DRY IRON)

COMMENTS

This specification was given on the August 1966 Exam, and the examinees were asked to criticize defective claims, rather than to prepare claims to a structure as had been customary in the past. The "sample claims to be criticized" used here are similar to those used on the Exam, but not identical.

The following list covers errors and debatable points which were intentionally made in the "sample" claims. There may be other errors.

Claim 1, in general. As an overall criticism, this claim does not set forth all of the elements necessary to "the invention," as defined in the specification. In particular, there is no specific description of the main point of the invention, which has to do with supplying steam selectively through front and rear ports as the iron is moved forward and back, by manipulating the handle to actuate valves. Thus, the claim is "incomplete" (see section 66) and "inconsistent with the disclosure" (section 18).

Claim 1, line 3, the claim consists of two sentences rather than one. (See section 4A.)

Lines 3 and 5, "plurality of openings" are made "elements" of the claim. (See section 26.) Holes should not be positively recited. This should read, for example, "a bottom member having a plurality of openings . . . [etc.]."

Lines 4 and 6, "bottom *plate*" is "indefinite" (section 23). This should read bottom "member," as in line 3. One must use consistent terminology for the same element throughout the claim.

Lines 4 and 6, no antecedent for "*the* forward portion" or "*the* rear section." It is at least debatable whether or not "bottom members" inherently have forward or rear sections. (See section 19 and section 16.) Better practice is, for example, "a bottom plate having a forward portion . . . etc."

Line 6, no connection of the second plurality of openings with the rear steam chamber. Also, no connection between the water chamber and the steam chamber, and nothing about heating the water. Thus, the claim is drawn, in part, to a "catalog of elements" (section 28).

Line 7, "toggle member." Mechanically this is not a "toggle member" but even if the student did not know this, the word "toggle" does not appear anywhere in the specification. Terms and phrases used in the claims must find clear support or antecedent basis in the specification. (See Rule 75(d) and section 18.) If this type of question is given, read the specification fairly closely and watch for inconsistencies in terminology.

Line 7, "connected to." It is doubtful whether this phrase sets forth enough structural cooperation with the other elements. (See section 30.) There is insufficient structure recited to support the functional statement.

Lines 7 and 8, "*the valve means.*" No antecedent. This should have been made an element of the claim. (See section 23.)

Lines 8 and 9, "whereby." The function immediately following "whereby" has nothing to do with the claimed structure in that all ordinary irons may be operated either forwardly or backwardly. The statement about ironing more effectively does necessarily follow from the previously recited structure. (See section 32.)

Also, laudatory expressions of this type ("more effectively than heretofore") are not permitted. This is "surplusage" (section 9).

Claim 2, line 1. It seems unclear whether "*push-pull* valve means" has any meaning, and this language is not used in the specification. This clause is vague and indefinite (section 67).

Line 1, this iron does not work "automatically." Thus, the claim is "misdescriptive" and "inconsistent with the specification."

Line 1, the claim is a "single means" claim. (See section 34.) The statute (35 U.S.C. § 112) sanctions "mean plus function" clauses only in claims to *combinations*. Also, the claim may be objectionable as being too broad, in that the broad means plus function language comes at the point of novelty (sections 34 and 31).

Line 1, the transition "including" is acceptable (section 7). However, "comprising" is preferred.

Claim 3, line 1, "claims 1 *or* 2." Rule 75(c) permits multiple dependent claims. (See section 12.) But, note section for a format for such claims.

Line 2, *omitting* the water chamber. See above, a dependent claim must *further restrict* the preceding claim. Thus elements cannot be subtracted, because this is a broadening of the claims.

Line 2 and 3, steam boiler and water hose. This runs afoul of rule 83, that the drawing must show every feature of the invention specified in the claims (section 18). Also, this is not described in the excerpts from the specification which were given (although it was described in the full specification as a conventional technique for commercial establishments).

Line 2, "steam *is supplied*." This sounds like a method limitation, and would be better defined (if included at all) in such terms as ". . . further comprising a central steam boiler, and a flexible hose . . . etc."

Claim 4, line 1, no preamble. Claims normally have some form of preamble, and it may be improper to omit it altogether. (See sections 6 and 15.)

Lines 1-4, reference numerals. There is no objection to the use of reference characters in claims, but this is done very rarely. However, when used, the characters should be enclosed in parentheses. This is provided on an optional basis in a notice "Guidelines for Drafting a Model Patent Application under the Revised Rules," 832 O.G. 5 (November 1, 1966) (section 19).

Lines 1-4. The claim is merely a "catalog" of elements, with no structural or operational cooperation set forth. (See section 28.) The claim must be drawn to an assembled, operable combination. This type of claim is often called an "aggregation," meaning as claimed (section 64).

Lines 2 and 3, *"selected from the group . . ."* This uses Markush language (see section 50) for mechanical elements, which is proper. The Markush type of alternative phraseology is useful for chemical cases where no generic expression is available but is also useful for mechanical cases. Also, the complete expression is alternative, which is improper. (See section 24.) Note also that weights and levers are not disclosed or shown, which is improper, as noted earlier, because it lacks "support in the description."

Line 4, the steam "ports" (holes) are claimed positively.

Claim 5, line 1, the *"preceding* claim (4) is not a method claim. It is an improper dependent claim because it is "inconsistent" with its parent claim.

Lines 2 and 3. The step added by the subclaim is only the overall step of moving the iron in the conventional manner. It is probably objectionable, or at least poor practice, to add dependent claims which add only highly conventional steps (section 61).

Claim 6. This is a dependent *method* claim adding *only* further details of *structure*, which is improper. Dependent method claims should add method steps or further define method steps. Also, apparatus limitations should be avoided as far as possible in method claims. (See sections 56 and 41.)

Line 2. There is no antecedent for "when the handle is pivoted," *in either Claim 6 or "parent" Claims* 5 or 4.

Claim 7. This is a so-called "omnibus" claim, which is improper under 35 U.S.C. § 112. Such claims have been held not "to particularly point out and distinctly claim" the invention (section 2).

GENERAL APPROACH TO "SLOPPY CLAIMS" QUESTIONS OF THIS TYPE

Given the first drawing, specification and sloppy claims, skim the claims first to see what they cover, generally, and mark obvious or trivial errors. (Here, unlike the previous case, the possible errors were not underlined.) Then read the specification fairly carefully against the claims. You must understand the main points of the invention fairly well to find some of the more sophisticated errors (incomplete, omits essential elements, reads on admitted prior art, etc.).

Underline the main elements (from the claims) in the specification, and make sure all are described in the same or consistent terminology. Make sure that everything in the claims is described, and that all structure claimed is shown in the drawings.

Then, of course, all of the formal, grammatical, and language errors described in the book must be found and identified, and answers written along the lines suggested in the previous problem.

One had approximately one and one-half hours to answer this type of question.

Case 28
CRITICIZING "SLOPPY CLAIMS"
(Bomb-Proof Coating)

PROTECTION DEVICE AGAINST AERIAL AND OTHER BOMBARDMENT

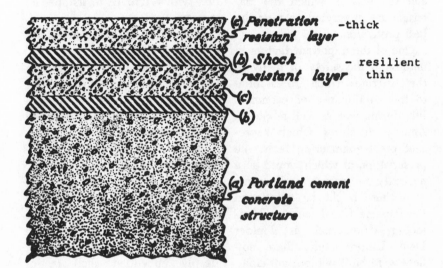

(c) *Penetration resistant layer* -thick

(b) *Shock resistant layer* - resilient thin

(c)

(b)

(a) *Portland cement concrete structure*

This invention relates to the safeguarding of structures and various objects of importance from the destructive effects of aerial or other bombardment. The invention also relates to the composition of materials which are used, and the way in which the materials are integrated to give the best protection.

One of the important factors in defense is the safety of many of the structures which are essential to the continuance of economic life, during was as well as peace. Among structures which represent great engineering feats, the preservation of which would be a necessity in waging a defensive war, there might be mentioned the Panama Canal locks and numerous dams, such as Boulder Dam. Unfortunately, these edifices were built without anticipating the effectiveness of aerial bombardment, and must now be considered with reference to their vulnerability to attack.

An object of the present invention, therefore, is to provide a method whereby not only structures already completed may be rapidly safeguarded, but also the protection of structures yet to be completed, such as forts, etc., of the new defense bases along the coasts of the United States and at various points in the Caribbean and Hawaiian Islands.

A further object of my invention is to provide protection of other than stationary objects, since protection against the shattering effects of bombs on the steel decks of battleships, for instance, may be obtained by using a material having a high degree of protection with reference to its specific gravity.

The effects of bombardment are essentially twofold:

(1) The penetrating effect due to the kinetic energy possessed by the projectiles, and

(2) The shattering effect caused by the rapid expansion and production of gases from the explosive contained in the shell.

The importance of the penetration factor varies, being dependent on the speed of the shell, and whether the shell is equipped with a delayed timing detonator. A deeply imbedded shell is, of course, much more effective than one which explodes on the surface. In constructing any protection against bombardment, therefore, one must consider primarily the two effects enumerated above.

My invention resides in the utilization of a covering material composed of layers, each layer being characterized by either its shock-absorbing powers or its resistance to penetration. Such a structure would include comparatively thin layers of shock resistent material while the penetration resistant layer would be comparatively thick. As shown in the drawing: *a* is a portion of a concrete dam or fortification, *b* is composed of a resilient material, while *c* is penetration resistant material. The number of layers need not be restricted, as shown.

Furthermore, the shock absorbent layer *b* may be continuous, or it may be honeycombed with air spaces to give a waffle-like structure, as long as there is sufficient material to act as a support for the upper layer. This form has shock absorbent powers not realized in the solid continuous form, since air is an ideal shock absorber. Again, this structure has the advantage of being capable of diffusing the shock waves so that their destructive effect is minimized.

As examples of shock absorbent materials which are resistant to shattering and spalling I wish to list particularly bituminous materials of all kinds, including air-blown, steam blown and filled asphalts; mixtures of asphalt with rock, sand and dust which have a high proporton of asphalt, and bituminous saturated roofing felt. However, besides bituminous materials I may use rubber and rubber compounds, cork and, in fact, any similar material which has a minimum capacity of transmitting shock waves. The materials need not necessarily be resilient, since a shattering or spalling resistance may even be obtained by including a layer of Cellophane between layers of cement, the desired effect here not being due to the Cellophane, but to its producing a discontinuity in the concrete structure, which in turn interrupts the shock waves. A preferred asphalt which has maximum shock absorbing qualities and yet has sufficient supporting strength is one with a melting point of 225° F.-325° F. and a penetration of 77° F. (100 g.–5 sec.) of 0.-20. The invention need not be limited to the examples of compositions just enumerated, since the essence of the invention is in the use of the two materials having the herein described characteristics and their use in conjunction with one another.

In general, a first layer of a resilient shock absorbing substance, such as air-blown asphalt of a high melting point, or mineral rubber. Cellophane, felt containing asphalt, etc., is placed next to the structure to be protected using some suitable thickness which has been determined to suit the properties of the materials used in each of the layers. The second, or penetration resistant layer *e*, is then applied. As example of penetration resistant materials which may be used in this layer are Portland cement concrete, steel, brick, sand, rock, hard asphalting concrete and the like, although I prefer to use hard asphaltic concrete, which comprises a mixture of steam blown or air-blown asphalt with a suitable quantity of graded sand and/or rock dust.

The advantage of using asphalt compositions in preference to Portland cement mixtures in protection for fortifications and the like, is evident because of several outstanding reasons. One of these is that asphalt mastic mixtures reach their final condition of maximum strength as soon as they have cooled, while the average Portland cement concrete requires a twenty-eight day period before approaching its maximum strength. This is important especially in picking possible effective emergency repairs. Freshly poured asphaltic mixtures bond perfectly to old asphaltic mixtures, thus if a portion of the structure is partially destroyed, it can be repaired quickly by merely filling the crater and cracks with a fresh asphaltic mixture. On the other hand, it is not feasible to obtain a good bond between cured and fresh Portland cement concrete. A damaging shrapnel effect following explosions is avoided, since

an asphalt mixture of good strength can be made without using large proportions of relatively coarse rock. Asphaltic mixtures do not split out large fragments on the surface when a direct hit is made and, furthermore, when an indirect hit is made the cushioning effect of the rubbery plastic binder in the asphalt mastic is of benefit because the asphalt resists shock relatively well. Besides these characteristics, certain types of asphaltic mastic compositions resist penetration of high impact missiles to about the same extent as well-cured Portland cement concrete.

In order to test materials for shock absorbent power, the following method can be employed:

A piece of material to be tested is placed on a smooth surface of a lead block and a half stick of dynamite is then placed on the test material. The depth of the impression produced by detonation of the dynamite serves as a measure of the shock absorbent power of the material. Table I gives the materials used as absorbers and the corresponding impression made on lead by the explosion.

Table I

Material description	Thickness, inches	Depth of impression, inches
	*	*
Air		
Pine		
Mineral rubber—300 M. P. oxidized asphalt		
Asphalt mortar—9% steam blown— penetration (at 100 g. and 5 sec.)— 150-200, remainder sand		
Saturated felt—6 plys of $\frac{1}{18}''$ felt, saturated with asphalt		
Tile		

The penetration resistance of various compositions is conveniently tested by simply firing rifle bullets at the test substance perpendicular to the surface of this material. The Springfield 30-06 rifle bullet fired point blank at fifty feet using different compositions penetrates as indicated below in Table II.

Table II

Material	Thickness of specimen, in.	Penetration, in. *	Spall crater area, sq. in.	Spall crater depth, in.
	*		*	*
Asphaltic concrete				
Portland cement concrete				
Steel				
Sand				
Oak				

*[Ed. Note: The copy of the specifications from which this material was set was insufficiently clear to complete the tables. The textual disclosure suffices for the problem.]

The asphaltic concrete 2½ inches thick was composed of 43 parts 10-28 mesh gravel, 62 parts 33-80 mesh sand, 4 parts rock dust finer than 80 mesh, 10 parts rock larger than 10 mesh, and 29 parts asphalt having a penetration of 80-80 at 77° F. (100 g.-5 sec.). The 8 inches thick sample of asphaltic concrete was prepared using 17.1 parts asphalt and 120 parts allicious concrete sand. The asphalt had a penetration value of 150-200 (100 g.—5 sec.) at 77° F., while the sand used had the following characteristics: passed 200 mesh—1.4 parts; 80 to 200 mesh—2.4 parts; 28 to 80 mesh—52 parts; 10 to 28 mesh—48 parts; retained on 10 mesh—10.3 parts; diatomaceous earth—6.3 parts. All quantities given are parts by weight.

The Portland cement concrete was a mix containing 1 part of Portland cement, 2 parts sand (10-80 mesh) and 4 parts rock (retained on 10 mesh).

The asphaltic mixture compositions may be further improved to give them more resistivity to penetration, mainly by varying the type of filler used. In the case of the Portland cement concrete, the spall crater was very large or about 5-10 times greater in diameter than that produced in the asphalt composition having the penetration resistance given in the examples described herein. As the resistance to penetration is increased in the asphaltic concrete, i.e., up to a value equal to that characteristic of a Portland cement concrete, the brittleness increases and the spalls from a rifle bullet shot being thrown several feet. These two opposed qualities of low spalling and low penetration resistance may be compromised by varying the composition at will. The compositions may be varied considerably by using asphalts having wide ranges of properties and by using different kinds of sand and rock. For instance, the shock resistant layer may contain 8-25% asphalt having a "normal" penetration at 77° F. (100 g. at 5 sec.) of 10-300 and the penetration resistant layer may contain 3-15% asphalt having approximately the same specifications.

Tests were also carried out to demonstrate the greatly improved resistance of a Portland cement concrete structure to explosives when it is protected using the method herein described.

Two blocks, each 5 ft. x 5 ft. x 3½ ft. were employed in the test. One block was not protected in any way, while the second one was covered with asphalt saturated paper followed by a 12 inch layer of 9% asphalt concrete. The asphalt concrete was composed of about four parts 10-50 mesh decomposed granite, four parts less than No. 10 mesh decomposed granite, one part greater than 80 mesh decomposed granite and limestone dust, and ½ part asphalt. This asphalt had the specification: Melting point of 95-105° F.; penetration at 77° F. (100 g.—5 sec.) of 150-200.

To simulate a hit by an aerial bomb, the blocks were subjected to repeated blastings using three sticks of Hercules straight 60% nitroglycerin dynamite at a time. The sticks weighed 6 ounces apiece, and the bundle was placed each time in the crater produced by the preceding explosion. After five charges, no shattering of the asphalt block had occurred, while after four charges, long cracks were produced in the Portland cement concrete block. After seven blastings the Portland cement block was seriously cracked all over the top and down the sides, the top foot of the block having no supporting value at all. Although seven blasts finally had split the asphalt covering into four segments, the Portland ce-

ment concrete block beneath was undamaged.

This experiment also presented an opportunity to show clearly the reduced spalling which occurs in the asphalt mastics as compared to the Portland cement concrete. At the end of the sixth blasting, the crater in the Portland cement concrete block measured 34 x 29 inches at the surface of the block and was 9¾ inches deep, while the crater in the protective covering of asphalt mastic at the end of the sixth blasting measured only 13 x 13 inches at the surface and was 9¼ inches deep. The reduction in spalling of the asphalt compositions in comparison to the Portland cement mixture is shown in Table II, where rifle fire was the method of testing employed.

It is understood that the above description is merely illustrative of preferred embodiments of my invention of which many variations may be made within the scope of the following claims without departing from the spirit thereof.

Problem*

Read Instructions Carefully

This part of the examination requires analysis of 5 claims proposed to be added to an application having the accompanying specification and drawing. Certain words and phrases in the claims have been underlined and numerically designated. *Most, but not all,* of the underlined portions represent instances wherein the claims fail to comply with United States patent law or accepted claim writing practices. In addition to the 10 numbered items in the claims, there are 2 additional instances involving deficiencies in the claims in substance or form. These instances should be listed as items 11 and 12 in your answer. For each number in each claim and for items 11 and 12, make a short statement as to why the underlined portion does represent a defect, if such is the case.

6. (1) A *bombardment-resistant coating for structures* which comprises an (2) *inner layer of shock resistant material and a thick external layer* formed of (3) *asphaltic concrete containing mineral fibers.*

7. (4) A *structure having thereon a coating* comprising layers of material (5) *such as* (6) *mineral rubber* combined

---

*Reprinted as given on the Feb. 13, 1968, Exam.

with layers of penetration resistant materials selected from (7) *the group consisting of steel, cement concrete, and asphalt concrete.*

8. (8) A *new process for rendering a structure resistant to penetration and shattering by bombardment* which comprises covering the externally exposed surfaces of said structure with an inner layer $\frac{1}{16}$-$\frac{1}{2}$ inch thick of (9) *paper saturated with asphalt or felt saturated with asphalt,* and applying to said inner layer at least six inches thick of penetration-resistant hard asphalt concrete.

9. A structure having thereon (10) *a coating essentially as described in the drawing.*

10. A bombardment-resistant structure consisting of the product of the method set forth in claim 8.

Case 28

CRITICIZING "SLOPPY CLAIMS"
(BOMB-PROOF COATING)

COMMENTS*

1. (a) Claiming a coating without claiming the combination with the base material
   (b) No antecedent basis in specification for "bombardment-resistant coating".
   (c) O.K.
2. Indefinite—unbased comparative "thick."
3. No disclosure of "concrete containing mineral fibers."
4. O.K.
5. Indefinite or alternative.
6. O.K.
7. The members are a proper group in Markush form, because they share a common relevant characteristic.
8. The term "new" in the claim in unnecessary and surplusage.
9. Indefinite because alternative.
10. Claim may not refer to the drawing and is indefinite as defining structure only be reference to the drawing.

Answers for 11 and 12 (unnumbered deficiencies).

(a) Claim 10 obviously nonstatutory because the structure can be defined other than by reference to the method.
(b) Claim 8 drawn to an obvious method.
(c) Claim 8—the range ($\frac{1}{16}$"-$\frac{1}{2}$") lacks antecedent support in the specification.

---

*Quoted from Patent Office Approved answers. There are fewer errors here than in the previous two problems, but they are more sophisticated. Also, many more require knowledge of the law.

Case 29
CRITICIZING "SLOPPY CLAIMS"
(Self-Priming Pump)

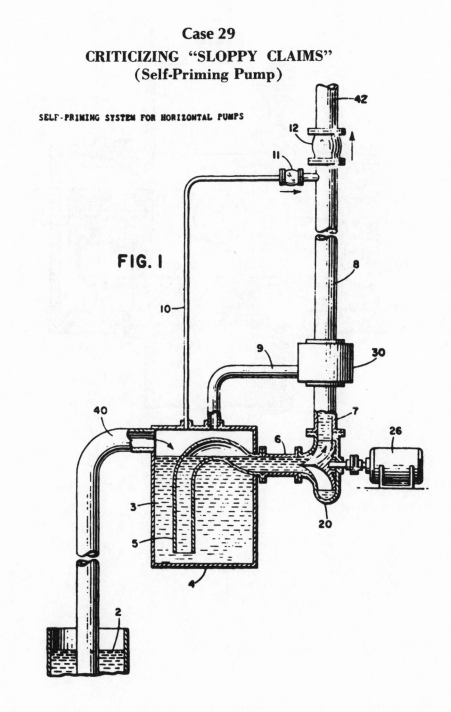

SELF-PRIMING SYSTEM FOR HORIZONTAL PUMPS

FIG. 1

FIG. 2

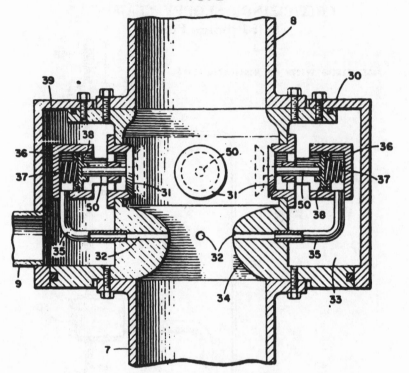

SELF-PRIMING SYSTEM FOR HORIZONTAL PUMPS
ABSTRACT OF THE DISCLOSURE

During repriming of a horizontal pump by recycling liquid from the discharge conduit of the pump to the suction well for the pump, air is displaced from the suction well through an air vent. Air may also be bled from the impeller casing of the pump, preferably by a conduit leading to the upper portion of the suction well.

Background of the invention

The present invention relates to a self-priming pumping system. In the past, there have been many different devices developed to automatically prime a liquid pump when the pump runs dry due to an insufficient amount of liquid being present at the pump inlet and to prevent air from being introduced to the suction side of the pump. These devices are essential to the efficient operation of a pumping system, since, as is well known, once air is admitted to the suction passage in sufficient quantities to allow the pump to exhaust the supply of liquid in the suction well, the pump no longer is able to maintain suction to pump the liquid. Consequently, the pumping operation would be stopped and the attention of an operator would be required if no automatic means for repriming the system is provided.

Summary of the invention

In accordance with the present invention, a horizontal pump is primed by liquid from a suction well or reservoir located at the pump inlet. The suction well is normally supplied with liquid to be pumped by a suction line communicating with the liquid source of pumpage. A repriming valve is located in the pump discharge column to allow automatic recycling of liquid from the discharge line to the suction well when the pump has lost suction. A one-way check value is positioned downstream from the repriming valve and allows fluid movement only in the downstream direction, and thus limits the quantity of liquid which may be recycled to that in the system between the repriming valve and the check valve. An air relief line with a one-way check valve connects the top of the suction well to the discharge column intermediate the first mentioned check valve and the repriming valve. Air is displaced from the suction well through the air relief line by the liquid which is recycled from the discharge column through the repriming valve to the suction well. When a portion of the recycled liquid flows from the suction well into the pump inlet, the liquid will be pumped into the discharge column causing the repriming valve to close. If the pump is not fully reprimed, the repriming valve will thereafter again allow the same liquid to be recycled to the suction well. This recycling will continue in this fashion until the normal pumping cycle is restored.

The present invention is designed for automatically repriming single or multi-stage pumps employing any reasonable length suction line. In the event of loss of suction head due to the pump running dry, there is no danger of pump damage since the system will continue to reprime itself.

According to a further feature of the invention, an air relief line may vent air from the impeller inlet casing. It has been found that when liquid in the suction well is exhausted and air is sucked into the pump, an air lock may be formed between the inlet of the pump intake line and the impeller. This entrapped air may keep liquid from reaching that point in the impeller section of the pump where sufficient velocity can be imparted to it to force the liquid and the entrapped air into the discharge column. By the use of an air relief line extending through the casing of the pump impeller chamber, a path is provided for venting such entrapped air when the repriming fluid flows into the pump inlet.

It is a principal object of the present invention to provide novel apparatus for automatically repriming a pumping system which is fed by a suction intake line.

Another object of the present invention is to provide a self-priming pumping system for a horizontal pump capable of developing a suction head by recycling its priming fluid.

Another object is to provide a self-priming pumping system capable of repeatedly developing a suction head to draw liquid up through a relatively long suction line.

A further object of the invention is to provide a self-priming pumping system wherein the component parts, including the pump, can be conveniently located to facilitate replacement or servicing, if necessary.

A still further object of the invention is to provide a self-priming pumping system that is rugged, positive in operation, and capable of pumping any sort of pumpage without becoming clogged or jammed.

An even further object of the present invention is to provide a self-priming pumping system for a horizontal pump that is compact, contains a minimum of moving parts, and is economical to manufacture.

The above and still further objects, features, and advantages of the present invention will become more apparent as this description proceeds.

Brief description of the drawing

FIGURE 1 is a side elevational view, partially in section, illustrating one embodiment of the present invention.

FIGURE 2 is a vertical sectional view of the repriming valve employed as part of the present invention.

Description of the preferred embodiments

Referring to FIGURE 1, reference numeral 4 designates a suction well or casing which acts as a reservoir for priming liquid 3. In normal operation, liquid 3 is supplied to the suction well through a suction line 40 which has its other end immersed in pumpage 2. A suction skirt 5 is positioned with its lower end adjacent the bottom of suction well 4, and is connected at its other end to an inlet 6 of a horizontal pump 20 which is driven by a motor 26. In the illustrated embodiment, suction skirt 5 has a curved upper portion, the lower inner surface of which is approximately level with the upper inner surface of the eye of the impeller, i.e., the horizontal inlet 6. A small aperture may be provided in the curved upper portion of the skirt 5 to function as an air bleed between this portion of the skirt and the top of the suction well 4. It is also possible to connect the vertically extending portion of skirt 5 to the pump inlet without elevating the upper portion of the skirt above the pump inlet 6, for example, by means of a 90° pipe elbow.

Pump 20 pumps fluid through an outlet 7, and a repriming valve assembly 30 to be described hereinafter into a discharge column 8. A one-way check valve 12 is positioned at the upper end of the discharge column 8 and connects the discharge column to a discharge line 42. A drain pipe 9 leads from valve 30 to the top of the suction well 4 so that liquid may be recycled in a manner to be described hereinafter to reprime the pump 20. The liquid in discharge column 8 and the quantity of liquid in repriming valve 30 above the level of drain pipe 9 are available to reprime the pump. Therefore, the discharge column 8 and the above mentioned portion of repriming valve 30 effectively function as a reservoir for repriming liquid. The volumetric capacity of this reservoir is at least sufficient to ensure that the quantity of liquid available to reprime the pump is sufficient to fill the pump inlet, inlet 6, skirt 5 and suction well 4 to a level corresponding to the level of the eye of the pump impeller.

An air relief conduit 10 leads from the top of the enclosed suction well 4 to the upper end of the discharge column 8 upstream from the check valve 12. A one-way check valve 11 in conduit 10 allows fluid movement only in a direction towards discharge column 8 to prevent liquid in column 8 from returning to the suction well via conduit 10.

FIGURE 2 illustrates a presently preferred repriming valve assembly 30. Valve assembly 30 basically comprises an inner casing 34 which has a lower portion in the shape of a venturi. The upper portion of the casing part of the reservoir section for the repriming liquid forms a cage structure for a plurality of peripherally spaced poppet valves 31 and the associated valve seats. A tube 35 is connected from each of four openings 32 in the throat of the venturi to a chamber formed by a cylinder 36 and a cooperating piston 38 which is connected to a valve 31 by a valve stem 50. A spring 37 between the head of each cylinder 36 and the associated piston 38 functions to normally bias each poppet valve 31 towards its open position which is shown by dashed lines in FIGURE 2. A jacket 39 surrounds the valve assembly and together with casing 34 forms an enclosed space 33 which is in communication with the drain pipe 9.

When liquid is being pumped during normal operation, the poppet valves 31 are maintained in their closed position by a pres-sure differential between the liquid in the upper portion of casing 34 and the liquid in cylinders 36, which pressure differential is of sufficient magnitude to overcome the bias of the springs 37. This pressure differential is established by the venturi in the lower section of casing 34 and control tubes 35 leading from openings 32 in the venturi to the cylinders 36. Since the tubes 35 communicate with the venturi, the static pressure in the venturi is present in the tubes, and in the cylinders 36. Due to the magnitude of the dynamic pressure factor flowing through the venturi which is proportional to the square of the velocity of the liquid, the static pressure in the venturi and hence in cylinders 36 is less than the static pressure acting upon the poppet valves 31 in the enlarged upper portion of casing 34. It is evident that the velocity of the liquid in the venturi is greater than the ambient velocity in the upper portion of casing 34 and therefore the pressure in conduits 35 is lower than the ambient pressure in the upper portion of the casing 34. Thus, a drop in pressure is created in cylinder 36 which permits pressure against valves 31 to force the valves 31 against their valve seats in opposition to the bias of springs 37. When the velocity of liquid flowing through the repriming valve reaches a predetermined low value, for example, when air is introduced into the system, and the pressure differential is sufficiently reduced in magnitude, the bias of springs 37 is effective to open the poppet valves 31. When the poppet valves open, liquid may flow through the valve ports into the space 33 and then into drain pipe 9.

The operation of the FIGURE 1 embodiment will now be described. With the suction well 4 filled with liquid to a level above the pump inlet 6, liquid pumped into discharge column 8 by pump 20 creates a suction which draws more liquid into the suction well from suction line 40. As long as liquid flow continues, repriming valve 30 and check valve 11 remain closed.

However, if air or other gas enters the suction well and suction is lost, the pumping action stops when the liquid in the suction well is depleted. When the liquid flow from the outlet 7 of the pump stops, the pressure differential holding the poppet valves 31 in their closed positions is reduced, and the valves are opened by springs 37. Liquid now flows out of valve assembly 30 and discharge column 8 through the ports associated with poppet valves 31, into space 33, and through drain pipe 9 back to the suction well 4. As the repriming liquid enters the suction well, air

is displaced through air relief conduit 10 and check valve 11 into the now empty upper end of discharge column 8. When the repriming fluid from the suction well passes through the suction skirt 5 into the pump inlet 6, the pump 20 then draws the repriming liquid out of the suction well and pumps it into the discharge column 8. The flow of the repriming liquid from the pump outlet reestablishes the pressure differential which causes the poppet valves 31 to move to the closed position. Check valve 11 closes as the liquid enters the discharge column 8, and the air which has entered the discharge column is now forced through check valve 12 into discharge line 42. The removal of liquid from the suction well 4 reduces the pressure at the opening of suction line 40 so that liquid is drawn upward therein. When the repriming liquid is depleted, the cycle is repeated until suction is reestablished for the pump 20. Factors such as the length in diameter of the suction line 40 will determine how many times the pump will be reprimed before full pumpage flow is reestablished.

In one of the embodiments tested, a suction line 22 feet long and 14 inches in diameter achived full discharge after three repriming cycles which took place in less than a minute.

Problem*

This part of the examination requires analysis of the four following claims proposed to be added to an application having the accompanying specification and drawings. The claims all would be subject to rejection.

Identify the portions or attributes of each claim that afford grounds for rejection and make a short statement for each as to why rejection is in order.

5. A self-priming pump system comprising a pump, an inlet for said pump, an outlet therefor, and means automatically supplying liquid to prime said pump when insufficient liquid is present at the pump inlet, said means including a suction well and an automatic valve regulating the flow of repriming liquid to said well.

6. A self-priming pump system comprising a pumpage supply (2), a suction casing (4), a pump (20), a drive motor (26), an automatic valve (30), and a drain pipe (9) communicating with the said valve.

7. A self-priming pump system comprising a pump having a horizontal inlet and an outlet, a suction well having a cavity which is partially below said inlet, the suction line opening into the suction well at a level above said inlet

---

*Reprinted as given on the Nov. 19, 1968, Exam.

to supply liquid to the cavity, a suction skirt having a lower end positioned in said cavity below said inlet and having an upper end connected to said inlet. A portion of said upper end is elevated above said inlet, reservoir means for repriming liquid having an upstream end connected to said outlet of said pump, a repriming valve connected to said pump outlet, a drain conduit connecting said valve to said suction well, means in the inlet of said valve for detecting a drop in liquid velocity, a valve device within the repriming valve biased to closed position, a discharge column leading from said valve, and an air relief conduit extending from said discharge column to a point upstream of said inlet.

8. A self-priming pump system as described in claim 7 in which said upper end of said suction skirt extends up to but not above the pump inlet and in which the said fluid responsive detecting means includes a Venturi passage.

Case 29

CRITICIZING "SLOPPY CLAIMS"
(SELF-PRIMING PUMP)

COMMENTS*

(Claim 5) Failure to point out novel combination in view of admitted prior art (under "Background of the Invention"). Also full credit for recognition of lack of structural relationship of suction well and automatic valve to remaining elements of claim.

(Claim 6) Mere catalog of elements, claim is incomplete in not setting forth relationship between elements. Use of reference numerals is not a defect. Section 608.01(m).

(Claim 7)

    (a) no antecedent for suction line.
    (b) use of period improper.
    (c) not supported by disclosure, inaccurate.
    (d) double inclusion, the valve casing and discharge pipe serve as the reservoir previously claimed.
    (e) indefinite as to which valve is antecedent.
    (f) indefinite as to which inlet is antecedent.

(Claim 8) Improper dependent claim is not including all elements of base claim, i.e. dependent claim is inconsistent with base claim. No proper antecedent for "said fluid responsive detecting means" since original claim called only for detecting means.

---

*Quoted from Patent Office Approved Answers. Some of these errors required careful study of the specifications and a good knowledge of how the device works.

Case 30

CRITICIZING "SLOPPY CLAIMS"
(Coated Pipe)

FIG.1.

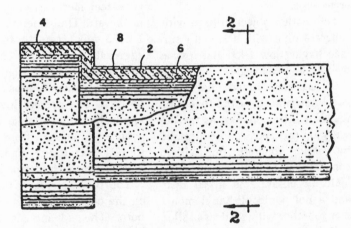

FIG.2.

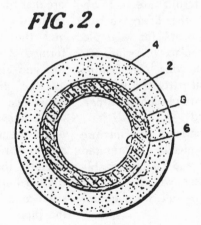

PIPE AND METHOD
OF MAKING SAME

This invention relates to the coating of concrete pipe.

It is an object of the present invention to increase the wear resistance of concrete pipe.

A further object is to increase the chemical resistance of concrete pipe.

Yet another object to to provide concrete pipe with a smooth surface having low frictional loss as well as low cleavage.

It has been found that these and other objects of the invention which will be apparent as the description proceeds can be attained by coating concrete pipe with a composition comprising an ethylenically unsaturated alkyd resin and a polymerizable vinyl monomer together with sand as a filler.

It is important to use sand as satisfactory results are not obtained when other fillers, such as calcium carbonate for example, are used to replace the sand.

In the following specification and claims all parts and percentages are by weight unless otherwise indicated.

For convenience the mixture of an ethylenically unsaturated alkyd resin and polymerizable vinyl monomer will hereinafter alternatively be called a polyester resin.

The coating composition of the polyester resin and sand should contain 50-90% of sand and 10-50% of resin. Preferably, the sand and resin are used in a ratio of 3.8 parts of sand to one part of resin.

The concrete pipe employed is of the conventional type and can be either reinforced or unreinforced. When reinforced pipe is employed, the reinforcing agent is a steel mesh, as is understood in the art. The concrete can be a 1:2.5:5 mix (cement to sand to aggregate), although any conventional concrete that is used to make concrete pipe can also be used. The present invention is applicable to all standard sizes of concrete pipe, e.g., from 4 inches to 12½ feet inside diameter and lengths up to 16 feet or longer.

The pipe can be coated either on the outside or on the inside or both. The advantages obtained by coating the pipe on the inside are that there is a marked increase in the wear resistance of the pipe, and the very smooth surfaces formed result in low frictional loss and also result in low cleavage, i.e., there is prevented the adherence to the pipe of salts and other materials which come out of the liquids which are transmitted through the pipe. Additionally, the polyester and sand coating imparts high chemical resistance to the inside surface of the pipe.

The primary purpose of applying an outside coating of the resin-sand coating composition is to impart high chemical resistance. Without such a coating the concrete pipe is completely unsuitable, for example, to be buried in soils of high acid content. Where there is no problem of chemical attack, however, the outside coating of polyester resin-sand can be omitted. Similarly, where the only problem is attack of the external environment of the pipe, then the internal polyester resin-sand coating can be omitted.

The polyester resin-sand coating can be applied externally by means of a spray gun or paint brush or by trowelling. An internal coating can be applied by the same methods or by extruding the resin-sand composition on the internal surface of the pipe while at the same time imparting a rotation to the pipe. In this latter case, the rotation speed is slow until the resin-sand composition has been inserted and then the speed is increased to uniformly spread the resin-sand coating.

In the drawings:

Figure 1 is a vertical section of a concrete pipe having both an internal and an external coating of the polyester resin-sand composition; and

Figure 2 is a section along the line 2–2 of Figure 1.

Referring more specifically to the drawings, there is shown a concrete pipe 2 having a conventional flange 4 at one end. The pipe throughout its length has an internal coating 6 of polyester resin-sand and an external coating 3 of the same polyester resin-sand composition.

The polyester resin-sand composition normally is applied internally to a thickness of $\frac{1}{16}$ to $\frac{1}{4}$ inch, and externally to the same thickness. Larger thicknesses can be imparted although they are not normally necessary and have the disadvantage of unduly increasing the cost of the finished product.

The polyester resins are a class of resins with which the resin chemist is familiar. The preferred resins of this class for employment in the coating compositions of the invention are the polymeric ester reaction products of one or more dicarboxylic acids and one or more polyhydric alcohols. Desirably one or more of these reactants shall contain a reactive double bond or ethylenic linkage. Among the dicarboxylic acids which may be used are phthalic, malic, maleic, fumaric, adipic, pimelic, suberic, sebacic, itaconic, citraconic, and succinic acids and their anhydrides. It is essential that some of the dicarboxylic acid component of the polyester resin contain an unsaturated ethylenic linkage. For this reason, maleic and fumaric acids are most desirable. Among the polyhydric alcohols which may be used are ethylene glycol, diethylene glycol and propylene glycol. A mixture of propylene glycol and dipropylene glycol is the most satisfactory polyhydric alcohol. One may use an unsaturated monohydric alcohol in place of part of the polyhydric alcohol. A typical example of such an alcohol is allyl alcohol which produces an allyl ester of the dicarboxylic acid. The polyester resins may be suitably modified or plasticized by the incorporation of alcohols, fatty acids, etc., to modify the chemical and physical characteristics as desired. The polyesters should comprise upward from about 15 or 30% and preferably 50% to 85% by weight of the resin and resin forming component, e.g., styrene, of the coating composition.

The resin component of the coating composition should also contain a non-volatile, monomeric, crosslinking solvent for the polyester resin. The function of this solvent is to make the polyester resin more fluid and also to crosslink the polyester resin at the time of curing to produce a crosslinked, or three dimensional resin with the polyester resin which is thermosetting in character. This monomeric solvent is an important member of the resin component, for it provides the necessary fluidity to the resin compo-

nent, imparts thermosetting characteristics to the cured resin and is consumed during the curing of the resin without forming volatile materials. This freedom from volatility is highly important for otherwise the release of volatile matter would produce bubbles, voids or pinholes on the surface and throughout the finished coating of the pipe. The lack of volatile matter permits curing when under pressure without requiring provision for vents, etc., in the molds. Also, escaping combustible, volatile matter may produce explosions, or fire hazards.

Among the monomeric polymerizable solvents which may be used are the hydrocarbons: styrene, vinyl toluene, e.g., o-vinyl toluene, p-vinyl toluene, and m-vinyl toluene, cyclo-pentadiene; vinyl acetate; diallyl esters, e.g., diallyl phthalate and triallyl cyanurate, as well as alpha methyl styrene. Styrene has produced the most satisfactory results thus far.

When produced commercially, these resin compositions also contain a small amount of a polymerization inhibitor so as to prevent gelation during storage prior to usage. Such inhibitors include the well known antioxidants; hydroquinone, t-butyl catechol, quinone, etc.

Polyester resins of the character contemplated for use in the present invention are sold in the trade and identified as "Paraplex" or "Vibrin" resins. In general, these resins are unsaturated high molecular weight polymers made by reacting one or more acids or a blend of acids, such as maleic or fumaric acid, with a dihydroxy alcohol, such as ethylene glycol. The specific properties of these resins vary depending largely upon the type and amount of each constituent in the combination. For best results, I prefer to employ a mixture of two different types of such resins. Certain of these resins form masses upon curing that are very rigid or inflexible, while others form more flexible rubbery masses. For the coating composition of my invention, I prefer to use a mixture of the rigid and flexible resins, and have found that with resins commercially available about 2 to 5 parts of rigid resin and 1 part of flexible resin produce excellent results. These proportions may, of course, be varied within wide limits depending upon the particular properties desired for the cured coating layer and the properties of the resins that are mixed.

I mix the resin and monomeric polymerizable solvent, such as styrene or other othylenically unsaturated monomer, e.g., vinyl acetate or vinyl toluene, with the finely divided sand filler to form a coating composition having the consistency of a thick slurry. The monomer is used in an amount of 15-85% or occasionally slightly more of the total of resin solids and monomer. Preferably, the monomer is employed in an amount of 50-85% of this resin solids-monomer liquid mix. About 40% resin solids and 60% styrene has been found to give a good workable consistency when employed with the sand, especially when the ratio of sand to polyester resin is about 3.8 to 1. The sand filler is finely divided silica which can be obtained from any source as silica. While sand is the preferred filler because of its chemical inertness and hardness, it is also possible to use other finely divided acid-resistant crushed rock as fillers, e.g., gravel.

The sand increases the hardness and strength of the coated surface. While it is possible to employ irregularly shaped particles of sand, it is preferable to use rounded particles of the sand filler.

While the sand can be of uniform particle size, e.g., between 30 and 200 mesh (U.S. Standard Sieve Series), it is preferable to employ sand having a gradation of particle size. When there is a gradation of particle size of the sand filler, there preferably is a gradual diminution in the quantity of material (by weight) corresponding to each sieve size as one goes from larger to smaller

Standard Sieve sizer.

In practice, satisfactory results may be obtained by using particles having at least two general particle size classifications, one of which may be said to be of large size (in the order of 30-70 mesh) and another of small size (in the order of 100-325 mesh). It has been found desirable to employ a major proportion, and preferably 60% or more, by weight, of the large size particles. One particularly successful gradation has been one in which about 65% by weight of the filler is of sand of approximately 40-70 mesh and 35% is of 70-140 mesh size. I have found also that a gradation of 80% of the former mesh size and 20% of the latter is equally satisfactory.

In addition to using a gradation of particle size of filler material, I prefer to use some filler of extremely small particle size, in the order of 325-mesh or smaller. Such material is sold under the designation "silica flour" or "Surfex." I prefer to add this material to the liquid resin component of the coating composition.

If desired, it is possible to add pigments and dyes for decorative purposes, but normally there is no need to utilize such materials. Either just prior to or just subsequent to mixing the polyester resin with the filler, a suitable polymerization catalyst should be added. The mixture of polyester resin, sand and catalyst is then applied to the pipe in one of the manners previously set forth. The resin is cured on the pipe at a temperature from room temperature up to about 350° F. To obtain a quick cure, temperatures in the upper range, e.g., 325-350° F., are preferable. Where time is not of the essence, lower temperatures can be satisfactorily employed.

As the catalysts there can be utilized numerous oxidizing catalysts, such as cumene hydroperoxide, dicumyl peroxide, benzoyl peroxide, and methyl ethyl ketone peroxide. The catalyst is usually employed in an amount of 0.4-4% of the polyester resin. Preferably, there is utilized with the catalyst a metallic drier such as manganese or cobalt naphthenate, for example. A typical example of a satisfactory catalyst-drier combination is 2% benzoyl peroxide, .75% manganese naphthenate and .75% cobalt naphthenate based on the polyester resin when using a cure in the upper end of the temperature range previously set forth.

On occasion it has been found advantageous to incorporate into the coating slurry a small percent, e.g. 1½-2% by weight of the total slurry of a cation modified clay, such as those disclosed in Hauser Patent 2,531,427. A preferred material of this class is dimethyl-dioctadecylammonium bentonite which is sold under the name "Bentone 34."

Typical examples of polyester resin-sand compositions which may be employed in forming the inside or the outside coating on the pipe are given below.

Example 1

A coating composition was prepared by stirring in a mixing vessel just prior to the coating operation an initial mixture having the following composition:

A mixture of about 27% by weight of polyester resins made up of 3 parts of rigid type polyester resin (Paraplex P43, believed to be a condensation product of propylene glycol and dipropylene glycol in the ratio of 1 to 3 with phthalic anhydride and maleic anhydride in ratio of 3 to 2) and 1 part of flexible type polyester resin (Paraplex P13, believed to be a condensation product of ethylene glycol and diethylene glycol with phthalic anhydride, maleic anhydride and adipic acid), 23% by weight of styrene monomer, 5% by weight of titanium dioxide as a pigment, and about 45% by weight of #325-mesh asbestine ....lbs.. 25.5

To this initial mixture were added the following:

Styrene monomer (solvent) .... lbs..	6.5
Bentone 34 (dimethyldioctadecylammonium bentonite) .... lbs..	0.5
Methyl ethyl ketone peroxide (catalyst) .... cc..	250
Manganese naphthenate (catalyst) .... lbs..	0.4

The resulting mix was agitated and to it was added promptly the following fillers:

86 lbs. crystal silica sand having the following approximate sieve analysis—

	Approx.
Sieve sizes:	percentages
No. 40	38.0
No. 50	41.0
No. 70	14.0
No. 100	4.0

22 lbs. banding sand having the following approximate sieve analysis—

	Approx.
Sieve sizes:	percentages
No. 50	0.9
No. 70	20.0
No. 100	48.2
No. 140	20.9
No. 200	7.0
No. 270	2.5

Example 2

	Parts by weight
Rigid type polyester resin (Paraplex P43)	45
Flexible type polyester resin (Paraplex P13)	15
Methyl ethyl ketone peroxide (catalyst)	2
Manganese naphthenate (catalyst)	2
Titanium dioxide (pigment)	12
Resin coated calcium carbonate (Surfex, believed to be calcium carbonate coated with polydimethyl siloxane resin) (filler)	19
Bentono 34 (dimethyldioctadecylammonium bentonite)	2
Monomeric styrene (solvent)	3
Total	100

To this mixture was added about 2 parts of silica sand to 1 part of the mixture. This silica sand was composed of about 65% by weight of particles of about 40 to 50 sieve size and 35% of about 100 sieve size.

Example 3

A solid polyester resin was prepared from 1266 pounds phthalic anhydride, 636 pounds maleic anhydride, 501 pounds dipropylene glycol and 855 pounds of propylene glycol. This resin which possessed an acid number of 35, was admixed with 1.32 pounds of hydroquinone as an inhibitor. This mixture of resin and inhibitor was diluted with 1284 pounds of styrene.

To 52 pounds of this resin, inhibitor and styrene mixture, there were added 1.5 pounds of benzoyl peroxide and 1.5 pounds of methyl ethyl ketone peroxide as well as 1.5 pounds of manganese naphthenate, 0.5 pound of cobalt naphthenate, 4.5 pounds of titanium dioxide (pigment), 1.5 pounds of Bentone 34, 5 pounds of antimony trioxide, 10 pounds of solid chlorinated paraffin and 18 pounds of styrene.

To one pound of the above composition, there is added 3.8 pounds of graded silica sand (of the same composition as in Example 1).

Example 4

The coating composition prepared in Example 1 was applied to the interior of the reinforced concrete pipe of 6 feet internal diameter by employing a spray gun. The coating was smoothed out by applying a sheet of cellophane over the coating and allowing the cellophane to remain until the coating composition had cured at room temperature. This took about 24 hours. The cellophane was then removed and the resulting coating on the interior of the pipe had a smooth surface.

The same procedure was employed to coat the exterior of the pipe with the composition of Example 1 and in similar fashion the coating was made smooth by the use of a cellophane covering which was subsequently removed after the resin had cured.

The finished product after removal of the cellophane is illustrated in Figure 1.

Example 5

A reinforced concrete pipe of 12 feet internal diameter and 2 feet in length was placed on rollers which were suitably connected to a variable speed motor. The resin-sand composition prepared in Example 3 was introduced to the interior of the pipe through a flexible hose. The hose was attached to a piston which was actuated by a cylinder containing compressed air. The piston was of sufficient length that the hose could travel from one end of the pipe to the other. The variable speed motor was started so that the pipe rotated at a speed of about ⅓ of a revolution per minute, and the resin was allowed to drip into the pipe through the hose. Simultaneously, the piston was actuated so that the resin composition was supplied throughout the length of the pipe. After three minutes, the resin had been supplied to the entire pipe and the piston and hose were removed from the interior of the pipe. The variable speed motor was then adjusted so that the pipe rotated at about 80 r.p.m. and this speed of rotation was continued for about three minutes in order to make the coating uniform throughout the pipe. The motor was then shut off.

Next, there were inserted into the pipe 2 split hemispherical steel molds which were kept apart by a jack. These molds were covered with cellophane as a parting agent and the jack was raised so that the cellophane coating on the split mold contacted the coating composition. The coating composition was then allowed to cure for about 24 hours at room temperature and the jack released so that the mold could be removed. The resulting coating on the interior of the pipe was smooth. In this example the split mold could be made of wood, metal or other material, and the parting agent could be a polytetrafluoroethylene coating or a silicon, e.g., a polymeric dimethyl-siloxane coating.

Example 6

Example 5 was repeated but the curing time was reduced to 30 minutes by placing the entire assembly of pipe and split molds in an oven heated to 325° F.

Example 7

An unreinforced concrete pipe of 6 inch internal diameter and 3 feet in length was coated on the outside with the composition of Example 2 by the brush method. A cellophane film was applied over the coating to smooth out the same and the pipe was then placed in an oven at 350° F. for 30 minutes in order to cure the resin. After removal from the oven, the cellophane film was taken off. The resulting pipe had a smooth, hard coating of the polyester resin-sand composition.

Problem*

This part of the examination requires analysis of 6 claims proposed to be added to an application having the accompanying specification and drawing. Certain words and phrases in the claims have been underlined, and designated by a number in parentheses. *Most, but not all* of the underlined portions represent instances wherein the claims fail to comply with United States patent law or accepted claim writing practice. For each number before an underlined section, make a short statement as to why the underlined portion does represent one or more defects, if such is the case.

7. (1) *a pipe having chemical and heat resistant properties* comprising a base pipe material and (2) *a coating applied on the exterior, on the interior, or on both the exterior and interior of the concrete base,* said coating being formed from a composition consisting of a polyester resin, (3) *a granular filler material,* a polymerization catalyst, and (4) *a polymerization inhibitor selected from the group comprising hydroquinone, t-butyl catechol, or quinone.*

8. A pipe as defined in claim 7 in which the granular filler material (5) *is sand.*

---

*Reprinted as given on Aug. 26, 1969, Exam.

9. A method of treating a concrete pipe to impart wear resistance which comprises (6) *the steps of coating the inner surfaces of the pipe with a composition comprising an unsaturated polyester resin, styrene monomer, and* (7) *a catalyst selected from the group consisting of dicumyl peroxide and benzoyl peroxide, applying sand of 40-140 mesh size to the coating on the pipe, and curing the coating at 325° F.*

10. (8) *A pipe as defined in claim 8 in which the sand is used in a ratio of 3.8 parts to one part of resin.*

11. A pipe as described in claim 7 in which the composition includes (9) *a pigment to impart a desired color to the pipe.*

12. (10) *A novel pipe comprising concrete, and a composition of polyester resin, sand, and a catalyst curing agent.*

Case 30

CRITICIZING "SLOPPY CLAIMS"
(COATED PIPE)

COMMENTS

1. (a) Lower case "a" improper as first word.
   (b) No support for "heat resistant."
2. (a) Alternative expression is indefinite.
   (b) No antecedent for "concrete."
3. "Granular material" is too broad since specification indicates that only certain materials (e.g. sand, gravel) will yield satisfactory results.
4. Improper Markush claiming by reason of (a) "comprising" and (b) "or."
5. No error involved.
6. Sequence of steps not supported by disclosure—sand is incorporated in composition prior to application to pipe.
7. No error—proper Markush group.
8. Claim 10 is an improper dependent claim because it is separated from a previous dependent claim. MPEP 608.01(n).
9. Addition of pigment renders the claim inconsistent with parent claim in which the composition is limited ("consisting of") to certain stated components.
10. (a) "Novel" is surplusage.
    (b) Mere catalog of elements—does not set forth structural relationship of concrete and composition.

---

*Quoted from Patent Office Approved Answers.

Case 31

CRITICIZING "SLOPPY CLAIMS"
(Golf Ball Cleaner)

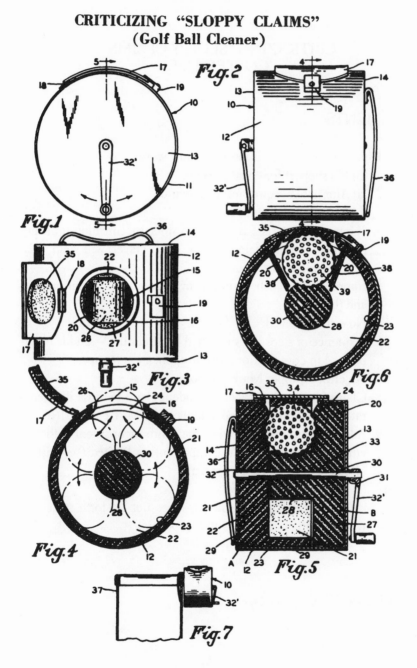

BALL WASHING APPARATUS

Our present invention relates to ball washing apparatus and more particularly and specifically to a portable golf ball washer which may be conveniently attached to a golf bag, wheeled caddy or the like in a readily available position for use by a golfer during play, and a washer which may be easily and conveniently stored in a pocket of the golf bag during periods of non-use.

Generally, certain golf ball washing apparatus constructions have been used heretofore for the purposes of cleaning dirt, grass stains and the like from the covers of golf balls. However, such prior apparatus as has been heretofore provided has had numerous disadvantages both from the standpoint of construction as well as from the standpoint of function and availability of use.

Certain of these prior golf ball washer constructions include a container provided with a pair of spaced brushes fixed in the container and a paddle like golf ball holder reciprocably supported between the brushes for the purpose of moving a golf ball back and forth in contact with the brush surfaces for cleaning the same.

In these prior constructions, the cleaning of golf balls is accomplished by the brushing action on the ball covers accompanied by the application to the balls of a liquid detergent solution which is carried in the container to a depth of approximately one-half the height of the brushes therein.

In the use of such prior constructions as those above noted, it has been discovered that during the hot days normal to the golfing season the detergent solution contained in the washers will evaporate rapidly thus necessitating constant refilling of the washers by golf course personnel in order to maintain the washers in satisfactorily operable condition. Unfortunately, the time and labor requirements necessary to maintain a program of refilling for washers of this type has resulted in a great laxity toward that end, thereby leaving such ball washers unattended and as such substantially useless to golfers.

Certain other types of prior constructions have been tried, but all of such constructions have required the maintenance of a liquid detergent level therein at all times in order to render the construction operative. Thus all prior constructions have the inherent disadvantages common to those above denoted relative to the evaporation of the cleaning solutions.

Another disadvantage in the use of prior constructions is inherent in the fact that such constructions are bulky and thus require stationary foundations for placement at intervals about a golf course where they are available to golfers. However, it has been the practice because of the costs involved in the provision of such washers as well as in the necessity that their placement be at points of normal congregation of all golfers to restrict the placement of such prior apparatus to points adjacent tees or greens about the course. Further, it has been an unfortunate practice for golf courses of the unusual management to space stationary washers of the type above noted at intervals of every other or every third tee about the course because of the requirements noted as well as the initial costs of installation.

Thus, the average golfer is confronted with a lack of facility to properly wash or clean dirty golf balls at points about the course other than those widely spaced stationary washers of the type above noted.

It is a general object of the present invention to provide a golf ball washer which substantially eliminates those disadvantages inherent in both the construction, use and availability of prior known apparatus.

Another object of the present invention lies in the provision of a portable golf ball washer which may be carried by each individual golfer in his golf bag with a minimum requirement of storage space, and a washer which may be quickly and easily attached to the golf bag or on a wheeled caddy in a position of ready availability for use at any time and at any point in his travels about a course.

Still another object of the present invention resides in the provision of a portable golf ball washer which eliminates the necessity of maintaining free liquid in the washer for washing purposes thus avoiding the spilling of detergent solutions in or on the golf bag of the user, and a washer which will remain in operable washing condition for long periods of time without the necessity of reconditioning the same by the addition of washing solutions.

Still a further object is to provide a golf ball washer which may be removably attached to a golf bag, a wheeled caddy or the like in such a position as to make it readily available for use by either right or left handed persons at any time.

Still another important object of the present invention is to provide a portable golf ball washer which is of substantially simple and inexpensive design and manufacture and which is highly efficient and easily operable in use for the purpose of cleaning those dirty substances from golf balls which are normally incurred with the use of the same.

These and other objects are accomplished by the .parts, constructions, arrangements, combinations and subcombinations comprising the present invention, the nature of which is set forth in the following general statement, and preferred embodiments of which—illustrative of the best modes in which applicants have contemplated applying the principles—are set forth in the following description and illustrated in the accompanying drawings, and which are particularly and distinctly pointed out and set forth in the appended claims forming a part hereof.

The nature of the present invention may be stated in general terms as including a cylindrical container taking the form of a housing, a pair of members of a spongy, liquid absorbent material substantially filling the housing, an arcuate passage formed in said spongy material between said members, said passage being of slightly lesser breadth than the diameter of a golf ball, an opening in said housing communicating with said passage to permit the insertion of a golf ball into said passage and its removal therefrom, a portion of said spongy material defining said passage being mounted for rotation relative to said container and said golf ball, whereupon a golf ball inserted in said passage will be resiliently abraded by those areas of the spongy material defining the passage, a hand crank means on said container having operable engagement with said movable portion of said spongy material, closure means on said container for said opening, and clip means on said container for removably securing the container to a golf bag, wheeled caddy or the like.

In the accompanying drawings in which like numerals designate similar parts throughout the several views:

Figure 1 is a side elevation of the washer;

Fig. 2 is an end view of the washer;

Fig. 3 is a plan view of the washer with the closure member in open condition;

Fig. 4 is a vertical section on line 4–4, Fig. 2 with the closure member in open condition;

Fig. 5 is a vertical section on line 5–5, Fig. 1 looking in the direction indicated;

Fig. 6 is a vertical section similar to Fig. 4 illustrating a modified construction of the washer; and

Fig. 7 is a pictorial illustration of the washer attached to a golf bag.

Referring now in particular to the accompanying drawings, the ball washer constituting the present invention is generally indicated at 10 and includes a cylindrical container 11 forming a housing having a continuous cylindrical wall 12 closed at each end by end walls 13 and 14. The cylindrical wall 12 is provided with a substantially circular access opening 15 therein which opening is of a slightly greater diameter than the diameter of a golf ball. The peripheral edges of the opening 15 are finished off with a circular rubber grommet 16 which is of general U-shaped configuration in cross section and which is applied as an edging strip to the container edges defining the opening. A curved or arcuate cover plate 17 is hinged as at 18 to the continuous cylindrical wall of the housing to form a closure member for the access opening 15. A suitable releasable catch member 19 is secured to the housing in such a manner as to selectively engage that edge of the cover plate opposite its hinged connection to lock the cover plate in closed condition over the access opening.

Interiorly the housing is provided with separate, complementary portions of a spongy, liquid absorbent material 20, which portions are so arranged within the container so as to define generally between them an annular passage 21 which is located within the container concentrically of the cylindrical wall thereof and which

is centered substantially equidistant between the end walls of the container, as is best seen in Fig. 5.

Referring to Fig. 5, one of those portions A of the spongy, liquid absorbent material 20 located in the washer housing takes the form of a circular cup 21 having a circular body portion 22 provided with a perpendicular ring flange or rim 23 extending outwardly about the entire circumference of the body portion except where it is broken off to provide a channel 24 therethrough, having tapered edges 26, (Fig. 4) to coincide with the peripheral edges of the access opening 15 in the container. A second portion B of the spongy liquid absorbent material takes the form of a circular disc 27 provided with a circular hub 28 extending outwardly centrally from one face of the disc 27, said circular hub extending outwardly from the disc a distance substantially equal to the depth of the peripheral rim flange 23 of the cup member 21.

The cup member 21 is disposed with the base portion thereof against the inner face of the end wall 14 of the housing to which it is secured by suitable adhesive means 29 and which disposition places the outer face of the rim flange 23 thereof in juxtaposition with the inner face of the cylindrical wall 12 of the housing substantially centrally between the ends thereof with the channel 26 in the rim flange coinciding with the access opening 15 in the container as is best seen in Fig. 4. The outer face of the rim flange 23 is also connected as at 29 to the inner face of the cylindrical wall 12.

A shaft 30 is extended through said container on the longitudinal axis thereof and is journaled in bearings 31 and 32 carried by the end walls 13 and 14 of the container respectively. Externally of the container wall 13, and beyond the bearing 31, the shaft 30 is provided with a crank handle 32′ for manual rotation of the shaft 30 in the bearing.

The second portion B of the spongy material is mounted on the shaft 30 with the shaft extending centrally through the hub portion 28. The mounting of sponge portion B on shaft 30 positions hub 28 centrally within the cup-shaped member 21. The disc 27 and hub member 28 constituting the second spongy portion B are cemented as at 33 to the shaft 30 to space the extended end of the hub portion at a slight clearance from the base portion of the circular cup member 21, and to cause rotation of the disc and hub with the shaft. The aforedescribed complementary assembly of the first sponge portion A and the second sponge portion B

provides for the formation of the annular passage 21 defined in cross section between the base portion and the rim flange of the sponge portion A and the disc portion and extended hub of the sponge portion B.

The cross sectional area of the annular passage 21 is such that when a golf bag 34 is placed downwardly through the access opening 15 of the container into the passage through the channel 26 in the rim flange 23 of the first sponge portion A, limited areas of the ball cover will resiliently embed themselves in the spongy material in the portions A and B as is best seen in Fig. 5.

A section of spongy, liquid absorbent material of general circular configuration is applied as at 35 to the inner face of the cover plate 17 so that when said cover plate is closed this section of spongy material will complete the continuity of the circular rim flange 23 on the sponge portion A by filling in the channel 26 therein.

Thus, when a ball is inserted into the annular passage 21 and the cover is closed, those portions of the golf ball immediately surrounding the intersecting perpendicular axes of the ball will be impressed into the spongy material and will be subject to resilient abrasion upon relative movement of the ball and portions of said spongy material.

To complete the construction of the ball washer as described heretofore, a resilient, substantially U-shaped clip 36 is secured to the outer face of the end wall 14 of the housing for the purposes of permitting detachable connection of the washer housing to a golf bag by any one of several possible modes of connection, one of such modes being illustrated in Fig. 7 where the clip is inserted downwardly over the top edge of a golf bag 37 adjacent the inner face of the bag with the washer 10 disposed adjacent the outer face of the bag with the access opening 15 therein disposed upwardly for the convenient insection of a ball thereinto, and with the handle 32′ disposed outwardly away from the bag to facilitate rotation of the shaft 30 and rotation of the sponge portion B and the golf ball 34.

To condition the ball washer for use, a liquid detergent solution is introduced into the container wherein the spongy material portions A and B absorb a substantial portion of such detergent solution for retention therein.

After completely wetting the spongy portions within the container, all free liquid remaining in the container is emptied out and the cover is closed and secured thus permitting the easy

storage and transportation of the ball washer. The closure plate 17 also substantially seals the housing preventing loss of the detergent solution through evaporation.

When the washer is attached to a golf bag, as shown in Fig. 7, the cover plate 17 may be opened and one or more golf balls 34 inserted into the annular passage 21 in the container through the access opening 15. These golf balls will be moved through the annular passage 21 in either a clockwise or counterclockwise direction, as indicated by arrows in Fig. 4, dependent upon the direction of operation of the crank handle 32′ by the resilient, frictional movement of the disc 27 and the hub 28 in engagement with the ball 34. When such ball or balls return to a position immediately beneath the access opening 15 the resilience of the central hub portion 28 will cause the balls to spring upwardly to positions partially clear of the access opening 15 permitting their ready removal from the washer.

During movement of the golf balls 34 through the annular passage, the balls will be oscillated and rotated without any uniform pattern by reason of the frictional braking action applied to the ball by the stationary cup member 21 and the frictional impelling action of the disc 27 and hub 28 whereby all surface areas of the ball cover will be resiliently abraded or rubbed by the detergent solution bearing spongy material thereby cleaning all foreign substances from the cover of the ball.

Referring to Fig. 6, a modification of the present ball washer is shown wherein the construction of the container and the spongy portions therein are identical with those aforedescribed. In this modified construction, a pair of stop members or gates 38 are secured to the inner face of the container at spaced positions on either side of the access opening 15 in the general direction of the annular passage. The stop members 38 are faced with spongy material 20. These stops extend substantially radially inwardly into the annular passage 21 to restrict movement of a golf ball 39 positioned in said passage and to maintain the ball within a fixed region immediately below the access opening 15 in the container. In this modified construction, a ball positioned in the annular passage 21 between the stop members or gates 38 will, when the cover plate 17 is closed and locked, have portions thereof embedded on all sides in spongy material 20, as aforedescribed relative to the previously disclosed construction, and rotation of the sponge portion B will cause oscillation, twisting and rotation of the ball

in contact with the spongy material thereby cleaning all foreign substances from the cover of the ball. Upon opening of the cover plate 17 there will be a resilient projection of the ball by hub 28 upwardly and outwardly of the access opening 15 for its removal from the container.

While in the instant disclosures the annular passage 21 is shown with a rectangular cross section, since such a configuration constitutes the most economical construction, it is fully contemplated that the sponge portions defining the annular passage could be so shaped as to provide an annular passage of round or oval cross-sectional configuration without departing from the spirit and scope of this invention.

It is further contemplated that any wet retaining material such as sponge rubber, neoprene or the like could be utilized as the abrading detergent holding means within the container of the washer construction shown and described.

Accordingly, a portable golf ball washer is provided which has inherently all those attributes, objects and advantages set forth above, and which provides an extremely new and useful article of manufacture of a type and function unique in the light of prior constructions.

In the foregoing description,

certain terms have been used for brevity, clearness and understanding, but no unnecessary limitations are to be implied therefrom beyond the requirements of the prior art, because such words are used for descriptive purposes herein and are intended to be broadly construed.

Moreover, the embodiments of the improved construction illustrated and described herein are by way of example, and the scope of the invention is not limited to the exact details of construction.

Having now described the invention, the construction, the operation and use of preferred embodiments thereof, and the advantageous new and useful results obtained thereby; the new and useful construction, and reasonable mechanical equivalents thereof obvious to those skilled in the art, are set forth in the appended claims.

PROBLEM*

This part of the examination requires analysis of 5 claims proposed to be added to an application having the accompanying specification and drawing. Certain phrases in the claims have been *underlined* and designated by a number in parenthesis. Most, but not all of the underlined portions represent instances wherein the claims fail to comply with United States patent law or accepted claim writing practice. For each number before an underlined section, make a short statement as to why the underlined portion does represent a defect, if such is the case.

3. A golf ball washer comprising (1) *a first housing,* said housing having (2) *at least one access opening* therethrough, means for selectively closing said opening, a first body of absorbent material fixed to a portion of said housing (3) *by adhesively securing* said first body to said housing on the inside thereof, a second body of

absorbent material within (4) *said cylindrical housing,* means including a shaft mounting (5) *one of said first and second bodies for rotation* relative to said housing, said bodies defining an annular chamber therebetween, and means attached to said shaft for manually rotating said rotatable body; (6) *a detergent solution is contained within the absorbent material of said first and second bodies.*

4. A washer as set forth in claim 3 wherein (7) *the first and second bodies cooperate with one another to form an annular chamber.*

5. A washer as defined in claim 3 wherein (8) *the means for rotating said rotatable body is omitted.*

6. A washer as recited in claim 3 in which the absorbent material of both said first and second bodies is (9) *selected from the group consisting of neoprene and sponge rubber.*

7. A washer as defined in claim 3 wherein said means for rotating said rotatable body includes a crank attached to said shaft and (10) *means for rotating said crank.*

---

*Reprinted as given on March 31, 1970, Exam.

Case 31

CRITICIZING "SLOPPY CLAIMS"
(GOLF BALL CLEANER)

COMMENTS*

1. "First" is surplusage.
2. "At least one" is improper since there is no support in the disclosure for more than one.
3. Improper method limitation.
4. "Cylindrical" does not have antecedent basis in the claim.
5. The recitation is inaccurate and inconsistent with the preceding recitations in the claim, since the first body has previously been defined as being fixed; accordingly, only the second body may rotate. [Here use of "is" causes the problem.]
6. The recitation is improper, since a claim must be the object of a single sentence starting with "I (or We) claim" (or the equivalent).
7. The recitation is a double inclusion of the previously recited element in Claim 3.
8. A dependent claim is not proper if it expressly omits a previously recited element since an essential characteristic of a proper dependent claim is that it shall include every limitation of the claim from which it depends. **
9. No error; proper Markush group.
10. The recitation is unsupported in the specification because there is no disclosure of structural means for rotating the crank. The specification only discloses the operator's hand for rotating the crank which cannot be claimed.

---

*Quoted from Patent Office Approved Answers.
**Full credit was given for alternate answer drawn to claim 5 being incomplete because it omits an essential element of the invention.

Case 32
CRITICIZING "SLOPPY CLAIMS"
(Foam Breaking)

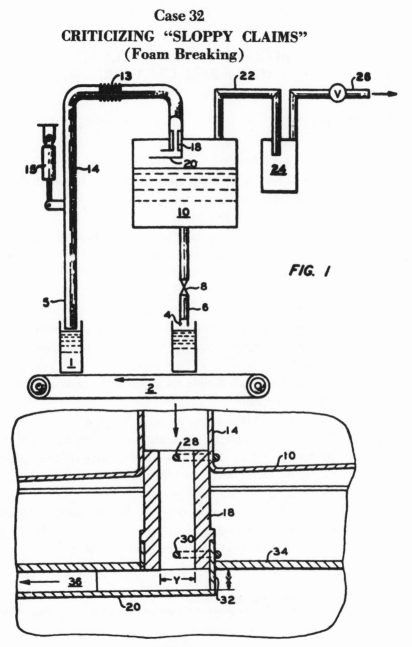

FIG. 1

FIG. 2

FOAM BREAKING

ABSTRACT
OF THE DISCLOSURE

Foam is passed through a cylindrical constriction and directed against a solid plate surface positioned substantially perpendicularly to the line of flow of the impinging foam, at a velocity sufficiently great to break down the foam. The ratio of the distance between the effluent end of the constriction and the solid plate surface to the diameter of the constriction is in the range of 0.25 to 1.

This invention relates to foam breaking. In one of its aspects, it relates to a method and apparatus for converting foam to a liquid by impinging the foam on a surface at such a force that the foam is thereby substantially destroyed and converted to liquid.

A milk filling apparatus for filling paper milk cartons uses one or more sets of piston and valve arrangements to pump a metered volume of milk into the cartons. This method and apparatus create foam on top of the liquid, which foam must be removed prior to the closing of the top of the cartons.

Many methods of breaking foam have been devised. Naucler 2,184,195 discloses a method of breaking foam in which foam is taken from a tank and passed through a pump to increase the pressure thereon and the foam is then sprayed back into the tank through a nozzle which emits the foam in a conical spray so that the individual froth bubbles travel in diverse directions to stretch the froth layer until the bubbles burst. This apparatus, due to the pump, subjects the foam material to contamination and is expensive. Further it is relatively inefficient.

One system for removing foam from the top of milk cartons is to direct a blast of live steam into the carton or in the filler bowl to eliminate rather than remove the foam. This method adequately eliminates the foam but is undesirable because live steam is dangerous. Further, there is some degree of water dilution to the milk, milk particles become cooked and give milk an off-flavor, and this method is expensive to incorporate into a commercial operation.

It was thought that the problem of foam formation in the top of the milk cartons could be overcome by drawing off the foam and returning it to the filler tank. However, the foam builds up in the tank to the point that it discharges from the blower used to draw the foam into the tank and must be trapped in a can. Using this method, about 100 to 200 gallons of milk per day will be trapped; however, this milk cannot be used as premium grade milk but must be reprocessed and used as a by-product.

I have now discovered that milk foam can be broken without loss of quality of material and with a minimum of equipment by impinging the foam against a solid surface at such a velocity that the foam is thereby broken.

By various aspects of this invention one or more of the following or other objects can be obtained.

It is an object of this invention to provide a novel process and apparatus for breaking foam.

It is a further object of this invention to provide a novel process and apparatus for recovering milk foam resulting from the filling of milk cartons.

It is a still further object of this invention to provide an economical process and apparatus for recovering milk foam from a filling operation without loss of quality of the removed product.

Other aspects, objects, and the several advantages of this invention are apparent to one skilled in the art from a study of this disclosure, the drawings, and the appended claims.

According to the invention, a foamed liquid is converted back into the liquid state by impinging the liquid against a surface at such a velocity that the form is thereby broken. This process is advantageously employed in breaking milk foam which results from filling of milk cartons.

In one embodiment the foam is drawn through a constriction prior to being impinged on the surface. In another embodiment the surface is perpendicular to the direction of flow of the foam at the surface.

The invention will now be described with reference to the accompanying drawings in which FIGURE 1 schematically shows an embodiment of the invention and FIGURE 2 is a detailed view of a portion of the apparatus schematically shown in FIGURE 1.

Referring now to the drawings, a plurality of cartons 1 traveling on conveyor 2 are systematically filled by filling spout 4 which has supplied to it milk which passes through line 6 from tank 10. A valve 8 is advantageously provided in line 6 to stop the flow of milk into the cartons at fixed periods of time or after a predetermined quantity of milk has been discharged. Milk is maintained in tank 10 at a predetermined level schematically shown in FIGURE 1. After the cartons have been filled and some foam remains on top, valve 8 is closed. The filled carton is then conveyed to a foam removal station and foam removal nozzle 5 is lowered into the carton by means 15 such as an air cylinder and a vacuum source 26 draws foam from carton 1 through nozzle 5, line 14, flexible connection 13 through restriction 18 in line 14, and impinges the foam against surface 20. The impingement of foam against surface 20 is at such a velocity that the foam will be converted to milk and fall back down into the tank. A suitable draw-off conduit 22 with trap-out tank 24 it provided for vacuum source 26.

Referring now to FIGURE 2 wherein a detailed version of the restriction means 18 and plate 20 is seen. As can be seen from the drawing, the restriction means 18 comprises a cylindrical tube through which the foam passes. This restriction increases the velocity of the foam through line 14. Restriction 18 has pin 28 which extends through line 14 to hold restriction 18 in line 14. Another pin 30 attaches to member 32, which is in turn attached to plate 20, and to restriction 18. Member 32, the bottom portion of which is U-shaped, has an outlet at 36. As can be seen from the figure the plate 20 is substantially perpendicular to the line of flow of the foam at plate 20. Other supporting means such as a baffle 34 can be employed to maintain restriction 18 and member 32 in place.

The distance between plate 20 and the end of restriction 18 is designated by the letter X, The diameter of the constriction is designated by Y. The ratio of X to Y can be important in breaking the foam. As is understood by one skilled in the art there is a minimum velocity of the foam which is required, however. This velocity is achieved by the suction means 26. Generally, the suction means must be less than 5, preferably in the range of 8 to 10 inches of Hg below atmospheric pressure. For a suction within the tank below the minimum value and within the preferred range, the ratio of X to Y will advantageously be in the range of .25 to 1, preferably .50 to .60.

Although the invention has been described with relation to impinging the foam against a surface which is perpendicular to the direction of flow at the surface, it is obvious that the surface could be slightly inclined as long as the flow is impinged against the surface at such velocity that the foam is thereby broken. Of course, it is preferred that the surface be perpendicular to the flow of foam so that a minimum velocity will be required.

It has been found that milk foam from milk cartons has been broken very effectively using an apparatus such as that hereinbefore described with the use of an American Blower Company, Size D, centrifugal fan with a 14 inch fan and a 3 inch pipe operating at a speed of 3600 r.p.m. Under these conditions the vacuum pulled in the tank 10 was in the range of 8 to 10 inches of Hg below atmospheric pressure and the velocity of the foam was estimated to be between 40 to 80 feet per second, probably about 60 feet per second.

Whereas the invention has been described with relation to having the impinging surface within the tank, it is obvious that the surface can be without the tank and a conduit can be used to drain the liquid into tank 10 from the surface.

Whereas the invention has been described with relation to breaking milk foam, it is obvious that other types of foams can be broken by the use of the invention. Other foams include beer, soap and the like.

---

*Excerpted from instructions given on Sept. 15, 1970, Exam.

PROBLEM*

This part of the examination requires analysis of claims proposed to be added to an application already on file in the United States Patent Office from which claims 1-9 have been cancelled and having the [accompanying] specification and drawings directed to "Foam Breaking."

Certain words and phrases in the claims have been underlined and designated by number in parenthesis.

Some, but not all, of the underlined portions represent instances wherein the claims fail to comply with United States Patent Law or accepted claim writing practice.

. . . [S]tate whether each items (1) through (12) is "proper" or "improper" and if "improper" why so.

10. An apparatus for converting foam to a liquid comprising a tank means to hold a quantity of liquid, (1) *outlet means or equivalent means* at the bottom of said tank means to pass liquid from said tank, said outlet means adapted to fill a container and (2) *draw liquid therefrom,* conduit means to remove foam from (3) *said filled containers,* said conduit means leading to said tank means, a solid plate having a surface thereof positioned substantially perpendicularly to the line of flow of said conduit means, (4) *means to draw said foam* through said conduit means at such a velocity that said

foam impinges on said surface and will thereby be converted to (5) *fluid,* a constriction provided within said conduit means adjacent the outlet end thereof and adjacent said surface, the ratio of the distance from the end of said constriction to said surface to the diameter of said constriction being in the range of 0.25 to 1.

11. (6) *An apparatus for converting foam to a liquid comprising a tank means to hold a quantity of liquid, outlet means at the bottom of said tank means to pass liquid from said tank means, said outlet means adapted to fill a milk carton, conduit means to remove foam from milk carton, said conduit leading to said tank, and means to draw said foam through said conduit.*

12. A method of converting (7) *liquid to a foam* which comprises passing said foam through a substantially cylindrical constriction to increase the velocity of the foam passing therethrough and impinging the effluent from said constriction against a solid plate positioned substantially perpendicular to the line of flow of the impinging foam, at a velocity sufficiently great to break down the foam, (8) *the ratio of the distance between the effluent end of said constriction and said solid plate surface to the diameter of said constriction being in the range of 0.2 to 1.*

13. (9) *The product produced by the process of claim 12.*

14. The method of claim 11 wherein (10) *said ratio is in the range of 0.4 to 0.6.*

Case 32

CRITICIZING "SLOPPY CLAIMS"
(FOAM BREAKING)

COMMENTS*

1. The recitation is improper because of the inclusion therein of "or equivalent means." Such inclusion is improper because (i) the expression is thus rendered alternative, MPEP 706.03(d), or (ii) the meaning of "equivalents thereof" is not necessary to cover the invention (2 points).

2. The phrase is improper because it is vague and indefinite, MPEP 706.03(d), or no antecedent for "outlet means" (2 points).

3. The phrase is improper because there is no antecedent basis therefor or because the scope is vague and indefinite. MPEP 706.03(d) (2 points).

4. The phrase is considered proper (2 points).

5. The phrase is improper. The term "fluid" is broader than the written disclosure. The term should be "liquid" because fluid includes gases. Also, no antecedent basis for "fluid" exists (2 points).

6. This phrase is improper because (i) it reads on the prior art described in the specification or (ii) it omits material limitations or (iii) it is misdescriptive (4 points).

7. The phrase is improper because the process described in the specification converts a foam to a liquid and not a liquid to a foam (2 points).

8. The phrase is considered proper (2 points).

---

*Quoted from Patent Office Approved Answers.

9. The phrase is a proper product by process. MPEP 706.03 (e), but is so broad now that it reads on the prior art since it covers nothing more than a carton of liquid, such as milk (4 points).

10. The phrase is improper because it contains new matter 35 U.S.C. section 132, last sentence. The limitation "0.4" is not found in the specification and therefore cannot appear in the claims. MPEP 706.03(o) (2 points). In addition full credit was given if it was noted that claim 11 was not a method claim or there is no antecedent basis in claim 11 for the underlined portion.

REVIEW AND CATALOG OF "SLOPPY CLAIMS" ERRORS

The following chart lists the type of claim errors, or problems that were not errors, including the seven prior Agents Exam questions given in the preceding examples, (Appendix B cases 26-32). Also listed are a few additional types of errors not included in the Exam questions. The chart keys the errors to the pertinent sections of this book, and to each case 26 to 32 where the error or possible error appeared.

TYPE OF ERROR   APPENDIX B—CASES

	Book Section	26 Suction Cleaner	27 Steam and Dry Iron	28 Bomb-Proof Coating	29 Self-Priming Pump	30 Coated Pipe	31 Golf Ball Cleaner	32 Foam Breaking
1. Claim in two sentences	4, 10	√	√		√		√	
2. Wrong verb form ("A suction cleaner includes. . . .") or improper punctuation	4, 7, 10	√			√			
3. Nonstatutory claim:	1		√	√				
a. Omnibus claim ("The invention as shown and described.")	2		√					
b. Referring to drawing where unnecessary ("A_____ as shown in the drawing.")	2, and see 54			√				
4. Lack of antecedent and/or support in claim		√	√		√	√		√
a. Inferential—adding limitations not previously introduced (". . . rear pair of wheels . . ." where number not previously recited)	20, 23	√	√		√		√	√
b. Inferential—adding element not previously introduced (". . . connected to said gear. . . ." where gear not previously introduced)	23	√	√		√	√		
5. Indefinite	67	√	√	√	√	√		√
a. Unclear which of two previous elements reference is being made to ("front and rear wheels" previously introduced; reference is to "said wheel")	23	√	√		√			
b. Alternative expressions ("such as")	24		√	√		√		√

TYPE OF ERROR   APPENDIX B—CASES

	Book Section	26 Suction Cleaner	27 Steam and Dry Iron	28 Bomb-Proof Coating	29 Self-Priming Pump	30 Coated Pipe	31 Golf Ball Cleaner	32 Foam Breaking
c. Different names for same elements	19, 23		√					
d. Referring to previously introduced element as though it were a new element ("a handle" previously recited; later on, claim recites "a handle" again— unclear if same or new handle)	23		√					
e. Basically not clear								√
f. Unbased comparative ("thick")	25				√			
6. Lack of antecedent and/or support in specification	18, 19	√	√	√	√			√
a. Not described at all	18, 19	√	√	√		√		√
b. Inconsistent with specification	18, 19	√			√	√	√	√
c. Misdescriptive	18, 19		√			√	√	√
d. Omits material limitations								√
7. Lack of antecedent and/or support in drawings	18	√	√					
8. Catalog of elements —Lack of cooperation	28-33 64	√	√		√			
a. Whole claim is mere catalogue	28	√	√		√	√		
b. Only some elements not connected (especially in dependent claims)	28	√	√		√			
9. Functional—too broad	30, 31	√	√		√			

TYPE OF ERROR   APPENDIX B—CASES

	Book Section	26 Suction Cleaner	27 Steam and Dry Iron	28 Bomb-Proof Coating	29 Self-Priming Pump	30 Coated Pipe	31 Golf Ball Cleaner	32 Foam Breaking
a. No structure to support function ("adapted to be reciprocated")	30, 31	✓	✓					
b. Single "means" claim	34	·	✓					
c. Claiming result only	31							
d. "Whereby" clause which does not necessarily follow from rest of claims	32		✓					
e. Failure to distinguish over prior art set forth in specification		✓				✓		✓
10. Double inclusion of elements (especially in dependent claims—claim previously recites "reservoir," then recites "casing" and "pipe," which are "the reservoir")	31, 34 56	✓	✓		✓		✓	
11. Surplusage (laudatory statements, *i.e.*, "new," "better," etc.)	9		✓	✓		✓	✓	✓
12. Markush	50		✓	✓		✓		
a. Mechanical group	50	✓						
b. Chemicals not in art-recognized class	50			✓				
13. Product-by-process is proper although product can be described otherwise	46			✓				✓
14. Obvious method of making product (*i.e.*, novelty only in product)	39			✓				
15. Trademark and proprietary material	51							

TYPE OF ERROR	Book Section	26 Suction Cleaner	27 Steam and Dry Iron	28 Bomb-Proof Coating	29 Self-Priming Pump	30 Coated Pipe	31 Golf Ball Cleaner	32 Foam Breaking
					APPENDIX B—CASES			
16. Positively reciting workpiece	16							
17. Positively reciting holes, grooves, etc.	26		√					
18. Dependent claim errors	11							
a. Inconsistent with parent	11	√	√				√	√
b. Alternative (*i.e.*, depends on more than one independent claim)	11	√	√					
c. Incorrect statutory class—adding method limitation to apparatus claim and vice versa	11		√					
d. Improper location (not sufficiently close to parent claim)	5			√		√		
e. Refers to element absent in parent (see 4.b., *supra*)	23, 11		√					√
f. Deletes element from parent							√	
19. Incomplete claim—claim lacks an element the specification and/or preamble require to yield proper combination. Omits element specification says is "essential." See 8 and 9, *supra*.	28-33 66							√
20. Negative limitations—may be O.K.	17							
21. Reference numerals in claim—O.K., if parenthesized	22							
22. Unnecessary apparatus limitation in method claim—questionable in view of elimination of "method functional of the apparatus" rejection	40-41							

TYPE OF ERROR	Book Section	26 Suction Cleaner	27 Steam and Dry Iron	28 Bomb-Proof Coating	29 Self-Priming Pump	30 Coated Pipe	31 Golf Ball Cleaner	32 Foam Breaking
		APPENDIX B—CASES						
23. Mental steps—may be O.K. if proper apparatus required to effect the steps	44							
24. Design claim in terms of structure instead of formalistic (See 3, *supra*.)	47							
25. Old combination	63							
26. Duplicate claiming—two claims differ only trivially or by very old matter	61							
27. Old material claimed per se, instead of in method (*i.e.*, "new use")	55							
28. Attempting to expand Markush grouping, esp. in dependent claim (Markush group: "A, B, and C"; dependent claim says element may also be "D")	8, 50					✓		
29. Unnecessary method limitation in apparatus claim							✓	

Appendix C

THE ART OF DESCRIBING STRUCTURES IN PATENT DRAWINGS INCLUDING A GLOSSARY OF MECHANICAL TERMS

By Louis B. Applebaum*

The effective communication of facts and ideas is the essence of the role of the patent attorney or agent. As amanuensis ("the hand of another") of the inventor, the patent attorney must select from the vast wealth that constitutes the words and phrases of the language, to convey the precise meaning that is appropriate to the application at hand, in the light of the prior art of record.

Three "languages"—three stylized forms of communication—are prescribed by the Rules of Practice: The specification must fully, clearly and concisely describe the invention (rule 71) and thus constitutes our primary language. The claims must particularly point out and distinctly claim what the *applicant* (not someone else) regards as his invention (rule 75), thus being a precis of the salient portions of the specification. And, third, the drawing must show every feature of the invention claimed (rule 83), depicting what is essential in the specification and claims. It thus becomes necessary for patent students to acquire facility in each of these three "languages," and to be able to translate from one to another.

No one of the three "languages" is a logical starting point for the

*Reprinted with permission from material prepared for the Practising Law Institute's Patent Agent's Examination Review Course. Mr. Applebaum is Patent Counsel, United States Navy Applied Science Laboratory. Edited by John D. Kaufmann.

translation process. However, since the pictorial is a fundamental base, we can ideally commence with a drawing and translate the invention shown therein to the language of claims. The development will, however, be limited to the translation from drawings to a detailed description (or specification) to avoid premature and incomplete treatment of the substantive and procedural complexities of claim drafting, which are discussed in this book.

This process of translating from drawings to words involves the understanding of the elements of patent drawings (as distinguished from other drawing formats), the understanding of the elements of mechanics, and the establishment or reinforcement of a basic and minimal vocabulary. With this learned, the words can be put together to provide a coherent and clear description.

First, it *must* be noted that patent drawings are stylized, simple and generally pictorial: Extracting pertinent phrases from the Rules of Practice, the drawing:

- Must shown every feature of the invention.
- When the invention is an improvement, the drawing must show the invention disconnected from the old structure, and in another view must show so much only of the old structure as will suffice to show the connection of the invention with what is old.
- Surface shading should be open.
- Sectional shading is by oblique parallel lines.
- Solid black should not be used for sectional or surface shading.
- Drawings should have the fewest lines possible consistent with clearness.
- The plane on which a sectional view is taken should be indicated on the general view by a broken or dotted line, designated by numerals corresponding to the number of the sectional view.

- Heavy lines on the shade side of objects should be used; light comes at 45° from the upper left hand corner.
- The same numeral is a reference to the same part.
- Certain symbols, illustrated in the Rules of Practice are accepted as conventional (these should be known).

A description of structure, in the language we call a "specification," is a grouping of words and phrases (each word or phrase being identifiable as an *element* or "island"), at times qualified by modifying appendage words and phrases (sub-elements or "peninsulas" of the island) AND LINKING WORDS AND PHRASES, COUPLING OR PROVIDING A BRIDGE FROM ONE ISLAND TO AT LEAST ONE OTHER ISLAND. Without this coupling or bridging, an "island" is left floating, and is not a proper part of the description: merely listing the "islands" *without including the coupling bridges*, results in a fatally defective description, in that it is no more than a listing or cataloging. (For example, do *not* say ". . . a motor, a rotary cam and a cam follower. . . ." Instead, say ". . . a motor, a rotary cam driven by the motor, and a cam follower engaging the cam. . . ." Note especially the terms below under the heading "Placement (relation)." One may find the following useful in successfully erecting and coupling together an integral empire of islands, peninsulas and bridges:

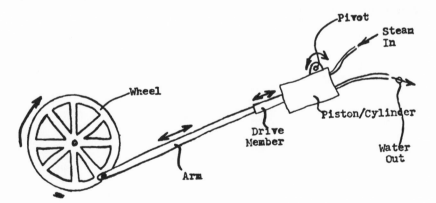

FOUR QUESTIONS

1. What is it? What is the element's name?
   > *EXAMPLE:* "*An arm. . . .*"
2. Where is it located?
   > *EXAMPLE:* "An arm . . . *having one end . . . mounted on . . . said flywheel and the other end . . . mounted . . . on said drive member. . . .*"
3. What does it do?
   > *EXAMPLE:* "An arm . . . having one end . . . mounted on . . . said flywheel and the other end . . . mounted . . . on said drive member, *for rotating said flywheel upon reciprocation of said drive member. . . .*"
4. How does it do what it does?
   > *EXAMPLE:* "An arm *freely reciprocable* having one end *pivotally* mounted on *the periphery of* said flywheel and the other end *fixedly* mounted *for reciprocation therewith* on said drive member, for rotating said flywheel upon reciprocation of said drive member. . . ."

NOTE: The "arm" as described is really a "pitman" or connecting rod as it operates, *e.g.*, on a steam locomotive. Similar descriptive language for the wheel and drive member must have preceded the description of the arm.

To build this description of structure from the drawings, the writer must have a vocabulary of general and "mechanical" words to constitute his translation of the elements and connectives or "bridges" he sees in the drawing. The following terms, grouped loosely by function, are probably a fairly comprehensive vocabulary of many terms used in the mechanical arts and patents.

GENERAL AND MECHANICAL TERMS

The following terms are grouped loosely by function. The list is illustrative rather than comprehensive.

Structure

arm
bail
band
base
beam
  cantilever
  simple
belt
blade
blower
body
boom
branch
carriage
case
chute
column
container
conveyor
cover
device
die
drum
enclosure
finger
frame
gauges
handle

head
housing
jacket
jaw
leg
member
neck
object
particle
partition
platform
plug
rib
ring
rod
shell
shoe
shoulder
sleeve
step
strut
track
truss
upright
wall

Mounting Method
attach
bolt

couple
demountably
engage
fix
hold
lock
mount
secure
set
weld

Fastener
bolt
cable
clamp
connection
coupling
dowel
hold down
hook
joint
  universal
keeper
key
latch
lock
lug
nail
nut

pin
rivet
screw
seam

Bearing
  antifriction
    ball
    needle
    roller
      tapered
  bushing
  fulcrum
  guide
  journal
  pivot
  radial
  seal
  seat
  sliding
  support
  thrust

Spring
  air
  bias
    element
  coil
  helical
    compression
    tension
  leaf
  torsional

Numbers
  multiplicity
  plurality

Placement
(relation)
  adjacent
  aligned
  attached
  axial
  complementary
  concentric
    eccentric
  contiguous
  distal-proximate
  divided
  engaged
  extended
  integral
  intermediate
  interposed
  juxtaposed
  located
  mating
  meshing
  offset
  opposed
  overlapping
  perpendicular
  parallel
  positioned
  projecting
  removable
  resting

retractable
spacer
staggered
superposed
supported
surrounding
symmetrical

Voids (having a void)
  aperture
  bore
  cavity
  chamber
    duct
  groove
  hole
  hollow
  notch
  opening
  orifice
  passage
  slit
  slot

Shape
  A- . . . Z- (etc.)
    ("a C-shaped
    member")
  annular
  arch
  arcuate
  barrel
  bucket
  channel

circular
concave-convex
conical
corrugated
cup
cylinder
depression
disc
dome
elliptical
fin
flange
fold
fork
helical
hook
notch
oblong
oval
parabolic
plane
rectangular
round
sheet
shelf
sinusoidal
spherical
square
taper
triangular
trough
tubular
twist
web

wedge

Material properties
dense
elastic
enlarged
flexible
foraminous
insulation
opaque
porous
resilient
rigid
translucent
transparent

Optical
bezel
bulb
    fluorescent
    incandescent
lamp
light
    beam
    ray
reflection
refraction
transmission
window

Fluid Flow
accumulator
aspirator
bellows

conduit
connector
convection
cylinder
    piston
    rod
dashpot
diaphragm
discharge
dispenser
filter
fitting
flue
gasket
hose
hydraulic
medium
nozzle
outlet
pipe
plunger
port
    inlet
    outlet
pump
    centrifugal
    gear
    piston
    vane
reservoir
seal
siphon
tank
tube

valve
  ball-check
  control
  gate
  shut-off

Position
  angle
    oblique
    obtuse
  bottom-top
  close-open
  crest
  edge
  external-internal
  face
  film
  horizontal-vertical
  layer
  lower-upper
  normal to-parallel
  rim
  section
  slant
  surface
  tilt

Materials
  adhesive
  concrete
  cork
  fabric
  fibre
  insulation

liquid
metal
plastic
refractory
rubber
sand
screen
wood

Electrical
  contact
  electrode
  electromagnet
  filament
  insulator
  lead
  line cord
  motor
  power supply
  resistance
  socket
  solenoid
  switch
  transformer
  wire

Rotation to translation
  bell crank
  cam
  connecting rod
  crank arm
  jack
  radius bar
  screw

winch
yoke

Translation to translation
  inclined plane
  lever
  linkage
    parallel
  straight line
    motion
  toggle
  wedge

Sequence
  alternate
  cyclic
  interval
  lag-lead

Movement
  compression
  downward-upward
  drag
  eccentric
  emergent
  extensible
  extrude
  grinding
  impact
  inertia
  longitudinal
  meeting
  pressing
  propelling

pulverize	clutch	pinion
sagging	centrifugal	right angle
severing	sprag	spur
slidable	toothed	worm and wheel
terminating	one-way	intermittent
torque	drive	escapement
transverse	belt	geneva
traversing	pulley	pawl and
vibrating	sheave	ratchet
	toothed	pendulum
Rotation to rotation	friction	journal
brake	gear	variable speed
band	bevel	flexible coupling
disc	crown	sprocket
shoe	internal	
chain	non-circular	

If one knew all of these terms and what they meant, he would be well able to write the vast majority of mechanical patent claims; *i.e.*, to translate these key words and phrases for naming the elements (section 19) and their connectives and interrelationships (sections 28-30) into good mechanical *combination* claims.

No two writers need generate descriptions from drawings in the same manner. But these procedural steps may be useful in writing mechanical claims.

1. Start with a title. Name or define generically the thing to be described (section 19).

2. List the elements and the subelements of the thing (section 16). This list can be tabular, or can be marked on the drawing, with lead lines to the part or the coupling element defined.

3. Note particularly how the elements are combined or associated with each other (sections 28-30). This is a vital step. The

description must include the structure that establishes how the elements function and cooperate with each other. Otherwise, it is a mere catalog of elements (sections 26 and 64).

4. Numerate where numeration is significant: "One, two, etc."; "a pair"; "a plurality"; "at least two"; a "first—" and later a "second—" etc. are very useful descriptions (section 20). ". . ." when any number, one or more, will do.

Finally, and most important: Recite the elements and their connectives in a logical order, rather than at random (section 27). There are many possible logical orders: Recite from the base up, as the thing might be erected. Recite in the probable sequence of assembly of the thing. Recite elements and their connectives in the order of their operation. Or recite the main body element, followed by a systematic description of the appendage elements—making certain to include the connective elements. And, usually, try to avoid describing the thing when it is in motion—try to describe it when it is at a rest point.

Of course, avoid all of the negative caveats as best you can: alternatives (section 24); negative limitations except for emergencies (section 17); "unduly functional" expressions (section 31); "vague and indefinite" expressions, including ambiguous words or "unbased comparatives" such as "large" (sections 23 and 67); the twin evils of incompleteness (section 66) and unnecessary, superfluous, needless, redundant prolixity (section 68); and all the other evils described in the book.

In gaining skill in translating drawings to descriptions, there is no substitute for practice. Write—and then critically review your writing. Write—and critically review the writing of another as he reviews your description. The reward will be improved skill in the most vital of our efforts, which fundamentally comes down to the communication of intelligence.

Appendix D

Primary Sources

Part One

Title 35 United States Code

35 U.S.C. 100 Definitions

When used in this title unless the context otherwise indicates—

(a) The term "invention" means invention or discovery.

(b) The term "process" means process, art or method, and includes a new use of a known process, machine, manufacture, composition of matter, or material.

(c) The terms "United States" and "this country" mean the United States of America, its territories and possessions.

(d) The word "patentee" includes not only the patentee to whom the patent was issued but also the successors in title to the patentee.

(e) The term "third-party requester" means a person requesting ex parte reexamination under section 302 or inter partes reexamination under section 311 who is not the patent owner.

35 U.S.C. 101 Inventions patentable

Whoever invents or discovers any new and useful process, machine, manufacture, or composition of matter, or any new and useful improvement thereof, may obtain a patent therefor, subject to the conditions and requirements of this title.

35 U.S.C. 102 Conditions for patentability; novelty and loss of right to patent

A person shall be entitled to a patent unless—

(a) the invention was known or used by others in this country, or patented or described in a printed publication in this or a foreign country, before the invention thereof by the applicant for patent, or

(b) the invention was patented or described in a printed publication in this or a foreign country or in public use or on sale in this country, more than one year prior to the date of the application for patent in the United States, or

(c) he has abandoned the invention, or

(d) the invention was first patented or caused to be patented, or was the subject of an inventor's certificate, by the applicant or his legal representatives or assigns in a foreign country prior to the date of the application for patent in this country on an application for patent or inventor's certificate filed more than twelve months before the filing of the application in the United States, or

(e) the invention was described in a patent granted on an application for patent by another filed in the United States before the invention thereof by the applicant for patent, or on an international application by another who has fulfilled the requirements of paragraphs (1), (2), and (4) of section 371 (c) of this title before the invention thereof by the applicant for patent, or

(f) he did not himself invent the subject matter sought to be patented, or

(g) (1) during the course of an interference conducted under section 135 or section 291, another inventor involved therein establishes, to the extent permitted in section 104, that before such person's invention thereof the invention was made by such other inventor and not abandoned, suppressed, or concealed, or (2) before such person's invention thereof, the invention was made in this country by another inventor who had not abandoned, suppressed, or concealed it. In determining priority of invention under this subsection, there shall be considered not only the respective dates of conception and reduction to practice of the invention, but also the reasonable diligence of one who was first to conceive and last to reduce to practice, from a time prior to conception by the other.

35 U.S.C. 103 Conditions for patentability; non-obvious subject matter

(a) A patent may not be obtained though the invention is not identically disclosed or described as set forth in section 102 of this title, if the differences between the subject matter sought to be patented and the prior art are such that the subject matter as a whole would have been obvious at the time the invention was made to a person having ordinary skill in the art to which said subject matter pertains. Patentability shall not be negatived by the manner in which the invention was made.

(b) (1) Notwithstanding subsection (a), and upon timely election by the applicant for patent to proceed under this subsection, a biotechnological process using or resulting in a composition of matter that is novel under section 102 and nonobvious under subsection (a) of this section shall be considered nonobvious if—

> (A) claims to the process and the composition of matter are contained in either the same application for patent or in separate applications having the same effective filing date; and

> (B) the composition of matter, and the process at the time it was invented, were owned by the same person or subject to an obligation of assignment to the same person.

(2) A patent issued on a process under paragraph (1)—

> (A) shall also contain the claims to the composition of matter used in or made by that process, or

> (B) shall, if such composition of matter is claimed in another patent, be set to expire on the same date as such other patent, notwithstanding section 154.

(3) For purposes of paragraph (1), the term "biotechnological process" means—

> (A) a process of genetically altering or otherwise inducing a single- or multi-celled organism to—

> > (i) express an exogenous nucleotide sequence,

> > (ii) inhibit, eliminate, augment, or alter expression of an endogenous nucleotide sequence, or

(iii) express a specific physiological characteristic not naturally associated with said organism;

(B) cell fusion procedures yielding a cell line that expresses a specific protein, such as a monoclonal antibody; and

(C) a method of using a product produced by a process defined by subparagraph (A) or (B), or a combination of subparagraphs (A) and (B).

(c) Subject matter developed by another person, which qualifies as prior art only under one or more of subsections (e), (f), and (g) of section 102 of this title, shall not preclude patentability under this section where the subject matter and the claimed invention were, at the time the invention was made, owned by the same person or subject to an obligation of assignment to the same person.

35 U.S.C. 112 Specification

The specification shall contain a written description of the invention, and of the manner and process of making and using it, in such full, clear, concise, and exact terms as to enable any person skilled in the art to which it pertains, or with which it is most nearly connected, to make and use the same, and shall set forth the best mode contemplated by the inventor of carrying out his invention.

The specification shall conclude with one or more claims particularly pointing out and distinctly claiming the subject matter which the applicant regards as his invention.

A claim may be written in independent or, if the nature of the case admits, in dependent or multiple dependent form.

Subject to the following paragraph, a claim in dependent form shall contain a reference to a claim previously set forth and then specify a further limitation of the subject matter claimed. A claim in dependent form shall be construed to incorporate by reference all the limitations of the claim to which it refers.

A claim in multiple dependent form shall contain a reference, in the alternative only, to more than one claim previously set forth and then specify a further limitation of the subject matter claimed. A multiple dependent claim shall not serve as a basis for any other multiple dependent claim. A multiple claim shall be construed to incorporate by reference all the limitations of the particular claim in relation to which it is being considered.

An element in a claim for a combination may be expressed as a means or step for performing a specified function without the recital of structure, material, or acts in support thereof, and such claim shall be construed to cover the corresponding structure, material, or acts described in the specification and equivalents thereof.

35 U.S.C. 119 Benefit of earlier filing date; right of priority

(a) An application for patent for an invention filed in this country by any person who has, or whose legal representatives or assigns have, previously regularly filed an application for a patent for the same invention in a foreign country which affords similar privileges in the case of applications filed in the United States or to citizens of the United States, or in a WTO member country, shall have the same effect as the same application would have if filed in this country on the date on which the application for patent for the same invention was first filed in such foreign country, if the application in this country is filed within twelve months from the earliest date on which such foreign application was filed; but no patent shall be granted on any application for patent for an invention which had been patented or described in a printed publication in any country more than one year before the date of the actual filing of the application in this country, or which had been in public use or on sale in this country more than one year prior to such filing.

(b) No application for patent shall be entitled to this right of priority unless a claim therefor and a certified copy of the original foreign application, specification and drawings upon which it is based are filed in the Patent and Trademark Office before the patent is granted, or at such time during the pendency of the application as required by the Commissioner not earlier than six months after the filing of the application in this country. Such certification shall be made by the patent office of the foreign country in which filed and show the date of the application and of the filing of the specification and other papers. The Commissioner may require a translation of the papers filed if not in the English language and such other information as he deems necessary.

(c) In like manner and subject to the same conditions and requirements, the right provided in this section may be based upon a subsequent regularly filed application in the same foreign country instead of the first filed foreign application, provided that any foreign application filed prior to such subsequent application has been withdrawn, abandoned, or otherwise disposed of, without having been laid open to public inspection and without leaving any rights outstanding, and has not served, nor thereafter shall serve, as a basis for claiming a right of priority.

(d) Applications for inventors' certificates filed in a foreign country in which applicants have a right to apply, at their discretion, either for a patent or for an inventor's certificate shall be treated in this country in the same manner and have the same effect for purpose of the right of priority under this section as applications for patents, subject to the same conditions and requirements of this section as apply to applications for patents, provided such applicants are entitled to the benefits of the Stockholm Revision of the Paris Convention at the time of such filing.

(e) (1) An application for patent filed under section 111(a) or section 363 of this title for an invention disclosed in the manner provided by the first paragraph of section 112 of this title in a provisional application filed under section 111(b) of this title, by an inventor or inventors named in the provisional application, shall have the same effect, as to such invention, as though filed on the date of the provisional application filed under section 111(b) of this title, if the application for patent filed under section 111(a) or section 363 of this title is filed not later than 12 months after the date on which the provisional application was filed and if it contains or is amended to contain a specific reference to the provisional application.

(2) A provisional application filed under section 111(b) of this title may not be relied upon in any proceeding in the Patent and Trademark Office unless the fee set forth in subparagraph (A) or (C) of section 41(a)(1) of this title has been paid.

(3) If the day that is 12 months after the filing date of a provisional application falls on a Saturday, Sunday, or Federal holiday within the District of Columbia, the period of pendency of the provisional application shall be extended to the next succeeding secular or business day.

(f) Applications for plant breeder's rights filed in a WTO member country (or in a foreign UPOV Contracting Party) shall have the same effect for the purpose of the right of priority under subsections (a) through (c) of this section as applications for patents, subject to the same conditions and requirements of this section as apply to applications for patents.

(g) As used in this section—

(1) the term "WTO member country" has the same meaning as the term is defined in section 104(b)(2) of this title; and

(2) the term "UPOV Contracting Party" means a member of the International Convention for the Protection of New Varieties of Plants.

35 U.S.C. 121 Divisional applications

If two or more independent and distinct inventions are claimed in one application, the Director may require the application to be restricted to one of the inventions. If the other invention is made the subject of a divisional application which complies with the requirements of section 120 of this title it shall be entitled to the benefit of the filing date of the original application. A patent issuing on an application with respect to which a requirement for restriction under this section has been made, or on an application filed as a result of such a requirement, shall not be used as a reference either in the Patent and Trademark Office or in the courts against a divisional application or against the original application or any patent issued on either of them, if the divisional application is filed before the issuance of the patent on the other application. If a divisional application is directed solely to subject matter described and claimed in the original application as filed, the Director may dispense with signing and execution by the inventor. The validity of a patent shall not be questioned for failure of the Commissioner to require the application to be restricted to one invention.

35 U.S.C. 134 Appeal to the Board of Patent Appeals and Interferences

a) Patent applicant. An applicant for a patent, any of whose claims has been twice rejected, may appeal from the decision of the administrative patent judge to the Board of Patent Appeals and Interferences, having once paid the fee for such appeal.

(b) Patent owner. A patent owner in any reexamination proceeding may appeal from the final rejection of any claim by the administrative patent judge to the Board of Patent Appeals and Interferences, having once paid the fee for such appeal.

(c) Third-party. A third-party requester in an inter partes proceeding may appeal to the Board of Patent Appeals and Interferences from the final decision of the administrative patent judge favorable to the patentability of any original or proposed amended or new claim of a patent, having once paid the fee for such appeal. The third-party requester may not appeal the decision of the Board of Patent Appeals and Interferences.

35 U.S.C. 161 Patents for plants

Whoever invents or discovers and asexually reproduces any distinct and new variety of plant, including cultivated sports, mutants, hybrids, and newly found seedlings, other than a tuber propagated plant or a plant found in an uncultivated state, may obtain a patent therefor, subject to the conditions and requirements of this title.

The provisions of this title relating to patents for inventions shall apply to patents for plants, except as otherwise provided.

35 U.S.C. 162 Description, claim

No plant patent shall be declared invalid for noncompliance with section 112 of this title if the description is as complete as is reasonably possible.

The claim in the specification shall be in formal terms to the plant shown and described.

35 U.S.C. 171 Patents for designs

Whoever invents any new, original and ornamental design for an article of manufacture may obtain a patent therefor, subject to the conditions and requirements of this title.

The provisions of this title relating to patents for inventions shall apply to patents for designs, except as otherwise provided.

35 U.S.C. 271 Infringement of patent

(a) Except as otherwise provided in this title, whoever without authority makes, uses, offers to sell, or sells any patented invention, within the United States or imports into the United States any patented invention during the term of the patent therefor, infringes the patent.

(b) Whoever actively induces infringement of a patent shall be liable as an infringer.

(c) Whoever offers to sell or sells within the United States or imports into the United States a component of a patented machine, manufacture, combination or composition, or a material or apparatus for use in practicing a patented process, constituting a material part of the invention, knowing the same to be especially made or especially adapted for use in an infringement of such patent, and not a staple article or commodity of commerce suitable for substantial noninfringing use, shall be liable as a contributory infringer.

(d) No patent owner otherwise entitled to relief for infringement or contributory infringement of a patent shall be denied relief or deemed guilty of misuse or illegal extension of the patent right by reason of his having done one or more of the following: (1) derived revenue from acts which if performed by another without his consent would constitute contributory infringement of the patent; (2) licensed or authorized another to perform acts which if performed without his consent would constitute contributory infringement of the patent; (3) sought to enforce his patent rights against infringement or contributory infringement; (4) refused to license or use any rights to the patent; or (5) conditioned the license of any rights to the patent or the sale of the patented product on the acquisition of a license to rights in another patent or purchase of a separate product, unless, in view of the circumstances, the patent owner has market power in the relevant market for the patent or patented product on which the license or sale is conditioned.

(e) (1) It shall not be an act of infringement to make, use, offer to sell, or sell within the United States or import into the United States a patented invention (other than a new animal drug or veterinary biological product (as those terms are used in the Federal Food, Drug, and Cosmetic Act and the Act of March 4, 1913) which is primarily manufactured using recombinant DNA, recombinant RNA, hybridoma technology, or other processes involving site specific genetic manipulation techniques) solely for uses reasonably related to the development and submission of information under a Federal law which regulates the manufacture, use, or sale of drugs or veterinary biological products.

(2) It shall be an act of infringement to submit—

(A) an application under section 505(j) of the Federal Food, Drug, and Cosmetic Act or described in section 505(b)(2) of such Act for a drug claimed in a patent or the use of which is claimed in a patent, or

(B) an application under section 512 of such Act or under the Act of March 4, 1913 (21 U.S.C. 151-158) for a drug or veterinary biological product which is not primarily manufactured using recombinant DNA, recombinant RNA, hybridoma technology, or other processes involving site specific genetic manipulation techniques and which is claimed in a patent or the use of which is claimed in a patent,

if the purpose of such submission is to obtain approval under such Act to engage in the commercial manufacture, use, or sale of a drug or veterinary biological product claimed in a patent or the use of which is claimed in a patent before the expiration of such patent.

(3) In any action for patent infringement brought under this section, no injunctive or other relief may be granted which would prohibit the making, using, offering to sell, or selling within the United States or importing into the United States of a patented invention under paragraph (1).

(4) For an act of infringement described in paragraph (2)—

(A) the court shall order the effective date of any approval of the drug or veterinary biological product involved in the infringement to be a date which is not earlier than the date of the expiration of the patent which has been infringed,

(B) injunctive relief may be granted against an infringer to prevent the commercial manufacture, use, offer to sell, or sale within the United States or importation into the United States of an approved drug or veterinary biological product, and

(C) damages or other monetary relief may be awarded against an infringer only if there has been commercial manufacture, use, offer to sell, or sale within the United States or importation into the United States of an approved drug or veterinary biological product.

The remedies prescribed by subparagraphs (A), (B), and (C) are the only remedies which may be granted by a court for an act of infringement described in paragraph (2), except that a court may award attorney fees under section 285.

(f) (1) Whoever without authority supplies or causes to be supplied in or from the United States all or a substantial portion of the components of a patented invention, where such components are uncombined in whole or in part, in such manner as to actively induce the combination of such components outside of the United States in a manner that would infringe the patent if such combination occurred within the United States, shall be liable as an infringer.

(2) Whoever without authority supplies or causes to be supplied in or from the United States any component of a patented invention that is especially made or especially adapted for use in the invention and not a staple article or commodity of commerce suitable for substantial noninfringing use, where such component is uncombined in whole or in part, knowing that such component is so made or adapted and intending that such component will be combined outside of the United States in a manner that would infringe the patent if such combination occurred within the United States, shall be liable as an infringer.

(g) Whoever without authority imports into the United States or offers to sell, sells, or uses within the United States a product which is made by a process patented in the United States shall be liable as an infringer, if the importation, offer to sell, sale, or use of the product occurs during the term of such process patent. In an action for infringement of a process patent, no remedy may be granted for infringement on account of the noncommercial use or retail sale of a product unless there is no adequate remedy under this title for infringement on account of the importation or other use, offer to sell, or sale of that product. A product which is made by a patented process will, for purposes of this title, not be considered to be so made after—

(1) it is materially changed by subsequent processes; or

(2) it becomes a trivial and nonessential component of another product.

(h) As used in this section, the term "whoever" includes any State, any instrumentality of a State, and any officer or employee of a State or instrumentality of a State acting in his official capacity. Any State, and any such instrumentality, officer, or employee, shall be subject to the provisions of this title in the same manner and to the same extent as any nongovernmental entity.

(i) As used in this section, an "offer for sale" or an "offer to sell" by a person other than the patentee, or any designee of the patentee, is that in which the sale will occur before the expiration of the term of the patent.

35 U.S.C. 281 Remedy for infringement of patent

A patentee shall have remedy by civil action for infringement of his patent.

35 U.S.C. 282 Presumption of validity; defenses

A patent shall be presumed valid. Each claim of a patent (whether in independent, dependent, or multiple dependent form) shall be presumed valid independently of the validity of other claims; dependent or multiple dependent claims shall be presumed valid even though dependent upon an invalid claim. Notwithstanding the preceding sentence, if a claim to a composition of matter is held invalid and that claim was the basis of a determination of nonobviousness under section 103(b)(1), the process shall no longer be considered nonobvious solely on the basis of section 103(b)(1). The burden of establishing invalidity of a patent or any claim thereof shall rest on the party asserting such invalidity.

The following shall be defenses in any action involving the validity or infringement of a patent and shall be pleaded:

(1) Noninfringement, absence of liability for infringement or unenforceability,

(2) Invalidity of the patent or any claim in suit on any ground specified in part II of this title as a condition for patentability,

(3) Invalidity of the patent or any claim in suit for failure to comply with any requirement of sections 112 or 251 of this title.

(4) Any other fact or act made a defense by this title.

In actions involving the validity or infringement of a patent the party asserting invalidity or noninfringement shall give notice in the pleadings or otherwise in writing to the adverse party at least thirty days before the trial, of the country, number, date, and name of the patentee of any patent, the title, date, and page numbers of any publication to be relied upon as anticipation of the patent in suit or, except in actions in the United States Claims Court [United States Court of Federal Claims], as showing the state of the art, and the name and address of any person who may be relied upon as the prior inventor or as having prior knowledge of or as having previously used or offered for sale the invention of the patent in suit. In the absence of such notice proof of the said matters may not be made at the trial except on such terms as the court requires. Invalidity of the extension of a patent term or any portion thereof under section 154(b) or 156 of this title because of the material failure—

(1) by the applicant for the extension, or

(2) by the Director,

to comply with the requirements of such section shall be a defense in any action involving the infringement of a patent during the period of the extension of its term and shall be pleaded. A due diligence determination under section 156(d)(2) is not subject to review in such an action.

35 U.S.C. 283 Injunction

The several courts having jurisdiction of cases under this title may grant injunctions in accordance with the principles of equity to prevent the violation of any right secured by patent, on such terms as the court deems reasonable.

35 U.S.C. 284 Damages

Upon finding for the claimant the court shall award the claimant damages adequate to compensate for the infringement, but in no event less than a reasonable royalty for the use made of the invention by the infringer, together with interest and costs as fixed by the court.

When the damages are not found by a jury, the court shall assess them. In either event the court may increase the damages up to three times the amount found or assessed.

The court may receive expert testimony as an aid to the determination of damages or of what royalty would be reasonable under the circumstances.

Appendix D

Primary Sources

Part Two

Rules of Practice

37 C.F.R. § 1.16   National application filing fees

(a) Basic fee for filing each application for an original patent, except provisional, design, or plant applications:

> By a small entity (§ 1.27(a))—$ 355.00

> By other than a small entity—$ 710.00

(b) In addition to the basic filing fee in an original application, except provisional applications, for filing or later presentation of each independent claim in excess of 3:

> By a small entity (§ 1.27(a))—$ 40.00

> By other than a small entity—$ 80.00

(c) In addition to the basic filing fee in an original application, except provisional applications, for filing or later presentation of each claim (whether independent or dependent) in excess of 20 (Note that § 1.75(c) indicates how multiple dependent claims are considered for fee purposes.):

> By a small entity (§ 1.27(a))—$ 9.00

> By other than a small entity—$ 18.00

(d) In addition to the basic filing fee in an original application, except provisional applications, if the application contains, or is amended to contain, a multiple dependent claim(s), per application:

> By a small entity (§ 1.27(a))—$ 135.00

> By other than a small entity—$ 270.00

(e) Surcharge for filing the basic filing fee or oath or declaration on a date later than the filing date of the application, except provisional applications:

  By a small entity (§ 1.27(a)) $65.00

  By other than a small entity $130.00

(f) Basic fee for filing each design application:

  By a small entity (§ 1.27(a))—$ 160.00

  By other than a small entity—$ 320.00

(g) Basic fee for filing each plant application, except provisional applications:

  By a small entity (§ 1.27(a))—$ 245.00

  By other than a small entity—$ 490.00

(h) Basic fee for filing each reissue application:

  By a small entity (§ 1.27(a))—$ 355.00

  By other than a small entity—$ 710.00

(i) In addition to the basic filing fee in a reissue application, for filing or later presentation of each independent claim which is in excess of the number of independent claims in the original patent:

  By a small entity (§ 1.27(a))—$ 40.00

  By other than a small entity—$ 80.00

(j) In addition to the basic filing fee in a reissue application, for filing or later presentation of each claim (whether independent or dependent) in excess of 20 and also in excess of the number of claims in the original patent (Note that § 1.75(c) indicates how multiple dependent claims are considered for fee purposes.):

  By a small entity (§ 1.27(a))—$ 9.00

  By other than a small entity—$ 18.00

(k) Basic fee for filing each provisional application:

  By a small entity (§ 1.27(a)) .... $ 75.00

  By other than a small entity $150.00

(l) Surcharge for filing the basic filing fee or cover sheet (§ 1.51(c)(1)) on a date later than the filing date of the provisional application:

  By a small entity (§ 1.27(a))—$ 25.00

By other than a small entity—$ 50.00

(m) If the additional fees required by paragraphs (b), (c), (d), (i) and (j) of this section are not paid on filing or on later presentation of the claims for which the additional fees are due, they must be paid or the claims must be canceled by amendment, prior to the expiration of the time period set for reply by the Office in any notice of fee deficiency.

NOTE: See §§ 1.445, 1.482 and 1.492 for international application filing and processing fees.

37 C.F.R. § 1.51   General requisites of an application

(a) Applications for patents must be made to the Commissioner of Patents and Trademarks.

(b) A complete application filed under § 1.53(b) or § 1.53(d) comprises:

> (1) A specification as prescribed by 35 U.S.C. 112, including a claim or claims, see §§ 1.71 to 1.77;

> (2) An oath or declaration, see §§ 1.63 and 1.68;

> (3) Drawings, when necessary, see §§ 1.81 to 1.85; and

> (4) The prescribed filing fee, see § 1.16.

(c) A complete provisional application filed under § 1.53(c) comprises:

> (1) A cover sheet identifying:

>> (i) The application as a provisional application,

>> (ii) The name or names of the inventor or inventors, (see § 1.41(a)(2)),

>> (iii) The residence of each named inventor,

>> (iv) The title of the invention,

>> (v) The name and registration number of the attorney or agent (if applicable),

>> (vi) The docket number used by the person filing the application to identify the application (if applicable),

>> (vii) The correspondence address, and

(viii) The name of the U.S. Government agency and Government contract number (if the invention was made by an agency of the U.S. Government or under a contract with an agency of the U.S. Government);

(2) A specification as prescribed by the first paragraph of 35 U.S.C. 112, see § 1.71;

(3) Drawings, when necessary, see §§ 1.81 to 1.85; and

(4) The prescribed filing fee, see § 1.16.

(d) Applicants are encouraged to file an information disclosure statement in nonprovisional applications. See § 1.97 and § 1.98. No information disclosure statement may be filed in a provisional application.

37 C.F.R. § 1.58   Chemical and mathematical formulae and tables

(a) The specification, including the claims, may contain chemical and mathematical formulas, but shall not contain drawings or flow diagrams. The description portion of the specification may contain tables; claims may contain tables either if necessary to conform to 35 U.S.C. 112 or if otherwise found to be desirable.

(b) Tables that are submitted in electronic form (§§ 1.96(c) and 1.821(c)) must maintain the spatial relationships (e.g., columns and rows) of the table elements and preserve the information they convey. Chemical and mathematical formulae must be encoded to maintain the proper positioning of their characters when displayed in order to preserve their intended meaning.

(c) Chemical and mathematical formulae and tables must be presented in compliance with § 1.52 (a) and (b), except that chemical and mathematical formulae or tables may be placed in a landscape orientation if they cannot be presented satisfactorily in a portrait orientation. Typewritten characters used in such formulae and tables must be chosen from a block (nonscript) type font or lettering style having capital letters which are at least 0.21 cm. (0.08 inch) high (e.g., elite type). A space at least 0.64 cm. (1/4 inch) high should be provided between complex formulae and tables and the text. Tables should have the lines and columns of data closely spaced to conserve space, consistent with a high degree of legibility.

37 C.F.R. § 1.71   Detailed description and specification of the invention

(a) The specification must include a written description of the invention or discovery and of the manner and process of making and using the same, and is required to be in such full, clear, concise, and exact terms as to enable any person skilled in the art or science to which the invention or discovery appertains, or with which it is most nearly connected, to make and use the same.

(b) The specification must set forth the precise invention for which a patent is solicited, in such manner as to distinguish it from other inventions and from what is old. It must describe completely a specific embodiment of the process, machine, manufacture, composition of matter or improvement invented, and must explain the mode of operation or principle whenever applicable. The best mode contemplated by the inventor of carrying out his invention must be set forth.

(c) In the case of an improvement, the specification must particularly point out the part or parts of the process, machine, manufacture, or composition of matter to which the improvement relates, and the description should be confined to the specific improvement and to such parts as necessarily cooperate with it or as may be necessary to a complete understanding or description of it.

(d) A copyright or mask work notice may be placed in a design or utility patent application adjacent to copyright and mask work material contained therein. The notice may appear at any appropriate portion of the patent application disclosure. For notices in drawings, see § 1.84(s). The content of the notice must be limited to only those elements provided for by law. For example, "copyright 1983 John Doe" (17 U.S.C. 401) and " *M* John Doe" (17 U.S.C. 909) would be properly limited and, under current statutes, legally sufficient notices of copyright and mask work, respectively. Inclusion of a copyright or mask work notice will be permitted only if the authorization language set forth in paragraph (e) of this section is included at the beginning (preferably as the first paragraph) of the specification.

(e) The authorization shall read as follows:

A portion of the disclosure of this patent document contains material which is subject to (copyright or mask work) protection.

The (copyright or mask work) owner has no objection to the facsimile reproduction by anyone of the patent document or the patent disclosure, as it appears in the Patent and Trademark Office patent file or records, but otherwise reserves all (copyright or mask work) rights whatsoever.

37 C.F.R. § 1.77   Arrangement of application elements

(a) The elements of the application, if applicable, should appear in the following order:

(1) Utility application transmittal form.

(2) Fee transmittal form.

(3) Application data sheet (see § 1.76).

(4) Specification.

(5) Drawings.

(6) Executed oath or declaration.

(b) The specification should include the following sections in order:

(1) Title of the invention, which may be accompanied by an introductory portion stating the name, citizenship, and residence of the applicant (unless included in the application data sheet).

(2) Cross-reference to related applications (unless included in the application data sheet).

(3) Statement regarding federally sponsored research or development.

(4) Reference to a "Sequence Listing," a table, or a computer program listing appendix submitted on a compact disc and an incorporation-by-reference of the material on the compact disc (see § 1.52(e)(5)). The total number of compact discs including duplicates and the files on each compact disc shall be specified.

(5) Background of the invention.

(6) Brief summary of the invention.

(7) Brief description of the several views of the drawing.

(8) Detailed description of the invention.

(9) A claim or claims.

(10) Abstract of the disclosure.

(11) "Sequence Listing," if on paper (see §§ 1.821 through 1.825).

(c) The text of the specification sections defined in paragraphs (b)(1) through (b)(11) of this section, if applicable, should be preceded by a section heading in uppercase and without under-lining or bold type.

37 C.F.R. § 1.126 Numbering of claims

The original numbering of the claims must be preserved throughout the prosecution. When claims are canceled the remaining claims must not be renumbered. When claims are added, they must be numbered by the applicant consecutively beginning with the number next following the highest numbered claim previously presented (whether entered or not). When the application is ready for allowance, the examiner, if necessary, will renumber the claims consecutively in the order in which they appear or in such order as may have been requested by applicant.

37 C.F.R. § 1.141 Different inventions in one national application

(a) Two or more independent and distinct inventions may not be claimed in one national application, except that more than one species of an invention, not to exceed a reasonable number, may be specifically claimed in different claims in one national application, provided the application also includes an allowable claim generic to all the claimed species and all the claims to species in excess of one are written in dependent form (§ 1.75) or otherwise include all the limitations of the generic claim.

(b) Where claims to all three categories, product, process of making, and process of use, are included in a national application, a three way requirement for restriction can only be made where the process of making is distinct from the product. If the process of making and the product are not distinct, the process of using may be joined with the claims directed to the product and the process of making the product even though a showing of distinctness between the product and process of using the product can be made.

37 C.F.R. § 1.146 Requirement for restriction

In the first action on an application containing a generic claim to a generic invention (genus) and claims to more than one patentably distinct species embraced thereby, the examiner may require the applicant in the reply to that action to elect a species of his or her invention to which his or her claim will be restricted if no claim to the genus is found to be allowable. However, if such application contains claims directed to more than a reasonable number of species, the examiner may require restriction of the claims to not more than a reasonable number of species before taking further action in the application.

37 C.F.R. § 1.151 Rules applicable

The rules relating to applications for patents for other inventions or discoveries are also applicable to applications for patents for designs except as otherwise provided.

37 C.F.R. § 1.153 Title, description and claim, oath or declaration

(a) The title of the design must designate the particular article. No description, other than a reference to the drawing, is ordinarily required. The claim shall be in formal terms to the ornamental design for the article (specifying name) as shown, or as shown and described. More than one claim is neither required nor permitted.

(b) The oath or declaration required of the applicant must comply with § 1.63.

37 C.F.R. § 1.154 Arrangement of application elements

(a) The elements of the design application, if applicable, should appear in the following order:

(1) Design application transmittal form.

(2) Fee transmittal form.

(3) Application data sheet (see § 1.76).

(4) Specification.

(5) Drawings or photographs.

(6) Executed oath or declaration (see § 1.153(b)).

(b) The specification should include the following sections in order:

(1) Preamble, stating the name of the applicant, title of the design, and a brief description of the nature and intended use of the article in which the design is embodied.

(2) Cross-reference to related applications (unless included in the application data sheet).

(3) Statement regarding federally sponsored research or development.

(4) Description of the figure or figures of the drawing.

(5) Feature description.

(6) A single claim.

37 C.F.R. § 1.164 Claim

The claim shall be in formal terms to the new and distinct variety of the specified plant as described and illustrated, and may also recite the principal distinguishing characteristics. More than one claim is not permitted.

37 C.F.R. § 1.173 Specification

(a) Contents of a reissue application. An application for reissue must contain the entire specification, including the claims, and the drawings of the patent. No new matter shall be introduced into the application. No reissue patent shall be granted enlarging the scope of the claims of the original patent unless applied for within two years from the grant of the original patent, pursuant to 35 U.S.C. 251.

(1) Specification, including claims. The entire specification, including the claims, of the patent for which reissue is requested must be furnished in the form of a copy of the printed patent, in double column format, each page on only one side of a single sheet of paper. If an amendment of the reissue application is to be included, it must be made pursuant to paragraph (b) of this section. The formal requirements for papers making up the reissue application other

than those set forth in this section are set out in § 1.52. Additionally, a copy of any disclaimer (§ 1.321), certificate of correction (§§ 1.322 through 1.324), or reexamination certificate (§ 1.570) issued in the patent must be included. (See also § 1.178).

(2) Drawings. Applicant must submit a clean copy of each drawing sheet of the printed patent at the time the reissue application is filed. If such copy complies with § 1.84, no further drawings will be required. Where a drawing of the reissue application is to include any changes relative to the patent being reissued, the changes to the drawing must be made in accordance with paragraph (b)(3) of this section. The Office will not transfer the drawings from the patent file to the reissue application.

(b) Making amendments in a reissue application. An amendment in a reissue application is made either by physically incorporating the changes into the specification when the application is filed, or by a separate amendment paper. If amendment is made by incorporation, markings pursuant to paragraph (d) of this section must be used. If amendment is made by an amendment paper, the paper must direct that specified changes be made.

(1) Specification other than the claims. Changes to the specification, other than to the claims, must be made by submission of the entire text of an added or rewritten paragraph, including markings pursuant to paragraph (d) of this section, except that an entire paragraph may be deleted by a statement deleting the paragraph without presentation of the text of the paragraph. The precise point in the specification must be identified where any added or rewritten paragraph is located. This paragraph applies whether the amendment is submitted on paper or compact disc (see §§ 1.52(e)(1) and 1.821(c), but not for discs submitted under § 1.821(e)).

(2) Claims. An amendment paper must include the entire text of each claim being changed by such amendment paper and of each claim being added by such amendment paper. For any claim changed by the amendment paper, a parenthetical expression "amended," "twice amended," etc., should follow the claim number. Each changed patent claim and each added claim must include markings pursuant to

paragraph (d) of this section, except that a patent claim or added claim should be canceled by a statement canceling the claim without presentation of the text of the claim.

(3) Drawings. Any change to the patent drawings must be submitted as a sketch on a separate paper showing the proposed changes in red for approval by the examiner. Upon approval by the examiner, new drawings in compliance with § 1.84 including the approved changes must be filed. Amended figures must be identified as "Amended," and any added figure must be identified as "New." In the event that a figure is canceled, the figure must be surrounded by brackets and identified as "Canceled."

(c) Status of claims and support for claim changes. Whenever there is an amendment to the claims pursuant to paragraph (b) of this section, there must also be supplied, on pages separate from the pages containing the changes, the status (i.e., pending or canceled), as of the date of the amendment, of all patent claims and of all added claims, and an explanation of the support in the disclosure of the patent for the changes made to the claims.

(d) Changes shown by markings. Any changes relative to the patent being reissued which are made to the specification, including the claims, upon filing, or by an amendment paper in the reissue application, must include the following markings:

(1) The matter to be omitted by reissue must be enclosed in brackets; and

(2) The matter to be added by reissue must be underlined, except for amendments submitted on compact discs (§§ 1.96 and 1.821(c)). Matter added by reissue on compact discs must be preceded with "<U>" and end with "</U>" to properly identify the material being added.

(e) Numbering of patent claims preserved. Patent claims may not be renumbered. The numbering of any claim added in the reissue application must follow the number of the highest numbered patent claim.

(f) Amendment of disclosure may be required. The disclosure must be amended, when required by the Office, to correct inaccuracies of description and definition, and to secure substantial correspondence between the claims, the remainder of the specification, and the drawings.

(g) Amendments made relative to the patent. All amendments must be made relative to the patent specification, including the claims, and drawings, which are in effect as of the date of filing of the reissue application.

37 C.F.R. § 1.181 Petition to the Commissioner

(a) Petition may be taken to the Commissioner: (1) From any action or requirement of any examiner in the ex parte prosecution of an application, or in the ex parte or inter partes prosecution of a reexamination proceeding which is not subject to appeal to the Board of Patent Appeals and Interferences or to the court; (2) in cases in which a statute or the rules specify that the matter is to be determined directly by or reviewed by the Commissioner; and (3) to invoke the supervisory authority of the Commissioner in appropriate circumstances. For petitions in interferences, see § 1.644.

(b) Any such petition must contain a statement of the facts involved and the point or points to be reviewed and the action requested. Briefs or memoranda, if any, in support thereof should accompany or be embodied in the petition; and where facts are to be proven, the proof in the form of affidavits or declarations (and exhibits, if any) must accompany the petition.

(c) When a petition is taken from an action or requirement of an examiner in the ex parte prosecution of an application, or in the ex parte or inter partes prosecution of a reexamination proceeding, it may be required that there have been a proper request for reconsideration (§ 1.111) and a repeated action by the examiner. The examiner may be directed by the Commissioner to furnish a written statement, within a specified time, setting forth the reasons for his other decision upon the matters averred in the petition, supplying a copy to the petitioner.

(d) Where a fee is required for a petition to the Commissioner the appropriate section of this part will so indicate. If any required fee does not accompany the petition, the petition will be dismissed.

(e) Oral hearing will not be granted except when considered necessary by the Commissioner.

(f) The mere filing of a petition will not stay any period for reply that may be running against the application, nor act as a stay of other proceedings. Any petition under this part not filed within two months of the mailing date of the action or notice from which relief is requested may be dismissed as untimely, except as otherwise provided. This two-month period is not extendable.

(g) The Commissioner may delegate to appropriate Patent and Trademark Office officials the determination of petitions.

Appendix D

Primary Sources

Part Three

Manual of Patent Examining Procedure

506   Completeness of Original Application

37 CFR 1.53. Application number, filing date, and completion of application.

(a) Application number. Any papers received in the Patent and Trademark Office which purport to be an application for a patent will be assigned an application number for identification purposes.

(b) Application filing requirements — Nonprovisional application. The filing date of an application for patent filed under this section, except for a provisional application under paragraph (c) of this section or a continued prosecution application under paragraph (d) of this section, is the date on which a specification as prescribed by 35 U.S.C. 112 containing a description pursuant to § 1.71 and at least one claim pursuant to § 1.75, and any drawing required by § 1.81(a) are filed in the Patent and Trademark Office. No new matter may be introduced into an application after its filing date. A continuing application, which may be a continuation, divisional, or continuation-in-part application, may be filed under the conditions specified in 35 U.S.C. 120, 121 or 365(c) and § 1.78(a).

> (1) A continuation or divisional application that names as inventors the same or fewer than all of the inventors named in the prior application may be filed under this paragraph or paragraph (d) of this section.

> (2) A continuation-in-part application (which may disclose and claim subject matter not disclosed in the prior application) or a continuation or divisional application naming an inventor not named in the prior application must be filed under this paragraph.

(c) Application filing requirements — Provisional application. The filing date of a provisional application is the date on which a specification as prescribed by the first paragraph of 35 U.S.C. 112, and any drawing required by § 1.81(a) are filed in the Patent and Trademark Office. No amendment, other than to make the provisional application comply with the patent statute and all applicable regulations, may be made to the provisional application after the filing date of the provisional application.

(1) A provisional application must also include the cover sheet required by § 1.51(c)(1) or a cover letter identifying the application as a provisional application. Otherwise, the application will be treated as an application filed under paragraph (b) of this section.

(2) An application for patent filed under paragraph (b) of this section may be converted to a provisional application and be accorded the original filing date of the application filed under paragraph (b) of this section,

(i) Provided that a petition requesting the conversion, with the fee set forth in § 1.17(q), is filed prior to the earliest of:

(A) Abandonment of the application filed under paragraph (b) of this section;

(B) Payment of the issue fee on the application filed under paragraph (b) of this section;

(C) Expiration of twelve months after the filing date of the application filed under paragraph (b) of this section; or

(D) The filing of a request for a statutory invention registration under § 1.293 in the application filed under paragraph (b) of this section.

(ii) The grant of any such petition will not entitle applicant to a refund of the fees which were properly paid in the application filed under paragraph (b) of this section.

(3)   A provisional application is not entitled to the right of priority under 35 U.S.C. 119 or 365(a) or § 1.55, or to the benefit of an earlier filing date under 35 U.S.C. 120, 121 or 365(c) or § 1.78 of any other application. No claim for pri-

ority under § 1.78(a)(3) may be made in a design application based on a provisional application. No request under § 1.293 for a statutory invention registration may be filed in a provisional application. The requirements of §§ 1.821 through 1.825 regarding application disclosures containing nucleotide and/or amino acid sequences are not mandatory for provisional applications.

(d) Application filing requirements — Continued prosecution (nonprovisional) application.

(1) A continuation or divisional application (but not a continuation-in-part) of a prior nonprovisional application may be filed as a continued prosecution application under this paragraph, provided that:

(i) The prior nonprovisional application is either:

(A) Complete as defined by § 1.51(b) ; or

(B) The national stage of an international application in compliance with 35 U.S.C. 371; and

(ii) The application under this paragraph is filed before the earliest of:

(A) Payment of the issue fee on the prior application, unless a petition under § 1.313(b)(5) is granted in the prior application;

(B) Abandonment of the prior application; or

(C) Termination of proceedings on the prior application.

(2) The filing date of a continued prosecution application is the date on which a request on a separate paper for an application under this paragraph is filed. An application filed under this paragraph:

(i) Must identify the prior application;

(ii) Discloses and claims only subject matter disclosed in the prior application;

(iii) Names as inventors the same inventors named in the prior application on the date the application under this paragraph was filed, except as provided in paragraph (d)(4) of this section;

(iv) Includes the request for an application under this paragraph, will utilize the file jacket and contents of the prior application, including the specification, drawings and oath or declaration from the prior application, to constitute the new application, and will be assigned the application number of the prior application for identification purposes; and

(v) Is a request to expressly abandon the prior application as of the filing date of the request for an application under this paragraph.

(3) The filing fee for a continued prosecution application filed under this paragraph is:

(i) The basic filing fee as set forth in § 1.16; and

(ii) Any additional § 1.16 fee due based on the number of claims remaining in the application after entry of any amendment accompanying the request for an application under this paragraph and entry of any amendments under § 1.116 unentered in the prior application which applicant has requested to be entered in the continued prosecution application.

(4) An application filed under this paragraph may be filed by fewer than all the inventors named in the prior application, provided that the request for an application under this paragraph when filed is accompanied by a statement requesting deletion of the name or names of the person or persons who are not inventors of the invention being claimed in the new application. No person may be named as an inventor in an application filed under this paragraph who was not named as an inventor in the prior application on the date the application under this paragraph was filed, except by way of a petition under § 1.48.

(5) Any new change must be made in the form of an amendment to the prior application as it existed prior to the filing of an application under this paragraph. No amendment in an application under this paragraph (a continued prosecution application) may introduce new matter or matter that would have been new matter in the prior application. Any new specification filed with the request for an application under this paragraph will not be considered part of the orig-

inal application papers, but will be treated as a substitute specification in accordance with § 1.125.

(6) The filing of a continued prosecution application under this paragraph will be construed to include a waiver of confidentiality by the applicant under 35 U.S.C. 122 to the extent that any member of the public, who is entitled under the provisions of § 1.14 to access to, copies of, or information concerning either the prior application or any continuing application filed under the provisions of this paragraph, may be given similar access to, copies of, or similar information concerning the other application or applications in the file jacket.

(7) A request for an application under this paragraph is the specific reference required by 35 U.S.C. 120 to every application assigned the application number identified in such request. No amendment in an application under this paragraph may delete this specific reference to any prior application.

(8) In addition to identifying the application number of the prior application, applicant should furnish in the request for an application under this paragraph the following information relating to the prior application to the best of his or her ability:

    (i) Title of invention;

    (ii) Name of applicant(s); and

    (iii) Correspondence address.

(9) Envelopes containing only requests and fees for filing an application under this paragraph should be marked "Box CPA." Requests for an application under this paragraph filed by facsimile transmission should be clearly marked "Box CPA."

(e) Failure to meet filing date requirements.

(1) If an application deposited under paragraph (b), (c), or (d) of this section does not meet the requirements of such paragraph to be entitled to a filing date, applicant will be so notified, if a correspondence address has been provided, and given a time period within which to correct the filing error.

(2) Any request for review of a notification pursuant to paragraph (e)(1) of this section, or a notification that the original application papers lack a portion of the specification or drawing(s), must be by way of a petition pursuant to this paragraph. Any petition under this paragraph must be accompanied by the fee set forth in § 1.17(i) in an application filed under paragraphs (b) or (d) of this section, and the fee set forth in § 1.17(q) in an application filed under paragraph (c) of this section. In the absence of a timely (§ 1.181(f)) petition pursuant to this paragraph, the filing date of an application in which the applicant was notified of a filing error pursuant to paragraph (e)(1) of this section will be the date the filing error is corrected.

(3) If an applicant is notified of a filing error pursuant to paragraph (e)(1) of this section, but fails to correct the filing error within the given time period or otherwise timely (§ 1.181(f)) take action pursuant to this paragraph, proceedings in the application will be considered terminated. Where proceedings in an application are terminated pursuant to this paragraph, the application may be disposed of, and any filing fees, less the handling fee set forth in § 1.21(n), will be refunded.

(f) *Completion of application subsequent to filing — Nonprovisional (including continued prosecution) application.* If an application which has been accorded a filing date pursuant to paragraph (b) of this section, including a continuation, divisional, or continuation-in-part application, does not include the appropriate filing fee or an oath or declaration by the applicant pursuant to § 1.63 or § 1.175, or, if an application which has been accorded a filing date pursuant to paragraph (d) of this section does not include the appropriate filing fee, applicant will be so notified, if a correspondence address has been provided, and given a period of time within which to file the fee, oath or declaration, and the surcharge as set forth in § 1.16(e) in order to prevent abandonment of the application. See § 1.63(d) concerning the submission of a copy of the oath or declaration from the prior application for a continuation or divisional application. If the required filing fee is not timely paid, or if the processing and retention fee set forth in § 1.21(l) is not paid within one year of the date of mailing of the notification required by this paragraph, the application may be disposed of. The notification pursuant to this paragraph may be made simultaneously with any notification pursuant to paragraph (e) of this section. If no correspondence address is included in the application, applicant has two months from the filing date to file the basic filing fee, the oath or declaration in an application under paragraph (b) of this section, and the surcharge as set forth in § 1.16(e) in order to prevent abandonment of the application; or, if no basic filing fee has been paid, one year from the filing date to pay the processing and retention fee set forth in § 1.21(l) to prevent disposal of the application.

(g) Completion of application subsequent to filing -Provisional application. If a provisional application which has been accorded a filing date pursuant to paragraph (c) of this section does not include the appropriate filing fee or the cover sheet required by § 1.51(c)(1), applicant will be so notified, if a correspondence address has been provided, and given a period of time within which to file the fee, cover sheet, and the surcharge as set forth in § 1.16(l) in order to prevent abandonment of the application. If the required filing fee is not timely paid, the application may be disposed of. The notification pursuant to this paragraph may be made simultaneously with any notification pursuant to paragraph (e) of this section. If no correspondence address is included in the application, applicant has two months from the filing date to file the basic filing fee, cover sheet, and the surcharge as set forth in § 1.16(l) in order to prevent abandonment of the application.

(h) Subsequent treatment of application — Nonprovisional (including continued prosecution) application. An application for a patent filed under paragraphs (b) or (d) of this section will not be placed on the files for examination until all its required parts, complying with the rules relating thereto, are received, except that certain minor informalities may be waived subject to subsequent correction whenever required.

> (i) Subsequent treatment of application — Provisional application. A provisional application for a patent filed under paragraph (c) of this section will not be placed on the files for examination and will become abandoned no later than twelve months after its filing date pursuant to 35 U.S.C. 111(b)(1).

(j) Filing date of international application. The filing date of an international application designating the United States of America is treated as the filing date in the United States of America under PCT Article 11(3), except as provided in 35 U.S.C. 102(e).

INCOMPLETE NONPROVISIONAL APPLICATIONS FILED UNDER 37 CFR 1.53(b)

If the nonprovisional application papers filed under 37 CFR 1.53(b) do not include at least a specification containing a description and at least one claim and a drawing, if necessary under 35 U.S.C. 113 (first sentence), or if the submitted application papers are too informal to be given a filing date, the case is held in the Office of Initial Patent Examination (OIPE) as an incomplete application and the applicant is informed of the shortcomings of the papers. No filing date is granted until the incompleteness is corrected.

Form PTO-1123, Notice of Incomplete Application, is prepared and mailed by the OIPE when nonprovisional application papers filed under 37 CFR 1.53(b) are deemed incomplete under 35 U.S.C. 111(a).

Such incompleteness may consist of the omission of any one of the following parts of an application. The component parts of a nonprovisional application filed under 37 CFR 1.53(b) necessary to obtain a filing date are:

A specification as prescribed by 35 U.S.C. 112 and 37 CFR 1.71.

A claim as prescribed by 35 U.S.C. 112 and 37 CFR 1.75.

A drawing, if necessary under 35 U.S.C. 113 (first sentence) and 37 CFR 1.81(a).

See 37 CFR 1.53(b).

Even though an application purports to include the component parts necessary to obtain a filing date, the application will still be held to be incomplete and a filing date will be refused if the component parts fail to satisfy the require-ments set forth above.

For example, if the documents purporting to be a specification are so obviously informal and incoherent that they would clearly not constitute a specification as required by 35 U.S.C. 112 and 37

CFR 1.71, the application would not be acceptable for examination and would not be accorded a filing date until corrections are made. The filing date of the application would be the date the corrections were made.

Filing dates are accorded to nonprovisional applications filed under 37 CFR 1.53(b) submitted without the names of all the inventors, the basic filing fee and/or the oath or declaration. In such cases, a notice is mailed by the OIPE requiring that at least the basic filing fee and the oath or declaration (which must include the names of all the inventors) be filed, accompanied by a surcharge (37 CFR 1.16(e)). In those cases where the basic filing fee is paid, but additional fees are required, a notice is mailed by the examining group, requiring that the balance of the fee be paid. See 37 CFR 1.53(f).

Occasionally, nonprovisional applications filed under 37 CFR 1.53(b) which have already been signed by the inventors contain informal claims that the attorney or agent feels should not be present in the application upon filing. However, since alteration after execution by the inventor and before filing is prohibited, such applications must be filed by the attorney or agent in the form in which they were executed by the inventors. A nonprovisional application filed under 37 CFR 1.53(b) may be filed with a preliminary amendment which is limited to the cancellation of claims. This will diminish the number of claims to be considered for calculation of the filing fee. Any other changes to the application should be the subject of a separate amendment which may be entered after the filing fee has been calculated and the filing date granted. If a preliminary amendment which cancels claims does not accompany the application at the time the application is filed, the notification of insufficient fee will inform the inventor, attorney, or agent of the possibility of correcting the insufficient payment by either (1) paying the additional required fee amount, or (2) filing an amendment which cancels claims to where the remaining claims are covered by the fee submitted upon filing. However, no refund will be made once the fee for claims is properly paid, even though claims are later canceled.

In the past, the OIPE has reviewed the claimed subject matter of newly filed nonprovisional applications to determine whether a filing date should be granted. Such applications included those drawn to perpetual motion devices and methods of doing business and applications for reissue signed by assignees or filed more than 2 years after the grant of the patent which appear to contain broadened reissue claims.

Under the current practice, a filing date is normally granted in such cases if the nonprovisional application filed under 37 CFR 1.53(b) is otherwise sufficient and then forwarded to the examiner for consideration and decision during the regular course of examination.

INCOMPLETE PROVISIONAL APPLICATIONS

If the provisional application papers do not include at least a specification containing a description and a drawing, if necessary under 35 U.S.C. 113 (first sentence) or if the submitted application papers are too informal to be given a filing date, the case is held in the OIPE as an incomplete application and the applicant is informed of the shortcomings of the papers. No filing date is granted until the incompleteness is corrected.

Such incompleteness may consist of the omission of any one of the following parts of an application. The component parts of a provisional application necessary to obtain a filing date are:

A specification as prescribed by 35 U.S.C. 112, first paragraph, and 37 CFR 1.71.

A drawing, if necessary under 35 U.S.C. 113 (first sentence) and 37 CFR 1.81(a).

Even though an application purports to include the com-ponent parts necessary to obtain a filing date, the application will still be held to be incomplete and a filing date will be refused if the component parts fail to satisfy the requirements set forth above. For example, if the documents purporting to be a specification are so obviously informal and incoherent that they would clearly not constitute a specification as required by 35 U.S.C. 112, first paragraph, and 37 CFR 1.71, the application would not be acceptable and would not be accorded a filing date until corrections are made. The filing date of the application would be the date the corrections were made. A provisional application will not be examined. However, a provisional application which does not include a cover sheet or letter identifying the application as a provisional application will be treated as a nonprovisional application filed under 37 CFR 1.53(b). See 37 CFR 1.53(c)(1).

NOTE: No amendment, other than to make the provisional application comply with all the applicable reglations, may be made to the provisional application after the filing date of the provisional application. See 37 CFR 1.53(c).

INFORMAL APPLICATIONS

An application is informal if it is typed on both sides of the paper, or is not permanent, legible, or reproducible. If such informalities are timely corrected, the application is given the filing date on which the original informal papers were filed.

The OIPE accords a filing date, as of the date indicated by the "Office Date" stamp (see MPEP § 505), to application papers which include a specification containing a description and at least one claim (nonprovisional applications filed under 37 CFR 1.53(b)), and a drawing, if necessary under 35 U.S.C. 113 (first sentence) but are informal because they do not comply with the rules or notices. In such applications, the OIPE prepares form PTO-152, Notice of Informal Application, indicating the informality and places it in the file wrapper. The examining group mails the letter to applicant. Failure to correct the informality within the specified time results in abandonment of the application.

The letter of transmittal accompanying the filing of continuing applications should include such additional information as the identification by application number of a provisional or parent application, its status, and location (if known) in the Patent and Trademark Office. The supplying of this information will simplify the processing of these applications.

601.01(b) Provisional Applications Filed Under 35 U.S.C. 111(b) [R-1]

A provisional application will be given a filing date in accordance with 37 CFR 1.53(c) as of the date the written description and any necessary drawings are filed in the Office. The filing date requirements for a provisional application set forth in 37 CFR 1.53(c) parallel the requirements for a nonprovisional application set forth in 37 CFR 1.53(b), except that no claim is required. Amendments, other than those required to make the provisional application comply with applicable regulations, are not permitted after the filing date of the provisional application.

When the specification or drawing are omitted, 37 CFR 1.53(e) requires that the applicant be notified and given a time period in which to submit the missing element to complete the filing. **See MPEP § 601.01(f) and § 601.01(g) for treatment of applications filed without drawings, or filed without all figures of drawings, respectively.

37 CFR 1.53(c)(1) requires all provisional applications be filed with a cover sheet or cover letter identifying the application as a provisional application. The Office will treat an application as having been filed under paragraph (b), unless the application is clearly identified as a provisional application. A provisional application, which is identified as such, but which does not have a complete cover sheet as required by 37 CFR 1.51(c)(1) will be treated as a provisional application. However, the complete cover sheet and a surcharge will be required to be submitted at a later date in conformance with 37 CFR 1.53(g).

When the provisional application does not have a complete cover sheet or the appropriate fee, the applicant will be notified pursuant to 37 CFR 1.53(g) and given a time period in which to provide the necessary fee or cover sheet and to pay the surcharge as set forth in 37 CFR 1.16(l) in order to prevent abandonment of the application. The time period will usually be set at 2 months from the date of notification. This time period may be extended under 37 CFR 1.136(a). If the filing fee is not timely paid, the provisional application will be disposed of. If no correspondence address has been provided, applicant has 2 months from the filing date to file the basic filing fee, cover sheet, and to pay the surcharge as set forth in 37 CFR 1.16(l) in order to prevent abandonment of the provisional application. Copies of a provisional application will be provided by the PTO upon request and payment of the fee set forth in 37 CFR 1.19(b) unless the provisional application has been disposed of (see 37 CFR 1.53(e) and (g)).

The basic filing fee must be paid in a provisional appli-cation, if any claim for benefits under 35 U.S.C. 119(e) based on that application is made in a subsequently filed copending nonprovisional application. 37 CFR 1.78(a)(3).

37 CFR 1.53(e)(2) requires that any request for review of a re-fusal to accord an application a filing date be made by way of a petition accompanied by the fee set forth in 37 CFR 1.17(q) (see MPEP § 506.02).

608.01(m) Form of Claims [R-1]

The claim or claims must commence on a separate sheet and should appear after the detailed description of the invention. While there is no set statutory form for claims, the present Office practice is to insist that each claim must be the object of a sentence starting with "I (or we) claim", "The invention claimed is" (or the equivalent). If, at the time of allowance, the quoted terminology is not present, it is inserted by the clerk. Each claim begins with a capital letter and ends with a period. Periods may not be used else-where in the claims except for abbreviations. See Fressola v. Man-beck, 36 USPQ2d 1211 (D.D.C. 1995). Where a claim sets forth a plurality of elements or steps, each element or step of the claim should be separated by a line indentation, 37 CFR 1.75(i).

There may be plural indentations to further segregate subcom-binations or related steps. In general, the printed patent copies will follow the format used but printing difficulties or expense may prevent the duplication of unduly complex claim formats.

Reference characters corresponding to elements recited in the detailed description and the drawings may be used in conjunction with the recitation of the same element or group of elements in the claims. The reference characters, however, should be enclosed within parentheses so as to avoid confusion with other numbers or characters which may appear in the claims. The use of reference characters is to be considered as having no effect on the scope of the claims.

Many of the difficulties encountered in the prosecution of patent applications after final rejection may be alleviated if each applicant includes, at the time of filing or no later than the first reply, claims varying from the broadest to which he or she believes he or she is entitled to the most detailed that he or she is willing to accept.

Claims should preferably be arranged in order of scope so that the first claim presented is the least restrictive. All dependent claims should be grouped together with the claim or claims to which they refer to the extent practicable. Where separate species are claimed, the claims of like species should be grouped together where possible. Similarly, product and process claims should be separately grouped. Such arrangements are for the purpose of facilitating classification and examination.

The form of claim required in 37 CFR 1.75(e) is particularly adapted for the description of improvement-type inventions. It is to be considered a combination claim. The preamble of this form of claim is considered to positively and clearly include all the elements or steps recited therein as a part of the claimed combination.

For rejections not based on prior art, see MPEP § 706.03.

The following form paragraphs may be used to object to the form of the claims.

§ 6.18.01 Claims: Placement

The claims in this application do not commence on a separate sheet in accordance with 37 CFR *1.52(b), the examiner should attempt to seek clarification from the applicant. Before sending out an Office action or notice setting a new time period for reply, the examiner should first attempt to call the applicant to determine whether the applicant intends the underlining and/or bracketing to appear in the issued patent. The substance of the interview must be made of record. The above form paragraph restarting the time period should only be used in such cases where the examiner is unable to obtain clarification from the applicant by telephone.

> 5. This form paragraph should not be used in a reissue application or a reexamination proceeding.

608.01(n)   Dependent Claims [R-1]

I. MULTIPLE DEPENDENT CLAIMS

37 CFR 1.75. Claim(s).

*****

(c) One or more claims may be presented in dependent form, referring back to and further limiting another claim or claims in the same application. Any dependent claim which refers to more than one other claim ("multiple dependent claim") shall refer to such other claims in the alternative only. A multiple dependent claim shall not serve as a basis for any other multiple dependent claim. For fee calculation purposes under § 1.16, a multiple dependent claim will be considered to be that number of claims to which direct reference is made therein. For fee calculation purposes, also, any claim depending from a multiple dependent claim will be considered to be that number of claims to which direct reference is made in that multiple dependent claim. In addition to the other filing fees, any original application which is filed with, or is amended to include, multiple dependent claims must have paid therein the fee set forth in § 1.16(d). Claims in dependent form shall be construed to include all the limitations of the claim incorporated by reference into the dependent claim. A multiple dependent claim shall be construed to incorporate by reference all the limitations of each of the particular claims in relation to which it is being considered.

*****

Generally, a multiple dependent claim is a dependent claim which refers back in the alternative to more than one preceding independent or dependent claim.

The second paragraph of 35 U.S.C. 112 has been revised in view of the multiple dependent claim practice introduced by the Patent Cooperation Treaty. Thus 35 U.S.C. 112 authorizes multiple dependent claims in applications filed on and after January 24, 1978, as long as they are in the alternative form (e.g., "A machine according to claims 3 or 4, further comprising — "). Cumulative claiming (e.g., "A machine according to claims 3 and 4, further comprising —") is not permitted. A multiple dependent claim may refer in the alternative to only one set of claims. A claim such as "A device as in claims 1, 2, 3, or 4, made by a process of claims 5, 6, 7, or 8" is improper. 35 U.S.C. 112 allows reference to only a particular claim. Furthermore, a multiple dependent claim may not serve as a basis for any other multiple dependent claim, either directly or indirectly. These limitations help to avoid undue confusion in determining how many prior claims are actually referred to in a multiple dependent claim.

A multiple dependent claim which depends from another multiple dependent claim should be objected to by using Form Paragraph 7.45.

§ 7.45 Improper Multiple Dependent Claims

Claim [1] objected to under 37 CFR 1.75(c) as being in improper form because a multiple dependent claim [2]. See MPEP § 608.01(n). Accordingly, the claim [3] not been further treated on the merits.

Examiner Note:

1. In bracket 2, insert —should refer to other claims in the alternative only—, and/or, —cannot depend from any other multiple dependent claim—.

2. Use this paragraph rather than 35 U.S.C. 112, fifth paragraph.

3. In bracket 3, insert —has— or —s have—.

Assume each claim example given below is from a different application.

A. Acceptable Multiple Dependent Claim Wording

Claim 5. A gadget according to claims 3 or 4, further comprising —

Claim 5. A gadget as in any one of the preceding claims, in which —

Claim 3. A gadget as in either claim 1 or claim 2, further comprising —

Claim 4. A gadget as in claim 2 or 3, further comprising —

Claim 16. A gadget as in claims 1, 7, 12, or 15, further comprising —

Claim 5. A gadget as in any of the preceding claims, in which —

Claim 8. A gadget as in one of claims 4-7, in which —

Claim 5. A gadget as in any preceding claim, in which —

Claim 10. A gadget as in any of claims 1-3 or 7-9, in which —

Claim 11. A gadget as in any one of claims 1, 2, or 7-10 inclusive, in which —

B. Unacceptable Multiple Dependent Claim Wording

1. Claim Does Not Refer Back in the Alternative Only

Claim 5. A gadget according to claim 3 and 4, further comprising —

Claim 9. A gadget according to claims 1-3, in which —

Claim 9. A gadget as in claims 1 or 2 and 7 or 8, which —

Claim 6. A gadget as in the preceding claims in which —

Claim 6. A gadget as in claims 1, 2, 3, 4 and/or 5, in which —

Claim 10. A gadget as in claims 1-3 or 7-9, in which —

2. Claim Does Not Refer to a Preceding Claim

Claim 3. A gadget as in any of the following claims, in which —

Claim 5. A gadget as in either claim 6 or claim 8, in which —

3. Reference to Two Sets of Claims to Different Features

Claim 9. A gadget as in claim 1 or 4 made by the process of claims 5, 6, 7, or 8, in which —

4. Reference Back to Another Multiple Dependent Claim

Claim 8. A gadget as in claim 5 (claim 5 is a multiple dependent claim) or claim 7, in which —

35 U.S.C. 112 indicates that the limitations or elements of each claim incorporated by reference into a multiple dependent claim must be considered separately. Thus, a multiple dependent claim, as such, does not contain all the limitations of all the alternative claims to which it refers, but rather contains in any one embodiment only those limitations of the particular claim referred to for the embodiment under consideration. Hence, a multiple dependent claim must be considered in the same manner as a plurality of single dependent claims.

C. Restriction Practice

For restriction purposes, each embodiment of a multiple dependent claim is considered in the same manner as a single dependent claim. Therefore, restriction may be required between the embodiments of a multiple dependent claim. Also, some embodiments of a multiple dependent claim may be held withdrawn while other embodiments are considered on their merits.

D. Handling of Multiple Dependent Claims by the Office of Initial Patent Examination

The Office of Initial Patent Examination (OIPE) is responsible for verifying whether multiple dependent claims filed with the application are in proper alternative form, that they depend only upon prior independent or single dependent claims and also for calculating the amount of the filing fee. A new form, PTO-1360, has been designed to be used in conjunction with the current fee calculation form PTO-875.

E. Handling of Multiple Dependent Claims by the Examining Group Technical Support Staff

The examining group technical support staff is responsible for verifying compliance with the statute and rules of multiple dependent claims added by amendment and for calculating the amount of any additional fees required. This calculation should be performed on form PTO-1360.

There is no need for an examining group technical support staff to check the accuracy of the initial filing fee since this has already been verified by the Office of Initial Patent Examination when granting the filing date.

If a multiple dependent claim (or claims) is added in an amendment without the proper fee, either by adding references to prior claims or by adding a new multiple dependent claim, the amendment should not be entered until the fee has been received. In view of the requirements for multiple dependent claims, no amendment containing new claims or changing the dependency of claims should be entered before checking whether the paid fees cover the costs of the amended claims. The applicant, or his or her attorney or agent, should be contacted to pay the additional fee. Where a letter is written in an insufficient fee situation, a copy of the multiple dependent claim fee calculation, form PTO-1360, should be included for applicant's information.

If an application filed prior to October 1, 1982, is amended on or after October 1, 1982, to include a proper multiple dependent claim for the first time, the fee set forth in § 1.16(d) must be paid.

If such an application contained a proper multiple dependent claim prior to October 1, 1982, the fee set forth in § 1.16(d) does not apply.

Where the examining group technical support staff notes that the reference to the prior claims is improper in an added or amended multiple dependent claim, a notation should be made in the left margin next to the claim itself and the number 1, which is inserted in the "Dep. Claim" column of that amendment on form PTO-1360, should be circled in order to call this matter to the examiner's attention.

F. Handling of Multiple Dependent Claims by the Examiner

Public Law 94-131, the implementing legislation for the Patent Cooperation Treaty amended 35 U.S.C. 112 to state that "a claim in dependent form shall contain a reference to a claim previously set forth." The requirement to refer to a previous claim had existed only in 37 CFR 1.75(c) before.

The following procedures are to be followed by examiners when faced with claims which refer to numerically succeeding claims:

If any series of dependent claims contains a claim with an improper reference to a numerically following claim which cannot be understood, the claim referring to a following claim should normally be objected to and not treated on the merits.

However, in situations where a claim refers to a numerically following claim and the dependency is clear, both as presented and as it will be renumbered at issue, all claims should be examined on the merits and no objection as to form need be made. In such cases, the examiner will renumber the claims into proper order at the time the application is allowed. (See Example B, below.)

Any unusual problems should be brought to the supervisor's attention.

Example A

(Claims 4 and 6 should be objected to as not being understood and should not be treated on the merits.)

1. Independent
2. Dependent on claim 5
3. Dependent on claim 2
4. ". . . as in any preceding claim"
5. Independent
6. Dependent on claim 4

Example B

Note: Parenthetical numerals represent the claim numbering for issue should all claims be allowed.

(All claims should be examined.)

1. (1) Independent
2. (5) Dependent on claim 5 (4)
3. (2) Dependent on claim 1 (1)
4. (3) Dependent on claim 3 (2)
5. (4) Dependent on either claim 1 (1) or claim 3 (2)

The following practice is followed by patent examiners when making reference to a dependent claim either singular or multiple:

(A) When identifying a singular dependent claim which does not include a reference to a multiple dependent claim, either directly or indirectly, reference should be made only to the number of the dependent claim.

(B) When identifying the embodiments included within a multiple dependent claim, or a singular dependent claim which includes a reference to a multiple dependent claim, either directly or indirectly, each embodiment should be identified by using the number of the claims involved, starting with the highest, to the extent necessary to specifically identify each embodiment.

(C) When all embodiments included within a multiple dependent claim or a singular dependent claim which includes a reference to a multiple dependent claim, either directly or indirectly, are subject to a common rejection, objection, or requirement, reference may be made only to the number of the dependent claim.

The following table illustrates the current practice where each embodiment of each claim must be treated on an individual basis:

Claim No.	Claim Dependency	Identification	
		All Claims	Approved practice
1	Independent	1	1
2	Depends from 1	2/1	2
3	Depends from 2	3/2/1	3
4	Depends from 2 or 3	4/2/1 4/3/2/1	4/2 4/3
5	Depends from 3	5/3/2/1	5
6	Depends from 2, 3, or 5	6/2/1 6/3/2/1 6/5/3/2/1	6/2 6/3 6/5

Claim No.	Claim Dependency	Identification	
		All Claims	Approved practice
7	Depends from 6	7/6/2/1 7/6/3/2/1 7/6/5/3/2/1	7/6/2 7/6/3 7/6/5

When all embodiments in a multiple dependent claim situation (claims 4, 6, and 7 above) are subject to a common rejection, objection, or requirements, reference may be made to the number of the individual dependent claim only. For example, if 4/2 and 4/3 were subject to a common ground of rejection, reference should be made only to claim 4 in the statement of that rejection.

The provisions of 35 U.S.C. 132 require that each Office action make it explicitly clear what rejection, objection and/or requirement is applied to each claim embodiment.

G. Fees for Multiple Dependent Claims

1. Use of Form PTO-1360

To assist in the computation of the fees for multiple dependent claims, a separate "Multiple Dependent Claim Fee Calculation Sheet," form PTO-1360, has been designed for use with the current "Patent Application Fee Determination Record," form PTO-875. Form PTO-1360 will be placed in the file wrapper by the Office of Initial Patent Examination (OIPE) where multiple dependent claims are in the application as filed. If multiple dependent claims are not included upon filing, but are later added by amendment, the examining group technical support staff will place the form in the file wrapper. If there are multiple dependent claims in the application, the total number of independent and dependent claims for fee purposes will be calculated on form PTO-1360 and the total number of claims and number of independent claims is then placed on form PTO-875 for final fee calculation purposes.

2. Calculation of Fees

(a) Proper Multiple Dependent Claim

35 U.S.C. 41(a), provides that claims in proper multiple dependent form may not be considered as single dependent claims for the purpose of calculating fees. Thus, a multiple dependent claim is considered to be that number of dependent claims to which it refers. Any proper claim depending directly or indirectly from a multiple dependent claim is also considered as the number of dependent claims as referred to in the multiple dependent claim from which it depends.

(b) Improper Multiple Dependent Claim

If any multiple dependent claim is improper, OIPE may indicate that fact by placing an encircled numeral "1" in the "Dep. Claims" column of form PTO-1360. The fee for any improper multiple dependent claim, whether it is defective for either not being in the alternative form or for being directly or indirectly dependent on a prior multiple dependent claim, will only be one, since only an objection to the form of such a claim will normally be made. This procedure also greatly simplifies the calculation of fees. Any claim depending from an improper multiple dependent claim will also be considered to be improper and be counted as one dependent claim.

(c) Fee calculation example

i) Comments On Fee Calculation Example

Claim 1 — This is an independent claim; therefore, a numeral "1" is placed opposite claim number 1 in the "Ind." column.

Claim 2 — Since this is a claim dependent on a single independent claim, a numeral "1" is placed opposite claim number 2 of the "Dep." column.

Claim 3 — Claim 3 is also a single dependent claim, so a numeral "1" is placed in the "Dep." column.

Claim 4 — Claim 4 is a proper multiple dependent claim. It refers directly to two claims in the alternative, namely, claim 2 or 3. Therefore, a numeral "2" to indicate direct reference to two claims is placed in the "Dep." column opposite claim number 4.

Claim 5 — This claim is a singularly dependent claim depending from a multiple dependent claim. For fee calculation purposes, such a claim is counted as being that number of claims to which direct reference is made in the multiple dependent claim from which it depends. In this case, the multiple dependent claim number 4 it depends from counts as 2 claims; therefore, claim 5 also counts as 2 claims. Accordingly, a numeral "2" is placed opposite claim number 5 in the "Dep." column.

Claim 6 — Claim 6 depends indirectly from a multiple dependent claim 4. Since claim 4 counts as 2 claims, claim 6 also counts as 2 dependent claims. Consequently, a numeral "2" is placed in the "Dep." column after claim 6.

Claim 7 — This claim is a multiple dependent claim since it refers to claims 4, 5, or 6. However, as can be seen by looking at the "2" in the "Dep." column opposite claim 4, claim 7 depends from a multiple dependent claim. This practice is improper under 35 U.S.C. 112 and 37 CFR 1.75(c). Following the procedure for calculating fees for improper multiple dependent claims, a numeral "1" is placed in the "Dep." column with a circle drawn around it to alert the examiner that the claim is improper.

Claim 8 — Claim 8 is improper since it depends from an improper claim. If the base claim is in error, this error cannot be corrected by adding additional claims depending therefrom. Therefore, a numeral "1" with a circle around it is placed in the "Dep." column.

Claim 9 — Here again we have an independent claim which is always indicated with a numeral "1" in the "Ind." column opposite the claim number.

Claim 10 — This claim refers to two independent claims in the alternative. A numeral "2" is, therefore, placed in the "Dep." column opposite claim 10.

Claim 11 — Claim 11 is a dependent claim which refers to two claims in the conjunctive ("1" and "9") rather than in the alternative ("1" or "9"). This form is improper under 35 U.S.C. 112 and 37 CFR 1.75(c). Accordingly, since claim 11 is improper, an encircled number "1" is placed in the "Dep." column opposite Claim 11.

ii) Calculation of Fee in Fee Example

After the number of "Ind." and "Dep." claims are noted on form PTO-1360, each column is added. In this example, there are

2 independent claims and 13 dependent claims or a total of 15 claims. The number of independent and total claims can then be placed on form PTO-875 and the fee calculated.

II. TREATMENT OF IMPROPER DEPENDENT CLAIMS

The initial determination, for fee purposes, as to whether a claim is dependent must be made by persons other than examiners; it is necessary, at that time, to accept as dependent virtually every claim which refers to another claim, without determining whether there is actually a true dependent relationship. The initial acceptance of a claim as a dependent claim does not, however, preclude a subsequent holding by the examiner that a claim is not a proper dependent claim. Any claim which is in dependent form but which is so worded that it, in fact is not, as, for example, it does not include every limitation of the claim on which it depends, will be required to be canceled as not being a proper dependent claim; and cancelation of any further claim depending on such a dependent claim will be similarly required. Where a claim in dependent form is not considered to be a proper dependent claim under 37 CFR 1.75(c), the examiner should object to such claim under 37 CFR 1.75(c) and require cancellation of such improper dependent claim or rewriting of such improper dependent claim in independent form. See Ex parte Porter, 25 USPQ2d 1144, 1147 (Bd. of Pat. App. & Inter. 1992) (A claim determined to be an improper dependent claim should be treated as a formal matter, in that the claim should be objected to and applicant should be required to cancel the claim (or replace the improper dependent claim with an independent claim) rather than treated by a rejection of the claim under 35 U.S.C. 112, fourth paragraph.). The applicant may thereupon amend the claims to place them in proper dependent form, or may redraft them as independent claims, upon payment of any necessary additional fee.

Note, that although 37 CFR 1.75(c) requires the dependent claim to further limit a preceding claim, this rule does not apply to product-by-process claims.

Claims which are in improper dependent form for failing to further limit the subject matter of a previous claim should be objected to under 37 CFR 1.75(c) by using Form Paragraph 7.36.

§ 7.36 Objection, 37 CFR 1.75(c), Improper Dependent Claim

Claim [1] objected to under 37 CFR 1.75(c), as being of improper dependent form for failing to further limit the subject matter of a previous claim. Applicant is required to cancel the claim(s), or amend the claim(s) to place the claim(s) in proper dependent form, or rewrite the claim(s) in independent form. [2].

Examiner Note:

1. In bracket 2, insert an explanation of what is in the claim and why it does not constitute a further limitation.

2. Note Ex parte Porter, 25 USPQ2d 1144 (Bd. Pat. App. & Inter. 1992) for situations where a method claim is considered to be properly dependent upon a parent apparatus claim and should not be objected to or rejected under 35 U.S.C. 112, fourth paragraph. See also MPEP § 608.01(n), "Infringement Test" for dependent claims. The test for a proper dependent claim is whether the dependent claim includes every limitation of the parent claim. The test is not whether the claims differ in scope. A proper dependent claim shall not conceivably be infringed by anything which would not also infringe the basic claim.

III. INFRINGEMENT TEST

The test as to whether a claim is a proper dependent claim is that it shall include every limitation of the claim from which it depends (35 U.S.C. 112, fourth paragraph) or in other words that it shall not conceivably be infringed by anything which would not also infringe the basic claim.

A dependent claim does not lack compliance with 35 U.S.C. 112, fourth paragraph, simply because there is a question as to (1) the significance of the further limitation added by the dependent claim, or (2) whether the further limitation in fact changes the scope of the dependent claim from that of the claim from which it depends. The test for a proper dependent claim under the fourth paragraph of 35 U.S.C. 112 is whether the dependent claim includes every limitation of the claim from which it depends. The test is not one of whether the claims differ in scope.

Thus, for example, if claim 1 recites the combination of elements A, B, C, and D, a claim reciting the structure of claim 1 in which D was omitted or replaced by E would not be a proper dependent claim, even though it placed further limitations on the remaining elements or added still other elements.

Examiners are reminded that a dependent claim is directed to a combination including everything recited in the base claim and what is recited in the dependent claim. It is this combination that must be compared with the prior art, exactly as if it were presented as one independent claim.

The fact that a dependent claim which is otherwise proper might relate to a separate invention which would require a separate search or be separately classified from the claim on which it depends would not render it an improper dependent claim, although it might result in a requirement for restriction.

The fact that the independent and dependent claims are in different statutory classes does not, in itself, render the latter improper. Thus, if claim 1 recites a specific product, a claim for the method of making the product of claim 1 in a particular manner would be a proper dependent claim since it could not be infringed without infringing claim 1. Similarly, if claim 1 recites a method of making a product, a claim for a product made by the method of claim 1 could be a proper dependent claim. On the other hand, if claim 1 recites a method of making a specified product, a claim to the product set forth in claim 1 would not be a proper dependent claim if the product might be made in other ways.

IV. CLAIM FORM AND ARRANGEMENT

A singular dependent claim 2 could read as follows:

2. The product of claim 1 in which . . . .

A series of singular dependent claims is permissible in which a dependent claim refers to a preceding claim which, in turn, refers to another preceding claim.

A claim which depends from a dependent claim should not be separated therefrom by any claim which does not also depend from said "dependent claim." It should be kept in mind that a dependent claim may refer back to any preceding independent claim. These are are the only restrictions with respect to the sequence of claims and, in general, applicant's sequence should not be changed. See MPEP § 608.01(j). Applicant may be so advised by using Form Paragraph 6.18.

§ 6.18 Series of Singular Dependent Claims

A series of singular dependent claims is permissible in which a dependent claim refers to a preceding claim which, in turn, refers to another preceding claim.

A claim which depends from a dependent claim should not be separated by any claim which does not also depend from said dependent claim. It should be kept in mind that a dependent claim may refer to any preceding independent claim. In general, applicant's sequence will not be changed. See MPEP § 608.01(n).

During prosecution, the order of claims may change and be in conflict with the requirement that dependent claims refer to a preceding claim. Accordingly, the numbering of dependent claims and the numbers of preceding claims referred to in dependent claims should be carefully checked when claims are renumbered upon allowance.

V. REJECTION AND OBJECTION

If the base claim has been canceled, a claim which is directly or indirectly dependent thereon should be rejected as incomplete. If the base claim is rejected, the dependent claim should be objected to rather than rejected, if it is otherwise allowable.

Form Paragraph 7.43 can be used to state the objection.

§ 7.43 Objection to Claims, Allowable Subject Matter

Claim [1] objected to as being dependent upon a rejected base claim, but would be allowable if rewritten in independent form including all of the limitations of the base claim and any intervening claims.

608.01(o)   Basis for Claim Terminology in Description

The meaning of every term used in any of the claims should be apparent from the descriptive portion of the specification with clear disclosure as to its import; and in mechanical cases, it should be identified in the descriptive portion of the specification by reference to the drawing, designating the part or parts therein to which the term applies. A term used in the claims may be given a special meaning in the description. No term may be given a meaning repugnant to the usual meaning of the term.

Usually the terminology of the original claims follows the nomenclature of the specification, but sometimes in amending the claims or in adding new claims, new terms are introduced that do not appear in the specification. The use of a confusing variety of terms for the same thing should not be permitted.

New claims and amendments to the claims already in the case should be scrutinized not only for new matter but also for new terminology. While an applicant is not limited to the nomenclature used in the application as filed, he or she should make appropriate amendment of the specification whenever this nomenclature is departed from by amendment of the claims so as to have clear support or antecedent basis in the specification for the new terms appearing in the claims. This is necessary in order to insure certainty in construing the claims in the light of the specification, Ex parte Kotler, 1901 C.D. 62, 95 O.G. 2684 (Comm'r Pat. 1901). See 37 CFR 1.75, MPEP § 608.01(i) and § 1302.01.

The specification should be objected to if it does not provide proper antecedent basis for the claims by using Form Paragraph 7.44.

§ 7.44 Claimed Subject Matter Not in Specification

The specification is objected to as failing to provide proper antecedent basis for the claimed subject matter. See 37 CFR 1.75(d)(1) and MPEP § 608.01(o). Correction of the following is required: [1]

608.01(p)   Completeness [R-1]

Newly filed applications obviously failing to disclose an invention with the clarity required are discussed in MPEP § 702.01.

A disclosure in an application, to be complete, must contain such description and details as to enable any person skilled in the art or science to which the invention pertains to make and use the invention as of its filing date. In re Glass, 492 F.2d 1228, 181 USPQ 31 (CCPA 1974).

While the prior art setting may be mentioned in general terms, the essential novelty, the essence of the invention, must be described in such details, including proportions and techniques, where necessary, as to enable those persons skilled in the art to make and utilize the invention.

Specific operative embodiments or examples of the invention must be set forth. Examples and description should be of sufficient scope as to justify the scope of the claims. Markush claims must be provided with support in the disclosure for each member of the Markush group. Where the constitution and formula of a chemical compound is stated only as a probability or speculation, the disclosure is not sufficient to support claims identifying the compound by such composition or formula.

A complete disclosure should include a statement of utility. This usually presents no problem in mechanical cases. In chemical cases, varying degrees of specificity are required.

A disclosure involving a new chemical compound or composition must teach persons skilled in the art how to make the compound or composition. Incomplete teachings may not be completed by reference to subsequently filed applications.

For "Guidelines For Examination Of Applications For Compliance With The Utility Requirement of 35 U.S.C. 101," see MPEP § 706.03(a)(1).

For "General Principles Governing Utility Rejections," see MPEP § 2107.

For a discussion of the utility requirement under 35 U.S.C. 112, first paragraph, in drug cases, see MPEP § 2107.02 and § 2164.06(a).

For "Procedural Considerations Related to Rejections for Lack of Utility," see MPEP § 2107.01.

For "Special Considerations for Asserted Therapeutic or Pharmacological Utilities," see MPEP § 2107.02.

I. INCORPORATION BY REFERENCE

The Commissioner has considerable discretion in determining what may or may not be incorporated by reference in a patent application. General Electric Co. v. Brenner, 407 F.2d 1258, 159 USPQ 335 (D.C. Cir. 1968). The incorporation by reference practice with respect to applications which issue as U.S. patents provides the public with a patent disclosure which minimizes the public's burden to search for and obtain copies of documents incorporated by reference which may not be readily available. Through the Office's incorporation by reference policy, the Office ensures that reasonably complete disclosures are published as U.S. patents. The following is the manner in which the Commissioner has elected to exercise that discretion. Section A provides the guidance for incorporation by reference in applications which are to issue as U.S. patents. Section B provides guidance for incorporation by reference in benefit applications; i.e., those domestic (35 U.S.C. 120) or foreign (35 U.S.C. 119(a)) applications relied on to establish an earlier effective filing date.

A. *Review of Applications Which Are To Issue as Patents.*

An application as filed must be complete in itself in order to comply with 35 U.S.C. 112. Material nevertheless may be incorporated by reference, Ex parte Schwarze, 151 USPQ 426 (Bd. App. 1966). An application for a patent when filed may incorporate "essential material" by reference to (1) a U.S. patent or (2) a pending U.S. application, subject to the conditions set forth below.

"Essential material" is defined as that which is necessary to (1) describe the claimed invention, (2) provide an enabling disclosure of the claimed invention, or (3) describe the best mode (35 U.S.C. 112). In any application which is to issue as a U.S. patent, essential material may not be incorporated by reference to (1) patents or applications published by foreign countries or a regional patent office, (2) non-patent publications, (3) a U.S. patent or application which itself incorporates "essential material" by reference, or (4) a foreign application.

Nonessential subject matter may be incorporated by reference to (1) patents or applications published by the United States or foreign countries or regional patent offices, (2) prior filed, commonly owned U.S. applications, or (3) non-patent publications however, hyperlinks and/or other forms of browser executable code cannot be incorporated by reference. See MPEP § 608.01

Mere reference to another application, patent, or publication is not an incorporation of anything therein into the application containing such reference for the purpose of the disclosure required by 35 U.S.C. 112, first paragraph. In re de Seversky, 474 F.2d 671, 177 USPQ 144 (CCPA 1973). In addition to other requirements for an application, the referencing application should include an identification of the referenced patent, application, or publication. Particular attention should be directed to specific portions of the referenced document where the subject matter being incorporated may be found. Guidelines for situations where applicant is permitted to fill in a number for Application No. _____ left blank in the application as filed can be found in In re Fouche, 439 F.2d 1237, 169 USPQ 429 (CCPA 1971) (Abandoned applications less than 20 years old can be incorporated by reference to the same extent as copending applications; both types are open to the public upon the referencing application issuing as a patent. See MPEP § 103).

1. Complete Disclosure Filed

If an application is filed with a complete disclosure, essential material may be canceled by amendment and may be substituted by reference to a U.S. patent or an earlier filed pending U.S. application. The amendment must be accompanied by an affidavit or declaration signed by the applicant, or a practitioner representing the applicant, stating that the material canceled from the application is the same material that has been incorporated by reference.

If an application as filed incorporates essential material by reference to a U.S. patent or a pending and commonly owned U.S. application, applicant may be required prior to examination to furnish the Office with a copy of the referenced material together with an affidavit or declaration executed by the applicant, or a practitioner representing the applicant, stating that the copy consists of the same material incorporated by reference in the referencing application. However, if a copy of a printed U.S. patent is furnished, no affidavit or declaration is required.

Prior to allowance of an application that incorporates essential material by reference to a pending U.S. application, the examiner shall determine if the referenced application has issued as a patent. If the referenced application has issued as a patent, the examiner shall enter the U.S. Patent No. of the referenced application in the specification of the referencing application (see MPEP § 1302.04). If the referenced application has not issued as a patent, applicant will be required to amend the disclosure of the referencing application to include the material incorporated by reference. The amendment must be accompanied by an affidavit or declaration executed by the applicant, or a practitioner representing the applicant, stating the amendatory material consists of the same material incorporated by reference in the referencing application.

2. Improper Incorporation

The filing date of any application wherein essential material is improperly incorporated by reference to a foreign application or patent or to a publication will not be affected because of the reference. In such a case, the applicant will be required to amend the specification to include the material incorporated by reference. The following form paragraphs may be used.

§ 6.19 Incorporation by Reference, Foreign Patent or Application

The incorporation of essential material in the specification by reference to a foreign application or patent, or to a publication is improper. Applicant is required to amend the disclosure to include the material incorporated by reference. The amendment must be accompanied by an affidavit or declaration executed by the applicant, or a practitioner representing the applicant, stating that the amendatory material consists of the same material incorporated by reference in the referencing application. In re Hawkins, 486 F.2d 569, 179 USPQ 157 (CCPA 1973); In re Hawkins, 486 F.2d 579, 179 USPQ 163 (CCPA 1973); In re Hawkins, 486 F.2d 577, 179 USPQ 167 (CCPA 1973).

§ *6.19.01 Improper Incorporation by Reference, General*

The attempt to incorporate subject matter into this application by reference to [1] is improper because [2].

Examiner Note:

1. In bracket 1, identify the document such as an application or patent number or other identification.

2. In bracket 2, give reason why it is improper.

The amendment must be accompanied by an affidavit or declaration executed by the applicant, or a practitioner representing the applicant, stating that the amendatory material consists of the same material incorporated by reference in the referencing application. In re Hawkins, 486 F.2d 569, 179 USPQ 157 (CCPA 1973); In re Hawkins, 486 F.2d 579, 179 USPQ 163 (CCPA 1973); In re Hawkins, 486 F.2d 577, 179 USPQ 167 (CCPA 1973).

Reliance on a commonly assigned copending application by a different inventor may ordinarily be made for the purpose of completing the disclosure. See In re Fried, 329 F.2d 323, 141 USPQ 27 (CCPA 1964), and General Electric Co. v. Brenner, 407 F.2d 1258, 159 USPQ 335 (D.C. Cir. 1968).

Since a disclosure must be complete as of the filing date, subsequent publications or subsequently filed applications cannot be relied on to establish a constructive reduction to practice or an enabling disclosure as of the filing date. White Consol. Indus., Inc. v. Vega Servo-Control, Inc., 713 F.2d 788, 218 USPQ 961 (Fed. Cir. 1983); In re Scar-brough, 500 F.2d 560, 182 USPQ 298 (CCPA 1974); In re Glass, 492 F.2d 1228, 181 USPQ 31 (CCPA 1974).

B. Review of Applications Which Are Relied on To Establish an Earlier Effective Filing Date.

The limitations on the material which may be incorporated by reference in U.S. patent applications which are to issue as U.S. patents do not apply to applications relied on only to establish an earlier effective filing date under 35 U.S.C. 119 or 35 U.S.C. 120. Neither 35 U.S.C. 119(a) nor 35 U.S.C. 120 places any restrictions or limitations as to how the claimed invention must be disclosed in the earlier application to comply with 35 U.S.C. 112, first paragraph. Accordingly, an application is entitled to rely upon the filing date of an earlier application, even if the earlier application itself incorporates essential material by reference to another document. See Ex parte Maziere, 27 USPQ2d 1705, 1706-07 (Bd. Pat. App. & Inter. 1993).

The reason for incorporation by reference practice with respect to applications which are to issue as U.S. patents is to provide the public with a patent disclosure which minimizes the public's burden to search for and obtain copies of documents incorporated by reference which may not be readily available. Through the Office's incorporation by reference policy, the Office ensures that reasonably complete disclosures are published as U.S. patents. The same policy concern does not apply where the sole purpose for which an applicant relies on an earlier U.S. or foreign application is to establish an earlier filing date. Incorporation by reference in the earlier application of (1) patents or applications published by foreign countries or regional patent offices, (2) non-patent publications, (3) a U.S. patent or application which itself incorporates "essential material" by reference, or (4) a foreign application, is not critical in the case of a "benefit" application.

When an applicant, or a patent owner in a reexamination or interference, claims the benefit of the filing date of an earlier application which incorporates material by reference, the applicant or patent owner may be required to supply copies of the material incorporated by reference. For example, an applicant may claim the benefit of the filing date of a foreign application which itself incorporates by reference another earlier filed foreign application. If necessary, due to an intervening reference, applicant should be required to supply a copy of the earlier filed foreign application, along with an English language translation. A review can then be made of the foreign application and all material incorporated by reference to determine whether the foreign application discloses the invention sought to be patented in the manner required by the first paragraph of 35 U.S.C. 112 so that benefit may be accorded. In re Gosteli, 872 F.2d 1008, 10 USPQ2d 1614 (Fed. Cir. 1989).

II. SIMULATED OR PREDICTED TEST RESULTS OR PROPHETIC EXAMPLES

Simulated or predicted test results and prophetical examples (paper examples) are permitted in patent applications. Working examples correspond to work actually performed and may describe tests which have actually been conducted and results that were achieved. Paper examples describe the manner and process of making an embodiment of the invention which has not actually been conducted. Paper examples should not be represented as work actually done. No results should be represented as actual results unless they have actually been achieved. Paper examples should not be described using the past tense.

For problems arising from the designation of materials by trademarks and trade names, see MPEP § 608.01(v).

608.01(q)   Substitute or Rewritten Specification [R-1]

37 CFR 1.125. Substitute specification.

(a) If the number or nature of the amendments or the legibility of the application papers renders it difficult to consider the application, or to arrange the papers for printing or copying, the Office may require the entire specification, including the claims, or any part thereof, be rewritten.

(b) A substitute specification, excluding the claims, may be filed at any point up to payment of the issue fee if it is accompanied by:

> (1) A statement that the substitute specification includes no new matter; and

> (2) A marked-up copy of the substitute specification showing the matter being added to and the matter being deleted from the specification of record.

(c) A substitute specification submitted under this section must be submitted in clean form without markings as to amended material.

(d) A substitute specification under this section is not permitted in a reissue application or in a reexamination proceeding.

The specification is sometimes in such faulty English that a new specification is necessary; in such instances, a new specification should be required.

Form Paragraph 6.28 may be used where the specification is in faulty English.

§ 6.28 Idiomatic English

A substitute specification in proper idiomatic English and in compliance with 37 CFR 1.52(a) and (b) is required. The substitute specification filed must be accompanied by a statement that it contains no new matter.

37 CFR 1.125(a) applies to a substitute specification required by the Office. If the number or nature of the amendments or the legibility of the application papers renders it difficult to consider the application, or to arrange the papers for printing or copying, the Office may require the entire specification, including the claims, or any part thereof be rewritten.

Form Paragraph 6.28.01 may be used where the examiner, for reasons other than faulty English, requires a substitute specification.

**

§ 6.28.01 Substitute Specification Required by Examiner

A substitute specification [1] the claims is required pursuant to 37 CFR 1.125(a) because [2].

A substitute specification filed under 37 CFR 1.125(a) must only contain subject matter from the original specification and any previously entered amendment under 37 CFR 1.121. If the substitute specification contains additional subject matter not of record, the substitute specification must be filed under 37 CFR 1.125(b) and must be accompanied by: 1) a statement that the substitute specification contains no new matter; and 2) a marked-up copy showing the amendments to be made via the substitute specification relative to the specification at the time the substitute specification is filed.

Examiner Note:

1. In bracket 1, insert either — excluding— or — including—
    .
2. In bracket 2, insert clear and concise examples of why a new specification is required.
3. A new specification is required if the number or nature of the amendments render it difficult to consider the application or to arrange the papers for printing or copying, 37 CFR 1.125.
4. See also form paragraph 13.01 for partial rewritten specification.
5. 37 CFR 1.125(b) provides applicants with the right of entry of substitute specifications, under the conditions set forth in the section, in applications other than reissue applications (37 CFR 1.125(d)) that have not been required by the examiner.

37 CFR 1.125(b) applies to a substitute specification voluntarily filed by the applicant. A substitute specification, excluding claims, may be voluntarily filed by the applicant at any point up to the payment of the issue fee provided it is accompanied by (1) a statement that the substitute specification includes no new matter, and (2) a marked-up copy of the substitute specification showing the matter being added to and the matter being deleted from the specification of record. 37 CFR 1.125(b). The Office will accept a substitute specification voluntarily filed by the applicant if the requirements of 37 CFR 1.125(b) are satisfied.

37 CFR 1.125(c) requires a substitute specification filed under 37 CFR 1.125(a) or (b) be submitted in clean form without markings as to amended material.

* * *

A substitute specification filed under 37 CFR 1.125(b) must be accompanied by a statement indicating that no new matter was included. There is no obligation on the examiner to make a detailed comparison between the old and the new specifications for determining whether or not new matter has been added. If, however, an examiner becomes aware that new matter is present, objection thereto should be made.

The filing of a substitute specification rather than amending the original application has the advantage for applicants of eliminating the need to prepare an amendment of the specification. If word processing equipment is used by applicants, substitute specifications can be easily prepared. The Office receives the advantage of saving the time needed to enter amendments in the specification and a reduction in the number of printing errors. A substitute specification is not permitted in a reissue application or in a reexamination proceeding. 37 CFR 1.125(d).

A substitute specification **which complies with 37 CFR 1.125 should normally be entered. The examiner should write "Enter" or "OK to Enter" and his or her initials in ink in the left margin of the first page of the substitute specification. A substitute specification which is denied entry should be so marked.

Form Paragraph 6.28.02 may be used to notify applicant that a substitute specification submitted under 37 CFR 1.125(b) has not been entered.

§ 6.28.02 *Substitute Specification Filed Under 37 CFR 1.125(b) Not Entered.*

The substitute specification filed [1] has not been entered because it does not conform to 37 CFR 1.125(b) because: [2]

Examiner Note:

1. In bracket 2, insert statement of why the substitute specification is improper, for example:

    — the statement as to a lack of new matter under 37 CFR 1.125(b) is missing—,

    — a marked-up copy of the substitute specification has not been supplied (in addition to the clean copy)—;

    — a clean copy of the substitute specification has not been supplied (in addition to the marked-up copy)—; or,

    — the substitute specification has been filed:

    — in a reissue application or in a reexamination proceeding, 37 CFR 1.125(d)-, or

    — after payment of the issue fee—, or

    — containing claims (to be amended) —.

See MPEP § 714.20 regarding entry of amendments which include an unacceptable substitute specification.

For new matter in amendment, see MPEP § 608.04.

For application prepared for issue, see MPEP § 1302.02.

608.01(r)   Derogatory Remarks About Prior Art in Specification

The applicant may refer to the general state of the art and the advance thereover made by his or her invention, but he or she is not permitted to make derogatory remarks concerning the inventions of others. Derogatory remarks are statements disparaging the products or processes of any particular person other than the applicant, or statements as to the merits or validity of applications or patents of another person. Mere comparisons with the prior art are not considered to be disparaging, per se.

608.01(s)   Restoration of Canceled Matter

Canceled text in the specification can be reinstated only by a subsequent amendment presenting the previously canceled matter as a new insertion. 37 CFR 1.121(a)(1)(iii). A claim canceled by amendment, which was not deleted and rewritten, can be reinstated only by a subsequent amendment presenting the claim as a new claim with a new claim number. 37 CFR 1.121(a)(2)(ii). See MPEP § 714.24.

608.01(t)   Use in Subsequent Application

A reservation for a future application of subject matter disclosed but not claimed in a pending application will not be permitted in the pending application. 37 CFR 1.79; MPEP § 608.01(e).

No part of a specification can normally be transferred to another application. Drawings may be transferred to another application only upon the granting of a petition filed under the provisions of 37 CFR 1.182.

608.01(u) Use of Formerly Filed Incomplete Application

Parts of an incomplete application which have been retained by the Office may be used as part of a complete application if the missing parts are later supplied. See MPEP § 506 and § 506.01.

608.01(v) Trademarks and Names Used in Trade

The expressions "trademarks" and "names used in trade" as used below have the following meanings:

Trademark: a word, letter, symbol, or device adopted by one manufacturer or merchant and used to identify and distinguish his or her product from those of others. It is a proprietary word, letter, symbol, or device pointing distinctly to the product of one producer.

Names Used in Trade: a nonproprietary name by which an article or product is known and called among traders or workers in the art, although it may not be so known by the public, generally. Names used in trade do not point to the product of one producer, but they identify a single article or product irrespective of producer.

Names used in trade are permissible in patent applications if:

(A) Their meanings are established by an accompanying definition which is sufficiently precise and definite to be made a part of a claim, or

(B) In this country, their meanings are well-known and satisfactorily defined in the literature.

Condition (A) or (B) must be met at the time of filing of the complete application.

TRADEMARKS

The relationship between a trademark and the product it identifies is sometimes indefinite, uncertain, and arbitrary. The formula or characteristics of the product may change from time to time and yet it may continue to be sold under the same trademark. In patent specifications, every element or ingredient of the product should be set forth in positive, exact, intelligible language, so that there will be no uncertainty as to what is meant. Arbitrary trademarks which are liable to mean different things at the pleasure of manufacturers do not constitute such language. Ex Parte Kattwinkle, 12 USPQ 11 (Bd. App. 1931).

However, if the product to which the trademark refers is set forth in such language that its identity is clear, the examiners are authorized to permit the use of the trademark if it is distinguished from common descriptive nouns by capitalization. If the trademark has a fixed and definite meaning, it constitutes sufficient identification unless some physical or chemical characteristic of the article or material is involved in the invention. In that event, as also in those cases where the trademark has no fixed and definite meaning, identification by scientific or other explanatory language is necessary. In re Gebauer-Fuelnegg, 121 F.2d 505, 50 USPQ 125 (CCPA 1941).

The matter of sufficiency of disclosure must be decided on an individual case-by-case basis. In re Metcalfe, 410 F.2d 1378, 161 USPQ 789 (CCPA 1969).

Where the identification of a trademark is introduced by amendment, it must be restricted to the characteristics of the product known at the time the application was filed to avoid any question of new matter.

If proper identification of the product sold under a trademark, or a product referred to only by a name used in trade, is omitted from the specification and such identification is deemed necessary under the principles set forth above, the examiner should hold the disclosure insufficient and reject on the ground of insufficient disclosure any claims based on the identification of the product merely by trademark or by the name used in trade. If the product cannot be otherwise defined, an amendment defining the process of its manufacture may be permitted. Such amendments must be supported by satisfactory showings establishing that the specific nature or process of manufacture of the product as set forth in the amendment was known at the time of filing of the application.

Although the use of trademarks having definite meanings is permissible in patent applications, the proprietary nature of the marks should be respected. Trademarks should be identified by capitalizing each letter of the mark (in the case of word or letter marks) or otherwise indicating the description of the mark (in the case of marks in the form of a symbol or device or other nontextual form). Every effort should be made to prevent their use in any manner which might adversely affect their validity as trademarks.

Form Paragraph 6.20 may be used.

§ 6.20 *Trademarks and Their Use*

The use of the trademark [1] has been noted in this application. It should be capitalized wherever it appears and be accompanied by the generic terminology.

Although the use of trademarks is permissible in patent applications, the proprietary nature of the marks should be respected and every effort made to prevent their use in any manner which might adversely affect their validity as trademarks.

Examiner Note:

Capitalize each letter of the word in the bracket or include a proper trademark symbol, such as § or § following the word.

The examiner should not permit the use of language such as "the product X (a descriptive name) commonly known as Y (trademark)" since such language does not bring out the fact that the latter is a trademark. Language such as "the product X (a descriptive name) sold under the trademark Y" is permissible.

The use of a trademark in the title of an application should be avoided as well as the use of a trademark coupled with the word "type", e.g., "Band-Aid type bandage."

In the event that the proprietary trademark is a "symbol or device" depicted in a drawing, either the brief description of the drawing or the detailed description of the drawing should specify that the "symbol or device" is a registered trademark of Company X.

The owner of a trademark may be identified in the specification.

Group directors should reply to all trademark misuse complaint letters and forward a copy to the editor of this manual.

See Appendix I for a partial listing of trademarks and the particular goods to which they apply.

INCLUSION OF COPYRIGHT OR MASK WORK NOTICE IN PATENTS

37 CFR 1.71. Detailed description and specification of the invention

*****

(d) A copyright or mask work notice may be placed in a design or utility patent application adjacent to copyright and mask work material contained therein. The notice may appear at any appropriate portion of the patent application disclosure. For notices in drawings, see § 1.84(s). The content of the notice must be limited to only those elements provided for by law. For example, "?1983 John Doe" (17 U.S.C. 401) and "*M* John Doe" (17 U.S.C. 909) would be properly limited and, under current statutes, legally sufficient notices of copyright and mask work, respectively. Inclusion of a copyright or mask work notice will be permitted only if the authorization language set forth in paragraph (e) of this section is included at the beginning (preferably as the first paragraph) of the specification.

(e) The authorization shall read as follows:

A portion of the disclosure of this patent document contains material which is subject to (copyright or mask work) protection. The (copyright or mask work) owner has no objection to the facsimile reproduction by anyone of the patent document or the patent disclosure, as it appears in the Patent and Trademark Office patent file or records, but otherwise reserves all (copyright or mask work) rights whatsoever.

37 CFR 1.84. Standards for drawings

*****

(s)   Copyright or Mask Work Notice. A copyright or mask work notice may appear in the drawing, but must be placed within the sight of the drawing immediately below the figure representing the copyright or mask work material and be limited to letters having a print size of .32 cm. to .64 cm. (1/8 to 1/4 inches) high. The content of the notice must be limited to only those elements provided for by law. For example, "?1983 John Doe" (17 U.S.C. 401) and "*M* John Doe" (17 U.S.C. 909) would be properly limited and, under current statutes, legally sufficient notices of copyright and mask work, respectively. Inclusion of a copyright or mask work notice will be permitted only if the authorization language set forth in § 1.71(e) is included at the beginning (preferably as the first paragraph) of the specification.

*****

The Patent and Trademark Office will permit the inclusion of a copyright or mask work notice in a design or utility patent application, and thereby any patent issuing therefrom,which discloses material on which copyright or mask work protection has previously been established, under the following conditions:

(A) The copyright or mask work notice must be placed adjacent to the copyright or mask work material. Therefore, the notice may appear at any appropriate portion of the patent application disclosure, including the drawing. However, if appearing in the drawing, the notice must comply with 37 CFR 1.84(s). If placed on a drawing in conformance with these provisions, the notice will not be objected to as extraneous matter under 37 CFR 1.84.

> (B) The content of the notice must be limited to only those elements required by law. For example, "?1983 John Doe"(17 U.S.C. 401) and "*M* John Doe" (17 U.S.C. 909) would be properly limited, and under current statutes, legally sufficient notices of copyright and mask work respectively.

> (C) Inclusion of a copyright or mask work notice will be permitted only if the following authorization in 37 CFR 1.71(e) is included at the beginning (preferably as the first paragraph) of the specification to be printed for the patent:

A portion of the disclosure of this patent document contains material which is subject to (copyright or mask work) protection. The (copyright or mask work) owner has no objection to the facsimile reproduction by any one of the patent disclosure, as it appears in the Patent and Trademark Office patent files or records, but otherwise reserves all (copyright or mask work) rights whatsoever.

(D) Inclusion of a copyright or mask work notice after a Notice of Allowance has been mailed will be permitted only if the criteria of 37 CFR 1.312 have been satisfied.

The inclusion of a copyright or mask work notice in a design or utility patent application, and thereby any patent issuing therefrom, under the conditions set forth above will serve to protect the rights of the author/inventor, as well as the public, and will serve to promote the mission and goals of the Patent and Trademark Office. Therefore, the inclusion of a copyright or mask work notice which complies with these conditions will be permitted. However, any departure from these conditions may result in a refusal to permit the desired inclusion. If the authorization required under condition (C) above does not include the specific language "(t)he (copyright or mask work) owner has no objection to the facsimile reproduction by anyone of the patent document or the patent disclosure, as it appears in the Patent and Trademark Office patent files or records, ..." the notice will be objected to as improper by the examiner of the application. If the examiner maintains the objection upon reconsideration, a petition may be filed in accordance with 37 CFR 1.181.

608.02   Drawing [R-1]

35 U.S.C. 113. Drawings.

The applicant shall furnish a drawing where necessary for the understanding of the subject matter to be patented. When the nature of such subject matter admits of illustration by a drawing and the applicant has not furnished such a drawing, the Commissioner may require its submission within a time period of not less than two months from the sending of a notice thereof. Drawings submitted after the filing date of the application may not be used (i) to overcome any insufficiency of the specification due to lack of an enabling disclosure or otherwise inadequate disclosure therein, or (ii) to supplement the original disclosure thereof for the purpose of interpretation of the scope of any claim.

37 CFR 1.81. Drawings required in patent application.

(a) The applicant for a patent is required to furnish a drawing of his or her invention where necessary for the understanding of the subject matter sought to be patented; this drawing , or a high quality copy thereof, must be filed with the application. Since corrections are the responsibility of the applicant, the original drawing(s) should be retained by the applicant for any necessary future correction.

(b) Drawings may include illustrations which facilitate an understanding of the invention (for example, flow sheets in cases of processes, and diagrammatic views).

(c) Whenever the nature of the subject matter sought to be patented admits of illustration by a drawing without its being necessary for the understanding of the subject matter and the applicant has not furnished such a drawing, the examiner will require its submission within a time period of not less than two months from the date of the sending of a notice thereof.

(d) Drawings submitted after the filing date of the application may not be used to overcome any insufficiency of the specification due to lack of an enabling disclosure or otherwise inadequate disclosure therein, or to supplement the original disclosure thereof for the purpose of interpretation of the scope of any claim.

37 CFR 1.84. Standards for drawings.

(a) Drawings. There are two acceptable categories for presenting drawings in utility patent applications:

(1) Black ink. Black and white drawings are normally required. India ink, or its equivalent that secures solid black lines, must be used for drawings, or

(2) Color. On rare occasions, color drawings may be necessary as the only practical medium by which to disclose the subject matter sought to be patented in a utility patent application or the subject matter of a statutory invention registration. The Patent and Trademark Office will accept color drawings in utility patent applications and statutory invention registrations only after granting a petition filed under this paragraph explaining why the color drawings are necessary. Any such petition must include the following:

(i) The fee set forth in § 1.17(i);

(ii) Three (3) sets of color drawings; and

(iii) The specification must contain the following language as the first paragraph in that portion of the specification relating to the brief description of the drawing:

The file of this patent contains at least one drawing executed in color. Copies of this patent with color drawing(s) will be provided by the Patent and Trademark Office upon request and payment of the necessary fee.

If the language is not in the specification, a proposed amendment to insert the language must accompany the petition.

(b) Photographs.

(1) Black and white. Photographs are not ordinarily permitted in utility patent applications. However, the Office will accept photographs in utility patent applications only after the granting of a petition filed under this paragraph which requests that photographs be accepted. Any such petition must include the following:

(i) The fee set forth in § 1.17(i); and

(ii) Three (3) sets of photographs. Photographs must either be developed on double weight photographic paper or be permanently mounted on bristol board. The photographs must be of sufficient quality so that all details in the drawings are reproducible in the printed patent.

(2) Color. Color photographs will be accepted in utility patent applications if the conditions for accepting color drawings have been satisfied. See paragraph (a)(2) of this section.

(c) Identification of drawings. Identifying indicia, if provided, should include the application number or the title of the invention, inventor's name, docket number (if any), and the name and telephone number of a person to call if the Office is unable to match the drawings to the proper application. This information should be placed on the back of each sheet of drawings a minimum distance of 1.5 cm. (5/8 inch) down from the top of the page. In addition, a reference to the application number, or, if an application number has not been assigned, the inventor's name, may be included in the left-hand corner, provided that the reference appears within 1.5 cm. (5/8 inch) from the top of the sheet.

(d) Graphic forms in drawings. Chemical or mathematical formulae, tables, and waveforms may be submitted as drawings and are subject to the same requirements as drawings. Each chemical or mathematical formula must be labeled as a separate figure, using brackets when necessary, to show that information is properly integrated. Each group of waveforms must be presented as a single figure, using a common vertical axis with time extending along the horizontal axis. Each individual waveform discussed in the specification must be identified with a separate letter designation adjacent to the vertical axis.

(e) Type of paper. Drawings submitted to the Office must be made on paper which is flexible, strong, white, smooth, non-shiny, and durable. All sheets must be free from cracks, creases, and folds. Only one side of the sheet shall be used for the drawing. Each sheet must be reasonably free from erasures and must be free from alterations, overwritings, and interlineations. Photographs must either be developed on double weight photographic paper or be permanently mounted on bristol board. See paragraph (b) of this section for other requirements for photographs.

(f) Size of paper. All drawing sheets in an application must be the same size. One of the shorter sides of the sheet is regarded as its top. The size of the sheets on which drawings are made must be:

> (1) 21.0 cm. by 29.7 cm. (DIN size A4), or
>
> (2) 21.6 cm. by 27.9 cm. (8 1/2 by 11 inches).

(g) Margins. The sheets must not contain frames around the sight (i.e., the usable surface), but should have scan target points (i.e., crosshairs) printed on two catercorner margin corners. Each sheet must include a top margin of at least 2.5 cm. (1 inch), a left side margin of at least 2.5 cm. (1 inch), a right side margin of at least 1.5 cm. (5/8 inch), and a bottom margin of at least 1.0 cm. (3/8 inch), thereby leaving a sight no greater than 17.0 cm. by 26.2 cm. on 21.0 cm. by 29.7 cm. (DIN size A4) drawing sheets, and a sight no greater than 17.6 cm. by 24.4 cm. (6 15/16 by 9 5/8 inches) on 21.6 cm. by 27.9 cm. (8 1/2 by 11 inch) drawing sheets.

(h) Views. The drawing must contain as many views as necessary to show the invention. The views may be plan, elevation, section, or perspective views. Detail views of portions of elements, on a larger scale if necessary, may also be used. All views of the drawing must be grouped together and arranged on the sheet(s) without wasting space, preferably in an upright position, clearly separated from one another, and must not be included in the sheets containing the specifications, claims, or abstract. Views must not be connected by projection lines and must not contain center lines. Waveforms of electrical signals may be connected by dashed lines to show the relative timing of the waveforms.

(1) Exploded views. Exploded views, with the separated parts embraced by a bracket, to show the relationship or order of assembly of various parts are permissible. When an exploded view is shown in a figure which is on the same sheet as another figure, the exploded view should be placed in brackets.

(2) Partial views. When necessary, a view of a large machine or device in its entirety may be broken into partial views on a single sheet, or extended over several sheets if there is no loss in facility of understanding the view. Partial views drawn on separate sheets must always be capable of being linked edge to edge so that no partial view contains parts of another partial view. A smaller scale view should be included showing the whole formed by the partial views and indicating the positions of the parts shown. When a portion of a view is enlarged for magnification purposes, the view and the enlarged view must each be labeled as separate views.

(i) Where views on two or more sheets form, in effect, a single complete view, the views on the several sheets must be so arranged that the complete figure can be assembled without concealing any part of any of the views appearing on the various sheets.

(ii) A very long view may be divided into several parts placed one above the other on a single sheet. However, the relationship between the different parts must be clear and unambiguous.

(3) Sectional views. The plane upon which a sectional view is taken should be indicated on the view from which the section is cut by a broken line. The ends of the broken line should be designated by Arabic or Roman numerals corre-

sponding to the view number of the sectional view, and should have arrows to indicate the direction of sight. Hatching must be used to indicate section portions of an object, and must be made by regularly spaced oblique parallel lines spaced sufficiently apart to enable the lines to be distinguished without difficulty. Hatching should not impede the clear reading of the reference characters and lead lines. If it is not possible to place reference characters outside the hatched area, the hatching may be broken off wherever reference characters are inserted. Hatching must be at a substantial angle to the surrounding axes or principal lines, preferably 45?. A cross section must be set out and drawn to show all of the materials as they are shown in the view from which the cross section was taken. The parts in cross section must show proper material(s) by hatching with regularly spaced parallel oblique strokes, the space between strokes being chosen on the basis of the total area to be hatched. The various parts of a cross section of the same item should be hatched in the same manner and should accurately and graphically indicate the nature of the material(s) that is illustrated in cross section. The hatching of juxtaposed different elements must be angled in a different way. In the case of large areas, hatching may be confined to an edging drawn around the entire inside of the outline of the area to be hatched. Different types of hatching should have different conventional meanings as regards the nature of a material seen in cross section.

(4) Alternate position. A moved position may be shown by a broken line superimposed upon a suitable view if this can be done without crowding; otherwise, a separate view must be used for this purpose.

(5) Modified forms. Modified forms of construction must be shown in separate views.

> (i) Arrangement of views. One view must not be placed upon another or within the outline of another. All views on the same sheet should stand in the same direction and, if possible, stand so that they can be read with the sheet held in an upright position. If views wider than the width of the sheet are necessary for the clearest illustration of the invention, the sheet

may be turned on its side so that the top of the sheet, with the appropriate top margin to be used as the heading space, is on the right-hand side. Words must appear in a horizontal, left-to-right fashion when the page is either upright or turned so that the top becomes the right side, except for graphs utilizing standard scientific convention to denote the axis of abscissas (of X) and the axis of ordinates (of Y).

(j) View for Official Gazette. One of the views should be suitable for publication in the Official Gazette as the illustration of the invention.

(k) Scale.

(1) The scale to which a drawing is made must be large enough to show the mechanism without crowding when the drawing is reduced in size to two-thirds in reproduction. Views of portions of the mechanism on a larger scale should be used when necessary to show details clearly. Two or more sheets may be used if one does not give sufficient room. The number of sheets should be kept to a minimum.

(2) When approved by the examiner, the scale of the drawing may be graphically represented. Indications such as "actual size" or "scale 1/2" on the drawings, are not permitted, since these lose their meaning with reproduction in a different format.

(3) Elements of the same view must be in proportion to each other, unless a difference in proportion is indispensable for the clarity of the view. Instead of showing elements in different proportion, a supplementary view may be added giving a larger-scale illustration of the element of the initial view. The enlarged element shown in the second view should be surrounded by a finely drawn or "dot-dash" circle in the first view indicating its location without obscuring the view.

(l) Character of lines, numbers, and letters. All drawings must be made by a process which will give them satisfactory reproduction characteristics. Every line, number, and letter must be durable, clean, black (except for color drawings), sufficiently dense and dark, and uniformly thick and well-defined. The weight of all lines and letters must be heavy enough to permit adequate reproduction. This requirement applies to all lines however fine, to shading, and to lines representing cut surfaces in sectional views. Lines and strokes of different thicknesses may be used in the same drawing where different thicknesses have a different meaning.

(m) Shading. The use of shading in views is encouraged if it aids in understanding the invention and if it does not reduce legibility. Shading is used to indicate the surface or shape of spherical, cylindrical, and conical elements of an object. Flat parts may also be lightly shaded. Such shading is preferred in the case of parts shown in perspective, but not for cross sections. See paragraph (h)(3) of this section. Spaced lines for shading are preferred. These lines must be thin, as few in number as practicable, and they must contrast with the rest of the drawings. As a substitute for shading, heavy lines on the shade side of objects can be used except where they superimpose on each other or obscure reference characters. Light should come from the upper left corner at an angle of 45?. Surface delineations should preferably be shown by proper shading. Solid black shading areas are not permitted, except when used to represent bar graphs or color.

(n) Symbols. Graphical drawing symbols may be used for conventional elements when appropriate. The elements for which such symbols and labeled representations are used must be adequately identified in the specification. Known devices should be illustrated by symbols which have a universally recognized conventional meaning and are generally accepted in the art. Other symbols which are not universally recognized may be used, subject to approval by the Office, if they are not likely to be confused with existing conventional symbols, and if they are readily identifiable.

(o) Legends . Suitable descriptive legends may be used, or may be required by the Examiner, where necessary for understanding of the drawing, subject to approval by the Office. They should contain as few words as possible.

(p) Numbers, letters, and reference characters.

(1) Reference characters (numerals are preferred), sheet numbers, and view numbers must be plain and legible, and must not be used in association with brackets or inverted commas, or enclosed within outlines, e.g., encircled. They must be oriented in the same direction as the view so as to

avoid having to rotate the sheet. Reference characters should be arranged to follow the profile of the object depicted.

(2) The English alphabet must be used for letters, except where another alphabet is customarily used, such as the Greek alphabet to indicate angles, wavelengths, and mathematical formulas.

(3) Numbers, letters, and reference characters must measure at least .32 cm. (1/8 inch) in height. They should not be placed in the drawing so as to interfere with its comprehension. Therefore, they should not cross or mingle with the lines. They should not be placed upon hatched or shaded surfaces. When necessary, such as indicating a surface or cross section, a reference character may be underlined and a blank space may be left in the hatching or shading where the character occurs so that it appears distinct.

(4) The same part of an invention appearing in more than one view of the drawing must always be designated by the same reference character, and the same reference character must never be used to designate different parts.

(5) Reference characters not mentioned in the description shall not appear in the drawings. Reference characters mentioned in the description must appear in the drawings.

(q) Lead lines. Lead lines are those lines between the reference characters and the details referred to. Such lines may be straight or curved and should be as short as possible. They must originate in the immediate proximity of the reference character and extend to the feature indicated. Lead lines must not cross each other. Lead lines are required for each reference character except for those which indicate the surface or cross section on which they are placed. Such a reference character must be underlined to make it clear that a lead line has not been left out by mistake. Lead lines must be executed in the same way as lines in the drawing. See paragraph (l) of this section.

(r) Arrows. Arrows may be used at the ends of lines, provided that their meaning is clear, as follows:

(1) On a lead line, a freestanding arrow to indicate the entire section towards which it points;

(2) On a lead line, an arrow touching a line to indicate the surface shown by the line looking along the direction of the arrow; or

(3) To show the direction of movement.

(s) Copyright or Mask Work Notice. A copyright or mask work notice may appear in the drawing, but must be placed within the sight of the drawing immediately below the figure representing the copyright or mask work material and be limited to letters having a print size of .32 cm. to .64 cm. (1/8 to 1/4 inches) high. The content of the notice must be limited to only those elements provided for by law. For example, "?1983 John Doe" (17 U.S.C. 401) and "M. John Doe" (17 U.S.C. 909) would be properly limited and, under current statutes, legally sufficient notices of copyright and mask work, respectively. Inclusion of a copyright or mask work notice will be permitted only if the authorization language set forth in § 1.71(e) is included at the beginning (preferably as the first paragraph) of the specification.

(t) Numbering of sheets of drawings. The sheets of drawings should be numbered in consecutive Arabic numerals, starting with 1, within the sight as defined in paragraph (g) of this section. These numbers, if present, must be placed in the middle of the top of the sheet, but not in the margin. The numbers can be placed on the right-hand side if the drawing extends too close to the middle of the top edge of the usable surface. The drawing sheet numbering must be clear and larger than the numbers used as reference characters to avoid confusion. The number of each sheet should be shown by two Arabic numerals placed on either side of an oblique line, with the first being the sheet number and the second being the total number of sheets of drawings, with no other marking.

(u) Numbering of views.

(1) The different views must be numbered in consecutive Arabic numerals, starting with 1, independent of the numbering of the sheets and, if possible, in the order in which they appear on the drawing sheet(s). Partial views intended to form one complete view, on one or several sheets, must be identified by the same number followed by a capital letter. View numbers must be preceded by the abbreviation "FIG." Where only a single view is used in an application to illus-

trate the claimed invention, it must not be numbered and the abbreviation "FIG." must not appear.

(2) Numbers and letters identifying the views must be simple and clear and must not be used in association with brackets, circles, or inverted commas. The view numbers must be larger than the numbers used for reference characters.

(v) Security markings. Authorized security markings may be placed on the drawings provided they are outside the sight, preferably centered in the top margin.

(w) Corrections. Any corrections on drawings submitted to the Office must be durable and permanent.

(x) Holes. No holes should be made by applicant in the drawing sheets. (See § 1.152 for design drawings, § 1.165 for plant drawings, and § 1.174 for reissue drawings.)

Drawings on paper are acceptable as long as they are in compliance with 37 CFR 1.84. Corrections thereto must be made in the form of replacement sheets since the Office does not release drawings for correction. See 37 CFR 1.85.

Good quality copies made on office copiers are acceptable if the lines are uniformly thick, black, and solid. Facsimile copies of drawings however, are not acceptable (37 CFR 1.6(d)(4)).

Drawings are currently accepted in two different size formats. It is, however, required that all drawings in a particular application be the same size for ease of handling and reproduction.

For examples of proper drawings, in addition to selected rules of practice related to patent drawings and interpretations of those rules, see the "Guide for the Preparation of Patent Drawings" which is available from the Superintendent of Documents (see MPEP Introduction).

For information regarding certified copies of an application-as-filed which does not meet the sheet size/margin and quality requirements of 37 CFR 1.52, 1.84(f), and 1.84(g), see MPEP § 608.01.

For design patent drawings, 37 CFR 1.152, see MPEP § 1503.02.

For plant patent drawings, 37 CFR 1.165, see MPEP § 1606.

For reissue application drawings, see MPEP § 1413.

For correction of drawings, see MPEP § 608.02(p). For prints, preparation and distribution, see MPEP § 508 and § 608.02(m). For prints, return of drawings, see MPEP § 608.02(y).

For pencil notations of classification and name or initials of assistant examiner to be placed on drawings, see MPEP § 719.03.

The filing of a divisional or continuation case under the provisions of 37 CFR 1.53(b) (unexecuted case) does not obviate the need for formal drawings. See MPEP § 608.02(b).

DEFINITIONS

A number of different terms are used when referring to drawings in patent applications. The following definitions are used in this Manual.

Original drawings: The drawing submitted with the application when filed. It may be either a formal or an informal drawing.

Substitute drawing: A drawing filed later than the filing date of an application. Usually submitted to replace an original informal drawing.

Formal drawing: A drawing in a form that complies with 37 CFR 1.84. Formal drawings are stamped "approved" by the Draftsperson.

Informal drawing: A drawing which does not comply with the form requirements of 37 CFR 1.84 or which is declared as informal when filedDraftsperson on form PTO-948. A drawing declared as informal by the applicant when filed is not reviewed by the Draftsperson for compliance with 37 CFR 1.84. A substitute form PTO-948 is placed in the file to indicate that the drawings were filed as informal.

Drawing print: This term is used for the white paper print prepared by the *Scanning Division of the Office of Initial Patent Examination (OIPE) of all original drawings. The drawing prints contain the **application number near the left-hand margin. Drawing prints should be placed on the top on the right-hand flap of the application file wrapper.

Interference print: This term is used to designate the copy prepared of the original drawings filed in file cabinets separate from the file wrappers and are used to make interference searches.

Plan: This term is used to illustrate the top view.

Elevation: This term is used to illustrate views showing the height of objects.

The following Form Paragraphs should be used when notifying applicants of drawing corrections.

§ 6.38 Acknowledgment of Proposed Drawing Correction

The proposed drawing correction and/or the proposed substitute sheets of drawings, filed on [1] have been [2].

Examiner Note:

1. In bracket 2, insert either —approved— or —disapproved—.
2. If approved, form paragraph 6.39 and one or more of paragraphs 6.40 or 6.41 or 6.44 must follow.
3. If disapproved, an explanation must be provided.

§ 6.38.01 Proposed Drawing Correction Disapproved, Changes Not Highlighted

The proposed drawing correction filed on [1] has been disapproved because it is not in the form of a pen-and-ink sketch showing changes in red ink or with the changes otherwise highlighted. See MPEP

§ 608.02(v).

§ 6.38.02 Proposed Drawing Correction Disapproved, New Matter

The proposed drawing correction and/or the proposed substitute sheets of drawings, filed on [1] have been disapproved because they introduce new matter into the drawings. 37 CFR 1.121(a)(6) states that no amendment may introduce new matter into the disclosure of an application. The original disclosure does not support the showing of [2].

Examiner Note:

In bracket 2, explain which feature(s) of the proposed drawing correction constitute(s) new matter.

§ 6.39 PTO No Longer Makes Drawing Changes

The Patent and Trademark Office no longer makes drawing changes. See 1017 O.G. 4. It is applicant's responsibility to ensure that the drawings are corrected. Corrections must be made in accordance with the instructions below.

Examiner Note:

This paragraph is to be used whenever the applicant has filed a request for the Office to make drawing changes. Form paragraph 6.40 must follow.

§ 6.40 Information on How To Effect Drawing Changes

INFORMATION ON HOW TO EFFECT DRAWING CHANGES

1. Correction of Informalities — 37 CFR 1.85; 1097 O.G. 36

New formal drawings must be filed with the changes incorporated therein. The art unit number, application number (including series code) and number of drawing sheets should be written on the reverse side of the drawings. Applicant may delay filing of the new drawings until receipt of the "Notice of Allowability" (PTOL-37 or PTO-37). If delayed, the new drawings MUST be filed within the THREE MONTH shortened statutory period set for reply in the "Notice of Allowability" to avoid extension of time fees. Extensions of time may be obtained under the provisions of 37 CFR 1.136(a) for filing the corrected drawings (but not for payment of the issue fee). The drawings should be filed as a separate paper with a transmittal letter addressed to the Official Draftsperson.

2. Corrections other than Informalities Noted by Draftsperson on form PTO-948.

All changes to the drawings, other than informalities noted by the Draftsperson, MUST be made in the same manner as above except that, normally, a highlighted (preferably red ink) sketch of the changes to be incorporated into the new drawings MUST be approved by the examiner before the application will be allowed. No changes will be permitted to be made, other than correction of informalities, unless the examiner has approved the proposed changes.

Timing of Corrections

Applicant is required to submit acceptable corrected drawings within the three month shortened statutory period set in the "Notice of Allowability". Within that three month period, two weeks should be allowed for review of the new drawings by the Office. If a correction is determined to be unacceptable by the Office, applicant must arrange to have an acceptable correction re-submitted within the original three month period to avoid the necessity of obtaining an extension of time with extension fees. Therefore, applicant should file corrected drawings as soon as possible.

Failure to take corrective action within the set (or extended) period will result in ABANDONMENT of the application.

§ 6.41 *Reminder That PTO No Longer Makes Drawing Changes*

Applicant is reminded that the Patent and Trademark Office no longer makes drawing changes and that it is applicant's responsibility to ensure that the drawings are corrected in accordance with the instructions set forth in Paper No. [1], mailed on [2].

Examiner Note:

This paragraph is to be used when the applicant has been previously provided with information on how to effect drawing changes (i.e., either by way of form paragraph 6.40 or a PTO-948 has been previously sent).

§ 6.42 *Reminder That Applicant Must Make Drawing Changes*

Applicant is reminded that in order to avoid an abandonment of this application, the drawings must be corrected in accordance with the instructions set forth in Paper No. [1], mailed on [2].

Examiner Note:

This paragraph is to be used when allowing the application and when applicant has previously been provided with information on how to effect drawing changes (i.e., by way of form paragraph 6.40 or a PTO-948 has been previously sent).

§ 6.43 Drawings Contain Informalities, Application Allowed

The drawings filed on [1] are acceptable subject to correction of the informalities indicated on the attached "Notice of Draftsperson's Patent Drawing Review," PTO-948. In order to avoid abandonment of this application, correction is required.

Examiner Note:

Use this paragraph when allowing the application, particularly at time of first action issue. Form paragraph 6.40 or 6.41 must follow.

§ 6.44 Drawing Informalities Previously Indicated

In order to avoid abandonment, the drawing informalities noted in Paper No. [1], mailed on [2], must now be corrected. Correction can only be effected in the manner set forth in the above noted paper.

Examiner Note:

Use this paragraph when allowing the application and applicant has previously been informed of informalities in the drawings.

§ 6.47 Examiner's Amendment Involving Drawing Changes

The following changes to the drawings have been approved by the examiner and agreed upon by applicant: [1]. In order to avoid abandonment of the application, applicant must make these agreed upon drawing changes.

Examiner Note:

1. In bracket 1, insert the agreed upon drawing changes.

2. Form paragraphs 6.39 and 6.40 **should follow, as appropriate For examples of suitable symbols and legends,

see the "Guide for the Preparation of Patent Drawings" available from the Superintendent of Documents (see MPEP Introduction).

The publications listed below have been reviewed by the Office and the symbols therein are considered to be generally acceptable in patent drawings. Although the Office will not "approve" all of the listed symbols as a group because their use and clarity must be decided on a case-by-case basis, these publications may be used as guides when selecting graphic symbols. Overly specific symbols should be avoided. Symbols with unclear meanings should be labeled for clarification.

These publications are available from the American National Standards Institute Inc., 11 West 42nd Street, New York, New York 10036.

The publications reviewed are the following:

Y32.2-1970 Graphic Symbols for Electrical & Electronics Diagrams

Y32.10-1967 (R1994) Graphic Symbols for Fluid Power Diagrams

Y32.11-1961 (R1993) Graphic for Process Flow Diagrams in the Petroleum & Chemical Industries

Y32.14-1962 Graphic Symbols for Logic Diagrams

Z32.2.3-1949 (R1994) Graphical Symbols for Pipe Fittings, Valves and Piping

Z32.2.4-1949 (R1953) Graphic Symbols for Heating, Ventilating & Air Conditioning

Z32.2.6-1950 (R1993) Graphic Symbols for Heat-Power Apparatus

The following symbols should be used to indicate various materials where the material is an important feature of the invention. The use of conventional features is very helpful in making prior art searches.

See MPEP § 601.01(f) for treatment of applications filed without drawings and MPEP § 601.01(g) for treatment of applications filed without all figures of drawings.

ILLUSTRATION SUBSEQUENTLY REQUIRED

The acceptance of an application without a drawing does not preclude the examiner from requiring an illustration in the form of a drawing under 37 CFR 1.81(c) or 37 CFR 1.83(c). In requiring such a drawing, the examiner should clearly indicate that the requirement is made under 37 CFR 1.81(c) or 37 CFR 1.83(c) and be careful not to state that he or she is doing so "because it is necessary for the understanding of the invention," as that might give rise to an erroneous impression as to the completeness of the application as filed. Examiners making such requirements are to specifically require, as a part of the applicant's next reply, at least an ink sketch or permanent print of any drawing proposed in reply to the requirement, even though no allowable subject matter is yet indicated. This will afford the examiner an early opportunity to determine the sufficiency of the illustration and the absence of new matter. See 37 CFR 1.121 and 37 CFR 1.81(d). The description should of course be amended to contain reference to the new illustration. This may obviate further correspondence where an amendment places the case in condition for allowance, except for the formal requirement relating to the drawing. In the event of a final determination that there is nothing patentable in the case, a formal drawing will not be required.

BLACK AND WHITE PHOTOGRAPHS

37 CFR 1.84. Standards for drawings.

* * * * *

(b) Photographs.

(1) Black and white. Photographs are not ordinarily permitted in utility patent applications. However, the Office will accept photographs in utility patent applications only after the granting of a petition filed under this paragraph which requests that photographs be accepted. Any such petition must include the following:

(i) The fee set forth in § 1.17(i); and

(ii) Three (3) sets of photographs. Photographs must either be developed on double weight photographic paper or be permanently mounted on bristol board. The photographs must be of sufficient quality so that all details in the drawings are reproducible in the printed patent.

*****

Photographs ** or photomicrographs (not photolithographs or other reproductions of photographs made by using screens) printed on sensitized paper are accceptable as final drawings, in lieu of India ink drawings, to illustrate inventions which are incapable of being accurately or adequately depicted by India ink drawings, e.g., crystalline structures, metallurgical microstructures, textile fabrics, grain structures and ornamental effects. The photographs or photomicrographs must show the invention more clearly than they can be done by India ink drawings and otherwise comply with the rules concerning such drawings.

Photographs submitted in lieu of ink drawings must comply with 37 CFR 1.84(b). However, the requirement of 37 CFR 1.84(b)(1) for a petition, petition fee, and three sets of black and white photographs has been waived. For black and white photographs, there is no requirement for a petition or petition fee, and only one set of photographs is required. See 1213 O.G. 108 (Aug. 4, 1998) and 1211 O.G. 34 (June 9, 1998).

Such photographs to be acceptable must be made on photographic paper having the following characteristics which are generally recognized in the photographic trade: double weight paper with a surface described as smooth; tint, white, or be photographs mounted on proper size bristol board.

See MPEP § 1503.02 for discussion of photographs used in design patent applications.

COLOR DRAWINGS OR COLOR PHOTOGRAPHS

37 CFR 1.84. Standards for drawings.

(a) Drawings. There are two acceptable categories for presenting drawings in utility patent applications:

* * * * *

(2) Color. On rare occasions, color drawings may be necessary as the only practical medium by which to disclose the subject matter sought to be patented in a utility patent application or the subject matter of a statutory invention registration. The Patent and Trademark Office will accept color drawings in utility patent applications and statutory invention registrations only after granting a petition filed under this paragraph explaining why the color drawings are necessary. Any such petition must include the following:

(i) The fee set forth in § 1.17(i);

(ii) Three (3) sets of color drawings; and

(iii) The specification must contain the following language as the first paragraph in that portion of the specification relating to the brief description of the drawing:

The file of this patent contains at least one drawing executed in color. Copies of this patent with color drawing(s) will be provided by the Patent and Trademark Office upon request and payment of the necessary fee.

If the language is not in the specification, a proposed amendment to insert the language must accompany the petition.

(b) Photographs.

* * * * *

(2) Color. Color photographs will be accepted in utility patent applications if the conditions for accepting color drawings have been satisfied. See paragraph (a)(2) of this section.

* * * * *

Limited use of color drawings in utility patent applications is provided for in 37 CFR 1.84(a)(2) and (b)(2). Unless a petition is filed and granted, the Draftsperson will not approve color drawings or color photographs in a utility or design patent application. The examiner must object to the color drawings or color photographs as being improper and require applicant either to cancel the drawings or to provide substitute black and white drawings

Under 37 CFR 1.84(a)(2) and (b)(2), the applicant must file a petition with fee requesting acceptance of the color drawings or color photographs. The petition is decided by a Supervisory Patent Examiner. See MPEP § 1002.02(d).

Where color drawings or color photographs are filed in a continuing application, applicant must renew the petition under 37 CFR 1.84(a)(2) and (b)(2) even though a similar petition was filed in the prior application. Until the renewed petition is granted, the examiner must object to the color drawings or color photographs as being improper.

In light of the substantial administrative and economic burden associated with printing a utility patent with color drawings or color photographs, the patent copies which are printed at issuance of the patent will depict the drawings in black and white only. However, a set of color drawings or color photographs will be attached to the Letters Patent. Moreover, copies of the patent with color drawings or color photographs attached thereto will be provided by the Patent and Trademark Office upon special request and payment of the fee necessary to recover the actual costs associated therewith.

Accordingly, the petition must also be accompanied by a proposed amendment to insert the following language as the first paragraph in the portion of the specification containing a brief description of the drawings:

> The file of this patent contains at least one drawing executed in color. Copies of this patent with color drawing(s) will be provided by the Patent and Trademark Office upon request and payment of the necessary fee.

It is anticipated that such a petition will be granted only when the Patent and Trademark Office has determined that a color drawing or color photograph is the only practical medium by which to disclose in a printed utility patent the subject matter to be patented.

It is emphasized that a decision to grant the petition should not be regarded as an indication that color drawings or color photographs are necessary to comply with a statutory requirement. In this latter respect, clearly it is desirable to file any desired color drawings or color photographs as part of the original application papers in order to avoid issues concerning statutory defects (e.g., lack of enablement under 35 U.S.C. 112 or new matter under 35 U.S.C. 132). The filing of the petition, however, may be deferred until acceptable formal drawings are required by the examiner.

NOTIFYING APPLICANT

If the original drawings are informal but may be admitted for examination purposes, the Draftsperson indicates on a 2-part form, PTO-948, what the informalities are and that new corrected drawings are required. In either case, the informal drawings are accepted as satisfying the requirements of 37 CFR 1.51.

The examiners are directed to advise the applicants by way of form PTO-948 (see MPEP § 707.07(a)) in the first Office action of the conditions which the Draftsperson considers to render the drawing informal.

Drawing corrections should be made when the application is in condition for allowance unless the examiner requires correction at an earlier date.

If the examiner discovers a defect in the content of the drawing, the applicant should be notified by using a Form Paragraph, where appropriate.

§ 6.21 *New Drawings, Competent Draftsperson*

New formal drawings are required in this application because [1]. Applicant is advised to employ the services of a competent patent draftsperson outside the Office, as the Patent and Trademark Office no longer prepares new drawings.

§ 6.22 Drawings Objected To

The drawings are objected to because [1]. Correction is required.

Examiner Note:

Follow with paragraph 6.27, if appropriate.

§ 6.22.01 Drawings Objected To, Details Not Shown

The drawings are objected to under 37 CFR 1.83(a) because they fail to show [1] as described in the specification. Any structural detail that is essential for a proper understanding of the disclosed invention should be shown in the drawing. MPEP § 608.02(d). Correction is required.

Examiner Note:

1. In bracket 1, identify the structural details not shown in the drawings.

2. Follow with form paragraph 6.27, if appropriate.

§ 6.22.02 Drawings Objected to, Different Numbers Refer to Same Part

The drawings are objected to as failing to comply with 37 CFR 1.84(p)(4) because reference characters "[1]" and "[2]" have both been used to designate [3]. Correction is required.

Examiner Note:

1. In brackets 1 and 2, identify the numbers which refer to the same part.

2. In bracket 3, identify the part which is referred to by different numbers.

3. Follow with form paragraph 6.27, if appropriate.

§ 6.22.03 Drawings Objected to, Different Parts Referred to by Same Number

The drawings are objected to as failing to comply with 37 CFR 1.84(p)(4) because reference character "[1]" has been used to designate both [2] and [3]. Correction is required.

Examiner Note:

1. In bracket 1, identify the number which refers to the different parts.

2. In brackets 2 and 3, identify the parts which are referred to by the same number.

3. Follow with form paragraph 6.27, if appropriate.

§ 6.22.04 Drawings Objected to, Incomplete

The drawings are objected to under 37 CFR 1.83(b) because they are incomplete. 37 CFR 1.83(b) reads as follows:

When the invention consists of an improvement on an old machine the drawing must when possible exhibit, in one or more views, the improved portion itself, disconnected from the old structure, and also in another view, so much only of the old structure as will suffice to show the connection of the invention therewith. Correction is required.

Examiner Note:

1. Supply a full explanation, if it is not readily apparent how the drawings are incomplete.

2. Follow with form paragraph 6.27, if appropriate.

§ 6.22.05 Drawings Objected to, Modifications in Same Figure

The drawings are objected to under 37 CFR 1.84(h)(5) because Figure [1] show(s) modified forms of construction in the same view. Correction is required.

Examiner Note:

1. In *bracket 1, insert the appropriate Figure number(s).

2. Follow with form paragraph 6.27, if appropriate.

§ 6.22.06 Drawings Objected to, Reference Numbers Not in Drawings

The drawings are objected to as failing to comply with 37 CFR 1.84(p)(5) because they do not include the following reference sign(s) mentioned in the description: [1]. Correction is required.

Examiner Note:

> 1. In bracket 1, specify the reference characters which are not found in the drawings, including the page and line number where they first occur in the specification.

> 2. Follow with form paragraph 6.27, if appropriate.

§ 6.22.07 Drawings Objected to, Reference Numbers Not in Specification

The drawings are objected to as failing to comply with 37 CFR 1.84(p)(5) because they include the following reference sign(s) not mentioned in the description: [1]. Correction is required.

Examiner Note:

> 1. In bracket 1, specify the reference characters which are not found in the specification, including the figure in which they occur.

> 2. Follow with form paragraph 6.27, if appropriate.

§ 6.23 Subject Matter Admits of Illustration

The subject matter of this application admits of illustration by a drawing to facilitate understanding of the invention. Applicant is required to furnish a drawing under 37 CFR 1.81. No new matter may be introduced in the required drawing.

Examiner Note:

When requiring drawings before examination use form paragraph 6.23.01 with a PTOL-90 or PTO-90C form as a cover sheet.

§ 6.23.01 Subject Matter Admits of Illustration (No Examination of Claims)

The subject matter of this application admits of illustration by a drawing to facilitate understanding of the invention. Applicant is required to furnish a drawing under 37 CFR 1.81. No new matter may be introduced in the required drawing.

Applicant is given a TWO MONTH time period to submit a drawing in compliance with 37 CFR 1.81. Extensions of time may be obtained under the provisions of 37 CFR 1.136(a). Failure to timely submit a drawing will result in ABANDONMENT of the application.

Examiner Note:

1. Use of this form paragraph should be extremely rare and limited to those instances where no examination can be performed due to lack of an illustration of the invention resulting in a lack of understanding of the claimed subject matter.

2. Use a PTOL-90 or PTO-90C form as a cover sheet for this communication.

§ 6.24 Informal Drawings

This application has been filed with informal drawings which are acceptable for examination purposes only. Formal drawings will be required when the application is allowed.

§ 6.24.01 Color Photographs and Color Drawings, Petition Required

**Color photographs and color drawings are acceptable only for examination purposes unless a petition filed under 37 CFR 1.84(a)(2) or *(b)(2) is granted permitting their use as formal drawings. In the event applicant wishes to use the drawings currently on file as formal drawings, a petition must be filed for acceptance of the color photographs or color drawings as formal drawings. Any such petition must be accompanied by the appropriate fee as set forth in 37 CFR 1.17(i), three sets of color drawings or color photographs, as appropriate, and ** an amendment to the first paragraph of the brief description of the drawings section of the specification which states:

The file of this patent contains at least one drawing executed in color. Copies of this patent with color drawing(s) will be provided by the Patent and Trademark Office upon request and payment of the necessary fee.

Color photographs will be accepted if the conditions for accepting color drawings have been satisfied.

Examiner Note:

> 1. color photographs or color drawings as the drawings required by 37 CFR 1.81.

> 2. Do not use this form paragraph for black and white photographs. The requirement of 37 CFR 1.84(b)(1) for a petition, petition fee, and three sets of black and white photographs has been waived. For black and white photographs, there is no requirement for a petition or petition fee, and only one set of photographs is required. See 1213 O.G. 108 (Aug. 4, 1998) and 1211 O.G. 34 (June 9, 1999).

§ 6.25.01 *Formal Drawings Suggested, Allowable Subject Matter Indicated*

Since allowable subject matter has been indicated, applicant is encouraged to submit formal drawings in response to this Office action. The early submission of formal drawings will permit the Office to review the drawings for acceptability and to resolve any informalities remaining therein before the application is passed to issue. This will avoid possible delays in the issue process.

§ 6.26 *Informal Drawings Do Not Permit Examination*

The informal drawings are not of sufficient quality to permit examination. Accordingly, new drawings are required in reply to this Office action.

Applicant is given a TWO MONTH time period to submit new drawings in compliance with 37 CFR 1.81. Extensions of time may be obtained under the provisions of 37 CFR 1.136(a). Failure to timely submit new drawings will result in ABANDONMENT of the application.

Examiner Note:

> 1. Use of this form paragraph should be extremely rare and limited to those instances where no examination can be performed due to the poor quality of the drawings resulting in a lack of understanding of the claimed subject matter.

> 2. Use a PTOL-90 or PTO-90C form as a cover sheet for this communication.

§ 6.27 *Correction Held in Abeyance*

Applicant is required to submit a proposed drawing correction in reply to this Office action. However, formal correction of the noted defect can be deferred until the application is allowed by the examiner.

DRAWING REQUIREMENTS

The first sentence of 35 U.S.C. 113 requires a drawing to be submitted upon filing where such drawing is necessary for the understanding of the invention. In this situation, the lack of a drawing renders the application incomplete and, as such, the application cannot be given a filing date until the drawing is received. The second sentence of 35 U.S.C. 113 deals with the situation wherein a drawing is not necessary for the understanding of the invention, but the case admits of illustration and no drawing was submitted on filing. The lack of the drawing in this situation does not render the application incomplete but rather is treated much in the same manner as an informality. The examiner should require such drawings in almost all such instances. Such drawings could be required during the processing of the application but do not have to be furnished at the time the application is filed. The applicant is allowed at least 2 months from the date of the letter requiring drawings to submit them.

Handling of Drawing Requirements Under the First Sentence of 35 U.S.C. 113

The Office of Initial Patent Examination (OIPE) will make the initial decision in all new applications as to whether a drawing is "necessary" under the first sentence of 35 U.S.C. 113. A drawing will be considered necessary under the first sentence of 35 U.S.C. 113 in all cases where the drawing is referred to in the specification and one or more figures have been omitted.

The determination under 35 U.S.C. 113 (first sentence) as to when a drawing is necessary will be handled in OIPE according to the following procedure. OIPE will make the initial determination whether or not drawings are required for the understanding of the subject matter of the invention. ** When no drawings are included in the application as filed and drawings are required, the application is treated as incomplete and the applicant is so informed by OIPE. The filing date will not be granted and applicant will be notified to complete the application (37 CFR 1.53(e)). ** If a drawing is later furnished, a filing date may be granted as of the date of receipt of such drawing.

An OIPE formality examiner should not treat an application without drawings as incomplete if drawings are not required. A drawing is not required for a filing date under 35 U.S.C. 111 and 113 if the application contains:

(1) at least one process claim including the term "process" or "method" in its introductory phrase;

(2) at least one composition claim including the term "composition," "compound," "mixture" or "pharmaceutical" in its introductory phrase;

(3) at least one claim directed to a coated article or product or to an article or product made from a particular material or composition (i.e., an article of known and conventional character (e.g., a table), coated with or made of a particular composition (e.g., a specified polymer such as polyvinylchloride);

(4) at least one claim directed to a laminated article or product (i.e., a laminated article of known and conventional character (e.g., a table)); or

(5) at least one claim directed to an article, apparatus, or system where the sole distinguishing feature is the presence of a particular material e.g., a hydraulic system using a particular hydraulic fluid, or a conventional packaged suture using a particular material).

For a more complete explanation about when a drawing is required, see MPEP § 601.01(f). For applications submitted without all of the drawings described in the specification, see MPEP § 601.01(g).

If an examiner feels that a filing date should not have been granted in an application because it does not contain drawings, the matter should be brought to the attention of the supervisory patent examiner (SPE) for review. If the SPE decides that drawings are required to understand the subject matter of the invention, the SPE should return the application to OIPE with a typed, signed, and dated memorandum requesting cancellation of the filing date and identifying the subject matter required to be illustrated.

706.03(c)   Rejections Under 35 U.S.C. 112, First Paragraph

Rejections based on the first paragraph of 35 U.S.C. 112 are discussed in MPEP § 2161–§ 2165.04. For a discussion of the utility requirements of 35 U.S.C. 112, first paragraph, and 35 U.S.C. 101, see MPEP § 706.03(a)(1) and § 2107–§ 2107.02. The appropriate form paragraphs 7.30.01 and 7.31.01 through 7.33.01 should be used in making rejections under 35 U.S.C. 112, first paragraph.

§ 7.30.01 Statement of Statutory Basis, 35 U.S.C. 112, First Paragraph

The following is a quotation of the first paragraph of 35 U.S.C. 112:

The specification shall contain a written description of the invention, and of the manner and process of making and using it, in such full, clear, concise, and exact terms as to enable any person skilled in the art to which it pertains, or with which it is most nearly connected, to make and use the same and shall set forth the best mode contemplated by the inventor of carrying out his invention.

Examiner Note:

> 1. The statute is no longer being re-cited in all Office actions. It is only required in first actions on the merits and final rejections. Where the statute is not being cited in an action on the merits, use paragraph 7.103.

> 2. Paragraphs 7.30.01 and 7.30.02 are to be used ONLY ONCE in a given Office action.

§ 7.31.01 Rejection, 35 U.S.C. 112, 1st Paragraph, Description Requirement, Including New Matter Situations

Claim [1] rejected under 35 U.S.C. 112, first paragraph, as containing subject matter which was not described in the specification in such a way as to reasonably convey to one skilled in the relevant art that the inventor(s), at the time the application was filed, had possession of the claimed invention. [2]

Examiner Note:

1. This rejection must be preceded by form paragraph 7.30.01 or 7.103.

2. In bracket 2, identify (by suitable reference to page and line numbers and/or drawing figures) the subject matter not properly described in the application as filed, and provide an explanation of your position. The explanation should include any questions the examiner asked which were not satisfactorily resolved and consequently raise doubt as to possession of the claimed invention at the time of filing.

Form Paragraph 7.31.02 should be used when it is the examiner's position that nothing within the scope of the claims is enabled. In such a rejection, the examiner should explain all the reasons why nothing within the scope of the claim is enabled. To make sure all relevant issues are raised, this should include any issues regarding the breadth of the claims relative to the guidance in the disclosure.

§ 7.31.02 Rejection, 35 U.S.C. 112, 1st Paragraph: Enablement

Claim [1] rejected under 35 U.S.C. 112, first paragraph, as containing subject matter which was not described in the specification in such a way as to enable one skilled in the art to which it pertains, or with which it is most nearly connected, to make and/ or use the invention. [2]

Examiner Note:

1. This rejection must be preceded by form paragraph 7.30.01 or 7.103.

2. If the problem is one of scope, form paragraph 7.31.03 should be used.

3. In bracket 2, identify the claimed subject matter for which the specification is not enabling along with an explanation as to why the specification is not enabling. The explanation should include any questions the examiner may have asked which were not satisfactorily resolved and consequently raise doubt as to enablement.

4. Where an essential component or step of the invention is not recited in the claims, use form paragraph 7.33.01.

Form paragraph 7.31.03 should be used when it is the examiner's position that something within the scope of the claims is enabled but the claims are not limited to that scope.

§ 7.31.03 Rejection, 35 U.S.C. 112, 1st Paragraph: Scope of Enablement

Claim [1] rejected under 35 U.S.C. 112, first paragraph, because the specification, while being enabling for [2], does not reasonably provide enablement for [3]. The specification does not enable any person skilled in the art to which it pertains, or with which it is most nearly connected, to [4] the invention commensurate in scope with these claims. [5]

Examiner Note:

1. This rejection must be preceded by form paragraph 7.30.01 or 7.103.

2. This paragraph is to be used when the scope of the claims is not commensurate with the scope of the enabling disclosure.

3. In bracket 2, identify the claimed subject matter for which the specification is enabling. This may be by reference to specific portions of the specification.

4. In bracket 3, identify aspect(s) of the claim(s) for which the specification is not enabling.

5. In bracket 4, fill in only the appropriate portion of the statute, i.e., one of the following: —make—, —use—, or —make and use—.

6. In bracket 5, identify the problem along with an explanation as to why the specification is not enabling. The expla-

nation should include any questions posed by the examiner which were not satisfactorily resolved and consequently raise doubt as to enablement.

§ 7.31.04 Rejection, 35 U.S.C. 112, 1st Paragraph: Best Mode Requirement

Claim [1] rejected under 35 U.S.C. 112, first paragraph, because the best mode contemplated by the inventor has not been disclosed. Evidence of concealment of the best mode is based upon [2].

Examiner Note:

1. This rejection must be preceded by form paragraph 7.30.01 or 7.103.

2. In bracket 2, insert the basis for holding that the best mode has been concealed, e.g., the quality of applicant's disclosure is so poor as to effectively result in concealment.

3. Use of this form paragraph should be rare. See MPEP §§ 2165- 2165.04.

Form paragraph 7.33.01 should be used when it is the examiner's position that a feature considered critical or essential by applicant to the practice of the claimed invention is missing from the claim.

§ 7.33.01 Rejection, 35 U.S.C. 112, 1st Paragraph, Essential Subject Matter Missing From Claims (Enablement)

Claim [1] rejected under 35 U.S.C. 112, first paragraph, as based on a disclosure which is not enabling. [2] critical or essential to the practice of the invention, but not included in the claim(s) is not enabled by the disclosure. See In re Mayhew, 527 F.2d 1229, 188 USPQ 356 (CCPA 1976). [3]

Examiner Note:

1. This rejection must be preceded by form paragraph 7.30.01 or 7.103.

2. In bracket 2, recite the subject matter omitted from the claims.

3. In bracket 3, give the rationale for considering the omitted subject matter critical or essential.

4. The examiner shall cite the statement, argument, date, drawing, or other evidence which demonstrates that a particular feature was considered essential by the applicant, is not reflected in the claims which are rejected.

706.03(d) Rejections Under 35 U.S.C. 112, Second Paragraph

Rejections under 35 U.S.C. 112, second paragraph, are discussed in MPEP § 2171–§ 2174. Form paragraphs 7.30.02 and 7.34 through 7.35.01 should be used to reject under 35 U.S.C. 112, second paragraph.

§ 7.30.02 Statement of Statutory Basis, 35 U.S.C. 112, Second Paragraph

The following is a quotation of the second paragraph of 35 U.S.C. 112:

The specification shall conclude with one or more claims particularly pointing out and distinctly claiming the subject matter which the applicant regards as his invention.

Examiner Note:

1. The statute is no longer being re-cited in all Office actions. It is only required in first actions on the merits and final rejections. Where the statute is not being cited in an action on the merits, use paragraph 7.103.

2. Paragraphs 7.30.01 and 7.30.02 are to be used ONLY ONCE in a given Office action.

§ 7.34 Rejection, 35 U.S.C. 112, 2nd Paragraph, Failure To Claim Applicant's Invention Claim [1] rejected under 35 U.S.C. 112, second paragraph, as failing to set forth the subject matter which applicant(s) regard as their invention. Evidence that claim [2] fail(s) to correspond in scope with that which applicant(s) regard as the invention can be found in Paper No. [3] filed [4]. In that paper, applicant has stated [5], and this statement indicates that the invention is different from what is defined in the claim(s) because [6].

Examiner Note:

1. This rejection must be preceded by form paragraph 7.30.02 or 7.103.

2. This paragraph is to be used only where applicant has stated, somewhere other than in the application, as filed, that the invention is something different from what is defined in the claim(s).

3. In brackets 3 and 4, identify the submission by applicant (which is not the application, as filed, but may be in the remarks by applicant, in the brief, in an affidavit, etc.) by Paper No. and the date the paper was filed in the PTO.

4. In bracket 5, set forth what applicant has stated in the submission to indicate a different invention.

5. In bracket 6, explain how the statement indicates an invention other than what is being claimed.

§ 7.34.01 Rejection, 35 U.S.C. 112, 2nd Paragraph, Failure To Particularly Point out and Distinctly Claim (Indefinite)

Claim [1] rejected under 35 U.S.C. 112, second paragraph, as being indefinite for failing to particularly point out and distinctly claim the subject matter which applicant regards as the invention.

Examiner Note:

1. This rejection must be preceded by form paragraph 7.30.02 or 7.103.2. This paragraph should be followed by one or more of the following form paragraphs 7.34.02–7.34.06, as applicable. If none of these form paragraphs are appropriate, a full explanation of the deficiency of the claims should be supplied. Whenever possible, identify the particular term(s) or limitation(s) which render the claim(s) indefinite and state why such term or limitation renders the claim indefinite. If the scope of the claimed subject matter can be determined by one having ordinary skill in the art, a rejection using this form paragraph would not be appropriate. See MPEP §§ 2171–2174 for guidance. See also form paragraph 17.07 for Pro Se applicants.

§ 7.34.02 Terminology Used Inconsistent with Accepted Meaning

While applicant may be his or her own lexicographer, a term in a claim may not be given a meaning repugnant to the usual meaning of that term. See In re Hill, 161 F.2d 367, 73 USPQ 482 (CCPA 1947). The term "[1]" in claim [2] is used by the claim to mean "[3]", while the accepted meaning is "[4]."

Examiner Note:

> 1. In bracket 3, point out the meaning that is assigned to the term by applicant's claims, taking into account the entire disclosure.

> 2. In bracket 4, point out the accepted meaning of the term. Support for the examiner's stated accepted meaning should be provided through the citation of an appropriate reference source, e.g., textbook or dictionary. See MPEP § 2173.05(a).

> 3. This form paragraph must be preceded by form paragraph 7.34.01.

§ 7.34.03 Relative Term — Term of Degree Rendering Claim Indefinite

The term "[1]" in claim [2] is a relative term which renders the claim indefinite. The term "[1]" is not defined by the claim, the specification does not provide a standard for ascertaining the requisite degree, and one of ordinary skill in the art would not be reasonably apprised of the scope of the invention. [3]

Examiner Note:

> 1. In bracket 3, explain which parameter, quantity, or other limitation in the claim has been rendered indefinite by the use of the term appearing in bracket 1.

> 2. This form paragraph must be preceded by form paragraph 7.34.01.

§ 7.34.04 Broader Range/Limitation And Narrow Range/Limitation in Same Claim

A broad range or limitation together with a narrow range or limitation that falls within the broad range or limitation (in the same claim) is considered indefinite, since the resulting claim does not clearly set forth the metes and bounds of the patent protection desired. Note the explanation given by the Board of Patent Appeals and Interferences in Ex parte Wu, 10 USPQ2d 2031, 2033 (Bd. Pat. App. & Inter. 1989), as to where broad language is followed by "such as" and then narrow language. The Board stated that this can render a claim indefinite by raising a question or doubt as to whether the feature introduced by such language is (a) merely exemplary of the remainder of the claim, and therefore not required, or (b) a required feature of the claims. Note also, for example, the decisions of Ex parte Steigewald, 131 USPQ 74 (Bd. App. 1961); Ex parte Hall, 83 USPQ 38 (Bd. App. 1948); and Ex parte Hasche, 86 USPQ 481 (Bd. App. 1949). In the present instance, claim [1] recites the broad recitation [2], and the claim also recites [3] which is the narrower statement of the range/limitation.

Examiner Note:

1. In bracket 2, insert the broader range/limitation and where it appears in the claim; in bracket 3, insert the narrow range/limitation and where it appears. This form paragraph may be modified to fit other instances of indefiniteness in the claims.

2. This form paragraph must be preceded by form paragraph 7.34.01.

§ 7.34.05 Lack of Antecedent Basis in the Claims

Claim [1] recites the limitation [2] in [3]. There is insufficient antecedent basis for this limitation in the claim.

Examiner Note:

1. In bracket 2, insert the limitation which lacks antecedent basis, for example —said lever— or —the lever—.

2. In bracket 3, identify where in the claim(s) the limitation appears, for example, —line 3—, —the 3rd paragraph of the claim—, —the last 2 lines of the claim—, etc.

3. This form paragraph should ONLY be used in aggravated situations where the lack of antecedent basis makes the scope of the claim indeterminate. It must be preceded by form paragraph 7.34.01.

§ 7.34.06 Use Claims

Claim [1] provides for the use of [2], but, since the claim does not set forth any steps involved in the method/process, it is unclear what method/process applicant is intending to encompass. A claim is indefinite where it merely recites a use without any active, positive steps delimiting how this use is actually practiced. Claim [3] is rejected under 35 U.S.C. 101 because the claimed recitation of a use, without setting forth any steps involved in the process, results in an improper definition of a process, i.e., results in a claim which is not a proper process claim under 35 U.S.C. 101. See for example Ex parte Dunki, 153 USPQ 678 (Bd. App. 1967) and Clinical Products, Ltd. v. Brenner, 255 F. Supp. 131, 149 USPQ 475 (D.D.C. 1966).

Examiner Note:

1. In bracket 2, insert what is being used. For example, insert —the monoclonal antibodies of claim 4—, where the claim recites "a method for using monoclonal antibodies of claim 4 to purify interferon."

2. See MPEP § 2173.05(q).

3. This form paragraph must be preceded by form paragraph 7.34.01.

§ 7.34.07 Claims Are a Literal Translation

The claims are generally narrative and indefinite, failing to conform with current U.S. practice. They appear to be a literal translation into English from a foreign document and are replete with grammatical and idiomatic errors.

Examiner Note:

This form paragraph must be preceded by form paragraph 7.34.01.

§ 7.34.08 Indefinite Claim Language: "For Example"

Regarding claim [1], the phrase "for example" renders the claim indefinite because it is unclear whether the limitation(s) following the phrase are part of the claimed invention. See MPEP § 2173.05(d).

Examiner Note:

This form paragraph must be preceded by form paragraph 7.34.01.

§ 7.34.09 Indefinite Claim Language: "Or The Like"

Regarding claim [1], the phrase "or the like" renders the claim(s) indefinite because the claim(s) include(s) elements not actually disclosed (those encompassed by "or the like"), thereby rendering the scope of the claim(s) unascertainable. See MPEP § 2173.05(d).

Examiner Note:

This form paragraph must be preceded by form paragraph 7.34.01.

§ 7.34.10 Indefinite Claim Language: "Such As"

Regarding claim [1], the phrase "such as" renders the claim indefinite because it is unclear whether the limitations following the phrase are part of the claimed invention. See MPEP § 2173.05(d).

Examiner Note:

This form paragraph must be preceded by form paragraph 7.34.01.

§ 7.34.11 Modifier of "Means" Lacks Function

Regarding claim [1], the word "means" is preceded by the word(s) "[2]" in an attempt to use a "means" clause to recite a claim element as a means for performing a specified function. However, since no function is specified by the word(s) preceding "means," it is impossible to determine the equivalents of the element, as required by 35 U.S.C. 112, sixth paragraph. See Ex parte Klumb, 159 USPQ 694 (Bd. App. 1967).

Examiner Note:

1. It is necessary for the words which precede "means" to convey a function to be performed. For example, the phrase "latch means" is definite because the word "latch" conveys the function "latching." In general, if the phrase can be restated as "means for _____," and it still makes sense, it is definite. In the above example, "latch means" can be restated as "means for latching." This is clearly definite. However, if "conduit means" is restated as "means for conduiting," the phrase makes no sense because the word "conduit" has no functional connotation, and the phrase is indefinite.

2. This form paragraph must be preceded by form paragraph 7.34.01.

§ *7.34.12 Essential Steps Omitted*

Claim [1] rejected under 35 U.S.C. 112, second paragraph, as being incomplete for omitting essential steps, such omission amounting to a gap between the steps. See MPEP § 2172.01. The omitted steps are: [2]

Examiner Note:

1. This rejection must be preceded by form paragraph 7.30.02 or 7.103.

2. In bracket 2, recite the steps omitted from the claims.

3. Give the rationale for considering the omitted steps critical or essential.

§ *7.34.13 Essential Elements Omitted*

Claim [1] rejected under 35 U.S.C. 112, second paragraph, as being incomplete for omitting essential elements, such omission amounting to a gap between the elements. See MPEP § 2172.01. The omitted elements are: [2]

Examiner Note:

1. This rejection must be preceded by form paragraph 7.30.02 or 7.103.

2. In bracket 2, recite the elements omitted from the claims.

3. Give the rationale for considering the omitted elements critical or essential.

§ 7.34.14 *Essential Cooperative Relationships Omitted*

Claim [1] rejected under 35 U.S.C. 112, second paragraph, as being incomplete for omitting essential structural cooperative relationships of elements, such omission amounting to a gap between the necessary structural connections. See MPEP § 2172.01. The omitted structural cooperative relationships are: [2]

Examiner Note:

1. This rejection must be preceded by form paragraph 7.30.02 or 7.103.

2. In bracket 2, recite the structural cooperative relationships of elements omitted from the claims.

3. Give the rationale for considering the omitted structural cooperative relationships of elements being critical or essential.

§ 7.35 *Rejection, 35 U.S.C. 112, 2nd Paragraph, Failure To Particularly Point Out And Distinctly Claim — Omnibus Claim*

Claim [1] rejected under 35 U.S.C. 112, second paragraph, as being indefinite in that it fails to point out what is included or excluded by the claim language. This claim is an omnibus type claim.

Examiner Note:

1. This rejection must be preceded by form paragraph 7.30.02 or 7.103.

2. Use this paragraph to reject an "omnibus" type claim. No further explanation is necessary.

3. See MPEP § 1302.04(b) for cancellation of such a claim by examiner's amendment upon allowance.

4. An example of an omnibus claim is: "A device substantially as shown and described."

§ 7.35.01 Trademark or Trade Name as a Limitation in the Claim

Claim [1] contains the trademark/trade name [2]. Where a trademark or trade name is used in a claim as a limitation to identify or describe a particular material or product, the claim does not comply with the requirements of 35 U.S.C. 112, second paragraph. See Ex parte Simpson, 218 USPQ 1020 (Bd. App. 1982). The claim scope is uncertain since the trademark or trade name cannot be used properly to identify any particular material or product. A trademark or trade name is used to identify a source of goods, and not the goods themselves. Thus, a trademark or trade name does not identify or describe the goods associated with the trademark or trade name. In the present case, the trademark/trade name is used to identify/describe [3] and, accordingly, the identification/description is indefinite.

Examiner Note:

1. In bracket 2, insert the trademark/trade name and where it is used in the claim.

2. In bracket 3, specify the material or product which is identified or described in the claim by the trademark/trade name.

[no 706.03 (e), (f), (g), (h), (i), or (j)]

706.03(k) Duplicate Claims

Inasmuch as a patent is supposed to be limited to only one invention or, at most, several closely related indivisible inventions, limiting an application to a single claim, or a single claim to each of the related inventions might appear to be logical as well as convenient. However, court decisions have confirmed applicant's right to restate (i.e., by plural claiming) the invention in a reasonable number of ways. Indeed, a mere difference in scope between claims has been held to be enough.

Nevertheless, when two claims in an application are duplicates, or else are so close in content that they both cover the same thing, despite a slight difference in wording, it is proper after allowing one claim to object to the other claim under 37 CFR 1.75 as being a substantial duplicate of the allowed claim.

Form paragraphs 7.05.05 and 7.05.06 may be used where duplicate claims are present in an application.

§ 7.05.05 Duplicate Claims, Warning

Applicant is advised that should claim [1] be found allowable, claim [2] will be objected to under 37 CFR 1.75 as being a substantial duplicate thereof. When two claims in an application are duplicates or else are so close in content that they both cover the same thing, despite a slight difference in wording, it is proper after allowing one claim to object to the other as being a substantial duplicate of the allowed claim. See MPEP § 706.03(k).

Examiner Note:

1. Use this form paragraph whenever two claims are found to be substantial duplicates, but they are not allowable. This will give the applicant an opportunity to correct the problem and avoid a later objection.

2. If the claims are allowable, use form paragraph 7.05.06.

§ 7.05.06 Duplicate Claims, Objection

Claim [1] objected under 37 CFR 1.75 as being a substantial duplicate of claim [2]. When two claims in an application are duplicates or else are so close in content that they both cover the same thing, despite a slight difference in wording, it is proper after allowing one claim to object to the other as being a substantial duplicate of the allowed claim. See MPEP § 706.03(k).

Examiner Note:

If the duplicate claims are not allowable, use form paragraph 7.05.05.

See MPEP § 804 for double patenting rejections of inventions not patentable over each other.

[no 706.03(l)]

706.03(m)   Nonelected Inventions

See MPEP § 821 to § 821.03 for treatment of claims held to be drawn to nonelected inventions.

[no 706.03(n)]

706.03(o) New Matter

35 U.S.C. 132. Notice of rejection; reexamination.

Whenever, on examination, any claim for a patent is rejected, or any objection or requirement made, the Commissioner shall notify the applicant thereof, stating the reasons for such rejection, or objection or requirement, together with such information and references as may be useful in judging of the propriety of continuing the prosecution of his application; and if after receiving such notice, the applicant persists in his claim for a patent, with or without amendment, the application shall be reexamined. No amendment shall introduce new matter into the disclosure of the invention.

In amended cases, subject matter not disclosed in the original application is sometimes added and a claim directed thereto. Such a claim is rejected on the ground that it recites elements without support in the original disclosure under 35 U.S.C. 112, first paragraph, Waldemar Link, GmbH & Co. v. Osteonics Corp. 32 F.3d 556, 559, 31 USPQ2d 1855, 1857 (Fed. Cir. 1994); In re Rasmussen, 650 F.2d 1212, 211 USPQ 323 (CCPA 1981). See MPEP § 2163.06–§ 2163.07(b) for a discussion of the relationship of new matter to 35 U.S.C. 112, first paragraph. New matter includes not only the addition of wholly unsupported subject matter, but may also include adding specific percentages or compounds after a broader original disclosure, or even the omission of a step from a method. See MPEP § 608.04 to § 608.04(c). See In re Wertheim, 541 F.2d 257, 191 USPQ 90 (CCPA 1976) and MPEP § 2163.05 for guidance in determining whether the addition of specific percentages or compounds after a broader original disclosure constitutes new matter.

In the examination of an application following amendment thereof, the examiner must be on the alert to detect new matter. 35 U.S.C. 132 should be employed as a basis for objection to amendments to the abstract, specification, or drawings attempting to add new disclosure to that originally disclosed on filing.

If subject matter capable of illustration is originally claimed and it is not shown in the drawing, the claim is not rejected but applicant is required to add it to the drawing. See MPEP

§ 608.01(l).

If new matter is added to the specification, it should be objected to by using Form Paragraph 7.28.

§ 7.28 *Objection to New Matter Added to Specification*

The amendment filed [1] is objected to under 35 U.S.C. 132 because it introduces new matter into the disclosure. 35 U.S.C. 132 states that no amendment shall introduce new matter into the disclosure of the invention. The added material which is not supported by the original disclosure is as follows: [2].

Applicant is required to cancel the new matter in the reply to this Office action.

Examiner Note:

1. This form paragraph is not to be used in reissue applications; use form paragraph 14.22.01 instead.

2. In bracket 2, identify the new matter by page and the line numbers and/or drawing figures and provide an appropriate explanation of your position. This explanation should address any statement by applicant to support the position that the subject matter is described in the specification as filed. It should further include any unresolved questions which raise a doubt as to the possession of the claimed invention at the time of filing.

3. If new matter is added to the claims, or affects the claims, a rejection under 35 U.S.C. 112, first paragraph, using form paragraph 7.31.01 should also be made. If new matter is added only to a claim, an objection using this paragraph should not be made, but the claim should be rejected using form paragraph 7.31.01. As to any other appropriate prior art or 35 U.S.C. 112 rejection, the new matter must be considered as part of the claimed subject matter and can not be ignored.

[no 706.03(p), (q), or (r)]

706.03(s) Foreign Filing Without License

35 U.S.C. 182. Abandonment of invention for unauthorized disclosure.

The invention disclosed in an application for patent subject to an order made pursuant to section 181 of this title may be held abandoned upon its being established by the Commissioner that in violation of said order the invention has been published or disclosed or that an application for a patent therefor has been filed in a foreign country by the inventor, his successors, assigns, or legal representatives, or anyone in privity with him or them, without the consent of the Commissioner. The abandonment shall be held to have occurred as of the time of violation. The consent of the Commissioner shall not be given without the concurrence of the heads of the departments and the chief officers of the agencies who caused the order to be issued. A holding of abandonment shall constitute forfeiture by the applicant, his successors, assigns, or legal representatives, or anyone in privity with him or them, of all claims against the United States based upon such invention.

35 U.S.C. 184. Filing of application in foreign country.

Except when authorized by a license obtained from the Commissioner a person shall not file or cause or authorize to be filed in any foreign country prior to six months after filing in the United States an application for patent or for the registration of a utility model, industrial design, or model in respect of an invention made in this country. A license shall not be granted with respect to an invention subject to an order issued by the Commissioner pursuant to section 181 of this title without the concurrence of the head of the departments and the chief officers of the agencies who caused the order to be issued. The license may be granted retroactively where an application has been filed abroad through error and without deceptive intent and the application does not disclose an invention within the scope of section 181 of this title.

The term "application" when used in this chapter includes applications and any modifications, amendments, or supplements thereto, or divisions thereof.

The scope of a license shall permit subsequent modifications, amendments, and supplements containing additional subject matter if the application upon which the request for the license is based is not, or was not, required to be made available for inspection under section 181 of this title and if such modifications, amendments, and supplements do not change the general nature of the invention in a manner which would require such application to be made available for inspection under such section 181. In any case in which a license is not, or was not, required in order to file an application in any foreign country, such subsequent modifications, amendments, and supplements may be made, without a license, to the application filed in the foreign country if the United States application was not required to be made available for inspection under section 181 and if such modifications, amendments, and supplements do not, or did not, change the general nature of the invention in a manner which would require the United States application to have been made available for inspection under such section 181.

35 U.S.C. 185. *Patent barred for filing without license.*

Notwithstanding any other provisions of law any person, and his successors, assigns, or legal representatives,shall not receive a United States patent for an invention if that person, or his successors, assigns, or legal representatives shall, without procuring the license prescribed in section 184 of this title, have made, or consented to or assisted another's making, application in a foreign country for a patent or for the registration of a utility model, industrial design, or model in respect of the invention. A United States patent issued to such person, his successors, assigns, or legal representatives shall be invalid, unless the failure to procure such license was through error and without deceptive intent, and the patent does not disclose subject matter within the scope of section 181 of this title.

If, upon examining an application, the examiner learns of the existence of a corresponding foreign application which appears to have been filed before the United States application had been on file for 6 months, and if the invention apparently was made in this country, he shall refer the application to Licensing and Review Section of Group 3640, calling attention to the foreign application. Pending investigation of the possible violation, the application may be returned to the examining group for prosecution on the merits. When it is otherwise in condition for allowance, the application will be again submitted to Licensing and Review Section of Group 3640 unless the latter has already reported that the foreign filing involves no bar to the United States application.

If it should be necessary to take action under 35 U.S.C. 185, Licensing and Review Section of Group 3640 will request transfer of the application to it.

[no 706.03(t)]

706.03(u) Disclaimer

Claims may be rejected on the ground that applicant has disclaimed the subject matter involved. Such disclaimer may arise, for example, from the applicant's failure to:

> (A) make claims suggested for interference with another application under 37 CFR 1.605 (See MPEP § 2305.02),
>
> (B) copy a claim from a patent when suggested by the examiner (MPEP § 2305.02), or
>
> (C) respond or appeal, within the time limit fixed, to the examiner's rejection of claims copied from a patent (see MPEP § 2307.02).

The rejection on disclaimer applies to all claims not patentably distinct from the disclaimed subject matter as well as to the claims directly involved.

Rejections based on disclaimer should be made by using one of Form Paragraphs 7.48 and 7.49.

§ 7.48 *Failure To Present Claims for Interference*

Claim [1] rejected under 35 U.S.C. [2] based upon claim [3] of Patent No. [4].

Failure to present claims and/or take necessary steps for interference purposes after notification that interfering subject matter is claimed constitutes a disclaimer of the subject matter. This amounts to a concession that, as a matter of law, the patentee is the first inventor in this country. See In re Oguie, 517 F.2d 1382, 186 USPQ 227 (CCPA 1975).

Examiner Note:

1. This paragraph should be used only after applicant has been notified that interference proceedings must be instituted before the claims can be allowed and applicant has refused to copy the claims.

2. In bracket 2, insert —102(g)— or —102(g)/103(a)—.

3. In bracket 4, insert the patent number, and —in view of _____— if another reference is also relied upon. When the rejection is under 35 U.S.C. 103(a), the examiner's basis for a finding of obviousness should be included. Note that interferences may include obvious variants, see MPEP § 2306.

§ 7.49 Rejection, Disclaimer, Failure To Appeal

Claim [1] stand finally disposed of for failure to reply to or appeal from the examiner's rejection of such claim(s) presented for interference within the specified time. See 37 CFR 1.661 and 1.663.

706.03(v)   After Interference or Public Use Proceeding

For rejections following an interference, see MPEP § 2363.03.

The outcome of public use proceedings may also be the basis of a rejection. See 37 CFR 1.292 and In re Kaslow, 707 F.2d 1366, 217 USPQ 1089 (Fed. Cir. 1983).

Upon termination of a public use proceeding including a case also involved in an interference, in order for a prompt resumption of the interference proceedings, a notice should be sent to the Board of Patent Appeals and Interferences notifying them of the disposition of the public use proceeding.

706.03(w)   Res Judicata

Res judicata may constitute a proper ground for rejection. However, as noted below, the Court of Customs and Patent Appeals has materially restricted the use of res judicata rejections. It should be applied only when the earlier decision was a decision of the Board of Appeals or any one of the reviewing courts and when there is no opportunity for further court review of the earlier decision.

The timely filing of a second application copending with an earlier application does not preclude the use of res judicata as a ground of rejection for the second application claims.

When making a rejection on res judicata, action should ordinarily be made also on the basis of prior art, especially in continuing applications. In most situations the same prior art which was relied upon in the earlier decision would again be applicable.

In the following cases a rejection of a claim on the ground of res judicata was sustained where it was based on a prior adjudication, against the inventor on the same claim, a patentably nondistinct claim, or a claim involving the same issue.

In re Freeman, 30 F.3d 1459, 31 USPQ 2d 1444 (Fed. Cir. 1994).

Edgerton v. Kingland, 168 F. 2d 121, 75 USPQ 307 (D.C. Cir. 1947).

In re Szwarc, 319 F.2d 277, 138 USPQ 208 (CCPA 1963).

In re Katz, 467 F.2d 939, 167 USPQ 487 (CCPA 1970) (prior decision by District Court).

In the following cases for various reasons, res judicata rejections were reversed.

In re Fried, 312 F.2d 930, 136 USPQ 429 (CCPA 1963) (differences in claims).

In re Szwarc, 319 F.2d 277, 138 USPQ 208 (CCPA 1963) (differences in claim).

In re Hellbaum, 371 F.2d 1022, 152 USPQ 571 (CCPA 1967) (differences in claims).

In re Herr, 377 F.2d 610, 153 USPQ 548 (CCPA 1967) (same claims, new evidence, prior decision by CCPA).

In re Kaghan, 387 F.2d 398, 156 USPQ 130 (CCPA 1967) (prior decision by Board of Appeals, final rejection on prior art withdrawn by examiner "to simplify the issue," differences in claims; holding of waiver based on language in MPEP at the time).

In re Craig, 411 F.2d 1333, 162 USPQ 157 (CCPA 1969) (Board of Appeals held second set of claims patentable over prior art).

In re Fisher, 427 F.2d 833, 166 USPQ 18 (CCPA 1970) (difference in claims).

In re Russell, 439 F.2d 1228, 169 USPQ 426 (CCPA 1971) (new evidence, rejection on prior art reversed by court).

In re Ackermann, 444 F.2d 1172, 170 USPQ 340 (CCPA 1971) (prior decision by Board of Appeals, new evidence, rejection on prior art reversed by court).

Plastic Contact Lens Co. v. Gottschalk, 484 F.2d 837, 179 USPQ 262 (D.C. Cir. 1973) (follows In re Kaghan).

706.03(x)   Reissue

The examination of reissue applications is covered in MPEP Chapter 1400.

35 U.S.C. 251 forbids the granting of a reissue "enlarging the scope of the claims of the original patent" unless the reissue is applied for within 2 years from the grant of the original patent. This is an absolute bar and cannot be excused. This prohibition has been interpreted to apply to any claim which is broader in any respect than the claims of the original patent. Such claims may be rejected as being barred by 35 U.S.C. 251. However, when the reissue is applied for within 2 years, the examiner does not go into the question of undue delay.

The same section permits the filing of a reissue application by the assignee of the entire interest only in cases where it does not "enlarge the scope of the claims of the original patent." Such claims which do enlarge the scope may also be rejected as barred by the statute. In In re Bennett, 766 F.2d 524, 226 USPQ 413 (Fed. Cir. 1985), however, the court permitted the erroneous filing by the assignee in such a case to be corrected.

A defective reissue oath affords a ground for rejecting all the claims in the reissue application. See MPEP § 1444.

Note that a reissue application is "special" and remains so even if applicant does not make a prompt reply.

803.02 Restriction—Markush Claims

PRACTICE RE MARKUSH-TYPE CLAIMS

If the members of the Markush group are sufficiently few in number or so closely related that a search and examination of the entire claim can be made without serious burden, the examiner must examine all claims on the merits, even though they are directed to independent and distinct inventions. In such a case, the examiner will not follow the procedure described below and will not require restriction.

Since the decisions in In re Weber, 580 F.2d 455, 198 USPQ 328 (CCPA 1978) and In re Haas, 580 F.2d 461, 198 USPQ 334 (CCPA 1978), it is improper for the Office to refuse to examine that which applicants regard as their invention, unless the subject matter in a claim lacks unity of invention. In re Harnish, 631 F.2d 716, 206 USPQ 300 (CCPA 1980); and Ex parte Hozumi, 3 USPQ2d 1059 (Bd. Pat. App. & Int. 1984). Broadly, unity of invention exists where compounds included within a Markush group (1) share a common utility and (2) share a substantial structural feature disclosed as being essential to that utility.

This subsection deals with Markush-type generic claims which include a plurality of alternatively usable substances or members. In most cases, a recitation by enumeration is used because there is no appropriate or true generic language. A Markush-type claim can include independent and distinct inventions. This is true where two or more of the members are so unrelated and diverse that a prior art reference anticipating the claim with respect to one of the members would not render the claim obvious under 35 U.S.C. 103 with respect to the other member(s). In applications containing claims of that nature, the examiner may require a provisional election of a single species prior to examination on the merits. The provisional election will be given effect in the event that the Markush-type claim should be found not allowable. Following election, the Markush-type claim will be examined fully with respect to the elected species and further to the extent necessary to determine patentability. If the Markush-type claim is not allowable over the prior art, examination will be limited to the

Markush-type claim and claims to the elected species, with claims drawn to species patentably distinct from the elected species held withdrawn from further consideration.

As an example, in the case of an application with a Markush-type claim drawn to the compound C-R, wherein R is a radical selected from the group consisting of A, B, C, D, and E, the examiner may require a provisional election of a single species, CA, CB, CC, CD, or CE. The Markush-type claim would then be examined fully with respect to the elected species and any species considered to be clearly unpatentable over the elected species. If on examination the elected species is found to be anticipated or rendered obvious by prior art, the Markush-type claim and claims to the elected species shall be rejected, and claims to the nonelected species would be held withdrawn from further consideration. As in the prevailing practice, a second action on the rejected claims would be made final.

On the other hand, should no prior art be found that anticipates or renders obvious the elected species, the search of the Markush-type claim will be extended. If prior art is then found that anticipates or renders obvious the Markush-type claim with respect to a nonelected species, the Markush-type claim shall be rejected and claims to the nonelected species held withdrawn from further consideration. The prior art search, however, will not be extended unnecessarily to cover all nonelected species. Should applicant, in response to this rejection of the Markush-type claim, overcome the rejection, as by amending the Markush-type claim to exclude the species anticipated or rendered obvious by the prior art, the amended Markush-type claim will be reexamined. The prior art search will be extended to the extent necessary to determine patentability of the Markush-type claim. In the event prior art is found during the reexamination that anticipates or renders obvious the amended Markush-type claim, the claim will be rejected and the action made final. Amendments submitted after the final rejection further restricting the scope of the claim may be denied entry.

806.04 Independent Inventions

If it can be shown that the two or more inventions are in fact independent, applicant should be required to restrict the claims presented to but one of such independent inventions. For example:

(A) Two different combinations, not disclosed as capable of use together, having different modes of operation, different functions or different effects are independent. An article of apparel such as a shoe, and a locomotive bearing would be an example. A process of painting a house and a process of boring a well would be a second example.

(B) Where the two inventions are process and apparatus, and the apparatus cannot be used to practice the process or any part thereof, they are independent. A specific process of molding is independent from a molding apparatus which cannot be used to practice the specific process.

(C) Where species under a genus are independent, for example, a genus of paper clips having species differing in the manner in which a section of the wire is formed in order to achieve a greater increase in its holding power.

SPECIES ARE TREATED EXTENSIVELY IN THE FOLLOWING SECTIONS.

806.04(a) Species — Genus

35 U.S.C. 121 provides that restriction may be required to one of two or more independent and distinct inventions. However, 37 CFR 1.141 provides that a reasonable number of species may still be claimed in one application if the other conditions of the rule are met.

806.04(b) Species May Be Related Inventions

Species, while usually independent, may be related under the particular disclosure. Where inventions as disclosed and claimed are both (A) species under a claimed genus and (B) related, then the question of restriction must be determined by both the practice applicable to election of species and the practice applicable to other types of restrictions such as those covered in MPEP Section 806.05–Section 806.05(i). If restriction is improper under either practice, it should not be required.

For example, two different subcombinations usable with each other may each be a species of some common generic invention. In Ex parte Healy, 1898 C.D. 157, 84 O.G. 1281 (Comm'r Pat. 1898), a clamp for a handle bar stem and a specifically different clamp for a seat post both usable together on a bicycle were claimed. In his decision, the Commissioner considered both the restriction practice under election of species and the practice applicable to restriction between combination and subcombinations.

As a further example, species of carbon compounds may be related to each other as intermediate and final product. Thus, these species are not independent and in order to sustain a restriction requirement, distinctness must be shown. Distinctness is proven if it can be shown that the intermediate product is useful other than to make the final product. Otherwise, the disclosed relationship would preclude their being issued in separate patents.

Form Paragraph 8.14 may be used in intermediate — final product restriction requirements.

8.14 Intermediate-Final Product

Inventions [1] and [2] are related as mutually exclusive species in an intermediate-final product relationship. Distinctness is proven for claims in this relationship if the intermediate product is useful to make other than the final product (MPEP Section 806.04(b), 3rd paragraph), and the species are patentably distinct (MPEP Section 806.04(h)). In the instant case, the intermediate product is deemed to be useful as [3] and the inventions are deemed patentably distinct since there is nothing on this record to show them to be obvious variants. Should applicant traverse on the ground that the species are not patentably distinct, applicant should submit evidence or identify such evidence now of record showing the species to be obvious variants or clearly admit on the record that this is the case. In either instance, if the examiner finds one of the inventions anticipated by the prior art, the evidence or admission may be used in a rejection under 35 U.S.C. 103(a) of the other invention.

Examiner Note:

> 1. This form paragraph is to be used when claims are presented to both an intermediate and final product (MPEP Section 806.04(b)).

> 2. Conclude restriction requirement with one of form paragraphs 8.21.01 through 8.21.03.

The intermediate and final product must have a mutually exclusive species relationship and as with all species restrictions, must be patentably distinct.

Typically, the intermediate loses its identity in the final product.

Additionally, the intermediate must be shown to be useful to make other than the final product. The examiner must give an example of an alternative use but need not provide documentation. Applicant then has the burden to prove or provide a convincing argument that the intermediate does not have the suggested use.

806.04(c) Subcombination Not Generic to Combination

The situation is frequently presented where two different combinations are disclosed, having a subcombination common to each. It is frequently puzzling to determine whether a claim readable on two different combinations is generic thereto.

This was recognized in Ex parte Smith, 1888 C.D. 131, 44 O.G.1183 (Comm'r Pat. 1888), where it was held that a subcombination was not generic to the different combinations in which it was used.

To exemplify, a claim that defines only the subcombination, e.g., the mechanical structure of a joint, is not a generic or genus claim to two different combinations, e.g., a doughnut cooker and an automobile transmission, each of which utilizes the same form of joint.

806.04(d) Definition of a Generic Claim

In an application presenting three species illustrated, for example, in Figures 1, 2, and 3, respectively, a generic claim should read on each of these views; but the fact that a claim does so read is not conclusive that it is generic. It may define only an element or sub-combination common to the several species.

It is not possible to define a generic claim with that precision existing in the case of a geometrical term. In general, a generic claim should include no material element additional to those recited in the species claims, and must comprehend within its confines the organization covered in each of the species.

For the purpose of obtaining claims to more than one species in the same case, the generic claim cannot include limitations not present in each of the added species claims. Otherwise stated, the claims to the species which can be included in a case in addition to a single species must contain all the limitations of the generic claim.

Once a claim that is determined to be generic is allowed, all of the claims drawn to species in addition to the elected species which include all the limitations of the generic claim will ordinarily be obviously allowable in view of the allowance of the generic claim, since the additional species will depend thereon or otherwise include all of the limitations thereof. When all or some of the claims directed to one of the species in addition to the elected species do not include all the limitations of the generic claim, then that species cannot be claimed in the same case with the other species. See MPEP Section 809.02(c).

806.04(e) Claims Restricted to Species

Claims are definitions of inventions. Claims are never species. Claims may be restricted to a single disclosed embodiment (i.e., a single species, and thus be designated a specific species claim), or a claim may include two or more of the disclosed embodiments within the breadth and scope of definition (and thus be designated a generic or genus claim).

Species are always the specifically different embodiments.

Species are usually but not always independent as disclosed (see MPEP Section 806.04(b)) since there is usually no disclosure of relationship therebetween. The fact that a genus for two different embodiments is capable of being conceived and defined, does not affect the independence of the embodiments, where the case under consideration contains no disclosure of any commonality of operation, function or effect.

806.04(f) Claims Restricted to Species, by Mutually Exclusive Characteristics

Claims to be restricted to different species must be mutually exclusive. The general test as to when claims are restricted, respectively, to different species is the fact that one claim recites limitations which under the disclosure are found in a first species but not in a second, while a second claim recites limitations disclosed only for the second species and not the first. This is frequently expressed by saying that claims to be restricted to different species must recite the mutually exclusive characteristics of such species.

[no 806.04(g)]

806.04(h) Species Must Be Patentably Distinct From Each Other

Where an applicant files a divisional application claiming a species previously claimed but nonelected in the parent case, pursuant to and consonant with a requirement to restrict, there should be no determination of whether or not the species claimed in the divisional application is patentable over the species retained in the parent case since such a determination was made before the requirement to restrict was made.

In a national application containing claims directed to more than a reasonable number of species, the examiner should not require restriction to a reasonable number of species unless he or she is satisfied that he or she would be prepared to allow claims to each of the claimed species over the parent case, if presented in a divisional application filed according to the requirement. Restriction should not be required if the species claimed are considered clearly unpatentable over each other.

In making a requirement for restriction in an application claiming plural species, the examiner should group together species considered clearly unpatentable over each other, with the statement that restriction as between those species is not required.

Where generic claims are allowed in a national application, applicant may claim in the same application additional species as provided by 37 CFR 1.141.

Where, however, an applicant optionally files another national application with claims to a different species, or for a species disclosed but not claimed in a parent case as filed and first acted upon by the examiner, there should be close investigation to determine the presence or absence of patentable difference. See MPEP Section 804.01 and Section 804.02.

806.04(i) Generic Claims Presented for First Time After Issue of Species

The Office no longer follows the practice of prohibiting the allowance of generic claims that are presented for the first time after the issuance of a copending application claiming plural species. Instead, the Office may reject the generic claims on the grounds of obviousness-type double patenting. Applicant may overcome such a rejection by filing a terminal disclaimer. See In re Braithwaite, 379 F.2d 594, 154 USPQ 29 (CCPA 1967).

806.05 Related Inventions

Where two or more related inventions are being claimed, the principal question to be determined in connection with a requirement to restrict or a rejection on the ground of double patenting is whether or not the inventions as claimed are distinct. If they are distinct, restriction may be proper. If they are not distinct, restriction is never proper. If nondistinct inventions are claimed in separate applications or patents, double patenting must be held, except where the additional applications were filed consonant with a requirement to restrict in a national application.

The various pairs of related inventions are noted in the following sections.

806.05(a) Combination and Subcombination or Element

A combination is an organization of which a subcombination or element is a part.

Relative to questions of restriction where a combination is alleged, the claim thereto must be assumed to be allowable (novel and unobvious) as pointed out in MPEP Section 806.02, in the absence of a holding by the examiner to the contrary. When a claim is found in a patent, it has already been found by the Office to be allowable and must be treated on that basis.

806.05(b) Old Combination—Novel Subcombination

Restriction is ordinarily not proper between a combination (AB) that the examiner holds to be old and unpatentable and the subcombination (B) in which the examiner holds the novelty, if any, to reside. Ex parte Donnell, 1923 C.D. 54, 315 O.G. 398 (Comm'r Pat.1923). See MPEP Section 820.01.

806.05(c) Criteria of Distinctness for Combination, Subcombination, or Element of a Combination

In order to establish that combination and subcombination inventions are distinct, two-way distinctness must be demonstrated.

To support a requirement for restriction, both two-way distinctness and reasons for insisting on restriction are necessary, i.e., separate classification, status, or field of search. See MPEP Section 808.02.

The inventions are distinct if it can be shown that a combination as claimed:

> (A) does not require the particulars of the subcombination as claimed for patentability (to show novelty and unobviousness), and

> (B) the subcombination can be shown to have utility either by itself or in other and different relations. When these factors cannot be shown, such inventions are not distinct.

The following examples are included for general guidance.

I. SUBCOMBINATION NOT ESSENTIAL TO COMBINATION

AB br/B sp Restriction Proper

Where a combination as claimed does not set forth the details of the subcombination as separately claimed and the subcombination has separate utility, the inventions are distinct and restriction is proper if reasons exist for insisting upon the restriction; i.e., separate classification, status, or field of search.

This situation can be diagramed as combination ABbr ("br" is an abbreviation for "broad"), and subcombination Bsp ("sp" is an abbreviation for "specific"). Bbr indicates that in the combination the subcombination is broadly recited and that the specific characteristics set forth in the subcombination claim Bsp are not set forth in the combination claim.

Since claims to both the subcombination and combination are presented and assumed to be patentable, the omission of details of the claimed subcombination Bsp in the combination claim ABbr is evidence that the patentability of the combination does not rely on the details of the specific subcombination.

II. SUBCOMBINATION ESSENTIAL TO COMBINATION

AB sp/B sp No Restriction

If there is no evidence that combination ABsp is patentable without the details of Bsp, restriction should not be required. Where the relationship between the claims is such that the separately claimed subcombination Bsp constitutes the essential distinguishing feature of the combination ABsp as claimed, the inventions are not distinct and a requirement for restriction must not be made, even though the subcombination has separate utility.

III. SOME COMBINATION CLAIMS RECITE SPECIFIC FEATURES OF THE SUBCOMBINATION BUT OTHER COMBINATION CLAIMS GIVE EVIDENCE THAT THE SUBCOMBINATION IS NOT ESSENTIAL TO THE COMBINATION.

AB sp/AB br (Evidence Claim)/B sp Restriction Proper

Claim ABbr is an evidence claim which indicates that the combination does not rely upon the specific details of the subcombination for its patentability. If claim ABbr is subsequently found to be unallowable, the question of rejoinder of the inventions restricted must be considered and the letter to the applicant should so state. Therefore, where the combination evidence claim ABbr does not set forth the details of the subcombination Bsp and the subcombination Bsp has separate utility, the inventions are distinct and restriction is proper if reasons exist for insisting upon the restriction.

In applications claiming plural inventions capable of being viewed as related in two ways, for example, as both combination-subcombination and also as different statutory categories, both applicable criteria for distinctness must be demonstrated to support a restriction requirement.

See also MPEP Section 806.04(b).

Form Paragraph 8.15 may be used in combination-subcombination restriction requirements.

8.15 Combination-Subcombination

Inventions [1] and [2] are related as combination and subcombination. Inventions in this relationship are distinct if it can be shown that (1) the combination as claimed does not require the particulars of the subcombination as claimed for patentability, and (2) that the subcombination has utility by itself or in other combinations (MPEP Section 806.05(c)). In the instant case, the combination as claimed does not require the particulars of the subcombination as claimed because [3]. The subcombination has separate utility such as [4].

Examiner Note:

1. This form paragraph is to be used when claims are presented to both combination(s) and subcombination(s) (MPEP Section 806.05(c)).

2. In situations involving evidence claims, see MPEP Section 806.05(c), example 3, and explain in bracket 3.

3. In bracket 4, suggest utility other than used in the combination.

4. Conclude restriction requirement with one of form paragraphs 8.21.01 through 8.21.03.

The burden is on the examiner to suggest an example of separate utility.

If applicant proves or provides an argument supported by facts, that the other utility, suggested by the examiner, cannot be accomplished, the burden shifts to the examiner to document a viable separate utility or withdraw the requirement.

904.01   Analysis of Claims [R-1]

The breadth of the claims in the application should always be carefully noted; that is, the examiner should be fully aware of what the claims do not call for, as well as what they do require. **During patent examination, the claims are given the broadest reasonable interpretation consistent with the specification. See In re Morris, 127 F.3d 1048, 44 USPQ2d 1023 (Fed. Cir. 1997). See MPEP § 2111–§ 2116.01 for case law pertinent to claim analysis.

904.01(a)   Variant Embodiments Within Scope of Claim [R-1]

Substantially, every claim includes within its breadth or scope ** one or more variant embodiments that are not disclosed **in the application, but which would anticipate the **claimed invention if found in a referenceshould be recognized**.

In each type of subject matter capable of such treatment (e.g., a machine or other apparatus), the subject matter as defined by the claim may be sketched or diagrammed in order to clearly delineate the limitations of the claim. Two or more sketches, each of which is as divergent from the particular disclosure as is permitted by claim recitation, will assist the examiner in determining the claim's actual breadth or scope. However, an applicant will not be required to submit such sketches of claim structure. In re Application filed November 16, 1945, 89 USPQ 280, 1951 C.D. 1, 646 O.G. 5 (Comm'r Pat. 1951).

904.01(b)   Equivalents [R-1]

All subject matter that is the * equivalent of the subject matter as defined in the claim, even though specifically different from the definition in the claim, must be considered unless expressly excluded by the claimed subject matterwhat arts are analogous to a particular claimed invention is at times difficult. It depends upon the necessary essential function or utility of the subject matter covered by the claims, and not upon what it is called by the applicantboth relate to the mixing art, this being the necessary function of each. Similarly a brick-cutting machine and a biscuit cutting machine have the same necessary function. See MPEP § 2141.01(a) for a discussion of analogous and nonanalogous art in the context of establishing a prima facie case of obviousness under 35 U.S.C. 103. See MPEP § 2131.05 for a discussion of analogous and nonanalogous art in the context of 35 U.S.C. 102.

904.01(c)   Analogous Arts [R-1]

Not only must the art be searched within which the invention claimed is classifiable, but also all analogous arts regardless of where classified.

The determination of *what arts are analogous to a particular claimed invention is at times difficult. It depends upon the necessary essential function or utility of the subject matter covered by the claims, and not upon what it is called by the applicant

For example, a tea mixer and a concrete mixer ** both relate to the mixing art, this being the necessary function of each. Similarly a brick-cutting machine and a biscuit cutting machine have the same necessary function. See MPEP § 2141.01(a) for a discussion of analogous and nonanalogous art in the context of establishing a prima facie case of obviousness under 35 U.S.C. 103. See MPEP § 2131.05 for a discussion of analogous and nonanalogous art in the context of 35 U.S.C. 102.

1605　　Specification and Claim [R-1]

35 U.S.C. 162. Description, claim.

No plant patent shall be declared invalid for noncompliance with section 112 of this title if the description is as complete as is reasonably possible.

The claim in the specification shall be in formal terms to the plant shown and described.

37 CFR 1.163. Specification and arrangement of application elements.

(a) The specification must contain as full and complete a disclosure as possible of the plant and the characteristics thereof that distinguish the same over related known varieties, and its antecedents, and must particularly point out where and in what manner the variety of plant has been asexually reproduced. In the case of a newly found plant, the specification must particularly point out the location and character of the area where the plant was discovered.

(b) Two copies of the specification (including the claim) must be submitted, but only one signed oath or declaration is required.

(c) The elements of the plant application, if applicable, should appear in the following order:

   (1)　Plant Application Transmittal Form.

   (2)　Fee Transmittal Form.

   (3)　Title of the invention.

   (4)　Cross-reference to related applications.

   (5)　Statement regarding federally sponsored research or development.

   (6)　Background of the invention.

   (7)　Brief summary of the invention.

   (8)　Brief description of the drawing.

   (9)　Detailed Botanical Description.

   (10) A single claim.

   (11) Abstract of the Disclosure.

   (12) Drawings (in duplicate).

(13) Executed oath or declaration.

(14) Plant color coding sheet.

(d) A plant color coding sheet as used in this section means a sheet that specifies a color coding system as designated in a color dictionary, and lists every plant structure to which color is a distinguishing feature and the corresponding color code which best represents that plant structure.

37 CFR 1.164. Claim.

The claim shall be in formal terms to the new and distinct variety of the specified plant as described and illustrated, and may also recite the principal distinguishing characteristics. More than one claim is not permitted.

The specification should include a complete detailed description of the plant and the characteristics thereof that distinguish the same over related known varieties, and its antecedents, expressed in botanical terms in the general form followed in standard botanical textbooks or publications dealing with the varieties of the kind of plant involved (evergreen tree, dahlia plant, rose plant, apple tree, etc.), rather than a mere broad non-botanical characterization such as commonly found in nursery or seed catalogs. The specification should also include the origin or parentage and the genus and species designation of the plant variety sought to be patented and must particularly point out where, e.g., location or place of business, and in what manner the variety of plant has been asexually reproduced.

Form Paragraphs 16.01, 16.09, and 16.10 may be used to object to the disclosure under 37 CFR 1.163(a).

§ 16.01 Specification, *Manner of Asexually Reproducing*

The application is objected to under 37 CFR 1.163(a) because the specification does not "particularly point out where and in what manner the variety of plant has been asexually reproduced". Correction is required.

§ 16.09 Specification, *Less Than Complete Description*

The disclosure is objected to under 37 CFR 1.163(a) because the specification presents less than a full and complete botanical description and the characteristics which distinguish over related known varieties. More specifically: [1].

§ 16.10 Specification, Location of Plant Not Disclosed

The disclosure is objected to under 37 CFR 1.163(a) because the specification does not particularly point out the location and character of the area where the plant was discovered.

Where color is a distinctive feature of the plant, the color should be positively identified in the specification by reference to a designated color as given by a recognized color dictionary or color chart ** . The application may optionally include a plant color coding sheet (e.g., Form PTO/SB/20, Plant Color Coding Sheet), as this provides a means for applicants to uniformly convey color characteristics of the plant. The plant color coding sheet is a sheet that specifies a color coding system as designated in a color dictionary, and lists every plant structure to which color is a distinguishing feature and the corresponding color code which best represents the color of that plant structure. **

Form paragraphs 16.02 and 16.03 may be used to object to the disclosure or reject the claim, respectively, because of a lack of a clear and complete disclosure with regard to colors.

Form PTO/SB/20. Plant Color Coding Sheet

§ 16.02 Colors Specified Do Not Correspond With Those Shown

The disclosure is objected to under 35 U.S.C. 112, first paragraph, because the [1] colors specified fail to correspond with those shown.

§ 16.03 Rejection, 35 U.S.C. 112, 1st Paragraph, Non-Support for Colors

The claim is rejected under 35 U.S.C. 112, first paragraph, as being unsupported by a clear and complete disclosure with regard to [1] colors, for the following reasons: [2].

If the written description of a plant is deficient in certain respects (see, e.g., In re Greer, 484 F.2d 488, 179 USPQ 301 (CCPA 1973))may be submitted in reply to an Office action. Such submission will not constitute new matter under 35 U.S.C. 132. *Jessel v. Newland, 195 USPQ 678, 684 (Dep. Comm'r Pat. 1977).

The rules on Deposit of Biological Materials, 37 CFR 1.801-1.809, do not apply to plant patent applications in view of the reduced disclosure requirements of 35 U.S.C. 162, even where a deposit of a plant has been made in conjunction with a utility application (35 U.S.C. 101).

A plant patent is granted only on the entire plant. It, therefore, follows that only one claim is necessary and only one is permitted. A method claim in a plant patent application is improper. An example of a proper claim would be "A new and distinct variety of hybrid tea rose plant, substantially as illustrated and described herein."

2105 Patentable Subject Matter — Living Subject Matter [R-1]

The decision of the Supreme Court in Diamond v. Chakrabarty, 447 U.S. 303, 206 USPQ 193 (1980), held that microorganisms produced by genetic engineering are not excluded from patent protection by 35 U.S.C. 101. It is clear from the Supreme Court decision and opinion that the question of whether or not an invention embraces living matter is irrelevant to the issue of patentability. The test set down by the Court for patentable subject matter in this area is whether the living matter is the result of human intervention.

In view of this decision, the Office has issued these guidelines as to how 35 U.S.C. 101 will be interpreted.

The Supreme Court made the following points in the Chakrabarty opinion:

> 1. "Guided by these canons of construction, this Court has read the term `manufacture' in § 101 in accordance with its dictionary definition to mean `the production of articles for use from raw materials prepared by giving to these materials new forms, 'nsqualities, properties, or combinations whether by hand labor or by machinery.'"

> 2. "In choosing such expansive terms as 'manufacture' and 'composition of matter,' modified by the comprehensive 'any,' Congress plainly contemplated that the patent laws would be given wide scope."

3. "The Act embodied Jefferson's philosophy that 'ingenuity should receive a liberal encouragement.' 5 Writings of Thomas Jefferson, at 75-76. See Graham v. John Deere Co., 383 U.S. 1, 7-10 (1966). Subsequent patent statutes in 1836, 1870, and 1874 employed this same broad language. In 1952, when the patent laws were recodified, Congress replaced the word 'art' with 'process,' but otherwise left Jefferson's language intact. The Committee Reports accompanying the 1952 act inform us that Congress intended statutory subject matter to 'include any thing under the sun that is made by man.' S. Rep. No. 1979, 82d Cong., 2d Sess., 5 (1952)."

4. "This is not to suggest that § 101 has no limits or that it embraces every discovery. The laws of nature, physical phenomena, and abstract ideas have been held not patentable."

5. "Thus, a new mineral discovered in the earth or a new plant found in the wild is not patentable subject matter. Likewise, Einstein could not patent his celebrated law that E=mc2 ; nor could Newton have patented the law of gravity."

6. "His claim is not to a hitherto unknown natural phenomenon, but to a nonnaturally occurring manufacture or composition of matter __ a product of human ingenuity 'having a distinctive name, character [and] use.'"

7. "Congress thus recognized that the relevant distinction was not between living and inanimate things, but between products of nature, whether living or not, and human-made inventions. Here, respondent's microorganism is the result of human ingenuity and research."

8. After reference to Funk Seed Co. & Kalo Co., 333 U.S.127 (1948), "Here, by contrast, the patentee has produced a new bacterium with markedly different characteristics from any found in nature and one having the potential for significant utility. His discovery is not nature's handiwork, but his own; accordingly it is patentable subject matter under § 101."

A review of the Court statements above as well as the whole Chakrabarty opinion reveals:

(A) That the Court did not limit its decision to genetically engineered living organisms;

(B) The Court enunciated a very broad interpretation of "manufacture" and "composition of matter" in 35 U.S.C. 101 (Note esp. quotes 1, 2, and 3 above);

(C) The Court set forth several tests for weighing whether patentable subject matter under 35 U.S.C. 101 is present stating (in quote 7 above) that:

The relevant distinction was not between living and inanimate things but between products of nature, whether living or not, and human-made inventions.

The tests set forth by the Court are (note especially the italicized portions):

(A) "The laws of nature, physical phenomena and abstract ideas" are not patentable subject matter.

(B) A "nonnaturally occurring manufacture or composition of matter — a product of human ingenuity -having a distinctive name, character, [and] use" is patentable subject matter.

(C) "[A] new mineral discovered in the earth or a new plant found in the wild is not patentable subject matter. Likewise, Einstein could not patent his celebrated E=mc2; nor could Newton have patented the law of gravity. Such discoveries are 'manifestations of . . . nature, free to all men and reserved exclusively to none.'"

(D) "[T]he production of articles for use from raw materials prepared by giving to these materials new forms, qualities, properties, or combinations whether by hand labor or by machinery" [emphasis added] is a "manufacture" under 35 U.S.C. 101.

In analyzing the history of the Plant Patent Act of 1930, the Court stated: "In enacting the Plant Patent Act, Congress addressed both of these concerns [the concern that plants, even those artificially bred, were products of nature for purposes of the patent law and the concern that plants were thought not amenable to the written description]. It explained at length its belief that the work of the plant breeder 'in aid of nature' was patentable invention. S. Rep. No. 315, 71st Cong., 2d Sess., 6-8 (1930); H.R. Rep. No. 1129, 71st Cong., 2d Sess., 7-9 (1930)."

The Office will decide the questions as to patentable subject matter under 35 U.S.C. 101 on a case-by-case basis following the tests set forth in Chakrabarty, e.g., that "a nonnaturally occurring manufacture or composition of matter" is patentable, etc. It is inappropriate to try to attempt to set forth here in advance the exact parameters to be followed.

The standard of patentability has not and will not be lowered. The requirements of 35 U.S.C. 102 and 103 still apply. The tests outlined above simply mean that a rational basis will be present for any 35 U.S.C. 101 determination. In addition, the requirements of 35 U.S.C. 112 must also be met. In this regard, see MPEP § 608.01(p).

Following this analysis by the Supreme Court of the scope of 35 U.S.C. 101, **the Federal Circuit held that patentable subject matter under 35 U.S.C. 101 includes seeds and seed-grown plants, even though plant protection is also available under the Plant Patent Act (35 U.S.C. 161–164) and the Plant Variety Protection Act (7 U.S.C. 2321 et. seq.). Pioneer Hi-Bred International Inc. v. J.E.M. AG Supply Inc., 200 F.3d 1374, 53 USPQ2d 1440, 1442-43 (Fed. Cir. 2000)(Title 35 and the Plant Variety Protection Act are not in conflict; there is simply a difference in the rights and obligations of each statute.). See also Ex parte Hibberd, 227 USPQ 443 (Bd. Pat. App. & Inter. 1985) wherein the Board held that plant subject matter may be the proper subject of a patent under 35 U.S.C. 101 even though such subject matter may be protected under the Plant Patent Act ** or the Plant Variety Protection Act **. Following the reasoning in Chakrabarty, the Board of Patent Appeals and Interferences has also determined that animals are patentable subject matter under 35 U.S.C. 101. In Ex parte Allen, 2 USPQ2d 1425 (Bd. Pat. App. & Inter. 1987), the Board decided that a polyploid Pacific coast oyster could have been the proper subject of a patent under 35 U.S.C. 101 if all the criteria for patentability were satisfied. Shortly after the Allen decision, the Commissioner of Patents and Trademarks issued a notice (Animals — Patentability, 1077 O.G. 24, April 21, 1987) that the Patent and Trademark Office would now consider nonnaturally occurring, nonhuman multicellular living organisms, including animals, to be patentable subject matter within the scope of 35 U.S.C. 101.

If the broadest reasonable interpretation of the claimed invention as a whole encompasses a human being, then a rejection under 35 U.S.C. 101 must be made indicating that the claimed invention is directed to nonstatutory subject matter. Furthermore, the claimed invention must be examined with regard to all issues pertinent to patentability, and any applicable rejections under 35 U.S.C. 102, 103, or 112 must also be made.

2106   Patentable Subject Matter — Computer-Related Inventions [R-1]

I. INTRODUCTION

These Examination Guidelines for Computer-Related Inventions ("Guidelines") are to assist Office personnel in the examination of applications drawn to computer-related inventions. "Computer-related inventions" include inventions implemented in a computer and inventions employing computer-readable media. The Guidelines are based on the Office's current understanding of the law and are believed to be fully consistent with binding precedent of the Supreme Court, the Federal Circuit and the Federal Circuit's predecessor courts.

These Guidelines do not constitute substantive rulemaking and hence do not have the force and effect of law. These Guidelines have been designed to assist Office personnel in analyzing claimed subject matter for compliance with substantive law. Rejections will be based upon the substantive law and it is these rejections which are appealable. Consequently, any failure by Office personnel to follow the Guidelines is neither appealable nor petitionable.

The Guidelines alter the procedures Office personnel will follow when examining applications drawn to computer-related inventions and are equally applicable to claimed inventions implemented in either hardware or software. The Guidelines also clarify the Office's position on certain patentability standards related to this field of technology. Office personnel are to rely on these Guidelines in the event of any inconsistent treatment of issues between these Guidelines and any earlier provided guidance from the Office.

**

Office personnel should no longer rely on the Freeman-Walter-Abele test to determine whether a claimed invention is directed to statutory subject matter. State Street Bank & Trust Co. v. Signature Financial Group Inc., 149 F. 3d 1368, 1374, 47 USPQ2d 1596, 1601-02 (Fed. Cir. 1998) ("After Diehr and Chakrabarty, the Freeman-Walter-Abele test has little, if any, applicability to determining the presence of statutory subject matter.").

Office personnel have had difficulty in properly treating claims directed to methods of doing business. Claims should not be categorized as methods of doing business. Instead, such claims should be treated like any other process claims, pursuant to these Guidelines when relevant. See, e.g., State Street, 149 F.3d at 1374-75, 47 USPQ2d at 1602 (Fed. Cir. 1998); In re Toma, 575 F.2d 872, 877-78, 197 USPQ 852, 857 (CCPA 1978); In re Musgrave, 431 F.2d 882, 893, 167 USPQ 280, 289-90 (CCPA 1970). See also In re Schrader, 22 F.3d 290, 297-98, 30 USPQ2d 1455, 1461-62 (Fed. Cir. 1994) (Newman, J., dissenting); Paine, Webber, Jackson & Curtis, Inc. v. Merrill Lynch, Pierce, Fenner & Smith, Inc., 564 F. Supp. 1358, 1368-69, 218 USPQ 212, 220 (D. Del. 1983).

The appendix which appears at the end of this section includes a flow chart of the process Office personnel will follow in conducting examinations for computer-related inventions.

II. DETERMINE WHAT APPLICANT HAS INVENTED AND IS SEEKING TO PATENT

It is essential that patent applicants obtain a prompt yet complete examination of their applications. Under the principles of compact prosecution, each claim should be reviewed for compliance with every statutory requirement for patentability in the initial review of the application, even if one or more claims are found to be deficient with respect to some statutory requirement. Thus, Office personnel should state all reasons and bases for rejecting claims in the first Office action. Deficiencies should be explained clearly, particularly when they serve as a basis for a rejection. Whenever practicable, Office personnel should indicate how rejections may be overcome and how problems may be resolved. A failure to follow this approach can lead to unnecessary delays in the prosecution of the application.

Prior to focusing on specific statutory requirements, Office personnel must begin examination by determining what, precisely, the applicant has invented and is seeking to patent, and how the claims relate to and define that invention. (As the courts have repeatedly reminded the Office: "The goal is to answer the question" 'What did applicants invent?' " In re Abele, 684 F.2d *902, 907, 214 USPQ *682, 687. Accord, e.g., Arrhythmia Research Tech. v. Corazonix Corp., 958 F.2d 1053, 1059, 22 USPQ2d 1033, 1038 (Fed. Cir. 1992).) Consequently, Office personnel will no longer begin examination by determining if a claim recites a "mathematical algorithm." Rather they will review the complete specification, including the detailed description of the invention, any specific embodiments that have been disclosed, the claims and any specific utilities that have been asserted for the invention.

A.   Identify and Understand Any Practical Application Asserted for the Invention

**

The claimed invention as a whole must accomplish a practical application. That is, it must produce a "useful, concrete and tangible result." State Street, 149 F.3d at 1373, 47 USPQ2d at 1601-02. The purpose of this requirement is to limit patent protection to inventions that possess a certain level of "real world" value, as opposed to subject matter that represents nothing more than an idea or concept, or is simply a starting point for future investigation or research (Brenner v. Manson, 383 U.S. 519, 528-36, 148 USPQ 689, 693-96); In re Ziegler, 992, F.2d 1197, 1200-03, 26 USPQ2d 1600, 1603-06 (Fed. Cir. 1993)). Accordingly, a complete disclosure should contain some indication of the practical application for the claimed invention, i.e., why the applicant believes the claimed invention is useful.

Apart from the utility requirement of 35 U.S.C. 101, usefulness under the patent eligibility standard requires significant functionality to be present to satisfy the useful result aspect of the practical application requirement. See Arrhythmia, 958 F.2d at 1057, 22 USPQ2d at 1036. Merely claiming nonfunctional descriptive material stored in a computer-readable medium does not make the invention eligible for patenting. For example, a claim directed to a word processing file stored on a disk may satisfy the utility requirement of 35 U.S.C. 101 since the information stored may have some "real world" value. However, the mere fact that the claim may satisfy the utility requirement of 35 U.S.C. 101 does not mean that a useful result is achieved under the practical application requirement. The claimed invention as a whole must produce a "useful, concrete and tangible" result to have a practical application.

A process that consists solely of the manipulation of an abstract idea is not concrete or tangible. See In re Warmerdam, 33 F.3d 1354, 1360, 31 USPQ2d 1754, 1759 (Fed. Cir. 1994). See also Schrader, 22 F.3d at 295, 30 USPQ2d at 1459. Office personnel have the burden to establish a prima facie case that the claimed invention as a whole is directed to solely an abstract idea or to manipulation of abstract ideas or does not produce a useful result. Only when the claim is devoid of any limitation to a practical application in the technological arts should it be rejected under 35 U.S.C. 101. Compare Musgrave, 431 F.2d at 893, 167 USPQ at 289; In re Foster, 438 F.2d 1011, 1013, 169 USPQ 99, 101 (CCPA 1971). Further, when such a rejection is made, Office personnel must expressly state how the language of the claims has been interpreted to support the rejection.

The applicant is in the best position to explain why an invention is believed useful. Office personnel should therefore focus their efforts on pointing out statements made in the specification that identify all practical applications for the invention. Office personnel should rely on such statements throughout the examination when assessing the invention for compliance with all statutory criteria. An applicant may assert more than one practical application, but only one is necessary to satisfy the utility requirement. Office personnel should review the entire disclosure to determine the features necessary to accomplish at least one asserted practical application.

B.   Review the Detailed Disclosure and Specific Embodiments of the Invention to Determine What the Applicant Has Invented

The written description will provide the clearest explanation of the applicant's invention, by exemplifying the invention, explaining how it relates to the prior art and explaining the relative significance of various features of the invention. Accordingly, Office personnel should begin their evaluation of a computer-related invention as follows:

— determine what the programmed computer does when it performs the processes dictated by the software (i.e., the functionality of the programmed computer) (Arrhythmia, 958 F.2d at 1057, 22 USPQ at 1036, "It is of course true that a modern digital computer manipulates data, usually in binary form, by performing mathematical operations, such as addition, subtraction, multiplication, division, or bit shifting, on the data. But this is only how the computer does what it does. Of importance is the significance of the data and their manipulation in the real world, i.e., what the computer is doing.");

— determine how the computer is to be configured to provide that functionality (i.e., what elements constitute the programmed computer and how those elements are configured and interrelated to provide the specified functionality); and

— if applicable, determine the relationship of the programmed computer to other subject matter outside the computer that constitutes the invention (e.g., machines, devices, materials, or process steps other than those that are part of or performed by the programmed computer). (Many computer-related inventions do not consist solely of a computer. Thus, Office personnel should identify those claimed elements of the computer-related invention that are not part of the programmed computer, and determine how those elements relate to the programmed computer. Office personnel should look for specific information that explains the role of the programmed computer in the overall process or machine and how the programmed computer is to be integrated with the other elements of the apparatus or used in the process.)

Patent applicants can assist the Office by preparing applications that clearly set forth these aspects of a computer-related invention.

C. Review the Claims

The claims define the property rights provided by a patent, and thus require careful scrutiny. The goal of claim analysis is to identify the boundaries of the protection sought by the applicant and to understand how the claims relate to and define what the applicant has indicated is the invention. Office personnel must first determine the scope of a claim by thoroughly * analyzing the language of *the claim before determining if the claim complies with each statutory requirement for patentability. See In re Hiniker Co., 150 F.3d 1362, 1369, 47 USPQ2d 1523, 1529 (Fed. Cir. 1998) ("[T]he name of the game is the claim.").

Office personnel should begin claim analysis by identifying and evaluating each claim limitation. For processes, the claim limitations will define steps or acts to be performed. For products, the claim limitations will define discrete physical structures or materialsor materials may be comprised of hardware or a combination of hardware and software.

Office personnel are to correlate each claim limitation to all portions of the disclosure that describe the claim limitation. This is to be done in all cases, i.e., whether or not the claimed invention is defined using means or step plus function language. The correlation step will ensure that Office personnel correctly interpret each claim limitation.

The subject matter of a properly construed claim is defined by the terms that limit its scope. It is this subject matter that must be examined. As a general matter, the grammar and intended meaning of terms used in a claim will dictate whether the language limits the claim scope. Language that suggests or makes optional but does not require steps to be performed or does not limit a claim to a particular structure does not limit the scope of a claim or claim limitation. The following are examples of language that may raise a question as to the limiting effect of the language in a claim:

(A) statements of intended use or field of use,

(B) "adapted to" or "adapted for" clauses,

(C) "wherein" clauses, or

(D) "whereby" clauses.

This list of examples is not intended to be exhaustive.

Office personnel must rely on the applicant's disclosure to properly determine the meaning of terms used in the claims. Markman v. Westview Instruments, 52 F.3d 967, 980, 34 USPQ2d 1321, 1330 (Fed. Cir.) (en banc), aff'd, U.S. , 116 S. Ct. 1384 (1996). An applicant is entitled to be his or her own lexicographer, and in many instances will provide an explicit definition for certain terms used in the claims. Where an explicit definition is provided by the applicant for a term, that definition will control interpretation of the term as it is used in the claim. Toro Co. v. White Consolidated Industries Inc., 199 F.3d 1295, 1301, 53 USPQ2d 1065, 1069 (Fed. Cir. 1999) (meaning of words used in a claim is not construed in a "lexicographic vacuum, but in the context of the specification and drawings."). Office personnel should determine if the original disclosure provides a definition consistent with any assertions made by applicant. See, e.g., In re Paulsen, 30 F.3d 1475, 1480, 31 USPQ2d 1671, 1674 (Fed. Cir. 1994) (inventor may define specific terms used to describe invention, but must do so "with reasonable clarity, deliberateness, and precision" and, if done, must " `set out his uncommon definition in some manner within the patent disclosure' so as to give one of ordinary skill in the art notice of the change" in meaning) (quoting Intellicall, Inc. v. Phonometrics, Inc., 952 F.2d 1384, 1387-88, 21 USPQ2d 1383, 1386 (Fed. Cir. 1992)). Any special meaning assigned to a term "must be sufficiently clear in the specification that any departure from common usage would be so understood by a person of experience in the field of the invention." Multiform Desiccants Inc. v. Medzam Ltd., 133 F.3d 1473, 1477, 45 USPQ2d 1429, 1432 (Fed. Cir. 1998). If an applicant does not define a term in the specification, that term will be given its "common meaning." Paulsen, at 30 F. 3d 1480, 31 USPQ2d at 1674.

If the applicant asserts that a term has a meaning that conflicts with the term's art-accepted meaning, Office personnel should encourage the applicant to amend the claim to better reflect what applicant intends to claim as the invention. If the application becomes a patent, it becomes prior art against subsequent applications. Therefore, it is important for later search purposes to have the patentee employ commonly accepted terminology, particularly for searching text-searchable databases.

Office personnel must always remember to use the perspective of one of ordinary skill in the art. Claims and disclosures are not to be evaluated in a vacuum. If elements of an invention are well known in the art, the applicant does not have to provide a disclosure that describes those elements. In such a case the elements will be construed as encompassing any and every art-recognized hardware or combination of hardware and software technique for implementing the defined requisite functionalities.

Office personnel are to give claims their broadest reasonable interpretation in light of the supporting disclosure. In re Morris, 127 F.3d 1048, 1054-55, 44 USPQ2d 1023, 1027-28 (Fed. Cir. 1997). Limitations appearing in the specification but not recited in the claim are not read into the claim. In re Prater, 415 F.2d 1393, 1404-05, 162 USPQ 541, 550-551 (CCPA 1969). See *also In re Zletz, 893 F.2d 319, 321-22, 13 USPQ2d 1320, 1322 (Fed. Cir. 1989) ("During patent examination the pending claims must be interpreted as broadly as their terms reasonably allow. . . . The reason is simply that during patent prosecution when claims can be amended, ambiguities should be recognized, scope and breadth of language explored, and clarification imposed. . . . An essential purpose of patent examination is to fashion claims that are precise, clear, correct, and unambiguous. Only in this way can uncertainties of claim scope be removed, as much as possible, during the administrative process.").

Where means plus function language is used to define the characteristics of a machine or manufacture invention, claim limitations must be interpreted to read on only the structures or materials disclosed in the specification and "equivalents thereof." (Two en banc decisions of the Federal Circuit have made clear that the Office is to interpret means plus function language according to 35 U.S.C. 112, sixth paragraph. In the first, In re Donaldson, 16 F.3d 1189, 1193, 29 USPQ2d 1845, 1848 (Fed. Cir. 1994), the court held:

The plain and unambiguous meaning of paragraph six is that one construing means-plus-function language in a claim must look to the specification and interpret that language in light of the corresponding structure, material, or acts described therein, and equivalents thereof, to the extent that the specification provides such disclosure. Paragraph six does not state or even suggest that the PTO is exempt from this mandate, and there is no legislative history indicating that Congress intended that the PTO should be. Thus, this court must accept the plain and precise language of paragraph six.

Consistent with Donaldson, in the second decision, In re Alappat, 33 F.3d *1526, 1540, 31 USPQ2d *1545, 1554 (Fed. Cir. 1994) (in banc), the Federal Circuit held:

Given Alappat's disclosure, it was error for the Board majority to interpret each of the means clauses in claim 15 so broadly as to "read on any and every means for performing the function" recited, as it said it was doing, and then to conclude that claim 15 is nothing more than a process claim wherein each means clause represents a step in that process. Contrary to suggestions by the Commissioner, this court's precedents do not support the Board's view that the particular apparatus claims at issue in this case may be viewed as nothing more than process claims.

Disclosure may be express, implicit or inherent. Thus, at the outset, Office personnel must attempt to correlate claimed means to elements set forth in the written description. The written description includes the original specification and the drawings. Office personnel are to give the claimed means plus function limitations their broadest reasonable interpretation consistent with all corresponding structures or materials described in the specification and their equivalents. Further guidance in interpreting the scope of equivalents is provided in MPEP § 2181 through § 2186.

While it is appropriate to use the specification to determine what applicant intends a term to mean, a positive limitation from the specification cannot be read into a claim that does not impose that limitation. A broad interpretation of a claim by Office personnel will reduce the possibility that the claim, when issued, will be interpreted more broadly than is justified or intended. An applicant can always amend a claim during prosecution to better reflect the intended scope of the claim.

Finally, when evaluating the scope of a claim, every limitation in the claim must be considered. Office personnel may not dissect a claimed invention into discrete elements and then evaluate the elements in isolation. Instead, the claim as a whole must be considered. See, e.g., Diamond v. Diehr, 450 U.S. at 188-89, 209 USPQ at 9 ("In determining the eligibility of respondents' claimed process for patent protection under 101, their claims must be considered as a whole. It is inappropriate to dissect the claims into old and new elements and then to ignore the presence of the old elements in the analysis. This is particularly true in a process claim because a new combination of steps in a process may be patentable even though all the constituents of the combination were well known and in common use before the combination was made.").

III. CONDUCT A THOROUGH SEARCH OF THE PRIOR ART

Prior to classifying the claimed invention under 35 U.S.C. 101, Office personnel are expected to conduct a thorough search of the prior art. Generally, a thorough search involves reviewing both U.S. and foreign patents and nonpatent literature. In many cases, the result of such a search will contribute to Office personnel's understanding of the invention. Both claimed and unclaimed aspects of the invention described in the specification should be searched if there is a reasonable expectation that the unclaimed aspects may be later claimed. A search must take into account any structure or material described in the specification and its equivalents which correspond to the claimed means plus function limitation, in accordance with 35 U.S.C. 112, sixth paragraph and MPEP § 2181 through § 2186.

IV. DETERMINE WHETHER THE CLAIMED INVENTION COMPLIES WITH 35 U.S.C. 101

A. Consider the Breadth of 35 U.S.C. 101 Under Controlling Law

As the Supreme Court has held, Congress chose the expansive language of 35 U.S.C. 101 so as to include "anything under the sun that is made by man." Diamond v. Chakrabarty, 447 U.S. 303, 308-09, 206 USPQ 193, 197 (1980). Accordingly, section 101 of title 35, United States Code, provides:

Whoever invents or discovers any new and useful process, machine, manufacture, or composition of matter, or any new and useful improvement thereof, may obtain a patent therefor, subject to the conditions and requirements of this title.

In Diamond, 477 U.S. at 308-309, 206 USPQ at 197, the court stated:

In choosing such expansive terms as "manufacture" and "composition of matter," modified by the comprehensive "any," Congress plainly contemplated that the patent laws would be given wide scope. The relevant legislative history also supports a broad construction. The Patent Act of 1793, authored by Thomas Jefferson, defined statutory subject matter as "any new and useful art, machine, manufacture, or composition of matter, or any new or useful improvement [thereof]." Act of Feb. 21, 1793, ch. 11, § 1, 1 Stat. 318. The Act embodied Jefferson's philosophy that "ingenuity should receive a liberal encouragement." V Writings of Thomas Jefferson, at 75-76. See Graham v. John Deere Co., 383 U.S. 1, 7-10 (148 USPQ 459, 462-464) (1966). Subsequent patent statutes in 1836, 1870, and 1874 employed this same broad language. In 1952, when the patent laws were recodified, Congress replaced the word "art" with "process," but otherwise left Jefferson's language intact. The Committee Reports accompanying the 1952 Act inform us that Congress intended statutory subject matter to "include anything under the sun that is made by man." S. Rep. No. 1979, 82d Cong., 2d Sess., 5 (1952); H.R. Rep. No. 1923, 82d Cong., 2d Sess., 6 (1952). [Footnote omitted]

This perspective has been embraced by the Federal Circuit:

The plain and unambiguous meaning of section 101 is that any new and useful process, machine, manufacture, or composition of matter, or any new and useful improvement thereof, may be patented if it meets the requirements for patentability set forth in Title 35, such as those found in sections 102, 103, and 112. The use of the expansive term "any" in section 101 represents Congress's intent not to place any restrictions on the subject matter for which a patent may be obtained beyond those specifically recited in section 101 and the other parts of Title 35. . . . Thus, it is improper to read into section 101 limitations as to the subject matter that may be patented where the legislative history does not indicate that Congress clearly intended such limitations.

Alappat, 33 F.3d at 1542, 31 USPQ2d at 1556.

As cast, 35 U.S.C. 101 defines four categories of inventions that Congress deemed to be the appropriate subject matter of a patent; namely, processes, machines, manufactures and compositions of matter. The latter three categories define "things" while the first category defines "actions" (i.e., inventions that consist of a series of steps or acts to be performed). See 35 U.S.C. 100(b) ("The term 'process' means process, art, or method, and includes a new use of a known process, machine, manufacture, composition of matter, or material.").

Federal courts have held that 35 U.S.C. 101 does have certain limits. First, the phrase "anything under the sun that is made by man" is limited by the text of 35 U.S.C. 101, meaning that one may only patent something that is a machine, manufacture, composition of matter or a process. See, e.g., Alappat, 33 F.3d at 1542, 31 USPQ2d at 1556; ** Warmerdam, 33 F.3d *at 1358, 31 USPQ2d *at 1757 (Fed. Cir. 1994). Second, 35 U.S.C. 101 requires that the subject matter sought to be patented be a "useful" invention. Accordingly, a complete definition of the scope of 35 U.S.C. 101, reflecting Congressional intent, is that any new and useful process, machine, manufacture or composition of matter under the sun that is made by man is the proper subject matter of a patent.**

The subject matter courts have found to be outside the four statutory categories of invention is limited to abstract ideas, laws of nature and natural phenomena. While this is easily stated, determining whether an applicant is seeking to patent an abstract idea, a law of nature or a natural phenomenon has proven to be challenging. These three exclusions recognize that subject matter that is not a practical application or use of an idea, a law of nature or a natural phenomenon is not patentable. See, e.g., Rubber-Tip Pencil Co. v. Howard, 87 U.S. (20 Wall.) 498, 507 (1874) ("idea of itself is not patentable, but a new device by which it may be made practically useful is"); Mackay Radio & Telegraph Co. v. Radio Corp. of America, 306 U.S. 86, 94, 40 USPQ 199, 202 (1939) ("While a scientific truth, or the mathematical expression of it, is not patentable invention, a novel and useful structure created with the aid of knowledge of scientific truth may be."); Warmerdam, 33 F.3d at 1360, 31 USPQ2d at 1759 ("steps of 'locating' a medial axis, and 'creating' a bubble hierarchy . . . describe nothing more than the manipulation of basic mathematical constructs, the paradigmatic 'abstract idea'").

Courts have expressed a concern over "preemption" of ideas, laws of nature or natural phenomena. The concern over preemption was expressed as early as 1852. See Le Roy v. Tatham, 55 U.S. 156, 175 (1852) ("A principle, in the abstract, is a fundamental truth; an original cause; a motive; these cannot be patented, as no one can claim in either of them an exclusive right."); Funk Brothers Seed Co. v. Kalo Inoculant Co., 333 U.S. 127, 132, 76 USPQ 280, 282 (1948) (combination of six species of bacteria held to be nonstatutory subject matter). The concern over preemption serves to bolster and justify the prohibition against the patenting of such subject matter. In fact, such concerns are only relevant to claiming a scientific truth or principle. Thus, a claim to an "abstract idea" is nonstatutory because it does not represent a practical application of the idea, not because it would preempt the idea.

B. Classify the Claimed Invention as to Its Proper Statutory Category

To properly determine whether a claimed invention complies with the statutory invention requirements of 35 U.S.C. 101, Office personnel should classify each claim into one or more statutory or nonstatutory categories. If the claim falls into a nonstatutory category, that should not preclude complete examination of the application for satisfaction of all other conditions of patentability. This classification is only an initial finding at this point in the examination process that will be again assessed after the examination for compliance with 35 U.S.C. 102, 103, and 112 is completed and before issuance of any Office action on the merits.

If the invention as set forth in the written description is statutory, but the claims define subject matter that is not, the deficiency can be corrected by an appropriate amendment of the claims. In such a case, Office personnel should reject the claims drawn to nonstatutory subject matter under 35 U.S.C. 101, but identify the features of the invention that would render the claimed subject matter statutory if recited in the claim.

1. Nonstatutory Subject Matter

Claims to computer-related inventions that are clearly nonstatutory fall into the same general categories as nonstatutory claims in other arts, namely natural phenomena such as magnetism, and abstract ideas or laws of nature which constitute "descriptive material." Abstract ideas, Warmerdam, 33 F.3d at 1360, 31 USPQ2d at 1759, or the mere manipulation of abstract ideas, Schrader, 22 F.3d at 292-93, 30 USPQ2d at 1457-58, are not patentable. Descriptive material can be characterized as either "functional descriptive material" or "nonfunctional descriptive material." In this context, "functional descriptive material" consists of data structures and computer programs which impart functionality when **employed as a computer component Warmerdam, 33 F.3d at 1360, 31 USPQ2d at 1759. When functional descriptive material is recorded on some computer-readable medium it becomes structurally and functionally interrelated to the medium and will be statutory in most cases since use of technology permits the function of the descriptive material to be realizedstored on a computer readable medium that increases computer efficiency held statutory) and Warmerdam, 33 F.3d at 1360-61, 31 USPQ2d at 1759 (claim to computer having specific memory held statutory product-by-process claim) with Warmerdam, 33 F.3d at 1361, 31 USPQ2d at 1760 (claim to a data structure per se held nonstatutory). When nonfunctional descriptive material is recorded on some computer-readable medium, it is not **statutory since no requisite functionality is present to satisfy the practical application requirementis not a computer component and it does not become statutory by merely recording it on a compact disk. Protection for this type of work is provided under the copyright law.

Claims to processes that do nothing more than solve mathematical problems or manipulate abstract ideas or concepts are more complex to analyze and are addressed below. * *

If the "acts" of a claimed process manipulate only numbers, abstract concepts or ideas, or signals representing any of the foregoing, the acts are not being applied to appropriate subject matter. Schrader, 22 F.3d at 294-95, 30 USPQ2d at 1458-59. Thus, a process consisting solely of mathematical operations, i.e., converting one set of numbers into another set of numbers, does not manipulate appropriate subject matter and thus cannot constitute a statutory process.

In practical terms, claims define nonstatutory processes if they:

— consist solely of mathematical operations without some claimed practical application (i.e., executing a "mathematical algorithm"); or

— simply manipulate abstract ideas, e.g., a bid (Schrader, 22 F.3d at 293-94, 30 USPQ2d at 1458-59) or a bubble hierarchy (Warmerdam, 33 F.3d at 1360, 31 USPQ2d at 1759), without some claimed practical application.

Cf. Alappat, 33 F.3d at 1543 n.19, 31 USPQ2d at 1556 n.19 in which the Federal Circuit recognized the confusion:

The Supreme Court has not been clear . . . as to whether such subject matter is excluded from the scope of 101 because it represents laws of nature, natural phenomena, or abstract ideas. See Diehr, 450 U.S. at 186 (viewed mathematical algorithm as a law of nature); Gottschalk v. Benson, 409 U.S. 63, 71-72 (1972) (treated mathematical algorithm as an "idea"). The Supreme Court also has not been clear as to exactly what kind of mathematical subject matter may not be patented. The Supreme Court has used, among others, the terms "mathematical algorithm," "mathematical formula," and "mathematical equation" to describe types of mathematical subject matter not entitled to patent protection standing alone. The Supreme Court has not set forth, however, any consistent or clear explanation of what it intended by such terms or how these terms are related, if at all.

Certain mathematical algorithms have been held to be nonstatutory because they represent a mathematical definition of a law of nature or a natural phenomenon. For example, a mathematical algorithm representing the formula E = mc2 is a "law of nature" — it defines a "fundamental scientific truth" (i.e., the relationship between energy and mass).

To comprehend how the law of nature relates to any object, one invariably has to perform certain steps (e.g., multiplying a number representing the mass of an object by the square of a number representing the speed of light). In such a case, a claimed process which consists solely of the steps that one must follow to solve the mathematical representation of E = mc2 is indistinguishable from the law of nature and would "preempt" the law of nature. A patent cannot be granted on such a process.

(a) Functional Descriptive Material: "Data Structures" Representing Descriptive Material Per Se or Computer Programs Representing Computer Listings Per Se

Data structures not claimed as embodied in computer-readable media are descriptive material per se and are not statutory because they are * * not capable of causing functional change in the computer "things." They are neither computer components nor statutory processes, as they are not "acts" being performed. Such claimed computer programs do not define any structural and functional interrelationships between the computer program and other claimed * *elements of a computer which permit the computer program's functionality to be realized. In contrast, a claimed computer-readable medium encoded with a computer program is a computer element which defines structural and functional interrelationships between the computer program and the *rest of the computer which permit the computer program's functionality to be realized, and is thus statutory. Accordingly, it is important to distinguish claims that define descriptive material per se from claims that define statutory inventions.

Computer programs are often recited as part of a claim. Office personnel should determine whether the computer program is being claimed as part of an otherwise statutory manufacture or machine. In such a case, the claim remains statutory irrespective of the fact that a computer program is included in the claim. The same result occurs when a computer program is used in a computerized process where the computer executes the instructions set forth in the computer program. Only when the claimed invention taken as a whole is directed to a mere program listing, i.e., to only its description or expression, is it descriptive material per se and hence nonstatutory.

Since a computer program is merely a set of instructions capable of being executed by a computer, the computer program itself is not a process and Office personnel should treat a claim for a computer program, without the computer-readable medium needed to realize the computer program's functionality, as nonstatutory functional descriptive material. When a computer program is claimed in a process where the computer is executing the computer program's instructions, Office personnel should treat the claim as a process claim. See Sections IV.B.2(b)-(e). When a computer program is recited in conjunction with a physical structure, such as a computer memory, Office personnel should treat the claim as a product claim. See Section IV.B.2(a).

(b) Nonfunctional Descriptive Material

Descriptive material that cannot exhibit any functional interrelationship with the way in which computing processes are performed does not constitute a statutory process, machine, manufacture or composition of matter and should be rejected under 35 U.S.C. 101. Thus, Office personnel should consider the claimed invention as a whole to determine whether the necessary functional interrelationship is provided.

Where certain types of descriptive material, such as music, literature, art, photographs and mere arrangements or compilations of facts or data, are merely stored so as to be read or outputted by a computer without creating any functional interrelationship, either as part of the stored data or as part of the computing processes performed by the computer, then such descriptive material alone does not impart functionality either to the data as so structured, or to the computer. Such "descriptive material" is not a process, machine, manufacture or composition of matter. (Data consists of facts, which become information when they are seen in context and convey meaning to people. Computers process data without any understanding of what that data represents. Computer Dictionary 210 (Microsoft Press, 2d ed. 1994).)

The policy that precludes the patenting of nonfunctional descriptive material would be easily frustrated if the same descriptive material could be patented when claimed as an article of manufacture. For example, music is commonly sold to consumers in the format of a compact disc. In such cases, the known compact disc acts as nothing more than a carrier for nonfunctional descriptive material. The purely nonfunctional descriptive material cannot alone provide the practical application for the manufacture.

Office personnel should be prudent in applying the foregoing guidance. Nonfunctional descriptive material may be claimed in combination with other functional descriptive multi-media material on a computer-readable medium to provide the necessary functional and structural interrelationship to satisfy the requirements of 35 U.S.C. 101. The presence of the claimed nonfunctional descriptive material is not necessarily determinative of nonstatutory subject matter. For example, a computer that recognizes a particular grouping of musical notes read from memory and upon recognizing that particular sequence, causes another defined series of notes to be played, defines a functional interrelationship among that data and the computing processes performed when utilizing that data, and as such is statutory because it implements a statutory process.

(c) Natural Phenomena Such as Electricity and Magnetism

Claims that recite nothing but the physical characteristics of a form of energy, such as a frequency, voltage, or the strength of a magnetic field, define energy or magnetism, per se, and as such are nonstatutory natural phenomena. O'Reilly v. Morse, 56 U.S. (15 How.) at 112-114. However, a signal claim directed to a practical application of **electromagnetic energy** is statutory. Id. at 114-119.

2. Statutory Subject Matter

For the purposes of a 35 U.S.C. 101 analysis, it is of little relevance whether the claim is directed to a machine or a process. The legal principles are the same. AT&T Corp. v. Excel Communications, Inc., 172 F.3d 1352, 1357, 50 USPQ2d 1447, 1451 (Fed. Cir. 1999).

(a) Statutory Product Claims

Products may be either machines, manufactures of compositions of matter.

A machine is "a concrete thing, consisting of parts or of certain devices and combinations of devices." Burr v. Duryee, 68 U.S. (1 Wall.) 531, 570 (1863).

A manufacture is "the production of articles for use from raw or prepared materials by giving to these materials new forms, qualities, properties or combinations, whether by hand labor or by machinery." Diamond v. Chakrabarty, 447 U.S. at 308, 206 USPQ at 196-97 (quoting American Fruit Growers, Inc. v. Brogdex Co., 283 U.S. 1, 11 (1931).

A composition of matter is "a composition[] of two or more substances [or] . . . a[] composite article[], whether [it] be the result of chemical union, or of mechanical mixture, whether . . . [it]be [a] gas[], fluid[], powder[], or solid[]." Diamond v. Chakrabarty, 447 U.S. at 308, 206 USPQ at 197 (quoting Shell Development Co. v. Watson, 149 F. Supp. 279, 280, 113 USPQ 265, 266 (D.D.C. 1957), aff'd per curiam, 252 F.2d 861, 116 USPQ 428 (D.C. Cir. 1958).

If a claim defines a useful machine or manufacture by identifying the physical structure of the machine or manufacture in terms of its hardware or hardware and software combination, it defines a statutory product. See, e.g., Lowry, 32 F.3d at 1583, 32 USPQ2d at 1034-35; Warmerdam, 33 F.3d at 1361-62, 31 USPQ2d at 1760.

**

Office personnel must treat each claim as a whole. The mere fact that a hardware element is recited in a claim does not necessarily limit the claim to a specific machine or manufacture. Cf. In re Iwahashi, 888 F.2d 1370, 1374-75, 12 USPQ2d 1908, 1911-12 (Fed. Cir. 1989), cited with approval in Alappat, 33 F.3d at 1544 n.24, 31 USPQ2d at 1558 n.24. **

A claim limited to a * machine or manufacture, which has a practical application in the technological arts, is statutory. In most cases, a claim to a specific machine or manufacture will have a practical application in the technological arts. See Alappat, 33 F.3d at 1544, 31 USPQ2d at 1557 ("the claimed invention as a whole is directed to a combination of interrelated elements which combine to form a machine for converting discrete waveform data samples into anti-aliased pixel illumination intensity data to be displayed on a display means. This is not a disembodied mathematical concept which may be characterized as an 'abstract idea,' but rather a specific machine to produce a useful, concrete, and tangible result."); and State Street, 149 F.3d at 1373, 47 USPQ2d at 1601 ("the transformation of data, representing discrete dollar amounts, by a machine through a series of mathematical calculations into a final share price, constitutes a practical application of a mathematical algorithm, formula, or calculation, because it produces `a useful, concrete and tangible result' — a final share price momentarily fixed for recording and reporting purposes and even accepted and relied upon by regulatory authorities and in subsequent trades."). Also see AT&T, 172 F.3d at 1358, 50 USPQ2d at 1452 (Claims drawn to a long-distance telephone billing process containing mathematical algorithms were held patentable subject matter because the process used the algorithm to produce a useful, concrete, tangible result without preempting other uses of the mathematical principle.).

**

(b) Statutory Process Claims

A claim that requires one or more acts to be performed defines a process. However, not all processes are statutory under 35 U.S.C. 101. Schrader, 22 F.3d at 296, 30 USPQ2d at 1460. To be statutory, a claimed computer-related process must either: (A) result in a physical transformation outside the computer for which a practical application in the technological arts is either disclosed in the specification or would have been known to a skilled artisan (discussed in i) below), or (B) be limited ** to a practical application within the technological arts (discussed in ii) below). See Diamond v. Diehr, 450 U.S. at 183-84, 209 USPQ at 6 (quoting

Cochrane v. Deener, 94 U.S. 780, 787-88 (1877)) ("A [statutory] process is a mode of treatment of certain materials to produce a given result. It is an act, or a series of acts, performed upon the subject-matter to be transformed and reduced to a different state or thing. . . . The process requires that certain things should be done with certain substances, and in a certain order; but the tools to be used in doing this may be of secondary consequence."). See also Alappat, 33 F.3d at 1543, 31 USPQ2d at 1556-57 (quoting Diamond v. Diehr, 450 U.S. at 192, 209 USPQ at 10). See also id. at 33 F.3d 1569, 31 USPQ2d at 1578-79 (Newman, J., concurring) ("unpatentability of the principle does not defeat patentability of its practical applications") (citing O'Reilly v. Morse, 56 U.S. (15 How.) at 114-19). ** If a physical transformation occurs outside the computer** a disclosure that permits a skilled artisan to practice the claimed invention, i.e., to put it to a practical use, is sufficient. On the other hand, it is necessary to claim the practical application if there is no physical transformation or if the process merely manipulates concepts or converts one set of numbers into another.

A claimed process is clearly statutory if it results in a physical transformation outside the computer, i.e., falls into one or both of the following specific categories ("safe harbors").

i) Safe Harbors

— Independent Physical Acts (Post-Computer Process Activity)

A process is statutory if it requires physical acts to be performed outside the computer independent of and following the steps to be performed by a programmed computer, where those acts involve the manipulation of tangible physical objects and result in the object having a different physical attribute or structure. Diamond v. Diehr, 450 U.S. at 187, 209 USPQ at 8. Thus, if a process claim includes one or more post-computer process steps that result in a physical transformation outside the computer (beyond merely conveying the direct result of the computer operation, ** the claim is clearly statutory.

Examples of this type of statutory process include the following:

— A method of curing rubber in a mold which relies upon updating process parameters, using a computer processor to determine a time period for curing the rubber, using the computer processor to determine when the time period has been reached in the curing process and then opening the mold at that stage.

— A method of controlling a mechanical robot which relies upon storing data in a computer that represents various types of mechanical movements of the robot, using a computer processor to calculate positioning of the robot in relation to given tasks to be performed by the robot, and controlling the robot's movement and position based on the calculated position.

Examples of claimed processes that do not achieve a practical application include:

— step of "updating alarm limits" found to constitute changing the number value of a variable to represent the result of the calculation (Parker v. Flook, 437 U.S. 584, 585, 198 USPQ 193, 195 (1978));

— final step of "equating" the process outputs to the values of the last set of process inputs found to constitute storing the result of calculations (Gelnovatch, 595 F.2d at 41 n.7, 201 USPQ at 145 n.7); and

— step of "transmitting electrical signals representing" the result of calculations (In re De Castelet, 562 F.2d 1236, 1244, 195 USPQ 439, 446 (CCPA 1977) ("That the computer is instructed to transmit electrical signals, representing the results of its calculations, does not constitute the type of `post solution activity' found in Flook, [437 U.S. 584, 198 USPQ 193 (1978)], and does not transform the claim into one for a process merely using an algorithm. The final transmitting step constitutes nothing more than reading out the result of the calculations.")).

— Manipulation of Data Representing Physical Objects or Activities (Pre-Computer Process Activity)

Another statutory process is one that requires the measurements of physical objects or activities to be transformed outside of the computer into computer data (In re Gelnovatch, 595 F.2d 32,

41 n.7, 201 USPQ 136, 145 n.7 (CCPA 1979) (data-gathering step did not measure physical phenomenon); Arrhythmia, 958 F.2d at 1056, 22 USPQ2d at 1036Examples of claimed processes that independently limit the claimed invention to safe harbor include:

— a method of conducting seismic exploration which requires generating and manipulating signals from seismic energy waves before "summing" the values represented by the signals (Taner, 681 F.2d at 788, 214 USPQ at 679); and

— a method of displaying X-ray attenuation data as a signed gray scale signal in a "field" using a particular algorithm, where the antecedent steps require generating the data using a particular machine (e.g., a computer tomography scanner). Abele, 684 F.2d at 908, 214 USPQ at 687 ("The specification indicates that such attenuation data is available only when an X-ray beam is produced by a CAT scanner, passed through an object, and detected upon its exit. Only after these steps have been completed is the algorithm performed, and the resultant modified data displayed in the required format.").

Examples of claimed processes that do not limit the claimed invention to pre-computing safe harbor include:

— "perturbing" the values of a set of process inputs, where the subject matter "perturbed" was a number and the act of "perturbing" consists of substituting the numerical values of variables (Gelnovatch, 595 F.2d at 41 n.7, 201 USPQ at 145 n.7 ("Appellants' claimed step of perturbing the values of a set of process inputs (step 3), in addition to being a mathematical operation, appears to be a data-gathering step of the type we have held insufficient to change a nonstatutory method of calculation into a statutory process?. In this instance, the perturbed process inputs are not even measured values of physical phenomena, but are instead derived by numerically changing the values in the previous set of process inputs.")); and

— selecting a set of arbitrary measurement point values (Sarkar, 588 F.2d at 1331, 200 USPQ at 135).

If a claim does not clearly fall into one or both of the safe harbors, the claim may still be statutory if it is limited ** to a practical application in the technological arts.

ii) Computer-Related Processes Limited to a Practical Application in the Technological Arts

There is always some form of physical transformation within a computer because a computer acts on signals and transforms them during its operation and changes the state of its components during the execution of a process. Even though such a physical transformation occurs within a computer, such activity is not determinative of whether the process is statutory because such transformation alone does not distinguish a statutory computer process from a non-statutory computer process. What is determinative is not how the computer performs the process, but what the computer does to achieve a practical application. See Arrhythmia, 958 F.2d at 1057, 22 USPQ2d at 1036.

A process that merely manipulates an abstract idea or performs a purely mathematical algorithm is nonstatutory despite the fact that it might inherently have some usefulness. In Sarkar, 588 F.2d at 1335, 200 USPQ at 139, the court explained why this approach must be followed:

No mathematical equation can be used, as a practical matter, without establishing and substituting values for the variables expressed therein. Substitution of values dictated by the formula has thus been viewed as a form of mathematical step. If the steps of gathering and substituting values were alone sufficient, every mathematical equation, formula, or algorithm having any practical use would be per se subject to patenting as a "process" under 101. Consideration of whether the substitution of specific values is enough to convert the disembodied ideas present in the formula into an embodiment of those ideas, or into an application of the formula, is foreclosed by the current state of the law.

For such subject matter to be statutory, the claimed process must be limited to a practical application of the abstract idea or mathematical algorithm in the technological arts. See Alappat, 33 F.3d at 1543, 31 USPQ2d at 1556-57 (quoting Diamond v. Diehr, 450 U.S. at 192, 209 USPQ at 10). See also Alappat at 1569, 31 USPQ2d at 1578-79 (Newman, J., concurring) ("unpatentability of the principle does n. .feat patentability of its practical applications") (citing O'Rei , v. Morse, 56 U.S. (15 How.) at 114-19). A claim is limited to a practical application when the method, as claimed, produces a concrete, tangible and useful result; i.e., the method recites a step or act of producing something that is concrete, tangible and useful. See AT&T, 172 F.3d at 1358, 50 USPQ2d at 1452. Likewise, a machine claim is statutory when the machine, as claimed, produces a concrete, tangible and useful result (as in State Street, 149 F.3d at 1373, 47 USPQ2d at 1601) and/or when a specific machine is being claimed (as in Alappat, 33 F.3d at 1544, 31 USPQ2d at 1557 (in banc). For example, a computer process that simply calculates a mathematical algorithm that models noise is nonstatutory. However, a claimed process for digitally filtering noise employing the mathematical algorithm is statutory.

Examples of this type of claimed statutory process include the following:

— A computerized method of optimally controlling transfer, storage and retrieval of data between cache and hard disk storage devices such that the most frequently used data is readily available.

— A method of controlling parallel processors to accomplish multi-tasking of several computing tasks to maximize computing efficiency. See, e.g., In re Bernhart, 417 F.2d 1395, 1400, 163 USPQ 611,616 (CCPA 1969).

— A method of making a word processor by storing an executable word processing application program in a general purpose digital computer's memory, and executing the stored program to impart word processing functionality to the general purpose digital computer by changing the state of the computer's arithmetic logic unit when program instructions of the word processing program are executed.

— A digital filtering process for removing noise from a digital signal comprising the steps of calculating a mathematical algorithm to produce a correction signal and subtracting the correction signal from the digital signal to remove the noise.

V. EVALUATE APPLICATION FOR COMPLIANCE WITH 35 U.S.C. 112

Office personnel should begin their evaluation of an application's compliance with 35 U.S.C. 112 by considering the requirements of 35 U.S.C. 112, second paragraph. The second paragraph contains two separate and distinct requirements: (A) that the claim(s) set forth the subject matter applicants regard as the invention, and (B) that the claim(s) particularly point out and distinctly claim the invention. An application will be deficient under 35 U.S.C. 112, second paragraph when (A) evidence including admissions, other than in the application as filed, shows applicant has stated that he or she regards the invention to be different from what is claimed, or when (B) the scope of the claims is unclear.

After evaluation of the application for compliance with 35 U.S.C. 112, second paragraph, Office personnel should then evaluate the application for compliance with the requirements of 35 U.S.C. 112, first paragraph. The first paragraph contains three separate and distinct requirements:

(A) adequate written description,

(B) enablement, and

(C) best mode.

An application will be deficient under 35 U.S.C. 112, first paragraph when the written description is not adequate to identify what the applicant has invented, or when the disclosure does not enable one skilled in the art to make and use the invention as claimed without undue experimentation. Deficiencies related to disclosure of the best mode for carrying out the claimed invention are not usually encountered during examination of an application because evidence to support such a deficiency is seldom in the record. Fonar Corp. v. General Electric Co., 107 F.3d 1543, 1548-49, 41 USPQ2d 1801, 1804 (Fed. Cir. 1997)

If deficiencies are discovered with respect to 35 U.S.C. 112, Office personnel must be careful to apply the appropriate paragraph of 35 U.S.C. 112.

A. Determine Whether the Claimed Invention Complies with 35 U.S.C. 112, Second Paragraph Requirements

1. Claims Setting Forth the Subject Matter Applicant Regards as Invention

Applicant's specification must conclude with claim(s) that set forth the subject matter which the applicant regards as the invention. The invention set forth in the claims is presumed to be that which applicant regards as the invention, unless applicant considers the invention to be something different from what has been claimed as shown by evidence, including admissions, outside the application as filed. An applicant may change what he or she regards as the invention during the prosecution of the application.

2. Claims Particularly Pointing Out and Distinctly Claiming the Invention

Office personnel shall determine whether the claims set out and circumscribe the invention with a reasonable degree of precision and particularity. In this regard, the definiteness of the language must be analyzed, not in a vacuum, but always in light of the teachings of the disclosure as it would be interpreted by one of ordinary skill in the art. Applicant's claims, interpreted in light of the disclosure, must reasonably apprise a person of ordinary skill in the art of the invention. However, the applicant need not explicitly recite in the claims every feature of the invention. For example, if an applicant indicates that the invention is a particular computer, the claims do not have to recite every element or feature of the computer. In fact, it is preferable for claims to be drafted in a form that emphasizes what the applicant has invented (i.e., what is new rather than old). In re Dossel, 115 F.3d 942, 946, 42 USPQ2d 1881, 1884 (Fed. Cir. 1997).

A means plus function limitation is distinctly claimed if the description makes it clear that the means corresponds to well-defined structure of a computer or computer component implemented in either hardware or software and its associated hardware platform. Atmel Corp. v. Information Storage Devices Inc., 198 F.3d 1374, 1380, 53 USPQ2d 1225, 1229 (Fed. Cir. 1999); B. Braun Medical, Inc. v. Abbott Labs., 124 F.3d 1419,

1424, 43 USPQ2d 1896, 1899 (Fed. Cir. 1997). Such means may be defined as:

— a programmed computer with a particular functionality implemented in hardware or hardware and software;

— a logic circuit or other component of a programmed computer that performs a series of specifically identified operations dictated by a computer program; or

— a computer memory encoded with executable instructions representing a computer program that can cause a computer to function in a particular fashion.

The scope of a "means" limitation is defined as the corresponding structure or material (e.g., a specific logic circuit) set forth in the written description and equivalents. See MPEP § 2181 through § 2186. Thus, a claim using means plus function limitations without corresponding disclosure of specific structures or materials that are not well-known fails to particularly point out and distinctly claim the invention. Dossel, 115 F.3d at 946-47, 42 USPQ2d at 1884-85. For example, if the applicant discloses only the functions to be performed and provides no express, implied or inherent disclosure of hardware or a combination of hardware and software that performs the functions, the application has not disclosed any "structure" which corresponds to the claimed means. Office personnel should reject such claims under 35 U.S.C. 112, second paragraph. B. Braun Medical, 124 F.3d at 1424, 43 USPQ2d at 1899. The rejection shifts the burden to the applicant to describe at least one specific structure or material that corresponds to the claimed means in question, and to identify the precise location or locations in the specification where a description of at least one embodiment of that claimed means can be found. In contrast, if the corresponding structure is disclosed to be a memory or logic circuit that has been configured in some manner to perform that function (e.g., using a defined computer program), the application has disclosed "structure" which corresponds to the claimed means.

When a claim or part of a claim is defined in computer program code, whether in source or object code format, a person of skill in the art must be able to ascertain the metes and bounds of the claimed invention. In certain circumstances, as where self-documenting programming code is employed, use of programming language in a claim would be permissible because such program source code presents "sufficiently high-level language and descriptive identifiers" to make it universally understood to others in the art without the programmer having to insert any comments. See Computer Dictionary 353 (Microsoft Press, 2ed. 1994) for a definition of "self-documenting code." Applicants should be encouraged to functionally define the steps the computer will perform rather than simply reciting source or object code instructions.

B. Determine Whether the Claimed Invention Complies with 35 U.S.C. 112, First Paragraph Requirements

1. Adequate Written Description

The satisfaction of the enablement requirement does not satisfy the written description requirement. See In re Barker, 559 F.2d 588, 591, 194 USPQ 470, 472 (CCPA 1977)** (a specification may be sufficient to enable one skilled in the art to make and use the invention, but still fail to comply with the written description requirement). See also In re DiLeone, 436 F.2d 1404, 1405, 168 USPQ 592, 593 (CCPA 1971). For the written description requirement, an applicant's specification must reasonably convey to those skilled in the art that the applicant was in possession of the claimed invention as of the date of invention. Regents of the University of California v. Eli Lilly & Co., 119 F.3d 1559, 1568, 43 USPQ2d 1398, 1405 (Fed. Cir. 1997). The claimed invention subject matter need not be described literally, i.e., using the same terms, in order for the disclosure to satisfy the description requirement.

2. Enabling Disclosure

An applicant's specification must enable a person skilled in the art to make and use the claimed invention without undue experimentation. The fact that experimentation is complex, however, will not make it undue if a person of skill in the art typically engages in such complex experimentation. For a computer-related invention, the disclosure must enable a skilled artisan to configure the computer to possess the requisite functionality, and, where applicable, interrelate the computer with other elements to yield the claimed invention, without the exercise of undue experimentation. The specification should disclose how to configure a computer to possess the requisite functionality or how to integrate the programmed computer with other elements of the invention, unless a skilled artisan would know how to do so without such disclosure. See, e.g., Dossel, 115 F.3d at 946-47, 42 USPQ2d at 1884-85; Northern Telecom v. Datapoint Corp., 908 F.2d 931, 941-43, 15 USPQ2d 1321, 1328-30 (Fed. Cir.1990

2111   Claim Interpretation; Broadest Reasonable Interpretation [R-1]

CLAIMS MUST BE GIVEN THEIR BROADEST REASONABLE INTERPRETATION

During patent examination, the pending claims must be "given the broadest reasonable interpretation consistent with the specification." Applicant always has the opportunity to amend the claims during prosecution and broad interpretation by the examiner reduces the possibility that the claim, once issued, will be interpreted more broadly than is justified. In re Prater, 415 F.2d 1393, 1404-05, 162 USPQ 541, 550-51 (CCPA 1969) (Claim 9 was directed to a process of analyzing data generated by mass spectrographic analysis of a gas. The process comprised selecting the data to be analyzed by subjecting the data to a mathematical manipulation. The examiner made rejections under 35 U.S.C. 101 and 102. In the section 102 rejection, the examiner explained that the claim was anticipated by a mental process augmented by pencil and paper markings. The court agreed that the claim was not limited to using a machine to carry out the process since the claim did not explicitly set forth the machine. The court explained that "reading a claim in light of the specification, to thereby interpret limitations explicitly recited in the claim, is a quite different thing from `reading limitations of the specification into a claim,' to thereby narrow the scope of the claim by implicitly adding disclosed limitations which have no express basis in the claim." The court found that applicant was advocating the latter, e.g., the impermissible importation of subject matter from the specification into the claim.). See also In re Morris, 127 F.3d 1048, 1054-55, 44 USPQ2d 1023, 1027-28 (Fed. Cir. 1997) (The court held that the PTO is not required, in the course of prosecution, to interpret claims in applications in the same manner as a court would in interpreting claims in an infringement suit. Rather, the "PTO applies to verbiage of the proposed claims the broadest reasonable meaning of the words in their ordinary usage as they would be understood by one of ordinary skill in the art, taking into account whatever enlightenment by way of definitions or otherwise that may be afforded by the written description contained in applicant's specification.").

The broadest reasonable interpretation of the claims must also be consistent with the interpretation that those skilled in the art would reach. In re Cortright, 165 F.3d 1353, 1359, 49 USPQ2d 1464, 1468 (Fed. Cir. 1999)(The Board's construction of the claim limitation "restore hair growth" as requiring the hair to be returned to its original state was held to be an unreasonably broad interpretation of the limitation. The court held that, consistent with applicant's disclosure and the disclosure of three patents from analogous arts using the same phrase to require only some increase in hair growth, one of ordinary skill would construe "restore hair growth" to mean that the claimed method increases the amount of hair grown on the scalp, but does not necessarily produce a full head of hair.)

2111.01   Plain Meaning [R-1]

THE WORDS OF A CLAIM MUST BE GIVEN THEIR "PLAIN MEANING" UNLESS THEY ARE DEFINED IN THE SPECIFICATION

While the meaning of claims of issued patents are interpreted in light of the specification, prosecution history, prior art and other claims, this is not the mode of claim interpretation to be applied during examination. During examination, the claims must be interpreted as broadly as their terms reasonably allow. This means that the words of the claim must be given their plain meaning unless applicant has provided a clear definition in the specification. In re Zletz, 893 F.2d 319, 321, 13 USPQ2d 1320, 1322 (Fed. Cir. 1989)(discussed below). One must bear in mind that, especially in nonchemical cases, the words in a claim are generally not limited in their meaning by what is shown or disclosed in the specification. It is only when the specification provides definitions for terms appearing in the claims that the specification can be used in interpreting claim language. In re Vogel, 422 F.2d 438, 441, 164

USPQ 619, 622 (CCPA 1970). There is one exception and that is when an element is claimed using language falling under the scope of 35 U.S.C. 112, 6th paragraph (often broadly referred to as means or step plus function language). In that case, the specification must be consulted to determine the structure, material, or acts corresponding to the function recited in the claim. In re Donaldson, 16 F.3d 1189, 29 USPQ2d 1845 (Fed. Cir. 1994)(see MPEP § 2181- § 2186).

In In re Zletz, supra, the examiner and the Board had interpreted claims reading "normally solid polypropylene" and "normally solid polypropylene having a crystalline polypropylene content" as being limited to "normally solid linear high homopolymers of propylene which have a crystalline polypropylene content." The court ruled that limitations, not present in the claims, were improperly imported from the specification. See also In re Marosi, 710 F.2d 799,218 USPQ 289 (Fed. Cir. 1983) ("Claims are not to be read in a vacuum, and limitations therein are to be interpreted in light of the specification in giving them their 'broadest reasonable interpretation." 710 F.2d at 802, 218 USPQ at 292 (quoting In re Okuzawa, 537 F.2d 545, 548, 190 USPQ 464, 466 (CCPA 1976))(emphasis in original). The court looked to the specification to construe "essentially free of alkali metal" as including unavoidable levels of impurities but no more.). Compare In re Weiss, 989 F.2d 1202, 26 USPQ2d 1885 (Fed. Cir. 1993) (unpublished decision — cannot be cited as precedent) (The claim related to an athletic shoe with cleats that "break away at a preselected level of force" and thus prevent injury to the wearer. The examiner rejected the claims over prior art teaching athletic shoes with cleats not intended to break off and rationalized that the cleats would break away given a high enough force. The court reversed the rejection stating that when interpreting a claim term which is ambiguous, such as 'a preselected level of force,' we must look to the specification for the meaning ascribed to that term by the inventor." The specification had defined "preselected level of force..." as that level of force at which the breaking away will prevent injury to the wearer during athletic exertion. It should be noted that the limitation was part of a means plus function element.)

"PLAIN MEANING" REFERS TO THE MEANING GIVEN TO THE TERM BY THOSE OF ORDINARY SKILL IN THE ART

When not defined by applicant in the specification, the words of a claim must be given their plain meaning. In other words, they must be read as they would be interpreted by those of ordinary skill in the art. In re Sneed, 710 F.2d 1544, 218 USPQ 385 (Fed. Cir. 1983) (The applicants had argued in an amendment after final rejection that the term "flexible plastic pipe," as used in the claims, pertained only to pipes of 2-inch diameter and 3-inch diameter and not to a pipe of 1.5 inch diameter. This definition of "flexible" was also advanced in an affidavit. The prior art, however, described 1.5 inch pipe as flexible. The court held that the specification and the evidence (the prior art) failed to support the gloss appellants sought to put on the term "flexible." Note that applicant had not defined "flexible plastic pipe" in the specification.); In re Barr, 444 F.2d 588, 597, 170 USPQ 330, 339 (CCPA 1971) ("The specification in this case attempts no definition of the claim language 'a phenyl radical.' Accordingly we must presume that the phrase was used in its commonly accepted technical sense.... Applicants] have not referred us to any standard work on chemistry which indicates that the commonly accepted technical meaning of the words 'a phenyl radical', without more, would encompass the hydroxyphenyl radical. On the contrary, Hackh's [Chemical Dictionary] quite plainly defines 'phenyl' as 'the monovalent radical... derived from benzene... or phenol.'").

APPLICANT MAY BE OWN LEXICOGRAPHER

Applicant may be his or her own lexicographer as long as the meaning assigned to the term is not repugnant to the term's well known usage. In re Hill, 161 F.2d 367, 73 USPQ 482 (CCPA 1947). Any special meaning assigned to a term "must be sufficiently clear in the specification that any departure from common usage would be so understood by a person of experience in the field of the invention." Multiform Desiccants Inc. v. Medzam Ltd., 133 F.3d 1473, 1477, 45 USPQ2d 1429, 1432 (Fed. Cir. 1998).

2111.02   Weight of Preamble

PREAMBLE IS NONLIMITING UNLESS IT BREATHES LIFE AND MEANING INTO THE CLAIM

The preamble is not given the effect of a limitation unless it breathes life and meaning into the claim. In order to limit the claim, the preamble must be "essential to point out the invention defined by the claim." Kropa v. Robie, 187 F.2d 150, 152, 88 USPQ 478, 481 (CCPA 1951) (discussed below). In claims directed to articles and apparatus, any phraseology in the preamble that limits the structure of that article or apparatus must be given weight. In re Stencel, 828 F.2d 751, 4 USPQ2d 1071 (Fed. Cir. 1987) (discussed below). On the other hand, a preamble is generally not accorded any patentable weight where it merely recites the purpose of a process or the intended use of a structure, and where the body of the claim does not depend on the preamble for completeness but, instead, the process steps or structural limitations are able to stand alone. In re Hirao, 535 F.2d 67, 190 USPQ 15 (CCPA 1976) (process claims, discussed below); Kropa v. Robie, 187 F.2d at 152, 88 USPQ at 481 (claims directed to apparatus, products, chemical structure, etc., as discussed below).

In In re Hirao, 535 F.2d 67, 190 USPQ 15 (CCPA 1976), the claim preamble set forth "A process for preparing foods and drinks sweetened mildly, and protected against discoloration, Streckler's reaction, and moisture absorption." The body of the claim recited two steps directed to the formation of high purity maltose and a third step of adding the maltose to foods and drinks as a sweetener. The court held that the preamble was only directed to the purpose of the process, the steps could stand alone and did not depend on the preamble for completeness.

In Kropa v. Robie, 187 F.2d 150, 152, 88 USPQ 478, 481 (CCPA 1951), a preamble reciting "An abrasive article" was deemed essential to point out the invention defined by claims to an article comprising abrasive grains and a hardened binder and the process of making it. The court said that "it is only by that phrase that it can be known that the subject matter defined by the claims is comprised as an abrasive article. Every union of substances capable inter alia of use as abrasive grains and a binder is not an `abrasive article.' " Id. at 481, 187 F.2d at 152. Therefore, the preamble served to further define the structure of the article produced.

In In re Stencel, 828 F.2d 751, 4 USPQ2d 1071 (Fed. Cir. 1987), the claim was directed to a driver for setting a joint of a threaded collar. The claim did not directly include the structure of the collar as part of the claimed article. The preamble did set forth the structure of the collar but the examiner had not given this recitation any weight. The court found that the collar structure could not be ignored. While the claim was not directly limited to the collar, the collar structure recited in the preamble did limit the structure of the driver. The court stated that "the framework — the teachings of the prior art — against which patentability is measured is not all drivers broadly, but drivers suitable for use in combination with this collar, for the claims are so limited." Id. at 1073, 828 F.2d at 754.

COMPOSITION CLAIMS—THE PREAMBLE IS GENERALLY NONLIMITING IF THE PREAMBLE MERELY RECITES AN INHERENT PROPERTY

When the claim is directed to a product, the preamble is generally nonlimiting if the body of the claim is directed to an old composition and the preamble merely recites a property inherent in the old composition. Kropa v. Robie, 187 F.2d at 152, 88 USPQ at 480-81.

THE INTENDED USE MAY FURTHER LIMIT THE CLAIM IF IT DOES MORE THAN MERELY STATE PURPOSE OR INTENDED USE

Intended use recitations and other types of functional language cannot be entirely disregarded. However, in apparatus, article, and composition claims, intended use must result in a structural difference between the claimed invention and the prior art in order to patentably distinguish the claimed invention from the prior art. If the prior art structure is capable of performing the intended use, then it meets the claim. In a claim drawn to a process of making, the intended use must result in a manipulative difference as compared to the prior art. In re Casey, 370 F.2d 576, 152 USPQ 235 (CCPA 1967); In re Otto, 312 F.2d 937, 938, 136 USPQ 458, 459 (CCPA 1963) (The claims were directed to a core member for hair curlers and a process of making a core member for hair curlers. Court held that the intended use of hair curling was of no significance to the structure and process of making.)

2111.03   Transitional Phrases [R-1]

The transitional phrases "comprising", "consisting essentially of" and "consisting of" define the scope of a claim with respect to what unrecited additional components or steps, if any, are excluded from the scope of the claim.

The transitional term "comprising", which is synonymous with "including," "containing," or "characterized by," is inclusive or open-ended and does not exclude additional, unrecited elements or method steps. Moleculon Research Corp. v. CBS, Inc., 793 F.2d 1261, 229 USPQ 805 (Fed. Cir. 1986); In re Baxter, 656 F.2d 679, 686, 210 USPQ 795, 803 (CCPA 1981); Ex parte Davis, 80 USPQ 448, 450 (Bd. App. 1948)("comprising" leaves "the claim open for the inclusion of unspecified ingredients even in major amounts").

The transitional phrase "consisting of" excludes any element, step, or ingredient not specified in the claim. In re Gray, 53 F.2d 520, 11 USPQ 255 (CCPA 1931); Ex parte Davis, 80 USPQ 448, 450 (Bd. App. 1948)("consisting of" defined as "closing the claim to the inclusion of materials other than those recited except for impurities ordinarily associated therewith."). Transitional phrases such as "composed of," "having," or "being" must be interpreted in light of the specification to determine whether open or closed claim language is intended. See, e.g., Regents of the Univ. of Cal. v. Eli Lilly & Co., 119 F.3d 1559, 1573, 43 USPQ2d 1398, 1410 (Fed. Cir. 1997), cert. denied, 118 S. Ct. 1548 (1998)(In the context of a cDNA having a sequence coding for human PI, the term "having" still permitted inclusion of other moieties.). A claim which depends from a claim which "consists of" the recited elements or steps cannot add an element or step. When the phrase "consists of" appears in a clause of the body of a claim, rather than immediately following the preamble, it limits only the element set forth in that clause; other elements are not excluded from the claim as a whole. Mannesmann Demag Corp. v. Engineered Metal Products Co., 793 F.2d 1279, 230 USPQ 45 (Fed. Cir. 1986).

The transitional phrase "consisting essentially of" limits the scope of a claim to the specified materials or steps "and those that do not materially affect the basic and novel characteristic(s)" of the claimed invention. In re Herz, 537 F.2d 549, 551-52, 190 USPQ 461, 463 (CCPA 1976) (emphasis in original)(Prior art hydraulic fluid required a dispersant which appellants argued was excluded from claims limited to a functional fluid "consisting essentially of" certain components. In finding the claims did not exclude the prior art dispersant, the court noted that appellants' specification indicated the claimed composition can contain any well-nown additive such as a dispersant, and there was no evidence that the presence of a dispersant would materially affect the basic and novel characteristic of the claimed invention. The prior art composition had the same basic and novel characteristic (increased oxidation resistance) as well as additional enhanced detergent and dispersant characteristics.). "A 'consisting essentially of' claim occupies a middle ground between closed claims that are written in a 'consisting of' format and fully open claims that are drafted in a 'comprising' format." PPG Industries v. Guardian Industries, 156 F.3d 1351, 1354, 48 USPQ2d 1351, 1353-54 (Fed. Cir. 1998). See also Atlas Powder Co. v. E.I. duPont de Nemours & Co., 750 F.2d 1569, 224 USPQ 409 (Fed. Cir. 1984); In re Janakirama-Rao, 317 F.2d 951, 137 USPQ 893 (CCPA 1963); Water Technologies Corp. v. Calco, Ltd., 850 F.2d 660, 7 USPQ2d 1097 (Fed. Cir. 1988). For search and examination purposes, absent a clear indication in the specification of what the basic and novel characteristics actually are, "consisting essentially of" will be construed as equivalent to "comprising." See, e.g., PPG, 156 F.3d at 1355, 48 USPQ at 1355 ("PPG could have defined the scope of the phrase 'consisting essentially of' for purposes of its patent by making clear in its specification what it regarded as constituting a material change in the basic and novel characteristics of the invention."). When an applicant contends that additional steps or materials in the prior art are excluded by the recitation of "consisting essentially of," applicant has the burden of showing that the introduction of additional steps or components would materially change the characteristics of applicant's invention. In re De Lajarte, 337 F.2d 870, 143 USPQ 256 (CCPA 1964). See also Ex parte Hoffman, 12 USPQ2d 1061, 1063-64 (Bd. Pat. App. & Inter. 1989)("Although 'consisting essentially of' is typically used and defined in the context of compositions of matter, we find nothing intrinsically wrong with the use of such language as a modifier of method steps. . . [rendering] the claim open only for the inclusion of steps which do not materially affect the basic and novel characteristics of the claimed method. To determine the steps included versus excluded the claim must be read in light of the specification. . . . [I]t is an applicant's burden to establish that a step practiced in a prior art method is excluded from his claims by 'consisting essentially of' language.").

2112.02   Process Claims

PROCESS CLAIMS—PRIOR ART DEVICE ANTICIPATES A CLAIMED PROCESS IF THE DEVICE CARRIES OUT THE PROCESS DURING NORMAL OPERATION

Under the principles of inherency, if a prior art device, in its normal and usual operation, would necessarily perform the method claimed, then the method claimed will be considered to be anticipated by the prior art device. When the prior art device is the same as a device described in the specification for carrying out the claimed method, it can be assumed the device will inherently perform the claimed process. In re King, 801 F.2d 1324, 231 USPQ 136 (Fed. Cir. 1986) (The claims were directed to a method of enhancing color effects produced by ambient light through a process of absorption and reflection of the light off a coated substrate. A prior art reference to Donley disclosed a glass substrate coated with silver and metal oxide 200-800 angstroms thick. While Donley disclosed using the coated substrate to produce architectural colors, the absorption and reflection mechanisms of the claimed process were not disclosed. However, King's specification disclosed using a coated substrate of Donley's structure for use in his process. The Federal Circuit upheld the Board's finding that "Donley inherently performs the function disclosed in the method claims on appeal when that device is used in 'normal and usual operation'" and found that a prima facie case of anticipation was made out. Id. at 138, 801 F.2d at 1326. It was up to applicant to prove that Donley's structure would not perform the claimed method when placed in ambient light.). See also In re Best, 562

F.2d 1252, 1255, 195 USPQ 430, 433 (CCPA 1977) (Applicant claimed a process for preparing a hydrolytically-stable zeolitic aluminosilicate which included a step of "cooling the steam zeolite ... at a rate sufficiently rapid that the cooled zeolite exhibits a X-ray diffraction pattern ...." All the process limitations were expressly disclosed by a U.S. patent to Hansford except the cooling step. The court stated that any sample of Hansford's zeolite would necessarily be cooled to facilitate subsequent handling. Therefore, a prima facie case under 35 U.S.C. 102/103 was made. Applicant had failed to introduce any evidence comparing X-ray diffraction patterns showing a difference in cooling rate between the claimed process and that of Hansford or any data showing that the process of Hansford would result in a product with a different X-ray diffraction. Either type of evidence would have rebutted the prima facie case under 35 U.S.C. 102. A further analysis would be necessary to determine if the process was unobvious under 35 U.S.C. 103.); Ex parte Novitski, 26 USPQ2d 1389 (Bd. Pat. App. & Inter. 1993) (The Board rejected a claim directed to a method for protecting a plant from plant pathogenic nematodes by inoculating the plant with a nematode inhibiting strain of P. cepacia. A U.S. patent to Dart disclosed inoculation using P. cepacia type Wisconsin 526 bacteria for protecting the plant from fungal disease. Dart was silent as to nematode inhibition but the Board concluded that nematode inhibition was an inherent property of the bacteria. The Board noted that applicant had stated in the specification that Wisconsin 526 possesses an 18% nematode inhibition rating.).

PROCESS OF USE CLAIMS — NEW AND UNOBVIOUS USES OF OLD STRUCTURES AND COMPOSITIONS MAY BE PATENTABLE

The discovery of a new use for an old structure based on unknown properties of the structure might be patentable to the discoverer as a process of using. In re Hack, 245 F.2d 246, 248, 114 USPQ 161, 163 (CCPA 1957). However, when the claim recites using an old composition or structure and the "use" is directed to a result or property of that composition or structure, then the claim is anticipated. In re May, 574 F.2d 1082, 1090, 197 USPQ 601, 607 (CCPA 1978) (Claims 1 and 6, directed to a method of effecting nonaddictive analgesia (pain reduction) in animals, were found to be anticipated by the applied prior art which disclosed the same compounds for effecting analgesia but which was silent as to addiction. The court upheld the rejection and stated that the applicants had merely found a new property of the compound and such a discovery did not constitute a new use. The court went on to reverse the rejection of claims 2-5 and 7-10 which recited a process of using a new compound. The court relied on evidence showing that the nonaddictive property of the new compound was unexpected.).

See also In re Tomlinson, 363 F.2d 928, 150 USPQ 623 (CCPA 1966) (The claim was directed to a process of inhibiting light degradation of polypropylene by mixing it with one of a genus of compounds, including nickel dithiocarbamate. A reference taught mixing polypropylene with nickel dithiocarbamate to lower heat degradation. The court held that the claims read on the obvious process of mixing polypropylene with the nickel dithiocarbamate and that the preamble of the claim was merely directed to the result of mixing the two materials. "While the references do not show a specific recognition of that result, its discovery by appellants is tantamount only to finding a property in the old composition." 363 F.2d at 934, 150 USPQ at 628 (emphasis in original).).

2113   Product-by-Process Claims

PRODUCT-BY-PROCESS CLAIMS ARE NOT LIMITED TO THE MANIPULATIONS OF THE RECITED STEPS, ONLY THE STRUCTURE IMPLIED BY THE STEPS

"[E]ven though product-by-process claims are limited by and defined by the process, determination of patentability is based on the product itself. The patentability of a product does not depend on its method of production. If the product in the product-by-process claim is the same as or obvious from a product of the prior art, the claim is unpatentable even though the prior product was made by a different process." In re Thorpe, 777 F.2d 695, 698, 227 USPQ 964, 966 (Fed. Cir. 1985) (citations omitted) (Claim was directed to a novolac color developer. The process of making the developer was allowed. The difference between the inventive process and the prior art was the addition of metal oxide and carboxylic acid as separate ingredients instead of adding the more expensive pre-reacted metal carboxylate. The product-by-process claim was rejected because the end product, in both the prior art and the allowed process, ends up containing metal carboxylate. The fact that the metal carboxylate is not directly added, but is instead produced in-situ does not change the end product.).

ONCE A PRODUCT APPEARING TO BE SUBSTANTIALLY IDENTICAL IS FOUND AND A 35 U.S.C. 102/103 REJECTION MADE, THE BURDEN SHIFTS TO THE APPLICANT TO SHOW AN UNOBVIOUS DIFFERENCE

"The Patent Office bears a lesser burden of proof in making out a case of prima facie obviousness for product-by-process claims because of their peculiar nature" than when a product is claimed in the conventional fashion. In re Fessmann, 489 F.2d 742, 744, 180 USPQ 324, 326 (CCPA 1974). Once the Examiner provides a rationale tending to show that the claimed product appears to be the same or similar to that of the prior art, although produced by a different process, the burden shifts to applicant to come forward with evidence establishing an unobvious difference between the claimed product and the prior art product. In re Marosi, 710 F.2d 798, 802, 218 USPQ 289, 292 (Fed. Cir. 1983) (The claims were directed to a zeolite manufactured by mixing together various inorganic materials in solution and heating the resultant gel to form a crystalline metal silicate essentially free of alkali metal. The prior art described a process of making a zeolite which, after ion exchange to remove alkali metal, appeared to be "essentially free of alkali metal." The court upheld the rejection because the applicant had not come forward with any evidence that the prior art was not "essentially free of alkali metal" and therefore a different and unobvious product.).

Ex parte Gray, 10 USPQ2d 1922 (Bd. Pat. App. & Inter. 1989) (The prior art disclosed human nerve growth factor (b-NGF) isolated from human placental tissue. The claim was directed to b-NGF produced through genetic engineering techniques. The factor produced seemed to be substantially the same whether isolated from tissue or produced through genetic engineering. While the applicant questioned the purity of the prior art factor, no concrete evidence of an unobvious difference was presented. The Board stated that the dispositive issue is whether the claimed factor exhibits any unexpected properties compared with the factor disclosed by the prior art. The Board further stated that the applicant should have made some comparison between the two factors to establish unexpected properties since the materials appeared to be identical or only slightly different.).

THE USE OF 35 U.S.C. 102/103 REJECTIONS FOR PRODUCT-BY-PROCESS CLAIMS HAS BEEN APPROVED BY THE COURTS

"[T]he lack of physical description in a product-by-process claim makes determination of the patentability of the claim more difficult, since in spite of the fact that the claim may recite only process limitations, it is the patentability of the product claimed and not of the recited process steps which must be established. We are therefore of the opinion that when the prior art discloses a product which reasonably appears to be either identical with or only slightly different than a product claimed in a product-by-process claim, a rejection based alternatively on either section 102 or section 103 of the statute is eminently fair and acceptable. As a practical matter, the Patent Office is not equipped to manufacture products by the myriad of processes put before it and then obtain prior art products and make physical comparisons therewith." In re Brown, 459 F.2d 531, 535, 173 USPQ 685, 688 (CCPA 1972).

2114   Apparatus and Article Claims — Functional Language [R-1]

For a discussion of case law which provides guidance in interpreting the functional portion of means-plus-function limitations see MPEP § 2181–§ 2186.

APPARATUS CLAIMS MUST BE STRUCTURALLY DISTINGUISHABLE FROM THE PRIOR ART

Claims directed to apparatus must be distinguished from the prior art in terms of structure rather than function. In re Danly, 263 F.2d 844, 847, 120 USPQ 528, 531 (CCPA 1959). "[A]pparatus claims cover what a device is, not what a device does." (emphasis in original) Hewlett-Packard Co. v. Bausch & Lomb Inc., 909 F.2d 1464, 1469, 15 USPQ2d 1525, 1528 (Fed. Cir. 1990).

MANNER OF OPERATING THE DEVICE DOES NOT DIFFERENTIATE APPARATUS CLAIM FROM THE PRIOR ART

A claim containing a "recitation with respect to the manner in which a claimed apparatus is intended to be employed does not differentiate the claimed apparatus from a prior art apparatus" if the prior art apparatus teaches all the structural limitations of the claim. Ex parte Masham, 2 USPQ2d 1647 (Bd. Pat. App. & Inter. 1987) (The preamble of claim 1 recited that the apparatus was "for mixing flowing developer material" and the body of the claim recited "means for mixing ..., said mixing means being stationary and completely submerged in the developer material". The claim was rejected over a reference which taught all the structural limitations of the claim for the intended use of mixing flowing developer. However, the mixer was only partially submerged in the developer material. The Board held that the amount of submersion is immaterial to the structure of the mixer and thus the claim was properly rejected.).

A PRIOR ART DEVICE CAN PERFORM ALL THE FUNCTIONS OF THE APPARATUS CLAIM AND STILL NOT ANTICIPATE THE CLAIM

Even if the prior art device performs all the functions recited in the claim, the prior art cannot anticipate the claim if there is any structural difference. It should be noted, however, that means plus function limitations are met by structures which are equivalent to the corresponding structures recited in the specification. In re Ruskin, 347 F.2d 843, 146 USPQ 211 (CCPA 1965) as implicitly modified by In re Donaldson, 16 F.3d 1189, 29 USPQ2d 1845 (Fed. Cir. 1994). See also In re Robertson, 169 F.3d 743, 745, 49 USPQ2d 1949, 1951 (Fed. Cir. 1999)(The claims were drawn to a disposable diaper having three fastening elements. The reference disclosed two fastening elements that could perform the same function as the three fastening elements in the claims. The court construed the claims to require three separate elements and held that the reference did not disclose a separate third fastening element, either expressly or inherently.).

2115   **Material or Article Worked Upon by Apparatus**

MATERIAL OR ARTICLE WORKED UPON DOES NOT LIMIT APPARATUS CLAIMS

"Expressions relating the apparatus to contents thereof during an intended operation are of no significance in determining patentability of the apparatus claim." Ex parte Thibault, 164 USPQ 666, 667 (Bd. App. 1969). Furthermore, "Inclusion of material or article worked upon by a structure being claimed does not impart patentability to the claims." In re Young, 75 F.2d 966, 25 USPQ 69 (CCPA 1935) (as restated in In re Otto, 312 F.2d 937, 136 USPQ 458, 459 (CCPA 1963)).

In In re Young, a claim to a machine for making concrete beams included a limitation to the concrete reinforced members made by the machine as well as the structural elements of the machine itself. The court held that the inclusion of the article formed within the body of the claim did not, without more, make the claim patentable.

In In re Casey, 370 F.2d 576, 152 USPQ 235 (CCPA 1967), an apparatus claim recited "A taping machine comprising a supporting structure, a brush attached to said supporting structure, said brush being formed with projecting bristles which terminate in free ends to collectively define a surface to which adhesive tape will detachably adhere, and means for providing relative motion between said brush and said supporting structure while said adhesive tape is adhered to said surface." An obviousness rejection was made over a reference to Kienzle which taught a machine for perforating sheets. The court upheld the rejection stating that "the references in claim 1 to adhesive tape handling do not expressly or impliedly require any particular structure in addition to that of Kienzle." The perforating device had the structure of the taping device as claimed, the difference was in the use of the device, and "the manner or method in which such machine is to be utilized is not germane to the issue of patentability of the machine itself."

Note that this line of cases is limited to claims directed to machinery which works upon an article or material in its intended use, it does not apply to product claims or kit claims (i.e., claims directed to a plurality of articles grouped together as a kit).

2116 Material Manipulated in Process

The materials on which a process is carried out must be accorded weight in determining the patentability of a process. Ex parte Leonard, 187 USPQ 122 (Bd. App. 1974).

2116.01 Novel, Unobvious Starting Material or End Product

All the limitations of a claim must be considered when weighing the differences between the claimed invention and the prior art in determining the obviousness of a process or method claim. See MPEP § 2143.03.

In re Ochiai, 71 F.3d 1565, 37 USPQ2d 1127 (Fed. Cir. 1995) and In re Brouwer, 77 F.3d 422, 37 USPQ2d 1663 (Fed. Cir. 1996) addressed the issue of whether an otherwise conventional process could be patented if it were limited to making or using a nonobvious product. In both cases, the Federal Circuit held that the use of per se rules is improper in applying the test for obviousness under 35 U.S.C. 103. Rather, 35 U.S.C. 103 requires a highly fact-dependent analysis involving taking the claimed subject matter as a whole and comparing it to the prior art. To support a rejection under 35 U.S.C. 103, the collective teachings of the prior art must have suggested to one of ordinary skill in the art that, at the time the invention was made, applicant's claimed invention would have been obvious. In applying this test to the claims on appeal in Ochiai and Brouwer, the court held that there simply was no suggestion or motivation in the prior art to make or use novel, nonobvious products in the claimed processes. Consequently, the court overturned the rejections based upon 35 U.S.C. 103.

Interpreting the claimed invention as a whole requires consideration of all claim limitations. Thus, proper claim construction requires treating language in a process claim which recites the making or using of a nonobvious product as a material limitation. Motivation to make or use the nonobvious product must be present in the prior art for a 35 U.S.C. 103 rejection to be sustained. The decision in Ochiai specifically dispelled any distinction between processes of making a product and methods of using a product with regard to the effect of any product limitations in either type of claim.

As noted in Brouwer, 77 F.3d at 425, 37 USPQ2d at 1666, the inquiry as to whether a claimed invention would have been obvious is "highly fact-specific by design". Accordingly, obviousness must be assessed on a case-by-case basis. The following decisions are illustrative of the lack of per se rules in applying the test for obviousness under 35 U.S.C. 103 and of the fact intensive comparison of claimed processes with the prior art: In re Durden, 763 F.2d 1406, 226 USPQ 359 (Fed. Cir. 1985) (The examiner rejected a claim directed to a process in which patentable starting materials were reacted to form patentable end products. The prior art showed the same chemical reaction mechanism applied to other chemicals. The court held that the process claim was obvious over the prior art.); In re Albertson, 332 F.2d 379, 141 USPQ 730 (CCPA 1964)(Process of chemically reducing one novel, nonobvious material to obtain another novel, nonobvious material was claimed. The process was held obvious because the reduction reaction was old.); In re Kanter, 399 F.2d 249, 158 USPQ 331 (CCPA 1968) (Process of siliconizing a patentable base material to obtain a patentable product was claimed. Rejection based on prior art teaching the siliconizing process as applied to a different base material was upheld.); Cf. In re Pleuddemann, 910 F.2d 823, 15 USPQ2d 1738 (Fed. Cir. 1990) (Methods of bonding polymer and filler using a novel silane coupling agent held patentable even though methods of bonding using other silane coupling agents were well known because the process could not be conducted without the new agent); In re Kuehl, 475 F.2d 658, 177 USPQ 250 (CCPA 1973) (Process of cracking hydrocarbons using novel zeolite catalyst found to be patentable even though catalytic cracking process was old. "The test under 103 is whether in view of the prior art the invention as a whole would have been obvious at the time it was made, and the prior art here does not include the zeolite, ZK-22. The obviousness of the process of cracking hydrocarbons with ZK-22 as a catalyst must be determined without reference to knowledge of ZK-22 and its properties." 475 F.2d at 664-665, 177 USPQ at 255.); and In re Mancy, 499 F.2d 1289, 182 USPQ 303 (CCPA 1974) (Claim to a process for the production of a known antibiotic by cultivating a novel, unobvious microorganism was found to be patentable.).

2129   Admissions as Prior Art [R-1]

ADMISSIONS BY APPLICANT CONSTITUTE PRIOR ART

When applicant states that something is prior art, it is taken as being available as prior art against the claims. Admitted prior art can be used in obviousness rejections. In re Nomiya, 509 F.2d 566, 184 USPQ 607, 610 (CCPA 1975) (Figures in the application labeled "prior art" held to be an admission that what was pictured was prior art relative to applicant's invention.).

A JEPSON CLAIM RESULTS IN AN IMPLIED ADMISSION THAT PREAMBLE IS PRIOR ART

The preamble elements in a Jepson-type claim (i.e., a claim of the type discussed in 37 CFR 1.75(e); see MPEP § 608.01(m)) "are impliedly admitted to be old in the art, ... but it is only an implied admission." In re Ehrreich, 590 F.2d 902, 909-910 200 USPQ 504, 510 (CCPA 1979) (emphasis in original) (citations omitted). See also Sjolund v. Musland, 847 F.2d 1573, 1577, 6 USPQ2d 2020, 2023 (Fed. Cir. 1988); Pentec, Inc. v. Graphic Controls Corp., 776 F.2d 309, 315, 227 USPQ 766, 770 (Fed. Cir. 1985); and Reading & Bates Construction Co. v. Baker Energy Resources Corp., 748 F.2d 645, 650, 223 USPQ 1168, 1172 (Fed. Cir. 1984). Claims must be read in light of the specification. Where the specification confirms that the subject matter of the preamble was invented by another before applicant's invention, the preamble is treated as prior art. However, certain art may be prior art to one inventive entity, but not to the public in general. In re Fout, 675 F.2d 297, 300-301, 213 USPQ 532, 535-36 (CCPA 1982). This is the case when applicant has made an improvement on his or her own prior invention. An applicant's own foundational work should not, unless there is a statutory bar, be treated as prior art solely because knowledge of this work is admitted. Therefore, when applicant explains that the Jepson format is being used to avoid a double patenting rejection over *the applicant's own copending application, the implication that the *preamble is admitted prior art is overcome. Reading & Bates Construction Co. v. Baker Energy Resources Corp., 748 F.2d 645, 650, 223 USPQ 1168, 1172 (Fed. Cir. 1984). Compare In re Fout, 675 F.2d 297, 300-01, 213 USPQ 532, 535-36 (CCPA 1982) (The court held that the preamble was admitted prior art because the specification explained that Paglaro, a different inventor, had invented the subject matter described in the preamble.).

2164.08(a)   Single Means Claim

A single means claim, i.e., where a means recitation does not appear in combination with another recited element of means, is subject to an undue breadth rejection under 35 U.S.C. 112, first paragraph. In re Hyatt, 708 F.2d 712, 714-715, 218 USPQ 195, 197 (Fed. Cir. 1983) (A single means claim which covered every conceivable means for achieving the stated purpose was held nonenabling for the scope of the claim because the specification disclosed at most only those means known to the inventor.). When claims depend on a recited property, a fact situation comparable to Hyatt is possible, where the claim covers every conceivable structure (means) for achieving the stated property (result) while the specification discloses at most only those known to the inventor.

2171   Two Separate Requirements for Claims Under 35 U.S.C. 112, Second Paragraph

The second paragraph of 35 U.S.C. 112 is directed to requirements for the claims:

The specification shall conclude with one or more claims particularly pointing out and distinctly claiming the subject matter which the applicant regards as his invention.

There are two separate requirements set forth in this paragraph:

(A) the claims must set forth the subject matter that applicants regard as their invention; and

(B) the claims must particularly point out and distinctly define the metes and bounds of the subject matter that will be protected by the patent grant.

The first requirement is a subjective one because it is dependent on what the applicants for a patent regard as their invention. The second requirement is an objective one because it is not dependent on the views of applicant or any particular individual, but is evaluated in the context of whether the claim is definite — i.e., whether the scope of the claim is clear to a hypothetical person possessing the ordinary level of skill in the pertinent art.

Although an essential purpose of the examination process is to determine whether or not the claims define an invention that is both novel and nonobvious over the prior art, another essential purpose of patent examination is to determine whether or not the claims are precise, clear, correct, and unambiguous. The uncertainties of claim scope should be removed, as much as possible, during the examination process.

The inquiry during examination is patentability of the invention as applicant regards it. If the claims do not particularly point out and distinctly claim that which applicants regard as their invention, the appropriate action by the examiner is to reject the claims under 35 U.S.C. 112, second paragraph. In re Zletz, 893 F.2d 319, 13 USPQ2d 1320 (Fed. Cir. 1989). If a rejection is based on 35 U.S.C. 112, second paragraph, the examiner should further explain whether the rejection is based on indefiniteness or on the failure to claim what applicants regard as their invention. Ex parte Ionescu, 222 USPQ 537, 539 (Bd. App. 1984).

2172   Subject Matter Which Applicants Regard as Their Invention

I. FOCUS FOR EXAMINATION

A rejection based on the failure to satisfy this requirement is appropriate only where applicant has stated, somewhere other than in the application as filed, that the invention is something different from what is de fined by the claims. In other words, the invention set forth in the claims must be presumed, in the absence of evidence to the contrary, to be that which applicants regard as their invention. In re Moore, 439 F.2d 1232, 169 USPQ 236 (CCPA 1971).

II. EVIDENCE TO THE CONTRARY

Evidence that shows that a claim does not correspond in scope with that which applicant regards as applicant's invention may be found, for example, in contentions or admissions contained in briefs or remarks filed by applicant, In re Prater, 415 F.2d 1393, 162 USPQ 541 (CCPA 1969), or in affidavits filed under 37 CFR 1.132, In re Cormany, 476 F.2d 998, 177 USPQ 450 (CCPA 1973). The content of applicant's specification is not used as evidence that the scope of the claims is inconsistent with the subject matter which applicants regard as their invention. As noted in In re Ehrreich, 590 F.2d 902, 200 USPQ 504 (CCPA 1979), agreement, or lack thereof, between the claims and the specification is properly considered only with respect to 35 U.S.C. 112, first paragraph; it is irrelevant to compliance with the second paragraph of that section.

III. SHIFT IN CLAIMS PERMITTED

The second paragraph of 35 U.S.C. 112 does not prohibit applicants from changing what they regard as their invention during the pendency of the application. In re Saunders, 444 F.2d 599, 170 USPQ 213 (CCPA 1971) (Applicant was permitted to claim and submit comparative evidence with respect to claimed subject matter which originally was only the preferred embodiment within much broader claims (directed to a method).). The fact that claims in a continuation application were directed to originally disclosed subject matter which applicants had not regarded as part of their invention when the parent application was filed was held not to prevent the continuation application from receiving benefits of the filing date of the parent application under 35 U.S.C. 120. In re Brower, 433 F.2d 813, 167 USPQ 684 (CCPA 1970).

2172.01   Unclaimed Essential Matter

A claim which omits matter disclosed to be essential to the invention as described in the specification or in other statements of record may be rejected under 35 U.S.C. 112, first paragraph, as not enabling. In re Mayhew, 527 F.2d 1229, 188 USPQ 356 (CCPA 1976). See also MPEP § 2164.08(c). Such essential matter may include missing elements, steps or necessary structural cooperative relationships of elements described by the applicant(s) as necessary to practice the invention.

In addition, a claim which fails to interrelate essential elements of the invention as defined by applicant(s) in the specification may be rejected under 35 U.S.C. 112, second paragraph, for failure to point out and distinctly claim the invention. See In re Venezia, 530 F.2d 956, 189 USPQ 149 (CCPA 1976); In re Collier, 397 F.2d 1003, 158 USPQ 266 (CCPA 1968).

2173   Claims Must Particularly Point Out and Distinctly Claim the Invention

The primary purpose of this requirement of definiteness of claim language is to ensure that the scope of the claims is clear so the public is informed of the boundaries of what constitutes infringement of the patent. A secondary purpose is to provide a clear measure of what applicants regard as the invention so that it can be determined whether the claimed invention meets all the criteria for patentability and whether the specification meets the criteria of 35 U.S.C. 112, first paragraph with respect to the claimed invention.

2173.01   Claim Terminology

A fundamental principle contained in 35 U.S.C. 112, second paragraph is that applicants are their own lexicographers. They can define in the claims what they regard as their invention essentially in whatever terms they choose so long as the terms are not used in ways that are contrary to accepted meanings in the art. Applicant may use functional language, alternative expressions, negative limitations, or any style of expression or format of claim which makes clear the boundaries of the subject matter for which protection is sought. As noted by the Court in In re Swinehart, 439 F.2d 210, 160 USPQ 226 (CCPA 1971), a claim may not be rejected solely because of the type of language used to define the subject matter for which patent protection is sought.

2173.02   Clarity and Precision

The examiner's focus during examination of claims for compliance with the requirement for definiteness of 35 U.S.C. 112, second paragraph is whether the claim meets the threshold requirements of clarity and precision, not whether more suitable language or modes of expression are available. When the examiner is satisfied that patentable subject matter is disclosed, and it is apparent to the examiner that the claims are directed to such patentable subject matter, he or she should allow claims which define the patentable subject matter with a reasonable degree of particularity and distinctness. Some latitude in the manner of expression and the aptness of terms should be permitted even though the claim language is not as precise as the examiner might desire. Examiners are encouraged to suggest claim language to applicants to improve the clarity or precision of the language used, but should not reject claims or insist on their own preferences if other modes of expression selected by applicants satisfy the statutory requirement.

The essential inquiry pertaining to this requirement is whether the claims set out and circumscribe a particular subject matter with a reasonable degree of clarity and particularity. Definiteness of claim language must be analyzed, not in a vacuum, but in light of:

(A) The content of the particular application disclosure;

(B) The teachings of the prior art; and

(C) The claim interpretation that would be given by one possessing the ordinary level of skill in the pertinent art at the time the invention was made.

If the scope of the invention sought to be patented cannot be determined from the language of the claims with a reasonable degree of certainty, a rejection of the claims under 35 U.S.C. 112, second paragraph is appropriate. In re Wiggins, 488 F.2d 538, 179 USPQ 421 (CCPA 1973).

2173.03 Inconsistency Between Claim and Specification Disclosure or Prior Art

Although the terms of a claim may appear to be definite, inconsistency with the specification disclosure or prior art teachings may make an otherwise definite claim take on an unreasonable degree of uncertainty. In re Cohn, 438 F.2d 989, 169 USPQ 95 (CCPA 1971); In re Hammack, 427 F.2d 1378, 166 USPQ 204 (CCPA 1970). In Cohn, the claim was directed to a process of treating a surface with a corroding solution until the metallic appearance is supplanted by an "opaque" appearance. Noting that no claim may be read apart from and independent of the supporting disclosure on which it is based, the court found that the description, definitions and examples set forth in the specification relating to the appearance of the surface after treatment were inherently inconsistent and rendered the claim indefinite.

2173.04   Breadth Is Not Indefiniteness

Breadth of a claim is not to be equated with indefiniteness. In re Miller, 441 F.2d 689, 169 USPQ 597 (CCPA 1971). If the scope of the subject matter embraced by the claims is clear, and if applicants have not otherwise indicated that they intend the invention to be of a scope different from that defined in the claims, then the claims comply with 35 U.S.C. 112, second paragraph.

Undue breadth of the claim may be addressed under different statutory provisions, depending on the reasons for concluding that the claim is too broad. If the claim is too broad because it does not set forth that which applicants regard as their invention as evidenced by statements outside of the application as filed, a rejection under 35 U.S.C. 112, second paragraph would be appropriate. If the claim is too broad because it is not supported by the original description or by an enabling disclosure, a rejection under 35 U.S.C. 112, first paragraph would be appropriate. If the claim is too broad because it reads on the prior art, a rejection under either 35 U.S.C. 102 or 103 would be appropriate.

2173.05   Specific Topics Related to Issues Under 35 U.S.C. 112, Second Paragraph

The following sections are devoted to a discussion of specific topics where issues under 35 U.S.C. 112, second paragraph have been addressed. These sections are not intended to be an exhaustive list of the issues that can arise under 35 U.S.C. 112, second paragraph, but are intended to provide guidance in areas that have been addressed with some frequency in recent examination practice. The court and Board decisions cited are representative. As with all appellate decisions, the results are largely dictated by the facts in each case. The use of the same language in a different context may justify a different result.

2173.05(a)   New Terminology

THE MEANING OF EVERY TERM SHOULD BE APPARENT

The meaning of every term used in a claim should be apparent from the prior art or from the specification and drawings at the time the application is filed. Applicants need not confine themselves to the terminology used in the prior art, but are required to make clear and precise the terms that are used to define the invention whereby the metes and bounds of the claimed invention can be ascertained. During patent examination, the pending claims must be given the broadest reasonable interpretation consistent with the specification. In re Prater, 415 F.2d 1393, 162 USPQ 541 (CCPA 1969). See also MPEP § 2111–§ 2111.01. When the specification states the meaning that a term in the claim is intended to have, the claim is examined using that meaning, in order to achieve a complete exploration of the applicant's invention and its relation to the prior art. In re Zletz, 893 F.2d 319, 13 USPQ2d 1320 (Fed. Cir. 1989).

THE REQUIREMENT FOR CLARITY AND PRECISION MUST BE BALANCED WITH THE LIMITATIONS OF THE LANGUAGE

Courts have recognized that it is not only permissible, but often desirable, to use new terms that are frequently more precise in describing and defining the new invention. In re Fisher, 427 F.2d 833, 166 USPQ 18 (CCPA 1970). Although it is difficult to compare the claimed invention with the prior art when new terms are used that do not appear in the prior art, this does not make the new terms indefinite.

New terms are often used when a new technology is in its infancy or is rapidly evolving. The requirements for clarity and precision must be balanced with the limitations of the language and the science. If the claims, read in light of the specification, reasonably apprise those skilled in the art both of the utilization and scope of the invention, and if the language is as precise as the subject matter permits, the statute (35 U.S.C. 112, second paragraph) demands no more. Shatterproof Glass Corp. v. Libbey Owens Ford Co., 758 F.2d 613, 225 USPQ 634 (Fed. Cir. 1985) (interpretation of "freely supporting" in method claims directed to treatment of a glass sheet); Hybritech, Inc. v. Monoclonal Antibodies,

Inc., 802 F.2d 1367, 231 USPQ 81 (Fed. Cir. 1986) (interpretation of a limitation specifying a numerical value for antibody affinity where the method of calculation was known in the art at the time of filing to be imprecise). This does not mean that the examiner must accept the best effort of applicant. If the proposed language is not considered as precise as the subject matter permits, the examiner should provide reasons to support the conclusion of indefiniteness and is encouraged to suggest alternatives that are free from objection.

A TERM MAY NOT BE GIVEN A MEANING REPUGNANT TO ITS USUAL MEANING

While a term used in the claims may be given a special meaning in the description of the invention, generally no term may be given a meaning repugnant to the usual meaning of the term. In re Hill, 161 F.2d 367, 73 USPQ 482 (CCPA 1947). However, it has been stated that consistent with the well-established axiom in patent law that a patentee is free to be his or her own lexicographer, a patentee may use terms in a manner contrary to or inconsistent with one or more of their ordinary meanings. Hormone Research Foundation Inc. v. Genentech Inc., 904 F.2d 1558, 15 USPQ2d 1039 (Fed. Cir. 1990). Accordingly, when there is more than one definition for a term, it is incumbent upon applicant to make clear which definition is being relied upon to claim the invention. Until the meaning of a term or phrase used in a claim is clear, a rejection under 35 U.S.C. 112, second paragraph is appropriate. It is appropriate to compare the meaning of terms given in technical dictionaries in order to ascertain the accepted meaning of a term in the art. In re Barr, 444 F.2d 588, 170 USPQ 330 (CCPA 1971).

2173.05(b) Relative Terminology

The fact that claim language, including terms of degree, may not be precise, does not automatically render the claim indefinite under 35 U.S.C. 112, second paragraph. Seattle Box Co., v. Industrial Crating & Packing, Inc., 731 F.2d 818, 221 USPQ 568 (Fed. Cir. 1984). Acceptability of the claim language depends on whether one of ordinary skill in the art would understand what is claimed, in light of the specification.

WHEN A TERM OF DEGREE IS PRESENT, DETERMINE WHETHER A STANDARD IS DISCLOSED OR WHETHER ONE OF ORDINARY SKILL IN THE ART WOULD BE APPRISED OF THE SCOPE OF THE CLAIM

When a term of degree is presented in a claim, first a determination is to be made as to whether the specification provides some standard for measuring that degree. If it does not, a determination is made as to whether one of ordinary skill in the art, in view of the prior art and the status of the art, would be nevertheless reasonably apprised of the scope of the invention. Even if the specification uses the same term of degree as in the claim, a rejection may be proper if the scope of the term is not understood when read in light of the specification. While, as a general proposition, broadening modifiers are standard tools in claim drafting in order to avoid reliance on the doctrine of equivalents in infringement actions, when the scope of the claim is unclear a rejection under 35 U.S.C. 112, second paragraph is proper. See In re Wiggins, 488 F. 2d 538, 541, 179 USPQ 421, 423 (CCPA 1973).

When relative terms are used in claims wherein the improvement over the prior art rests entirely upon size or weight of an element in a combination of elements, the adequacy of the disclosure of a standard is of greater criticality.

REFERENCE TO AN OBJECT THAT IS VARIABLE MAY RENDER A CLAIM INDEFINITE

A claim may be rendered indefinite by reference to an object that is variable. For example, the Board has held that a limitation in a claim to a bicycle that recited "said front and rear wheels so spaced as to give a wheelbase that is between 58 percent and 75 percent of the height of the rider that the bicycle was designed for" was indefinite because the relationship of parts was not based on any known standard for sizing a bicycle to a rider, but on a rider of unspecified build. Ex parte Brummer, 12 USPQ2d 1653 (Bd. Pat. App. & Inter. 1989). On the other hand, a claim limitation specifying that a certain part of a pediatric wheelchair be "so dimensioned as to be insertable through the space between the doorframe of an automobile and one of the seats" was held to be definite. Orthokinetics, Inc. v. Safety Travel Chairs, Inc., 806 F.2d 1565, 1 USPQ2d 1081 (Fed. Cir. 1986). The court stated that the phrase "so dimensioned" is as accurate as the subject matter permits, noting that the patent law does not require that all possible lengths corresponding to the spaces in hundreds of different automobiles be listed in the patent, let alone that they be listed in the claims.

A. "About"

The term "about" used to define the area of the lower end of a mold as between 25 to about 45% of the mold entrance was held to be clear, but flexible. Ex parte Eastwood, 163 USPQ 316 (Bd. App. 1968). Similarly, in W.L. Gore & Associates, Inc. v. Garlock, Inc., 721 F.2d 1540, 220 USPQ 303 (Fed. Cir. 1983), the court held that a limitation defining the stretch rate of a plastic as "exceeding about 10% per second" is definite because infringement could clearly be assessed through the use of a stopwatch. However, the court held that claims reciting "at least about" were invalid for indefiniteness where there was close prior art and there was nothing in the specification, prosecution history, or the prior art to provide any indication as to what range of specific activity is covered by the term "about." Amgen, Inc. v. Chugai Pharmaceutical Co., 927 F.2d 1200, 18 USPQ2d 1016 (Fed. Cir. 1991).

B. "Essentially"

The phrase "a silicon dioxide source that is essentially free of alkali metal" was held to be definite because the specification contained guidelines and examples that were considered sufficient to enable a person of ordinary skill in the art to draw a line between unavoidable impurities in starting materials and essential ingredients. In re Marosi, 710 F.2d 799, 218 USPQ 289 (CCPA 1983). The court further observed that it would be impractical to require applicants to specify a particular number as a cutoff between their invention and the prior art.

C. "Similar"

The term "similar" in the preamble of a claim that was directed to a nozzle "for high-pressure cleaning units or similar apparatus" was held to be indefinite since it was not clear what applicant intended to cover by the recitation "similar" apparatus. Ex parte Kristensen, 10 USPQ2d 1701 (Bd. Pat. App. & Inter. 1989).

A claim in a design patent application which read: "The ornamental design for a feed bunk or similar structure as shown and described." was held to be indefinite because it was unclear from the specification what applicant intended to cover by the recitation of "similar structure." Ex parte Pappas, 23 USPQ2d 1636 (Bd. Pat. App. & Inter. 1992).

D. "Substantially"

The term "substantially" is often used in conjunction with another term to describe a particular characteristic of the claimed invention. It is a broad term. In re Nehrenberg, 280 F.2d 161, 126 USPQ 383 (CCPA 1960). The court held that the limitation "to substantially increase the efficiency of the compound as a copper extractant" was definite in view of the general guidelines contained in the specification. In re Mattison, 509 F.2d 563, 184 USPQ 484 (CCPA 1975). The court held that the limitation "which produces substantially equal E and H plane illumination patterns" was definite because one of ordinary skill in the art would know what was meant by "substantially equal." Andrew Corp. v. Gabriel Electronics, 847 F.2d 819, 6 USPQ2d 2010 (Fed. Cir. 1988).

E. "Type"

The addition of the word "type" to an otherwise definite expression (e.g., Friedel-Crafts catalyst) extends the scope of the expression so as to render it indefinite. Ex parte Copenhaver, 109 USPQ 118 (Bd. App. 1955). Likewise, the phrase "ZSM-5-type aluminosilicate zeolites" was held to be indefinite because it was unclear what "type" was intended to convey. The interpretation was made more difficult by the fact that the zeolites defined in the dependent claims were not within the genus of the type of zeolites defined in the independent claim. Ex parte Attig, 7 USPQ2d 1092 (Bd. Pat. App. & Inter. 1986).

F. Other Terms

The phrases "relatively shallow," "of the order of," "the order of about 5mm," and "substantial portion" were held to be indefinite because the specification lacked some standard for measuring the degree intended and, therefore, properly rejected as indefinite under 35 U.S.C. 112, second paragraph. Ex parte Oetiker, 23 USPQ2d 1641 (Bd. Pat. App. & Inter. 1992).

The term "or like material" in the context of the limitation "coke, brick, or like material" was held to render the claim indefinite since it was not clear how the materials other than coke or brick had to resemble the two specified materials to satisfy the limitations of the claim. Ex parte Caldwell, 1906 C.D. 58 (Comm'r Pat. 1906).

The terms "comparable" and "superior" were held to be indefinite in the context of a limitation relating the characteristics of the claimed material to other materials — "properties that are superior to those obtained with comparable" prior art materials. Ex parte Anderson, 21 USPQ2d 1241 (Bd. Pat. App. & Inter. 1991). It was not clear from the specification which properties had to be compared and how comparable the properties would have to be to determine infringement issues. Further, there was no guidance as to the meaning of the term "superior."

2173.05(c)   Numerical Ranges and Amounts Limitations

Generally, the recitation of specific numerical ranges in a claim does not raise an issue of whether a claim is definite.

I. NARROW AND BROADER RANGES IN THE SAME CLAIM

Use of a narrow numerical range that falls within a broader range in the same claim may render the claim indefinite when the boundaries of the claim are not discernible. Description of examples and preferences is properly set forth in the specification rather than in the claims. If stated in the claims, examples and preferences lead to confusion over the intended scope of a claim. In those instances where it is not clear whether the claimed narrower range is a limitation, a rejection under 35 U.S.C. 112, second paragraph should be made. The Examiner should analyze whether the metes and bounds of the claim are clearly set forth. Examples of claim language which have been held to be indefinite are (A) "a temperature of between 45 and 78 degrees Celsius, preferably between 50 and 60 degrees Celsius"; and (B) "a predetermined quantity, for example, the maximum capacity."

II. OPEN-ENDED NUMERICAL RANGES

Open-ended numerical ranges should be carefully analyzed for definiteness. For example, when an independent claim recites a composition comprising "at least 20% sodium" and a dependent claim sets forth specific amounts of nonsodium ingredients which add up to 100%, apparently to the exclusion of sodium, an ambiguity is created with regard to the "at least" limitation (unless the percentages of the nonsodium ingredients are based on the weight of the nonsodium ingredients). On the other hand, the court held that a composition claimed to have a theoretical content greater than 100% (i.e., 20-80% of A, 20-80% of B, and 1-25% of C) was not indefinite simply because the claims may be read in theory to include compositions that are impossible in fact to formulate. It was observed that subject matter which cannot exist in fact can neither anticipate nor infringe a claim. In re Kroekel, 504 F.2d 1143, 183 USPQ 610 (CCPA 1974).

In a claim directed to a chemical reaction process, a limitation required that the amount of one ingredient in the reaction mixture should "be maintained at less than 7 mole percent" based on the amount of another ingredient. The examiner argued that the claim was indefinite because the limitation sets only a maximum amount and is inclusive of substantially no ingredient resulting in termination of any reaction. The court did not agree be cause the claim was clearly directed to a reaction process which did not warrant distorting the overall meaning of the claim to preclude performing the claimed process. In re Kirsch, 498 F.2d 1389, 182 USPQ 286 (CCPA 1974).

Some terms have been determined to have the following meanings in the factual situations of the reported cases: the term "up to" includes zero as a lower limit, In re Mochel, 470 F.2d 638, 176 USPQ 194 (CCPA 1974); and "a moisture content of not more than 70% by weight" reads on dry material, Ex parte Khusid, 174 USPQ 59 (Bd. App. 1971).

III. "EFFECTIVE AMOUNT"

The common phrase "an effective amount" may or may not be indefinite. The proper test is whether or not one skilled in the art could determine specific values for the amount based on the disclosure. See In re Mattison, 509 F.2d 563, 184 USPQ 484 (CCPA 1975). The phrase "an effective amount . . . for growth stimulation" was held to be definite where the amount was not critical and those skilled in the art would be able to determine from the written disclosure, including the examples, what an effective amount is. In re Halleck, 422 F.2d 911, 164 USPQ 647 (CCPA 1970). The phrase "an effective amount" has been held to be indefinite when the claim fails to state the function which is to be achieved and more than one effect can be implied from the specification or the relevant art. In re Fredericksen 213 F.2d 547, 102 USPQ 35 (CCPA 1954). The more recent cases have tended to accept a limitation such as "an effective amount" as being definite when read in light of the supporting disclosure and in the absence of any prior art which would give rise to uncertainty about the scope of the claim. In Ex parte Skuballa, 12 USPQ2d 1570 (Bd. Pat. App. & Inter. 1989), the Board held that a pharmaceutical composition claim which recited an "effective amount of a compound of claim 1" without stating the function to be achieved was definite, particularly when read in light of the supporting disclosure which provided guidelines as to the intended utilities and how the uses could be effected.

2173.05(d) Exemplary Claim Language ("for example," "such as")

Description of examples or preferences is properly set forth in the specification rather than the claims. If stated in the claims, examples and preferences lead to confusion over the intended scope of a claim. In those instances where it is not clear whether the claimed narrower range is a limitation, a rejection under 35 U.S.C. 112, second paragraph should be made. The Examiner should analyze whether the metes and bounds of the claim are clearly set forth. Examples of claim language which have been held to be indefinite because the intended scope of the claim was unclear are:

(A) "R is halogen, for example, chlorine";

(B) "material such as rock wool or asbestos" Ex parte Hall, 83 USPQ 38 (Bd. App. 1949);

(C) "lighter hydrocarbons, such, for example, as the vapors or gas produced" Ex parte Hasche, 86 USPQ 481 (Bd. App. 1949); and

(D) "normal operating conditions such as while in the container of a proportioner" Ex parte Steigerwald, 131 USPQ 74 (Bd. App. 1961).

2173.05(e) Lack of Antecedent Basis

A claim is indefinite when it contains words or phrases whose meaning is unclear. The lack of clarity could arise where a claim refers to "said lever" or "the lever," where the claim contains no earlier recitation or limitation of a lever and where it would be unclear as to what element the limitation was making reference. Similarly, if two different levers are recited earlier in the claim, the recitation of "said lever" in the same or subsequent claim would be unclear where it is uncertain which of the two levers was intended. A claim which refers to "said aluminum lever," but recites only "a lever" earlier in the claim, is indefinite because it is uncertain as to the lever to which reference is made. Obviously, however, the failure to provide explicit antecedent basis for terms does not always render a claim indefinite. If the scope of a claim would be reasonably ascertainable by those skilled in the art, then the claim is not indefinite. Ex parte Porter, 25 USPQ2d 1144, 1145 (Bd. Pat. App. & Inter. 1992) ("controlled stream of fluid" provided reasonable antecedent basis for "the controlled fluid"). Inherent components of elements recited have antecedent basis in the recitation of the components themselves. For example, the limitation "the outer surface of said sphere" would not require an antecedent recitation that the sphere has an outer surface.

EXAMINER SHOULD SUGGEST CORRECTIONS TO ANTECEDENT PROBLEMS

Antecedent problems in the claims are typically drafting oversights that are easily corrected once they are brought to the attention of applicant. The examiner's task of making sure the claim language complies with the requirements of the statute should be carried out in a positive and constructive way, so that minor problems can be identified and easily corrected, and so that the major effort is expended on more substantive issues. However, even though indefiniteness in claim language is of semantic origin, it is not rendered unobjectionable simply because it could have been corrected. In re Hammack, 427 F.2d 1384 n.5, 166 USPQ 209 n.5 (CCPA 1970).

A CLAIM TERM WHICH HAS NO ANTECEDENT BASIS IN THE DISCLOSURE IS NOT NECESSARILY INDEFINITE

The mere fact that a term or phrase used in the claim has no antecedent basis in the specification disclosure does not mean, necessarily, that the term or phrase is indefinite. There is no requirement that the words in the claim must match those used in the specification disclosure. Applicants are given a great deal of latitude in how they choose to define their invention so long as the terms and phrases used define the invention with a reasonable degree of clarity and precision.

2173.05(f)   Reference to Limitations in Another Claim

A claim which makes reference to a preceding claim to define a limitation is an acceptable claim construction which should not necessarily be rejected as improper or confusing under 35 U.S.C. 112, second paragraph. For example, claims which read: "The product produced by the method of claim 1." or "A method of producing ethanol comprising contacting amylose with the culture of claim 1 under the following conditions ....." are not indefinite under 35 U.S.C. 112, second paragraph, merely because of the reference to another claim. See also Ex parte Porter, 25 USPQ2d 1144 (Bd. Pat. App. & Inter. 1992) where reference to "the nozzle of claim 7" in a method claim was held to comply with 35 U.S.C. 112, second paragraph. However, where the format of making reference to limitations recited in another claim results in confusion, then a rejection would be proper under 35 U.S.C. 112, second paragraph.

2173.05(g)   Functional Limitations

A functional limitation is an attempt to define something by what it does, rather than by what it is (e.g., as evidenced by its specific structure or specific ingredients). There is nothing inherently wrong with defining some part of an invention in functional terms. Functional language does not, in and of itself, render a claim improper. In re Swinehart, 439 F.2d 210, 169 USPQ 226 (CCPA 1971).

A functional limitation must be evaluated and considered, just like any other limitation of the claim, for what it fairly conveys to a person of ordinary skill in the pertinent art in the context in which it is used. A functional limitation is often used in association with an element, ingredient, or step of a process to define a particular capability or purpose that is served by the recited element, ingredient or step. Whether or not the functional limitation complies with 35 U.S.C. 112, second paragraph is a different issue from whether the limitation is properly supported under 35 U.S.C. 112, first paragraph or is distinguished over the prior art. A few examples are set forth below to illustrate situations where the issue of whether a functional limitation complies with 35 U.S.C. 112, second paragraph was considered.

It was held that the limitation used to define a radical on a chemical compound as "incapable of forming a dye with said oxidizing developing agent" although functional, was perfectly acceptable because it set definite boundaries on the patent protection sought. In re Barr, 444 F.2d 588, 170 USPQ 33 (CCPA 1971).

In a claim that was directed to a kit of component parts capable of being assembled, the Court held that limitations such as "members adapted to be positioned" and "portions . . . being resiliently dilatable whereby said housing may be slidably positioned" serve to precisely define present structural attributes of interrelated component parts of the claimed assembly. In re Venezia, 530 F.2d 956, 189 USPQ 149 (CCPA 1976).

2173.05(h) Alternative Limitations

I. MARKUSH GROUPS

Alternative expressions are permitted if they present no uncertainty or ambiguity with respect to the question of scope or clarity of the claims. One acceptable form of alternative expression, which is commonly referred to as a Markush group, recites members as being "selected from the group consisting of A, B and C." See Ex parte Markush, 1925 C.D. 126 (Comm'r Pat. 1925).

Ex parte Markush sanctions claiming a genus expressed as a group consisting of certain specified materials. Inventions in metallurgy, refractories, ceramics, pharmacy, pharmacology and biology are most frequently claimed under the Markush formula but purely mechanical features or process steps may also be claimed by using the Markush style of claiming. See Ex parte Head, 214 USPQ 551 (Bd. App. 1981); In re Gaubert, 524 F.2d 1222, 187 USPQ 664 (CCPA 1975); and In re Harnisch, 631 F.2d 716, 206 USPQ 300 (CCPA 1980). It is improper to use the term "comprising" instead of "consisting of." Ex parte Dotter, 12 USPQ 382 (Bd. App. 1931).

The use of Markush claims of diminishing scope should not, in itself, be considered a sufficient basis for objection to or rejection of claims. However, if such a practice renders the claims indefinite or if it results in undue multiplicity, an appropriate rejection should be made.

Similarly, the double inclusion of an element by members of a Markush group is not, in itself, sufficient basis for objection to or rejection of claims. Rather, the facts in each case must be evaluated to determine whether or not the multiple inclusion of one or more elements in a claim renders that claim indefinite. The mere fact that a compound may be embraced by more than one member of a Markush group recited in the claim does not necessarily render the scope of the claim unclear. For example, the Markush group, "selected from the group consisting of amino, halogen, nitro, chloro and alkyl" should be acceptable even though "halogen" is generic to "chloro."

The materials set forth in the Markush group ordinarily must belong to a recognized physical or chemical class or to an art-recognized class. However, when the Markush group occurs in a claim reciting a process or a combination (not a single compound), it is sufficient if the members of the group are disclosed in the specification to possess at least one property in common which is mainly responsible for their function in the claimed relationship, and it is clear from their very nature or from the prior art that all of them possess this property. While in the past the test for Markush-type claims was applied as liberally as possible, present practice which holds that claims reciting Markush groups are not generic claims (MPEP § 803) may subject the groups to a more stringent test for propriety of the recited members. Where a Markush expression is applied only to a portion of a chemical compound, the propriety of the grouping is determined by a consideration of the compound as a whole, and does not depend on there being a community of properties in the members of the Markush expression.

When materials recited in a claim are so related as to constitute a proper Markush group, they may be recited in the conventional manner, or alternatively. For example, if "wherein R is a material selected from the group consisting of A, B, C and D" is a proper limitation, then "wherein R is A, B, C or D" shall also be considered proper.

Subgenus Claim

A situation may occur in which a patentee has presented a number of examples which, in the examiner's opinion, are sufficiently representative to support a generic claim and yet a court may subsequently hold the claim invalid on the ground of undue breadth. Where this happens the patentee is often limited to species claims which may not provide him with suitable protection.

The allowance of a Markush-type claim under a true genus claim would appear to be beneficial to the applicant without imposing any undue burden on the Patent and Trademark Office or in any way detracting from the rights of the public. Such a subgenus claim would enable the applicant to claim all the disclosed operative embodiments and afford applicant an intermediate level of protection in the event the true genus claims should be subsequently held invalid.

The examiners are therefore instructed not to reject a Markush-type claim merely because of the presence of a true genus claim embracive thereof.

See also MPEP § 608.01(p) and § 715.03.

See MPEP § 803.02 for restriction practice re Markush-type claims.

II. "OR" TERMINOLOGY

Alternative expressions using "or" are acceptable, such as "wherein R is A, B, C, or D." The following phrases were each held to be acceptable and not in violation of 35 U.S.C. 112, second paragraph in In re Gaubert, 524 F.2d 1222, 187 USPQ 664 (CCPA 1975): "made entirely or in part of"; "at least one piece"; and "iron, steel or any other magnetic material."

III. "OPTIONALLY"

An alternative format which requires some analysis before concluding whether or not the language is indefinite involves the use of the term "optionally." In Ex parte Cordova, 10 USPQ2d 1949 (Bd. Pat. App. & Inter. 1989) the language "containing A, B, and optionally C" was considered acceptable alternative language because there was no ambiguity as to which alternatives are covered by the claim. A similar holding was reached with regard to the term "optionally" in Ex parte Wu, 10 USPQ2d 2031 (Bd. Pat. App. & Inter. 1989). In the instance where the list of potential alternatives can vary and ambiguity arises, then it is proper to make a rejection under 35 U.S.C. 112, second paragraph and explain why there is confusion.

2173.05(i) Negative Limitations

The current view of the courts is that there is nothing inherently ambiguous or uncertain about a negative limitation. So long as the boundaries of the patent protection sought are set forth definitely, albeit negatively, the claim complies with the requirements of 35

U.S.C. 112, second paragraph. Some older cases were critical of negative limitations because they tended to define the invention in terms of what it was not, rather than pointing out the invention. Thus, the court observed that the limitation "R is an alkenyl radical other than 2-butenyl and 2,4-pentadienyl" was a negative limitation that rendered the claim indefinite because it was an attempt to claim the invention by excluding what the inventors did not invent rather than distinctly and particularly pointing out what they did invent. In re Schechter, 205 F.2d 185, 98 USPQ 144 (CCPA 1953).

A claim which recited the limitation "said homopolymer being free from the proteins, soaps, resins, and sugars present in natural Hevea rubber" in order to exclude the characteristics of the prior art product, was considered definite because each recited limitation was definite. In re Wakefield, 422 F.2d 897, 899, 904, 164 USPQ 636, 638, 641 (CCPA 1970). In addition, the court found that the negative limitation "incapable of forming a dye with said oxidized developing agent" was definite because the boundaries of the patent protection sought were clear. In re Barr, 444 F.2d 588, 170 USPQ 330 (CCPA 1971).

Any negative limitation or exclusionary proviso must have basis in the original disclosure. See Ex parte Grasselli, 231 USPQ 393 (Bd. App. 1983), aff'd mem., 738 F.2d 453 (Fed. Cir. 1984). The mere absence of a positive recitation is not basis for an exclusion. Any claim containing a negative limitation which does not have basis in the original disclosure should be rejected under 35 U.S.C. 112, first paragraph as failing to comply with the written description requirement. Note that a lack of literal basis in the specification for a negative limitation may not be sufficient to establish a prima facie case for lack of descriptive support. Ex parte Parks, 30 USPQ2d 1234, 1236 (Bd. Pat. App. & Inter. 1993). See MPEP § 2163–§ 2163.07(b) for a discussion of the written description requirement of 35 U.S.C. 112, first paragraph.

2173.05(j) Old Combination

A CLAIM SHOULD NOT BE REJECTED ON THE GROUND OF OLD COMBINATION

With the passage of the 1952 Patent Act, the courts and the Board have taken the view that a rejection based on the principle of old combination is NO LONGER VALID. Claims should be considered proper so long as they comply with the provisions of 35 U.S.C. 112, second paragraph.

A rejection on the basis of old combination was based on the principle applied in Lincoln Engineering Co. v. Stewart-Warner Corp., 303 U.S. 545, 37 USPQ 1 (1938). The principle was that an inventor who made an improvement or contribution to but one element of a generally old combination, should not be able to obtain a patent on the entire combination including the new and improved element. A rejection required the citation of a single reference which broadly disclosed a combination of the claimed elements functionally cooperating in substantially the same manner to produce substantially the same results as that of the claimed combination. The case of In re Hall, 208 F.2d 370, 100 USPQ 46 (CCPA 1953) illustrates an application of this principle.

The court pointed out in In re Bernhardt, 417 F.2d 1395, 163 USPQ 611 (CCPA 1969) that the statutory language (particularly point out and distinctly claim) is the only proper basis for an old combination rejection, and in applying the rejection, that language determines what an applicant has a right and obligation to do. A majority opinion of the Board of Appeals held that Congress removed the underlying rationale of Lincoln Engineering in the 1952 Patent Act, and thereby effectively legislated that decision out of existence. Ex parte Barber, 187 USPQ 244 (Bd. App. 1974). Finally, the Court of Appeals for the Federal Circuit, in Radio Steel and Mfg. Co. v. MTD Products, Inc., 731 F.2d 840, 221 USPQ 657 (Fed. Cir. 1984), followed the Bernhardt case, and ruled that a claim was not invalid under Lincoln Engineering because the claim complied with the requirements of 35 U.S.C. 112, second paragraph. Accordingly, a claim should not be rejected on the ground of old combination.

2173.05(k) Aggregation

Rejections on the ground of aggregation should be based upon a lack of cooperation between the elements of the claim.

Example of aggregation: A washing machine associated with a dial telephone.

A claim is not necessarily aggregative because the various elements do not function simultaneously, e.g., a typewriter. In re Worrest, 201 F.2d 930, 96 USPQ 381 (CCPA 1953). Neither is a claim necessarily aggregative merely because elements which do cooperate are set forth in specific detail.

A rejection on aggregation should be made only after consideration of the court's comments in In re Gustafson, 331 F.2d 905, 141 USPQ 585 (CCPA 1964), wherein the court indicated it is improper to reject claims as "aggregative" without specifying the statutory basis of the rejection, i.e., an applicant is entitled to know whether his claims are being rejected under 35 U.S.C. 101, 103, or 112. In Gustafson, the court found that the real objection to the claims was that they failed to comply with 35 U.S.C. 112, second paragraph.

[no 2173.05(l)]

2173.05(m) Prolix

Examiners should reject claims as prolix only when they contain such long recitations or unimportant details that the scope of the claimed invention is rendered indefinite thereby. Claims are rejected as prolix when they contain long recitations or unimportant details which hide or obscure the invention. Ex parte Iagan, 1911 C.D. 10, 162 O.G. 538 (Comm'r Pat. 1910), expresses the thought that very long detailed claims setting forth so many elements that invention cannot possibly reside in the combination should be rejected as prolix. See also In re Ludwick, 4 F.2d 959, 1925 C.D. 306, 339 O.G. 393 (D.C. Cir. 1925).

2173.05(n) Multiplicity

37 CFR 1.75. Claim(s).

(a) The specification must conclude with a claim particularly pointing out and distinctly claiming the subject matter which the applicant regards as his invention or discovery.

(b) More than one claim may be presented provided they differ substantially from each other and are not unduly multiplied.

(c) One or more claims may be presented in dependent form, referring back to and further limiting another claim or claims in the same application. Any dependent claim which refers to more than one other claim ("multiple dependent claim") shall refer to such other claims in the alternative only. A multiple dependent claim shall not serve as a basis for any other multiple dependent claim. For fee calculation purposes under § 1.16, a multiple dependent claim will be considered to be that number of claims to which direct reference is made therein. For fee calculation purposes, also, any claim depending from a multiple dependent claim will be considered to be that number of claims to which direct reference is made in that multiple dependent claim. In addition to the other filing fees, any original application which is filed with, or is amended to include, multiple dependent claims must have paid the fee set forth in § 1.16(d). Claims in dependent form shall be construed to include all the limitations of the claim incorporated by reference into the dependent claim. A multiple dependent claim shall be construed to incorporate by reference all the limitations of each of the particular claims In relation to which it is being considered.

(d) (1) The claim or claims must conform to the invention as set forth in the remainder of the specification and the terms and phrases used in the claims must find clear support or antecedent basis in the description so that the meaning of the terms may be ascertained by reference to the description (See § 1.58(a)).

(2) See §§ 1.141 to 1.146 as to claiming different inventions in one application.

(e) Where the nature of the case admits, as in the case of an improvement, any independent claim should contain in the following order, (1) a preamble comprising a general description of all elements or steps of the claimed combination which are conventional or known, (2) a phrase such as "wherein the improvement comprises," and (3) those elements, steps, and/or relationships which constitute that portion of the claimed combination which the applicant regards as the new or improved portion.

(f) If there are several claims, they shall be numbered consecutively in Arabic numerals.

(g) The least restrictive claim should be presented as claim number 1, and all dependent claims should be grouped together with the claim or claims to which they refer to the extent practicable.

(h) The claim or claims must commence on a separate sheet.

(i) Where a claim sets forth a plurality of elements or steps, each element or step of the claim should be separated by a line indentation.

An unreasonable number of claims, that is, unreasonable in view of the nature and scope of applicant's invention and the state of the art, may afford a basis for a rejection on the ground of multiplicity. A rejection on this ground should include all the claims in the case inasmuch as it relates to confusion of the issue.

To avoid the possibility that an application which has been rejected on the ground of undue multiplicity of claims may be appealed to the Board of Patent Appeals and Interferences prior to an examination on the merits of at least some of the claims presented, the examiner should, at the time of making the rejection on the ground of multiplicity of claims, specify the number of claims which in his or her judgment is sufficient to properly define applicant's invention and require the applicant to select certain claims, not to exceed the number specified, for examination on the merits. The examiner should be reasonable in setting the number to afford the applicant some latitude in claiming the invention.

The earlier views of the Court of Customs and Patent Appeals on multiplicity were set forth in In re Chandler, 254 F.2d 396, 117 USPQ 361 (1958) and In re Chandler, 319 F.2d 211, 225, 138 USPQ 138, 148 (1963) (Applicant's latitude in stating their claims in regard to number and phraseology employed "should not be extended to sanction that degree of repetition and multiplicity which beclouds definition in a maze of confusion."). These views have been somewhat revised by its views in In re Flint, 411 F.2d 1353, 1357, 162 USPQ 228, 231 (CCPA 1969) ("The [42] claims differed from one another and we have no difficulty in understanding the scope of protection. Nor is it clear, on this record, that the examiner or board was confused by the presentation of claims in this case or that the public will be.") and In re Wakefield, 422 F.2d 897, 902, 164 USPQ 636, 639 (CCPA 1970) ("Examination of forty claims in a single application may be tedious work, but this is no reason for saying that the invention is obscured by the large number of claims. We note that the claims were clear enough for the examiner to apply references against all of them in his first action.").

If a rejection on multiplicity is in order the examiner should make a telephone call explaining that the claims are unduly multiplied and will be rejected on that ground. Note MPEP § 408. The examiner should request selection of a specified number of claims for purposes of examination.

If time for consideration is requested arrangements should be made for a second telephone call, preferably within three working days.

When claims are selected, a formal multiplicity rejection is made, including a complete record of the telephone interview, followed by an action on the selected claims.

When applicant refuses to comply with the telephone request, a formal multiplicity rejection is made. The applicant's reply to a formal multiplicity rejection of the examiner, to be complete, must either:

> (A) Reduce the number of claims presented to those selected previously by telephone, or if no previous selection has been made to a number not exceeding the number specified by the examiner in the Office action, thus overcoming the rejection based upon the ground of multiplicity, or

> (B) In the event of a traverse of said rejection applicant, besides specifically pointing out the supposed errors of the multiplicity rejection, is required to confirm the selection previously made by telephone, or if no previous selection has been made, select certain claims for purpose of examination, the number of which is not greater than the number specified by the examiner.

If the rejection on multiplicity is adhered to, all claims retained will be included in such rejection and the selected claims only will be additionally examined on their merits. This procedure preserves applicant's right to have the rejection on multiplicity reviewed by the Board of Patent Appeals and Interferences.

Also, it is possible to reject one claim on an allowed claim if they differ only by subject matter old in the art. This ground of rejection is set forth in Ex parte Whitelaw, 1915 C.D. 18, 219 O.G. 1237 (Comm'r Pat. 1914). The Ex parte Whitelaw doctrine is restricted to cases where the claims are unduly multiplied or are substantial duplicates. Ex parte Kochan, 131 USPQ 204, 206 (Bd. App. 1961).

2173.05(o) Double Inclusion

While the concept that double inclusion of an element in members of a Markush group recited in a claim is, per se, objectionable and renders a claim indefinite is supported by some of the older cases like Ex parte White, 759 O.G. 783 (Bd. App. 1958) and Ex parte Clark, 174 USPQ 40 (Bd. App. 1971), other decisions clearly hold that there is no per se rule of indefiniteness concerning overlapping members where alternatives are recited in a claim, e.g., members of a Markush group. In re Kelly, 305 F.2d 909, 134 USPQ 397 (CCPA 1962).

The facts in each case must be evaluated to determine whether or not the multiple inclusion of one or more elements in a claim gives rise to indefiniteness in that claim. The mere fact that a compound may be embraced by more than one member of a Markush group recited in the claim does not lead to any uncertainty as to the scope of that claim for either examination or infringement purposes. On the other hand, where a claim directed to a device can be read to include the same element twice, the claim may be indefinite. Ex parte Kristensen, 10 USPQ2d 1701 (Bd. Pat. App. & Inter. 1989).

2173.05(p) Claim Directed to Product-By-Process or Product and Process

I. PRODUCT-BY-PROCESS

There are many situations where claims are permissively drafted to include a reference to more than one statutory class of invention. A product-by-process claim, which is a product claim that defines the claimed product in terms of the process by which it is made, is proper. In re Moeller, 117 F.2d 565, 48 USPQ 542

(CCPA 1941); In re Luck, 476 F.2d 650, 177 USPQ 523 (CCPA 1973); In re Steppan, 394 F.2d 1013, 156 USPQ 143 (CCPA 1967); and In re Pilkington, 411 F.2d 1345, 162 USPQ 145 (CCPA 1969). A claim to a device, apparatus, manufacture, or composition of matter may contain a reference to the process in which it is intended to be used without being objectionable under 35 U.S.C. 112, second paragraph, so long as it is clear that the claim is directed to the product and not the process.

The fact that it is necessary for an applicant to describe his product in product-by-process terms does not prevent him from presenting claims of varying scope. Ex parte Pantzer, 176 USPQ 141 (Bd. App. 1972).

II. PRODUCT AND PROCESS IN THE SAME CLAIM

A single claim which claims both an apparatus and the method steps of using the apparatus is indefinite under 35 U.S.C. 112, second paragraph. In Ex parte Lyell, 17 USPQ2d 1548 (Bd. Pat. App. & Inter. 1990), a claim directed to an automatic transmission workstand and the method steps of using it was held to be ambiguous and properly rejected under 35 U.S.C. 112, second paragraph.

Such claims should also be rejected under 35 U.S.C. 101 based on the theory that the claim is directed to neither a "process" nor a "machine," but rather embraces or overlaps two different statutory classes of invention set forth in 35 U.S.C. 101 which is drafted so as to set forth the statutory classes of invention in the alternative only. Id. at 1551.

2173.05(q)   "Use" Claims

Attempts to claim a process without setting forth any steps involved in the process generally raises an issue of indefiniteness under 35 U.S.C. 112, second paragraph. For example, a claim which read: "A process for using monoclonal antibodies of claim 4 to isolate and purify human fibroblast interferon." was held to be indefinite because it merely recites a use without any active, positive steps delimiting how this use is actually practiced. Ex parte Erlich,

3 USPQ2d 1011 (Bd. Pat. App. & Inter. 1986).

Other decisions suggest that a more appropriate basis for this type of rejection is 35 U.S.C. 101. In Ex parte Dunki, 153 USPQ 678 (Bd. App. 1967), the Board held the following claim to be an improper definition of a process: "The use of a high carbon austenitic iron alloy having a proportion of free carbon as a vehicle brake part subject to stress by sliding friction." In Clinical Products Ltd. v. Brenner, 255 F. Supp. 131, 149 USPQ 475 (D.D.C. 1966), the district court held the following claim was definite, but that it was not a proper process claim under 35 U.S.C. 101: "The use of a sustained release therapeutic agent in the body of ephedrine absorbed upon polystyrene sulfonic acid."

Although a claim should be interpreted in light of the specification disclosure, it is generally considered improper to read limitations contained in the specification into the claims. See In re Prater, 415 F.2d 1393, 162 USPQ 541 (CCPA 1969) and In re Winkhaus, 527 F.2d 637, 188 USPQ 129 (CCPA 1975), which discuss the premise that one cannot rely on the specification to impart limitations to the claim that are not recited in the claim.

A "USE" CLAIM SHOULD BE REJECTED UNDER ALTERNATIVE GROUNDS BASED ON 35 U.S.C 101 AND 112

In view of the split of authority as discussed above, the most appropriate course of action would be to reject a "use" claim under alternative grounds based on 35 U.S.C. 101 and 112.

BOARD HELD STEP OF "UTILIZING" WAS NOT INDEFINITE

It is often difficult to draw a fine line between what is permissible, and what is objectionable from the perspective of whether a claim is definite. In the case of Ex parte Porter, 25 USPQ2d 1144 (Bd. Pat. App. & Inter. 1992), the Board held that a claim which clearly recited the step of "utilizing" was not indefinite under 35 U.S.C. 112, second paragraph. (Claim was to "A method for unloading nonpacked, nonbridging and packed, bridging flowable particle catalyst and bead material from the opened end of a reactor tube which comprises utilizing the nozzle of claim 7.").

2173.05(r)   Omnibus Claim

Some applications are filed with an omnibus claim which reads as follows: A device substantially as shown and described. This claim should be rejected under 35 U.S.C. 112, second paragraph because it is indefinite in that it fails to point out what is included or excluded by the claim language. See Ex parte Fressola, 27 USPQ2d 1608 (Bd. Pat. App. & Inter. 1993), for a discussion of the history of omnibus claims and an explanation of why omnibus claims do not comply with the requirements of 35 U.S.C. 112, second paragraph.

Such a claim can be rejected using Form Paragraph 7.35. See MPEP § 706.03(d).

For cancelation of such a claim by examiner's amendment, see MPEP § 1302.04(b).

2173.05(s)   Reference to Figures or Tables

Where possible, claims are to be complete in themselves. Incorporation by reference to a specific figure or table "is permitted only in exceptional circumstances where there is no practical way to define the invention in words and where it is more concise to incorporate by reference than duplicating a drawing or table into the claim. Incorporation by reference is a necessity doctrine, not for applicant's convenience." Ex parte Fressola, 27 USPQ2d 1608, 1609 (Bd. Pat. App. & Inter. 1993) (citations omitted).

Reference characters corresponding to elements recited in the detailed description and the drawings may be used in conjunction with the recitation of the same element or group of elements in the claims. See MPEP § 608.01(m).

2173.05(t)   Chemical Formula

Claims to chemical compounds and compositions containing chemical compounds often use formulas that depict the chemical structure of the compound. These structures should not be considered indefinite nor speculative in the absence of evidence that the assigned formula is in error. The absence of corroborating spectroscopic or other data cannot be the basis for finding the structure indefinite. See Ex parte Morton, 134 USPQ 407 (Bd. App.

1961), and Ex parte Sobin, 139 USPQ 528 (Bd. App. 1962), in this regard.

A claim to a chemical compound is not indefinite merely because a structure is not presented or because a partial structure is presented. For example, the claim language at issue in In re Fisher, 427 F.2d 833, 166 USPQ 18 (CCPA 1970) referred to a chemical compound as a "polypeptide of at least 24 amino acids having the following sequence." A rejection under 35 U.S.C. 112, second paragraph for failure to identify the entire structure was reversed and the court held: "While the absence of such a limitation obviously broadens the claim and raises questions of sufficiency of disclosure, it does not render the claim indefinite." Chemical compounds may be claimed by a name that adequately describes the material to one skilled in the art. See Martin v. Johnson, 454 F.2d 746, 172 USPQ 391 (CCPA 1972). A compound of unknown structure may be claimed by a combination of physical and chemical characteristics. See Ex parte Brian, 118 USPQ 242 (Bd. App. 1958). A compound may also be claimed in terms of the process by which it is made without raising an issue of indefiniteness.

2173.05(u) Trademarks or Trade Names in a Claim

The presence of a trademark or trade name in a claim is not, per se, improper under 35 U.S.C. 112, second paragraph, but the claim should be carefully analyzed to determine how the mark or name is used in the claim. It is important to recognize that a trademark or trade name is used to identify a source of goods, and not the goods themselves. Thus a trademark or trade name does not identify or describe the goods associated with the trademark or trade name. See definitions of trademark and trade name in MPEP § 608.01(v). A list of some trademarks is found in Appendix I.

If the trademark or trade name is used in a claim as a limitation to identify or describe a particular material or product, the claim does not comply with the requirements of the 35 U.S.C. 112, second paragraph. Ex parte Simpson, 218 USPQ 1020 (Bd. App. 1982). The claim scope is uncertain since the trademark or trade name cannot be used properly to identify any particular material or product. In fact, the value of a trademark would be lost to the extent that it became descriptive of a product, rather than used as an identification of a source or origin of a product. Thus, the use of a trademark or trade name in a claim to identify or describe a material or product would not only render a claim indefinite, but would also constitute an improper use of the trademark or trade name.

If a trademark or trade name appears in a claim and is not intended as a limitation in the claim, the question of why it is in the claim should be addressed. Does its presence in the claim cause confusion as to the scope of the claim§ If so, the claim should be rejected under 35 U.S.C. 112, second paragraph.

2173.05(v)   Mere Function of Machine

In view of the decision of the Court of Customs and Patent Appeals in In re Tarczy-Hornoch, 397 F.2d 856, 158 USPQ 141 (CCPA 1968), process or method claims are not subject to rejection by Patent and Trademark Office examiners under 35 U.S.C. 112, second paragraph, solely on the ground that they define the inherent function of a disclosed machine or apparatus. The court in Tarczy-Hornoch held that a process claim, otherwise patentable, should not be rejected merely because the application of which it is part discloses apparatus which will inherently carry out the recited steps.

2181   Identifying a 35 U.S.C. 112, Sixth Paragraph Limitation [R-1]

The purpose of this section is to set forth guidelines for the examination of 35 U.S.C. 112, sixth paragraph "means or step plus function" limitations in a claim. The Court of Appeals for the Federal Circuit, in its en banc decision In re Donaldson Co., 16 F.3d 1189, 29 USPQ2d 1845 (Fed. Cir. 1994), decided that a "means-or-step-plus-function" limitation should be interpreted in a manner different than patent examining practice had previously dictated. The Donaldson decision affects only the manner in which the scope of a "means or step plus function" limitation in accordance with 35 U.S.C. 112, sixth paragraph, is interpreted during examination. Donaldson does not directly affect the manner in which any other section of the patent statutes is interpreted or applied.

When making a determination of patentability under 35 U.S.C. 102 or 103, past practice was to interpret a "means or step plus function" limitation by giving it the "broadest reasonable interpretation." Under the PTO's long-standing practice this meant interpreting such a limitation as reading on any prior art means or step which performed the function specified in the claim without regard for whether the prior art means or step was equivalent to the corresponding structure, material or acts described in the specification. However, in Donaldson, the Federal Circuit stated:

Per our holding, the "broadest reasonable interpretation" that an examiner may give means-plus-function language is that statutorily mandated in paragraph six. Accordingly, the PTO may not disregard the structure disclosed in the specification corresponding to such language when rendering a patentability determination.

LANGUAGE FALLING WITHIN 35 U.S.C. 112, SIXTH PARAGRAPH

** The PTO must apply 35 U.S.C. 112, sixth paragraph in appropriate cases, and give claims their broadest reasonable interpretation, in light of and consistent with the written description of the invention in the application. See Donaldson, 16 F.3d at 1194, 29 USPQ2d at 1850 (stating that 35 U.S.C. 112, sixth paragraph "merely sets a limit on how broadly the PTO may construe means-plus-function language under the rubric of 'reasonable interpretation.'"). The Federal Circuit has held that applicants (and reexamination patentees) before the PTO have the opportunity and the obligation to define their inventions precisely during proceedings before the PTO. See In re Morris, 127 F.3d 1048, 1056-57, 44 USPQ2d 1023, 1029-30 (Fed. Cir. 1997) (35 U.S.C. 112, second paragraph places the burden of precise claim drafting on the applicant); In re Zletz, 893 F.2d 319, 322, 13 USPQ2d 1320, 1322 (Fed. Cir. 1989) (manner of claim interpretation that is used by courts in litigation is not the manner of claim interpretation that is applicable during prosecution of a pending application before the PTO). Applicants and reexamination patentees before the PTO have an opportunity and obligation to specify, consistent with these guidelines, when a claim limitation invokes 35 U.S.C. 112, sixth paragraph.

A claim limitation will be interpreted to invoke 35 U.S.C. 112, sixth paragraph if it meets the following 3-prong analysis:

(A) the claim limitations must use the phrase "means for" or "step for";

(B) the "means for" or "step for" must be modified by functional language; and

(C) the phrase "means for" or "step for" must not be modified by structure, material or acts for achieving the specified function.

With respect to the first prong of this analysis, a claim element that does not include the phrase "means for" or "step for" will not be considered to invoke 35 U.S.C. 112, sixth paragraph. If an applicant wishes to have the claim limitation treated under 35 U.S.C. 112, sixth paragraph, applicant must either: (A) amend the claim to include the phrase "means for" or "step for" in accordance with these guidelines; or (B) show that even though the phrase "means for" or "step for" is not used, the claim limitation is written as a function to be performed and does not provide any structure, material, or acts which would preclude application of 35 U.S.C. 112, sixth paragraph. While traditional "means for" or "step for" language does not automatically make an element a means-(or step-) plus-function element, conversely, lack of such language does not prevent a limitation from being construed as a means-(or step-) plus-function limitation. See Signtech USA, Ltd. v. Vutek, Inc., 174 F.3d 1352, 1356, 50 USPQ2d 1372, 1374-75 (Fed. Cir. 1999) ("ink delivery means positioned on ?" invokes 35 U.S.C. 112, sixth paragraph since the phrase "ink delivery means" is equivalent to "means for ink delivery"); SealFlex, Inc. v. Athletic Track and Court Construction, 172 F.3d 836, 850, 50 USPQ2d 1225, 1234 (Fed. Cir. 1999) (Radar, J., concurring) ("claim elements without express step-plus-function language may nevertheless fall within 112 § 6 if they merely claim the underlying function without recitation of acts for performing that function?In general terms, the 'underlying function' of a method claim element corresponds to what that element ultimately accomplishes in relationship to what the other elements of the claim and the claim as a whole accomplish. 'Acts,' on the other hand, correspond to how the function is accomplished?If the claim element uses the phrase 'step for,' then § 112, § 6 is presumed to apply?On the other hand, the term 'step' alone and the phrase 'steps of' tend to show that § 112, § 6 does not govern that limitation."); Personalized Media Communications LLC v. ITC, 161 F.3d 696, 703-04, 48 USPQ2d 1880, 1886-87 (Fed. Cir. 1998); Mas Hamilton Group v. LaGard Inc., 156 F.3d 1206, 1213, 48 USPQ2d 1010, 1016 (Fed. Cir. 1998) ("lever moving element for moving the lever" and "movable link member for holding the lever?and for releasing the lever" were construed as means-plus-function limitations invoking 35 U.S.C. 112, sixth paragraph since the claimed limitations were described in terms of their function not their mechanical structure); Ethicon, Inc. v. United States Surgical Corp., 135 F.3d 1456, 1463, 45 USPQ2d 1545, 1550 (Fed. Cir. 1998) ("use of the word 'means' gives rise to 'a presumption that the inventor used the term advisedly to invoke the statutory mandates for means-plus-function clauses'"); O.I. Corp. v. Tekmar, 115 F.3d 1576, 1583, 42 USPQ2d 1777, 1782 (Fed. Cir. 1997) (method claim that paralleled means-plus-function apparatus claim but lacked "step for" language did not invoke 35 U.S.C. 112, sixth paragraph). Thus, absent an express recitation of "means for" or "step for" in the limitation, the broadest reasonable interpretation will not be limited to "corresponding structure?and equivalents thereof." Morris, 127 F.3d at 1055, 44 USPQ2d at 1028 ("no comparable mandate in the patent statute that relates the claim scope of non-§ 112 § 6 claims to particular matter found in the specification").

With respect to the second prong of this analysis, see York Prod., Inc. v. Central Tractor Farm & Family Center, 99 F.3d 1568, 1574, 40 USPQ2d 1619, 1624 (Fed. Cir. 1996) (holding that a claim limitation containing the term "means" does not invoke 35 U.S.C. 112, sixth paragraph if the claim limitation does not link the term "means" to a specific function). It must be clear that the element in the claims is set forth, at least in part, by the function it performs as opposed to the specific structure, material, or acts that perform the function. See also Caterpillar Inc. v. Detroit Diesel Corp., 41 USPQ2d 1876, 1882 (N.D. Ind. 1996) (35 U.S.C. 112, sixth paragraph "applies to functional method claims where the element at issue sets forth a step for reaching a particular result, but not the specific technique or procedure used to achieve the result.");O.I. Corp., 115 F.3d at 1582-83, 42 USPQ2d at 1782 (With respect to process claims, "[35 U.S.C. 112, sixth paragraph] is implicated only when steps plus function without acts are present?If we were to construe every process claim containing steps described by an 'ing' verb, such as passing, heating, reacting, transferring, etc., into a step-plus-function, we would be limiting process claims in a manner never intended by Congress." (Emphasis in original).). However, "the fact that a particular mechanism?is defined in functional terms is not sufficient to convert a claim element containing that term into a 'means for performing a specified function' within the meaning of section 112(6)." Greenberg v. Ethicon Endo-Surgery, Inc., 91 F.3d 1580, 1583, 39 USPQ2d 1783, 1786 (Fed. Cir. 1996) ("detent mechanism" defined in functional terms was not intended to invoke 35 U.S.C. 112, sixth paragraph). See also Al-Site Corp. v. VSI International Inc., 174 F.3d 1308, 1318, 50 USPQ2d 1161, 1166-67 (Fed. Cir. 1999) (although the claim elements "eyeglass hanger member" and "eyeglass contacting member" include a function, these claim elements do not invoke 35 U.S.C. 112, sixth paragraph because the claims themselves contain sufficient structural limitations for performing those functions). Also, a statement of function appearing only in the claim preamble is generally insufficient to invoke 35 U.S.C. 112, sixth paragraph. O.I. Corp., 115 F.3d at 1583, 42 USPQ2d at 1782 ("[A] statement in a preamble of a result that necessarily follows from performing a series of steps does not convert each of those steps into step- plus-function clauses. The steps of 'passing' are not individually associated in the claims with functions performed by the steps of passing.").

With respect to the third prong of this analysis, see Seal-Flex, 172 F.3d at 849, 50 USPQ2d at 1234 (Radar, J., concurring) ("Even when a claim element uses language that generally falls under the step-plus-function format, however, 112 § 6 still does not apply when the claim limitation itself recites sufficient acts for performing the specified function."); Rodime PLC v. Seagate Technology, Inc., 174 F.3d 1294, 1303- 04, 50 USPQ2d 1429, 1435-36 (Fed. Cir. 1999) (holding "positioning means for moving" does not invoke 35 U.S.C. 112, sixth paragraph because the claim further provides a list of the structure underlying the means and the detailed recitation of the structure for performing the moving function removes this element from the purview of 35 U.S.C. 112, sixth paragraph); Cole v. Kimberly-Clark Corp., 102 F.3d 524, 531, 41 USPQ2d 1001, 1006 (Fed. Cir. 1996) (holding "perforation means?for tearing" does not invoke 35 U.S.C. 112, sixth paragraph because the claim describes the structure supporting the tearing function (i.e., perforation)). In other cases, the Federal Circuit has held otherwise. See Unidynamics Corp. v. Automatic Prod. Int'l, 157 F.3d 1311, 1319, 48 USPQ2d 1099, 1104 (Fed. Cir. 1998) (holding "spring means" does invoke 35 U.S.C. 112, sixth paragraph). Although use of the term "means" in a clause reciting predominantly structure does not evoke 35 U.S.C. 112, sixth paragraph, York Products, 99 F.3d at 1574, 40 USPQ2d at 1623, "[t]he recitation of some structure in a means plus function element does not preclude applicability of section 112(6)." During examination, however, applicants have the opportunity and the obligation to define their inventions precisely, including whether a claim limitation invokes 35 U.S.C. 112, sixth paragraph. Thus, if the phrase "means for" or "step for" is modified by structure, material or acts for achieving the specified function, the PTO will not apply 35 U.S.C. 112, sixth paragraph until such modifying language is deleted from the claim limitation. Laitram Corp. v. Rexnord, Inc., 939 F.2d 1533, 1536, 19 USPQ2d 1367, 1369 (Fed. Cir. 1991). It is necessary to decide on an element by element basis whether 35 U.S.C. 112, sixth paragraph applies. Each claim must be independently reviewed to determine the applicability of 35 U.S.C. 112, sixth paragraph, even where the application contains substantially similar process and apparatus claims. O.I. Corp., 115 F.3d at 1583-1584, 42 USPQ2d at 1782 ("We understand that the steps in the method claims are essentially in the same language as the limitations in the apparatus claim, albeit without the 'means for' qualification?Each claim must be independently reviewed in order to determine if it is subject to the requirements of section 112, § 6. Interpretation of claims would be confusing indeed if claims that are not means- or step- plus function were to be interpreted as if they were, only because they use language similar to that used in other claims that are subject to this provision.").

Accordingly, these guidelines provide applicants with the opportunity to either invoke or not invoke 35 U.S.C. 112, sixth paragraph based upon a clear and simple set of criteria.

Limitations that fall within the scope of 35 U.S.C. 112, sixth paragraph include:

(A) a jet driving device so constructed and located on the rotor as to drive the rotor . . . ["means" unnecessary]. The term "device" coupled with a function is a proper definition of structure in accordance with the last paragraph of 35 U.S.C. 112. The addition of the words "jet driving" to the term "device" merely renders the latter more definite and specific. Ex parte Stanley, 121 USPQ 621 (Bd. App. 1958);

(B) "printing means" and "means for printing" which would have the same connotations. Ex parte Klumb, 159 USPQ 694 (Bd. App. 1967). However, the terms "plate" and "wing," as modifiers for the structureless term "means," specify no function to be performed, and do not fall under the last paragraph of 35 U.S.C. 112;

(C) force generating means adapted to provide . . . . De Graffenreid v. United States, 20 Ct. Cl. 458, 16 USPQ2d 1321 (Ct. Cl. 1990);

(D) call cost register means, including a digital display for providing a substantially instantaneous display for . . . . Intellicall Inc. v. Phonometrics, Inc., 952 F.2d 1384, 21 USPQ2d 1383 (Fed. Cir. 1992);

(E) reducing the coefficient of friction of the resulting film [step plus function; "step" unnecessary], In re Roberts, 470 F.2d 1399, 176 USPQ 313 (CCPA 1973); and

(F) raising the pH of the resultant pulp to about 5.0 to precipitate . . . . Ex parte Zimmerley, 153 USPQ 367 (Bd. App. 1966).

In the event that it is unclear whether the claim limitation falls within the scope of 35 U.S.C. 112, sixth paragraph, a rejection under 35 U.S.C. 112, second paragraph may be appropriate.

PROCEDURES FOR DETERMINING WHETHER THE WRITTEN DESCRIPTION ADEQUATELY DESCRIBES THE

CORRESPONDING STRUCTURE, MATERIAL, OR ACTS NECESSARY TO SUPPORT A CLAIM LIMITATION WHICH INVOKES 35 U.S.C. 112, SIXTH PARAGRAPH

If a claim limitation invokes 35 U.S.C. 112, sixth paragraph, it must be interpreted to cover the corresponding structure, materials, or acts in the specification and "equivalents thereof." See 35 U.S.C. 112, sixth paragraph. See also B. Braun Medical, Inc. v. Abbott Lab., 124 F.3d 1419, 1424, 43 USPQ2d 1896, 1899 (Fed. Cir. 1997). If the written description fails to set forth the supporting structure, material or acts corresponding to the means- (or step-) plus-function, the claim may not meet the requirement of 35 U.S.C. 112, second paragraph:

Although [35 U.S.C. 112, sixth paragraph] statutorily provides that one may use means-plus- function language in a claim, one is still subject to the requirement that a claim 'particularly point out and distinctly claim' the invention. Therefore, if one employs means-plus-function language in a claim, one must set forth in the specification an adequate disclosure showing what is meant by that language. If an applicant fails to set forth an adequate disclosure, the applicant has in effect failed to particularly point out and distinctly claim the invention as required by [35 U.S.C. 112, second paragraph].

See Donaldson, 16 F.3d at 1195, 29 USPQ2d at 1850; see also B. Braun Medical, 124 F.3d at 1425, 43 USPQ2d at 1900; and In re Dossel, 115 F.3d 942, 946, 42 USPQ2d 1881, 1884-85 (Fed. Cir. 1997).

Whether a claim reciting an element in means- (or step-) plus-function language fails to comply with 35 U.S.C. 112, second paragraph because the specification does not disclose adequate structure (or material or acts) for performing the recited function is closely related to the question of whether the specification meets the description requirement in 35 U.S.C. 112, first paragraph. See In re Noll, 545 F.2d 141, 149, 191 USPQ 721, 727 (CCPA 1976) (unless the means-plus-function language is itself unclear, a claim limitation written in means-plus- function language meets the definiteness requirement in 35 U.S.C. 112, second paragraph so long as the specification meets the written description requirement in 35 U.S.C. 112, first paragraph). However, 35

U.S.C. 112, sixth paragraph does not impose any requirements in addition to those imposed by 35 U.S.C. 112, first paragraph. See In re Knowlton, 481 F.2d 1357, 1366, 178 USPQ 486, 492-93 (CCPA 1973). Conversely, the invocation of 35 U.S.C. 112, sixth paragraph does not exempt an applicant from compliance with 35 U.S.C. 112, first and second paragraphs. See Donaldson, 16 F.3d at 1195, 29 USPQ2d at 1850; Knowlton, 481 F.2d at 1366, 178 USPQ at 493.

The written description does not have to explicitly describe the structure (or material or acts) corresponding to a means- (or step-) plus-function limitation to particularly point out and distinctly claim the invention as required by 35 U.S.C. 112, second paragraph. See Dossel, 115 F.3d at 946, 42 USPQ2d at 1885. Under proper circumstances, drawings may provide a written description of an invention as required by 35 U.S.C. 112. Vas-Cath, Inc. v. Mahurkar, 935 F.2d 1555, 1565, 19 USPQ2d 1111, 1118 (Fed. Cir. 1991). Rather, disclosure of structure corresponding to a means-plus-function limitation may be implicit in the written description if it would have been clear to those skilled in the art what structure must perform the function recited in the means-plus-function limitation. See Atmel Corp. v. Information Storage Devices Inc., 198 F.3d 1374, ___, 53 USPQ2d 1225, 1229 (Fed. Cir. 1999); Dossel, 115 F.3d at 946-47, 42 USPQ2d at 1885 ("Clearly, a unit which receives digital data, performs complex mathematical computations and outputs the results to a display must be implemented by or on a general or special purpose computer (although it is not clear why the written description does not simply state 'computer' or some equivalent phrase.)"). However, the claims must still be analyzed to determine whether there exists corresponding adequate support for such claim under 35 U.S.C. 112, first paragraph. In considering whether there is 35 U.S.C. 112, first paragraph support for the claim limitation, the examiner must consider not only the original disclosure contained in the summary and detailed description of the invention portions of the specification, but also the original claims, abstract, and drawings. See In re Mott, 539 F.2d 1291, 1299, 190 USPQ 536, 542-43 (CCPA 1976) (claims); In re Anderson, 471 F.2d 1237, 1240, 176 USPQ 331, 333 (CCPA 1973) (claims); In re Armbruster, 512 F.2d 676, 678-79, 185 USPQ 152, 153-54 (CCPA 1975) (abstract);

Anderson, 471 F.2d at 1240, 176 USPQ at 333 (abstract); Vas-Cath Inc. v. Mahurkar, 935 F.2d at 1564, 19 USPQ2d at 1117 (drawings); In re Wolfensperger, 302 F.2d 950, 955-57, 133 USPQ 537, 541- 43 (CCPA 1962) (drawings).

Therefore, a means-(or step-) plus-function claim limitation satisfies 35 U.S.C. 112, second paragraph if: (A) the written description links or associates particular structure, materials, or acts to the function recited in a means- (or step-) plus-function claim limitation; or (B) it is clear based on the facts of the application that one skilled in the art would have known what structure, materials, or acts perform the function recited in a means- (or step-) plus-function limitation.

37 CFR 1.75(d)(1) provides, in part, that "the terms and phrases used in the claims must find clear support or antecedent basis in the description so that the meaning of the terms in the claims may be ascertainable by reference to the description." In the situation in which the written description only implicitly or inherently sets forth the structure, materials, or acts corresponding to a means- (or step-) plus-function, and the examiner concludes that one skilled in the art would recognize what structure, materials, or acts perform the function recited in a means- (or step-) plus-function, the examiner should either: (A) have the applicant clarify the record by amending the written description such that it expressly recites what structure, materials, or acts perform the function recited in the claim element; or (B) state on the record what structure, materials, or acts perform the function recited in the means- (or step-) plus-function limitation. Even if the disclosure implicitly sets forth the structure, materials, or acts corresponding to a means- (or step-) plus-function claim element in compliance with 35 U.S.C. 112, first and second paragraphs, the PTO may still require the applicant to amend the specification pursuant to 37 CFR 1.75(d) and MPEP § 608.01(o) to explicitly state, with reference to the terms and phrases of the claim element, what structure, materials, or acts perform the function recited in the claim element. See 35 U.S.C. 112, sixth paragraph ("An element in a claim for a combination may be expressed as a means or step for performing a specified function without the recital of structure, material, or acts in support thereof, and such claim shall be construed to cover the corresponding structure, material, or acts described in the

specification and equivalents thereof." (emphasis added)); see also B. Braun Medical, 124 F.3d at 1424, 43 USPQ2d at 1900 (holding that "pursuant to this provision [35 U.S.C. 112, sixth paragraph], structure disclosed in the specification is 'corresponding' structure only if the specification or prosecution history clearly links or associates that structure to the function recited in the claim. This duty to link or associate structure to function is the quid pro quo for the convenience of employing 112, paragraph 6."); Wolfensperger, 302 F.2d at 955, 133 USPQ at 542 (just because the disclosure provides support for a claim element does not mean that the PTO cannot enforce its requirement that the terms and phrases used in the claims find clear support or antecedent basis in the written description).

SINGLE MEANS CLAIMS

Donaldson does not affect the holding of In re Hyatt, 708 F.2d 712, 218 USPQ 195 (Fed. Cir. 1983) to the effect that a single means claim does not comply with the enablement requirement of 35 U.S.C. 112, first paragraph. As Donaldson applies only to an interpretation of a limitation drafted to correspond to 35 U.S.C. 112, sixth paragraph, which by its terms is limited to "an element in a claim to a combination," it does not affect a limitation in a claim which is not directed to a combination.

2184   **Determining Whether an Applicant Has Met the Burden of Proving Nonequivalence After a Prima Facie Case Is Made**

If the applicant disagrees with the inference of equivalence drawn from a prior art reference, the applicant may provide reasons why the applicant believes the prior art element should not be considered an equivalent to the specific structure, material or acts disclosed in the specification. Such reasons may include, but are not limited to:

(A) Teachings in the specification that particular prior art is not equivalent;

(B) Teachings in the prior art reference itself that may tend to show nonequivalence; or

(C) 37 CFR 1.132 affidavit evidence of facts tending to show nonequivalence.

TEACHINGS IN APPLICANT'S SPECIFICATION

When the applicant relies on teachings in applicant's own specification, the examiner must make sure that the applicant is interpreting the "means or step plus function" limitation in the claim in a manner which is consistent with the disclosure in the specification. If the specification defines what is meant by "equivalents" to the disclosed embodiments for the purpose of the claimed means or step plus function, the examiner should interpret the limitation as having that meaning. If no definition is provided, some judgment must be exercised in determining the scope of "equivalents." Generally, an "equivalent" is interpreted as embracing more than the specific elements described in the specification for performing the specified function, but less than any element that performs the function specified in the claim. To interpret "means plus function" limitations as limited to a particular means set forth in the specification would nullify the provisions of 35 U.S.C. 112 requiring that the limitation shall be construed to cover the structure described in the specification and equivalents thereof. D.M.I., Inc. v. Deere & Co., 755 F.2d 1570, 1574, 225 USPQ 236, 238 (Fed. Cir. 1985).

The scope of equivalents embraced by a claim limitation is dependent on the interpretation of an "equivalent." The interpretation will vary depending on how the element is described in the supporting specification. The claim may or may not be limited to particular structure, material or acts (e.g., steps) as opposed to any and all structure, material or acts performing the claimed function, depending on how the specification treats that question.

If the disclosure is so broad as to encompass any and all structure, material or acts for performing the claimed function, the claims must be read accordingly when determining patentability. When this happens the limitation otherwise provided by "equivalents" ceases to be a limitation on the scope of the claim in that an equivalent would be any structure, material or act other than the ones described in the specification that perform the claimed function. For example, this situation will often be found in cases where (A) the claimed invention is a combination of elements, one or more of which are selected from elements that are old, per se, or (B) apparatus claims are treated as indistinguishable from method claims. See, for example, In re Meyer, 688 F.2d 789, 215 USPQ 193 (CCPA 1982); In re Abele, 684 F.2d 902, 909, 214 USPQ 682, 688 (CCPA 1982); In re Walter, 618 F.2d 758, 767, 205 USPQ 397, 406-07 (CCPA 1980); In re Maucorps, 609 F.2d 481, 203 USPQ 812 (CCPA 1979); In re Johnson, 589 F.2d 1070, 200 USPQ 199 (CCPA 1978); and In re Freeman, 573 F.2d 1237, 1246, 197 USPQ 464, 471 (CCPA 1978).

On the other end of the spectrum, the "equivalents" limitation as applied to a claim may also operate to constrict the claim scope to the point of covering virtually only the disclosed embodiments. This can happen in circumstances where the specification describes the invention only in the context of a specific structure, material or act that is used to perform the function specified in the claim.

FACTORS TO BE CONSIDERED IN DECIDING EQUIVALENCE

When deciding whether an applicant has met the burden of proof with respect to showing nonequivalence of a prior art element that performs the claimed function, the following factors may be considered. First, unless an element performs the identical function specified in the claim, it cannot be an equivalent for the purposes of 35 U.S.C. 112, sixth paragraph. Pennwalt Corp. v. Durand-Wayland, Inc., 833 F.2d 931, 4 USPQ2d 1737 (Fed. Cir. 1987), cert. denied, 484 U.S. 961 (1988).

Second, while there is no litmus test for an "equivalent" that can be applied with absolute certainty and predictability, there are several indicia that are sufficient to support a conclusion that one element is or is not an "equivalent" of a different element in the context of 35 U.S.C. 112, sixth paragraph. Among the indicia that will support a conclusion that one element is or is not an equivalent of another are:

> (A) Whether the prior art element performs the function specified in the claim in substantially the same way, and produces substantially the same results as the corresponding element disclosed in the specification. Lockheed Aircraft Corp. v. United States, 193 USPQ 449, 461 (Ct. Cl.

1977). The concepts of equivalents as set forth in Graver Tank & Mfg. Co. v. Linde Air Products, 339 U.S. 605, 85 USPQ 328 (1950) are relevant to any "equivalents" determination. Polumbo v. Don-Joy Co., 762 F.2d 969, 975, n. 4, 226 USPQ 5, 8-9, n. 4 (Fed. Cir. 1985).

(B) Whether a person of ordinary skill in the art would have recognized the interchangeability of the element shown in the prior art for the corresponding element disclosed in the specification. Lockheed Aircraft Corp. v. United States, 193 USPQ 449, 461 (Ct. Cl. 1977); Data Line Corp. v. Micro Technologies, Inc., 813 F.2d 1196, 1 USPQ2d 2052 (Fed. Cir. 1987).

(C) Whether the prior art element is a structural equivalent of the corresponding element disclosed in the specification being examined. In re Bond, 910 F.2d 831, 15 USPQ2d 1566 (Fed. Cir. 1990). That is, the prior art element performs the function specified in the claim in substantially the same manner as the function is performed by the corresponding element described in the specification.

(D) Whether there are insubstantial differences between the prior art element and the structure, material or acts disclosed in the specification. Warner-Jenkinson Co. v. Hilton Davis Chemical Co., 117 S. Ct. 1040, 41 USPQ2d 1865, 1875 (1997); Valmont Industries, Inc. v. Reinke Mfg. Co., 983 F.2d 1039, 25 USPQ2d 1451 (Fed. Cir. 1993).

These examples are not intended to be an exhaustive list of the indicia that would support a finding that one element is or is not an equivalent of another element for the purposes of 35 U.S.C. 112, sixth paragraph. A finding according to any of the above examples would represent a sufficient, but not the only possible, basis to support a conclusion that an element is or is not an equivalent. There could be other indicia that also would support the conclusion.

MERE ALLEGATIONS OF NONEQUIVALENCE ARE NOT SUFFICIENT

In determining whether arguments or 37 CFR 1.132 evidence presented by an applicant are persuasive that the element shown in the prior art is not an equivalent, the examiner should consider and weigh as many of the above-indicated or other indicia as are presented by applicant, and should determine whether, on balance, the applicant has met the burden of proof to show nonequivalence. However, under no circumstance should an examiner accept as persuasive a bare statement or opinion that the element shown in the prior art is not an equivalent embraced by the claim limitation. Moreover, if an applicant argues that the "means" or "step" plus function language in a claim is limited to certain specific structural or additional functional characteristics (as opposed to "equivalents" thereof) where the specification does not describe the invention as being only those specific characteristics, the claim should not be allowed until the claim is amended to recite those specific structural or additional functional characteristics. Otherwise, a claim could be allowed having broad functional language which, in reality, is limited to only the specific structure or steps disclosed in the specification. This would be contrary to public policy of granting patents which provide adequate notice to the public as to a claim's true scope.

APPLICANT MAY AMEND CLAIMS

Finally, as in the past, applicant has the opportunity during proceedings before the Office to amend the claims so that the claimed invention meets all the statutory criteria for patentability. An applicant may choose to amend the claim by further limiting the function so that there is no longer identity of function with that taught by the prior art element, or the applicant may choose to replace the claimed means plus function limitation with specific structure, material or acts that are not described in the prior art.

Appendix E

Glossary and Index of Patent Terms
By John D. Kaufmann and Robert C. Faber

A/AN—(1) In a claim, the indefinite article A or AN connotes "one or more." (2) Also, the indefinite article A or AN is used as modifier of an ELEMENT the first time the ELEMENT is set forth (i.e., introduced) in a claim. See THE. (20, **23**)*

AGGREGATION—(1) A lack of structural and/or functional co-operation between the various parts of an assembly; the opposite of COMBINATION. A non-cooperating assembly of parts (strict-ly speaking, NON-STATUTORY subject matter)–an inherent de-fect in a structure, qua structure, which no claim, however well drafted, can cure. (2) A COMBINATION claimed without suffi-cient particularity and definiteness, so that the ELEMENTS of the claim, *as claimed,* do not cooperate. A structure is not necessarily an AGGREGATION solely because all of its ELEMENTS, either in fact or as claimed, do not function simultaneously (as in a type-writer). Recent cases cast doubt on the propriety of this ground of REJECTION. See MPEP 706.03(i) and Sections 28 and 64. (28, **64**, 65)

ALTERNATIVE EXPRESSION—The alternative setting forth in a claim of two ELEMENTS, either (and both) of which perform the same FUNCTION in the claim, instead of a single ELEMENT

---

* Numerals refer to sections of the book where the term is used expressly or implicitly; **boldface numerals** indicate sections where the term is defined or discussed in detail. Solid Caps designate terms defined in the glossary.

to perform the FUNCTION. For example: "a spring *or* piston-cylinder for moving the member." Usually, there is a GENERIC word covering the ALTERNATIVE ELEMENTS, in the case of the example "means for biasing," which should be used in the claim. ALTERNATIVE EXPRESSIONS *may* render a claim INDEFINITE. In some cases, ALTERNATIVE EXPRESSIONS are permissible, if the claim is not rendered INDEFINITE thereby. For example, "one *or* more arms" (but note the connotation of A and AN). The primary use of alternative elements is in MARKUSH groupings. See MPEP 706.03(d) and Sections 20, 24, 36 and 50. (20, **24**, 34, 36, 50, 58)

AMENDMENT—A change made in or to a patent application in response to (and hopefully to avoid) a REJECTION or OBJECTION by the EXAMINER. An AMENDMENT is part of a RESPONSE and may affect claims, the DESCRIPTION or the drawings. (6)

ANALOGOUS ART—A REFERENCE or some PRIOR ART directed to the same necessary FUNCTION or utility as is the subject matter set forth in a claim, either the entire claim or particular elements thereof, even though the environment differs. For example, a brick cutter shown in a REFERENCE may be ANALOGOUS ART with respect to a claimed dough cutter. See MPEP 904.01(c).

ANTECEDENT/ANTECEDENT BASIS—A claim must be consistent with the SPECIFICATION and with itself. That is, ELEMENTS recited in the claim must find ANTECEDENT BASIS in the DESCRIPTION and within the claim, if earlier recited therein. Therefore: (1) Support for; the quality of an ELEMENT which is set forth in (and supported by) the DESCRIPTION and which is then POSITIVELY recited in a claim. (2) A POSITIVELY recited, claimed ELEMENT to which later reference is made in the same (or in a DEPENDENT) claim. Absent an ANTECEDENT in the disclosure and/or claims as originally filed, a claim will be NEW MATTER. See Sections 18 and 23. (15, 16, **18**, 19, 20, **23**, 31, 33, 34, 36, 64, 67, 69)

ANTICIPATED—See FULLY MET.

APPARATUS—(1) An adjective meaning mechanical or MA-CHINE-like. (2) A noun meaning a MACHINE or DEVICE, including an electrical circuit, having cooperating parts and a "rule of operation" to accomplish a useful RESULT, usually some act or operation on an ARTICLE or WORKPIECE. Sometimes contrasted with an ARTICLE OF MANUFACTURE or a PRODUCT. (**Chapter III, 11,** 12, 13, 14, 15, 16, 32, 35, 37, 38, 40, 41, 42, 45)

APPARATUS LIMITATIONS IN METHOD CLAIMS—Section 41.

APPARATUS, METHOD FUNCTIONAL OF—Section 40.

ARBITRARY NAMES—Section 51.

ART—(1) A METHOD or PROCESS (pre-1952 usage). (2) Today, a field of technology, as in 35 U.S.C. § 103. See 35 U.S.C. § 100(b) and Section 36.

ARTICLE—A WORKPIECE. Distinguish from ARTICLE OF MANUFACTURE. (14, 15)

ARTICLE OF MANUFACTURE—One of the STATUTORY CLASSES of UTILITY PATENT. Broadly, any product made by man and having industrial utility. Similar to an APPARATUS or MACHINE, but usually having no moving parts or "rule of operation." The same as a MANUFACTURE. It is often difficult to tell whether a DEVICE is a MACHINE or an ARTICLE OF MANU-FACTURE, but this difficulty is immaterial. See Section 45. (**Chapter V,** 3, 42, **45,** 47, 50, 54, 57, 61, 62, 64, 65)

ARTICLE OF MANUFACTURE, OBVIOUS METHOD OF MAKING—Section 39.

BODY—of a CLAIM. Narrative expository prose following the PREAMBLE and the TRANSITION of a claim and reciting the ELEMENTS of the claimed INVENTION as well as a description of how these ELEMENTS cooperate to make up the operative COMBINATION recited in the PREAMBLE. See Section 9. (6, 7, **9,** 11, 14, 15, 34, 36, 57, 59)

BROAD/BROAD CLAIM—Relates to a claim which covers or READS ON a wide range and variety of DEVICES, PROCESSES, etc., because the claim contains only few, or only general, limitations. Sometimes called "wide," especially in British practice. A claim may be so BROAD as to be INDEFINITE (Section 31) or to READ ON the PRIOR ART. See NARROW. (5, 6, 7, 8, 15, 16, 17, 19, 31, 34, 35, 36, 46, 49, 60, 63, 67, 68)

CAFC—Abbreviation for the United States Court of Appeals for the Federal Circuit.

CATALOG—An AGGREGATION (Sense (2)) as claimed. See Sections 28 and 64. (**28**, 57, **64**)

CCPA—Abbreviation for the United States Court of Customs and Patent Appeals, superseded in 1982 by the CAFC.

CHEMICAL CLAIMS—See Chapter VI and Sections 42, 49 and 52.

CLAIM—A description of the INVENTION (Sense (2)) protected, located at the end of every patent SPECIFICATION. The protection afforded by a patent is measured by the CLAIMS which are similar to a real property deed in function, i.e., describing metes and bounds.

CLAUSE—In a CLAIM, the description of an element or elements between separating punctuation, commas, semi-colons.

CLOSED-ENDED—See CONSISTING ESSENTIALLY OF and CONSISTING OF. (8)

COLON-SEMICOLON FORM—A claim format in which a colon may be inserted after the TRANSITION and semicolons are used between the ELEMENTS. Such a claim format may be used: in the OUTLINE FORM; the SINGLE PARAGRAPH FORM; or in the SUB-PARAGRAPH FORM. See Section 10.

COINED NAME CLAIM—A hybrid type of FINGERPRINT CLAIM in which the COINED NAME is defined and its distinctive properties, structure and METHOD of production are set forth in the DESCRIPTION (Section 53). Such a claim may be proper in the event the COINED NAME was known in the PRI-OR ART before the application was filed (which occurs only rarely). (52, **53**, 54)

COMBINATION—(1) An interrelated group of ELEMENTS, structurally and FUNCTIONALLY tied together in a claim to an operative DEVICE to effect some useful FUNCTION or RESULT. Simultaneity of operation of the ELEMENTS is not necessary. See AGGREGATION and CATALOG. (2) A complete MACHINE, PROCESS, ARTICLE OF MANUFACTURE, COMPOSITION, etc., as distinguished from a SUBCOMBINATION thereof. See Sections 9, 28, 29, 30, 33, 35, 38, 45 and 64. (1, 6, 7, 8, 9, 10, 11, 12, 15, 16, 20, **28**, **29**, **30**, 33, 34, 35, 36, 42, 45, 49, 50, 56, 57, 59, 63, **64**, 65, 68)

COMPOSITION/COMPOSITION OF MATTER—PRODUCTS wherein the chemical nature of the substances or materials used, rather than the shape or form, is the distinguishing characteristic. A COMPOSITION may be a molecule, COMPOUND, solution, mixture, alloy, atom, etc. Sometimes contrasted with ARTICLE OF MANUFACTURE. See Section 49. (Chapter VI, 3, 11, 12, 41, 42, **49**, 51, 52, 54, 56, 57)

COMPOUND—Usually, a molecule, per se. See COMPOSITION. (49, 50, 52, 53)

COMPRISES/COMPRISING—TRANSITION words between the BODY of the claim and the PREAMBLE and within a clause in the body of the claim. The words mean "including the following ELEMENTS (in the BODY or the elements following the element preceeding that TRANSISTION word), but not excluding others." A claim or clause using either word is said to be OPEN-ENDED. Thus, "A COMPOSITION COMPRISING (or WHICH COMPRISES) A, B and C" *requires* the presence of A, B and C, but does *not* exclude other components. Hence, one who produces another COMPOSITION made up of A, B, C and D would INFRINGE. INCLUDES and HAS mean the same thing. See Section 7. (7, 15, 20, 36, 50, 57)

COMPUTER PROGRAMS—Section 44.

CONSISTING ESSENTIALLY OF—A TRANSITION between the PREAMBLE and BODY of a claim and within a clause in the body of the claim. The phrase means "excluding other ELEMENTS of any essential significance to the claimed COMBINATION." More NARROW than COMPRISES, but more BROAD than CONSISTING OF. Hence, one who adds an additional component to the claimed COMBINATION may or may not INFRINGE, depending on whether the additional component substantially alters the properties of the COMPOSITION. For example, where a claim calls for "a tough, impact-resistant COMPOSITION, CONSISTING ESSENTIALLY OF A, B and C," and another adds D to the COMPOSITION, if the addition results in a COMPOSITION which is extremely brittle (i.e., nonimpact-resistant) there is no INFRINGEMENT, because D's properties substantially changed the properties of the COMPOSITION. The line between CONSISTING ESSENTIALLY OF and CONSISTING OF is not clear. Use of either phrase results in what is termed a CLOSED-ENDED CLAIM. See Section 8.

CONSISTING OF—A TRANSITION between the PREAMBLE and BODY of a claim and within a clause in the body of the claim. The phrase means "excluding more than traces of other than the recited ingredients." Use of the phrase results in a CLOSED-ENDED claim. Thus, "A COMPOSITION CONSISTING OF A, B and C" *requires* the presence of A, B and C, and only A, B and C. One who produces a COMPOSITION of A, B, C and D would not INFRINGE. See COMPRISES, CONSISTING ESSENTIALLY OF and Section 8. (8, 11, 12, 50)

CONTRIBUTORY INFRINGEMENT/CONTRIBUTORY INFRINGER—INFRINGEMENT arising when one (the CONTRIBUTORY INFRINGER) sells a component of a patented INVENTION, or a material or APPARATUS for use in practicing a patented PROCESS, knowing the same to be especially made and adapted for use in an INFRINGEMENT of such patent, unless what is sold is a staple article of commerce suitable for substantial non-infringing use. 35 U.S.C. § 271(c).

COUNT—A claim defining the INVENTION the priority of which is being contested in an INTERFERENCE.

DEPENDENT CLAIM—A claim which refers back to and further restricts (i.e., makes more NARROW) a single preceding claim (the PARENT CLAIM), which may itself be a DEPENDENT CLAIM. 35 U.S.C. § 112, Rule 75(c) and Sections 11, 12. (5, **11**, **12**, 21, 23, 36, 41, 42, 57, 58, 60, 68)

DESCRIPTION—Often referred to as WRITTEN DESCRIPTION or "detailed DESCRIPTION." The SPECIFICATION of a patent or patent application is made up of drawings, a DESCRIPTION and claims. The DESCRIPTION describes the structure, composition, cooperation, function, embodiments, etc. of the INVENTION in a quite detailed, technical fashion and provides ANTECEDENT basis for the terms of the claims which define the INVENTION. (16, 18, 22, 48, 51)

DESIGN CLAIM—Section 45.

DEVICE—(1) A generalized word meaning "thing" or "item." (2) A MACHINE or APPARATUS. (14, 15)

DOCTRINE OF EQUIVALENTS—A legal tenet holding that where a DEVICE, etc., accused of INFRINGING a claim does not include each and every ELEMENT of the CLAIM in *haec verba*, it will still INFRINGE the claim if it includes for every ELEMENT thereof either such ELEMENT or the EQUIVALENT of ELEMENTS not precisely present. See FILE WRAPPER ESTOPPEL. (34)

DOUBLE INCLUSION—Setting forth in a claim precisely the same ELEMENT twice as two different ELEMENTS, usually under two different names. See Sections 11, 12, 21 and 34. (11, 12, **21**, 34)

DRAWINGS, REFERENCE TO IN CLAIMS—Section 54.

DUPLICATE CLAIM—A redundant CLAIM. A CLAIM that does not "differ substantially" from another claim in the same patent or patent application. See Rule 75(b), MPEP 706.03(k) and Section 61. (60, **61**)

ELECTRICAL CLAIMS—Section 35. (Circuit claims.)

ELECTRICAL METHODS—Section 43.

ELEMENTS—(1) In CLAIM terminology, those things which together constitute the claimed INVENTION. In APPARATUS and ARTICLE OF MANUFACTURE claims, the ELEMENTS are the main structural parts; in METHOD claims, the ELEMENTS are steps or acts, usually GERUND phrases and clauses; in COMPOSITION claims, the ELEMENTS are chemicals or molecules. See Sections 16, 18, 19, 20, 26, 27, 35 and 37. (7, 8, 9, 10, 11, 12, 14, **16**, 18, 19, 20, 21, 22, 23, 24, 25, 26, 27, 28, 29, 30, 34, 35, 36, 37, 38, 41, 45, 49, 57, 59, 60, 63, 66, 68). (2) The respective parts of an assembly.

ELEMENTS, FEATURES OF—Section 25.

ELEMENTS, NAMING OF—Section 19.

ELEMENTS, NUMBER OF—Section 20.

ELEMENTS, ORDER OF—Sections 27 and 38.

ELEMENTS, PARTS OF—Section 25.

ELEMENTS, STRUCTURAL CONNECTION OF—Chapter 29.

ELEMENTS, TYING TOGETHER—Section 28.

EQUIVALENT—An ELEMENT or group of ELEMENTS that either is not substantially different from, is interchangeable with, or that performs substantially the same FUNCTIONS in substantially the same manner to produce substantially the same RESULT as an ELEMENT, group of ELEMENTS or INVENTION set forth in a claim. See DOCTRINE OF EQUIVALENTS. (34, 40, 54)

EUROPEAN-TYPE CLAIM—A claim format, similar to a JEPSON claim format, and common in European patents. The format followed is usually: "A (name of the DEVICE and its FUNCTION) of the type having (recitation of the PRIOR ART, usually that found in a *single* REFERENCE) characterized in that (recitation of the improvement in the claim BODY)." See Section 57.

EXAMINATION/EXAMINER—The EXAMINER, a Patent Office employee, studies in detail patent applications to determine if the applicant is entitled to a patent under the STATUTE. Such study is called the EXAMINATION. (1, 4A, 66)

EXHAUSTED COMBINATION—See OLD COMBINATION. (63)

FILE WRAPPER—The official file of the Patent Office relating to the EXAMINATION of a patent application. It includes the application as filed, all formal papers and all correspondence (Office actions, RESPONSES, and the like) preceding the issuance of (or denial of) a patent. Often called PROSECUTION HISTORY. Sometimes called "file history."

FILE WRAPPER ESTOPPEL—If a patent applicant, whose claims are REJECTED (or sometimes OBJECTED to), NARROWS those claims (as by adding limiting language thereto or by making arguments interpreting the claim language in a restrictive manner) and thereafter obtains allowance of the formerly rejected claims, he may be strictly limited by the additional language or arguments, and will not be entitled to any EQUIVALENTS with respect thereto. Often called PROSECUTION HISTORY ESTOPPEL. See INFRINGE and DOCTRINE OF EQUIVALENTS.

FINGERPRINT CLAIM—A claim defining a chemical COMPOSITION in terms of its properties, such as X-ray diffraction, solubility, melting point, phase diagram, spectrum, etc., often as shown in the drawing. The use of such a claim is limited to emergency situations wherein the differences between the INVENTION and the PRIOR ART cannot be explained or described (and claimed) in the traditional terms of physical or chemical structure. Such a claim must, nevertheless, distinctly claim the INVENTION. See Sections 52, 53 and 54. (52, 53, 54)

FORM/FORMAT OF CLAIMS IN GENERAL—Chapter II and Section 10.

FORMAL REJECTION—A REJECTION (OBJECTION) made by the EXAMINER to the form, as opposed to the substance (novelty and/or unobviousness), of a claim. A NON-ART REJECTION. See Chapter X. (Chapter X, 60, 67)

FULLY MET—A phrase used to REJECT a claim which is completely anticipated by or shown in a single REFERENCE. This type of REJECTION is properly posited on 35 U.S.C. § 102, not on 35 U.S.C. § 103.

FUNCTION/FUNCTIONAL CLAUSE/LIMITATION—Describing an ELEMENT in terms of what it does, as opposed to what it is (i.e., its structure). See Section 30. At times a FUNCTIONAL LIMITATION may be expressed negatively, that is, by what the ELEMENT does not do. (**30**, 31, **33**, 34, 45, 49, 63, 67)

FUNCTIONAL ORDER—A logical ordering of the ELEMENTS of a claim which begins with the ELEMENT which first contacts the WORKPIECE. See STRUCTURAL ORDER and Section 27.

GAZETTE—See OG/OFFICIAL GAZETTE.

GENERIC/GENUS—A GENUS is a class BROADER than, or including, more than one SPECIES. "Primate" is a GENUS with respect to "man" and "ape" which are SPECIES thereof. A GENERIC claim includes within its SCOPE two or more disclosed embodiments (SPECIES). Such a claim must cover or READ ON what is comprehended in each of the SPECIES. See MPEP 806.02(d) and (e), and Section 58. (15, 19, 24, 34, 36, 45, 49, 50, 51, **58**)

GERUND—A verbal noun expressing the action of the verb in a generalized manner; a verbal noun, ending in "-ing" and performing the function of a substantive, often taking the case phrase construction, and at the same time showing the verbal features of tense and voice, taking adverbial modifiers, and governing objects. Usually, GERUNDS are the first words of METHOD steps, the basic ELEMENTS of a METHOD claim. See Section 36.

HAS/HAVING—TRANSITION words between the PREAMBLE and the BODY of a claim. Mean the same as COMPRISES/COMPRISING. (7, 57)

HOLE—Absence of material. HOLES, unlike most ELEMENTS, should usually be claimed INFERENTIALLY (Sense (1)), as "*a* lever having *a* hole." See Section 26. (25, **26**, 34)

IMPROVEMENT CLAIM—Section 57.

INCLUDES/INCLUDING—TRANSITION words between the PREAMBLE and BODY of a claim. Mean the same as COMPRISES/COMPRISING. (7, 57)

INCOMPLETE—Quality of a claim which omits essential ELEMENTS or cooperative relationships. See MPEP 706.03(f) and Section 66. (59, **66**, 67, 68)

INDEFINITE—(1) Lack of proper ANTECEDENT. (2) The quality of a claim which fails to accurately define the limits or boundaries of the INVENTION for any reason. (3) Not meeting the requirements of 35 U.S.C. § 112 to particularly point out and distinctly claim the INVENTION. See Section 67. (17, **23**, 24, 25, 34, 36, 50, **67**)

INDEPENDENT CLAIM—A claim that contains a complete description of the subject matter, without reference to any other claim. (See DEPENDENT CLAIM.) (11)

INDIRECT LIMITATION—Example: First reciting "a gear" and then reciting "said plastic gear" in a claim, where the same gear is meant in both instances. "Plastic" is an INDIRECT LIMITATION rendering the claim INDEFINITE. See ANTECEDENT, INFERENTIAL and POSITIVE, and MPEP 706.03(d) and Section 23.

INFERENTIAL—(1) In reference to the form of claims as such, an INFERENTIAL claim is one wherein a new ELEMENT is introduced in the middle of a clause which introduces and describes another ELEMENT. See Section 16. (2) The term is also used to refer to the setting forth of an ELEMENT (or a limitation or feature thereof) in a claim not found in the DESCRIPTION, or an ELEMENT (or limitation of an ELEMENT) set forth definitely in the claim ("*the* arm") where not set forth earlier in the claim. See INDIRECT LIMITATION and Sections 18, 23 and 67. (3) APPARATUS limitations are usually brought into METHOD claims INFERENTIALLY in the sense of meaning (1). See Section 41. (**16**, 18, 23, 41, 63, 67)

INFRINGE/INFRINGEMENT/INFRINGER—An INFRINGER INFRINGES a claim by making, using or selling in the United States that which is set forth in the claim without the authority of the patent owner. See 35 U.S.C. § 271 and DOCTRINE OF EQUIVALENTS. Normally, the DEVICE, etc., accused of being an INFRINGEMENT must contain each and every ELEMENT of the claim. (2, 11, 12, 16, 34, 35, 52, 53, 55, 56, 60)

INOPERATIVE—Incapable of performing an intended purpose. INOPERATIVENESS may reside in an INVENTION, *qua* INVENTION, or as claimed. See AGGREGATION.

IN ORDER TO—See WHEREBY. Often used in a manner different from WHEREBY in a MEANS-plus-FUNCTION clause, as: "means for rotating the wheel IN ORDER TO reciprocate the arm. . . ." Usually, "IN ORDER TO reciprocate the arm" will be considered as a STRUCTURAL/FUNCTIONAL limitation and may fall under 35 U.S.C. section 112, para. 6. (31, 34)

INTERFERENCE—A proceeding in the Patent Office to determine among (a) one or more patent applicants and one or more patentees, or (b) two or more applicants, claiming the same INVENTION, which of the parties was the first inventor. The claim defining the contested INVENTION is called a COUNT. (32, 55)

INTRODUCTION/INTRODUCTORY PHRASE— "I (or we) claim" or "What is claimed is." Each claim is the direct object of a SINGLE SENTENCE beginning with an INTRODUCTORY PHRASE, which appears only once, before the first claim. See Section 4. (4A, 14)

INVENTION—(1) As a legally significant act, the summation of conception and reduction to practice, actual or constructive. (2) Also, the thing or DEVICE invented and claimed in a patent or patent application. (3) Sometimes used (misused?) as meaning unobvious as in "what is the invention?"; meaning, what is the novel and unobvious feature(s) defined in the claim. See 35 U.S.C. § 103. (3, 11, 12, 16, 18, 34, 39, 49, 53, 55, 58, 60, 63, 64, 67, 68)

JEPSON CLAIM—A claim format for an improvement-type INVENTION wherein the old ELEMENTS are set forth in the PRE-

AMBLE of the claim and the new or modified ELEMENTS (or new or modified COMBINATIONS thereof) are set forth in the BODY of the claim. Similar to a EUROPEAN-TYPE CLAIM. See Section 57. (34, 57, 63). From a Patent Office decision involving an inventor named Jepson.

LABEL CLAIM—A type of NEW USE CLAIM wherein a statement of the intended use of a COMPOSITION is set forth in the PREAMBLE as a PREAMBLE LIMITATION and is relied on for novelty and/or unobviousness. See Section 56.

LAUDATORY STATEMENTS—Words such as "novel" or "efficiently" or "long wearing" which are generally not permitted in UTILITY claims. See Section 9. Sometimes called SURPLUSAGE. Permitted in plant patent claims. See Section 45. (9, 48)

MACHINE—One of the STATUTORY CLASSES of UTILITY PATENT. Often called "APPARATUS." A DEVICE usually having moving parts and a "rule of operation." Often contrasted with ARTICLE OF MANUFACTURE. (Chapter III, 3, 14, 15, 16, 45, 57, 64, 67)

MANUFACTURE—An ARTICLE OF MANUFACTURE. (3, 15, 64, 65)

MARKUSH CLAIM—A claim using special language as a permissible ALTERNATIVE EXPRESSION for a group of materials, articles, or steps operable therein. Used most in chemical claims but useful in mechanical, electrical, method and other types of claims. A contrived GENERIC expression where no true GENERIC expression exists. Example: "a metal selected from the group CONSISTING OF copper, silver and gold." Technically, but permissibly, violates the rule against ALTERNATIVE EXPRESSIONS. See Section 50. (24, 49, 50, 55). From a case, *Ex parte Markush*.

MEANS—A generalized and very BROAD word used to describe, in appropriate situations, an ELEMENT of a claim. See sixth paragraph of 35 U.S.C. § 112 and Section 34. (11, 12, 19, 21, 23, 24, 26, 29, 34, 35, 36, 45, 49, 50, 58). Properly phrased as "means for (performing a specified function)."

MENTAL STEPS—Sections 43 and 65.

METHOD—A procedure for transforming or reducing an ARTI-CLE, WORKPIECE or chemical substance to a different state or thing. METHOD, PROCESS and ART mean the same thing. METHOD is more common in mechanical and electrical claims; PROCESS is more common in chemical claims; ART today is more commonly used to mean "field of technology." See Chapter IV. (Chapter IV, 11, 12, **36**, 38, 39, 40, 43, 44, 52, 54, 56, 57)

METHOD CLAIMS, APPARATUS LIMITATIONS IN—Section 41.

METHOD, ELECTRICAL—Section 43.

METHOD FUNCTIONAL OF APPARATUS—Section 40.

METHOD OF MAKING AN ARTICLE OF MANUFACTURE, OBVIOUS—Section 39.

MPEP—The Manual of Patent Examining Procedure, a looseleaf booklet published by the Government Printing Office and available from the Superintendent of Documents, Box 1533, Washington, D.C. 20013. It is the EXAMINERS' "bible." (4A)

MULTIPLE DEPENDENT CLAIM—A DEPENDENT CLAIM which is DEPENDENT upon more than one other, preceding CLAIM or is dependent upon another MULTIPLE DEPENDENT CLAIM. (12)

MULTIPLICITY—A word connoting an indefinite number, two or more; usually a fairly large number. Often thought of as being greater than a PLURALITY. (20)

NARROW/NARROW CLAIM—A NARROW CLAIM covers or READS ON a restricted SCOPE of DEVICES, PROCESSES, etc., because it contains either many, or quite specific, limitations. A NARROW CLAIM is usually entitled only to a NARROW range of EQUIVALENTS. See BROAD CLAIM, OLD COMBINA-TION, PICTURE CLAIM (Sense (2)) and PROLIX. (5, 15, 16, 36, 46, 49, 60, 67, 68)

NEGATIVE LIMITATION—A claim limitation telling what an ELEMENT is not, instead of what it is; or what is does not do, instead of what it does. See Sections 17 and 45.

NEW MATTER—A term of art in Patent Law meaning any matter not "fairly" disclosed within the "four corners" (entire SPECIFICATION) of a patent application as filed. NEW MATTER may not be introduced into an application after it is filed. An ANTECEDENT for any element added to a claim after filing must be found in the original disclosure, or the claim will be, or be based upon, NEW MATTER. (51, 69)

NEW USE CLAIM—A claim to a METHOD involving some NEW USE of an old material or COMPOSITION, such as the killing of insects by spraying with DDT, DDT being old for *other* purposes. Traditionally (and under 35 U.S.C. § 100(b)), such a NEW USE may be claimed only in METHOD terminology, and the test of patentability is the novelty and unobviousness of the METHOD. See PREAMBLE LIMITATIONS; LABEL CLAIM and Section 56. (6, 42, 45, 49, 56, 59, 63)

NON-ART REJECTION—A REJECTION of a claim based, not on PRIOR ART (i.e., not on 35 U.S.C. §§ 102 and/or 103), but on the form of the claim. See FORMAL REJECTION and CHAPTER X. Includes REJECTIONS due to: METHOD functional of APPARATUS (Section 40), improper NEW USE (Section 64) and PRINTED MATTER limitations (Section 65), and other bases covered in Chapter X. (Chapter X, 44, 63)

NON-STATUTORY—(1) Quality of the subject matter of a purported INVENTION which is not patentable under 35 U.S.C. § 101, either by the precise terms thereof, or by case-law interpretation. See Sections 3 and 65. (2) Also used as a ground for REJECTION of a claim to an INVENTION where the claim is inherently defective, as an OMNIBUS CLAIM (Section 2), the claim sets forth a RESULT only (Section 31) or the claim depends solely on printed matter for patentability (Section 65). See FORMAL REJECTION and NON-ART REJECTION. (2, 3, 31, 44, 64, 65)

NUMBERING OF CLAIMS—Section 5.

NUMERALS, REFERENCE, IN CLAIMS—Section 22.

OBJECTION—A criticism by an EXAMINER to the form of a claim, as opposed to its substance. See NON-ART REJECTION and REJECTION. (17, 31)

OFFICIAL GAZETTE/OG—A weekly publication of the Patent Office, giving abstracts of and other information on all patents granted that week, as well as other information relating to patent and trademark practice. (17) Now split into two volumes, one for Patents, one for Trademarks.

OLD COMBINATION—Quality of a claim which recites an overall COMBINATION (including a SUBCOMBINATION) wherein the INVENTION resides in the SUBCOMBINATION which does not cooperate in some new and unobvious manner with the remainder of the COMBINATION. Sometimes called EXHAUSTED COMBINATION or OVERCLAIMING. A ground for REJECTION. See Section 63. (57, 59, **63**, 66)

OMNIBUS CLAIM—A claim in formal terms, such as "My IN-VENTION substantially as shown and described." Not permitted in Utility patents under 35 U.S.C. § 112. This form of claim is used in design patents, and in modified form in plant patents. See Sections 2, 47, 48, 52 and 54.

OPEN-ENDED—See COMPRISES.

ORDER OF CLAIMS—Sections 5 and 56.

OPERATIONAL EXPRESSIONS—Section 30.

OUTLINE FORMAT—A claim format in which each ELEMENT is introduced in its own SUBPARAGRAPH which may be identi-fied by a parenthesized number or letter. See Section 10. (**10**, 38)

OVERCLAIMING—See OLD COMBINATION. (31, **63**)

PARENT CLAIM—A main claim from which a DEPENDENT CLAIM depends. (11, 12, 23, 57) The parent claim may itself be INDEPENDENT or dependent.

PERIPHERAL CLAIM—The type of claim used in the United States. It defines the outer boundaries of the INVENTION. All that is within those boundaries (including all the claimed ELEMENTS and their EQUIVALENTS) will be READ ON by the claim; all that is outside the boundaries is not READ ON by the claim. See DOCTRINE OF EQUIVALENTS. (2)

PICTURE CLAIM—A claim reciting all significant structure disclosed in the description, omitting only "nuts and bolts." Thus, a very NARROW claim. (54, 60)

PLANT PATENT CLAIM—Section 48.

PLURALITY—An indefinite number, two or more. See MULTIPLICITY. (20)

POSITIVE/POSITIVELY—(1) The opposite of INFERENTIAL. A POSITIVE recitation of an ELEMENT means that the ELEMENT is introduced and fully described in a clause of a claim in which no other ELEMENT is introduced (except for a HOLE). See Sections 16, 18, 23, 37, 41 and 67. (2) The opposite of NEGATIVE. See NEGATIVE LIMITATION. (16, 17, 25, 34, 36, 57, 63)

PQ—See USPQ.

PREAMBLE—The initial part of a claim, the purpose of which is to name or define the thing being claimed. Often the environment in which the claimed thing will be used is set forth, as well as the WORKPIECE. See NEW USE CLAIM and Sections 6, 15, 16, and 56. (**6**, 7, 9, **11**, 12, 14, **15**, 16, 30, 34, 36, 49, 55, 56, 57, 59)

PREAMBLE LIMITATION—Descriptive statement in a PREAMBLE such as those related to the field of use, environment, etc. Possibly helpful in distinguishing a claim over PRIOR ART. See NEW USE CLAIM and Section 56. (**15**, 44, **56**, 59, 63)

PRINTED MATTER—See NON-ART REJECTION, NON-STATUTORY, and Section 65. (**44**, **65**)

PRIOR ART—All subject matter (patents, publications, etc.) bearing on the novelty and unobviousness of a claimed INVENTION pursuant, *inter alia*, to 35 U.S.C. §§ 102 and 103.

PROCESS—One of the STATUTORY CLASSES of UTILITY PATENT. See METHOD. (Chapter IV, 3, 5, 36, 47, 51, 53)

PROCESS, CHEMICAL—Section 42.

PRODUCT—Synonomous with ARTICLE OF MANUFACTURE and COMPOSITION. (5, 49)

PRODUCT-BY-PROCESS—A type of claim defining a PRODUCT in terms of the PROCESS by which it is made. Generally used when the PRODUCT cannot be defined in more traditional terms. This type of claim covers the PRODUCT *only* when made by the specified PROCESS. Novelty and unobviousness must reside in the PRODUCT and not merely in the PROCESS. See MPEP 706.03(e) and Section 43. (11, 12, 31, 45, **46**, 53, 56)

PROLIX—Quality of a claim which is "too complete" in that it sets forth long recitations of unimportant details which hide or obscure the INVENTION. See MPEP 706.03(g) and Section 68. (68)

PROSECUTION HISTORY—See FILE WRAPPER.

PROSECUTION HISTORY ESTOPPEL—See FILE WRAPPER ESTOPPEL.

PUNCTUATION OF CLAIMS—Section 10.

READ ON—To encompass, comprehend or give support to; to be within the terms of. If a claim READS ON a device accused of being an INFRINGEMENT thereof, the DEVICE does INFRINGE. If a claim READS ON a REFERENCE (or, *vice versa*) the claim is either unpatentable or invalid. A claim must READ ON the DESCRIPTION of the patent or application to which it is appended for the ELEMENTS of the claim to find ANTECEDENT basis therein. (18, 67)

REFERENCE—See PRIOR ART. Whether a REFERENCE is available as PRIOR ART depends on 35 U.S.C. §§ 102 and 103 and case-law interpretations thereof. PRIOR ART REFERENCES may be relied on by the EXAMINER or an accused INFRINGER to attack a claim.

REFERENCE NUMERALS IN CLAIMS—Section 22.

REJECTION—Disallowance of a claim by an EXAMINER because of its substance (lack of novelty; obvious). See OBJECTION and PRIOR ART. (17, 31, 40, 64, 66, 67, 68)

RESPONSE—An applicant's answer to an Office action. Attempts to meet REJECTIONS of and OBJECTIONS to claims either by AMENDMENT, or argument, or both.

RESTRICTION REQUIREMENT—Where the EXAMINER concludes that an application contains claims directed to more than one INVENTION, he may require the applicant to elect one INVENTION and to restrict his claims to such elected INVENTION. (58, 59)

RESULT—What the INVENTION is intended to accomplish. Claims setting forth only RESULTS are objectionable as too BROAD. See Sections 31 and 32. (31, 32, 34, 36)

SAID—THE. Used in claims to refer back to a claim element previously introduced. Preferable to use THE. "THE SAID" is a redundancy to be avoided. (23)

SCOPE—Breadth; the limits of the boundaries of a PERIPHERAL CLAIM. See BROAD and NARROW. (Chapter VIII, 5, 6, 11, 12, 16, 19, 22, 25, 34, 48, 49, 60, 63, 67, 68)

SCOPE OF CLAIMS, VARYING—Chapter VIII.

SINGLE ELEMENT CLAIM—A rare type of claim not to a COMBINATION but to one ELEMENT. Permissible if not a SINGLE MEANS CLAIM. (9)

SINGLE MEANS CLAIM—An impermissible claim not to a COMBINATION and having only one ELEMENT which is expressed in the form of "MEANS plus function." See Sections 34 and 36, and 38 U.S.C. § 112. (34, 36, 42, 57)

SINGLE PARAGRAPH FORM—A claim format in which the EL-EMENTS are not identified by indentation, letters or numerals, but are set off by commas. See COLON-SEMICOLON FORM, OUTLINE FORM, SUBPARAGRAPH FORM and Sections 10 and 14.

SINGLE SENTENCE RULE—In the United States, a claim must be a single sentence. See INTRODUCTION and Section 4A. (**4A**, 9, 26)

SO THAT—See IN ORDER TO and WHEREBY. (31, 33, 34)

SPECIES/SPECIFIC—A SPECIES is a member of a GENUS. A SPECIES is one of the two or more alternative and mutually exclusive embodiments of an INVENTION. The different SPECIES may be structures, steps, COMPOUNDS, chemicals, etc. See GENERIC/GENUS and Section 58. (11, 19, 24, 36, 50, 56, 58)

SPECIFICATION—The drawings, DESCRIPTION and claims of a patent application or patent. See NEW MATTER. (1, 16, 18, 19, 30, 34, 36, 44, 45, 51, 52, 53, 60, 63)

STATUTE—Title 35 of the United States Code (35 U.S.C.). (Chapter I, 1)

STATUTORY CLASSES—The main categories or "pigeonholes" into which a technical subject must fit in order to be potentially patentable. These categories are set forth in 35 U.S.C. §§ 101, 161 and 171 as interpreted by the case-law, and include PROCESS, MACHINE, MANUFACTURE, COMPOSITION OF MATTER, designs and plants. See Section 3. (3, 4A)

STEP—A generalized word used in appropriate situations as an ELEMENT of a METHOD CLAIM. Used in step-plus-function or step-for-performing-a-function claim ELEMENT. See sixth paragraph of 35 U.S.C. § 112 and Section 34.

STRUCTURAL CONNECTION—Section 29.

STRUCTURAL ORDER—A logical ordering of the ELEMENTS of a claim which begins with a base, power source or input and proceeds structurally to an ultimate ELEMENT or output. See FUNCTIONAL ORDER and Section 27.

SUBCOMBINATION—An ELEMENT or group of ELEMENTS that forms a part of a primary COMBINATION. If a SUBCOMBINATION has utility by itself, it may be claimed separately from the COMBINATION. See Section 59. (**59**, 63, 66)

SUBCOMBINATION FORMAT—A claim format for a SUBCOMBINATION: "In a (name of COMBINATION) for (COMBINATION'S FUNCTION), an X and a Y," where X, Y is the claimed SUBCOMBINATION. An exception to the "rule" that a TRANSITION should be between the PREAMBLE and BODY of a claim. (59)

SUBPARAGRAPH FORM—A claim format in which each ELEMENT is introduced and defined in its own indented subparagraph. See COLON-SEMICOLON FORM, OUTLINE FORM, SINGLE PARAGRAPH FORM and Section 10. (10, 14, 16, 38)

SUPPORT FOR CLAIMS IN SPECIFICATION AND DRAWINGS—See ANTECEDENT and Sections 18 and 23.

SURPLUSAGE—See LAUDATORY STATEMENTS. (9)

TABULAR FORM—Same as SUBPARAGRAPH FORM. (10)

THE—The definite article THE is used to refer to an ELEMENT which has been introduced earlier in a claim. Alternatively SAID may be used, meaning the same thing. (11, **23**)

THEREBY—See WHEREBY. (31, 32)

TRADEMARKED MATERIALS—Section 51.

TRANSITION/TRANSITIONAL PHRASE—Language between the PREAMBLE and BODY of a claim. May affect the SCOPE of the claim. See COMPRISES, CONSISTING OF, CONSISTING ESSENTIALLY OF, INCLUDES, HAS and Section 7. (7, 8, 9, 14, 59)

ULTIMATE SPECIES—A SPECIES which cannot be further divided into other SPECIES. (55, 58) Example: Silver is an ultimate species of the genus "conductive metals."

UNBASED COMPARATIVE—An adjective, such as "thick," "heavy," "small," etc., used in a claim wherein no basis for the use thereof (i.e., thicker, heavier, smaller than what?) is set forth. The remedy is to provide a basis or relation for comparison, such as "said second member being thicker than said first member." Many words, such as resilient, flexible, etc., while, strictly speaking, UNBASED, are usually accepted without question. An UNBASED COMPARATIVE is a ground for REJECTION or OBJECTION, because its use may render a claim INDEFINITE. See Section 25.

UNDUE MULTIPLICITY—Presentation of too many claims in view of the nature and SCOPE of the INVENTION. See Rule 75(b), MPEP 706.03(1) and Section 62. (11, 12, 50, 53, 60, 62)

USPQ—The *United States Patent Quarterly*, a case reporter published quarterly and advance sheets in a magazine published weekly by BNA, Inc., and covering cases on patents, trademarks, copyrights, intellectual property, etc., from any forum.

UTILITY PATENT—Patents defining INVENTIONS having industrial utility (METHOD, APPARATUS, ARTICLE OF MANUFACTURE, COMPOSITION OF MATTER) as distinguished from design patents (Section 47) and plant patents (Section 48). (2, 50)

VAGUE—See INDEFINITE. (25, 67)

VARYING SCOPE OF CLAIMS—Chapter VIII.

WHEREBY—When properly used in a claim, a word introducing a clause describing the FUNCTION or operation necessarily following from previously recited structure, whether a whole claim or an ELEMENT thereof. The phrase traditionally means "it necessarily follows from the foregoing that." Such a WHEREBY clause is improper when it is used to *imply* structural or cooperational relationships which are not positively recited in the claim. See Section 32. (31, **32**, 33, 36)

WORKPIECE—The thing or ARTICLE operated on, altered, changed or reduced by a claimed APPARATUS or METHOD. It should be introduced in the PREAMBLE of the claim, and/or introduced INFERENTIALLY in the BODY of the claim. See Sections 15, 16, and 37. (14, 15, 16, 27, 30, 36, 37)

WRITTEN DESCRIPTION—See DESCRIPTION.

Tables of Authorities

(References are to sections.)

Cases

N

O

P

Q

R

Union Carbide Corp. v. American Can Co., § 40

Union Carbide Corp. v. Borg Warner Corp., § 18

Union Carbide Corp. v. Filtrol, § 56

V

Valmont Ind., Inc. v. Reinke Mfg. Co., § 34

Vehicular Technologies Corp. v. Titan Wheel International, Inc., §§ 7, 8

Venezia, *In re*, §§ 23, 28, 30, 32, 45, 64

W

W.L. Gore Assocs. v. Garlock, Inc., § 19

Wakefield, *In re*, §§ 62, 68

Walter, *In re*, § 44

Warmedam, *In re*, § 44

Warner Jenkinson Co. v. Hilton Davis Chem. Co., § 34

Water Technologies Corp. v. Calco Ltd., § 8

Waterloo Furniture Components, Ltd. v. Haworth, Inc. § 34

Weber, *In re*, § 50

Weiss, *Ex parte*, § 48

Wells Mfg. Corp. v. Littelfuse Inc, § 57

Welstead, *In re*, § 50

Wilson, *In re*, §§ 23, 56

WMS Gaming, Inc. v. International Game Technology, § 34

Wolfrum and Gold, *In re*, §§ 24, 31, 67

Worrest, *In re*, § 64

Y

Yoder Bros. v. California-Fla. Plant Corp., § 48

York Prods., Inc. v. Central Tractor Farm & Family Ctr., § 34

Z

Zahn, *In re*, § 47

Ziegler v. Phillips Petroleum Co., § 8

Zimmerly, *Ex parte*, § 34

Manual of Patent Examining Procedure

SECTION

506, § 48A

601.01(b), § 48A

608.01(m), §§ 4A–6, 10, 22, 57

608.01(n), §§ 11–13

608.01(p)(C), § 72

608.01(v), § 51

608.02, § 54

706.02, § 23

706.03(a), §§ 63, 65

706.03(c), §§ 30–31, 34, 45

706.03(d), §§ 16, 17, 22–24

706.03(e), § 46

706.03(f), §§ 16, 23, 66

SECTION

706.03(g), § 68

706.03(i), §§ 28, 63, 64

706.03(j), § 63

706.03(k), §§ 60–61

706.03(l), § 62

706.03(n), § 18

706.03(o), §§ 18, 69

706.03(q), § 39

706.03(r), § 40

706.03(s), § 2

706.03(u), § 18

706.03(y), § 50

803.02, § 50

Patent Office Rules of Practice

Title 35, United States Code

Other Statutes

Index

(References are to sections.)